W9-BEU-021

HANDBOOK TO LIFE IN THE MEDIEVAL WORLD

VOLUME 3

MADELEINE PELNER COSMAN
AND LINDA GALE JONES

Facts On File
An imprint of Infobase Publishing

Handbook to Life in the Medieval World

Facts On File, Inc.
An imprint of Infobase Publishing
132 West 31st Street
New York NY 10001

Library of Congress Cataloging-in-Publication Data

Cosman, Madeleine Pelner.
   Handbook to life in the medieval world / Madeleine Pelner Cosman and Linda Gale Jones.
     p. cm.
   "Handbook to Life in the Medieval World, looks at the medieval period from the perspective of Christians, Jews, and Muslims who inherited and inhabited the Classical Roman Empire . . ."—Introd.
   Includes bibliographical references and index.
   ISBN-13: 978-0-8160-4887-8
   1. Civilization, Medieval. 2. Civilization, Christian. 3. Civilization, Islamic. 4. Jews—Civilization. I. Jones, Linda Gale. II. Title.
   CB351.C625 2007
   909.07—dc22   2007000887

Facts On File books are available at special discounts when purchased in bulk quantities for businesses, associations, institutions, or sales promotions. Please call our Special Sales Department in New York at (212) 967-8800 or (800) 322-8755.

You can find Facts On File on the World Wide Web at http://www.factsonfile.com

Text design by Cathy Rincon
Maps by Jeremy Eagle

Printed in the United States of America

VB Hermitage 10 9 8 7 6 5 4 3 2 1

This book is printed on acid-free paper and contains 30% post-consumer recycled content.

CONTENTS

LIST OF ILLUSTRATIONS   v

LIST OF MAPS   vi

ACKNOWLEDGMENTS   vii

INTRODUCTION   ix

VOLUME I

1   HISTORY   1
    Western Europe   3
    Byzantine Empire   43
    Islamic Empire   56
    Jews in the Medieval World   75
    Chronology   98
    Reading   104

2   SOCIETY   109
    Christian Society   110
    Muslim Society   138
    Jewish Society   161
    Reading   180

3   ECONOMY AND TRADE   185
    Economy and Trade in Christian Europe   189
    Economy and Trade in the Islamic
      Empire   213
    Jewish Economy and Trade   242
    Reading   256

4   WARFARE AND WEAPONS   261
    Christian Warfare and Weapons   262
    Islamic Jihad, Warfare, and Weapons   292
    Jewish Military Matters   311
    Reading   320

VOLUME II

5   PHILOSOPHY AND RELIGION   325
    Christian Theology and Philosophy   326
    Jewish Philosophy and Theology   365
    Islamic Philosophy and Theology   386
    Reading   409

6   MYSTICISM AND MAGIC   413
    Christian Mysticism and Magic   414
    Jewish Mysticism and Magic   439
    Islamic Mysticism and Magic   451
    Reading   464

7   MEDICINE, SCIENCE, AND
    TECHNOLOGY   469
    Medicine in Europe   470
    Science and Technology in Europe   503
    Jewish Contributions to Medicine
      and Science   514
    Medicine, Science, and Technology
      in the Islamic World   525
    Reading   546

8   ART AND ARCHITECTURE   551
      The Patronage of the Arts   552
      Christian Art and Architecture   554
      Jewish Art and Architecture   588
      Islamic Art and Architecture   603
      Reading   625

VOLUME III

9   LITERATURE   629
      Christian Literature   631
      Jewish Literature   665
      Islamic Literature   683
      Reading   708

10   MUSIC AND DANCE   713
      Christian Music and Dance   714
      Jewish Music and Dance   737
      Islamic Music and Dance   747
      Reading   759

11   HOLIDAYS AND FESTIVALS   763
      Christian Holidays and Festivals 764
      Jewish Weddings, Sabbaths, and
         Holidays   794
      Islamic Holidays and Festivals   813
      Reading   821

12   CLOTHING, COSTUME, AND
      TEXTILES   825
      Christian Clothing   826
      Jewish Costumes and Clothing   834
      Muslim Clothing and Textiles   845
      A Glossary of Christian, Jewish, and
         Muslim Hat Styles and Clothing 858
      Reading   870

BIBLIOGRAPHY   873

INDEX   935

LIST OF ILLUSTRATIONS

Council of Constance, Germany	25	Al-Idrisi's *Geographic Atlas*	224
Map of Thames at London	37	Umayyad mosque, Damascus	225
Prophet's Mosque in Medina	58	Gold dinar coin, Sulayhid dynasty, Yemen,	
Richard I and Saladin during the Third		1094	228
Crusade	73	Design of a threshing machine	232
Italian prayer book, 1492	80	Meir Magino	246
Burning of Jews and Christians	89	Maximilian I in an armorer's shop	267
Interrelatedness	112	Chain mail	271
Field workers	120	Bassinet and *camail*	272
A portable wooden tub	124	Gorget	272
A bathhouse scene	126	Jupon	274
Noble man and woman hunters	128	Caparisoned horse	275
Old man and young woman	134	Joan of Arc	282
Madrasa	147	First attack on Constantinople in 1453	301
Harim	154	Turkish shield	309
Panels with hunting and banquet scenes,		Knights dressed in chain mail	317
Fatimid Egypt	158	A warrior	318
Altneuschule in Prague, Czech Republic	167	Adam and Eve	328
Charity	168	Last Supper	330
Harvesting and a rural banquet	179	Twice-told Eve	332
Feast celebrating the crusaders' capture of		Presentation of Christ in the Temple	334
Jerusalem, 1099	187	*Virgin and Child*	335
Farm women	190	Allegorical feast	338
An itinerant Italian pastry cook on a street		Sloth	339
corner in Constance	196	Saint Jerome in his study	341
Fish market	199	Four Horsemen	344
Nest of weights	200	Hell	346
Steelyard scales	201	Aquinas confounds the heretics	352
Crescentius discussing herb planting	203	Aristotle's *Ethics* in Hebrew	366
Anti-Semitic Korn-Jude coin	204	Miniature from Moses Maimonides,	
View of Venice from Marco Polo's *Livres*		*Mishneh Torah*	377
du Graunt Caam	211	Page from the Quran	390
Allegory of human being adrift	212	Avicenna's *Canon of Medicine*	398
Ariadeno Barbarossa	216	Arius and Averroës	402
		Philosopher's furnace	426

Zodiac woman	431	Arches of the Great Mosque of Córdoba	610
Witch and devil	435	Calligraphic pages	615
Four witches	436	King Arthur	637
Witches at the Sabbath	437	A German minnesinger	641
Sefirotic tree	444	Christine de Pizan teaches the power of	
Rumi tomb	457	temperance	649
The Dance of the Dervishes	460	Dante's *Divine Comedy*	655
Examples of physiognomy	475	Christine de Pizan in her study	665
Physiognomy of foreheads	476	*North French Miscellany*	678
Nose surgery	482	Udhri poetry	687
Four humors	485	Al-Hariri's *Maqamat*	701
Pregnant woman	493	Tabriz carpet	704
Urinalysis	496	Music theory	716
Zodiac man	498	Feast music	723
Tactus eruditus	499	Musical instruments	730
Temperance with mechanical clock	504	Trumpets announce the emperor	731
Sewage system plan	507	*Dance macabre*	736
Worm condenser	511	Preparations for Passover	746
Distillation chambers	512	Mevlevi dervishes	757
Microcosm/macrocosm	522	Three musicians	759
Four humors	527	Table fountain	768
Jewish translation of Arab text	539	Mummers	778
Astrolabe	541	Jester	782
Colegiata de Santa Julia, Santillana del Mar,		Feast	790
Spain	556	Saint Elizabeth feeding the poor	793
Notre-Dame, Paris	560	Feast	794
Outside the monastery walls of the Grande		Sabbath lamp	800
Chartreuse	561	Shofar	802
Mont-Saint-Michel	564	Pilgrimage	815
Gold buckle	567	A bridal feast	831
Initial *W*	570	Chaperone	832
Initial *S*	571	Brocaded robe	833
Interlaced *ITA*	572	*Judenhut*	842
Old Testament	574	Fatimid earrings	849
Byzantine icon	586	Coptic cloth	857
Micrographic masorah	596	Frontlet	860
Moses depicted with horns	597	Emperor Maximilian I, Albrecht Dürer	864

LIST OF MAPS

Germanic Kingdoms, c. 500	6	Islamic Empire at Its Height	65
Holy Roman Empire, 1215–1250	11	Christian Persecutions, c. 1200–1500	85
Crusader States, 1098–1291	28	Main Eurasian Routes in Mongol Times	218
First European Universities	40	Trans-Saharan Trading Networks	220
Byzantine Empire under Justinian, 565	44	World of the Radhanites, Ninth Century	253
Byzantine Empire in the 11th and 12th Centuries	51		

9

LITERATURE

Most modern people know the European Middle Ages through medieval literature, rather than medieval art, philosophy, religion, or science. Modern ideas about courtly manners, courtly love, and chivalry customarily are based on literary depictions rather than historical treatises or visual icons. This continuing interest in the Middle Ages makes it especially fascinating to review the multiple types of medieval fiction and nonfiction that depicted medieval reality and transmitted medieval worldviews to subsequent centuries.

The first task at hand is to recognize the difficulties of classifying medieval literary production. To begin with, to the modern reader, one person, who reads a written text in silence, the term *literature* refers to original written compositions. In reality, much of medieval "literature" began as oral productions of lyrical poetry, verse, prose, and sermons that were recited or, in the case of lyric and verse, even sung in public before an audience. Neat modern divisions between fiction and nonfiction or religious and secular literature also break down upon closer inspection. Medieval romance blends historical figures and events concerning Alexander the Great, King Arthur, or Charlemagne with myths and legends. Royally commissioned historical chronicles interpolate biblical events and Greek or "pagan" mythical motifs with the feats of medieval kings. Religious literature, such as the lives of the saints genre, fused the facts of the saint's life with those of Greco-Roman or pagan heroes. The preservation of dozens or hundreds of distinct versions of the same cycle of epics or poems sometimes challenges the concept of individual authorship.

The second and perhaps more challenging task is to recognize the cultural plurality of the producers of medieval literature. Contemporary popular Western conceptions of the Middle Ages are overwhelmingly Christian. Western general audiences are undoubtedly familiar with the images of Muslims as the enemies of Christendom in the crusades or of Jews as the victims of Christian repression. Less well known are the Jewish and Muslim contributions to much of what composes medieval Christian "fiction and nonfiction," the literary production of Jews and Muslims themselves, and the often surprising instances of intertextuality whereby authors of one cultural tradition appropriate and reinvent the literary tropes of another for their own purposes.

Jewish Haggadic literature, which includes beast fables, frame tales, and exempla, found its way directly or indirectly into the literature of Christendom. By the same token, Jewish authors rewrote Christian *chansons de geste* and chivalric literature to respond to the needs and worldview of their readers. Similarly, Arabic court poetry, mirrors for princes and other instruction manuals, dream interpretation literature, and fiction such as the famous *The Thousand and One Nights* heavily influenced the literature produced in Christendom and the Jewish world. Such cultural borrowings were made possible because of several dynamic factors. In the first place, Jews, Christians, and Muslims alike inherited the legacy of classical Greek literature. Second, the translation of ancient Greek literature and of Arabic, Hebrew, Persian, Sanskrit, or Latin works into vernacular languages facilitated their appropriation by other cultural-linguistic groups. Finally, it must be remembered that the literary output of medieval Christians, Jews, and Muslims was also influenced by contacts among the three communities, whether through conversion from one religion to another, military conquests, diplomatic relations, courtly patronage, or the mere coexistence of bilingual Christians, Jews, and Muslims in the same geographical space, which allowed the purchase or commissioning of books by the "Other." Medieval literature is thus Christian, Jewish, and Muslim, and this chapter discusses the major contributions of each community, taking care to note what is unique or particular to each, but also to highlight instances of cultural borrowing or parallel developments.

Christian Literature

Literary creation during the Christian European Middle Ages displays a fascinating fusion of the religious and the secular, fact and fiction, and morality and the burlesque. The earliest surviving texts written in medieval Latin and the vernacular languages are sermons and hagiography (from the Greek: *hagio*, "holy," and *graphe*, "writing"), which include the "Lives of the Saints," collections of miracle tales, and accounts of the discovery of holy relics. Priests and monks incorporated these texts into the Christian liturgy of the mass and the celebration of saints' feast days to instill Christian doctrine and concepts of morality in their lay and religious audiences. The *chansons de geste* or epic songs of heroic exploits depicted the feats and adventures of Emperor Charlemagne and his Twelve Peers. This genre fused the feudal values of loyalty to the monarch with the religious values of fidelity to and defense of the Christian Church. Romances, the most famous of which pertain to King Arthur and his Knights of the Round Table, celebrated the ideals of chivalry and courtly love. Related to the romance were the *lais*, or short metrical romance poems, often set to music, such as those composed by Marie de France (c. 1160), and the Breton *Lais*, which included elements of Celtic mythology. The *fabliaux* (little fables) were comical rude, lewd stories written in verse that represented the antithesis of the chivalric romance. They graced the great halls of the nobility, taverns of townspeople, and fairgrounds for everyone from peasants to ladies, knights, and squires.

Lyric poetry, recited or sung by troubadours and minnesingers, described love as powerful suffering that either ennobled or destroyed the lover. Their depictions of love poetry affected our modern ideas of polite etiquette and the inspirational effects of love. Geoffrey Chaucer's *Canterbury Tales* and Boccaccio's *The Decameron* exemplify the brilliantly crafted, popular frame tales that employed the pilgrimage and banquet, respectively, as a literary pretext to unite diverse characters whose opposed interests, styles, language, and morals otherwise would make them absurdly incompatible.

Drama is another significant literary genre. Religious dramas such as the Passion Play, mystery play, miracle play, and morality play find their origins in the inherently theatrical short Latin dialogues within the Easter Mass, called *tropes*, as well as in the vast production of hagiography, especially the "Lives of the Saints." As noted, the sermons written for major feasts, such as Christmas, Easter Holy Week, and saints' festivals, contained many theatrical elements and often provided the script for religious drama. Mimes, minstrels, traveling jugglers, and *joculatores*—all survivals of ancient Greek and Roman performing arts—together with the folk rites and rituals of *mummings*, *masques*, and *morris dances* provided popular marketplace entertainment.

Devotional and moralistic literature served as important medieval tutors for Christian doctrine, morals, and norms of behavior aimed at different categories of people: rulers, laypersons, religious men and women. It comprises a number of disparate genres, including bestiaries, which featured endearing animal characters with human foibles and virtues in the tradition of the classical Aesop, and beast epics, such as the tales of Reynard the Fox and Ysengrimus the Wolf. Exempla were collections of tales demonstrating exemplary behavior that preachers incorporated in their sermons to instruct, edify, and entertain their audiences.

Instruction manuals comprise a wide array of secular and religious literature. A popular literary type, instruction books taught readers how to fight, rule, and love, and to live and die as good Christian men and women. To learn chivalry, one could consult *Le Livre des fais d'armes et de chevalerie* (*The Book of the Deeds of Arms and Chivalry*), written circa 1410 by Christine de Pizan. Rulers and administrators read "mirrors of princes," *miroirs des princes*, to learn the art of good government. Secular and ecclesiastical figures wrote manuals for the art of love, *ars amandi*. Women avidly read manuals of conduct to learn to lead devout, exemplary Christian lives. For the art of dying a good Christian death, a medieval man or woman could consult an *ars moriendi* book. The genre of dream visions, whose aims were also moralistic and exemplary, ranges from the imaginings in the poem *Pearl* written in alliterative Middle English to Dante's magisterial vision of the *Divine Comedy*, written in bravura Italian triple rhyme, *terza rima*. Riddles were another popular literary genre.

Last but not least, the secular and ecclesiastical authorities wrote or commissioned the writing of historical chronicles to document for posterity the history of their institutions and of key events such as the Crusades. The Venerable Bede's (d. 735) *Ecclesiastical History of the English People*, the 12th-century *Cronica Adefonsi Imperatoris* (*The Chronicle of Alfonso the Emperor of Spain*), and the Anonymous *Gesta Francorum et aliorum Hierosolymitanorum* (*The Deeds of the Franks and the Other Pilgrims to Jerusalem*) are just three examples of this prolific chronicler activity.

The chapter concludes with a brief glimpse of the multiple literary languages in a given medieval country. In England, for instance, Anglo-Saxon was the language for the epic *Beowulf* and such magnificent elegies as the *Wanderer, Seafarer*, and *Battle of Maldon*. Other authors after the 11th century selected Anglo-Norman and any one of four major Middle English dialects plus incursions of Danish in the area called the Danelaw. The Occitan language of Provençal left an indelible mark on the lyrical poetic production of southern France, the Iberian Peninsula, and Italy. Galaico-Portuguese and Arabic were the favored languages of poetic expression in Christian and Muslim Iberia, respectively, while Castilian reigned supreme in epic romances such as the 11th-century *Poema del Mío Cid*. Itinerant German minnesingers played a pivotal role in standardizing the Middle High German dialects prevalent in the high Middle Ages.

Hagiography and Devotional Literature

The church continued the late antiquity tradition of writing the *vita*, or "life," of a saint, which would be recited as part of the sermon for the saint's feast day. The earliest hagiographies were modeled after the canonical gospel and apocryphal versions of the life of Jesus, which in turn were derived from Greco-Roman biographies. The hagiographies of late antiquity celebrated the lives of Christian martyrs and hermits, such as the Greek patriarch Athanasius of Athena's (d. 373) *Life of Saint Anthony of Egypt* (d. 356). In the high and late Middle Ages hagiographies were composed for a variety of motives, including to harness lay piety and devotion away from heretical currents, to popularize a pilgrimage to a new saint's shrine, or even to help resolve political disputes. Examples of such works include *The Book of Saint Foy* (the anonymous Anglo-Norman *Vie de Sainte-Foi*), *La Vida de Santo Domingo de Silos* (Life of Saint Dominic), written by the Spanish poet and priest Gonzalo de Berceo (1190–

1264), the *First Life of Saint Francis of Assisi* (*Vita Prima*), by the Franciscan friar Thomas of Celano (c. 1200–c. 1260), and the *Life of Saint Thomas of Canterbury*, included in de Voragine's *Golden Legend*.

The *Legenda Aurea*, or *Golden Legend*, by the Dominican preacher and archbishop of Genoa Jacobus de Voragine (1230–98) was the most popular and widely diffused collection of saints' lives in the Middle Ages. Compiled circa 1260, the author's biographies combine the official version of the saint's life drawn from church liturgy with legends of the miracles produced by the saint's relics and other supernatural feats. Each biographical entry begins with an etymology of the meaning of the saint's name that allegorizes the hero's qualities. The immensely popular hagiographic romance *Barlaam and Josaphat* recounts the conversion of a fourth-century Indian prince, Josaphat, to Christianity after his encounter with the hermit Barlaam. The prince defies his father and renounces the throne in order to live a life of ascetic retreat beside his master Barlaam. Scholars agree that the story is a Christianized version of the Sanskrit story of the Buddha. The Byzantines translated an Arabic version of the story into Greek, which, in turn, was translated into Latin in the 11th century.

SPIRITUAL AUTOBIOGRAPHY

Following the late antiquity tradition of Saint Augustine's and Saint Patrick's *Confessions*, medieval Christian writers wrote spiritual autobiographies of their conversion to a more intensely lived Christian life of piety and devotion. The Benedictine monk, abbot, and historian Guibert of Nogent (France) (1053–1124) modeled his *De Vita sua* (*Memoirs*) on the *Confessions* of Saint Augustine, devoting great attention to his childhood, education, and renunciation of worldly vanities in order to devote himself fully to God. He and

his contemporary the Scholastic philosopher Peter Abelard (1079–1142), author of the autobiographical *Historia calamitatum* (*The Story of Calamities*), intended their life experiences to serve as an example for others. *The Book of Margery Kempe* is a remarkable autobiography written by an English laywoman, which narrates her spiritual conversion from housewife and mother to bride of Christ. A vision of Christ spurs her to renounce the "vanities" of the world and to lead a life of celibacy and pious devotion. Margery of Kempe (1373–1478) recounts her pilgrimages to Rome, Jerusalem, and Santiago de Compostela and her visionary, mystical conversations with Christ.

MYSTICAL AND VISIONARY LITERATURE

In the 14th and 15th centuries a number of women mystics wrote mystical treatises detailing the soul's journey to God. Notable examples of this visionary literature include Saint Catherine of Siena's (d. 1380) "Dialogue," or "Treatise on Divine Providence," and the anchoress Saint Julian of Norwich's "Sixteen Revelations of Divine Love," written circa 1393, when the author experienced intense visions of God while suffering from a severe illness. Julian's most famous saying, "All shall be well, and all shall be well, and all manner of things shall be well," reflects her mystical insight that suffering with joy and acceptance is a means of drawing nearer to God. The Swedish mystic Saint Birgitta (1303–73) recorded her visions of God, which were translated into Latin under the title *Revelationes coelestes* (*Celestial Visions*) and widely diffused in Europe.

DEVOTIONAL POETRY

Devotional poems composed in Latin and vernacular languages accompanied the celebration of religious feasts and were intended to strengthen Christian faith and instill feelings of contrition and piety. The 13th-century poetic hymn *Stabat Mater Dolorosa* (The sorrowful mother is standing) depicts the sorrow of the Virgin Mary as she stood by the cross witnessing Christ's crucifixion. The poem is attributed to Jacopone da Todi and was usually set to music for the observance of Easter. Legend has it that Saint Francis of Assisi (d. 1226) composed his *Cantico del Sole* (*Canticle to Brother Sun*) in his native Umbrian tongue while enraptured in mystical ecstasy. The *Dies Irae* (Days of wrath) was composed by the Franciscan friar Thomas of Celano (d. 1270), who was a disciple of Saint Francis, the founder of the Franciscan Order, and the author of the hagiographic *Life of Saint Francis* and the *Life of Saint Clare of Assisi*. The *Dies Irae* is an apocalyptic poem that describes the fate of souls on the day of judgment. As the *Stabat Mater*, it was set to music to accompany the liturgy of All Souls' Day (November 2). The increasing popular devotion to the Virgin Mary from the 13th century onward is reflected in the numerous vernacular litanies, songs, and poems of praise dedicated to her, of which the Spanish poet Gonzalo de Berceo's *Milagros de Nuestra Señora* (The miracles of Our Lady) and *Loores de la Virgen* (The praises of the Virgin) are prime representatives.

Chanson de Geste

Written in Old French, the *chanson de geste* (song of heroic deeds) was an epic poetic narrative of heroic exploits. It emerged in the late 11th-century Frankish kingdoms and lasted until the end of the 15th century, gaining in popularity throughout western Europe. The genre was based on fact but elaborated by legend and art and developed into three thematic cycles: the cycle of the king, or *Cicle du Roi*, referring principally to Charlemagne, but also

his heirs and their wars against the Saracens; the cycle of Doön de Mayence, which focuses on the exploits of the rebel barons of Narbonne who opposed the Carolingian dynasty; and the cycle of Garin de Montglane, which featured the exploits of knights who were younger royal sons. Barred from inheriting the throne, they sought glory and land fighting the "pagans." The most popular examples of the *chanson de geste* were *Le Chanson de Roland* (*The Song of Roland*), which belongs to the Charlemagne cycle, and *La Chançun de Guillelme* (*The Song of William*), which belongs to the cycle of Garin de Montglane. The *chansons de geste* were composed in decasyllabic monorhyme stanzas and typically were recited to music by minstrel poets called *trouvères* who played the fiddle (*vielle*) or violin (*viol*) as they performed. In addition to the Saracen foe, the *chansons de geste* featured mythical characters such as monsters and giants, and the use of magic.

Chanson de geste warriors at King Charlemagne's court, the Twelve Equals (*Douze Pers*), fought heroically for king and God rather than for love or prestige, and thus epitomized feudal and Christian ideals. These heroes brazenly tested body, weaponry, and martial strategy, rather than intellectual virtue or social finesse. The *Song of Roland*'s eponymous hero Roland was rash (*preux*) and physically and martially powerful, while his friend and artistic foil, Oliver, was learned and wise (*sage*). Paired opposites in literature, as in life, were depicted in separate characters, though ideally, as in Arthurian romance, they were united in a single, heroic human being, the rhetorical *topos* called wisdom and strength (*sapientia et fortitudo*).

The *Chanson de Roland*, composed or perhaps inscribed by a writer named Turoldus, between 1098 and 1100, and possibly connected to Roland exploits sung by the minstrel Taillefer in 1066 at the Battle of Hastings, was a powerful Christian epic commemorating

King Charlemagne's initial victory in war against the Muslims in Spain. The epic is based on the Battle of Roncesvaux in the Pyrenees Mountains in 778, during which Basque forces attacked the rear guard of Charlemagne's troops to ravenge the sacking of Pamplona. In the *Song of Roland* the Basques are transformed into Saracens, demons, and giants. The epic sets the city of Zaragoza as the last stronghold of the Muslim king Marsile. In a brilliant ruse, he pretends to submit to Charlemagne, swears to convert to Christianity, and pledges himself as vassal. When Charlemagne leaves the field, Marsile attacks the rear guard commanded by the impetuous knight Roland as the army crosses the Pyrenees Mountains.

Crying the battle cry *Montjoie*, Roland and the Christians kill hundreds or thousands of Muslims but lose many of their own warriors. Too late to call for reinforcements, Roland nevertheless blows his horn, Olifant, for help, but he and his forces are massacred. Baligant, the emir of Babylon, goes to the aid of Marsile and fights fierce hand-to-hand combat against King Charlemagne, who, though receiving a severe head wound, nevertheless strikes down the pagan foe. The fallen Roland rises to heaven and the angel Gabriel reassures King Charlemagne that his triumph was just. The *chanson de geste* appealed to the exclusively masculine world of heroic men who returned to their homeland with honor and glory even in defeat, with the promise of heavenly reward.

In the Iberian Peninsula the *Cantar del mío Cid* represents the most renowned example of the Castilian *cantar de gesta* (*chanson de geste*) genre of poetic verse. The literary tradition was more broadly known as the *Mester de juglaría* ("Ministry of jongleury") because the stories were recited or sung by *juglares* (jounglers). The *Cantar del mío Cid* narrates the true story of the Castilian warrior Rodrigo Díaz de Vivar (d. 1099), whose military exploits among the Christians and Muslims earned him the nickname *El Cid Campeador*. The name *El Cid* derives from the Arabic *al-sayyid*, an honorific title meaning "lord," and *Campeador* is an epithet bestowed upon the conqueror of a rival warrior leader. El Cid was a military general in the service of the king of Castile and Léon, Alfonso VI (r. 1065–1109). Spurned and dishonored because the king exiled him from the court in 1079, the Cid became a mercenary fighter in the service of Christian and Muslim monarchs, yet longed to regain his honor and place in Alfonso's court. He captured Valencia from the Almoravid emir al-Qadir in 1084 and established a small kingdom, although he officially ruled it on behalf of Alfonso VI.

The *Cantar del mío Cid* is traditionally divided into three plots: the *Cantar del destierro*, or "Song of Exile," describes his exile from Castile and his adventures fighting the Muslim emir of Zaragoza. The *Cantar de las Bodas* ("Wedding Song") narrates El Cid's capture of Valencia, his receipt of King Alfonso's forgiveness, and the marriage of his two daughters to the infantes of Carrión. The *Cantar de la Afrenta de Corpes* (The song of the affront to the daughters) relates that when the infantes abandon the daughters of the Cid, he restores the family honor and marries his daughters to the Infantes of Aragon and Navarre. The *Cantar del mío Cid* is an anonymous work that was transmitted orally and performed by *juglares* in palaces and public squares. It was transcribed for the first time in 1207 by Per Abad.

The Anglo-Saxons also produced epic poetry. *Beowulf* is the oldest and longest epic poem composed in Old English. Scholars continue to dispute the date of composition, placing it sometime between the late eighth and 10th centuries. The epic narrates the heroic exploits of Beowulf, a Germanic warrior from Sweden, who travels to Denmark at the behest of King Hrothgar to defeat the monster Grendel and avenge the killing of the king's warriors. As does *The Song of Roland*, *Beowulf* alludes to historical characters and events but blends them with fanciful legend. Though the characters featured lived in the sixth century, that is, prior to the conversion to Christianity of these Germanic tribes, they are all depicted as models or antitheses of Christian behavior. Even the villains, the monster Grendel and his mother, are portrayed as descendants of the biblical Cain.

The anonymous epic poem *Nibelungenlied* belongs to the Germanic poetic tradition. It celebrates the feats of the Burgundian kings, an East Germanic tribe from the area of Scandinavia. Composed sometime between 1190 and 1200, *Nibelungenlied* combines pre-Christian Teutonic and Nordic mythology with ancient Greek and Christian motifs, as well as the themes of courtly love (discussed later). *Nibelungenlied* probably influenced the composition of *Kudrun*, an anonymous epic poem written in Middle High German that appeared in the mid-13th century. This epic saga recounts the intrigues and romance adventures that intertwine the lives of three rival kings and their children. The epic centers upon Gudrun, the daughter of one of the kings, who is taken prisoner in a distant Norman castle and forced into servitude, and the 13-year Odyssey-like pursuit by her father and brother to rescue her.

Romance

The term *romance* derives from the French *roman* and refers to vernacular as opposed to Latin texts. As a literary genre it originated in the 12th century and designates a form of courtly narrative poetry composed in octosyllabic rhymed couplets or prose that depicted courtly love, tests of virtue, and triumphs over impossibilities, including magical and marvelous figures such as fiery dragons. Courtly love was understood as intense suffering derived from the sight or the contemplation of the

dearly beloved. It aroused in the lover confusion, forgetfulness, and life-threatening loss of appetite for food and for living, yet it also inspired his intellectual vigor and martial prowess. The court of Eleanor of Aquitaine (1122–1204), queen of France and England, patronized and promoted the ideals of courtly love. Her courtier Andreas Capellanus (Andrew the Chaplain) wrote the *Art of Courtly Love*, an instruction book for courtly adulterers. (*See* the section on instruction books, pages 646–651).

Romance subjects mirrored the customs and ethics of the audience. Inspiring people by moralizing and entertaining them with marvels, magic, and mysticism, romance subjects generally followed two *matters*, as the 13th-century writer Jean Bodel classed them. The matter of Britain concerned King Arthur and his Knights of the Round Table. The Matter of Greece and Rome encompassed tales of the Trojan War and the adventures of King Alexander the Great. Bodel's third literary subject is the matter of France, which solemnized the heritage of King Charlemagne and his Twelve Peers in the French *chansons de geste*.

KING ARTHUR AND HIS KNIGHTS OF THE ROUND TABLE

Arthurian romance written in prose or poetry almost always concerned King Arthur; his queen, Guinevere; and such knights of his Round Table as Sir Lancelot, Sir Gawain, Sir Perceval, and Sir Galahad. Lancelot was Guinevere's lover, and a vertiginous courtly love circle pivoted around their adulterous joy. The historical Arthur was a sixth-century fighter referred to as a *dux bellorum* whose exploits were recorded in works by the historians Gildus, Nennius, Geraldus Cambrensis, and Geoffrey of Monmouth. Arthur's exploits were embellished by writers of courtly romances in Old French, Middle High German, Middle English, Icelandic, Italian, and Welsh, most of which were written between the 12th and 15th centuries.

One of the best romancers was Chrétien de Troyes, a 12th-century poet writing in France under the patronage of Countess Marie de Champagne, the daughter of Queen Eleanor of Aquitaine. His romances *Cliges*, *Lancelot*, and *Perceval* were popular in their time and widely imitated. Though Chrétien's romances probably derived their magic, mysticism, and marvels from Celtic heritage, the intellectual discussions of love and its effects catered to contemporary life's elegance and interests in the brilliant courts of the art patrons Queen Eleanor of Aquitaine and her daughter, Marie of Champagne. Literature mirrored life and life mirrored art in such ideas as the service of love, love from afar, courtly love, human perfectibility, and virtue defined by trial. Love's suffering was a virtue best comprehended by testing it. Just as God required proof of Job's obedience and fidelity in the biblical Book of Job, so romance heroines required proof of faithful deference and submission from their knights.

Sir Gawain, Sir Perceval, and Sir Lancelot were subjects of separate romances in various languages. One of the most famous medieval knights and lovers was Sir Tristan, not technically an Arthurian since his beloved was Isolt, wife of King Mark of Cornwall. These knights as romance heroes shared patterns of adventures customarily beginning with a marvelous childhood. This *enfance* was a formulaic series of childhood exploits beginning with birth that prefigured and explained the knight's later feats. A medieval romancer justified his hero's extraordinary prowess by defining his early extraordinary promise.

Almost every important Arthurian hero first was a prodigious youth, notably precocious, like Tristan, or exceptionally naïve and foolish, like Perceval. Youthful portraits and childhood adventures occupied a prominent place in the total work of art. Between the hero's birth and

Arthur pulling the sword from the stone   HIP/Art Resource, NY.

the ceremony of his knighting, recurrent motifs, probably originating in Celtic or classical tradition, included the hero's incestuous, secret, or tragic birth; his upbringing with a foster parent; his temporary exile and eventual return to his patrimony; his namelessness or his belated discovery of his name; his mission to avenge iniquity or insult to his father; and his quest for advice. The childhood education of the hero was another theme that romances emphasized. Little bound by traditional proscription, the hero's learning provided the romance writer with an opportunity to dramatize ideals pleasing to his patrons or to his own imagination. Education predicted the hero's rescuing damsels in distress, relieving iniquities in towns, fighting inequities in castles, vanquishing fiery dragons, and dying magnificently.

Some romance knights were portrayed as learned and intellectual. Tristan's education suggested that knowledge of music and manners made the man. Thomas of Britain and

Gottfried von Strassburg depicted the development of the learned knight whose artistic and intellectual exploits were as important as his chivalric adventures. Likewise, learning was important in other versions of the Tristan romance, such as Eilhart von Oberg's *Tristrant*, the English *Sir Tristrem*, the French *prose Tristan*, and Malory's book of *Sir Tristriam of Lyones*.

Conversely, Perceval as hero began life as a naïve fool, guileless and ingenuous, possessing no knowledge or restraint. When he arrived at court, the people marveled at Perceval's stupidity, laughed at his ignorance, and derided him for his simplicity. In the great Perceval poems by Chretien de Troyes and Wolfram von Eschenbach, Sir Perceval was a brave man who only slowly gained wisdom. Yet Perceval's adventures in chivalry, in love, and in his quest for the Holy Grail demonstrated the power of inherent goodness and noble birth to respond to spiritual progress and chivalric development. Whereas Sir Tristan was a learned gentleman, artistic musician, and sensitive lover, his artistic cultivation served only one queen and the knight himself. In contrast, Perceval served the ideals of chivalry and all of Christianity through winning the Holy Grail. The Perceval tales placed knighthood in service to morality, as in five other popular versions of Perceval's adventures, *Peredur, Sir Perceval, Carduino, Bliocadran's Prologue*, and *The Lai of Tyolet*.

Passionate Sir Lancelot was best known through Chretien de Troyes's *Lancelot or the Knight of the Cart* (*Chevalier de la Charette*), Ulrich von Zatzikhoven's *Lanzelet*, and the *Prose Lancelot* by an anonymous French writer. Minor romances also depicted the hero's preparation for carrying out future feats of rescuing damsels, killing dragons, jousting, or fighing for justice, honor and love, as in the romances of *Galeran, Wigalois, Wigamur*, and *Sone de Nausai*.

GREECE AND ROME

The second subject matter of romance concerned Greece and Rome, which inspired romances of Achilles, Odysseus, Aeneas, Hector, and Alexander. In the 12th century Joseph of Exeter wrote a long Troy tale in Latin hexameters, and an even longer romance consisting of 30,000 octosyllabic lines was written by Benoît de Sainte-Maure. Boccaccio in his *Filostrato* and Chaucer in his *Troilius and Chryseide* were especially inventive in their versions of these classical themes.

The Alexander romances added to his life history much Eastern and Greek folklore and Byzantine exotica. The 10th-century *Historia de Preliis* by Archpresbyter Leo and the fragmentary romances by Albéric de Pisançon and Pfaffe Lamprecht do not equal the literary sophistication of the best Arthurian romances. But Alexander cycles written around the year 1200 provided elements the literary world has cherished. Alexander romances written in a 12-syllable line so influenced poets that the technique was called the *alexandrine*.

Another heritage of the Alexander romance was a codification of chivalric parallelisms exemplified in the *Nine Worthies*, a term coined by the 14th-century French author Jacques de Longuyon to exemplify the nine personages who best represented the ideals of chivalry. Jacques de Longuyon in his *Voeux du Paon* (*Vows of the Peacock*) celebrated the Three Jewish Worthies, King David, Joshua, and Judas Maccabaeus, who paralleled in character and acts the Three Classical Worthies, Hector of Troy, Alexander the Great, and Julius Caesar, who in turn synchronized exploits with the Three Christian Worthies, Charlemagne, King Arthur, and Godfrey of Bouillon, one of the crusader kings. This literary conceit affected art as well as literature, as in the tapestry cycles of the *Nine Worthies* still visible in New York City at the Cloisters

Museum and in the allusions made to them in later literary works such as Shakespeare's play *Love's Labour's Lost*.

A romance tale that rivaled the matters of Britain and Rome in popularity in the 13th and 14th centuries was the story of *Fleur et Blanchefleur*. The earliest surviving version is a late 12th-century French text, although Castilian, Italian, German, English, Dutch, and Norwegian versions attest to the story's immense popularity. Fleur ("belonging to the flower") and Blanchefleur ("white flower") are star-crossed lovers divided by religion. Fleur is the son of Fenix, Muslim king of Spain, and Blanchefleur is the granddaughter of a Christian knight. King Fenix attacks a group of pilgrims in Galicia on their way to the shrine of Santiago de Compostela. During the attack the Christian knight is killed and his widowed pregnant daughter is captured and taken prisoner to Naples, where she is made lady-in-waiting to Fenix's wife. There she and the king's Muslim pregnant wife give birth on the same day to Blanchefleur and Fleur, respectively. The two children grow up in the court together, and the Muslim king, fearing his son will fall in love with the Christian Fleur, sells her to merchants, who take her to the court of the emir of Cairo. The remainder of the story narrates Fleur's exploits to retrieve his love, rescuing her from the watch tower of the emir's castle. Moved by their love, the emir releases her, she and Fleur are married, Fleur converts to Christianity, and they return to Spain, where they inherit his father's kingdom and convert the population to Christianity.

The *Lai*

The *lai* was a Celtic British and Old French poetic genre closely related to the romance. Generally *lais* are much shorter than romances, 600 to 1,000 lines, as opposed to the 3,000 or more lines characteristic of medieval romance, but they treat the same themes of chivalry and courtly love and its vicissitudes. The rhymed verses of the *lai* are filled with magic, marvels, mystery, and fantastical transformations, such as shape shifting from human being to werewolf or from straw to gold, and similar motifs typical of Celtic fairy lore. Such transformations could be punishment for the violation of a taboo or a reward for virtue. The original Breton *lais* are no longer extant. They were composed in a Celtic language related to Welsh and Cornish, which was spoken by fifth- and sixth-century immigrants to northern France who were fleeing the Anglo-Saxons. Breton literature popularized the Celtic-British hero King Arthur, profoundly influencing subsequent Arthurian romance.

The Breton *lais* inspired the famous *Lais of Marie de France*, composed in Anglo-Norman in the 1170s, and Geoffrey Chaucer adopted the style in his exquisite "Franklin's Tale." Usually sung by a minstrel, troubadour, or jongleur, the *lai* was associated with the Old Irish *loid* and the Middle High German courtly love lyric, the *Lied*.

Lyric Poetry

Not all medieval lyrics were love poems, but love as a theme had multiple powerful forms: courtly love, cerebral love, sensual love, sexual love, platonic love, distant love (*amor de longh*), epistolary love declared only in letters, love of woman, love of man, and love of God. The vast corpus of love poetry includes a preponderance of poems meant to be sung. Among the poets of the 10th through 14th centuries, the most prolific professional and semiprofessional love poets were the troubadours, the *trouvères*, the *minnesingers*, and the Italian writers of the *dolce stil nuovo*.

TROUBADOURS

Troubadours were poets, composers, and singers who flourished in the 12th and 13th centuries in the south of France. They wrote in the Provençal language, also called the *Langue d'oc* (from the Provençal word for "yes," in contrast to the northern French language, *Langue d'oïl*). Languedoc was the geographic area south of the Loire River. Troubadour love songs depicted courtly love in an ingenious, mannered, mathematically and metrically complex poetic form. Their repertoire consisted of several subgenres, notably the *alba, canzo, pastorella, sirventes,* and *tenson.*

alba   The *alba* was an especially popular song type. A morning song or dawn song, an *alba* (Provençal, "dawn") signaled the coming of daylight or of a jealous husband, thereby ending illicit lovers' amorous night. Sung by the man or woman, it lamented the arrival of dawn and loss of passion, and sung by a faithful lookout, it warned of danger. The customary *alba* refrain was, Dawn comes! *Et ades sera l'alba.*

canzo   The Provençal troubadour *canzo* was a musical poetic song with six or seven line stanzas in a tripartite metrical scheme. An initial section called the *frons* consisted of two *pedes* (Latin, "feet") followed by a *cauda.* The French trouvere *ballade* and German Minnesinger *bar song* were essentially identical.

pastorella   Another mannered love poem was the *pastorella*, detailing a sexual dalliance between a knight or nobleman and a shepherdess and celebrating country pleasures and erotic delights. If the woman was a willing partner, both exulted in natural sensuality; if she was seduced, she humiliatingly outwitted the man.

sirventes   The *sirventes* were satiric songs lambasting love rivals, enemies, and political events.

tenson   The *tenson* was a poetic debate or a quarrel poem, often an invective full of crude, yet incisively witty personal, social, and literary criticism.

Troubadours flourished in the courts of Queen Eleanor of Aquitane and her daughter Marie of Champagne. Notable poet composers included Count William IX, Bernart de Ventadorn, Marcabru, Jaufre Rudel, Arnaut Daniel, Bertrand de Born, and Peire Vidal.

Female troubadours, called *trobaritz*, included more than 20 intelligent, literate, artistically productive women writers who were active in Occitania, in the south of France. Among them were the countess of Dia, Castelloza, Isabella, Aralais, Garsenda, and many anonymous women who followed and amended the poetic conventions of courtly love. They wrote complicated rhythm schemes, formulaic phrases, strict rhythmic patterns and wonderful wordplays and exquisitely utilized stylistic trappings of the art of mannered passion.

Though stunningly popular in their time and influencing the trouvères in north France, the minnesingers in Germany, and practitioners of the "sweet new style," *dolce stil nuovo*, in Italy, the troubadours and their culture of courtly love were destroyed during the Albigensian Crusade. Heretical Albigensians were attacked between 1208 and 1229, devastating much of southern France and the major Provençal courts. These dualist Christians upheld ideas that profoundly threatened established church dogma. They rejected the material world as an evil creation of the devil, believed the New Testament was an allegory, spurned the sacraments, repudiated the resurrection, denied papal authority, and considered the cross a symbol of Satan's triumph over Christ. (*See* chapter 5, Philosophy and Religion). Pope Innocent III ordered the crusade and Simon of Montfort conducted it with exemplary ferocity.

TROUVÈRES AND THE
DOLCE STIL NUOVO

The trouvères were northern French poets, composers, and singers who wrote in Langue d'oïl and created not only courtly love lyrics but also heroic *chansons de geste*. In Tuscany, imitators of the Provençal troubadour courtly love poems wrote in the *dolce stil nuovo*. Dante in his own lyric cycle the *Vita nuova* dubbed the Provençal-influenced poems the "sweet new style," referring to the works of Guido Guinizelli of Bologna (c. 1230–76) and Guido Cavalcanti of Florence (1255–1300). These poems treated women and courtly, courteous conduct, although Cavalcanti's poems are markedly more pessimistic in tone. Francesco Petrarca (Petrarch) (d. 1374) introduced the dimension of the soul's exploration and the psychological effects of unrequited love in his two lyrical poems "I Trionfi" (Triumphs) and "Il Canzioniere" (The Songbook).

The "sweet new style" was new with respect to the traditional Italian lyric tradition that flourished in the Sicilian school from the 1230s under the impulse of Emperor Frederick II of Sicily. While the Sicilian school was also indebted to the Provençal lyric tradition, important innovations were also made especially by its schoolmaster (*caposcuole*) Giacomo da Lentini (13th century). Da Lentini invented the sonnet, the Sicilian version of the Provençal *canzo*. The sonnet is divided into two parts, each of which has a distinct rhyme: The first are octave rhymes ABABABAB and the second are sextet rhymes CDCDCD. In the same century a northern version of the Sicilian school was founded in Tuscany by Guittone d'Arezzo.

MINNESINGERS

Minnesingers flourished in Germany during the 12th through 14th centuries writing courtly love and practical songs called *Minnelieder*.

The Manessische Liederhandschrift (Manesse Codex), *probably compiled at the request of the Manesse family of Zürich, Switzerland, about 1300, contains 140 collections of love poems organized by the social status of the poets, beginning with Holy Roman Emperor Henry VI. The page shown here portraits Duke Heinrich IV of Schlesien-Breslau. The lozenges of the horse's caparison enclose the letters* AMOR *for this joust of love.* From the *Manessische Liederhandschrift,* German, 14th century, Cod. Pal. Germ. 848, fol. 11. Courtesy of the Bibliothek of the University of Heidelberg, Heidelberg, Germany.

Composers and poets were of noble descent or from the social class called *ministeriales*, knights bound to the service of an overlord or ruler. Their nobility was not based on land holdings and loyalty but rather on administrative skill, as they often served as managers of villages or manors and intellectual administrators at major courts. The *Minnelied*, written in Middle High German, emphasized a knight's adoration of a lady and a woman's passionate yearnings for her lover.

These love songs adhered to the traditional tripartite structure of the *bar form* and troubadour *canzo*. Minnesingers wrote crusading songs, hymns to the Virgin, and political and moralistic songs. Wolfram von Eschenbach wrote brilliant examples of the *Tagelied*, a dawn song comparable to the Provençal *alba*. The *Lied* was a typical courtly love lyric emulating the Provençal *canzo*. One of the greatest minnesingers was Walther von der Vogelweide, who excelled in all lieder forms but was especially accomplished in the satiric *Spruch*, similar to the Provençal *sirventes*.

Neidhart von Ruenthal's courtly love songs of "high love" (*Hohe Minne*) depicted love for a highborn lady, similar to the *domna* of the troubadours. His splendid "low love" (*Niedere Minne*) songs celebrated a lesser, earthier, common love in which the unspoiled, pastoral beautiful woman exuberantly sharing her lips and body welcomed the man to country pleasures. Another song type was a debate between a man and a woman, the *Wechsel*, a subgenre of which was a love message, a declaration of love transmitted through an intermediary, the *Botenlied*.

Other important minnesingers were Hartmann von Aue, Reinmar von Hagenau, Dietmar von Eist, Reinmar del Alta, and Heinrich von Morungen. The most famous Jewish minnesinger was Susskind von Trimburg.

ENGLISH LOVE LYRICS

English love and country life connected in one of the earliest Middle English songs, the delightful welcome to summer, "Sumer is ycumenn in," a charming invitation to seduction, also called "The Cuckoo Song." The refrain celebrating the cuckoo's loud singing confirms the message of cuckolding: Just as the summer birds mate, seeds grow, meadows blow, and buck and bullock couple with their mates, so ought lovers. Still other Middle English love lyrics were derived from Latin hymns to the Virgin Mary. The preeminent chief poet, the archipoeta, of the goliards or wandering poets writing primarily in Latin composed erotic, irreverent poems as well as contemplative, pious, bravura praises of the Virgin Mary. The Goliards' songs were later collected and preserved at the monastery of Benediktbeuern under the title *carmina burana*.

The Frame Tale

The frame tale, sometimes called framed tale, was a narrative structural device in which one overarching or frame story incorporated many smaller otherwise unrelated stories, characters, techniques, and styles. Its roots go back to India and to the Persian fables *Hazar Afsana* (*The Thousand Tales*), which were translated into Arabic in the eighth century and partly inspired the compilation of *The Thousand and One Nights*. Chaucer's *Canterbury Tales* was a splendid example of a frame tale, as were Boccaccio's *Decameron*, Sercambi's *Novella*, and *The Thousand and One Nights*.

In *The Decameron*, a group escaping from the plague assembles in a country house and whiles away the time telling tales to entertain one another. Chaucer's fictional pilgrimage to Canterbury, the shrine of Saint Thomas à Becket, united sundry folk and themes, remarkably diverse language styles and moralities. The ploy of framing disparity allowed writers to violate classical canons of decorum requiring the three unities, of time, place, and style, as well as permitting authors to dramatize the same subject from divergent viewpoints. A frame tale juxtaposed elegant courtly romance with hilarious beast epic with moral sermon with raunchy, exuberant fabliau.

THE CANTERBURY TALES

Chaucer's *Canterbury Tales* exemplified frame tale ingenuities. Pilgrims gathered at the Tabard Inn one April when lively fellowship beckoned them to Canterbury. The group included a Knight; a Squire; a regal Nun with her chaplain, three priests, and spoiled little dogs; a rotund Monk, a hunter who adored fine, fatty foods; a Friar; a Merchant; a Shipman; a young Clerk from Oxford University; a Sergeant of the Law, who sat at table with a wealthy landowner; a Franklin; elaborately costumed Guildsmen (a haberdasher, carpenter, weaver, dyer, and tapestry maker), who ostentatiously had their own Cook; and a Physician, who astrologically determined propitious times to administer gold cordials to his patients. A lusty, deaf cloth weaver, the Wife of Bath, who had married at least five husbands, sat beside a poor town Parson traveling with his brother, a Plowman, who spoke with a Reeve, a grain Miller, an ecclesiastical Summoner, a Pardoner, a Manciple from a law temple, and Chaucer himself. This stunningly diverse fictional social group allowed Chaucer to tell tales consistent with his characters' profession or personality. Splendid humor, language variations, philosophical antitheses, and artistic disjunctures merited John Dryden's description of Chaucer's frame tale as representing "God's plenty" (Dryden 531).

Recurring themes within Chaucer's *Canterbury Tales* provided structural unity within diversity. Husbands and wives, for instance, debated mastery in marriage. Three pilgrims told tales disparate in style but related in subject. "The Wife of Bath's Tale" dramatized the thesis that woman must have mastery over man while the "Clerk's Tale" depicted the antithesis that man should have absolute sovereignty over woman. Synthesis governed the "Franklin's Tale," in which gender relations are balanced, investing power in man and woman equally.

Similarly, *gentilesse*, an inherent nobility of spirit expressed in action, likewise pervaded many tales within Chaucer's frame. Not always associated with noble birth, gentility connoted a generosity of spirit that subjugated one's personal desires to a larger good or a common profit. This intrinsic graciousness also was called *freedom*. Dante in his *Convivio* discussed *gentilezza*, inherent, ethical courtesy displayed in all acts of life.

A related recurring concept was the *troth*, a pledge, promise, and verbal contract necessarily honored, no matter the cost, illogic, or violation of other imperatives, if one subscribed to *gentilesse*. In "The Franklin's Tale," for instance, beautiful Dorigen, importuned by an unwanted, unwelcome student suitor while her beloved merchant husband was away, in annoyed anguish rashly pledged to sleep with the suitor if he made the rocks and boulders disappear from the coastline of Brittany. The lovelorn scholar lavished his tuition money on employing a mighty magician from Italy to create an illusion of a clear coast and triumphantly demanded the pledged love. Who had the most generosity and graciousness of spirit, freedom, and *gentilesse*? Dorigen's husband adored his wife, respected her word, and mournfully assented. She so honored *troth* that even though magic tricked her, she was ready to fulfill word by her body. The young lover, observing such integrity, released Dorigen from her pledge, and the magician, seeing his illusion fail its intended goal, took only half his fee.

Drama and Theater

The pageantry and ceremony of the medieval Christian mass led directly to the development of modern drama as we celebrate it today. From simple tropes, the short dramatic scenes interpolated into Christian liturgy from secular sources, the pomp and ritual of the ecclesiastical mass became increasingly theatrical, instructing the pious in religious dogma and morality and stirring religious fervor. Drama that successfully united the paired opposites of *docere et delectare*, "to instruct and to delight," resulted in the best art. As Chaucer paraphrased Plato in the *Timaeus*, words must be perfect cousins to deeds. Elegant epic characters were expected to speak refined language, but rude, crude boors spouted lascivious obscenity. When too many bawdy, raucous elements were interpolated into the Easter mass liturgy, the church hierarchy expelled these protodramas from the church back to the marketplace where many of the cruder elements originated.

The *Quem quaeritis trope* is the earliest surviving example of medieval drama, a ninth-century manuscript from the monastery at Saint Gall. Its few powerful sentences, chanted or sung antiphonally, dramatize the story of the three Marys, the holy women who first discovered Christ's Resurrection from the sepulchre. The Virgin Mary, Mary Magdalene, and another Mary, Mary Cleophas or Mary Salome, went to Christ's tomb to anoint his body. They see the tombstone rolled back and angels ask them, "Servants of Christ, whom do you seek in the sepulchre?" (Latin, *Quem quaeritis in sepulchro o christicolae?*). The three Marys answer, "Servants of Heaven, we look for Jesus of Nazareth crucified!" (Latin, *Jesum Nazarenus, crucificum, O coelicolae!*).

This dramatic interchange was augmented theatrically with amusing, popular marketplace entertainers called *joculatores*, the heirs of the late Roman itinerant theater, players and entertainers who performed at markets, fairs, and church festivals. Their formulaic characterizations and predictable, amusing actions offered the pleasure of the familiar and a reestablishment of the idea of order in the world, *ordo mundi*. Stock characters included the ointment seller (the *unguentarius*) and the boasting soldier (the *miles gloriosus*). Another stock character, the superannuated lover (the *senex amans*), with his young, sexually exuberant wife also was inserted into sacred drama, as was the *unguentarius*'s shrewish, talkative wife, called the *gossip*. Combining the sacred and profane, the short Latin *Quem queritis trope* influenced the development of the Passion Play and miracle, mystery, and morality plays.

PASSION PLAY

A Passion Play was a drama about Christ's suffering, or Passion; his crucifixion; and his resurrection. The German Oberammergau Passion Play still is popular in the 21st century. The medieval Passion Plays dealt with some, many, or all of Christ's sufferings culminating in his crucifixion, through which Christians were redeemed. Usually complete with lugubrious detail, most Passion Plays included the instruments of Christ's Passion, such as nails, crown of thorns, lance, sponge, scourge, pillar, hammer, rope, and dice. Other customary props in the play were a portrait of Judas, who betrayed Jesus; a depiction of the hands that struck Christ; a representation of the rooster that crowed after Peter denied Christ; and a facsimile of Saint Veronica's veil, or *vernicle*, the holy relic that retained a likeness of Christ's face after Veronica wiped the blood and sweat from it on the road to Calvary.

The Passion Play symbolically recreated Christ's march to crucifixion on the path or road of anguish, the Via Dolorosa. Fourteen Stations of the Cross identified significant events along this perilous road. The Franciscans particularly popularized this road to Golgotha along which Jesus carried his cross. Customarily, the passion play enacted some or all of the 14 Stations of the Cross: (1) Christ's condemnation to death; (2) Christ's receiving the cross to carry; (3) Christ's first fall, of the three times he staggers under the cross's weight; (4) Christ's meeting his mother, the

Virgin Mary; (5) Simon of Cyrene's carrying the cross; (6) Saint Veronica's offering her veil, which becomes her *vernicle*; (7) Christ's second fall; (8) Jesus' meeting the woman of Jerusalem; (9) Christ's third stagger; (10) the stripping naked of Jesus; (11) the nailing to the cross; (12) the Crucifixion and Christ's dying; (13) the descent from the cross, the Pietà; (14) Christ's burial and entombment. Some Passion Plays also included moments from the childhood and early life history of Jesus Christ that foreshadowed his crucifixion.

MYSTERY PLAYS

Mystery plays were dramas on biblical subjects. The term *mystery* was initially thought to refer to God or Christ's intercession in the human world such as at the Creation, the Fall of mankind, the Flood, the Crucifixion, and the Redemption of humanity. Scholars now agree that the genre takes its name from the Latin *mysterium*, meaning "occupation or craft, art, or trade." Members of the same *mysterie* were guildsmen practicing the same craft, such as weavers, dyers, and bakers. Many mystery plays were organized into dramatic cycles, ranging from the Creation in the Old Testament to the Day of Judgment depicted in the Apocalypse of the New Testament. The English Wakefield, York, and Chester plays were written and performed by craft guildsmen who staged the dramas on movable pageant wagons. Their productions were portable and moved from town to town, allowing the theater to go to the audience rather than the pious to the proscenium. The anonymous 12th-century *Jeu d'Adam* was the most popular of the French mysteries.

MIRACLE PLAYS

Miracle plays were dramas about religious subjects drawn from Scripture and hagiographical sources that narrated the life and death of the saints. Miracle plays dramatized wondrous deeds, spectacular devotion, lugubriously detailed martyrdoms, and the meticulously described virtues of those who had imitated and suffered for Christ. The *Jeu de Saint-Nicholas* (*The Play of Saint Nicholas*) was written in the 13th century by the French poet Jean Bodel. Bodel's participation in Saint Louis's crusade to Egypt inspired this crusader drama, which ends with the conversion of the Muslims to Christianity after the miraculous intervention of Saint Nicholas. In the same century the Parisian Rutebeuf wrote the "Miracle of Theophilus," dramatizing the popular legend of an officer of the church of Adana in Cilicia who was relieved of his duties and bartered his soul to the devil in order to regain his post. A miraculous intervention of the Virgin Mary releases his soul from the devil's grasp. The Miracles of Our Lady, plays depicting the miraculous intervention of Mary, dominated religious theater in the 14th and 15th centuries. The tale of Saint Nicholas and His Three Balls, persisting in the modern golden globes arranged in the modified triangle of the pawnbroker's sign, described Saint Nicholas of Myra's bags of gold as dowry for each of three deserving poor girls.

MORALITY PLAYS

Contemporaneous with the mystery, passion, and miracle plays were the popular morality plays consisting of allegorical dramas in which personified virtues and vices competed for the hero's soul and played out their battle on the field of the mind. In the dramatic 15th-century morality play *Everyman*, the eponymous hero is summoned by Death. Of all his companions, Beauty, Kindred, Worldly Goods, and Good Deeds, only the latter fulfils his promise to go with the hero and be his guide, standing at his side, even on the very last steps of his final voyage to death and judgment. Other moralities included the *Castle of Perseverance, Mundus et Infans*, and early Faust plays in which an intelligent, studious hero sold his soul to the devil for short-lived youth and love.

OTHER DRAMATIC ENTERTAINMENT

Other dramatic and dance entertainments included the *Moresca, morris dances, maypoles, mumming plays, mattachins, masquerades*, and *masques*. (*See* chapter 10 on music and dance.)

Also crossing the boundaries between drama and music were the *Singspiele*, German for "song play." A dramatic music text was partly prose, partly verse, partly spoken, and partly sung. The French dramatist Adam de la Halle (c. 1240–87) wrote his charming *Robin and Marion* (*Le Jeu de Robin et Marion*), one of the earliest song plays. Called *chant fable* in French, this dramatic genre also included the delightful 13th-century play *Aucassin et Nicolette* (author unknown), which also combined prose, verse, declamation, and song.

Instruction Books

Our modern bookstores' impressive array of "how to" books finds its parallel in the medieval instruction manuals that taught people how to live and how to act according to an ideal type, often a religious or secular hero. Instruction books were startlingly diverse texts composed to educate people in ethics and morality, in working in crafts and professions, in personal behavior, and in refining the mind and the soul.

MIRROR OF PRINCES

Mirrors of princes were instruction books for responsible, courtly, humane rulers. Not only dedicated to those who literally were princes, the mirrors taught leadership to the nobility and etiquette to all who wished to imitate the noble. Originally derived from the classic treatise of Isocrates called *Ad Nicoclem* written in 374 B.C.E., this common literary genre exercised the minds and pens of Neoplatonist thinkers such as John of Salisbury, who wrote *Policraticus*, and William Perrault, Hugh of Fleury, and Aegidius Romanus. Mirrors of princes were popular in various versions and translations, serving people born to the court and nobility, and townsmen and dreamers imitating habits of the courtly.

THE ART OF LOVE

Seduction manuals, treatises on the art of love, and analyses of the art of courtly love pleased large numbers of readers both secular and clerical. Many of these medieval manuals were entitled *The Art of Love*, based on Ovid's Latin *Ars amatoria*. In the 12th century Andreas Capellanus wrote *De Amore libri tres* (*The Art of Courtly Love*), a book of three volumes that explained the nature and definition of courtly love, the rules of behavior in a courtly love affair, and the "rejection of love," or why courtly love should never be practiced. *The Art of Courtly Love* included wonderful descriptions of amorous etiquette, sexual politics, practical love lore, and techniques of psychological manipulation. Courtly love was always adulterous and initiated by the male lover. The married beloved or *domna* almost invariably was of a higher social rank than her lover and demanded from him the self-sacrificing "service of love," called *service d'amour* in French and *Minnedienst* in German. The courtly lover owed a double allegiance to his beloved and to God, or to the god of love.

Capellanus discussed in detail the stratagems of secrecy needed to present the public scandal of adultery. He suggested the use of code names and employment of a trusted servant to serve as the lovers' go-between. Alternatively, messages could be entrusted to a canine companion to carrying between lovers or console the grief of lovers separated. The literary motif of the romance dog companion derived from the friendly beast guides to the otherworld found in Greek mythology. In the Tristan legend, for instance, the canine companions were named Petit Cru and Husdan. Other sex manuals included recipes for aphrodisiacs and advice on precoital play.

Depictions of courtly love appear in Chaucer's "Wife of Bath's Tale." In that lusty story, a noble knight of King Arthur's court, Gawain, raped a maiden. Queen Guinevere as judge of the Court of Love imposed upon him the challenge of getting the correct answer to the question on mastery: "What do women most desire?" Incorrectly answering that question would cause Gawain to suffer decapitation. His answer that women desire mastery over men satisfied the court and saved his head.

HUNTING MANUALS

Hunting manuals were instruction books for both the ceremony and sport of hunting, including the methods of tracking, chasing, killing, and carving prey. Beyond their didactic purpose, these treatises provided the medieval aristocracy with the practical means to imitate the heroes of chivalric romance, who were often depicted engaging in hunting. Renowned hunting treatises were written by Gaston Phebus (1331–91) and King Frederick II of Sicily (1194–1250).

Many such hunt manuals included sections on falconry, the elaborate ceremonial technique of hunting game with birds of prey such as falcons and hawks. Well versed in Arabic, Frederick II wrote a famous book on falconry or hawking, *The Art of Hunting with Birds* (*Tractatus de arte venandi cum avibus*), which was based on an Arabic treatise on the topic.

Birds were trained to sit on the wrists, hoodwinked and held by gesses, and took flight at the sound of ceremonial musical calls. Falconry was as much a courtly exercise and entertainment as a practical acquisition technique for kitchen fowl. In addition to falconry, some hunting manuals included long sections on animal husbandry and veterinary science. Others depicted the medical uses of animals in the treatment and cure of human disease and injury. A prime example of this type of book is the *Historia Animalium* (*History of Animals*) by the Swiss naturalist Conrad Gessner (1516–65), which summarized all classical and contemporary knowledge about four-legged animals, amphibians, fowl and other birds, and fish and marine life. Magnificently illustrated, it was one of the earliest printed books. Abbreviated versions of the work were subsequently published by Gessner and other authors, including Rudolph Huësslin's *Vogel-Buch*, relating to medical uses of birds; the *Animal Book* (*Tier-Buch*) of Conrad Forer, which was a general study of mammals; and the *Fisch-Buch*, which treated marine life.

Gaston Phebus, count of Foix between 1387 and 1391, wrote a wonderful hunting guide, *Les Déduits de la chasse* (*The Hunting Book*), which included excellent advice on caring for hunting dogs. Maintaining that inactivity was deadly to the dogs, he recommended that the grooms take them out of their kennels each morning and night and run them around the enclosures. With curry combs, brushes, and straw, a good groom would prepare his hounds for presentation, walking them on leashes and picking the best laxative herbs to keep the animals' intestinal systems well regulated. If any dog suddenly became mute, debilitated, or sleepy; or lost its appetite, slavered, was weak on his legs; or if his bark was hoarse, then he might be suffering from rabies, which would be fatal. That dog's bite would endanger people. Therefore Gaston Phebus advised isolating the hound and using particular herbs and medications to cure him.

Long, tiring hunts subjected dogs to injuries of eye, ear, throat, and paws. If a dog had swollen paws, Gaston Phebus recommended soaking the paws in a vessel of warm water with leaves of lavender, rosemary, and chamomile. But special care was always to be lavished on dislocated shoulders, best handled by orthopedists and bonesetters, on broken limbs, best put in harnesses, and on protecting the dog's sexual organs.

Yet other hunting manuals were dedicated specially to the music that accompanied hunting. Because some medieval horns played only a single pitch, the talent of the hunting horn player depended upon rhythm, the length of the note, and the intensity of sound. Special names for particular hunting calls included the *mote*, blown at the uncoupling of the hounds. The *rechete* was blown to recall dogs or to urge them to the kill. The *mane* and *pryse* rhythmically suggested the animal's calm when prepared in the banquet hall. Harmonious hunting preceded healthful eating.

Hunting music inspired particular forms of song in which the music of the ceremonial pursuit of the animal was transformed into the pursuit of a desired lover. Therefore hunting music inspired such important poetic and musical forms as the *chasse*, *caccia*, and *catch*, early forms of polyphony (*see* chapter 10 on music and dance). Love allegories with variations upon the title "The Hunt of Love" used the language of the chase for depicting the art of courtly love. Poetry and song expressed passion for the beautiful woman or magnificent man by means of hunting rhetoric and hunting horn music. Fabliaux writers and the lusty devotees of *amor de con* (Provençal, "love of sexual intercourse") particularly delighted in exploiting the connections between sexual pursuit and consummation and the art of hunting. The noble Provençal troubadour William IX, duke of

Aquitaine and count of Poitiers (1071–1126), suggested in his poetry that love of sexual dalliance, *amor de con*, explained his own and other men's inexorable, insatiable, and intemperate love proclivities.

DANCE MANUALS

The *dance of love*, or *love's old dance*, was a euphemism for sexual dalliance. However, most dance manuals seriously taught the fine art of moving gracefully through space. Dance masters at major courts, such as Domenico da Piacenza (1390–1470), Antonio Cornazano (c. 1430–85), and Guglielmo Ebreo (1425–80) wrote important treatises on the art of the dance emphasizing the ways in which dance integrated physique, emotional control, and the art of living beautifully. Da Piacenza wrote the *De arte saltandi et choreas ducendi* (*The Book on the Art of Dancing*) circa 1455 while serving in the court of Milan and is the declared master of Guglielmo and Cornazano. The *Trattato dell'arte del ballo di Guglielmo Ebreo Pesarese* (*The Book on the Art of Dancing* by Guglielmo Ebreo) meticulously describes the dance steps of 17 *bassadanza*, a slow stately dance in one tempo featuring low as opposed to high steps, and 17 *ballo* dances. The *ballo* (pl. *balli*) is a lively, dramatic dance of multiple tempos for a prescribed number of male and female dancers. Cornazano devotes nearly half of his *Libro dell' arte del danzare* (*The Book on the Art of Dance*) to discussing the qualities needed to dance, including memory, measure, spirit, variety, and an adequate use of space. The remainder provides description of various dance forms, including *bassedanza* and *balli*.

INSTRUCTION BOOKS FOR WOMEN

Instruction books for secular women taught the proper decorum of behavior according to social status and religious condition. Male and female

One of the Seven Virtues, Temperance, along with Faith, Hope, Charity, Prudence, Fortitude, and Justice, was depicted as an elegant, learned woman. Like most allegorical figures, she personified an abstract idea and possessed an identifying attribute. Temperance, representing moderation, equilibrium, timing, and balance, had as her symbolic identifying device a mechanical clock. Just as Justice was portrayed wielding her scales, Temperance was associated with the time-measuring technological marvel of gears and escapement mechanisms, which in turn exemplified perfect, active heavenly order. Fiovanni da Dondi, a physician, astronomer, and clockmaker, created a magnificent clockwork in 1348 to measure hours, minutes, and planetary movements, representing the harmonies of the microcosm, the human body, with the macrocosm, the heavenly spheres in their orbits and rotations. Here Christine de Pizan teaches the power of temperance to four listening women. Her geared clock with an hour hand and a minute hand is surmounted by a bell for ringing the hours for prayer, for markets, and for life's ceremonial feasts. From Christine de Pizan's *Othea*, 15th century. Courtesy of the Bodleian Library, Oxford University, Oxford.

religious hermits attempting a life in imitation of Christ withdrew from the world. Some wrote instruction manuals for others to emulate them, such as the late 12th-century instruction book for female hermits called *Ancrene Wisse or Ancrene Riwle, The Anchoress's Rule.* The prolific 15th-century writer Christine de Pizan wrote several instruction books for women that touched upon all areas of public and private life, including *Le Livre de Trois Virtues* (*Book of the Three Virtues*) or (*The Treasury of the City of Ladies*), and her most acclaimed treatise, *Le Livre de la Cité des Dames* (*The Book of the City of Ladies*). De Pizan's writings responded to the misogynist representations of women as schemers of dubious morality that pervaded some courtly love literature, most notoriously the allegorical *Roman de la Rose* by the French author Jean de Meun (discussed later). The same countermisogynist impulse to reassert the nobility and Christian morality of women inspired the Spanish Augustinian monk and preacher Fray Martin of Córdoba (d. c. 1476) to write his *Jardín de Nobles Donzellas* (*The Garden of Noble Ladies*) and the Spanish Franciscan friar and preacher Francesc Eiximenis (1327–1409) to write his *Llibre de les Dones* (*The Book of Women*). The latter work spelled out the norms of living a Christian life according to the four social categories of women—religious, maiden, married, and widow.

ARS MORIENDI

Whereas the mission of the modern institution of the hospice is to allow the terminally ill to die with dignity, the medieval instruction book on *ars moriendi* ("the art of dying") taught the pious Christian how to prepare his or her soul for death. A devotional text and instruction book, the *ars moriendi* prepared a person for a model Christian death and a blissful passing to the next life. Teaching virtues as useful for living as for dying, such as patience in adversity, the *ars moriendi* were illustrated with depictions of vices to warn the reader of what the guilty soul would endure. An impatient patient in a Dutch *ars moriendi* dated 1465 extended his bony leg from under his bed cover and violently kicked his medical attendants, knocked over his medication table, and behaved fiendishly, egged on by a small devil hiding beneath his bed, ready to snatch his soul and carry it to hell the instant he released it at death.

Pictorial didactics included sculptured funerary books, the *transi*, or transitory, *tombs*. A *transi tomb* was a sarcophagus topped by a carved portrait of a corpse in a state ranging from peaceful repose to repulsive skeletal decay. The tomb was meant to be a *memento mori* (Latin, "reminder of death"). Early *transi tombs* appealed to the living to pray for the souls of the dead. Later medieval *transi tombs* became dramatic symbols for the wealthy and powerful for depicting death as resolving all conflict between pride and humility, earthly wealth and holy poverty.

Memento mori graced literature, art, and even personal jewelry, as in a bracelet's pendant charm in the form of an exquisitely carved ivory or boxwood skull. Thought neither morbid nor lugubrious, it was a reminder in the midst of frivolity that life's higher purposes or time's shortness must temper joy in earthly delights. Therefore in depictions of the dance of death, as in Jacob Meydenbach's 15th-century *Der Toten Tantz*, from Mainz, a skeleton viol player snatched a young lover, while another skeleton playing a cornet with a grave worm extruded from it regaled unwilling listeners. Once Death was ready to dance with someone, neither social status, moral virtue, age, wealth, nor political position could overpower or prevent it.

OTHER INSTRUCTION BOOKS

Medieval writers believing in the perfectibility of humankind taught by means of instruction books how best to live and die. A medieval reader could learn how to play chess. Performing magic required a *clavicula*, a small key or short treatise such as the *Clavicle of Moses* or *Clavicula Salomonis Regis* (*The Key of Solomon the King*). The means for stimulating and preserving good health could be learned from medical manuals of Salerno and the other hygiene and dietary texts. (*See* chapter 7, Medicine, Science, and Technology.) Preachers learned the finer points of composing and delivering a successful sermon from the *ars praedicandi*, while pious religious and lay persons learned the best way to pray to God by consulting the *ars orandi* ("art of praying") manuals.

Warfare treatises and military instruction books taught martial ideals as well as practical advice on weaponry ranging from swords to siege engines (*see* chapter 4, Warfare and Weapons). Ingenious mechanical military devices designed by the 14th-century physician and technologist Guido da Vigevano included catapults with prefabricated, portable, and multipurpose parts; paddle wheel boats; towers utilizing structural iron; and armored fighting wagons powered by crankshafts or windmills.

Epitoma de rei militaris (*A Summary of Military Matters*) by the Roman writer Flavius Vegetius inspired important military instrument design and strategy in the Middle Ages and influenced the 14th-century military engineer Konrad Keyser in writing his remarkable instruction manual *Bellifortis* on how to make weapons with multiple cannons. The prolific French woman author Christine de Pizan also drew extensively from the writings of Vegetius in composing her medieval "best-seller" on chivalry, *Livre de fais d' armes et de chivalries*, the *Book of Deeds of Arms and Chivalry*.

EXEMPLA

The *exemplum* is a brief didactic and moralizing tale that commonly was incorporated in religious and secular medieval literature in order to instruct the audience in proper conduct in an entertaining way. *Exempla* stem from diverse sources, notably *Aesop's Fables* and similar literature by other classical writers, Jewish exempla and haggadic literature, and Arabic folktales. The Spanish Jewish rabbi formerly known as Moses Sefardi who converted to Christianity in 1106, taking the name of Petrus Alfonsus, is recognized as a key figure responsible for the transmission of the Jewish and Arabic sources into Christian Europe. His *Disciplina clericalis* (*Ecclesiastical Discipline*), a collection of moralizing tales to guide the clergy, drew extensively on Jewish and Arabic sources and became a standard text for clerical instruction throughout Western Europe. Another Spanish author, Don Manuel of Castile (1283–1349), wrote the immensely popular *Libro de los exemplos del Conde Lucanor et de Patronio*. The *exempla* are recounted in the form of a conversation between the protagonist, Conde Lucanor, and his spiritual and moral adviser, Patronio, who provides him advice on how to act wisely.

An important number of exempla compilations were assembled in a clerical milieu to be used by preachers throughout the Latin West. Significant Spanish contributions include the *Libro de los Exenplos por A. B. C.* (*The Book of Exempla by A. B. C.*), compiled in 1435 by the archdeacon of Valderas in northern Spain, the 15th-century *Libro de los gatos* (*The Book of Cats*) and the 13th-century *Liber Exemplorum ad usum praedicantium saecula XIII compositus a quodam Fratre Minore Anglico de Provincia Hiberniae* ("The Book of Exempla for the Use of Preaching in the 13th Century, Compiled by the Friars Minor of the Iberian Peninsula"), the latter two anonymous. The *Exempla* from the "*Sermones vulgares*" of the Dominican preacher and inquisitor Jacques de Vitry (d. 1260) and the *Tractatus de diversis materiis praedicabilibus* (Treatise of diverse materials to be used for preaching) by the Dominican inquisitor Étienne de Bourbon (d. 1256) were especially designed for preaching against heresy. The *Noveletti, esempi morali e apologhi* ("Novelettes, Moral Exempla and Apologia"), by the charismatic 15th-century Italian preacher Bernadino of Siena (d. 1444), and the *Dialogus Miraculorum* (*Dialogue of Miracles*) by the monk Caesar of Heisterbach of Germany (1180 to before 1250) were also widely used by preachers across western Europe.

Beast Literature

Medieval affections for animals are evident in the copious hunting manuals and treatises on animal husbandry. The bestiary, the beast fable, and the beast epic were popular literary forms among all social classes at all levels of literacy. Beast literature pressed animal lore and natural history into the service of morality.

Domestic animals included such exotic breeds as monkeys. Gracing the shoulders of acrobats and entertainers in town squares and the laps of court ladies, monkeys were so commonplace that even toll collectors on bridges who solicited money from each person and for all merchandise allowed monkeys to pass free. On the toll bridges of Paris, a 14th-century merchant crossing a bridge with monkeys to sell paid four coins. But if the monkeys were pets for amusement, no toll was charged. In fact, monkeys performing before the toll guard enabled their keeper and everything that he carried to pass free.

BESTIARY

The *bestiary* was an unnatural natural history derived in part from an anonymous second-century work called the *Physiologus*, a didactic text describing characteristics of beasts while imparting moral or religious teachings. For instance, the fox is fraudulent and ingenious, duping others to feed him. Likewise the devil craftily deceives the unwary. Another tale unites bears and Jesus Christ. The mother bear licks into shape her bear cubs born blind and requiring her necessary to finish them. She transforms the inchoate bear into an actual animal, her caressing, creative tongue completing the bear shaping. Likewise, Christianity cares for Christians, truly refining and completing humankind.

Wildly extravagant beasts were created by conflation of travelers' reports about exotic local animals, such as the *camelelephantoleopard*. The elephant was thought the most pious of beasts because it kneeled. The salamander in those bestiaries following Pliny and Aristotle depicted a lizardlike amphibian that both withstood fire and fought it. Its dramatic poisonous properties enabled it to kill at once. If a salamander climbed a fruit tree, all fruits would instantly become infected with its venom, killing anyone who ate them. A salamander falling into a well poisoned it with its powerful toxin, slaying any who drank from the well. The salamander was common in the iconography of evil.

The caladrius bird was often depicted in bestiaries and in medical manuscripts. It also appeared in romances of Alexander the Great, who found these exquisite white birds at the court of Xerxes. Considered a prognosticator of death, the caladrius bird was taken to the hospital bed of patients. If the bird turned its face away, it predicted death. If the bird gazed at the ill person, the patient would recover. Its gaze also was said to cure jaundice. In the *Physiologus* the caladrius typified Jesus Christ. Another important inspiration of medieval bestiaries was the *Etymologiae* (Etymologies) of the Spanish archbishop Isidore of Seville (560–636), whose vast encyclopedic compendium of all knowledge was the standard reference throughout medieval Latin Europe. Many bestiaries were anonymous; however, some of the

most significant surviving examples by known authors include two French works, *Bestiare* of Pierre de Beauvais (d. 1475) and *Le Bestiare divin* of Guillaume le Clerc of Normandy (13th century); a Latin text of English origin, the *Bestiarius*, which was composed sometime between 1400 and 1425 and is attributed to a woman named Ann Walshe; and the 12th-century *Bestiare* of Philippe de Thaon, a Norman writer who composed the text in Anglo-Norman verse. Guillaume le Clerc and Ann Walshe consciously followed the classification scheme of information devised by Isidore of Seville, while Philippe de Thaon drew mostly from the *Physiologus*.

BEAST FABLES

Beast fables were meticulously crafted short stories or poems in which human foibles and vices were examined through the antics and actions of animals. At the end of the tale, a moral conveyed the wise message in a short pithy sentence. Beast fables were meant to teach by entertaining. Sometimes lavishly illustrated, fables were traceable to the great Greek collection of Aesop, collected in Latin in the first century by Phaedrus, and written by numerous known and unknown writers including the great French aristocrat Marie de France.

Consider Marie de France's rooster in her fable "The Fox and the Rooster," taken from her collection of *Fabliaux* (discussed later). A rooster was up on a dunghill singing. A fox came up to him and flattered him saying he had "never seen such a fine bird" except for his father who sang better because he closed his eyes. To which the rooster replied, "I can do the same." The fox then seized the rooster and carried him away to the forest. As the fox crossed the field all the shepherds and their dogs ran after him. Seizing his opportunity, the rooster said, "Go on, tell them that I'm yours and you'll never let me go!" But when the fox tried to speak, the rooster leapt out of his mouth, the fox then cursed his mouth for speaking when he should have been silent. The rooster replied, "I should do the same and curse the eyes that closed when they should have watched and been alert." Moral: Fools all speak when they should be quiet and hold their tongues when they should speak. (*The Fables of Marie de France*, trans. M. L. Martin, 1994. Available online. "Marie de France. Fable 60." URL: http://home.earthlink.net/~dianska/fable60.htm.)

BEAST EPIC

The beast epic was a popular satiric story utilizing language, episodes, and action suitable to classical epic but voiced and performed by animals. Beast epics achieved double mockery of the epic's high-flown subjects and precious style and of human foibles, follies, and vices. Traceable also to the traditions of Aesop, Phaedrus, the Eastern fables of *Bidpai*, and the 12th-century *Disciplina clericalis* (*Ecclesiastical Discipline*) by the Spanish theologian Petrus Alfonsus (d. 1110), beast epics included the 12th-century *Le Roman de Renart* (*The Romance of Reynard the Fox*), Heinrich de Glichezare's *Reinhart Fuchs*, and the many stories of Ysengrimus, the Wolf. Chaucer included a beast epic in the *Canterbury Tales*, the "Nun's Priest's Tale." The *Disciplina clericalis* was especially influential, having been translated into several languages and diffused throughout Europe. As noted, the author, a Jewish rabbi originally named Moses Sefardi who converted to Christianity in 1106, drew extensively on Arabic didactic sources and is responsible for introducing Christian Europe to fables of Eastern origin, such as *Bidpai*. The moralizing intent of these works made them especially popular among preachers, who incorporated them into their sermons.

Riddle

A popular, ancient literary game, a riddle gave a metaphoric clue to an object's or idea's identity without naming it. A riddle's intellectual delight was in its personification and paradox, its startling symmetry of word applicable in two opposing realms, reality and language. In the remarkable eighth-century Anglo-Saxon *Exeter Book*, 95 riddles include such commonplace subjects as a sword, shield, badger, cuckoo, storm, Moon, onion, and key. Riddle 45 is typical: "A moth ate songs—wolfed words! That seemed a weird dish—that a worm should swallow dumb thief in the dark, the songs of a man, his chants of glory, their place of strength. That thief-guest was no wiser for having swallowed words." (The Riddles from the *Exeter Book*. Available online. URL: http://www.kenyon.edu/AngloSaxonRiddles/texts.htm.)

Usually ingenious and containing *gnomic*, sententious proverbial sayings, riddles both taught and pleased.

Kenning

The kenning, the Anglo-Saxon and Old Germanic poetic technique of describing something without naming it, was related to the riddle. Two or more major qualities conjoined in a kenning described the unknown element. The ocean was the whale's road. A high-prowed sailing ship was the foamy-necked floater. The kenning for a well-wrought sword was hammer-leavings.

Fabliaux

Rude, crude, lewd tales, *fabliaux* depicted the adventures of ebullient philanderers, voluptuous women, and clever, bold, and bawdy wives of sexually senescent men. Witty and wily fabliaux women often cuckolded their elderly husbands, stock characters called the *senex amans*. The fabliaux wife sported with a sexually athletic young lover, sometimes a student. Lascivious clerics also were important fabliaux lovers of willing women congregants.

The fabliaux woman was the opposite of courtly love's *domna*, highborn, imperious, capricious inspiration for troubadour love from afar and service of love. The fabliaux woman not only willingly indulged in sex but initiated the wildest dances of love and celebrated her own sensuality.

Customarily the fabliaux were anonymous; however, the *Fabliaux* of Marie de France is one notable exception. Most likely their writers were learned, courtly men and women who delighted in the gossip and gusto of the marketplace and country bedroom.

Allegorical Writings

The animals in the beast literature that allegorize human vices and virtues represent one facet of the medieval penchant for allegorical writing. Medieval allegory finds its origins in the tradition of biblical interpretation that aimed to reconcile the Old Testament and New Testament texts. There were four types of allegorical interpretation: literal, typological, tropological, and anagogical. A literal interpretation understands the text at face value; there is no underlying or hidden meaning. The typological interpretation explains the persons and events of the Old Testament as figures or "types" that prefigure the events surrounding Christ as told in the New Testament. The tropological or moral interpretation reveals the moral lesson that should guide present conduct. Finally, the anagogical interpretation serves as a warning of the end of time and the last judgment. Second only to the Bible was the remarkable fifth-century allegory by the Roman poet Prudentius (d. c. 1413) called *Psychomachia*, which personified the Seven Deadly Sins and other abstract ideas later important to medieval literature and art. In this work allegory was "mind battle," a *psychomachia*, a war within the mind in which conflicting ideas struggled for the individual's personal choice.

DREAM VISION

Among the most significant genres of allegorical literature is the dream vision. The *Roman de la Rose*, Dante Alighieri's *Divine Comedy*, and the wonderful alliterative revival poems called *Pearl* and *Piers Plowman* are prime examples. Most of the characters in these works are allegorical or allegories, personifications of abstract ideas, vivifying, intensifying, and augmenting meaning. Almost every medieval dream vision one way or another was traceable to the startlingly influential fifth-century Roman author Macrobius, who wrote a commentary on Cicero's *Dream of Scipio* describing a theory of dreams, their causes, and effects. In the typical dream vision, a person fell asleep and dreamed a vision of past, present, or future love; religion; or politics. Usually a fictional persona dreamed the dream in which the author spoke as himself, using the familiar first-person singular tense in order to create verisimilitude.

The *Roman de la Rose*, a 13th-century poem written by Guillaume de Lorris circa 1230 and later amplified by Jean de Meun, relates the dream of a courtier who wants to win the affection of his ladylove, the Rose. He dreams that he is led into the garden of Pleasure by the Lusty Lady. He dances the dance of Time and is guided by Happiness, Love, Wealth, and Generosity. To win the Rose he must seek the help of Hope, Pleasant Thoughts, Charming Looks, and Sweet Words. The allegorical characters personify the ideals of courtly love. The second part of the poem challenges the lofty picture of courtly love and introduces elements of danger: Danger, Shame, Fear, and Death. In the end, the forces of Love overcome these dangers and the courtier wins the love of the Rose. This was one of the most popular allegorical poems in the Middle Ages; however, some of the female allegories were deemed misogynist by the aforementioned Christine de Pizan, who wrote her manuals of instructions for ladies as a reaction to the work.

In Dante's sublime *Divine Comedy*, Dante depicted himself voyaging under the guidance of Virgil to hell and to purgatory, and under the direction of his ladylove, Beatrice to heaven, respectively, in the three books of *Inferno*, *Purgatorio*, and *Paradiso*. Dante's guides Virgil and Beatrice are themselves allegories, the first representing human reason, and the second representing human race enlightened by revelation. This allegorical dream of the afterlife takes place during Easter Week, beginning on Holy Thursday, the eve of Christ's death and impending Resurrection. Virgil first guides Dante through the nine circles of hell, imagined in concentric circles with the innermost reserved for Satan. Each circle is inhabited by a category of persons and Dante is shown their fate. For instance, the first circle, limbo, is inhabited by the unbaptized and virtuous pagans who do not know Christ. They are condemned to exclusion from heaven. The sixth circle is inhabited by heretics, who are trapped eternally in blazing tombs, while the seventh circle is inhabited by those who did all manner of violence against their fellows or God. Among them are the blasphemers and sodomites, who are condemned to burn in a flaming desert. The ninth circle is reserved for the malicious sinners, such as the sowers of discord, the prophet Muhammad among them, who are condemned to be eternally ripped apart.

Fourteenth-century image of Dante and Virgil at the top of Purgatory, from Dante's Divine Comedy
Giraudon/Art Resource.

Dante and Virgil escape from the abode of hell before dawn on Easter Sunday and enter purgatory, an imposing mountain with seven terraces. Similarly to hell, each level represents one of the seven deadly sins and the means of expiating them is revealed. Thus, the first terrace, the sin of pride, must be purged by carrying heavy weights on the back. The second terrace, envy, must be expurgated by having the eyes sewn shut and wearing sackcloth. The third terrace, wrath, is purged by walking through fetid smoke. Sloth, the fourth terrace, must be expiated by continually running, while avarice, the fifth terrace, is overcome by prostrating on the ground. The sixth terrace, gluttony, is expurgated by fasting from food and drink, while the seventh terrace, lust, is purged by burning in flames.

The summit of the mountain of purgatory leads to the Garden of Paradise. Here Dante takes leave of his guide, Virgil, who as a pagan is barred from entering heaven. Dante's beloved Beatrice accompanies him through the heavenly bodies—the Moon, planets, and stars—until he reaches heaven. There Beatrice becomes almost like another Mary, interceding on his behalf so that he can obtain the vision of Christ and Mary and the realm of Empyrean Heaven, where he is face to face with the Almighty. This dazzling allegorical poem, composed in three-line rhyming iambic stanzas called *terza rima*, intricately linked stanza to stanza (ABA, BCB, CDC, DED) and though widely imitated was unequaled.

The *Piers Plowman*, an apocalyptic allegorical narrative composed in the late 14th century by the English author William Langland (d. c. 1385), stands second only to Chaucer's *The Canterbury Tales* in popularity. It relates the vision of a humble layman, a plowman called Will, and his search for Christ and the way to live a proper Christian life. The narrator has a series of eight visions in which he seeks out allegorical characters, such as the "Quest for Saint Truth" and "the Quest for Righteous Living" (Dowel), and is guided by the allegorized Reason, Conscience, and Alma, among others. Charity, the highest virtue, is planted like a tree in Man by God, and the Piers Plowman is its caretaker. Some of the visions reflect contemporary criticism of the clergy, such as in the Fifth Vision, when Anima (Soul) shows him that the friars who beg are not imitating Christ—they are merely lazy—and the corrupt clergy are likened to debased coinage. Also, in the eighth and final vision of the coming of the Antichrist the clergy are shown following the Antichrist and scorning Conscience and the Cardinal Virtues in exchange for wealth. Other visions reveal the anti-Semitism of 14th-century England, as when the Jews send a blind man to stab the crucified Christ with a spear. At the end of the vision Piers Plowman defeats Pride with the help of Grace.

Chronicles

The two great institutions of the Christian Middle Ages, the church and the monarchy, devoted special effort to recording the key events and persons of history, with special emphasis on the history of ruling dynasties, ecclesiastical rulers and religious orders, and the documentation of the Crusades. A sense of religious mission pervaded even the secular historical chronicles. Court historians located the reigning dynasty in a timeline stemming from the genesis of the world, with the kings portrayed as the heirs of biblical heroes. Similarly, crusader historians depicted events as happening at the hand of God. Chronicle writing was practiced among the Irish, the Anglo-Normans, the English, the French, the Iberians, the Danish, the Germans.

In his *Chronique* the French chronicler Enguerrand de Monstrelet (d. 1453) documented the Hundred Years' War and Joan of

Arc's interview with Philip the Good, duke of Burgundy (r. 1419–67), after her capture by the Burgundians (*see* chapter 1, History).

The acknowledged "father of English history" is the Venerable Bede (d. 735), a monk at the monastery of Saint Peter in Wearmouth, Northumbria. His *Historia ecclesiastica gentis Anglorum* (*The Ecclesiastical History of the English People*) covers the ecclesiastical and political history of English from the time of Caesar until the year 731. William of Malmesbury (d. 1143), English historian and monk of Malmesbury Abbey, wrote a series of English histories modeled after the Venerable Bede's *Historia*: *The Gesta regum anglorum* (*Deeds of the English kings*), which covers the years 449–1127, and the *Gesta pontificum anglorum* (*Deeds of the English bishops*) are his most significant works. Matthew Paris (d. 1259), abbot of Saint Albans Monastery and its official recorder of events, is considered the most comprehensive of the English historians. His *Chronica majorca* covered the major happenings from creation to 1066, the year of the Norman Conquest. The text known as the Warkworth's *Chronicle*, attributed to the master of Peterhouse in Cambridge, describes the events of the Wars of the Roses (1461–73), and the anonymous *Davies Chronicle* documents the reigns of the English monarchs Richard II, Henry IV, Henry V, and Henry VI, from 1377 to 1461.

The *Gesta Danorum* (*The Deeds of the Danes*), by the 12th-century writer Saxo the Grammarian, is the most ambitious account of Danish history, covering the events from the time of Christ until the reign of the Danish king Canute VI (r. 1182–1202). Among the Germanic chroniclers Otto von Freising (1115–58), a Cistercian abbot and bishop of Freising (Bavaria, Germany), wrote the *Gesta Friderici imperatoris* (*The Deeds of Emperor Frederick*) at the behest of the Hohenstaufen king Frederick I, the Holy Roman Emperor (r. 1152–90). Important events covered in the chronicle include the feud between the rival dynasties of the Guelfs and the Hohenstaufen.

Notable Christian chroniclers of the Iberian Peninsula include Saint Isidore of Seville (d. 636), author of the two works on the Christian history of the Peninsula, the *Chronicum maius* (*The Great Chronicle*) and the *Historia de regibus Gothorum, Vandalorum et Suevorum* (*A History of the Visigoths, Vandals, and Suebians*). Two anonymous eighth-century Latin chronicles, *The Arabic-Byzantine Chronicle of 741* and the *Mozarabic Chronicle of 754*, document the Muslim occupation of Spain in 711, the attendant establishment of the caliphate, and the emerging Christian kingdoms. The history of the Kingdoms of León and Castile, would-be heirs of the Visigothic kingdom, is told in the anonymous 12th-century *Chronica Adefonsi Imperatoris* (*The Chronicle of Alfonso the Emperor*), which documents the reign of Alfonso VII (1126–57), his self-proclamation as the Emperor of All of Spain, and his wars against the Almoravid Muslims. The *De rebus Hispanie* (*History of Hispania*) by the archbishop of Toledo and historian Rodrigo Jiménez de Rada (d. 1247) continued where Isidore of Seville left off, covering the history of the peninsula until the year in 1243. Alfonso X the Wise, king of Castile and León (1221–84), patronized and participated in the composition of two historical chronicles, the *Primera cronica general* and the *General estoria*. Both works were composed in Spanish rather than Latin and drew heavily upon a variety of sources, including biblical, classical, and Arabic works. Four important chronicles detail the history of the Crown of Aragon, the earliest of which is the *Llibre del rei en Pere d'Aragó e dels seus antecessors* ("The Book of King Peter of Aragon and His Predecessors"), written by the 13th-century Catalan chronicler Bernat Desclot. James I of Aragon "the Conqueror" (1208–76) is distinguished as the first monarch to write his own chronicle-autobiography, the *Llibre dels Feits* (*Book of*

Deeds). His descendant Peter IV of Aragon (1319–87) followed his example, writing his own *Cronica* a century later. Most unusual is the *Cronica* of Ramon Muntaner (1270–1336), a largely autobiographical account of the life of the author and his exploits as an *Almogavar*, a Catalan mercenary soldier who participated in the wars against the Turks in Constantinople.

The Italian monk and bishop Rogerius of Apulia (1205–66) devoted his *Carmen miserabile super destructione, Regni Hungariae per Tartaros* (*The Sad Song for the Destruction of the Kingdom of Hungary by the Tartars*) to describing the horrors of the Mongol-Tatar invasions of Germany and other European territories from 1223 onward. The Icelandic sagas, written in Old Norse in the 12th to 15th centuries, detail the major events of Scandinavian history beginning with the time of the settlement of Iceland in the ninth and 10th centuries. An important example is the *Njal's Saga*, which covers the events of 930 to 1020, including the conversion to Christianity in the year 1000.

CRUSADER CHRONICLES

Fulcher of Chartres stands out among crusader historians. He wrote his *Historia* of the First Crusade (1096–99) documenting his journey to the Holy Land in the company of Baldwin of Boulogne (d. 1112) and the establishment of the Kingdom of Jerusalem. Baldwin would become the first titled king of Jerusalem in 1101. Fulcher consulted the anonymous *Gesta Francorum et aliorum Hierosolimitanorum* (*The Deeds of the Franks and All the Pilgrims to Jerusalem*), a remarkable account of the First Crusade told from the point of view of a knight who fought in it. In turn, William, the archbishop of Tyre, drew upon Chartres's *Historia* to compile his all-important *Historia rerum in partibus transmarinis gestarum* (*History of Deeds beyond the Sea*), a history of the Latin Crusader Kingdom of Jerusalem. Anna Comnena (1083–1153)

was the daughter of the Byzantine emperor Alexius I (r. 1081–1118) and the first female historical chronicler. Her 15-volume family history, the *Alexiad*, preserves an eyewitness account of the First Crusade from the Byzantine perspective. Ambrose the Poet, a Norman poet who accompanied Richard I the Lionhearted on the Third Crusade to Jerusalem (1189–92), wrote *L'Estoire de la guerre sainte* (*The History of the Holy War*) in French rhymed verse as a biographical account of the king's deeds.

The Dominican inquisitor and preacher Jacques de Vitry, mentioned previously, is the author of *L'Historia Hierosolimitana abbreviata* (*The Abridged History of Jerusalem*), a two-volume history that treats the "Oriental history" of the rise of Islam and the causes of the Crusades, the history of the first three Crusades, and a description of Jerusalem. The second part, the "Occidental History," treats the Latin Church. An important Byzantine chronicle of the disastrous Fourth Crusade (1202–04) in which the Latin armies captured Constantinople is *The Sack of Constantinople* by the historian Nicetas Chroniates (1155–1216), a Constantinoplan eyewitness to the events. The Latin perspective is chronicled in the *De la conquête du Constantinople* (*On the Conquest of Constantinople*) by Geoffrey I Villehardouin (1160–1212), a French knight and historian who participated in the crusade.

Literary Languages

ENGLAND

Anglo-Saxon was the earliest English language spoken and written in England, from about 700 through 1100. Also called Old English, Anglo-Saxon had four major dialects. Northumbrian, an Anglian dialect, was spoken north of the Humber River. Mercian, also an

Anglian dialect, was spoken in that geographical area between the Thames River and the Humber. West Saxon, a Saxon dialect, was spoken south of the Thames. Kentish, in Kent and part of Surrey, was the dialect spoken by the Jute people.

The great epic *Beowulf*, the finest long poem in Anglo-Saxon, depicted adventures of the hero Beowulf against supernatural enemies of King Hrothgar and the warriors of his mead-hall, the monsters Grendal and his fierce mother. Exquisite Anglo-Saxon elegies called the *Wanderer* and the *Seafarer* also demonstrated the artistic vigor of that language, which repudiated rhyme in favor of strenuous rhythm and alliteration, the repeated initial consonants in sequential words (*fierce, foul, ferocious, fire-fuming dragon*). Important in Germanic and Anglo-Saxon literature, alliteration also served the writings of the alliterative revival in 14th-century England in the northwest Midlands dialect, a reestablishment of Anglo-Saxon poetic techniques that hitherto had been considered unfashionable because of their functional form. Authors wrote alliterative romances as well as such bravura poems as *Sir Gawain and the Green Knight, Pearl, Piers Plowman*, and the *Alliterative Morte Arthur.*

Old French and Anglo-Norman   Old French and Anglo-Norman creations at the English court were written in a Norman French dialect in England in the period between the Norman Conquest of 1066 and the 15th century. These refined, fashionable, courtly competitors of native Anglo-Saxon attitudes and literature included the imaginative *lais* and poetic tales of Marie de France, the pseudo-historical, self-congratulatory chronicles of Gaimar in his *L'estorie des Engleis* (*History of the English*), and Wace's story of Brutus, *Roman de Brut*, an Arthurian legend. Thomas of Britain wrote his romance of *Tristan* in Anglo-Norman. Although Chaucer's Middle English virtually was standard English in the 14th century, his contemporary John Gower proudly wrote his *Mirour de l'omne* (*The Mirror of Man*) in Anglo-Norman.

Middle English   Derived from Anglo-Saxon dialects, Middle English was the language favored in England during the years 1100 through 1500. Four major dialects of Middle English were Northern, Midland, Southern, and Kentish. But regional subdialects were popular, such as the Northwest Midlands.

Among Geoffrey Chaucer's remarkable poetic and political achievements was the regularization of both pronunciation and spelling of English at the royal court and among the citizenry. Formidable regional dialects and speech variations made Middle English not one but many languages. For instance, alliterative revival works written in Northwest Midlands dialect were not easily understood by those who spoke Kentish and read *Ancrene Wisse*, who could not easily understand the eastern Midland or London dialect of Chaucer's *Canterbury Tales*, whose speakers in turn found it difficult to comprehend Scandinavian language vestiges in the so-called Danelaw. Chaucer's exquisite style justifiably earned him the reputation as the father of the Middle English language.

Danelaw   In north, east, and central England, those parts of the island settled or controlled by the Danish invaders from the ninth century on, Danish custom and modified Saxon law were the law of the land. That Scandinavian heritage remains alive today in England's more than 1,400 placenames with such suffixes as *by*, meaning "farm," as in *Whitby, Rugby*, and *Grimsby*. Similarly, any placename ending with *thorpe*, meaning "village," as in *Bishopsthorpe, Lynnthorpe*, and *Althorpe*, or with the suffix *toft*, meaning "ground" or "earth mound," as in *Grimtoft, Easttoft*, and *Langtoft*, reflects the Danelaw tradition.

FRANCE

Various Celtic languages were spoken in the territory constituting France at the time of the Roman invasion of Gaul by Julius Caesar in 58–52 B.C. Vulgar Latin, the language spoken by Roman soldiers, settlers, and slaves, soon became the lingua franca of the region. All the Romance languages (meaning the language of the Romans) derive from Vulgar Latin, and all are characterized by the loss of the complicated declension system of Classical Latin, a resulting preference for a subject-verb-object sentence structure, and varying degrees of changes in vowel pronunciation. In the third and the fourth centuries Germanic tribes invaded Gaul and settled throughout the region, adopting the Gallo-Romance language but adapting it to their indigenous syntax and pronunciation patterns. These Germanic tribes included the Franks, who settled in northern Gaul; the Burgundians, who settled in the Rhone Valley; the Allemani, who settled on the Gallo-Germanic border; and the Visigoths, who settled in the Aquitaine and the Iberian Peninsula.

Langues d'Oïl An important consequence of the Germanic invasions was the division of the Gallo Romance language into two major linguistic variants, the Langues d'Oc and the Langues d'Oïl, so named for the manner in which each linguistic group said the word meaning "yes." The Langues d'Oc, or Occitan language, was spoken in the regions south of the Loire River and in parts of northern Spain, while the Langues d'Oïl, also referred to as Old French, was spoken in the northern region of France, Belgium, Switzerland, and Norman-controlled England. Burgundian, Anglo-Norman, Norman, Belgian (Walloon), and Parisian (Francien) are important variants of the Langues d'Oïl. Under the influence of the court of Charlemagne and particularly the succeeding Capetian dynasty, the Langues d'Oïl gained ground as the official language of the court and the language of national unity. Official documents, of the royal chancellery were composed in Old French. A papal decree issued in the year authorized priests to preach in the Vulgate languages to the masses. This gave rise to the composition of the hagiographies, such as the *La Cantilène de Sainte Eulalie* (11th c.) and the *Vie de Saint Alexis,* (11th c.) and to a vibrant Old French literary tradition that included such works as the chanson the geste, the "matter of Britain" and matter of Rome romances, and the Breton lais.

Langue d'Oc The Langue d'Oc, or Occitan, dialects were spoken in the regions south of the Loire River: Languedoc, Rousillon, Aquitaine, Provence, the Midi Pyrenees, Limousin, Poiteau, Gascony, and northeast Spain. The Occitan language was significantly influenced by the migration of Vascon tribes from northern Spain into southern France during the sixth and seventh centuries. Provençal, the Occitan dialect spoken in southwestern France is the language of the pontifical court at Avignon. It is also the language of the famed troubadour poets and jongleurs. The tradition of Provençal lyrical poetry began with William IX of Aquitaine (d. 1127) and flourished in the courts of Eleanor of Aquitaine and Richard the Lionhearted. Troubadour poets fled into neighboring Spain and Italy from the destabilization provoked by the Albigensian Crusade (1209–29) and the ensuing Inquisition. The 12th-century epic *Girart de Roussillon,* based on the real-life exploits of the ninth-century Burgundian count, is considered a masterpiece of Provençal *chanson de geste.*

IBERIAN PENINSULA

When the Roman legions completed their conquest of the Iberian Peninsula in 19 B.C.E., they encountered a medley of peoples—Iberians, Celts, Asturs, Carthagenians, Greeks, Basques, and others—and their distinctive languages. Latin became the lingua franca of all the territories of Hispania with the exception of the northern Basque territory. In the fourth and fifth centuries waves of Visigothic tribes invaded the peninsula, eventually seizing power after the sacking of Rome in 410, yet adopting Latin as the official language and retaining many Roman institutions. In the wake of the Arab occupation of the peninsula in the eighth century Arabic replaced Latin as the lingua franca in the territories under Muslim control. The demise of *The Latin language* vis-à-vis Arabic in the usage and prestige of favored the development of Romance languages throughout the Iberian Peninsula. Within less than a century of the Arab occupation Arabized Christians living under Muslim rule in al-Andalus, known pejoratively as Mozarabs, had adopted the Arabic language and developed their own hybrid Romance dialect known as Mozarabic. As the northern Christian kingdoms became consolidated in the ninth century onward, three major and distinct Romance languages evolved from the Vulgar Latin, Galaico-Portuguese, Castilian, and Catalan, which to varying degrees were influenced by the Arabic and Mozarabic languages. The Christian Reconquest of territories that would be absorbed into the Kingdoms of Castile and Aragon from the 13th century onward precipitated a "brain drain" as the wealthier and more cultivated elements of the Muslim population chose to emigrate to the southern regions still under Islamic rule. Over time, the Mudejar populations who remained in Christian Castile, Navarre, and Aragon became speakers of Aljamia, Castilian, and Aragonese Romance dialects heavily impregnated with Arabic vocabulary and written in the Arabic alphabet. Jewish populations living in the Iberian Peninsula adopted the dominant language used in the territories where they resided, preserving Hebrew primarily for religious literature.

Castilian   The Castilian language was born in the Burgos area of southern Cantabria in northern Spain. The earliest known writings in the Castilian language are the *Glosas Emilianenses* or "Glosses of [the Monastery of] San Millán de Cogolla," annotations made in the margins of a Latin liturgical text dated 964. The Castilian language spread laterally into the areas of Asturias and Leon and southward under the impetus of the conquest and repopulation of Muslim territories. During the reign of King Alfonso the Wise (1252–84) the Castilian language was standardized and catapulted into prominence as the language of official documentation and culture. Castilian literature composed prior to this period, such as the *Poema del Mío Cid* was written in one of the Castilian dialects. The Jewish scholars and translators working in Alfonso's court and the schools of translation, both based in Toledo, were particularly influential in promoting the use of vernacular Castilian in their translations. The Catholic monarchs Isabel of Castile and Ferdinand of Aragon made Castilian the official language of the entire kingdom.

Aragonese-Catalan   Variants of the Provençal language called Catalan, Aragonese, and Valencian, were spoken in the territories composing the Crown of Aragon, which included the Kingdoms of Aragon and Valencia and the Balearic Islands. The oldest surviving text written in a mixture of this language and Provençal is the group of sermons known as the *Homilies d'Organyà*, ("Homilies of Organyà") named after the northern town of Alt Urgell where they were found. The acknowledged master of Catalan literature is Ramon Llull (1235–1315) of Mallorca, a prolific writer, philosopher, and Franciscan lay preacher. Llull was fluent in Arabic, Latin, and Catalan, and his philosophical and fiction works display a clear Arabic influence. His main contribution to Catalan literature is *Blanquerna*, considered to be a precursor of the romantic novel. The distinction of writing the first truly modern novel in a European language belongs to Joanot Martorell (1413–68), a Valencian author of the novel *Tirant lo Blanc*, which relates the crusading and romantic adventures of a Catalan knight in the employ of the Byzantine army.

Galaico-Portugues Galaico-Portugues, or Galician Portuguese, was the Hispano-Romance language that evolved in the area of Galicia and northern Portugal in the ninth century. The oldest surviving Galician text is a devotional poem entitled "Ora faz ost'o Senhor de Navarre" by João Soares de Paiva, composed circa 1200. Galaico-Portugues as the language of culture, poetry, and religious expression par excellence, used even in the Kingdom of Castile. Alfonso the Wise, mentioned earlier as the promoter of the standardization of the Castilian language, composed his *Las Cantigas de Santa Maria (Songs to the Virgin Mary)* in Galician Portuguese. It was not until the year 1290 that the Portuguese king Dinis (r. 1261–1325) proclaimed Portuguese the official language of the realm.

ITALY

Italian is considered to be the closest to Latin of all the Romance languages. Medieval "Italian" is in fact not one standardized language but rather many regional dialects that developed in the Italian Peninsula, Sicily, Corsica, Sardinia, and the area the Italians call Ticino, nowadays in southern Switzerland. Each of the city-states had its own dialect. The northern and northwest dialects, which include Lombardo, Piemontese, Ligure, and Milanese, receive the name of *Gallo-Italian*, owing to the strong influence the Occitan language. Variants of the Venetian dialect predominated in

Venice and the northeast. Tuscan, Umbrian, Abbruzzian, Molisano, and Campano are the major dialects that evolved in the central peninsula. In the southern part of peninsular Italy Pugliese, Lucano, Maruggese, Salentino, and Calabrese form another cluster of dialects that differ substantially from the northern ones, as do the island dialects of Sicilian, Corsican, and Sardinian. Sicilian is heavily influenced by the Greek-Byzantine and Phoenician peoples who once ruled the island; it also absorbed many Arabic words as a result of Muslim domination from the eighth to 11th century.

After the fall of the Roman Empire in the fifth century and until the beginning of the 12th century, Classical and Vulgar Latin continued to be the principal official and literary languages used in the Italian Peninsula. During the end of this period Italian writers were strongly influenced by French Provençal writers, producing a number of court poets who composed *chanson de geste* and lyrical poetry in that language or using vocabulary combining hybrid elements of Latin, Italian vernaculars, and Provençal. The earliest text written in a recognizably Italian language are legal documents dating from the 10th century. The first true Italian literary movement emerged in 13th-century Sicily under the patronage of Emperor Frederick II and is known as "the Sicilian school." It was heavily indebted to Provençal courtly love poetry, and its major representatives are Giacomo da Lentini, Guido delle Colonne, and Pier della Vigna. Da Lentini is acknowledged as the inventor of the sonnet. This poetic trend quickly spread north and was developed further in Tuscany, where Tuscan poets such as Chiaro Davanzati and Compiuta Donzella expanded the thematic repertoire to include moral and political topics. In the 14th century Dante's *Commedia* firmly established his native Tuscan—albeit influenced by the Sicilian of the Sicilian school—as the standard literary language of Italy.

GERMANY

As is Italian, German is divided into clearly distinguished dialects, the principal ones West Germanic, East Germanic, and North Germanic. The North Germanic languages are spoken in the Scandinavian countries and include Icelandic, Norwegian, Danish, Swedish, and Faeroese. The West Germanic is the largest language group, originally spoken in the areas of the Rhine, the Alps, Elbe, and the North Sea. East Germanic is the language spoken by the eastern Germanic tribes who migrated from Scandinavia into eastern Germany between the sixth and third centuries B.C.E., who include the Lombards, Vandals, Goths, Burgundians, and Crimeans. The Western and Eastern Germanic languages are known jointly as the Southern Germanic languages.

Old High German and Middle High German   The waves of migrations of Germanic peoples into France and the Italian and Iberian Peninsulas that took place between the third and fifth centuries provoked important linguistic transformations in their spoken languages. Scholars commonly refer to the *High German consonant shift* or *second sound shift* to designate the sound changes in the central and southern parts of Germany that affected the southern Germanic dialects, giving rise to the development of Old High German. (The Germanic dialect spoken in the North German Lowlands not affected by this linguistic shift is called Low German.) The sound change affected the pronunciation of many consonants, for example, *p > f, pp > pf, t > ss, tt > ts, k > ch, kk > kch*. These differences can be appreciated by comparing certain modern English and German words, for example, *pound > Pfund, pipe > Pfeife, hope > hoffen, apple > Apfel, tide > Zeit, cat > Katze,* and *make > machen.* Old High German flourished from approximately the year 500 to the middle of the 11th century, although the earliest written texts date to the eighth century, and is characterized by a fully fledged noun declension and verb conjugations with distinctive endings. Old High German is not a single language but consisted of many dialects. In the areas of Speyer, Worms, Mainz, and Frankfurt Rhine Franconian was spoken, while Middle Franconian was spoken in Cologne and Trier. Alemannic was spoken in the regions of Strausbourg and Reichenau. Bavarian predominated in Freising, Passau, Regensburg, Ausburg, and Salzburg.

The surviving examples of Old High German literature are primarily Christian religious texts, such as the Bavarian ninth-century epic poem entitled *Muspilli*, about the Last Judgment, the meaning of which is unknown. Two notable exceptions to the ecclesiastical literature are the *Das Hildebrandslied* (*The Lay of Hildebrand*), a poetic dialogue between the hero Hildebrand and his estranged son Hadubrand, whom he tragically kills in a combat, and the *Die Merseburger Zaubersprüche* (The Merseburger Incantations), a rare ninth- or 10th-century manuscript of pre-Christian magic spells. A Latin–High Old German dictionary called the *Codex Abrogans* dates from the eighth century. The linguistic changes of all unstressed vowels to the vowel *e* and the simplification of the inflectional system that occurred in this period led to the emergence of Middle High German, the language of the minstrel poets.

It was the minstrel poets who first promoted the standardization of Middle High German in order to make their songs understood by the widest possible audience. To this end, they avoided using dialectical regionalisms and rhymes in their *Minnesangs*, which only make sense in particular dialects. Courtly romance authors and epic poets such as Hartmann von Aue of Swabia (d. 1230) and the minnesinger and lyrical poet von Eschenbach also composed their works in Middle High German. Johannes Gutenberg's invention of the printing press and Martin Luther's translation of the Bible into German fomented the diffusion of the German variant spoken in the central region of Wittenberg.

Yiddish Yiddish is a variety of Middle High German spoken by the Ashkenazic Jews and written in the Hebrew alphabet. It emerged in the 13th and 14th centuries with the rise of urban culture, most notably in Speyer, Maintz, and Worms. Its most important literary work is the 14th-century epic poem *Dukus Horant*.

Major Christian Writers

Alfonso X el Sabio (the Wise), king of Castile and León (r. 1221–1284; 1252–1284). Acclaimed patron of the famous schools of translation and a renowned poet and writer, best known for his poetic hymns to the Virgin Mary, *Cantigas de Santa Maria*, and two major historical chronicles, *Primera Crónica general* and the *Gran estoria*.

Giovanni Boccaccio (1313–1375). Scholar, diplomat, and one of the greatest Italian poets, whose *Decameron* helped elevate Italian vernacular poetry to the level of Classical Latin literature.

Geoffrey Chaucer (c. 1340–1400). The quintessential Middle English poet, best known as the author of the *Canterbury Tales*. Inspired by the Italian poets Dante, Petrarch, and Boccaccio, his other major works include *Parlement of Foules*, *Troilus and Criseyde*, and the *Legend of Good Women*.

Chrétien de Troyes (alive between 1160 and 1181). Court poet to Countess Marie de Champagne, author of the epic poems *Perceval*, *Lancelot, the King of the Cart*, and *Yvain, the King of the Lion*, which are considered the finest of the genre.

Dante Alighieri (1265–1321). Italian philosopher and political thinker, considered the single greatest poet of the Middle Ages, immortalized by his allegorical masterpiece *La Divina Commedia*.

Hildegarde of Bingen (1098–1179). Benedictine abbess, visionary mystic, poet, and musical composer, best known for her musical composition *Order of the Virtues* and her mystical writings, the *Illuminations* and *The Book of the Rewards of Life*.

Julian of Norwich (1342–c. 1416). Major English anchoress and mystical writer, best known for her account of her spiritual visions, the *Shewings* and *A Revelation of Love*.

Ramon Llull (1235–1315). Majorcan Franciscan lay preacher, mystic, philosopher, and author of the most important literary works written in Catalan, including the mystical novel *Blanquerna* and the mystical texts *The Book of the Lover and the Beloved* and *The Book of Marvels*.

Matthew Paris (1200–1259). English Benedictine monk and author of England's greatest medieval historical chronicles, the *Chronica majora*, *Historia Anglorum*, and the *Gesta abbatum monasterii Sancti Albani*.

Francesco Petrarca (Petrarch) (1304–1374). Influential Italian poet, writer, scholar, and cleric who is considered to be the founder of Renaissance humanism. His literary works include *The Ascent of Mount Ventoux* and the *Tale of Griselda*.

Christine de Pizan (1364–1430). One of the greatest and most prolific women prose writers, whose works, *The Book of the City of Ladies*, *The Book of the Three Virtues*, and *The Letter to the God of Love*, defended women's virtue against the misogynistic trends of courtly love literature.

With her pet dog observing, Christine de Pizan, the prolific 15th-century professional author, writes in her study, seated on a high-backed chair and working at a sloping desk. Natural light streams in through her window. Her hat is on, and her pen is in hand. A box with pen nibs and ink is open beside her book. Christine was said to be an excellent calligrapher and may have been her own scribe for some manuscripts among her 20 published books. From Christine de Pizan, *Collected Works*, 15th century. Courtesy of the British Library, London, Harley Manuscript 4431.

Hrsovitha von Gandersheim (d. 1200). This important Benedictine nun was mother superior of her house in Gandersheim in Saxony in the 10th century, poet, scholar, playwright, and physician. Her exquisite work was rediscovered and widely performed in the 20th century. Her Latin writings imitated those of Terence, Virgil, and Horace. She dramatically praised women's power, chastity, and fortitude. Greatly celebrated in her own time, her poems and theater were well known throughout Germany and Europe. Among her three most popular works were *Dulcitius*, *Sapientia*, and *Paphnutius*.

Juan Ruiz (1283–1350). Archpriest of Hita (Toledo) and acclaimed author, often compared to Geoffrey Chaucer; his ribald epic poem *The Book of Good Love* is a masterpiece of Castilian literature.

The writers of the European Christian Middle Ages did not compose their works in an environment hermetically sealed off from any influences of their Jewish and Muslim neighbors and rivals. The preceding discussion of frame tale, *exempla*, and mirror for princes literature indicates just some of the many examples of cultural exchange among the three religious communities. In the following section we shall see that Jewish writers produced a wealth of religious and devotional literature bearing witness to the particularities of the religious faith in a way parallel to that of Christian writers. On the other hand, religion is not entirely synonymous with culture and where the latter is concerned, it will become clear that the Jewish contribution to the narrative literary output of the dominant Christian or Muslim culture was significant.

Jewish Literature

Universal, Insular, and Particularist Literature

Resembling *Aesop's Fables*, the *Mishler Shualim* (The Fox Fables) was written in 12th-century

France in Hebrew by the Jewish Aesop, Bere-chiah ben Natronai Ha Nakdan. The author's techniques were typical of the best fable writers. Dramatic and amusing animal actions imitated human follies and vices in order to teach morality. Although the fables were written in Hebrew, their subject was universal and their audience, potentially, was all humanity, not simply Jews. Such universal qualities in medieval Jewish literature contrasted markedly with a second tendency of medieval Jewish authors in relation to their subjects and audiences: the insular.

One Jewish version of the Arthurian cycle focuses on the exploits of the faithful knight Sir Bove. As in the original versions, here, too, Sir Bove jousted valiantly in tournaments, fought bravely on the battlefield, rescued damsels in distress, and defeated fire-eating dragons. And yet, the characters greet one another saying "Shalom aleichem," (Heb.: Peace be with you), and they celebrate their victories in battle using the Hebrew expression, *"Mazel tov"* (Good luck, "May your planetary influences be favorable"). His faithful wife, Lady Druzane, follows him everywhere, but "lamented that in her wandering life she has not had the opportunity to circumcise her [sons] according to Jewish law, and her father consoles her by saying, 'Do not worry, dear. Tomorrow I will arrange a great circumcision feast.'" (Shandler, Jeffrey. "On the Frontiers of Ashkenaz: Translating into Yiddish, Then and Now." *Judaism: A Quarterly Journal of Jewish Life and Thought.* January 1, 2005. Available online. URL: http://www. encyclopedia.com/doc/1G1-138949894.html.)

The 16th-century Jewish author of that hilarious Arthurian romance adapted his source the Italian version of the Anglo-Roman romance *Sir Bevis of Hamilton* for a specifically Jewish audience: Elijah Levita wrote his *Bove Bukh* in Yiddish, a combination of Hebrew with German, decorating the Arthurian characters and actions with qualities of Jewish culture,

Yiddishkeit. Author, subject, and audience were unmistakably, unabashedly insular. The Arthurian world and the Round Table itself pivoted around a secular Jewish point. (*See* the discussion below on Heroic Romance).

Such artistic insularity differed not only from the universal type of medieval Jewish literature but also from the particularist. Jewish writers identified and particularized the Jewish experience, while integrating Jewishness with worldliness. Israel is to other peoples, says the Spanish philosopher and poet Judah Halevi (1080–1141), as the heart is to other parts of the body: It suffers for the whole and is more acutely pierced by grief than any other physical member.

Particularist Jewish writers explained centuries of suffering in the Diaspora, communal persecution, and private grief as the natural result of divine selection. Not for nothing did God speak to Israel, saying, "for you are a people holy to the Lord your God. Out of all the peoples on the face of the earth, the Lord has chosen you to be his treasured possession" (Deut. 14:2). Jewish particularist literature depicted the Jews as the special, chosen, people, particularly enjoying their elect status but particularly suffering the piercing pain of the Diaspora experience.

The universal, the insular, and the particularist artistic qualities conveniently classify the multiplicities of medieval secular Jewish literature. This tripartite classification gives an order to an otherwise unwieldy diversity of literary types, themes, and languages in Jewish literature of the 10th through 16th centuries written primarily in Hebrew but also in Arabic, Latin, Persian, Castilian, Ladino, Occitan, English, German, Yiddish, Italian, and such other vernaculars as Polish and Serbo-Croatian. Jewish literary texts are as diverse as the responsibilities of the Jews in the Christian and Islamic communities in which they thrived or perished. In addition to their own imaginative literature—a product of their world traveling as merchant adventurers, students, and rabbis—Jewish writers were commissioned by kings and caliphs to translate Latin and Arabic texts. Jews thus helped transmit Eastern science, philosophy, and literature to the European West. At the same time, they recorded for their own internal consumption the experiences of exile (Diaspora) and persecution in liturgical poetry and in their own crusader chronicles. And while the earliest Jewish literature is clearly religious in theme, the line between the religious and profane and the divisions between fiction and nonfiction writing were sometimes blurred, just as we saw in the discussion of Christian literature.

Haggadah and Halachah

Halachah is the collective corpus of the Jewish law, custom, or practice and comprises biblical strictures, binding legal tenets, and rabbinic commentaries that are believed to have the power of law inaugurated by God and enforced by his minions on Earth for correct regulation of human life. (*See* the discussion in chapter 5 on philosophy and religion.) The halachic legal corpus is complemented by nonlegalistic Haggadah literature, a vast corpus of rabbinic moral exhortations, biblical commentaries, legends, short stories, moral examples, humorous folktales, and mystical and erotic writings that enliven, explicate, and otherwise teach the word of law. Haggadic literature, though secular in subject, is ultimately moralistic, even pedagogical in intent. Certainly writers of Haggadah exulted in the humor, magic, or splendor of their materials. However, the essential purposes of their art were religious instruction and moral edification. As were the successful Christian dramatists of the era, the finest Jewish writers were able to combine Plato's otherwise antithetical ideas of teaching

and entertainment, *docere et delectare*: The best instruction was pleasing and the keenest delight informing.

Genres of Haggadic Literature

Unifying typical medieval opposites of teaching and pleasing were eight classes of Haggadic literature: beast fables, frame tales, heroic romances, chansons de geste, satires, poetry of love and war, instruction books, and exempla. All eight genres offer surprises to the modern audience expecting decorous pieties.

Particularly intriguing in medieval Jewish literature is a mannered battle between the sexes inextricably associated with vibrant eroticism. More astonishing is the prevalence of animals: animal heroes and heroines, beast companions, magical transformations between beasts and beings, and animal analogies, metaphors, and symbols. This literary ark of animals suggests a medieval Judaic belief in an interdependence between animalkind and humanity.

Even the most intellectual and sophisticated medieval Jews, as their contemporary Christian and Muslim neighbors, understood the life cycles of farm animals and were familiar with animal hunting and slaughtering. Such practical knowledge augmented the vast set of animal prescriptions, prohibitions, and hygienic, culinary, and koshering regulations derived from the biblical books of Leviticus and Deuteronomy and biblical commentaries.

Preoccupations with animals and with their association with sanctity or sin explain the prevalence of animals in Haggadic literature. Moreover, referring to the animal world to teach virtue and avoidance of vice in the human world was a classical teaching device, doubtlessly useful for its benevolent indirection. But medieval Jewish animal lore had even deeper roots, as we shall see, in Jewish apocalyptic mysticism.

Beast Fable

TOPICS

Beast fables were short poetic or prose works depicting exploits of clever or foolish, good or evil animals, followed by an explicit moral. Many were borrowed directly from Aesop's Fables, such as the tale of the "Lion and the Crane" and the "Fox in the Vineyard." One of the finest Jewish fabulists was the aforementioned 12th- to 13th-century exegete and grammarian Berechiah ben Natronai Ha Nakdan, whose collection of Hebrew fables entitled *Mishlei shualim* (*Fox Fables*) is as we have seen, a Jewish adaptation of tales from the acclaimed Aesop Fables and from Arabic sources. His tale of the fox, crow, and cheese reminds us of the universality of greed and the folly of pride. Others of Berechiah's more than 100 Hebrew fables taught similar personal lessons, counseling good behavior and reforming an individual's dangerous tendencies such as talking too much or trusting too uncritically.

Some fables taught turning apparent adversity to creative opportunity. Consider the tale of the thirsty bird of prey, the osprey, and the slender-necked pot. The parched bird underwent three days without drink until at last he spied cool water at the bottom of a long-necked flask. No matter how he turned the flask or contorted himself, he could not reach his eager beak down to the cool fluid. So he gathered pebbles and threw them carefully down the shaft until he caused the water level to rise to the top. Then he drank his fill.

The moral: Good sense, knowledge, and shrewd cunning are better than strength. Even without a strong neck and stalwart body, one obtains power by wisdom.

Beyond personal instruction, Berechiah's fables taught painful political lessons necessary for group protection. While forgiveness was a virtue and some transgressors might be per-fectible, beware! The man teaching a wolf the alphabet may get him to learn the *aleph*, *bet*, and *gimmel*, the first three Hebrew letters, but no matter how the wolf arranges those letters into a word they will always spell his primary desire: sheep.

Moral: Evil creatures seemingly susceptible to reform truly are not reformable. The eye and heart bent on wickedness ultimately declare it with the mouth. Alert your ear to listen for evil, and open your eye to see it.

Utilitarian political advice and personal moral instruction were the purposes of most medieval and Renaissance Jewish fables, luring the audience into passive tranquility with an entertaining story before shooting the barb of truth.

ANCIENT ROOTS

Well meriting the title of the Jewish Aesop, Berechiah wrote in the ancient traditions of Eastern and Western animal tales. His relationships with French Christian writers apparently were mutually respectful. In the writings of both Berechiah and the great noblewoman fabulist Marie de France there are 37 fables that are so close in matter and manner that Berechiah is likely to have read Marie's work and copied it, or she might have seen and imitated his. While for some popular tales both writers independently might have emended a third writer's original, 13 fables exist only in the writings of Berechiah and Marie, not in Latin, Greek, or contemporary medieval collections. These are so close in subject and style as to make intentional imitation inevitable.

Jewish fable writing is traceable at least to Rabbi Meir, a venerable second-century scholar in Asia Minor who adapted 300 animal fables combining beast action with specifically Jewish ethical tutelage. The 300 fables find their origins in the work of a first-century Greek rhetor, Nicostratus, who compiled

Aesop's Fables with the Fables of Kybises, the latter a Libyan writer who transmitted a collection of Indian fables into the Greek-speaking world circa the year 50. Closer to the more insular as opposed to universal fabulist heritage was the delightful collection of beast and bird stories by the 13th-century Spanish physician Isaac ibn Sahula. Ibn Sahula, who lived in Castile during the end of the reign of Alfonso X the Wise, composed his *Meshal Haqadmoni* ("The Tale of the Ancient One") in Hebrew in rhymed prose in the style of the Arabic *maqamat* (sessions) poets. (*See* the section on Islamic Literature.) The *Meshal haqadmoni* features a series of satirical debates between animal cynics and moralists, in which the moralists always triumph. His animals did not wear foreign garments but were robed in words of Torah. Their wise riddles and illusions were Talmudic.

Ibn Sahula's deer expounded Halachah and scriptural law. His self-righteous rooster cockadoodled biblical verse. As Chaucer's Chaunticleer did in the *Canterbury Tales*, this rooster discoursed delicately with his harem of hens. The rabidly rabbinic rabbit preached ethics. The long-legged stork, an astrologer-fatalist, debated a Jewish rationalist frog who paraphrased Maimonides. The hawk's masterly learned discourse split hairs on the Jewish law of damages, indulging the rabbinic technique analyzing opposing sides of an argument called *pilpulism*.

Isaac ibn Sahula's beast fables contained a treasury of winged and four-pawed expositions not only on human ethics but also on cosmography, philosophy, geography, climate, language development, and anatomy of the human eye. Loquacious and insularly Judaic, containing important medical and scientific information, Ibn Sahula's work was a self-consciously encyclopedic instruction book for anyone desiring to learn: man, woman, or child. So that children especially would love his book

and eagerly read it, he adorned it with beautiful illustrations.

KALILAH AND DIMNAH

The fabulists Berechiah Ha Nakdan and Isaac Ibn Sahula were indebted to the renowned *Kalilah and Dimnah*, also known as the *Fables of Bidpai*, an etiquette book of good counsel featuring both beast fable and frame tale. This art of statecraft expressed ideas of leadership and morality via the adventures of beasts, two of which were jackals named Kalilah and Dimnah. The book's arrival in the Western world itself was a source of wonderment and cross-cultural fertilization. The fables originated in Buddhist India sometime in the first millennium B.C.E. as a didactic manual of instruction for young Hindu princes called the *Panchatantra*. In the sixth century C.E., the Sassanian Persian king Khosroe (r. 531–79) acquired a Sanskrit copy of the tales and had it translated into Pahlavi. At this stage Persian fables that feature King Khosroe were added to the collection and the work was also translated into Old Syriac. In the eighth century the Iranian Muslim scholar Ibn al-Muqaffaa translated *Kalilah and Dimnah* into Arabic, adding an introduction and several more tales, which would become especially popular, such "The Ascetic and His Guest" and "Heron and the Duck." The subsequent versions that Ibn Sahula and Berechia Ha Nakdan had access to were Hebrew translations of this Indian-Persian-Arabic collection.

Kalilah and Dimnah has been translated into numerous languages, including Chinese, Tibetan, and Syriac. Translations of the work into Western languages were undertaken by Jewish authors on three different occasions, demonstrating a remarkable Jewish contribution to medieval world literature via the art and craft of translation. First was a Greek version by an 11th-century Jewish physician, Simeon son of Seth. In 12th-century Italy a certain Rabbi

Joel translated Ibn al-Muqaffaa version into Hebrew. This version was translated by John of Capua, a Jewish convert to Christianity, into Latin under the title *Directorum Vitae Humanae* (*Guide for Human Life*). A 13th-century grammarian from Toledo, Jacob ben Eleazar, produced a Hebrew version. The majority of other versions translated into vernacular Spanish, German, Italian, Dutch, and English derive from John of Capua's translation; however, in the 13th century King Alfonso X the Wise commissioned its translation into Castilian.

Why were Jews translating tales of beasts, birds, and fishes? Jacob ben Eleazar remarked that he translated *Kalilah and Dimnah* into rhymed Hebrew because the "law book" of the Indians, "their Torah and guiding star," first concealed and then revealed profoundest wisdom and mystery. The old and wise understood its hidden meanings. Children laughed at its lovely stories. Maturing youngsters would better appreciate its fundamental ethical teachings by indirection, charm, and grace.

The Frame Tale

MISHLE SENDEBAR

Mishle Sendebar (known as *The Book of Sindbad* in its Eastern version and *The Seven Sages of Rome* in the Christian West) were celebrated frame tales of remote Indian origin. *Mishle Sendebar* crossed seas and continents undergoing a prodigious number of translations similarly to of *Kalilah and Dimnah*. Abraham ibn Hasdai (d. 1240) of Barcelona was a learned writer, poet, and translator of many Arabic philosophical and medical texts into Hebrew. He translated the Arabic version of the *Book of Sindbad* (*Kitab Sindebar*) into Hebrew with the title *Mishle Sendebar*. Those clever short stories pertained directly or indirectly to power struggles between women and men.

The frame tale unfolds as a "mirror for princes," with the sage tutor Sendebar educating a young learned prince. At Sendebar's advice, the prince swears an oath not to speak for a week. But the prince attracts the eye of his aged father's new young wife, who speaks sweet words, bares her firm young breasts, and, as does Potiphar's wife, tries to cajole the prince to bed with her.

When he refuses, the young queen tousles her hair, tears her dress, and dashes to the king shouting that the prince tried to rape her. Since the prince dared not speak even to defend himself, his silence infuriated his father, who thought him guilty and was ready to put him to death. But seven sages saved the prince for seven days by telling stories about women's perfidy.

In "The Crafty Old Crone and Her Weeping Bitch" one sage told of an ugly old woman who was so crafty she could make an unwilling married woman accept a young lover while her husband was away. The old crone took her fat old bitch of a dog to the young woman's house and fed the animal bread soaked in garlic. The dog appeared to weep bitter tears.

The young woman asked why the dog was crying. The old crone replied that the dog was in fact her beautiful daughter who had been transformed into a weeping bitch for refusing the hand of a worthy man in marriage.

To prevent a similar dire fate, the once hesitant young wife now eagerly met her lover.

In "The Greedy Bathhouse Keeper's Sexually Hired Wife" a gigantically fat prince went daily to the bathhouse, where he disported himself naked in the warm heat. The bathhouse keeper thought the prince had no genitals since they were entirely covered by folds of fat. One day the bath man remarked that the kingdom was endangered if the prince could not create an heir to the throne. The prince replied that he would pay 1,000 gold coins to any woman who would spend the day and night with him in the bathhouse. He invited the worried bathhouse keeper to watch the sport.

Believing the prince a eunuch who could not harm a woman, the bathhouse keeper, greedy for the gold, recommended his own young, beautiful wife for the test.

He was horrified, but she was jubilant when the potent prince lay with her again and again. The husband, aghast, shouted, "Come out; come out!" But the young wife laughingly refused. She had pledged her honor to remain with the prince till the test was finished.

A third Sendebar tale, "The Everywhere Desiring Man," demonstrated how easily women deceive men. A man was given three precious wishes. He asked his wife's advice. She thought that since nothing pleased him as much as sexual intercourse, he ought to request wondrous potency and feeling. He so wished. Suddenly his whole body was covered with penises.

Now everywhere desiring, but not anywhere desirable, he wished to God to remove the penises. They all disappeared, including his own, and he became a eunuch.

With a final wish, he requested his own precious member be returned.

Although these stories seem to castigate women, the apparent misogynism of the *Mishle Sendebar* is now being reconsidered as not truly antifeminist. The women are cleverer and craftier than the men, often dominating them through their sexuality as well as their wit. They almost always cuckold their husbands, too foolish, jealous, old, or greedy to merit better. Compared to the earlier Eastern versions and to the later Western Sendebar tales, the Hebrew stories portrayed women as less governed by malice or evil, more celebrating their own female ingenuity and eroticism.

Though the *Mishle Sendebar* was common to many cultures and demonstrated a universality of subject, in the Hebrew version the language the characters spoke was not simply Hebrew but biblical paraphrase. Abraham ben Hasdai

cleverly interpolated references to biblical books (especially the Old Testament *Book of Esther*), to the Talmud, and to medieval commentators in every tale as puns or ingenious paraphrases.

Representing simultaneously the universal and the insular strains of Jewish literature, the *Sendebar* tales also asserted the critical importance of Jews as mediators between the folklore of the East and the literature of Western Europe.

SEFER SHAASHUIM

Another important frame tale that also integrated beast fables is the *Sefer shaashuim* (*Book of Delight*) written in the 12th century by Joseph ben Meir ibn Zabara, a physician, satirist, and poet in Barcelona. In the rhymed prose of the Arabic *maqamat* narrative genre (discussed later), this Spanish physician's imaginary voyage with a demon companion named Enan Hanatash led from Barcelona through the world of women, animals, magical beings, and brute good sense, then back again to Spain.

Before setting out, Joseph admitted to his unnatural guest: "I fear your face has more than a trace of evil and unworthiness. Therefore I guess I had best decline your fine invitation to travel through the world lest an arrow of fate be hurled, just as felled the leopard with the fox." (Abrahams, http://www.authorama.com/delight-2/) This statement cleverly introduced the first beast parable, followed by a leopard's wife's version of a fox and lion story, in turn linked to a fox's tale. When tired after a day of journeying, the doctor-narrator Joseph ibn Zabara and the demon Enan rested at an inn. There they engaged in medical disputes that became important repositories of Judaic science and medicine. Ibn Zabara created a treasury of popular attitudes toward health and hygiene, physicians and cures, psychology and physics, physiology and physiognomy.

As noted, this long chain of hilarious stories composed in rhymed prose was directly borrowed from the Arabic *maqamat* tradition. However, *Sefer shaashuim* digressed from the genre's origins, insofar as the author, Ibn Zabara, assumes the role of author, narrator, and protagonist, whereas in the Arabic works these three roles are assumed by different personages. Moreover, whereas the episodes of the Arabic *maqamat* occur in a cyclical fashion, in the *Book of Delights*, the episodes are arranged according to a linear structure. Charming, learned, fanciful, whimsical, and satiric, *Sefer shaashuim* castigated folly and counseled vigilance against exaggerated seriousness. For Ibn Zabara, as for most writers of *maqamat*, beast fables, and frame tales, humor was the net to snare the spirit.

MAQAMA

Ibn Sahul's *Meshel haqadamoni* and Ibn Zubara's *Sefer shaashuim* represent just two examples of the extensive corpus of Hispano-Judaic literature written in rhymed prose. Medieval Spanish Jews enthusiastically adopted the uniquely Arabic genre of rhymed prose narrative, the *maqama* (pl. *maqamat*-sessions) which emerged in 10th-century Iraq and quickly spread to Spain. A full discussion of the Arabic literary genre is contained in the section on Muslim literature. Here it suffices to note that the popularity of the Arabic prose narrative encouraged Jewish writers to extend the use of Hebrew to the composition of secular literature rather than to preserve it almost exclusively for religious and liturgical purposes as earlier. Circa the year 1218 the accomplished Spanish poet Judah al-Harizi (1165–1235) translated into Hebrew the *Maqamat* of Abu Muhammad al-Qasim al-Hariri of Basra (d. 1052), considered the most exquisite example of the new Arabic prose genre, before undertaking the challenge of writing his own *maqamat* in Hebrew, entitled *Sefer tahkemoni* (*The Book of Wisdom or the Heroic*).

Sefer tahkemoni bears all the hallmarks of a classic *maqama* genre: a narrator who relates the comical adventures of the wily roguish protagonist Hever the Kenite, who always manages to escape unscathed from a difficult situation thanks to his eloquent tongue, brilliant satire, and clever ingenuity. Hever the Kenite appears in 50 unlinked episodes or "gates" in the most varied situations, for example, in a dispute between a rabbi and a Karaite, on the battlefield in "Of Battle Lords and Dripping Swords," as a preacher in "Brimstone and Wrath against the Worldly Path," or as a beggar working the crowd in "Beggars' Hearts versus Frozen Hearts." Wearing a variety of guises and disguises— whether preacher, erudite teacher, knight, philosopher, or magician—the hero always manages to win over his audience with his verbal acrobatics.

Heroic Romance

German Jews spoke vernacular German and were well acquainted with the romance epics such as the King Arthur cycle that circulated throughout Western Europe. The 14th and 15th centuries witnessed the composition of hybrid (macaronic) songs and poems combining German and Hebrew vocabulary, which would give rise to the development of the Yiddish language. In tandem with this linguistic innovation was the emergence of Jewish troubadours who performed versions of Christian epic romances, which they adapted to their Jewish audiences. Such adaptations were achieved by making the heroes Jewish and introducing elements of Jewish religious culture and Hebrew vocabulary. The first Yiddish heroic romance, entitled *Dukus Horunt*, is an adaptation of *Kudrun*, the mid-13th-century German epic saga of three rival kings and the quest to rescue the princess Gudrun.

The most popular of the Yiddish heroic romances was undoubtedly the aforementioned *Bovo-Bukh*, composed by Elijah Bahur (1469–1549). *Bovo-Bukh* finds its origins in the 13th-century Anglo-Norman romance *Sir Bevis of Hampton*, which had been translated into Italian as *Buovo d'Antona*. *Bovo Bukh* is the story is a young prince who yearns to ravenge the death of his father at the hands of his mother and her lover. Forced to flee to Flanders, Bovo falls in love with Druzane, the daughter of the king, who is captured by the king of Babylonia. The romance tells of Bovo's exploits in rescuing Druzane, smiting the Babylonian king and his son "Lucifer," and avenging his father's death. Also extant is a long and complete 14th-century Yiddish romance, *King Arthur*. The prolific writer Abraham ibn Hasdai, mentioned earlier as the translator of *Mishlei Sendebar*, translated into Hebrew the *Alexander Romance*. The authors of these Jewish romances introduce decidedly Jewish motifs: In the Arthurian romance the delightful Yiddish Sir Bove was not the only knight of King Arthur's court who *shalomed* (Hebrew, "peace be with you") and *dovened* (Hebrew, "daily ritual prayer") his way from battles to enchanted castles in Jewish heroic romances, and traditional banquet scenes are filled with references to bar mitzvahs, kosher feasts, and wedding rings inscribed with *Mazel Tov*.

Chanson de Geste

Just as Sephardic Jews of Spain adopted and adapted Arabic literary genres such as the *maqama* to produce original and veritable masterpieces in the Hebrew language, so, too, Ashkenazic Jews residing in northern France, England, Germany, and Italy appropriated Christian European genres such as the French *chansons de geste*, lending their works a distinctively Jewish flavor. William in the Jewish *Song of William* was fashioned after the historic Count William of Toulouse, a warrior of the Jewish al-Makhir dynasty descended from the line of the Davidian kings and allegedly granted control of the principality in Narbonne, France, as a reward for helping Charles Martel in his wars against the Muslims. The Jewish principality is said to have survived from 768 to 900.

This Count William epitomizes the multiple and contested versions of European epic poetry. According to the Jewish *chanson de geste*, he was a loyal knight who fought for Charlemagne in the East, led Frankish forces to capture Barcelona, and was earlier sent from France to the caliph of Baghdad to obtain for King Charlemagne the proofs of his stewardship of the holy city of Jerusalem so that at his coronation in 800 he could rightly claim to be emperor of the Holy Roman lands. Amusing episodes describe him following Jewish customs and law both before and after battle. Before eating, William always carefully and ceremonially washed his hands, silently saying a Hebrew blessing for hand washing. Since the Talmud required a man to feed his beast before himself, in the *Song of William* the hero's wife, Guiburc, first feeds and covers her husband's worn and weary horse before she places food before her famished husband. Needless to say, in the Christian versions of the epic, the family's name is changed from *al-Makhir* to *Aimeri*, and Count William is transformed into an exemplary Christian knight, descendant of the royal house of Merovingian kings, who goes on to found a monastery where he retires to live out his last days as a monk and is later canonized as a saint.

The historical Solomon, marquis of the Spanish march and descendant of the Makhiri princes in feudal France, apparently was the inspiration for the hero of French heroic poems called Bueve Cornebut, in English Bovo Horn Buster and in Hebrew *Gad a-Keren*. The

Middle English romance *Sir Bevis of Hampton*, composed circa 1324, derives from the same tradition.

Satire

KALONYMOUS BEN KALONYMOUS

Kalonymous ben Kalonymous, the 13th-century satirist of Provence, gained fame as a scholar and prolific translator of philosophical, medical, and mathematical books from Arabic or Latin into Hebrew. From a prominent, learned family and bearing his father's title of honor, Ha Nasi (the prince), Kalonymous was commissioned by King Robert of Naples to go to Rome to translate Hebrew scientific books into Latin. His translations were monumental in intellectual range and elegance of style. Their voluminousness is astounding.

Kalonymous's satires endeared him to the Hebrew-reading public that shared his annoyance with sanctimoniousness, ignorance, and self-destructive vice. Kalonymous aimed his caustic, ironic barrage against anyone deserving it, such as rabbis not as sacred as they seem, young scholars reveling in secret debauchery, and wealthy evil people buying protection for their souls.

His most popular satire was *Eben Bochan* (*The Touchstone*). Humor and right reason aimed to restore sanity to those simultaneously flaunting their piety, complaining against Judaism's restrictive responsibilities, and envying women while condemning them. If being a man subject to the 613 Talmudic obligations for holiness was so painful, then Kalonymous recommended becoming transsexual: After all, it was far more pleasant to be able to spend the day sitting, knitting, laughing, and talking about dresses than pouring over Mosaic law, rabbinic lore, philosophy, and ethics.

Kalonymous intruded his specifically Jewish satire in unexpected places. Into his translation of an Arabic encyclopedia he slipped his own description of a verbal battle between men and birds, a debate judged by the king of the birds. Questions to be resolved were, Ought man dominate beasts? Does man have the right to control the created world? Addressing the king, a Hebrew scholar from the East defended Jewish humankind as surely superior to the birds. Jews possess prophets and sages giving wise laws to conduct life according to God's design. They have synagogues and temples to pray in, praising the creator. Jews celebrate holidays and feasts to re-create the body and soul and have fast days, as Yom Kippur, to atone for sins. Since birds have none of these, surely the chosen people ought to rule over the ignorant, deprived feathered creatures. Quite the contrary, argued the bird king. The fact of fast days and penitential prayer simply displays Jews' sinfulness, never equal to the bird's winged innocence. The bird temple is the immense universe, without walls or ceiling, needing no rabbis to counsel or chastise the flock. Finding food and shelter in fields and gardens, mountains and valleys, they sing God's praises daily through the year, needing no fixed festivals for their cheerful exultation of his name. Only mankind's wickedness in hunting birds and abusing their habitat interferes with avian devotions. Clearly man is inferior in God's praise and does not have the right to dominate beasts.

Not surprisingly, this learned argument is adjudicated in favor of the birds. It represents yet another aspect of Judaic reverence for animals as displayed in beast fable and frame tale. Here, as in Chaucer's *Parliament of Foules*, Kalonymous dramatizes the political implications of irrationality. He carries to ultimate logical conclusions unquestioned illogical attitudes. As with most fine satire, the listener's unwilling mind, enticed by humor, is readily convinced.

IMMANUEL OF ROME

Kalonymous ben Kalonymous was highly respected in Rome along with other 13th- and 14th-century writers in that wealthy, aristocratic, and politically significant Jewish community. Immanuel of Rome was one such fine satirist. He was superbly educated, medically trained, a friend of Dante, and a disciple of Maimonides. Immanuel was a masterly writer of lewdly erotic sonnets and wielder of a poetic "rod of anger" scourging stupidity. So impudent, independent, and infuriatingly exultant was Immanuel's satire that the Portuguese rabbi Joseph Karo (1488–1575) specifically mentions in his code of Jewish law, *Shulkhan Arukh* (*The Set Table*), that all of Immanuel's poetry should be forbidden definitively, effectively depriving pious Jews of reading the works of Immanuel of Rome for nearly 500 years.

Immanuel of Rome's *Mahberot* (*The Compositions of Immanuel*), the Hebrew name for the *maqama* genre of rhymed prose narrative) was deemed sinful reading because of the prohibition against sitting in "the seat of scorners," a reference to Psalms 1:1, which meant, among other things, avoiding associating with sinners who add insult to injury by scoffing, mocking, and "scorning" their sinfulness. Imitating Dante's *Divine Comedy* as a voyage to the otherworld, Immanuel peopled his heaven with skinny withered old women with warts on their noses who were pretentiously pure and sexually dry. Hell had the luscious honest whores, who revel in their active beauty, using breasts and vulvas for sharing pleasures and celebrating life.

But hell also contained pagan classical thinkers such as Plato, Aristotle, and Galen. In the deepest abyss walked a "band of blind people," leaders of the Jewish people who had physical eyes yet refused to see, who ridiculed knowledge and science, and who thus defrauded their people. Immanuel always vivified condemnation by his extraordinary wit. Dante's friend Busone da Gubbio called Immanuel's genius his "happily laughing soul." Even in Dante's literary heaven, prophets and patriarchs joyfully welcomed him from afar: "Immanuel is coming. We shall enjoy much laughter."

PURIM PARODIES

During the 12th to 14th centuries Jewish writers began to incorporate satirical parodies of the Purim liturgy into their celebration of that joyful and carnivelesque holiday. The rowdy German satirical Purim plays (*Purimspiel*) were possibly influenced by Christian carnival celebrations exulted in abundant wine drinking and merriment. In the 12th century Menachem ben Aaron composed the *Hymn for the Night of Purim*, a parody of a real hymn, the *Hymn for the First Night of Passover*, written by Meir ben Isaac, which is preserved in the *Mazhor Vitry*, a collection of juridical *responsa*, laws, and prayers compiled in the same century by Simhah ben Samuel in Vitry, France. Menachem ben Aaron's hymn is an ode to the joys of intoxication.

In the 14th century parody came into its own as a separate literary genre, and no religious feast or pietistic movement was deemed taboo. The anonymous *Megillat Setarim*, or *Scroll of Secrecy*, parodies the Talmudic *Megillat Esther*, or Scroll of Esther, which is read during the Purim liturgy. Kalonymous ben Kalonymous penned his *Masekhet Purim* (Purim Tractate), which also paradies the Scroll of Esther. The anonymous *Sefer Habakhuk ha Navi* (*Book of Habakhuk the Prophet*) also appeared in this century. An anonymous 15th-century satire from Provence also entitled *Masekhet* (*Purim Tractate*), features the fictitious election of a Purim king who will reign over Jewish towns for the month preceding the Purim festival.

The Purim parodies typically portray biblical and rabbinic characters in hilarious situations. Mordechai, one of the heroes of the Book of Esther, may be redrawn as a buffoon, while the villain of the story, Hamam, might reappear as a tragic figure. The real prophets Noah and Lot are shown as drunkards alongside fictitious characters such as "Prophet Habakbuk" (the Bottle) and Rabbi Shakhra (the Drunkard).

Poems of Love and War

IMMANUEL OF ROME

Proudly calling himself prince of poets, Immanuel of Rome wrote structurally dazzling and linguistically graceful poems. His poetry is also important in the sixth classification of Jewish literature: poems of love and war. Never hypocritically humble, Immanuel considered himself master of love and passion, meriting the royal crown for erotica.

His Italian sonnets voice lusty delight in physical pleasure. Elegantly insolent and nobly vulgar, his poetry, unfortunately, cannot be translated into English. Let one example suggest the richness of the original. Immanuel spent a jovial weekend at a villa enjoying both the hospitality and the secret bed of the noble lady. He said in farewell to her and her husband, "I could live forever in your quaint house." *Quaint* has five meanings: "charming," "beautifully used," "sensible and alive with experience," "valuable," and "vagina."

JUDAH HALEVI

Two earlier lyric poets of the golden age of Spanish Jewry (10th through 12th centuries) command attention for their versatility, learning, and rhapsodic magnificence. They are Judah Halevi and Samuel ibn Nagrela. Judah Halevi of Toledo (1075–1144) was an eminent court physician, a philosopher, and the author of more than 800 poems in Hebrew and Arabic expressing his profound yearning for the Jewish return to the Holy Land and his fervent love of God. Judah Halevi's ecstatic celebrations of Zion appear in modern Jewish prayer books. Devout scholars cherish his liturgical odes and nationalistic epistles. Yet this poet, philosopher, and physician also wrote secular love songs, wedding odes, satires, epigrams, riddles, and seafaring poems, although even these secular works were steeped in religious feeling. The German poet Heinrich Heine said of Judah Halevi that his poems were "God-kissed."

The most sensual love is inherently spiritual. Judah Halevi's "fire and dew" love poems depicted human love as beautiful earthly shadows of divine substance. Judah Halevi's language of love longing was the same whether his beloved was a beautiful woman, the city of Jerusalem, or God himself. His most famous poem "My Heart Is in the East," begins thus: "My heart is in the East and I in the uttermost West. How can I find savor in food? How shall it be sweet?" (Cited in http://www.myjewishlearning.com/ideas_belief/LandIsrael). After Judah Halevi laments, he sets out from Spain to the holy city. Is this true geography or metaphoric discovery of the intricacies of female anatomy? As John Donne centuries later praised his beloved in bed as his "America," his "new found land," so Judah Halevi depicts the ecstasy of divine love understood on Earth through the medium of sensual splendor.

No matter how universal the theme of desire, anguish, or unrequited love, Judah Halevi wrote with the particular passion of the Jew among the Others. Judah Halevi saw himself as a Spanish Jew fighting against the Christian Europeans, the Western Jew against the Eastern Muslims occupying the holy places. Although he was a privileged court physician in Córdoba, he was not immune to the suffering of his Jewish coreligionists under the Almoravid regime and at the hands of Christian crusaders in the East. Neither universalist nor insular, his poetry represents the medieval Judaic particularist trend. Unlike Maimonides, who demanded understanding God, Judah Halevi inspired loving God. Human kissing and acts of love merely transmitted the soul's language out from its inexpressible smoldering center. Bodily pleasures were the second concentric circle yearningly radiating out to the third of divine love.

SAMUEL IBN NAGRELA

One hundred years earlier in Andalusia, another Jewish poet combined the demands of public service with private art. With masterly control over languages, Samuel wrote poems in Hebrew, Arabic, and Castilian, displaying poetic virtuosity in at least 57 separate verse meters. Samuel ibn Nagrela (993–1056) was a "prince" or ruler of the Sephardic Jews in Muslim Spain. Not only leader of the Jewish community, Samuel Ha Nagid (Samuel the Prince), as he was called, was also appointed vizier in 1038 to the court of Granada and commander to the Zirid ruler Badis al-Muzaffar's armies. A skilled and canny statesman he was able to survive the intrigues of the Zirid court. (The same would not be true for his son, Yusuf, who succeeded him in the vizierate, who was assassinated in 1066 after rumors of corruption, along with other members of the Jewish community.) Samuel Ha Naguid was mystically inspired enough by his own talents to act with "God's assurance" as chosen protector to his people, and devoted and affectionate enough to write to his son from the battlefield tent poems of advice, fear, or triumph.

Samuel ibn Nagrela's war poems depicted the exhilaration of battle, the brave stuggles of strong horsemen. The poetry also chronicled the terrors and loneliness of the war fields, the battle camps at night, and the ruined citadels whose once proud warriors buried beneath the rubble reminded the author of his own mortality. The long battle poems are heroic in their description of daring deeds. But the Jewish prince always particularizes the events and his reactions as Jewish. He shines the light of his experience through a Jewish prism, bending every ray from the color of the universal to that of the particular.

Amid the cries of battle joy and the clashings of chain-mailed warriors with glistening shields, Samuel entreated the Jewish patriarchs and God for mercy prayed for salvation. Each battle day was another personal day of judgment and each assault or siege he survived demonstrated God's protective attention to his warrior minions.

Samuel strictly observed the Sabbath in the field. When work was forbidden he commanded his armies to rest from their toil. Seductive though it is, war always destroys: "War at first a beautiful maid / with whom every man flirts. At the end, she is a despised hag. All who meet her she grieves and hurts" (Weinberger 118).

When not acting as general, Samuel was a courtier and politician, prime minister of an Islamic realm. As the Toledan philosopher, astronomer, and historian Abraham ibn Daud Halevi (1110–80) described him, he merited all four crowns: the crown of Torah, the crown of power, the crown of Levite, and the crown of a good name. When Samuel died, his contemporary the great medieval Arab historian Ibn Hayyan of Córdoba (d. 1076), grudgingly admired him for his many qualities of moral perfection and probity.

Some of Samuel ibn Nagrela's love poems are almost never found in anthologies because of their blatantly sexual and homoerotic images. As passionate as they are mannered, these poems exhibit traditional Arabic structural formulas and wordplays. In the Taifa (Petty Kingdom) courts of 11th-century Islamic Spain, for example, it was customary to have as cup bearers young men usually addressed by animal names of endearment, such as Fawn, Hind, Doe, or Gazelle. These erotic entertainers often cultivated a lisp or stutter and spoke with sexually suggestive wordplay.

Religious Poetry

PIYYUT

Liturgical poetry, known as *piyyut* (pl. *piyyutim*), has been composed since Mishnaic times (from 200 C.E. onward) in Hebrew or Aramaic to be sung, chanted, or recited during religious services. Solomon ibn Gabriol (d. 1058), the renowned Jewish poet and philosopher of Spain, composed the "Adon Olam" (Lord of the World) in a rhyming iambic tetrameter, and remains one of the best loved poems often sung daily at the end of synagogue services or at the close of the Sabbath even today.

The *piyyut Maoz tzur*, "Rock of Ages," is a powerful liturgical poem recited or sung at Hanukkah. The origins and authorship are debated; however, the most likely theories date the poem to the martyrdom of Jews in Mainz, Germany, during the First Crusade in 1096 or during the Second Crusade (1145–48) and the author's first name is thought to be Mordecai. The first five stanzas of the poem are written in the past tense and recall the occasions in the Bible when God spared the Jews from the persecution of their enemies, such as the Exodus from Egypt, the end of the Babylonian captivity, and the miraculous delivery of the Persian Jews from the evil vizier Hamam (the Festival of Purim). The final stanzas are situated in the present time and the poet switches to the present tense to express his hopes that the Temple will be rebuilt in Jerusalem and that the enemies of the Jews will be defeated.

Despite the ban on reading Immanuel of Rome, his poetic version of the *Yigdal* (meaning "may God be hallowed"), an allusion to Maimonides' "Thirteen Articles of the Creed" written in the form of a sonnet, was allowed to be sung in the synagogues at the opening of the morning prayer and the close of evening services. An even more popular *Yigdal* was the *piyyut* composed by the liturgical poet Daniel ben Judah Dayyan of Rome in the early 15th century.

MARTYROLOGICAL POEMS

The 11th to 13th centuries saw the flourishing of a new genre of religious poetry among the Ashkenazic Jews in northern France and the

זה לויתן

Leviathan, c. 1280. Fish curving to form a circle. The Leviathan was, according to Talmudic sources, one of the mythical creatures that would be consumed at the messianic banquet awaiting the virtuous in the world to come. From the North French Miscellany, *a Hebrew manuscript written by Benjamin the Scribe.* HIP/Art Resource, NY.

Rhineland in Germany, the poetry of martyrdom. Written in Hebrew or in the European vernacular languages, the poetry finds its precedents in biblical descriptions of martyrdoms, such as the story of the Maccabees, and in rabbinical discussions of these biblical texts. Yet the martyrological laments were composed in response to real historical events: the mass pogroms and murders visited upon Jewish community in the wake of crusader fervor, the fanaticism aroused by the celebration of Easter, or the fury unleashed by unfounded rumors of Jews' desecrating the Christian host. Rabbi Meir of Rothenburg composed a moving lament to the Talmud after the burning of the Jewish Talmud in Paris in 1242. No fewer than seven martyrdom laments were composed to commemorate the terrible events surrounding the burning of 31 Jews in the French city of Blois in 1171, as revenge for the alleged murder of a Christian child.

Instruction Books

The seventh classification of Jewish secular literature are the ethical instruction books, the *musar*. While some were uninventive lists of exhortation to piety, the most popular instruction books combined the familiar medieval techniques of pleasing while teaching, instructing while delighting. Not surprisingly, animal tales and beast references were important literary devices and moral instructors.

SEFER HASIDIM

The most influential of all Jewish instruction books was the *Sefer hasidim* (*Book of the Pious*), which preserved both medieval ideas of Jewish piety and good conduct and ingenious methods for teaching it.

Though the *Book of the Pious* generally is ascribed to Judah the Pious Kalonymous

(d. 1217), it was probably written over the course of several generations by three men of the same Kalonymous family. Judah's father, Rabbi Samuel b. Kalonymous, also known as "the Pious," wrote much of the introduction, and a disciple and probable nephew, Eleazar the Pious of Worms, also participated in the composition. Their instruction manual represented the most radically particularist form of literature, since its aim was to draw a sharp dividing line between "the pious" and "the adversaries," the latter being "other Jews" rather than the Gentiles, as one might expect (Schafer 31).

Between the years 1150 and 1250 these men were leading figures in the new movement of pious asceticism that emerged among the so-called *Shum* communities, a Hebrew acronym for the German Jewish populations of Speyer, Worms, and Mainz. The movement was known as the "Pious of Ashkenaz" (*Hasidei Ashkenaz*), and it blended the old Palestinian-Babylonian *Merkavah* mysticism, which envisaged the mystical ascent as a journey upward toward the seven heavens to the divine throne, with a new radically moral asceticism aimed at the common folk. It should be noted that the term *Hasid* (pl. *Hasidim*) simply means "pious" and this 12th-century movement bears no direct relation to the later Hasidic movement that would emerge in modern Poland. This German *Book of the Pious* insisted that none of the world's people other than the Jews were commanded to sacrifice themselves for the sanctification of God's name. The reason for this redefinition of the phrase "chosen people" was to vindicate the superiority of Jewish piety in the face of the horrific treatment of the Jews after the Second Crusade and to counter contemporary Christian exaltation of their own martyrs. If each Jew was required to become a martyr for God's word, then he had better learn to love God better than he loved life, and the *Book of the Pious* provides clear instructions on how the pious Jew should conduct him- or herself when facing martyrdom. It also addresses the question of disguising oneself as a means of avoiding persecution, allowing, for example, beardless youths to dress as women or women to dress as males and carry a sword in order to avoid detection, but prohibiting disguising onslf as a monk or priest or wearing a cross.

Furthermore, a pious Jew dying for God's word had better understand it. Thus the *Book of the Pious* counseled prayer not in Hebrew but in the vernacular languages people spoke and understood, for if prayer were the heart's petition, how could it be successful if the heart did not understand what the lips spoke?

The *Sefer hasidim* preached ascetic freedom from the bonds of worldly goods. It counseled self-sacrificial concern for others' material necessities. What is mine is yours, and what is yours is yours. Such sensitivity pertained to emotion as well: Do not kiss your children in the synagogue, for a person having no children might be accidentally hurt and grieved by your joy.

The pious person did not deny himself sexuality. Hasidism was at once ascetic and sexually erotic. Human love was earthly intimation of heavenly passion for God. The body sometimes required abnegation but usually required celebration. Through its ecstasies one ascended to heavenly ideas. Through it, by descending to brute sense, one reaffirmed affinities to others of God's creatures, the animals.

Likewise, by humbling human pride the Hasid penitentially made restitution for human use and exploitation of animals. Furthermore, Hasidism preached a type of Jewish pantheism, describing God's presence in all creatures. For this reason, time and again, the *Book of the Pious* exhorted the pious to refrain from harming any living creature.

The *Sefer hasidim* also gave Jews clear advice about how to maintain the boundaries between them and their Christian neighbors. We find, for instance, that no window of a Jewish house or synagogue should look out upon a church, nor should a Jewish family reside in a part of town where it would have to share water with Christians. Other passages were unabashedly polemical: A Christian shows some Jews a garment that he claims was once worn by Jesus. He then tosses it into a fire and seeing that it does not burn, tries to convince the Jews to convert to Christianity. A Jewish sage has the garment taken to him, washes it with vinegar, then tosses it again into a fire, whereupon it is immediately consumed by the flames (Schafer 38). Yet many passages in the *Book of the Pious* reflect positive relations between Jews and Christians, giving guidance on how to pray together for rainfall in times of drought.

Exempla

Exempla were were short popular tales rabbis inserted in their homilies and lessons in order to explain the rudiments of Jewish law, generally arranged in manuscripts according to subject or a calendrical order of ritual prayer. A rabbi needing to expound upon a biblical point or Talmudic idea simply turned to the requisite section in his trusty book. For example, to explain the biblical concept "Cast your bread upon the waters" (Eccles. 11:1) a good exempla collection provided several explanatory tales taken from Haggadah beast fables, frame tales, or similar sources.

It was not at all unusual to find a beast fable amid the learned discourse of medieval rabbis. This type of exemplum was at once universal, insular, and particular. As were other examples of Haggadic medieval literature, exempla were characterized by whimsy, charm, virtuosic wordplay, and a plethora of intelligent animals. Beast adventures taught virtue. Beast advice prevented folly and vice. Medieval Jewish secular literature reaffirmed man's and woman's middle place in God's great chain of being, mediating gracefully between beasts and angels.

Works of Wisdom

The works of wisdom are numerous spiritual and moral writings that could be considered instruction manuals for the soul. The 11th-century Spanish moralist Bahya ibn Pakuda of Zaragoza is renowned for his *Hovot ha-levavot* (*Duties of the Heart*), which he wrote originally in Arabic in 1080 and later was translated into Hebrew. The eponymous "duties of the heart" that are meant to guide the moral life of Jews include a series of obligations to God and one's fellows, especially the belief in the existence and unity of God, trust in God, love and fear of God, and repentance, followed by a set of prohibitions, such as against bearing grudges or taking revenge. The work is clearly modeled upon contemporary Muslim spiritual and mystical works in which the reader must ascend through a series of 10 gates in the interior journey toward spiritual perfection.

Judah Halevi's philosophical novel *Ha Kuzari* expresses these yearnings for the land of Israel and his profound belief in the Jews as the chosen people and the Hebrew language as the chosen language of divine revelation. The novel, written in the form of a dialogue between the king and a Muslim, a Christian, and a Jewish philosopher, is based upon the true events surrounding the conversion of the Turkish tribe known as the Khazars to the Jewish religion. The dialogues that lead the king ultimately to choose the Jewish religion are simultaneously a manifestation of philosophical logic, a vindication of Judaism against its Muslim and Christian detractors, and a guide for spiritual perfection.

Jewish Crusader Chronicles

Jewish populations throughout Western Europe became the unwitting victims of Christian crusader fervor. In many cases even the protection of a Christian monarch himself was insufficient to spare the lives of entire communities. Jewish historians and eyewitnesses to these events left heart-wrenching chronicles of the heroic act of *qiddush ha-Shem*, or the "sanctifying of the holy name," the Jewish idiomatic expression for martyrdom. Solomon bar Samson, a German Jewish writer of whom little or nothing is known, wrote a chronicle in the year 1140 describing the horrors of the slaughter of Jews in Mainz who had taken refuge in the archepiscopal palace. The events described took place on May 27, 1096, during the First Crusade as Christian Knights and laypeople made their way to Jerusalem. Samson highlights the extraordinary courage of the women:

> The children of the holy covenant who were there, martyrs who feared the Most High, although they saw the great multitude, an army numerous as the sand on the shore of the sea, still clung to their Creator. Then young and old donned to their armor and girded on their weapons and at their head was Rabbi Kalonymus ben Meshullam, the chief of the community. Yet because of the many troubles and the fasts which they had observed they had no strength to stand up against the enemy. [They had fasted to avert the impending evils.] Then came gangs and bands, sweeping through like a flood until Mayence [Mainz] was filled from end to end.... The women there girded their loins with strength and slew their sons and their daughters and then themselves. Many men, too, plucked coverage and killed their wives, their sons, their infants. The tender and delicate mother slaughtered the babe she had played with, all of them, men and women arose and slaughtered one another. The maidens and the young brides and grooms looked out of the windows and in a loud voice cried: "Look and see, O our God, what we do for the sanctification of Thy great name in order not to exchange you for a hanged and crucified one." (J. Marcus, 1938, pp. 115–120)

Jewish historians also recorded the devastating impact of the bizarre Christian accusations of ritual murder that surfaced in the 12th century, claiming that the Jews murdered a Christian child in order to obtain its blood to be used in the celebration of the Passover. As the scholar Miri Rubin argues, such accusations were probably a reflection of Christian doubts and anxieties about the Christian doctrine of the transubstantiation and a tragic expression of extreme religious piety. A German Jewish talmudist, Ephraim ben Jacob (1132–1200), preserves an account of the burning of more than 30 Jewish men and women in the city of Blois that took place in May 1171. He writes in his *A Book of Historical Records*, "The Christian servants hastened back to his master and said, 'Here, my lord, what a certain Jew did. As I rode behind him toward the river in order to give your horses at drink, I saw him throw a little Christian child, whom the Jews have killed, into the water. When I saw this, I was horrified and hastened back quickly for fear he might kill me too'. . . . The next morning the master rode to the ruler of the city, to the cruel Theobald. . . . He was our ruler that listened to falsehood, for his servants were wicked. . . . When he heard this he became enraged and had all the Jews seized and thrown into prison." (J. Marcus, 1938, pp. 127–130)

In describing the murder by burning, the author records: "It was also reported in a letter that as the flames mounted high, the martyrs began to sing in unison a melody that began softly but ended up with a full voice. The Christian people came and asked us, 'What kind of a song is this for we have never heard such a sweet melody?' The author exclaims, 'O daughters of Israel, weep for the thirty-one souls that were burned for the sanctification of the Name, and let your brothers, the entire house of Israel, bewail the burning.'" (J. Marcus, 1938, pp. 127–130)

Major Jewish Writers

Judah Halevi (c. 1075–1141). Spanish rabbi, poet, and philosopher, best known for his remarkable philosophical novel *Sefer ha Kuzari*, which was inspired by the real conversion of a Turkic tribe to Judaism centuries earlier.

Berechiah Ha Nakdan (alive 12th–13th centuries). English Jewish exegete, moralist, grammarian, and translator, best known for his Hebrew work *Mishlei shualim*, or *Fox Fables*.

Judah al-Harizi (1165–1234). Spanish rabbi, translator of Maimonides' Arabic works into Hebrew, and acclaimed poet, best known for introducing the Arabic *maqamat* genre of rhymed prose fiction into Hebrew literature and author of the first Hebrew *maqama*, the *Book of Tahkemoni*.

Abraham ben Meir ibn Ezra (c. 1049–1164). Famous Spanish grammarian, biblical commentator, poet, philosopher, and astronomer; author of a massive *Diwan* (anthology of religious and secular poems). He is responsible for introducing Ashkenazic Jews to the scholarly and literary output of Arabic writing by Jews and Muslims.

Solomon ibn Gabriol (Avicebron) (c. 1021–1058). Major poet and philosopher in Malaga, Spain; author of numerous secular poems on love and nature, religious mystical poetry, he is best known for his magnum opus, the *Fons vitae* (*The Well of Life*), and his poetic anthology *The Improvement of the Moral Qualities*.

Samuel ibn Nagrela (993–1056). Vizier to the Zirid court of Granada, leader "prince" of the Sephardic community of Muslim Spain, and renowned poet whose *Diwan* (anthology) includes poems on platonic and erotic love, religion, and warfare.

Isaac ibn Sahula (alive 13th century). Castilian prose writer and court poet to Alfonso X, best known for his masterpiece of rhymed prose (*maqama*) *Meshel haqadmoni* (*The Tale of the Ancient One*).

Immanuel the Roman (c. 1265–1330). Renowned scholar and poet and infamous satirist, noted for having introduced the sonnet into Hebrew literature. His *Mahberot Immanuel* (*Compositions of Immanuel*) scandalized the pious Jewish community with their erotic and satirical content.

Numerous references in this chapter indicate the close literary ties connecting Jewish and Muslim writers. Spanish Jews played a leading role in translating Arabic scientific and literary works into Hebrew and European languages, making them known to Ashkenazic Jews and Christians throughout Europe. At the same time, Jewish writers were particularly inspired by Arabic poetry and prose writing, especially the *maqama* genre, and demonstrated time and again that they were as capable as their Muslim neighbors and rivals of producing masterful literary works in Arabic and especially in Hebrew. The following section discusses the Arabo-Muslim literature and its contribution to a universal medieval literature.

ISLAMIC LITERATURE

Medieval Arab-Islamic literature is an amalgam of the contributions of the literary genres and traditions of the peoples who inhabited the medieval Islamic world. Pride of place must be accorded to the Arabs, whose Classical Arabic language became the lingua franca of the Islamic world: the language of political administration and religion, as well as the language of cultural expression. The pure Arabic of the pre-Islamic Bedouins—preserved in poetry, proverbs, oratory, epic narratives, song, the Quran, and the sayings and speeches of Muhammad—served as the literary model for future generations of Arabs and non-Arabs. Persians, Egyptians, Indians, Berbers, and others adopted the language and literary customs of the Arabs, infusing them with their own indigenous genres. In turn, a variety of literary genres, including stories, fables, "mirrors for princes," and philosophical literature, were translated from Greek, Persian, Hindi, or Sanskrit into Arabic and subsequently into European languages.

Pre-Islamic Arabic Literary Genres: Poetry and Song

In their origins, pre-Islamic poetry and song are oral-literary genres, composed to be performed in public either by the poet himself (*shair*) or a professional reciter or bard, known as a *rawi*. Many poems were composed to be sung rather than recited, and these, together with conventional songs, were sung by a professional singer, called a *mughanni*. Desert warriors and nomads sang songs of their own noble heritage, their tribal virtues, and their heroic adventures. Some wrote panegyrics recording the feats of their patrons. Women poets sang mourning songs for dead relatives or friends. Female mourners were called *naihat* and performed the lamentation for the dead known as *nawh*.

Traditionally poetry has been called the *diwan al-Arab*, or "register of the Arabs," in reference to the singular social role and historical significance of poetry in Arabic societies, among the pre-Islamic Bedouins as well as the urbane medieval Arabs of Baghdad, Damascus, Córdova, and similar cultural centers. Poetry was the medium through which momentous events and the feats of important persons of a tribe or other social units were recorded and transmitted to future generations. In the medieval period, poetry inserted in historical chronicles, biographical dictionaries, and other genres of prose writing continued to serve this memorial function, testifying as well to the impact and perception of events on the persons involved.

QASIDA

Perhaps the most significant pre-Islamic poetic form is the *qasida*, or ode. The *qasida* was a poem consisting of between 60 and 100 lines with the same rhyme running throughout, and whose main theme was boasting or panegyric. It was composed in two hemstitches and the rhyme was maintained at first in both lines, and subsequently only in the second hemstitch. In addition to these aesthetic limitations in poetic form, the *qasida* was characterized by three parts or movements: (1) The *nasib*, or amatory prelude, evoked the painful separation of lovers from neighboring tribes that have settled briefly in the same camp in the desert but must go their separate ways. The hero tries to forget his beloved but lingers tearfully over all the details of her departure, tears streaming down his face. (2) On the dangerous journey, typically on camelback, the poet extols the strength of his camel, in the hope that it will be able to catch up with his lover. The poem may also extol the surrounding landscape, hunting, and other desert *topoi*. (3) In the self-praise or boasting (*mufakhara*) the poet would speak of his own heroism, generosity, courage, and fortitude, called in Arabic *sabr*, or a "panegyric" (*madih* or *madh*), in which he praises the virtues of his tribe. As an alternative to these panegyric themes, the final part might be an elegy of love (*ghazal*) or a satire (*hija*) of the enemies of the poet, his patron, or the tribe. The first two sections of the poem are considered a prelude to the final, most important part. These poems were not written in the pre-Islamic period, giving rise to the existence of several versions of a single *qasida*, since the *rawi*, or poet, was free to improvise. A particular group of poems, which were called the *Muallaqat*, or "Suspended Poems," gained the fame of representing the best examples of Arabic poetry.

A *qasida* of the sixth-century Yemeni poet-prince and reputed inventor of the genre Imrul al-Qays begins as follows:

> Stop, oh my friends, let us pause to weep
>   over the remembrance of my beloved.
> The traces of her encampment are not
>   wholly obliterated even now.
> For when the South wind blows the sand
>   over them the North wind sweeps it
>   away. . .
> On the morning of our separation it was
>   as if I stood in the gardens of our tribe,
> Amid the acacia-shrubs where my eyes
>   were blinded with tears by the smart
>   from the bursting pods of colocynth.

> ("The Poem of Imru-ul-Qais."
> Available online.URL: http://www.
> sacredtexts.com/isl/hanged.

In emblematic scenes, male pre-Islamic poets praised the landscape, beasts, women, and men (whether as lovers or friends). Women poets tended to excel in the subgenre of elegy, as the poetry of al-Khansa (600–670) illustrates. Al-Khansa, a noble Bedouin woman was a contemporary of the prophet Muhammad. Having lost brothers and sons in battle, her poetic lamentations beautifully express her sorrow. Her most famous poem is "Lament for Her Brother":

> In the evening remembrance keeps me
>   awake, and in the morning I am worn
>   out by the overwhelming disaster in
>   the case of Sakhr, and what youth is

there like Sakhr to deal with a day of
warring and skilful spear-thrust?
And to deal with tenacious opponents
when they transgress so that he can
assert the right of someone on whom
oppression has fallen?
I have not seen his like in the extent of
the disaster caused by his death, either
among *djinn* or among men. Truly
strong against the vicissitudes of
fortune and decisive in affairs, showing
no confusion. . . .
Ah, O Sakhr, I shall never forget you
until I part from my soul and my grave
is cut.
The rising of the sun reminds [me] of
Sakhr, and I remember him every time
the sun sets.

(Al Khansas's Lament for Her Brother.
Available online. URL: http://www.
westsa.edu/~mhamil/Khansa.html.)

Since the language of these pre-Islamic
poems and songs was useful for understanding
the difficult language of the Quran, in the eighth
century Muslim scholars began to edit and compile them into written anthologies and to cate-
gorize them according to periods of development.
The Abbasid prince and poet Ibn al-Mutazz (d.
908) was one of the first philologists to distinguish four periods of Arabic poetry, the pre-
Islamic poetry of *al-qudama*, "ancients"; the
period of the *mukhadram*, referring to poets of
the period straddling the Jahiliyya (pre-Islamic)
and early Islamic eras; the *awail al-islamiyyin*, literally, "first Islamic poets," referring to the
Umayyad composers; and the *muhdathun*, or
"modern poets," referring to those of the medieval period under the Abbasids.

Great ninth-century writers utilized the
Arabic past as well as the great renaissance of
classical philosophy and science in the many
Greek texts that in translation augmented the
magnificent Islamic libraries.

UMAYYAD AND ABBASID POETRY

Poetry under the Umayyads and the Abbasids
retained many of the features from the pre-
Islamic period: Most of the famous poets, Ghiyath ibn Ghawth ibn al-Salt, also known as
al-Akhtal ("the loquacious") (d. c. 710); Tammam ibn Ghalib, also known as al-Farazdaq
("the lump of dough") (d. c. 739), and Jarir ibn
Atiyya ibn al-Khatafa (d. 729), for example,
were all of Bedouin origin. They remained
faithful to the pre-Islamic conventions of the
qasida, although the court culture of Umayyad
Damascus and later Abbasid Baghdad favored
the prominence of the panegyric of the ruler
and other wealthy patrons over the ancient
themes of the desert journey or the praise of
one's tribe. Some important changes took
place, however, which particularly reflect the
influence of Islam, among them the heroic
ethos and the poetry expressing it. Pre-Islamic
poetry celebrated great deeds and triumphs
over adversaries both human and natural.
Death was the logical conclusion of heroic
honor. By contrast, the philosophically and
religiously puritanical Kharijites, for example,
wrote heroic poems, rejecting the ostentation
and secularity of the Islamic enterprise and
extolling the glories of martyrdom.

GOLDEN AGE OF ARABIC POETRY

The golden age of Arabic poetry generally
refers to the period spanning the final decades
of Umayyad rule (c. 720s–49) and the height of
the Abbasid period, from 750 to the end of the
11th century. Its literary center was the Abbasid
court at Baghdad, which attracted the best and
brightest luminaries of traditional Arabic poetry
as well as the vanguards of poetic and prose
innovations. Poetic output began to decline in
the Arab East when the Seljuk Turks overran
Baghdad in 1055 and then the Mongols sacked
the magnificent city in 1258, delivering the

coup de grace to its literary genius. Literary Baghdad was not easily equaled, except perhaps by the poets and prose writers of al-Andalus, whose golden age of the ninth and 10th centuries coincided with the zenith of the Umayyad dynasty. Though conventional rhythms, imagery, phrasing, and syntax guided and guarded much Arabic poetry, some descriptions were startlingly original.

Umayyad and Abbasid court poets marshalled their poetic skills to praise royal patrons and revile royal enemies, often providing valuable historical narratives of the events of their times. Abbasid poet al-Buhturi (d. 897) epitomizes the role of the poet-hero who extolled the religious and moral virtues of the Abbasid rulers vis-à-vis their Alid rivals. The murder of Caliph al-Mutawakkil in 867 prompted al-Buhturi to write:

> Will Time ever retrieve for me my days in white palaces and countyards?
> There's no union with them momentarily, nor do they have a minute for a visit.
> A moment of merriment is not renewed in memory without renewing my ardor for them.
> A yearning, among many, left me awake at night, as if it were one malady among many.

> (Samer Mahdy Ali 2005–06. Formerly available online. URL: http://www.uib. no/jais/v006ht/06-001-023Ali1PP. htm#_ftn27)

Poetic Genres

GHAZAL

Love poetry changed in a number of ways during the Islamic period. The initial amatory prelude to the pre-Islamic *qasida* (*nasib*), in which the hero mourned a past love that he strove to forget, was transformed into an erotic poem dedicated to the present object of his affections, often in the form of independent love poems called *ghazal*. Under the influence of Umayyad and especially Abbasid court culture, the *nasib* tended to give way to the panegyrics (*madih*) dedicated to the caliph or other patrons, while the raunchier erotic poems were sometimes known by the subgeneric name of *mujuniyyat*.

UDHRI POETRY

A major innovation of the Umayyad poets was the adaptation of love poetry to an independent love lyric that celebrated chaste, or *udhri*, love. This poetry took its name from the tribe of Udhra, nicknamed "those who die when they love." In *udhri* poetry the hero lover is intensely ardent, chaste, and so hopelessly enamored of his beloved—who may not even know of his existence or who cruelly rejects him—that he slowly wastes away and dies. While in the traditional qasida the pre-Islamic warrior hero rushes headlong into battle for honor and generosity of spirit, the *udhri* lover, such as depicted by the seventh-century poet Jamil ibn Abdallah ibn Mamar al-Udhri (d. 701), conceives of his love as a form of jihad, and the lover as a martyr who dies for love. Some scholars have suggested that Arabic *udhri* poetry may have influenced the courtly love lyric of the West, transmitted through the introduction of Muslim female court poets and singers into European courts.

Abbasid love poetry has many similarities to the Western 12th-century troubadour songs and courtly love songs in which fully requited love was socially impossible. The troubadour praised a high-born, imperious, exquisite, learned woman who was inaccessible because she was his social superior and another man's wife. Abu Nuwas, Abu l-Atahiya, and the other Abbasid poets praised intelligent, beautiful professional singers who as slaves were social inferiors yet socially inaccessible as another man's

بعدق ... كند از ماه مشك | مى افكند ان سرو برخاك خشك
... كفت فر باذ ازين يره بخت | كى اوكند برجاز من بند ...
... هجران براتش فكند ان ... | ... نم جه خواهذ هى ازين د
بزارى سوى اسمان كرد ست | ... هى كفت اى داو داذ كر
توداني كانت صبر مى طافتم | نوده سيدى زنر بذ زاح ...
كفت ازسهى سروادرزكنا | ... بوسيذ رحسار ان نو بهان ...

Scene from the only known illustrated manuscript of the poem the Romance of Varqa and Gulshah, *by Urwa b. Huzam al-Udhri, paintings by Abd al Mumin al-Khuwayyi. Varqa pays a farewell visit to his lover Gulshah before his departure for Yemen. The couple stand amongst trees and birds.* Werner Forman/ Art Resource.

property. In these poems it is the poet-lover who is the slave, for he invariably subjugates himself to his beloved and complies with her every whim. He is completely powerless against the overwhelming passion for his beloved and this passion consumes him unto death. The beloved's fickleness and her apparent pleasure in the lover's degradation only inflame the hero's ardor. Abu Nuwas claimed that even if his beloved Janan decided to walk on his face and tread on his cheek, he would have welcomed that degradation. Disparagement was better than silent contempt. He was glad everytime her lips uttered his name, even in abuse! The more fervent the poet's language and the more complex in meter, mode, and rhythm, the more valuable became his poetic output.

Khamriyyat The Abbasid poets excelled in the composition of "Bacchic" poetry devoted to the pleasures of drinking wine, in Arabic *khamr*, from which the name of this subgenre of poetry is derived. Given Islam's prohibition of wine drinking, it is no surprise that the first poets who developed the genre and its most illustrious authors are almost invariably associated with libertinism and antireligious sentiment or skepticism. This is true of the so-called libertines of Kufa, a veritable counterculture of poets who flourished in the eighth century, whose representatives include Muti ibn Iyas (d. 785) and Abu Dulama (d. c. 787), an African slave and court jester. An important transformation occurs in the poetic tropes under the influence of a certain eighth-century poet, Ahmad ibn Ishaq, who expanded the traditional theme of the pleasures of drinking wine to writing about his own public bouts of drunken debauchery and sexual libertinism. The poets following him imitated his example of recording their own drunken escapades in verse. The genre reached its epogee with the Iraqi court poet Abu Nuwas (d. c. 813) (discussed later), acclaimed for the eloquence and originality of his odes to wine and homosexual love.

Madih   The panegyric poem (*madih* or *madh*) best exemplifies the social reality of poetic composition both in the pre-Islamic period and during the golden age: that the vast majority of poetry was commissioned or under the patronage of a court. It was noted in the discussion of the pre-Islamic *qasida* that the third and most important part of the poem often consisted of a panegyric. In the Abbasid Golden Age the *madih* is transformed into an independent poetic genre. A beautifully written *madih* was usually the best way for an ambitious poet to gain entry into the prestigious Abbasid court in Baghdad or the Umayyad court in Spain. Abu Tayyib Ahmad ibn al-Husayn al-Jufi, al-Mutanabbi (915–955), perhaps the greatest of all the panegyrists, spent his career not

attached to one particular court, but rather as a troubadour under the patronage of wealthy and influential men in Iraq, Syria, Perisa, and Antioch.

The death of the sovereign or other patron would be the occasion to compose a mournful panegyric singing the praises of the deceased and lamenting his or her loss. Mournful laments (*marthiya*) expressing pain over the death of a loved one who died suddenly or violently are an important subgenre of *madih*. Panegyric extols the moral qualities of the patron: his intelligence, courage, justice, and modesty, and the nobility of his ancestry. Additionally a panegyrist might compose a *madih* to commemorate an important event, such as the birth of the sovereign's heir or a victory in battle. Poets also composed panegyrics to extol the virtues of one's tribe, land, or city.

Zuhdiyyat   *Zuhdiyyat*, or "ascetic poems," emerge as an autonomous poetic genre in the eighth century as an offshoot of the mournful lament (*marthiya*). The sudden death of a loved one, news of the heroic death on the battlefield of a boon companion, or the loss of an eminent poet or scholar provided the occasion for the poet to reflect upon the ephemerality of life, the inevitability of death, and one's fate in the afterlife. Abu Nuwas composed numerous ascetic poems; however, the true master of the genre is his contemporary Ismail ibn Qasim ibn Qaysan Abu l-Atahiyya of Kufa (748–826), whose *zuhdiyyat* are veritable sermons in verse describing in vivid detail the horrors of death, the true leveler of all, respecting neither social class nor wealth.

Poets of the Abbasid Court

The Abbasid court attracted numerous important poets such as Jarir ibn Atiyya ibn al-Khatafa (d. 729), Tammam ibn Ghalib al-Farazdaq (d. c. 739), Abu Nuwas, al-Buhturi, and Abu l-Atahiyya and paid them generously to write magnificent poems praising the court and caliphate with panegyric grandeur. They were also employed to write love poetry; panegyrics celebrating a patron's heroism, courage, and generosity; tributes to hunting; Bacchic poems in praise of wine (*khamriyyat*); and erotic poems (*mujuniyyat*) praising women, young boys, and singing girls. Many Muslim moralists defended these beautiful poems extolling forbidden excesses in wine, revelry, and a lascivious life by stating that the Quran allowed poets to say that which they do not do. Poetry was poetry, religion was religion, and therefore pagan sensual and sexual excesses could be acceptable in literary art.

Bashshar ibn Burd Bashshar ibn Burd (c. 714–737) wrote panegyrics, elegy, and satirical *qasidas* as well as fine amorous poems, dedicated mostly to a Basran woman named Abda. Though of humble origins, blind from birth, and infamous for his physical ugliness and caustic temper, Bashshar ibn Burd attracted the attention of the women of his day and first was admitted into the Umayyad court as official poet and subsequently gained the favor of the second Abbasid caliph, Abu Jafar Abdallah al-Mansur (r. 754–775). The pithiness of his epigrams, parodies, and amorous elegies and his inventive language gained him the reputation as one of the "great poets of Basra," and he influenced future generations of acclaimed Abbasid poets, including Abu l-Atahiya and Abu Nuwas.

Abu l-Atahiya Abu l-Atahiya, a pen name meaning "the father of craziness," was among the most celebrated of the Abbasid poets. His real name was Abu Ishaq Ismail ibn Qasim ibn Qaysan, and he was born in 748 in Kufa, south of Baghdad, Iraq, into a poor working-class family and died in 826. Abu l-Atahiya started life as a jar maker, son of a physician who earned his money by cupping. He learned the art of poetry from a prominent circle of poets in the city of Kufa that included the *ghazal* poet Waliba ibn al-Hubab (d. 786), with whom he frequented the mosques until he became a master of Arabic. With his companion, the Iraqi musician Ibrahim al-Mawsili (d. 804), Abu l-Atahiya traveled to Baghdad to join the rich court of the caliph. A panegyric poem in praise of Caliph Muhammad ibn Mansur al-Mahdi (r. 775–785) earned him a place in the Abbasid court. There he encountered the slave woman named Utbah who became the literary love of his life for 20 years.

Utbah initially was the slave to Rasta, the daughter of a certain Abu l-Abbas and wife of Caliph al-Mahdi. Abu l-Atahiya fell in love with Utbah at first sight. One version of the love story placed the poet as seeing Utbah on horseback in the court of Caliph al-Mahdi, where she was surrounded by a retinue of servants. He approached her and from that moment forward pursued her and composed poetry for her, skillfully using the poetic tropes and techniques of the day. His efforts, however, would be in vain.

Utbah treated Abu l-Atahiya with contempt and did not want to be driven from the prince's household. When it appeared that the caliph was willing to give her in marriage to the poet, she conceived a stratagem to make it appear that the poet was not after her but only after money. She contrived to have al-Mahdi's finance minister offer a bribe to the poet to induce him to leave her alone. The official offered Abu l-Atahiya 100,000 coins without specifying whether they were to be in dirhams or dinars, the former a silver unit of currency, the latter a gold unit of currency worth at least 10 times the dirham. The ruse worked because the caliph concluded that the poet had been seduced more by money than Utbah's charms.

Abu l-Atahiya blamed the caliph for Utbah's rejection and took his revenge by composing elegiac verses that could be interpreted negatively. Enraged, the caliph ordered him flogged and imprisoned. After al-Mahdi's death, Abu l-Atahiya's reputation was restored and he was summoned back to the court of al-Mahdi's successor, Harun al-Rashid (785–809) to compose *ghazals*. By this time, however, the poet had undergone a spiritual conversion and turned his talents to composing ascetic poetry, *zuhdiyyat*. These poems were essentially sermons in verse and spoke of the terrors of death from which no one, wealthy or poor, even the caliph, would escape.

Abu Nuwas Abu Nuwas (d. 817), whose full name was al-Hasan ibn Hani al-Hakami, rivals Bashshar ibn Burd in being considered the finest of the Arabic "modern" poets, the *muhdathun*. Born in Iran of an Arab father and Persian mother, Abu Nuwas went to school in Basra, then moved to Kufa, where he studied poetry with Waliba ibn al-Hubab, just as Abu l-Atahiya had. Abu Nuwas moved to Baghdad to join the court, where the musician Ishaq al-Mawsili (767–850), the son of the aforementioned Ibrahim al-Mawsili, introduced the young poet to Caliph Harun al-Rashid. There Abu Nuwas worked and thrived during the caliphate of al-Rashid's heir, Caliph Muhammad ibn Harun al-Amin (r. 809–813). Abu Nuwas's erotic poetry celebrated the love of young boys and of slave women; while his *khamriyyat* praised wild drinking in taverns, revelry, and the delights of pleasure gardens. Abu Nuwas's *qasidas* do not begin with the traditional mourning over the abandonment of the hero's dwelling place, but rather with the abandonment of the wine tavern! Abu Nuwas was most innovative, however, in the poems he dedicated to hunting, describing in vivid language falcons, hounds, horses, and game. Although images of hunting are found in pre-Islamic Bedouin poetry, which he studied, Abu Nuwas was the first poet to convert the hunting poem into an independent genre.

His poetry, mostly sung by him and set to music, was widely praised. It is possible that he was a Murjiite Muslim who believed that in the afterlife a Muslim might suffer painful punishment but ultimately would be forgiven and live in glory with God and the prophet Muhammad. Abu Nuwas died soon after al-Amin was murdered in 813. Reports of the poet's death attributed it to poison by victims of his venomous tongue, to overdrinking in a tavern, or to the harsh vicissitudes of prison life when he was jailed.

The vast majority of Abu Nuwas's erotic poetry praises the beauty and sensuality of young boys. Yet in the court of Harun al-Rashid, Abu Nuwas met the beautiful, witty, educated slave woman Janan, who in keeping with the thematic conventions of Abbasid erotic poetry, rejected the attentions of her admirer and intentionally humiliated him. Janan complained, showered him with imprecations because of his unwanted attentions, but ultimately softened because of his extraordinary perseverance in love despite her disdain.

Umayyad Spain

POETIC GENRES

Muwashshaha In Umayyad Córdoba a new Arabic poetic genre, known as *muwashshaha*, was said to have been invented by Muhammad ibn Mahmud al-Qabri (d. 911). The *muwashshaha* differs from the *qasida* in that it is a strophic poem, meaning that every line did not end in the same rhyme, but rather each series of lines (strophe) would follow a pattern of rhymes that was repeated throughout. Each strophe, in turn, was ended by an envoi (*kharja*). The language of the poem was Classical Arabic; however, the language of the *kharja* was often colloquial Arabic and, a very few cases a Romance language, giving rise to scholarly speculation that the poetic genre may be Romance in origin. This is unlikely, however, given that the language of the poems is predominantly classical Arabic and the themes treated are the same as those of the medieval classical Arabic tradition: love poetry (*ghazal*) and panegyric (*madih*). Moreover, the *muwashshaha*, shares many characteristics with another early Islamic poetic genre, the *musammat* or *qasida simtiyya*, which was also stanzaic, having a fixed number of lines that rhymed with each other, followed by stanza closing lines that rhyme with each other. (The earliest surviving examples of this genre belong to the Abbasid poet Abu Nuwas.) As was much poetry of the Abbasid period, the *muwashshaha* was composed to be set to music. Composers of *muwashshaha*, called *washshah*, also wrote wine poetry (*khamriyyat*) and ascetic, mystical, and religious poetry (*zuhdiyyat*).

Zajal Another strophic form, the *zajal*, emerged in the 11th century and became popular in Spain; as the *muwashshaha* did, it quickly spread and was imitated elsewhere. The most famous poet of *zajal* was Abu Bakr Muhammad ibn Quzman (d. 1160) of Córdoba. The *zajal* usually was composed in the Andalusi Arabic dialect and later in Aljamiado, a hybrid Hispano-Arabic dialect written in an adapted Arabic script. Ibn Quzman flourished at a time when the conservative Berber Almoravids had consolidated their power in al-Andalus, and thus he composed panegyrics for the wealthy Arab religious and political aristocracy, in addition to writing love and wine poetry.

Poets of Umayyad Spain

Ibn Khafaja of Valencia The Valencian-born Abu Ishaq ibn Ibrahim ibn Abi l-Fath ibn Khafaja (d. 1139) was regarded as one of the greatest poets of his time, not only in al-Andalus, but in the Islamic East as well. Born into a wealthy family, he was an independent spirit who spurned invitations to become a court poet and dedicated himself to writing poetry about nature. His poetic passion for trees, lakes, ponds, and flowers earned him the nickname "the Gardener" (*al-Jannan*).

Ibn Zaydun of Córdoba Abu l-Walid Ahmad ibn Abdallah ibn Zaydun of Córdoba (d. 1070) lived through a period of political turmoil and transition in al-Andalus as the Umayyad caliphate weakened and splintered into the Petty Kingdoms. His embroilment in political intrigues of Córdoba was such that he was nicknamed "the leader of the Córdoban *fitna*" (political strife). In his career he served as a preacher in the Umayyad court and later served many of the so-called petty kings of Spain. He earned his living as a panegyrist to his successive patrons, but he achieved fame for his amorous and literary relationship with the poet Princess Wallada, daughter of the Abbasid caliph al-Mustakfi (r. 902–908). Their poetic exchanges reflect a stormy and torrid relationship, which ends when she leaves him for his archenemy the Umayyad vizier Ibn Abdus.

Mystical Poetry

Many Sufi mystics articulated their yearnings for God, spiritual progression along the mystical path, and mystical visions in poetic verse. The Andalusian mystic Ibn al-Arabi (d. 1240) is regarded among the greatest and most original mystics. His collection of mystical odes, *Tarjuman al-ashwaq*, may likewise be interpreted as love poetry dedicated to his beloved, Nizam. The allegorical odes of the Persian Sufi Ibn al-Farid (d. 1235) depicted a deep yearning for a personal relationship with the divine. This desire for God was described as intoxication. Many pious poems were short and pithy. For instance, the blind Syrian poet Abu al Ala al-Maarri (d. 1057) wrote, "Make not, when you work a deed of shame, the scoundrel's plea, 'My forbears did the same.'" (al-Maarri. Available online. URL: www.humanistictexts.org/al_ma%27arri.htm.) Other poets, such as al-Mutanabbi (d. 965), wrote beautiful elegies. Panegyrics that praised the patron, the caliph's adventures, the caliph's heritage, and the caliphate often compared the earthly court to the heavenly paradise. The most talented poets united lofty subject with poetic grandeur.

Heroic Romance

Heroic romance is a narrative genre nearly as old and respected as poetry. Pre-Islamic bards would sing or recite the heroic exploits of their tribes. These epic romances, as did poetry, often recorded the exploits and adventures of real historical personalities, epic battles, tragic romances, and other monumental events, yet they embellished fact with elements of legend. The most singular works are the chivalric epics *Sirat Antar* (*The Romance of Antar*), a work comparable in stature to the *Song of Roland*; *Sirat al-amira Dhat al-Himma* (*The Romance of Princess Dhu al-Himma*); *Sirat Baybars* (*The Romance of Baybars*); and *Sirat Bani Hilal* (*The Romance of the Banu Hilal*); and the love story *Layla wa l-Majnun* (*Layla and the Madman*), a tragedy that would remind Western readers of Shakespeare's *Romeo and Juliet*.

SIRAT ANTAR

Portions of this anonymous chivalric epic romance date to the late eighth century; however, in its 12th-century version, the *Sirat Antar* it consisted of more than 10,000 lines of rhymed verse. The hero of the *Romance of Antar*

is the bastard son of a prominent member of the Arab tribe, the Banu Abs, and an enslaved African princess. The child is endowed from birth with superhuman physical strength and singlehandedly rescues the entire tribe during a raid by enemies. As a reward for his extraordinary bravery he is acknowledged by his father and made an honored member of the tribe, epitomizing the best of Arab masculine virtue. He falls in love with his cousin, the beautiful Arab princess Abla, and wants to marry her, but her father, Antar's uncle, demands that the hero successfully overcome a series of obstacles. The ensuing chivalric exploits take him to the battlefields of Syria, Iraq, Persia, the land of the Franks, and India, where we find the hero defeating Arab, Persian, and Indian kings and Byzantine and crusader knights.

DHU AL-HIMMA

In the prologue of the work *Dhu al-Himma* the author describes it as "the greatest history of the Arabs, and the Umayyad and Abbasid caliphs, comprising the history of the Arabs and their wars and their amazing conquests," thereby giving an idea of the scope of a chivalric saga that pits the forces of Islam against the Byzantine army. The epic centers upon the rivalry between two Arab tribes, the Banu Kilab and the Banu Sulaym, and their attempts to gain the favor of the Umayyad and subsequently Abbasid caliphs through their chivalric exploits in battles with the Byzantine Christians. The heroine of the romance, Dhu al-Himma, whose name means "the woman of noble purpose," is a princess of the Banu Kilab who is captured in a raid and raised by another tribe. While in captivity she develops Amazon-like powers, escapes and returns to her tribe, and persuades them to support the new Abbasid rulers. Although Dhu al-Himma marries her Arab cousin al-Harith, their child, Abd al-Wahhab, has African features as hero of the

Sirat Antar romance has. Abd al-Wahhab and his mother, Dhu al-Himma, are depicted as heroes playing crucial roles in the defeat of the Byzantine enemy.

SIRAT BANU HILAL

The composition of the epic romance, *Sirat Banu Hilal*, also known as *Taghribat Bani Hilal* (*The Western Migration of the Banu Hilal*) or *Sirat Abu Zayd al-Hilali* (*The Romance of Abu Zayd al-Hilali*), began sometime in the 11th century. It is based on the true events of the migration of the Banu Hilal (a tribe of Yemeni origin) from Egypt to Tunisia. When a famine ravished Fatimid Egypt during the 10th century, the leader of the Berber Zanata tribe in Tunisia seized the opportunity to rebel against the Fatimid caliph, al-Mustansir bi-Llah Abu Tamim ibn Ali al-Zahir (r. 1036–94). To regain control of the situation al-Mustansir dispatched the Banu Hilal tribe to Tunisia. The epic relates the story of their migration and heroic exploits of the tribal chief, Abu Zayd, who leads the Banu Hilal in victory against the rebel Berber Zanata.

SIRAT AL-SULTAN BAYBARS

Sirat al-Sultan Baybars, the Romance of Sultan Baybars, narrates the spectacular rise to power and exploits of the Mamluk sultan of Egypt and Syria al-Malik al-Zahir Rukun al-Din Baybars al-Bunduqdari (1223–77). Baybars's real life was indeed worthy of epic narration: Born a Kipchak Turk in Crimea, he was captured by Mongols at an early age and sold as a slave in Mamluk Syria. Sold again because his owner could not bear his ugly and imposing appearance, Baybars is bought by a Mamluk officer in Egypt, where he was stationed as a bodyguard of the Ayyubid ruler al-Salih al-Ayyub (1240–49). He fought heroically under the command of the Ayyub sultan Qutuz (d. 1260) against the crusaders and the Mongols. After the decisive defeat of the Mongols in the battle at the Palestinian town of Ayn Jalut in 1260, Baybars killed Sultan Qutuz and seized power, going on to win numerous battles against the crusaders. *The Romance of Sultan Baybars* remains tremendously popular today in Syria and Egypt, where it is performed by bards in cafes throughout those countries.

LAYLA AND MAJNUN

The precise origins of the Arabic romance *Layla and the Majnun* are unknown; however, references to real historical figures such as a governor of Medina who served in the late seventh to early eighth centuries situate the text in northern Arabia during the Umayyad period. The romance exists in various versions; each tells the tragic story of two star-crossed lovers, Qays ibn al-Mulawwa and his cousin, Layla. Separated by fate, Qays becomes crazed with love (*Majnun* means "madman") as he searches high and low to recover his true love.

In the most popular version of the romance Qays was a tribal prince, son of the great chieftain of the Banu Amir. Layla and Qays Majnun instantly fell in love as children sent to school under the tutelage of a learned master. Qays was intellectually so swift that he held a book in hand and could read it at once, speak words sweeter than the music of the lute, and demonstrate wit sharper than an arrow and wisdom more lustrous than a pearl. He was enraptured by the exquisite black-haired Layla and composed poems to her beauty and wit. He assumed the title of "madman" because he could not marry Layla, whose father had promised her in marriage to another man. After much wandering in the wilds and composing of exquisite poems that eventually reached Layla's hands, and after periods of lucidity in which the prince regained his sanity and acted with intelligence and magnificence with his friend Ibn Salam, the two lovers died side by side.

The tragedy and madness of Majnun's unfulfilled love portrayed in this heroic romance may be compared to the theme of the *udhri* poets of southern Arabia. *Layla and Majnun* was unrivaled as a heroic romance and was translated into many languages of the Islamic world, most notably Persian and Urdu.

Arabic Prose Literature

Arabic prose literature developed along with Islam's requirements in the eighth century for rulers to understand the events surrounding the beginnings of Islamic history and for scholars to preserve in meticulous fashion Muhammad's recitation of the Quran and his sayings or Hadith. Two major genres of historical writing, the *sira* (biography) and *tarikh* (historical chronicle), achieved prominence as Muslims sought to preserve the faithful memory of the beginning of Islam and its Prophet as part of universal history as well as the history of the peoples who were to form the Islamic world. Along with the establishment of the vast Islamic empire and the caliphate occurred the development of an extensive bureaucratic machine. The bureaucratic secretaries who had inheritated Sassanian protocol and business ethics wrote epistles (*risalas*) and instruction books combining practical and moral guidelines of government. Subsequently the *risala* was applied to writing treatises on a variety of subjects, covering literature, politics, society, and religion.

The writing of individual biographies or the biographies (*sira*) of a notable tribe evolved into the composition of biographical dictionaries preserving the biographical notices of peoples sharing the same profession or hailing from the same region. At the same time, the *sira* inspired autobiographical writing, some autonomous works, others in the form of lengthy prologues or appendices to other works. The Arabs also invented the genre of *adab*, referring to the "manners" or the sum knowledge of a topic, a profession, a social class, and so forth. Another literary genre, the *maqamat*, meaning "sessions," was spectacularly popular for the originality of its form and content, composed entirely in rhymed prose. Rhymed prose became the favored form in which authors composed two other popular genres: the beast fable and the frame tale.

RISALA

In its pre-Islamic origins a *risala* was a message, invariably delivered orally. However, toward the end of the Umayyad period and most especially under the impetus of the Abbasid caliphate, the *risala* was transformed from an oral message into a formal written genre, increasingly composed in ornate rhymed prose (*saj*) and sometimes containing poetic verse. Employing a letter framework in which the person addressed has requested the author to elucidate his thoughts upon a particular subject, the *risala* became a principal vehicle for the transmission of knowledge. The Umayyad caliph Abd al-Malik ibn Marwan (r. 685–705) wrote to a jurist of Medina, Urwa ibn al-Zubayr (d. c. 714), seeking information about the rise of Islam. The resulting epistles preserve precious information about the political institutions and worldview of the Umayyads.

Under the Abbasids the *risala* developed into a tool for the analysis of political, military, and social institutions and events and the exposition of one's personal thoughts and opinions on a given topic, as well as new and sometimes unconventional ideas. In these *risalas*, the person addressed is most often invented by the author, and thus the prologue explaining the motive for writing the text is a literary device that lends legitimacy to the author's opinions.

The *risala* was used to discuss all the major issues affecting Islamic society: philosophy, theology, politics, law, society and social institutions, grammar, and literature. The famous Abbasid poet and prose writer Abu l-Ala al-Maarri addressed his *Risalat al-sahil wa l-shahij* (Epistle of the horse and the mule) to the governor of Aleppo. The lowly and unfortunate mule, blindfolded and forced constantly to draw water to fill a cistern while never being allowed to drink, suddenly begins to speak and seeks the intervention of more noble animals—the horse, the camel, and others—to call his plight to the attention of the governor of Syria. Some of the most eminent philosophers, such as Abu Yusuf Yaqub ibn Ishaq al-Kindi (d. 866) and Muhammad Abu Bakr ibn Zakariyya al-Razi (d. 935), used the epistle form to explain their philosophical systems of thought. In the 10th century, the Ismaili Brethren of Purity (Ikwan al-Safa) composed their *Rasail*, which comprised 52 epistles on "all the profound realities of the universe" and the "hidden meanings of Revelation and the Law" to guide their Shiite-Neoplatonist adepts.

Many *risalas* were indeed personal letters, some of a confessional, even autobiographical, nature. The 10th-century man of letters and philosopher Abu Hayyan al-Tawhidi revealed his most intimate thoughts, state of mind, and motivations in his *Risalat al-ulum* (Epistle on the Sciences). In a series of letters written to his son, a certain Abu Hilal al-Sabi discloses that premonitions of his impending death had prompted him to render a balance of his life, loves, and personal and professional temptations and foibles, which might help advise his son.

INSTRUCTION BOOKS

One of the earliest and best instruction books is attributed to a Persian writer who was executed in 757, Ibn al-Muqaffaa. Employed first in the service of the Umayyads and later of the Abbasids, he is credited as being the first to translate works from the Iranian and Indian literary heritage into Arabic prose. One example of a genre that Ibn al-Muqaffaa introduced from the Iranian literary heritage is the "mirror of princes," a manual of practical ethics addressed to princes and courtiers. His *al-Adab al-kabir* (The Great book of manners) was a book of maxims and wisdom sayings offering advice and instruction on the art of combining ethics with political survival. How could an ethical man thrive in a suspicious despot's court? How could one remain tranquil and keep a cool head when one's best friend suddenly started consorting with the enemy? The *al-Adab al-kabir* and another work, the *Kitab maarif* (*The Book of Knowledge*), preserve excerpts from the Persian *Khudaynama*, which relates the epic tales from the military, political, and social history of ancient, pre-Islamic Iran. An even more important mirror of princes, the *Risala fi l-Sahaba* (Epistle on the Companions), addresses itself to an unnamed caliph, thought to be al-Mansur, and reflects upon the political and social problems associated with his caliphate, such as the treatment of the military elite and the choice of high officers.

HISTORICAL CHRONICLES: *SIRA* AND *TARIKH*

The *sira* is an Islamic genre of literature that narrates the momentous historical events in the life of a person, community, or political dynasty. Precedents for this genre are found in the pre-Islamic histories of the battles of the Arabs (*ayyam al-Arab*) and the Persian tradition of dynastic chronicles, such as that translated from the Persian into Arabic by Ibn al-Muqaffaa. The *sira* of the prophet Muhammad, originally composed by Ibn Ishaq in the eighth century and redacted by Ibn Hisham nearly a century later, served as a model for later chronicles of kings and dynasties.

Tarikh, which literally means "history," is closely related to the *sira;* however, emphasis is placed on world history, the history of a particular region or empire, the history of events, and the great men, usually prophets and kings, who participated in them. Historical writing in the Islamic world was initially inseparable from religious studies, as authors strove to justify Islam's place in world history, best exemplified by Muhammad ibn Jarir al-Tabari's (d. 923) monumental *History of the Prophets and Kings* (*Tarikh al-anbiya wa l-muluk*) and Ahmad ibn Yahya al-Baladhuri's (d. 892) *Futuh al-Buldan* (*The History of the [Islamic] Conquests*). A 10th-century history of the world starting from creation, entitled *The Golden Meadows* (*Muruj al-Dhahab*), by the historian and traveler Abu l-Hasan Ali al-Masudi (d. 956), had an exceptionally delightful literary quality. From the 10th century onward, however, historical writing became more scientific and dissociated from religious lore, as is seen in the production of numerous local histories and histories of major cities from al-Andalus and the Maghrib in the far west to the Central Asian lands of Dar al-Islam. Among the most significant contributions are those of al-Miskawayh (d. 1030) of Iraq and Ibn Hayyan (d. 1076) of Córdoba and *The History of India* (*Tarikh al-Hind*) by the acclaimed Iranian scholar Abu Rayhan al-Biruni (d. 1050).

Muslim authors related the crusades from their point of view. The earliest historical account was written by Abu Yala ibn Asad al-Tamimi, known as Ibn al-Qalanisi (d. 1166) of Damascus. His *Dhayl al-Tarikh* (*Appendix to the History of Damascus*) preserves his firsthand experience of the First and Second Crusades. Izz al-Din ibn al-Athir (d. 1233) of Iraq includes eyewitness accounts of the Third and Fourth Crusades in his historical magnum opus, *Kamil al-tawarikh* (*The Complete History*), a global history of the Muslim peoples from pre-Islamic times until his own day. Jamal al-Din ibn al-Wasil (d. 1298) was an officer in the Ayyubid and Mamluk armies, who wrote his *Mufarrij al-Kurub fi akhbar Bani Ayyub* ("The dissipator of anxieties concerning the history of the Ayyubids") to extol the feats of Saladin and his successors and is considered the most reliable source for the Fifth Crusade.

Special mention must be made of Abu l-Faraj al-Isfahani's (d. 967) magnum opus on the history of Arabic music from pre-Islamic times to the 10th century, *Kitab al-aghani* (*The Book of Songs*). At the behest of the Abbasid caliph Harun al-Rashid, Abu l-Faraj compiled and classified the select music of famous singers and the poets for whom they composed music. Contributions included those of Ibrahim al-Mawsili, Ismail ibn Jami, Fulayh ibn al-Awra, among others. *The Book of Songs* was expanded under the patronage of subsequent Abbasid caliphs. Abu l-Faraj provides precious biographical accounts of poets and songwriters, details about the life and times of ancient Arab tribes from which the poets hailed, and vivid accounts of court life and the musicians and singers in the Umayyad and Abbasid courts.

BIOGRAPHICAL DICTIONARIES

The chain of learning (*isnad*) characteristic of the study of the Hadith of the prophet Muhammad and the traditions of his companions required that each link be firm, reliable, verifiable, and connected in unbroken integrity to the one before and the one after. This need to verify the chain of transmission led to a unique type of Islamic literary genre called the biographical dictionary. In the collection of the Hadiths it was imperative to know who had transmitted each story or saying and from whom he had learned it, in order to verify its authenticity. Transmission was required to be continuous and each item transmitted both true and reliable. Legal scholars, physicians, Sufi masters, and local luminaries, both men and women, were listed in biographical dictionaries, making them a "Who's Who" for a particular city or region.

In the 11th century al-Khatib al-Baghdadi wrote an important biographical dictionary for the city of Baghdad. Others wrote for Damascus, Cairo, al-Andalus, and the Maghrib. Especially ambitious authors attempted biographical dictionaries of all Islamic history. Ahmad ibn Khallikan (d. 1282) recorded the biographies of rulers, ministers, poets, and religious scholars in his famous *Wafayat al-Ayan* (*Obituaries of Eminent Men*).

Modern readers in search of intimate details about a person's life may be somewhat disappointed, since most biographical dictionary entries are characteristically terse, as their aim is to provide the information most relevant to their intended scholarly audience. Medieval readers wanted to know the person's full name, dates of birth and death, professions exercised; the subjects, books, or Hadiths he or she studied and under which scholars; which *ijazas* (diplomas) he received, the persons to whom she or he in turn transmitted this knowledge; and the books or poetry that she or he composed. Excerpts of the latter might be included in the text, especially if the person was a famous poet. The main objective of the entries about scholars was to determine their intellectual genealogy. The biographical entry on a ruler, politician, or person caught up in important political or social events might detail some of the pertinent descriptions of these events.

Often an exception to this rule of brevity could be found in the biographical dictionaries dedicated to Sufi mystics or "saints," a subgenre known as *manaqib*. In these hagiographies the compiler provided fascinating anecdotes about the individual's personal life and inner thoughts, vivid accounts of the events leading up to his or her spiritual conversion, and the miracles or other prodigies performed by these persons.

AUTOBIOGRAPHICAL WRITING

Autobiography constitutes one of the most significant and enduring forms of the Arabic literary production. The unbroken 1,000-year history of Arabic autobiographical writing, beginning in the ninth century, proves the fallacy of Western origins of the genre. Arabic autobiography, often called *al-sira al-dhatyya* (personal history) or *tarjama nafsiyya* (interpretation of the self) by its authors, is related to historical and biographical writing. Indeed, many biographers drew upon circulating autobiographies in the compilation of their dictionaries.

Authors had many motivations for writing the story of their lives: The defense of one's reputation from calumny prompted Hunayn ibn Ishaq (d. 873), court physician to Caliph al-Mutawakkil Ala Allah Jafar ibn al-Mutasim (r. 821–861) and eminent translator of many important Greek scientific works (including those of Hippocrates and Galen), to write about his "trials and tribulations," which appear as a notice in the biographical dictionary of Ibn Abi Usaybia (d. 1270) entitled *Uyun al-anba fi tabaqat al-atibba* ("Sources of News on the Biographies of Doctors"). Abdallah ibn Buluggin, the last Zirid Berber prince of Granada, whom the Almoravids exiled to Morocco in 1090, composed his autobiography, *Kitab al-Tibyan* (*The Book of Memoirs*), as part of a larger history of his family's political dynasty. An overwhelming majority of these autobiographies were personal accounts of spiritual or mystical progress, such as the ninth-century Iraqi al-Muhasibi's *Kitab al-Nasiih* (*The Book of Advice*), which served as a model for later authors. Many prominent historians, such as Imad al-Din al-Isfahani (d. 1201), personal secretary to the Ayyubid sultan of Egypt, Saladin (Salah al-Din al-Ayyub) (d. 1193); the historian and court vizier Ibn al-Adim of Aleppo (d. 1262); and the great historian, protosociologist and philosopher Ibn Khaldun of Tunis (d. 1406), wrote their autobiographies, as did famous philosophers and physicians, including al-Razi (Rhazes) (d. 935) and Ibn Sina (Avicenna) (d. 1037).

Philosophy and travel literature combined with autobiography in Usama Ibn Munqidh's (d. 1188) *Kitab al-Itibar* (The contemplation of experience). Daily life is depicted though the eyes of this Syrian fighter and nobleman working with Saladin against the crusaders. Philosophy also united with autobiography in al-Ghazali's (d. 1111) *al-Munqidh min al-dalal* (*The Deliverer from Error*). This dramatic account, which may be compared with Augustine's *Confessions*, describes the theologian's intellectual crises that propelled him toward mysticism. The Jewish scholar Samawal al-Maghribi (d. 1174) and the 15th-century Christian author Fray Anselmo Turmeda (also known as Abdallah Turjuman) wrote autobiographies of their conversion to Islam, which they appended to polemical treatises denouncing their former religions.

ADAB LITERATURE

Adab, from the Arabic word meaning "habit, behavioral norms, or manners" and usually translated as "belles-lettres," was a novel medieval literary form that served as the humanistic complement to the religious control of conduct, similar to the *sunna*, in which one's behavior is the external manifestation of the believer's heart. Therefore, the same ethical standards governed the selection of a police chief or court secretary and the resignation of one's personal urges to the will of God. By extension, *adab* came to be synonymous with urbanity, good manners, civility, and etiquette in all human activities, ranging from personal habits such as eating, drinking, and dressing, to ethical and social matters such as friendship, politics, war, and study. A further nuance to the meaning of *adab* was the idea of the sum of knowledge or the art of a profession, such the *adab* of the secretary (*katib*), orator (*khatib*), or judge (*qadi*). Up until the Umayyad period, the practitioner of *adab*, the *adib*, was a person who had acquired the sum of knowledge as defined by the Arabic tradition. In this sense, the *adib* could be thought of as a precursor to the "Renaissance man": His expertise consisted in the mastery of the pre-Islamic and early Muslim poets, the epic histories and battles of the Arabs (*ayyam al-Arab*), and the maxims and proverbs that encoded Bedouin ethics. Developments in the Abbasid period reflect Arab contact with Hellenistic practical philosophy and ethics, Iranian epic, Indian fable, and the traditions of other foreign cultures, seen mainly in the contributions of non-Arabs who had adopted the Arab and Islamic cultures, such al-Jahiz and Ibn al-Muqaffaa.

Adab Authors

Al-Jahiz (d. 869)   Al-Jahiz stands out as one of the earliest, best, and most prolific authors of *adab* literature. Of African origin, he was brought up in Basra, Iraq, then the center of Arabic culture, and enjoyed the patronage of the Abbadid caliph Abu Jafar ibn Harun al-Mamun (r. 813–833). He is the author of more than 30 books, in which he displays his mastery of both the Arabic literary heritage of poetry, maxims, proverbs, and epics and the literary traditions of the Iranian epic, Indian fable, and Greek philosophy. He excelled in the art of combining instruction with entertainment and moral commentary, covering themes such as love and friendship, envy and pride, hypocrisy and sincerity. In a particularly popular section of one of his numerous masterpieces, *Kitab al-bayan wa l-tabyin* (*The Book of Clarity and Clarification*), he describes the eloquence of ascetics and the equally memorable eloquence of the insane.

Another of his great works was his bestiary, *Kitab al-hayawan* (*The Book of Animals*). The bestiary consists of magnificently incompatible subjects all mixed together in superb prose. Al-Jahiz moved effortlessly from hard observational science to legend, from zoology to mythology. Why is man the microcosm of the macrocosm? Why do babies cry? Why is fire hot? What is the psychology of the castrated eunuch? What unites the prostitute, lover, and pimp? That last question he answers in a disquisition called "On Singing Girls."

Kitab al-bukhala (*The Book of Misers*) presented a delightful set of characters to discuss the different categories of miserliness. Al-Jahiz belonged to the rationalist Mutazilite school. Though he maintained that God did not send anyone to hell, the sinner's inherent attraction to fire would ultimately make the sinner and fire unite in a single substance. Therefore the sinner would not suffer endless pain but rather *become* fire. This was either an idiosyncratic rational idea or irony.

Ibn Qutayba (d. 889)   Ibn Qutayba was another luminary in the field of *adab*. He was born in Kufa into an Arabized family of Iranian origin. He was a renowned Sunni theologian, being a disciple of Ahmad ibn Hanbal (d. 855), the founder of the Hanbali school of law, as well as an Arabic philologist. The author of several *adab* compendia, he is perhaps best known for his encyclopedic collection entitled *Uyun al-akhbar* (*The Sources of History*). The *Uyun al-akhbar* is divided into 10 sections devoted to distinct topics such as government, war, friendship, food, and women. As did al-Jahiz, Ibn Qutayba believed that instruction was best served and most efficacious when simultaneously pleasing. Accordingly, he favored the use of lists, maxims, and pithy sayings designed to make his orthodox Sunni-inspired morals memorable to his audience. In this Ibu al-Qutayba differs from his two great literary predecessors Ibu al-Muqaffaa and al-Jahiz, whose style was characteristically ornate and bombastic.

Ibn Qutayba best represents the transition in the meaning of *adab* from the summation of general knowledge (cf. the humanities) to the specialized knowledge necessary for given offices and social functions. His *Adab al-katib* (*The Book of the Secretary*) exemplifies this trend, which later authors would imitate, in for instance, the *Adab al-wazir* (*The Book of the Vizier*), and the *Adab al-qadi* (*The Book of the Judge*). Ibn al-Qutayba also wrote several *adab* treatises on literary topics, including his famous poetic anthology *Kitab al-shir wa l-shuara* (*The Book of Poetry and Poets*), as well as on astronomy and religion. Regarding the latter, Ibn Qutayba departed from al-Jahiz in style as well as substance. For whereas al-Jahiz followed the Mutazili school, Ibu Qutayba's religious writings exemplify the return to orthodox Sunnism in accordance with the Abbasid ruler's growing disdain for Mutazilism as official state doctrine.

Ibn Abd Rabbihi (d. 940)   The Spanish Muslim writer Ibn Abd Rabbihi, a noted poet in his own right, wrote *al-Iqd al-farid* (*The Unique Necklace*), a magnificent *adab* encyclopedia that drew upon materials from al-Jahiz and Ibn Qutayba. *Al-Iqd* is organized into 25 chapters, each named for a precious jewel and treating a different subject. The author covers an amazing variety of topics, for example, "How Kings Should Be Addressed," "Government," "War," "Religious Knowledge and the Principles of Good Conduct," "Music and Song," and "Women."

Ibn Hazm of Córdoba (d. 1064)   The art and etiquette of love are powerfully explored in *Tawq al-hammama* (*The Ringed Dove*) by Ibn Hazm of Córdoba. Ibn Hazm, a poet, jurist, historian, theologian, and philosopher, is one of the most significant figures of medieval Islamic history. Ibn Hazm grew up in a harem, a background that may explain his interest in the psychology of women and his penchant for erotic poetry. Ibn Hazm witnessed the downfall of the Cordovan caliphate and was a victim of the political turmoil leading up to it. A fervent defender of the Umayyad caliphate, he was imprisoned on several occasions. Disillusioned with politics, he retreated to Jativa and devoted himself to writing of poetry and intellectual activities. *The Ringed Dove* explained, among other things, that lovers who humbly submitted to the beloved were not unmanly but rather fashionable and elegant.

Types of *Adab* Literature

Beast Fables Here it is appropriate to mention the singular contribution of the Persian author Ibn al-Muqaffaa to the genre of *adab*. He wrote an Arabic version of a Middle Persian translation of an Indian set of fables of Bidpai called *Kalila wa Dimna*. This set of beast fables transmitted virtue and morality to the audience through the beautiful conceit of talking animals.

Books of Etiquette and Books of Anecdotes Other important subgenres of *adab* were the books of etiquette and books of anecdotes, which described types of people or events. Books devoted to different types of people treated madmen, fools, gullible people, clever people, and lovers. One of the most famous event books was al-Tanukhi's (d. 994) *Deliverance after Distress* (*al-Faraj bad al-shidda*).

Partisans on both sides of sectarian disputes also resorted to *adab* literature, which they filled with religious anecdotes. The zealous Hanbali jurisconsult, teacher, and preacher of Baghdad, Ibn al-Jawzi, wrote an anti-Sufi book of anecdotes called *Talbis iblis* (*The Devil's Deceit*). Al-Yafii (d. 1367) wrote the pro-Sufi (*Garden of Fragrant Plants*).

Philosophy *Adab* sometimes combined philosophy and theology. In *Kitab al-imta wa l-muanasa* (*The Book of Enjoyment and Conviviality*), the 10th-century author Abu Hayyan al-Tawhidi discusses free will, nature of the soul, and predestination in the course of 40 "nights" or gatherings devoted to the discussion of literary, philosophical, religious, grammatical, and other subjects. The Syrian poet al-Maarri (d.1057) wrote a set of conversations in heaven and hell with Arab poets. He called his erudite book *Risalat al-ghufran* (*The Epistle of Forgiveness*). The 10th-century philosophical encyclopedia written by the Brethren of Purity had a long discussion on the hierarchy of the created creatures, *"The Case of the Animals versus Man before the King of the Jinn."*

Maqama An important medieval Arabic fictional genre, called the *maqama* (pl. *maqamat*) ("assembly"), was characterized by a hero who expresses himself eloquently in rhymed prose (*saj*) in the hope of personal gain. According to Ibn Qutayba, the hero was usually a Bedouin or a shabbily dressed person who would deliver his speeches before an aristocratic audience. Alternatively, if the audience was of the popular classes, the hero would be a popular storytelling preacher (*qass*). As the genre developed, the hero evolved into both a *qass* and a wandering rogue, who would travel from place to place attracting audiences that would pay him generously for the eloquent tales he told.

The Iraqi philologist Badi al-Zaman al-Hamadhani (d. 1008) is credited with fully developing the genre's structure and content. The narrative form of the *Maqamat al-Hamadhani* (*Assemblies of al-Hamadhani*) is exclusively rhymed prose, and there are in fact two heroes: the narrator, or *rawi*, who narrates to the author the adventures and eloquent speeches of the protagonist, a wandering confidence man and cheerful vagabond who sleeps, eats, and cleverly talks his way through life with hilarious, erudite verse, and rhymed prose. It should be noted that al-Hamadhani's epithet, *Badi al-Zaman*, the "Innovator of His Time," was conferred upon him in recogni-

Farewells of Abou Zayd and al-Harith before the return to Mecca. From al-Hariri's Maqamat *(Assemblies, or Entertaining dialogues)*   Art Resource, NY.

cunning and wit to gain a monetary prize from his unsuspecting victims. The plot always climaxes when Abou Zayd reveals his ruse—after pocketing the money—with rhymed prose such as as the following:

> O Thou who, deceived
> By a tale, hast believed
> A mirage to be truly a lake,
>> Though I ne'er had expected
>> my fraud undetected,
> Or doubtful my meaning to make!
> I confess that I lied
> When I said that my bride
> And my first-born were Barrah and Zeid;
> But guile is my part;
> And deception my art,
> And by these are my gains ever made.

(Maqamat al-Hariri. Available online. URL: http://www.ebooksread.com/ authors-eng/warner/The-worlds-best-literature-ancient-and-modern-vol-2.887.shtml.)

tion of the innovations that he made in rhetorical style in Arabic literature. This new style, itself called *badi* ("innovative"), differed from earlier periods in its deliberate use of elaborate ornamental features and difficult and obscure vocabulary.

This new genre of literature and its ornate rhetorical style were imitated and transformed by numerous successors, the most important of whom was Abu Muhammad al-Qasim al-Hariri of Basra (d. 1052), whose *Maqamat* al-Hariri closely imitated the style and structure of his predecessor, but was infused with even more ornate language and verbal acrobatics. The audience for the *maqama* genre had to be intelligent and learned in order to appreciate the elaborate style and difficult language used to relate hilarious and ludicrous events. The juxtaposition made for humor and popularity of the style. The hero of al-Hariri's *Maqamat*, the wily Abou Zayd, is one of the most endearing characters of Arabic literature. Time and again we encounter him in disguise, employing his

The *maqama* was diffused to other Arabic-speaking areas of the Islamic world, such as al-Andalus and the Maghrib, where they were studied, commented upon, and imitated. So popular was the *maqama*, particularly of al-Hariri, that authors composed them in other languages as well, including Persian, of which the assemblies of Hamid al-Din al-Balki (d. 1156) is a prime example. As we have seen above, Sephardic Jews of Spain, such as Judah ben Shlomo ab Harizi (d. 1225) and Jacobo ben Eleazar (d. 13th century), translated the Arabic *maqama* literature into Hebrew and composed numerous *maqamat* in that language.

BEAST LITERATURE

Animal lore in Islam was well represented by such remarkable books as the Persian *Uses of Animals* (*Manafi al-hayawan*) by the

11th-century Syrian physician Ibn Bakhtisheu. A 13th-century example of the *Manafi* preserved in New York City's Pierpont Morgan Library described methods for creating medications compounded from the organs and bodily parts of many animals and included observations on their lives, habitats, and behavior. The elephant was said to be afraid of piglets, cocks, rams, mosquitoes, and mice. It so hated snakes that it would trample them to death. This way the elephant guarded its young from snakes. Deer also hated snakes and had carried mouthfuls of water to the snake holes to drive them out. Hunters cleverly outsmarted elephants by determining which tree the elephant leaned against in sleep at night by noting the great amount of dung found at the foot of the tree. The hunters then sawed that tree through to the middle so that when the elephant leaned against it at night for sleep, the tree would break, the elephant would fall, and the hunters could kill it.

There are notable similarities in the beliefs expressed by Arab, Persian, and European writers of bestiaries. In *The Uses of Animals* the mountain goat or ibex was said to drop itself from a huge height on a precipice, fall on its horns, restore its footing, and run off, unharmed. Likewise in English bestiaries the ibex or mountain goat could hurl itself from a mountain peak, leap huge distances, and preserve itself unhurt. Other remarkable beliefs that Eastern writers shared with European writers included that bears eat ants to cure illness, camels detest horses, dogs are faithful to their masters, and deer adore music and hear it when their ears are raised but are deaf to music when their ears are laid back. They also believed that the porcupine could throw its quills wherever it wished. Mice brilliantly stole eggs by teamwork: One mouse on its back would hold the egg in its paws while another would sled the egg holder away by pulling its tail. Teamwork in egg theft demonstrated rodent intelligence.

FRAME TALE

As we have seen from the discussions of Jewish and Christian literature, the frame tale, a literary device in which one overarching story incorporates many shorter, otherwise unrelated stories, is Indian in origin, as are many of the tales featuring animals. Its beginnings lie also in the Persian fables *Hazar afsana* (*The Thousand Tales*), which were translated into Arabic in the eighth century. Other Mesopotamian, Egyptian, Persian, and Arabic tales, including the Arabic cycle entitled *Kitab Sindibad* (*The Book of Sindbad*) were incorporated along with the *Hazar Afsana* into what would become *The Thousand and One Nights*. Far Eastern tales originating among the Turkic Mongols and Islamic countercrusade stories of Muslim heroism were appended to the stories in later centuries.

The Thousand and One Nights One of the best known Arabic literary compilations is the spectacular frame tale *The Thousand and One Nights*. The work cannot be attributed to a single author and is believed to be a compilation of stories stemming from several sources, including ancient Persian, Indian, and Arabian, and written in different periods and places. The thread that links the stories tells the story of Queen Scheherazade, who was condemned to death. She prevented her husband, the king of Samarkand, from killing her by telling 1,001 stories over 1,001 nights. Ultimately, the king was so entranced by her rhetoric and brilliance in tale telling that he relented, rescinded his death decree, and welcomed her back to life.

The power of Scheherazade's stories, as diffused through the translation into European languages since the 18th century, enabled them to endure through the centuries so that even today American children have heard of "Ali Baba and the Forty Thieves," "Sinbad the Sailor," and "Aladdin and His Magic Lamp."

Persian Literature in the Islamic World

Persian literature became world renowned after the Arab-Islamic invasions in 641. Persian culture influenced the court life of Abbasid and subsequent Persian rulers and many Persian government administrators perfected language and terminology in the cities in which they worked. Persian political power was restricted under the Seljuk Turks, who conquered the area in the 11th century, but Persian culture achieved new heights of excellence. Persian poetry, like Persian art, was decorative, ornamental, graceful, exquisite, intellectual, and passionate.

OMAR KHAYYAM (c. 1048–1131)

One of the greatest Persian poets was Omar Khayyam. Born in 11th-century Nishapur, this mathematician produced considerable scientific achievements that have been eclipsed by the popularity of his *Rubayyat*, a collection of epigrammatic verse quatrains. The *rubai* is a form of Persian poetry whose origins are in pre-Islamic times. It is readily identified by three basic elements: brevity, the use of a particular meter, and the use of a rhyme appropriate to its structure. Typically the rhyme scheme is AABA; however, in more elaborate versions the scheme may be extended to AABA, BBCB, CCDC, and so on. Omar Khayyam composed his famous quatrains during the Seljuk hegemony, which encouraged exquisite architecture, elegant textiles and pottery, new schools and universities, and poets, and poetry and exalted the position of the court poet. Yet his quatrains are somber and ascetic, even mystical in tone, reflecting upon the fickleness of life, and the ephemerality of its pleasures and expressing a regretful nostalgia and deep sorrow.

Three examples from the acclaimed translation of poet Edward Fitzgerald (d. 1888) follow:

Oh, threats of Hell and Hopes of Paradise!
To talk, one thing is certain, that life flies:
One thing is certain, and the rest is lies:
The flower that once has bloomed forever
   dies. (no. LXIII)

Then to this earthen bowl did I adjourn
My lip the secret well of life to learn;
And lip to lip it murmured "While you
   live, drink!
For once dead you never shall return."
   (no. XXXV)

The moving finger writes:
And having writ, moves on;
Nor all thy piety nor wit shall lure it back
   to cancel half a line
Nor all thy tears wash out a word of it.
   (no. LXXI)

(The Rubaiyat: http://etext.library.
adelaide.edu.au/)

NIZAMI GANJAWI (B.C.E. 1140)

One of the most significant Persian authors whose literature was translated into Arabic and enriched Arabic literature was Nizami Ganjawi (b. c. 1140). Nizami lived in a culturally sophisticated Caucasian outpost town called Ganjeh, now in Azerbaijan. Later given the honorific title of "learned doctor," *hakim*, Nizami refused the position of court poet. Unlike the panegyrics of his time, Nizami's poetry celebrated the artists and engineers associated with his country. He emphasized the engineering feats of Farhad, for example, rather than the courage or chivalry of the traditional hero. Nizami's epics celebrated the military and amorous exploits of men, but they are outstanding in their depiction of heroines as strong, dependable, subtle, intelligent, beautiful, and passionate. In Nizami's work the women are as capable as the men in power. Although faithful, when appropriate, they are treacherous, deceitful,

Tabriz hunt carpet. Border has excerpts from Omar Khayyam.   Art Resource, NY.

cantankerous, and ready to murder. Nizami is also unusual in his vivid portraits of ordinary people, artists and musicians as well as princes and kings.

Nizami gloried in extravagant splendor of princely gardens and courts and described with enthusiasm the jewels, perfumes, silks, and flamboyant colors of material life in this world just as he celebrated the natural world, history, mathematics, astronomy, medicine, and philosophy. The poet used elements of all of these disciplines in his romances. Five epic romances, collectively entitled *Khamseh* ("five"), in particular demonstrated Nizami's brilliance.

Khamseh   One of the best literary understandings of the human mind and emotions, *Khamseh* consisted of five epic poems called *masnavis*. The five poems are *The Treasury of Mysteries, Khosrow and Shirin, Layla and Majnun, The Seven Princesses,* and *Alexander the Great.*

The Treasury of Mysteries   *Treasury of Mysteries* is a philosophical-didactic poem with mystical overtones. The moral message is that of universal justice, as the verses urge the protection of the poor and the weak against the injustices of the wealthy and powerful. The transitory nature of life is the poet's warning to all.

Khosrow and Shirin   Long ago in the land of Persia lived King Hormuzd the Great, called "the Light of the World's Justice," who had as his heir and son a magnificent young man named Khosrow called Parvis, "the victorious one." The crown prince excelled in all he did and was schooled in all learned disciplines: a wizard with sword, spear, and arrow, and a master of the art of war. He learned the mysteries of the stars and the subtle ways of man and beast from the counselor Bozorg Omid and learned that "the rights of the ruled must always rule." He also had a dear close friend, the painter Shapur, who not only was a spec-

tacular draftsman and colorist but could make a head appear to move and a bird's wing appear to fly. He had traveled widely and told Khosrow of many marvels, including a woman of wealth and property, the Armenian queen Mihin Banu. Queen Banu had an enchanting niece named Shirin, who would make a fine wife for the prince, and a magical black horse named Shabdiz. After many extraordinary adventures in which Shirin became queen of Armenia and Khosrow king of Persia, the two lovers joined in ecstatic passion and ultimately death. When Khosrow was assassinated in a dungeon, Shirin covered his bloody body with kisses and stabbed herself as he had been stabbed and the two united in death for eternity.

Layla and Majnun   Ghanjawi's *Layla and Majnun* is a Persian translation of the Arabic romance about the Arab prince Qays who falls madly in love with his cousin, Layla, and becomes insane (*majnun*) when she is betrothed to another man. He wanders aimlessly, without eating or sleeping, subsisting only to compose love poetry to Layla. Starved and overcome with fever, he dies. Layla rushes to him, prostrates herself beside him, and dies of love at his side. Ghanjawi's version of the story ends on a note of hope: He introduces a dream sequence in which the two lovers are reunited in paradise, where they sit on sumptuous carpets embracing and drinking wine.

The Seven Princesses   *The Seven Princesses* (*Haft Paykar*) is an allegory of the seven pleasures of love, the seven stages in human life, the seven stages of the mystical journey of the soul. The hero of the story is Bahram Gur, the object of the affection of seven princesses, each of whom attempts to win his love by casting a spell upon him. The story unfolds over seven days as he visits each one of them in their respective pavilions. The mystical and the erotic are tastefully blended as the hero enters each dome-roofed pavilion, the dome representing celestial bodies and planets.

Alexander the Great   The magnificent story of Alexander the Great, *Iskandar-Nama*, told in two parts, portrays the Greek conqueror as a national hero of the Persian people. The first part, entitled *Sharaf-nama* (The Book of Honor), covers the story of Alexander from his birth through his unparalleled conquest of the world. The second part, *Iqbal-Nama* (*The Book of Wisdom*), transforms him into a philosopher and a prophet. Nizami depicts Alexander's quest for knowledge and his splendid collection of books as the epitome of the wise prophet and sage ruler.

FIRDAWSI (940–1020)

The 10th- to 11th-century poet and epic composer Mansur ibn Hasan Firdawsi wrote what has become Iran's national epic, *Shah-nameh* (*The Book of Kings*). At the beginning of his epic book, Firdawsi explained his philosophy and religious beliefs, which were steeped in Shii lore. He described a parable of doomed passengers aboard 70 ships carrying the 70 religions of mankind. He included devotees of African, Chinese, and European religions among the passengers. The largest, most beautiful ship carried the holy family of the Shia and, of course, on this ship, Firdawsi sailed. He was aware that all ships ultimately would founder in the stormy sea of eternity. Nevertheless, he gladly clutched the helping hands of the Prophet; his son-in-law and successor, Ali; and Ali's sons, Hassan and Huseyn.

Firdawsi described his inauspicious welcome to the court where he would create his masterpiece. Recently having arrived in Ghazna, he intruded on the three famous court poets of Sultan Mahmud (r. 998–1030). These venerable learned ones were disturbed by the young uninvited boorish stranger and refused to welcome Firdawsi until he passed the test of supplying the fourth line of a quatrain, a four-line poem that they had artfully devised with a terribly difficult rhyme. Firdawsi so brilliantly provided the necessary words that the poets were compelled to accept him and introduce him to the sultan, who commissioned him to write the *Shah-Nameh.* (Unfortunately for Firdawsi, his patron did not appreciate nor pay for the magnificent book until Firdawsi had died.)

The *Shah-Nameh* described the adventures and misadventures of historical figures and magical beings. From the introduction of evil into the world by demons to the patricidal villain named Zahhak who had two hungry snakes growing from his shoulders, the fabulous stories inspired some of Persia's most magnificent painting and exquisite books. A summary of four of these stories follows:

"Gayumarth, Shah of Iran"   Gayumarth, the legendary first shah of Iran, ruled an idyllic kingdom that was innocent and pure until a demon named Ahriman introduced evil into the world by plot and vicious intent. The angel Surush warned Gayumarth of impending trouble. In a huge battle against the Black Div (devil), son of Ahriman, the shah's own beloved son, Siyamak, was slain. In turn, Siyamak's son, Hushang, avenged his father's death by killing the Black Div. Hushang was assisted in his war against evil by an army of angels and animals. Leopards, lions, wolves, and deer had long been loyal retainers and fighters since the days of Gayumarth's kingdom atop Iran's loftiest mountain.

Meanwhile Zahhak murdered his father and became king in his place. Zahhak's hungry snakes required a daily diet of two young men's brains. Ultimately Zahhak's people revolted, led by the warrior Faridun, who chained the tyrant to the summit of Mount Damavand in order to prolong his agony.

At the court of Gayumarth the basic arts of life were discovered. Cultivation of food and the making of clothing from animal skins led to mutual reverence between animals and man. Hushang, who succeeded his father's 30-year reign, developed new arts such as mining, smithery, and animal husbandry. One day, wise and just Hushang threw a rock at a ferocious monster, which vanished. But the rock struck a boulder and sparks flared up. Hushang had discovered the divine gift of fire. He gathered his courtiers and animals to learn the potentialities of this divine gift, which all henceforth were to worship and celebrate in a feast called *sadeh*, a Zoroastrian festival still celebrated today.

Hushang's son, Tahmuras, improved upon the arts of his father and added weaving and many new arts that he learned not only from good spirits but from the *divs* (Farsi, "demons"). Tahmuras defeated Ahriman and the *divs* but spared the life of any demon who could teach him a new, valuable art. Tahmuras therefore learned the alphabet and the scripts for Greek, Arabic, Persian, Pahlavi, Sogdian, and Chinese.

"Zal, Son of Sam" A shah of Iran named Zal was the father of the most renowned hero of the *Shah-Nameh*, Rustam. Zal was the son of Sam and born with hair as white as snow. This was considered a bad omen and Sam exposed the infant to die on a distant mountain. But Zal did not die. He was adopted by a gigantic, monstrous bird called the Simurgh, a phoenix, who raised Zal in her nest with her own feathered youngsters. Years later a caravan of merchants noticed the precocious naked boy with his snowy mane in the bird's nest. Ultimately Sam heard about the boy and rescued his son. The white-haired prince and his powerful Simurgh mother tearfully parted but she gave Zal magic feathers to use to summon her if he needed her help upon his return to the human kingdom.

"Rustam, Son of Zal" The magi, Zoroastrian shamanic priests who presided over religious ceremonies and performed rituals and magic, are prominent characters in Ganjawi's saga. One of the magi told Zal about a remarkable descendant of the Persian king Faridun named Kay Qubad, who was endowed with grace, modesty, and excellence and had legal claim to the throne. Zal's son, Rustam, went to find this future king, who later became the founder of the Kayanian dynasty. Within one mile of Mount Alburz, Rustam came upon a magnificent garden with flowers, trees, and streams. A young man with his court of noblemen invited Rustam to drink a toast with them. Raising glasses in a toast "To the free," the young nobleman proved to be Kay Qubad and both rode off in order for him to take the throne of Iran, which he ruled well for 100 years.

One of the many adventures Rustam went through required him to fight a disguised *div* named Akvan who in the shape of an onager or wild ass had ravished the countryside, killing horses. Shah Kay Qubad understood that only a lionlike champion could overcome this ferocious enemy and invited Rustam to spur his horse, Rakhsh, to capture the onager and prevent it from further devastating the kingdom. Rustam slew the animal with his sword and carried the head to the shah.

"Adventures of Gushtasp and Sarkad" Shah Luhrasp disliked his son, Gushtasp, who left home for Rum in Turkey to seek his fortune. Gushtasp became a mighty warrior and huntsman. When the emperor of Rum set a series of trials for all who wished the hand of his magnificent daughter, Gushtasp, earned her love. Later he slew the horrid dragon of Mount Saqila so that his good friend could join the family by marrying yet another daughter of the emperor.

Persiflage and perfidy intruded upon the most harmonious royal courts. A court musician named Sarkad jealously guarded his position as chief singer by assuring that the shah would hear no professional singer's voice but his own. Shah Khusraw Parviz adored fine singing and rewarded it generously. An excellent musician named Barbad bribed a royal gardener to allow him to perch in a tree under which the shah was accustomed to picnic with his court. After a delectable meal was set, the concealed musician Barbad began to sing so rapturously that the shah offered to reward the man regaling his senses by stuffing his mouth with precious jewels and pearls. Barbad with his stringed instrument gracefully slid down from the tree and ultimately was appointed court musician in place of his jealous rival.

READING

Christian Literature

GENERAL

Brandle and Zippel 1947, Cook 1943, Coulton 1962, Farrar and Evans 1964, Loomis and Willard 1948, Patch 1927, Stone 1964: medieval literature, in general; Barratt 1992, Bornstein 1981, Cosman 2000, Ducket 1964, Ferrante 1976 and 1997: women writers; Ferrante 1975, Hays 1964, Hughes 1943, Kelly 1957, Patch 1927: women in literature.

RELIGIOUS AND DEVOTIONAL LITERATURE

Dyas et al. 2005, Goodrich, 2004, Head, 2000, Heffernan, 1988: hagiography; Messenger, 1948: Latin hymns; O'Sullivan, 2005: Marian devotion and French hymns; O'Callaghan, 1998: *Cantigas de Santa Maria*; Keller, 1978: Castilian and Galician religious verse; Alvilda Petroff 1986, Barrat 1992, Benedict, 2004,

Dronke 1984: women mystic writers; Julian of Norwich, 2005: *Showings*; Roman, 2005: Julian of Norwich and Margery Kempe; Jacobus de Voragine 1993, Jacques de Vitry 1890, Mosher 1911, Young and Gregg 1997, Zink 1977: *exempla*, sermons, didactic literature.

ROMANCE

Andreas Capellanus 1941, Bloch 1991, Dodd 1959, Dronke 1968, Ferrante and Economou 1975, Lewis 1958, Lochrie 1999, Marks 1975, Lacy 1996, Newman 1968, Wack 1990: courtly love; Chretien de Troyes 1975, Furman 1974, Gottfried von Strassburg 1960, Guillaume de Lorris and Jean de Meun 1962, Jackson 1960, Jost 1986, Lacy 1996, Loomis 1949 and 1959, Malory 1985, Owen 1968, Ruck 1991, Tolkien and Gordon 1955, Paris 1883: Arthurian romances; Andrew and Waldron 1978, Borroff 1967, Cawley and Anderson 1976, Tolkein and Gordon 1967: *Sir Gawain and the Green Knight*; Jackson 1960, Wolohojian 1969: Alexander and other classical heroes.

CHANSON DE GESTE

Luquiens 1952, Sayers 1957: *Song of Roland*; Fletcher 1989, Merwin 1959: *El Cid*.

FRAME TALE

Benson and Anderson 1971, Chaucer 1977, Curry 1960, Dodd 1959, Kelly 1973, Robertson 1957: Chaucer; Boccaccio 1999: *The Decameron*.

LOVE POETRY

Goldin 1973 and 1974, Kermode 1972, Marks 1975, Picot 1975, Ruck 1991, Stone 1964: love poetry; Bogin 1976, Briffault 1965, Cosman 1996, Goldin 1974, Nelli 1963: troubadours and trouvères; Goldin 1973, Hatto and Taylor 1958: German and Italian lyrics; Barratt 1992, Brandl and Zippel 1947, Cook 1943, Davis 1964, Loomis and Willard 1948: Middle English poetry.

DRAMA

Cooper and Worthan 1984: *Everyman*; Jacobus de Voragine 1969 and 1993: *Legenda Aurea*.

INSTRUCTION BOOK

Andreas Capellanus 1941, Shapiro and Wadsworth 1971: the art of love; Herrad of Landsberg 1977: the Garden of Delights; Bornstein 1981, Christine de Pizan 1908, 1932, and 1989, Cosman and Willard 1989: Christine de Pizan.

FABLIAUX AND LAIS

Aarne 1951, Benson and Anderson 1971, Cholakian and Cholakian 1962 and 1974, Harrison 1974, Hellman and Gorman 1965, Johnston and Owen 1957, Nykrog 1957, Tetel 1973: fabliaux; Marie de France, 1983: Fables of Marie de France; Berechia ha-Nakdan 1967: fables of a Jewish Aesop; Aarne 1951, Thompson 1989: *marchen* and folk motifs; Burgess 1987, Marie de France 1978 and 1983: Lais of Marie de France.

ALLEGORY

Dunbar 1929, Bloom 1987: general and Dante's *Divine Comedy*; Aers 1975, Salter and Pearsall 1969: *Piers Plowman*.

HISTORICAL CHRONICLES

France and Zajac 1998, Hallam 1989, Housley 1996, Shepkaru 2002, Stone 1939: crusader chronicles; Wolf 1990: medieval Spain; Swan (trans.) 1905: *Gesta Romanorum*; Savage 1997, Swanton 1996: *Anglo-Saxon Chronicles*; Bartlett 2000: Norman England; Shopkow, 1997: Norman and French history.

LITERARY LANGUAGES

Burnley 2000, Curran 2002, Gneuss 1996: Old and Middle English; Baker 1995, Fulk 1991: Beowulf; Nielsen 1985, Orwin 1992: Old English and German; Ewert 1969, Fox and Wood 1968, Holmes 1947, Rickard 1996. Entwistle 1936, Moreno-Fernández 2005: history of Iberian languages; Sánchez Sánchez 2000: early Spanish literature; González-Casanova 1995: Catalan and Ramon Llull; Devoto 1978, Grandgent 1927, Hainsworth 1988, Migliorini 1966: general history; Privitera 2004: Sicilian; Bonfante 1999, Janson 2004: Latin and Romance language history. Nielsen, 1985 and 1989, Orwin 1992, Strong 1886: Old English and German; Bernhardt and Davis 1997: High German; Stockman 1998: Low German; Geipel 1982, Herzog 2000: Yiddish.

MAJOR CHRISTIAN WRITERS

Dyas et al. 2005, Lees et al. 1994, Verbeke et al. 2005, Willaert et al. 2004.

Jewish Literature

GENERAL

Twersky and Harris 1979–2000: Jewish literature, general; Hadas 1967, Mansoor 1991: the Jewish Aesop, Berechiah ha Nakdan; Abrahams 1969, Baer 1961, Baron 1967, Constable 1997, Goldstein 1965 and 1971, Yerushalmi 1971: Haggadic literature.

BEAST FABLE

Hadas 1967: Berechiah ha Nakdan; Baron 1967, Ben-Amos 1999, Hadas 1967, Neumann 1969: beast fables by Berechiah ha Nakdan and Isaac Ibn Sahula; Neumann 1969: influence of *Kalilah and Dimnah*.

FRAME TALE

Baron 1967, Ben-Amos 1999, Constable 1997, Marcus 1938, Millas Villacrosa 1968: *Tales of Sendebar*; Abrahams 2007, Neumann 1969: Joseph ibn Zabara's *Book of Delight*.

HEROIC ROMANCE

Baron 1967, Lacy 1996, Modder 1960: *Sir Bove* and other Jewish Arthurian romances; Lacy 1996: Elijah Levita *Bove Bukh*; Fuks 1957, Stauch 1990: *Dukus Horant* epic; Przybilski 2002: Christian-Jewish cultural transfer.

CHANSON DE GESTE

Przybilski 2002: Christian-Jewish cultural transfer; Zuckerman 1972, *see also* chapter 1: Count William of Toulouse and the Makhir dynasty; Zuckerman 1972: the *Song of William*.

SATIRE

Baron 1967, Mansoor 1991, Yerushalmi 1971: Kalonymous ben Kalonymous and his book *The Touchstone*; Baron 1967, Mansoor 1991, Yerushalmi 1971: Immanuel of Rome's *Mahberot*.

POEMS OF LOVE AND WAR

Carmi 1981 and 2006, Caspi 1995, Constable 1997, García Gómez 1945, Goldstein 1965, Mansoor 1965, Millas Villacrosa 1968: poetry; Constable 1997, Goldstein 1965, Scheindlin 1999: Judah Halevi; Ibn Nagrela 1973, Scheindlin 1999, Shirmann 1951, Weinberger 1973: Samuel ibn Nagrela's love poetry; John Donne's poem "To His Mistress Going to Bed."

RELIGIOUS POETRY

Einbinder 2002, Marcus 1990: *piyyut* and martyrological poetry.

INSTRUCTION BOOK

Baron 1967, Bernavi 1992, Mansoor 1991, Schafer, 2004: the *Book of the Pious*; Shapiro and Wadsworth 1971: French guides to the art of love.

EXEMPLA

Baron 1967, Ben Amos 1999, Hadas 1967, Metzger and Metzger 1982: *exempla* collections.

MAQAMA

Hamilton et al. 2004: Hebrew and Arabic literature of Spain; Ibn Zabara 1931: *The Book of Delight*.

JEWISH CRUSADE CHRONICLES

Chazan 2000, G Cohen, 1999, J Cohen 1982, 1999, and 2006, Habermann 1971, Shepkaru 2002.

MAJOR JEWISH WRITERS

Ben, Amos 1999, Cluse 2004, Twersky and Harris 2002: Jewish literature, general.

Islamic Literature

PRE-ISLAMIC ARABIC LITERARY GENRES: POETRY AND SONG

Allen 2000, Farmer 1967, Hamori 1982, Hourani 1991: Arabic poetry, in general; Allen 2000, Stetkevych 2002: *qasida*.

UMAYYAD AND ABBASID POETRY

Allen 2000, Beeston et al. 2003, al-Freih and Halsall 1998, Hamori 1982: erotic poetry (Abu l-Atahiyah, Abu Nuwas, et al.) under the Abbasids.

UMAYYAD SPAIN

Abu-Haidar, 2001, Beeston et al. 2003, Jayyusi 1999, Menocal et al. 2000, Monroe 2004: Hispano-Arabic poetry; Stern 1972: *muwash-shaha* and *zajal*; Menocal 1987, Menocal et al. 2000, Nykl 1970: Hispano-Arabic poetry and French troubadours.

MYSTICAL POETRY

Hamori 1982, Homerin 1994, Smith 1950 and 1954, Schimmel 1982, Smith 1950 and 1954: mystical poetry.

HEROIC EPIC

Allen 1998 and 2000, Heath 1996: general and *Sirat Antar*; Reynolds 1995: general and *Sirat Bani Hilal*.

ARABIC PROSE LITERATURE

Allen 1998 and 2000, Chelkowski et al. 1975, Hourani 1991, Hamori 1982, Kennedy 2005: Arabic prose, in general.

BIOGRAPHY AND AUTOBIOGRAPHY

Allen 1998 and 2000, Hitti 2000: Usama ibn Munqidh; Hourani 1991: biographical dictionaries; Reynolds et al. 2001: biography and autobiography, Watt 1953: al-Ghazali.

SIRA AND HISTORICAL CHRONICLES

Hourani 1991, Hamori 1982: Arabic historians; Gabrielli 1984: Arab crusader historians; Hitti and Bulliet 2000: Usama ibn Munqidh.

ADAB AND BELLES-LETTRES

Allen 1998 and 2000, Malti-Douglas 1985, Kennedy 2005: general *adab*; Al-Jahiz 1980, Kennedy 2005, Pellat 1951 and 1969: the works of al-Jahiz; Ashtiany 1990, Kennedy 2005: Abbasid belles-lettres; Arazi and Ben-Shammay 1999, Bonebakker 1977, *risala*; Arberry 1955, Dawood 1973, Haddawy 1990, Horovitz 1927: Scheherazade and *The Thousand and One Nights*; Agajanian 1958: "Uses of Animals"; Kennedy 2005, Kops and Bodenheimer 1949, Lecomte 1999: Ibn Qutayba's stories; Margliouth 1922: Nishwar al-Muhadara's "Food for Entertainment"; Goodman 1978: "The Case of Animals versus Man before the King of the Jinn"; al-Tawhidi 1953: Abu Hayyan al-Tawhidi's *Book of Enjoyment and Conviviality (Kitab al-Imta wal-Muanasa)*; Gibb 1958: Ibn Battuta.

MAQAMA

Allen 1998 and 2000, Chenery and Steingass 1867–98, Gerhardt 1963, Halsall 1998, Prendergast 1915, Warner 2004, (Internet source http://www.ebooksread.com/authors-eng/warner/the-worlds-best-literature) *maqamat* or "assemblies"; Hamilton et al. 2004: Hebrew and Arabic literature of Spain.

PERSIAN LITERATURE IN THE ISLAMIC WORLD

Arberry 1994, Rypka 1968: Persian poetry and the *Khamseh* of Nizami; Arnold 1929, Arberry 1995, Ettinghausen 1972, Gray 1977, Martin 1912, Petrosyan and Akimushkin 1955, Welch 1973 and 1976, Welch and Dickson 1973: the Persian epic *Shah-Nameh*; Arberry 1952 and 1994, Esfandiary 1949, Fitzgerald 1884, Graves and Ali-Shah 1967, Saidi 1991: the *Rubaiyat* of Omar Khayyam; Arberry 1994, Elwell-Sutton 1975 and 1976: Persian *rubai*; Meisami 1993, *see* Readings for chapter 4: Nasir-i Khusraw's *Book of Travels*.

10

MUSIC AND DANCE

Music and literature were closely related in the sacred and secular songs of medieval Christians, Jews, and Muslims. Christian *troubadours*, *trouveres*, and *minnesingers* had their Jewish counterparts. Rhythms and instruments of the Muslim troubadour singers and court musicians found their way into the courtly music of the Christian realms of Spain and across the Pyrenees. Music in the theater was important in the earliest plays derived from the church liturgy and the antiphonal singing within the church. Likewise, music was an important element in Jewish liturgical and pious festival celebrations, and it was indispensable in fomenting religious ecstasy among Muslim Sufi mystics. Muslim and Christian military music had its marching songs, its rhythmic battle cries, and its songs to stimulate courage and victory. Hunting music was played on hunting horns from the moment the first hounds were uncoupled, to the horns urging both dogs and hunters to the kill, to the rhythmic presentation of meat in the banquet hall. All three communities lauded the therapeutic and medicinal properties of music: Banquet music was specifically created to stimulate good digestion while aesthetically pleasing musical tastes of the banqueters. Music in health spas was contrived to counteract the negative effects of disease or injury by utilizing rhythms associated with the patient's bodily type, determined by the *four temperaments* of humankind, the sanguine, the phlegmatic, the choleric, and the melancholic.

Dance was associated with music as an extension of musical rhythm by bodily movement for physical exercise, for refining ability to elegantly move through space, for pleasure and entertainment, for integrating exquisite movements of the human body with animal choreography, as in horse ballets, and for demonstrating education and social grace. Whoever did not know the current courtly dances was assumed to be ill with lumbago or gout or thought to be an imposter or spy. This chapter explores the exhilarating history of music and dance among medieval Christians, Jews, and Muslims.

CHRISTIAN MUSIC AND DANCE

Church Music

A seventh-century man who never could sing suddenly sang the sweetest, most inspirational, elegant songs. If this song-making brilliance of the earlier mute, unlettered herdsman named Caedmon (d. c. 679) truly was a miracle, then he who always had exited in shame from the beer halls whenever the harp was passed to him for singing would generate intellectual excellence, ecclesiastical renown, and cold cash to the monastery of Whitby. Abbess Hilda (d. 680), leader of the seventh-century coeducational monastery, carefully reviewed the evidence of transformation of the once ignorant man to the most spectacular poet in the English language. Abbess Hilda invited Caedmon to leave his worldly life to join the Whitby spiritual community as a monk. Thereafter the monastery joyously resounded with his songs and poems for the multitudes.

This story of the first Anglo-Saxon poet was transmitted by the Venerable Bede, himself a monk of the monastery at Jarrow, near Whitby, in his book the *Ecclesiastical History of the English People*, written in Latin, *Historia Ecclesiastica Gentis Anglorum*. Completed in the year 731, this tale reminds us of the all-pervasive power of medieval music. Not knowing how to make music was a serious social disability. Music was one of the mathematical arts of the seven liberal arts. Grammar, rhetoric, and logic composed the literary *trivium* while the mathematical and scientific studies of arithmetic, geometry, astronomy, and music were the *quadrivium* of the customary university curriculum. But even the unlearned could sing inspirationally to praise God. Song expressed sanctity.

Church music pervaded all aspects of ecclesiastical life. Though some of the greatest medieval ecclesiastical musical monuments were *masses*, these exquisite, formulaic praises of God were not as common as the stunning range of musical consecrations caused by the requirements to pray every three hours. Most secular people did not have the leisure to pray eight times daily. But professional churchmen and churchwomen who consecrated their lives to prayer such as the monks, nuns, friars, priests, and ecclesiastical figures supported by the Christian Church literally performed their work as prayer, and for many, prayer was their work. They performed the work of God, the *opus dei*, celebrating *the divine office*. The eight canonical hours into which the 24-hour day was separated for the Christian divine office were *matins, lauds, prime, terce, sext, nones, vespers,* and *compline*. Each hour's devotions consisted of several specific *psalms, canticles,* hymns, readings, *antiphons* (short scriptural texts sung by alternating pairs of choruses in a church or monastic chapel), and a short prayer called a *collect*, consisting of an invocation to God, a petition, and a concluding celebration of divine glory.

Gregorian chant was one of the four musical dialects of the church; the others were the *Ambrosian, Gallican,* and *Mozarabic chants, Gregorian chant,* or *plainsong,* contained formulaic configurations of musical tones called *church modes,* or scales, with repetitive, rhythmic musical patterns.

MUSIC THEORY AND WORLD ORDER

Such comprehensive celebration of music had its origins in theories of the world enunciated by such great sixth-century philosophers as Boethius of Rome, the Roman senator Cassiodorus, and Theodoricus de Campo (14th century). The order of the world (Latin, *ordo mundi*) was God's creation of a blessed interrelatedness of all created things. God's divine plan for perfect order in the universe was expressed in the *macrocosm*, the totality of creation consisting of four essential elements, earth, air, fire, and water, and their four essential contraries, hot, cold, moist, and dry. These qualities were reflected proportionally in the human being, the creation in small, the *microcosm*, whose disease fevers, menstrual cycles, and pulse music illustrated and imitated celestial harmonies in the healthy physique. Boethius, drawing on the works of earlier Greek musical theorists, explicated the ideas of the *ordo mundi* in his famous treatise *On Musical Theory* (*De Institutione musica*) in which he distinguished among the three classes of music.

Demonstrating perfect musical and mathematical order as well as the interconnectedness of creation, Boethius's first music was *musica mundana* (Latin, "world music"), the music of the celestial spheres. Planetary patterns were connected with the rhythms of the zodiac. This music of the spheres was intimately connected with the harmonies of the body in Boethius's second classification, *musica humana*. Periodic fevers, rhythms of the human pulse, male and female hormonal rhythms, and the many identifiable patterns of breathing and heartbeat were the constituents of human music. The only class of music actually heard by human ears was the last, *musica instrumentis*, music played on instruments or sung by the mortal voice.

Boethius, counselor to the Roman emperor Theoderic the Great (d. 526), was jailed for a false accusation of treachery and executed in 524. He was known for his musical studies and his influential book called the *Consolation of Philosophy* (*Consolatio Philosophiae*), which celebrated the unreliability and inscrutability of earthly fortune, and the human fall from prosperity to misery in tragedy. It was translated several times including by King Alfred of Wessex (d. 899), Geoffrey Chaucer, and Jean de Meun (d. 1305), author of the romance *Roman de la Rose*.

In the 14th century Theodoricos de Campo created another class of music based upon the Boethian *three classes*. Theodoricos's *four classes of music* included *musica mundana*, the harmony of the universe, and *musica humana*, the human bodily harmonies and soul rhythms. *Musica vocalis* pertained to animal and natural voices such as rushing water, clapping thunder, creaking trees in wind, and the sounds of the four winds (the rough north wind Boreas, the south wind Notus, the east wind called Euros or Argestes, and the mild west wind called Zephyr or Zephyrus, whose sweet breath inspired Chaucer's men and women to go on pilgrimages). The fourth class of music was *musica artificialis*, human vocal and instrumental sound.

The distinct musical forms also were thought associated with the *four seasons*, spring, summer, fall, and winter; with the *four stages of life*, infancy, youth, prime, and old age; along with the *four temperaments*, sanguine, choleric, phlegmatic, and melancholic, produced by the *four humors*, blood; yellow bile, or choler; phlegm; and black bile, or melancholia. These harmonies were represented in *cosmological diagrams*, circular designs demonstrating the world's harmonious unities.

THE CHURCH MASS

The *mass* was the liturgical celebration of Christ's Last Supper, or *Eucharist*, and the Crucifixion. The Last Supper was Christ's celebration in Jerusalem of the Jewish Passover, or Pesach meal, the seder, with his Twelve Apostles, foreshadowing his betrayal. During that festive meal, Jesus Christ consecrated the bread and wine, thereby initiating the first communion and the first *Eucharist*. The Eucharist in the Middle Ages was the major act of Christian thanksgiving in which the bread or wafer represented the body of Jesus Christ and the wine his blood by the process of *transubstantiation*, the theological doctrine that during the consecration in celebrating the Eucharist, the bread and wine actually were converted to Christ's body and blood. Transubstantiation in music was thought to be a *stimulus amorus*, Latin for "stimulation to love and veneration," as were the musical portraits of Jesus Christ's execution on the cross at Calvary, his crucifixion.

Music theory. A woodcut from Theorica musicae *(1492), by Franchino Gaffurio, showing experiments to establish the mathematical relationships between musical intervals.* [Ency Renaissance p 331. No credit listed.]

The word *mass* derived from the concluding benediction meaning, "Go; the congregation is dismissed," *ite missa est congregation*. Structurally, the mass consisted of the *proper*, the varying elements, and the *ordinary*, the constant elements. The mass sections, followed by the code letter *P* for "proper" and the constant elements *O* for "ordinary," are as follows: *introit* (P), *kyrie* (O), *gloria* (P), *gradual* (P), *alleluia* (P) or *tract* (P), *credo* (O), *offertory* (P), *sanctus* (O), *agnus dei* (O), *communion* (O), *ite missa est* or *benedictus* (O).

The *introit* was part of the proper, the ornate antiphonal first chant of the mass. *Kyrie*, from the Greek meaning "O Lord!" was a triple supplication to God sung three times as the first element of the ordinary of the mass, at the end of canonical hours, and elsewhere in the liturgy. The common chant phrase *Kyrie eleison, Christe eleison, Kyrie eleison* meant "Lord have mercy; Christ have mercy; Lord have mercy."

After the *kyrie* of the mass on certain feast days, *hymns* celebrating God were sung, such as the sublime *gloria in excelsis deo* (Latin, "glory to God on high"). This hymn, called the *angelic hymn*, was part of the *greater doxology*: the formulaic spoken or sung praise of God's glory dedicated to the *Holy Trinity*, God as Father, Son, and Holy Ghost. The *greater doxology* was in contrast to the *lesser doxology* with the formula *gloria patri* (Latin, "glory to the Father"), the beginning of the praises of the three members of the Trinity, *gloria patri et filio et spiritu sancto*, often ending hymns during the divine office. The *gloria* is part of the mass proper.

The *gradual*, also part of the *proper*, has its title derived from the Latin *gradus*, "step." This melodically florid responsorial chant originally was sung from the steps of the *ambo*, the pulpit in the center aisle of a church or cathedral from which the gospel lesson was read. The text taken mostly from the *psalms*, it was called the *responsorium gradual*.

The next part of the proper was the *alleluia* or the *tract*. Exultant music, it often contained *melismas*, musically fancy, emotionally expressive vocal elaborations of the single-syllable text in Gregorian chant and 13th-century polyphony. *Melismas* contrasted to the so-called syllabic style. The *jubilus* was a long exuberant *melisma* sung to the final *a* of an *alleluia*.

The liturgical *tract* was the chant sung or recited at mass on certain penitential days in place of the *alleluia*. Originally it was the psalm chanted after the second lesson, later superseded by the *alleluia*, though preserved on days of penitence and mourning. Differing from the *gradual*, the *tract* was chanted without a response. Some say the origin of the word was the Latin *tractim*, meaning "straight through," while others maintain it derived from the Greek word for "train" or "series," denoting a typical tune joining several parts of a hymn. The *tract* was sung on the first Sunday in Lent and on Palm Sunday and was usually said on Sundays between *Septuagesima* (Latin, "70th"), the 70 days beginning with the third Sunday before Lent and ending with the Saturday before Easter.

Next in order was the *credo* (Latin, "I believe"). A short, concise, formal statement of the fundamental dogmas of Christianity, the *credo* often was followed by the *offertory*. The credo would include the *Apostles' Creed*, the short statement of basic Christian beliefs thought originally formulated by the Twelve Apostles. Liturgically important in *baptism*, the creed also was said before *matins* and *prime* and after *compline*. The *offertory*, part of a proper of the mass, consisted of the priest's offering gifts of bread and wine as part of the Christian *Eucharist* ceremony. Or it was a donation of money provided by parishioners at mass for use by the clergy for themselves and for the poor and the sick.

The *sanctus* was the fourth element or the ordinary of the mass. The words in Latin *sanctus, sanctus, sanctus, . . . pleni sunt caeli et terra,* meaning "Holy Holy Holy, heaven and Earth are filled," were followed by *benedictus qui venit*, meaning "He is blessed who comes in God's name." *Agnes Dei* (Latin, "Lamb of God") was a section of the ordinary of the mass usually sung three times after the *consecration* and before *communion*. The Lamb of God was the graphic representation of the eschatological triumph of Christ according to the vision of the Apocalypse in the Book of Revelation 5:6 and John 1:29. *Communion*, also part of the ordinary, was the culminating rite of the mass, which realized spiritual union between a Christian and Christ in the celebration of the *Eucharist*. The eating of the spiritual food of souls—"He that eats me, the same also shall live by me"—(cf.: John 6:55–57) represents one of the seven sacraments of the Christian church. These seven sacraments were acts conferring Christian grace: *baptism, communion, confirmation, penitence (confession), extreme unction, holy orders* and *matrimony*.

The final element of the mass was the *ite missa est*, or the *benedictus*, also part of the ordinary, from the Latin *Benedictus qui venit*, "He is blessed who comes in the name of the Lord."

GREGORIAN CHANT

Of the four musical dialects of Western church music, one of the most familiar to modern ears is *Gregorian chant*, though the other three are equally fascinating, *Ambrosian chant, Gallican chant*, and *Mozarabic or Visigothic chant*. *Gregorian chant* was Roman liturgical *plainsong* or *chant*, traditionally thought arranged and codified in the seventh century under Pope Gregory I. *Plainsong*, from Latin *planus cantus*, "flat or level song," was the 13th-century name for monophonic, vocal, rhythmical free melodies. A short phrase or melody for singing psalms and canticles in public worship, *plainsong* had a long *reciting note* to which an indefinite number of syllables were sung, followed by a rhythmical *cadence*. Musical intoning was *single chant* when sung to one verse of a psalm, consisting of two strains of three and four bars, each beginning with a *reciting note. Double chant* was twice the length of a *single chant* and sung to two verses.

Plainsong was important for Christian *psalmody*. In the liturgy, songs were sung in one of three ways. Straight choral singing of the song was called *direct psalmody*. Alternation between chorus and soloist was called *responsorial singing*. Alternating between two choirs was *antiphonal singing. Psalmody* was descended from Hebrew *cantillation*, which was a solo chanting, musical recitation intoned in synagogues for prayers and Bible readings.

A *psalm* was a sacred song or hymn sung in private devotion during one of the eight *canonical hours* or in public prayer. Psalms also referred to the Old Testament *Psalms of David*. A *psalter* was a psalm book used both in church and in private prayer. A practical prayer book used during the *canonical hours*, it was a less comprehensive prayer text than a *breviary*, customarily used by the clergy, but for some patrons was as richly illuminated as the most sumptuous *books of hours*.

NOTRE DAME SCHOOL AND *ARS ANTIQUA*

The Notre Dame school was the spectacular 12th- and 13th-century center for church music at the Cathedral of Paris, Notre Dame. The school was important for its experiments in *counterpoint*, instrumental and vocal *polyphony* in which several separate instrumental or human voices sang at the same time in several distinct voices or parts, usually each with its own text, all simultaneously performed. The music was arranged to emphasize the importance of each part's melodic line. The conjunction of all intertwining musical voices produced dazzling sound. Composers created extravagant embellishments upon a single fixed melody, the *cantus firmus*, the base of the polyphonic composition to which voices were added in counterpoint.

The French great masters Leonin (d. c. 1201) and Perotin (c. 1160–1240) experimented with rhythm and created exquisite examples of *organum* and *motet*. The *organum* was an early type of polyphonic music that had been described in a famous ninth-century music book called *Musica enchiriadis*. Four types of *organum* evolved. The *parallel organum* during the ninth and 10th centuries developed into the *free organum* during the 11th and 12th centuries, then the *melismatic organum*, in the 12th century, culminating in the 13th-century *measured organum*. The best sources for the Notre Dame school compositions were the manuscripts of Montpellier, Bamberg, and Huelgas. Successors to Leonin, Perotin, and their contemporaries contemptuously referred to them as practitioners of the old art, the *ars antiqua*.

ARS NOVA

The new musical art of the 14th century, calling itself *ars nova* (Latin, "new art"), was a reaction against the old *ars antiqua*. The French musical theorist Philipe de Vitry (d. 1361) in 1325 wrote of the bold innovations of his contemporaries in his important musical theory text, *Ars nova*. In it he described the *ars nova* as characterized by brilliant polyphonic musical compositions, bravura performance, and precise notation, particularly in Italy and France. Poet composers also were mathematical experimenters. The luminary Guillaume de Machaut (c. 1300–77) created his spectacular *Mass of Notre Dame* and exquisite, complex, sometimes bawdy, secular songs. Giovanni da Cascia (active in the first half of the 14th century) and Jacobo da Bologna (d. after 1378), as did Machaut, wrote music incorporating harmonically interesting, bold dissonances, rhythmic complexities, audacious syncopation and beat displacement, and intellectually adventurous, rhapsodic melodies. They wrote ballads, *rondeaux*, beginning and ending with a bipartite refrain, and *virelais*, a popular song and dance form with a recurring refrain.

Musical Modes and Notations

MUSICAL MODES

Musical modes pertained to rhythm or tone. Repetitive rhythmic musical patterns were named after classical literary verse patterns. The *trochaic mode* consisted of a phrase of two syllables, the first stressed and the following unstressed. An example is the rhythm of the magnificent hymn called *Pange lingua* (Latin, "Sing, tongue"). One famous Latin hymn by that name was composed by Venantius Fortunatus in the sixth century. Another version was composed by the great theologian Saint Thomas Aquinas in the 13th century using the first line and trochaic meter of the Venantius hymn and embellishing them magnificently. The *iambic* meter consisted of a short followed by a long beat. The *dactylic* was the poetic meter consisting of a long beat followed by two short beats. Its opposite was the *anapestic*, two short beats followed by a long. The *spondaic* consisted of two adjacent long beats often used for elegies, funeral poems, and to signify conclusion, literally, the end. The *tribrachic* was a metrical mode consisting of phrases with three short syllables. All of these were typical of early mensural music developed in the 13th century in which every note had a strictly determined rhythmic value. Circa 1260 the German composer Franco of Cologne codified this system of musical time using written mensural notations in his treatise *Ars cantus mensurabilis* (*The Art of Measurable Song*).

Formulaic configurations of musical tones existed in Gregorian chant, specifically octave segments of the C-major scale. The range of tones, the *ambitus*, was an interval ranging from a fourth, as in a simple *antiphon*, to an octave or more, as in *graduals* and *alleluias*. The center tone was called the *finalis*; it was the tone upon which the melody ended. There were six *finalis* notes: D, E, F, G, A, and C.

Two subgroups of six modes were called the *authentic* and the *plagal*. In the *authentic* mode called *Dorian* the finalis was the note D. *Phrygian* had the *finalis* E; *Lydian*, G; *Aeolian* had the *finalis* A; *Ionian*, the *finalis* C. The *plagal* subgroups added the prefix *hypo-* to each of the six modes, as in *Hypo-Dorian*, *Hypo-Phrygian*, and *Hypo-Lydian*. In the *plagal* mode, the ambitus or range began with the fourth below and extended to the fifth above. *Ambrosian chant*, that elegantly florid liturgical chant established in the fourth century by Saint Ambrose, bishop of Milan, omitted *plagal modes* of *Gregorian chant*, as did *Mozarabic* chant in the Spanish Visigothic liturgical tradition, so named for the Christian populations who resided in Muslim Spain, known as the Mozarabs, from the Arabic *Mustarab*.

The 11th-century Italian Benedictine monk Guido d'Arezzo created a clever mnemonic for remembering musical pitch of the hexacord, the six-note scale, the important musical structure of six diatonic tones separated by a semitone interval, namely, C, D, E, G, and A. Guido recommended using the five digits of the hand, therefore pictorially and by reference, *Guido's hand*. The hand of the singer became a modulator with each tip and joint of each finger having an allocated note. The singer then could practice music and exercise singing at any time. Guido emended the earlier *tetrachord* theory and anticipated the modern *heptachord* system and the octave. The tetrachord was an ascending group of four tones with a specific interval structure.

Guido's brilliant technique of *solmization* is still taught today. In *The Sound of Music*, Maria's song "Do Re Mi" states a form of the monk Guido's 11th-century ideas. In the medieval original, pitch on the musical scale was represented by Guido's syllables, not letters, and his names for the tones C through A, *ut, re, mi, fa, so, la*, actually derived from the first two letters of successive words in a hymn to Saint John. Originally it looked like this: **Ut** *queante laxis.* **Re**sonare fibris. **Mi**ra gestorum. **Fa**muli tuorum. **Sol**ve polluti. **La**bii reatum. **S**ancte **J**oannes. The medieval student therefore could count on and sing on his fingers.

GOTHIC NEUMES AND HORSESHOE NAILS

Gothic neumes were the notation for Gregorian chant and plainsong as well as other 14th- and 15th-century music. A *neume* was a square or diamond-shaped musical notation sign for writing plainsong. Neumes gave pitch but not timing. Important from the eighth through the 14th century, this musical marking was also called *Nagelschrift* or *Hufnagelschrift* (*huf*, "hoof"; *nagel*, "nail"; *schrift*, "writing"), because the notation resembled horseshoe nails.

MENSURAL NOTATION

In opposition to the free rhythms of Gregorian chant or plainsong was *mensural music*, the 13th- through 16th-century polyphonic compositions with every note having a strictly determined rhythmic value. Therefore notation had to represent the appropriate timing. The system of musical notation called *mensural notation* was codified by Franco of Cologne in the 13th century. He asserted fixed time relationships among note values, as in *mimina, maxima, longa*, and *brevis*. Now a note indicated not only pitch but duration.

Secular Music

Secular music in medieval Europe included love songs, political satire, dances, and drama. During the 10th century jongleurs and minstrels, traveling vocal and instrumental performers, relied on oral tradition to entertain the crowd. Among the professional and semi-professional love poets of the 10th through 14th centuries were the troubadours, the *trouvères*, the *minnesingers*, and the Italian writers of the *dolce stil nuovo*, most of whose poems were meant to be sung (*see* chapter 9 on literature for more information on love poetry). During the 11th to 13th centuries the *Goliards*, wandering scholar poets, sang in Latin of life, love, chastity, drink, whores, sex, and obscenity.

Music was also an important form of entertainment for the nobility. A banqueter listening to music of lute, vielle, and cornet accompanying a fine dinner of roast beef, asparagus, and turnips beautifully cooked with chestnuts and cream would not be surprised if suddenly stimulated to amorous ideas. Attentive to the music, she or he would have eaten those foods known to be aphrodisiacs expecting either to indulge the effects of erotic music and titillating menu or to shift quickly to musical rhythm and melody correct for an ardor-cooling salad. In banquet hall and health spa, sensual stirrings of the lute might accompany erotic feasters from bath to bed.

MEDICAL MUSIC

Music of the hunt and banquet was allied to medicine because food was thought to stimulate the four major bodily fluids, the four humors, determining health or illness. Wedding feast melodies were the erotic stimulating sound of the *shivaree*, which in musical procession led the happy pair to the nuptial bedroom where musical echoes would later sound in the medical obstetric chamber. Such practical medical music expressed the harmonies of the medieval world order.

Medieval physicians would not perform elective surgery without the patient's prior preparation by diet and music therapy. If the patient's bodily type was choleric, the surgeon would attempt to regulate the patient's excitable, irascible constitution and calm the rhythm of pulse by tranquil music accompanying a diet including mild wine, boiled rice, barley cream, boiled veil and chicken, and, in season, baked pears and apples. Conversely, a melancholic patient before surgery would listen to sensual, joyous melody to accompany light cheese, eggs, custard, and diary products.

Medical theorists in their texts and practitioners with their patients utilized both musical idea and performance in diagnosis of disease, prognosis of cure or death, and treatment by medicine or surgery. Hospitals, clinics, and health spas sounded with rhythm and melody. Music was mood changer and antidote to poison. It promoted wound healing, and the elaborate mathematical theories of human pulse music required the medieval physician to cultivate a learned touch, a *tactus eruditus*, an ability to feel pulse music through fingers, perceiving rhythm, tempo, proportion, and meter.

The 12th-century chronicler Geraldus Cambrensis said that the sweet harmony of music not only affords pleasures but renders important services. It greatly cheers the drooping spirit, smoothes the wrinkled brow, and promotes hilarity. Nothing so enlivens the human heart, refreshes and delights the mind. Music draws forth the genius and by means of insensible things quickens the senses with sensible effect. Music soothes disease and pain. The sounds that strike the ear, operating within, either heal our maladies or enable us to bear them with greater patience. A comfort to all and an effectual remedy to many, music mitigates all sufferings and some it cures.

Mood music had a venerable tradition in Greek, Roman, and Arab thought. Musical mood changers were mediated to the Middle Ages by Isidore of Seville, fourth century; Cassiodorus, fifth century; and most importantly Boethius, born in 480. Boethius's treatise *On Music* was read in the medieval universities and medical schools. He quoted the method by which Pythagorus used spondaic melody to calm and restore to self-mastery a young man who was so agitated by the sound of the Phrygian mode that he nearly became insane. One night when the youth's mistress went to his rival's house and locked the door, the young man went into a frenzy, having been stimulated by his music, and was ready to set fire to the house. Resisting all restraint, he responded to reason only when his friends changed the mode of music and thus by rhythm and melody reduced his fury to perfect calm.

In medieval health handbooks such as Ibn Butlan's (11th century) *Taqwim al-sihha*, translated into Latin as *Tacuinum sanitatis* (*Tables of Health*), music could incite anger, useful for treating cases of hysterical paralysis. (*See* chapter 7 for more information on Ibn Butlan's treatise.) Music was thought effective antidote to poisonous bites and stings of reptiles and insects. A patient bitten by a scorpion was thought helped if the physician imitated in music the offending beast's rhythms. Physician and patient might therefore counteract the harmful affects of the arachnid's poison. The Italian *tarantela* dance was thought derived from a medical musical treatment for the bite of a tarantula. Scorning such ideas as ignorant superstition, William of Amara, in his 14th-century *Treatise on Poisons*, nevertheless recommended music as treatment for tarantula bite because the effect of its poison was severe melancholy, cured by joy, stimulated by stirring melody.

For phlebotomy and bloodletting, music directly and indirectly determined efficacy.

Depending upon the patient's ailment or astrological temperament, the music pulsed and throbbed in benevolent correlation. One of the most important medieval medical music forms was the music of the pulse. Physicians took patients' pulse either at the brachial artery or at the wrist. The physician calculated rhythm, tested pulse strength or irregularity, and compared this information to numerous pulse music treatises written by such venerable physicians as Galen, whose 16 books on pulse distinguished among 27 separate varieties of human pulse.

The physician, astrologer, and philosopher Peter of Abano (d. 1316), professor at Paris and Padua, required that medical practitioners know music theory and feel it in pulse. His widely published treatise called *The Conciliator* (*Concilator*) gave elegant music depictions of concordance, dissonance, mathematical musical proportions, semitones, the scale, the monochord, and the Greek diatonic, chromatic, and enharmonic tetrachords. Peter of Abano suggested that infants customarily have a *trochaic* pulse beat, whereas the aged have *iambotrochaic*. Special pulses were caused by climate, pregnancy, and disease. A sluggish pulse, *pulsus formicans*, crawled slowly as an ant. Leaping pounding pulse, *pulsus gazellans*, flew fleetingly fast as the gazelle. Just as music consisted of high and low notes arranged in proportion, so the pulse consisted of strokes of greater and lesser speed and intensity. Both music and pulse were characterized by rhythmic patterns of time intervals.

Medieval medicine justly has been called time medicine, *chronophysica*. Prior to surgical intervention the medieval physician and surgeon would use devices such as the *astrolabe* and *volvelle* to calculate the zodiacal configurations at the time of the patient's injury or onset of illness, along with the patient's time of birth, in order to determine the prognosis and the probabilities of survival. The *planespheric astrolabe* was not only a reckoner of time but a universal instrument and calculator for measuring heights, distances, and latitudes and reckoning positions of heavenly bodies. It was also used for horoscopy. In 1348 the physician, astronomer, and clock maker named Giovanni da Dondi invented an instrument that replicated the automatic rhythms of the human pulse and calculated the cyclic rhythms of the stars.

The year 1348 marked the height of the *Black Plague*, although epidemics had terrorized Europe earlier. In 1340, for example, the city of Florence buried one-sixth of its citizens, who had succumbed to the plague. Such death quotas extraordinarily affected the art, economics, philosophy, religion, and technology of the living. Chronometers were instruments of prediction, diagnosis, prognosis, and treatment of disease. Perfecting the accuracy of the machine might extend the life of the human being. Medieval physicians and scientists turned medical adversity into technological virtue. Prodigious clock makers such as the physician astrologers Jacob and his son Giovanni da Dondi and (d. 1359, 1389, respectively) and the physicians Simon Bredon (d. 1372) and Nicholas of Lynn (mid-14th century) made timing machines so that physicians might accurately time for healing. Hypocrites said that healing was a matter of timing. Clock makers used plague as an opportunity to harness time mechanically for healing. Physicians became great healers to the extent they allowed time as healer to heal and so long as they as healers accurately timed.

FEAST MUSIC

In the banquet hall feast music was important for ceremony and digestion. Fanfares and trumpets sounded to signal service of each dish and course of food. Since the food served was determined by the temperaments of the feasters, most dishes had appropriate musical

A 15th-century woodcut depicting a musical feast.   The Metropolitan Museum of Art, New York. Harris Brisbane Dick Fund, 1931.

accompaniments. Trumpets, pipes, bells, lutes, horns, shawms, and rolling drums provided aural splendor, stirring sound, and digestives. Discordant sound was thought to cause incomplete food metabolism. Feast music also was an antidote to banquet poisons. Peter de Marra said in his treatise dedicated to Pope Urban V (d. 1370) *Papal Garland Concerning Poisons* that joy derived from music might prevent poison from penetrating to the vitals.

For culinary music at the D'Este court of Ferrara, the chief cook, Christoforo da Messisbugo (d. 1548), author of *Banchetti, compositioni de vivande et apparecchio generale* ("*Banquets, the Composition of Victuals and General Appearance*"), listed for each fish course, meat, and wine its complement by viols, voice, and choir. While the noble guests washed hands with perfumed water, a musical performance by six singers, six viols, a lyre, a lute, a zither, a trombone, a recorder, a flute, and numerous keyboard instruments accompanied the 17th course.

HUNTING MUSIC

The animals on the medieval banquet tables had been hunted with special horns and melodic calls for particular animals, for specific types of hunt with dogs or birds, and for particular rituals within the hunt. It was believed that the more rhythmic the animal's catch and kill, the more healthful the quality of the meat. Since most 14th-century hunting horns played one pitch, hunting calls depended upon rhythm and intensity of sound. One call, the *mote*, was blown at the uncoupling of the hounds. The *rechete* re-called hounds or urged them to the kill. The *mane* and the *pryse* rhythmically portended the animals' calm in the banquet hall, since harmonious hunting prefigured healthful eating.

Hunting music inspired song forms with such names as *chasse*, *caccia*, and *catch*, early forms of *polyphony*, in which the music of the ceremonial pursuit of the animal was transferred to the pursuit of the desired lover. Hunt music indirectly affected sophisticated love allegories and love songs.

SEXUAL MUSIC

Sounding the spectacle of a newly married couple's march to the bedroom was the *shivaree*, erotic, stimulating music to assure their consummate coupling. The word *shivaree* probably derives from the French *charivari*, referring to the noisy mock-serenade music accompanying newlyweds to their bedroom. In the bedroom heavenly harmonies reflected in a mirror registering the Moon and the stars of the night sky would determine the exact propitious moment for sexual intercourse in order to conceive a remarkable child. This star rhythm reflecting glass was called a *conception time mirror*. Obstetric chambers had a *birth time mirror*. The moment a child was conceived and the time noted by a *conception time mirror* and the instant of birth reflected in the *birth time mirrors* enabled practitioners of *genethlialogy*, the study of the governing constellations, to predict the baby's physical nature, humoral balance, temperament, personality, predilections, even likely adult profession.

Song Collections

For both sacred and secular songs, more lyrics have survived the centuries as poems than as musical settings. Yet remarkable musical manuscripts still exist. The *Carmina burana* manuscript in the Munich Staatsbibliothek was the collection of songs of the Goliards. The text plus some musical notation also were preserved in the 12th- through 13th-century manuscript at Benedictbeuren in Bavaria. Satiric, anticlerical, erotic, often lewd Latin and vernacular verses were written and performed by the itinerant Goliards, who, as educated students, were intimately familiar with church ritual and prayer. Wittily sophisticated, ingeniously punning, musically dazzling songs of such writer-musicians as the 12th-century *Archipoeta* of Germany, one of the principal Goliardic singers, whose true name is unknown, celebrated learning, wine, women, and intense sexual pleasure.

The *Dodecachordon* (*Twelve Chords*) was a significant book of musical theory by the Swiss poet and musical theorist Henricus Glareanus (d. 1547), which expanded the traditional eight church modes to 12. The *Old Hall Manuscript* was a superb collection of 148 polyphonic musical compositions performed in the royal household chapel in 15th-century England, a precedent probably initiated by King Henry IV (r. 1413–22). The compositions included settings of the *ordinary* of the mass, *isorhythmic motets*, and *antiphons*. *Isorhythmic motets* were unaccompanied choral compositions with three groups of vocalists singing simultaneously one or more sacred texts intended for performance in church liturgy, especially at vespers.

Motets were a popular polyphonic musical pattern from the 13th century onward, with numerous secular and solo subtypes. The *isorhythmic motet* used repeated, identical musical rhythmic patterns called *taleae*, as in a liturgical *cantus firmus*, a fixed melody that served as the base of the *polyphonic* composition and to which other voices were added in *counterpoint*. This motet technique became particularly popular in 14th-century motets.

Other important medieval music texts were the anonymous ninth-century musical treatise describing polyphony entitled *Musica enchiriadis* (*Music Manual*), which emphasized the newly introduced portative organ. The *Lucidarium* was the title of a late 13th-century musical treatise on plain or unmeasured music by Marchettus of Padua. The *Trent Codices* were seven significant musical manuscripts containing 15th-century polyphonic compositions by John Dunstable (d. 1453), Guillaume Dufay (d. 1474), and Gilles Binchois (d. 1460). The *Colmar Songbook* from the early 15th century contains many types of songs including those of *minnesingers*.

Tropers were books of liturgical tropes and short distinctive *cadences* for use at the end of a melody. These phrases sung by the choir added embellishment to the text of a mass. From the 10th through the 12th century, the *Saint Martial School* at the abbey at Saint Martial in Limoges, France, created exquisite tropes, as well as many examples of the polyphonic *organum*, and *sequences*. A *sequence* was one of the most significant types of liturgical *Gregorian chant* tropes. Attached to the *alleluia*, the *sequence* was probably invented and certainly popularized by Notker Balbulus, a 10th-century monk of Saint Gall.

Love poems either secular or sacred musically set in counterpoint for several voices, usually five or six, singing polyphonically were called *madrigals*. Early versions were presented in the *Squarcialupi Codex*, the important 14th-century music collection now in Florence, including works of Francesco Landini. Landini was famous for his *Landini Cadence*, a musical feature in the *Ars nova*, particularly in the works of Guillaume de Machaut (d. 1377) and Burgundian composers. In this musical form, the sixth degree (A) was inserted between the leading tone (B) and octave (C), and the altered fourth (F sharp) served as a leading tone to the dominant (G).

Litanies (Greek, "supplication") were prayers of petition for peace, unity, good harvest, or protection from plague, usually followed by a response such as "Lord, have mercy!" Often chanted during processions, they were common before the celebration of Ascension. *Litanies to the Virgin* were popular responsorial supplications celebrating the virtues of the Virgin, invoking her as "Star of the Morning," "Star of the Sea," and "Queen of Angels." The customary response was "Pray for us!" A particularly popular *antiphon* to the Virgin was *Ave regina coelorum* (Latin, "Hail, Queen of Heaven"), an antiphon sung usually after the canonical hour of compline or as a vespers hymn. Dufay composed a mass around this chant melody. Yet another popular hailing of Mary was the *Ave Maris Stella* (Latin, "Hail, Star of the Sea"), a popular *Gregorian chant hymn* celebrating Mary and frequently used in *motets*.

Songs of the *troubadours*, *trouveres*, and *minnesingers*, and other secular songs often appeared simple and ecstatic yet were meticulous intellectual, often mathematical creations. Typical were songs of the minnesinger Neidhart von Reuental (d. c. 1245). Following Donates's terminology for the sections of the tripartite courtly song, Neidhart's splendid songs generally were composed of a *frons*, the poetic stanza consisting of two *pedes*, followed by a *cauda*, the musical tail or cadence to the song and instrumental composition. In German the name for the frons was the *Aufgesang*, consisting of two *Stollen* plus the *Abgesang*.

Neidhart's songs were of two types. Neidhart's vigorous, vivacious summer songs called *Reien* imitated rustic dance rhythms and celebrated simple, natural, pastoral gratifications, both aesthetic and sexual. Neidhart's winter songs were called *Tanze* and were stately metered melodies similar to the music of courtly indoor dancing. Neidhart would select a number that factored well, and then with dazzling ingenuity create a mathematically perfect version of the number either in the syllables within the complex stylistic form or in the rhythmic meter for singing. This early mannered music was melodically eccentric, rhythmically complex, though seemingly simple at first hearing, and by the time of the 14th century expressed exquisitely and idiosyncratically by Guillaume de Machaut.

Musical Instruments

Medieval musical instruments are fascinating in and of themselves as makers of sounds strident and exotic to modern ears and, to the modern eye, for their occasionally bizarre shapes. Some instruments were in families, such as the *recorder*, a beaked whistle flute, fashioned in six ranges also called *consorts*. The deepest sound was made by the double bass recorder, the next higher sound by the bass, followed by tenor, alto, soprano, and marvelously high-pitched sopranino. Likewise *viols* also had in families and particular variations. The *viola da braccio* (Italian,

"arm viol") was a small stringed instrument with steeply sloping shoulders and crescent-shaped sound holes played with a convex bow. The *viola da gamba* (Italian, "knee viol") was a large slender-necked stringed instrument held between the knees and bowed, the prototype of the cello. An alphabetical catalog of medieval musical instruments begins with the *arch lute* and arigot and ends with the *zampogna*.

arch lute The *arch lute* was a long, large *lute* with its base strings lengthened. The lute, derived from the Arabic *al-ud*, a plucked stringed musical instrument, had a body shaped like a pear half, its neck long and flat, having multiple frets, a pegboard perpendicular to the neck, and strings running parallel to the body. The arch lute had strings lengthened as in a *theorbo*. Possibly named after its inventor, the *theorbo* was a double-necked lute with two sets of tuning pegs, the lower holding the melody strings, and the upper the base strings. It became extremely popular by the 17th century.

Lute melodies were written in *tablature*, an early notational system for music in which tones were indicated by letters, figures, and symbols, rather than by *neumes*, the method for Gregorian chant melodies, also called the *Nagelschrift*. Tablature also differed from *mensural notation*, in that the tablature staff represented each lute string to be stopped for a particular pitch. For flute notation, a similar tablature indicated the holes on the flute.

arigot **and other pipes** The *pipe and tabor* were common in historical portraits of marketplaces, processions, and theatrical events in noble halls. The same musician played both musical instruments simultaneously. A particularly popular pipe was the *arigot*, a Provençal musical pipe related to the *flageolet*, a recorder-like wind instrument with four finger holes in front and two on the back. Its full range could be manipulated by one hand. The *tabor*, a drum, usually a light, small percussion instrument, was played while buckled onto the player's chest or left arm. One hand manipulated the pipe while the other beat the drum with a drumstick.

Panpipe was another name for the *syrinx*, a row of graduated pipes bound together, each with a different pitch. This pipe, usually played simultaneously with a *tabor* drum, was an early wind instrument. Associated with the pagan fertility god Pan, it was often portrayed in medieval bucolic scenes, associated also with Erato, Polyphemus, various elegant dancing fauns, as well as Poesia, the personification of poetry, and satyrs and with shepherds.

Bagpipes were especially popular among the Celtic populations of Scotland, Ireland, Wales, French Brittany, and northern Spain. Whereas in modern times the bagpipe is associated with funerals and solemn commemorations, in medieval times it was an orgiastic instrument connoting passion, vigorous sex, and inebriation. It was thought to be the medieval phonetic equivalent of the ancient Greek *aulos* and the Roman *tibia*. Nevertheless angels also frequently played bagpipes in musical scenes in painting, sculpture, graphic arts, and stained glass, not only as soloists but in angel concerts, particularly in sacred paintings. A bagpipe was a composite instrument attached to a windbag providing air power, with one or more reed pipes called *chanters*, which were the melody pipes, single or double reed, with finger holes. The other pipes produced a *drone*, a continuous single base *burdon*, consisting of a note of long duration sounded continuously against the melody played by the higher pipes.

Other drone instruments were the *hurdy-gurdy* and the bass-course *vielle*. The *hurdy-gurdy* is believed to have its origins in Spain, where it was called *zanfona* (from the Vulgar Latin, *symponia*). It was not a wind but rather a stringed instrument, also a composite. An unbowed, mechanical, stringed instrument with a keyboard, the hurdy-gurdy consisted of a revolving wheel cranked by a handle that touched internal strings and a set of stopping rods to sound several bass strings as a *drone*, or *burden*. Meanwhile other strings were activated by keys struck for the melody. The *hurdy-gurdy* also was called a *wheel fiddle* or a *vielle a roue*.

bassoon   The *bassoon*, a slightly conical, double-reeded musical instrument, the bass oboe, was constructed with its tube bent back on itself, and a crook containing the reed at right angles from its upper end. This early bassoon was derived from the earlier *curtal* and popular *dulcian*.

buccine   A *buccine* was a straight trumpet or trombone, a wind instrument for accompanying dances such as the extremely popular *canary*, a dance in three-four or six-four time, also accompanied by *castanets*, the small shell-shaped, hinged percussion instruments played with the thumb and first finger, to which they were secured by a thong.

cithera   A *cithera* was a triangular musical instrument having between seven and eleven strings. Derived from an ancient Greek instrument comparable to the *lyre* or *phorminx*, it was also called the *zither* and sometimes was played with a plectrum. The traditional zither, rather than triangular was customarily trapezoidal.

cittern   A *cittern* was a pear-shaped musical instrument with a particularly characteristic neck. The basse side was thinner than the treble, allowing the player's thumb easily to reach around the nine strings of the instrument clustered in four groups. There were similar configurations depending upon the country and century in which the cittern was played.

clarion   A *clarion* call sometimes referred to a stirring, thrilling, shrill trumpet call, or an early single-note trumpet.

clavichord The *clavichord* was a 15th-century stringed instrument consisting of a rectangular case with a keyboard whose hammers struck the strings to maintain pressure until they were released. It produced an exquisitely soft muted tone. Some clavichords were fretted. The composer Praetorius called for grouping instruments in consorts and *stimmwerke*. In medieval Christian iconography the *clavichord* was the instrument of choice for portraying Saint Cecilia (although sometimes she was portrayed with an organ or harp), just as King David was shown playing a harp or such other instruments as *lyre, rotta, kinnor,* and *lira da braccio.* The *kinnor* was probably not a harp but rather a *lyre,* a stringed instrument, either plucked or bowed, taken to western Europe from Byzantium, with a trapezoidal frame and five, seven, or nine strings, King David's signal instrument.

Wonderful depictions of medieval and Renaissance instruments appeared in the *intarsias* and other wood inlay extravagances in the Ducal Palace of Urbino, the principal residence of Federigo da Montefeltro (d. 1482), especially in his little study or *studiolo.* A masterpiece of the newly invented techniques of linear perspective, the *intarsia* (Latin, "inlay") portrayed a large *clavichord* with 47 keys, 29 long and 18 short, the long keys decorated with Gothic patterns. Like early clavichords, it was fretted, and the curvature of keys and their tangents drawn in precise perspective. The Metropolitan Museum of Art has a spectacular early clavichord created in 1537 by Alexander Trasontinus with the inscription "Just as the rose is the flower of flowers, this is the clavichord of clavichords" (*Ut rosa flos florum ita hoc clavile clavilium*). It possesses 36 keys, 21 long and 15 short.

The *studiolo* also had a nine-string lute side by side with a *lira da braccio,* with five strings, four stopped, one free basse string, with a round simple peg box, a flat belly, and side walls curving in between the belly and the back, because the side walls were much thicker than those of the later violin.

Related to the *clavichord* was the *harpsichord,* a keyboard stringed instrument in which the musician played black and white keys connected to levers in turn connected to jacks in turn having quills or leather points that plucked the strings and set them in vibration. The *double harpsichord* had an extra string to each key, sounding an octave higher than the others, and a second keyboard to control the extra strings. It was called a *double manual harpsichord.* The modern piano developed from both the clavichord and the harpsichord. Likewise the *virginal* had its strings excited by a jack or quill *plectrum.* Interestingly enough, the harpsichord, as the organ, imitated the drone of a *bagpipe* or *hurdy-gurdy* when it was important in the music to create a pastoral or sylvan mood.

cornetto The *cornetto* was a wooden, ivory, or leather musical wind instrument, a curved horn topped by a trumpetlike mouthpiece. It was fingered in the same way as a recorder. It also was called a *zink.* In the so-called *Dance of Death,* a popular 15th-century graphic depiction of life's uncertainties and death's inexorable arrival, a fearsome figure would compel the unwilling to dance. In a pair of woodcuts from *Der Toten Dantz* by Jacob Meydenbach (c. 1491), a dancing skeleton played a cornetto to regale unwilling listeners, and a vile worm descended from its bell. This *Dance of Death* was related to the *Dance macabre* and was a form of *memento mori,* a reminder of the certainty of death.

cracelle The *cracelle* was a rattle or ratchet noisemaker twirled on ceremonial occasions and churches in place of bells during Holy Week. It was comparable to the *gregor* sounded by Jews celebrating Purim, desiring to drown in cacophony the hated name of the villain Haman. Lepers walking in the streets used the cracelle to sound their malady music, warning others of their approach.

cromorne   In artistic representation as well as in musical references, the *cromorne* or *Krummhorn* (German, "bent horn") was an especially popular instrument, notably at feasts, played along with *shawms*. The *Krummhorn* was a slender, oboelike instrument, curved at its end to create a J-shaped horn. In French it was called *cormorne*, meaning "mournful horn," because of its nasal, strident, lamenting tone. It was sounded by a double reed in a capped mouthpiece.

curtal   The *curtal* was an early form of bassoon, related to the *dulcian*.

dulcimer   The *dulcimer* was a trapezoidal stringed musical instrument struck with hammers held in the player's hands, unlike the *psaltery*, which it resembled, which was plucked. The *psaltery* as plucked *zither* was commonly played not only in town and court; the art history record places the instrument in heaven with the players including angels, saints, King David, and the Nine Muses, the classical goddesses of the arts, daughters of Zeus and Mnemosyne, or Memory. The muses were all depicted with psalteries and were identified as follows: Dedicated to history was Cleo; to music and lyric poetry, Euterpe; to comedy and pastoral poetry, Thalia; to tragedy, Melpomene; to dance and song, Terpsichore; to lyric and love poetry, Erato; to astronomy, Urania; to epic poetry, Calliope; and to heroic hymns, Polyhymnia.

flute   The *flute* in the Middle Ages was similar to its modern form. This musical wind instrument as the *transverse flute* was held horizontally, the air blown across a hole. Pitch was determined by covering and unstopping holes. The flute is one of the oldest musical instruments known to mankind. In 12th-century Europe it was more used for military than artistic music, as was the end blown flute, the *recorder*.

gigue   The *gigue* (French *gigot*, "ham") was a ham-shaped or pear-shaped stringed instrument, usually bowed, and similar to the *rebec*, a slender-necked stringed instrument held at the chest or between the knees and bowed. The stunning *intarsia* study of Federigo da Montefeltro preserves a pear-shaped *rebec*, leaning beside its bow in a cupboard. It is notable for its distinctive sickle-shaped peg box rather than the more usual cucumber or boat shape. It has a long, thin fingerboard tapering gradually to a broad sound box with a rounded profile.

gregor   The *gregor*, like the *cracelle*, was a cacophonous instrument, a ratchet-rattle noisemaker, that Jews twirled on the holiday of Purim, while reciting the Book of Esther, to obliterate the sound of the name of hated Haman.

haut boy   A *haut boy* was an early name for the oboe.

idiophone   The *idiophone* was a self-sounder, a practical rather than an artistic musical instrument, such as a clapper, bones, bell chime, gong, gregor, cracelle, or noisemaker. Its purpose was to alert people to danger, to announce an entrance, or to stimulate animals to run or to fight.

monochord   Useful for music as well as a scientific instrument for investigation and demonstration of acoustical laws, the *monochord* was a single-string musical instrument consisting of a long wooden resonator along which a movable attached ridge varied the vibrating lengths of the string.

organistrum   An *organistrum* was similar to a *hurdy-gurdy*, probably originally meant to be played as an accompaniment for an *organum*, the early form of polyphonic music first described in the remarkable musical collection the *Musica enchiriadis*.

organ portative   A particularly exquisite *portative organ* or *organ portative* was depicted in the *intarsia* in the Gubbio study. The portative organ could be a small organ worn about the player's neck, the keyboard played with the right hand, the left hand working a triangular feeder bellows. Or the organ could be set on a stand with one person playing, another working the bellows from behind. Organ scales were not regularly diatonic or chromatic but selective, omitting notes unusual in particular types of music. The organ had as many keys as it had pipes and contained no stops.

piva   A *piva* was an Italian bagpipe. *Piva* also was the name for the fastest dance step, embellished by leaps and quick turns in the *basse dance*, and for a very energetic early Renaissance dance.

racket   A short, thick, reed-sounding wind instrument called the *racket* had wooden or ivory cylinders that were pierced lengthwise by cylindrical channels arranged in a circle. The central cylinder had a blowing cup called the *pirouette*, of one of five sizes. The treble created the highest tones, then alto, tenor, bass, and double bass.

Rauschpfeif   The *Rauschpfeif* was a small, reeded wind instrument consisting of one finger hole in the back and seven in the front that developed into the modern oboe.

regal   A *regal* was a small reed organ, the pipes of which were shaped like cylindrical clarinet beaks. The Bavarian Bible regal could be folded and packed into its book-shaped bellows. When closed, it resembled a large book of Scripture.

sackbut   A *sackbut* (from French *sacque boute*, "pull push") was an early trombone made in three distinct pitches, the alto, tenor, and bass.

shawm   A *shawm* was a double-reeded wind instrument with a slightly conical, narrow bore that produced a nasal and strident sound. The shawm was played at ceremonial events and particularly as signal of the conclusion of a fabulous feast. It, too, was often associated with the classical *aulos* and was an orgiastic instrument frequently in the pictorial representations of the Marsyas myth, a musical contest between Marsyas and Apollo.

Maximilian is surrounded by musicians practicing cornetto (top), clavichord (right), organ (left), and harp (foreground). On a table at the lower right lie a flute, a cromorne, a small shawm, and soprano and alto cylindrical recorders. A trumba marina, sackbut, and kettle drums lie scattered on the floor. "Maximilian with His Musicians," woodcut, from *Der Weisskunig* (1505–1516), Hans Burgmair (c. 1473–c. 1531). Vienna: Die Österreichische Nationalbibliothek, MS coll. no. 3032.

tambourine The medieval *tambourine*, from the Middle Persian *tambur*, retained its simple shape during the course of centuries as a musical instrument consisting of a membrane or skin stretched over one side of a stiff, round frame circled by metal disks that jingled when the tambourine was shaken or struck with the fingers. Of Middle Eastern origin, the *tambourine*, Arabic variants of which were the *riqq* and *daff*, was another instrument that became popular in Europe as a result of contacts between Christians and Muslims.

trumba marina The *trumba marina*, also called by its German name *Trumscheit*, meaning "drum log," was at least six feet long, triangular, a stringed instrument over which a single string was stretched. Inside the long sound box at least 20 sympathetic strings were tuned in unison to the outside playing string. A player used one hand to bow the string and the other to touch it lightly, thus producing harmonic notes. Additionally the inverted U-shaped bridge, with its left foot shorter than the right, freely vibrated against the soundboard, thereby creating a drumming noise.

trumpet The *trumpet* was an important military and ceremonial brass horn. Early trumpets did not have side holes, crooks, slide, and valves, which were added to later versions. Trumpets were used for fanfares, hunting calls, and the announcements and advertisements blown by waits, the civic singers hired by a town to announce important events musically, entertain at public celebrations, and chant the hours. The customary [time telling] of the waits also indicated state of peace or its violation as in "Nine of the clock and all is well!"

zampogna The *zampogna*, also called the *zamparella*, was an Italian bagpipe. Pictorially it was associated with sexual orgies.

With armorial banners pendant from their trumpets, heralds announce the emperor in procession with a royal retinue. From Ulrich von Richtenthal, *Beschreibung des Constanzer Conziliums*, German, 1450–1470. Courtesy of the New York Public Library.

BELLS

Bells were pervasive sounds in the medieval world. Large market bells tolled commercial hours. Municipal bells and church bells rang the time. For the eight canonical hours of the day, churches, cathedrals, and monasteries tolled the times for prayer. Bells announced political events such as a royal progress, a declaration of war, a signature of peace. Rites of passage, such as marriage or death, were announced by bells. Bells signaled alarm and alarmed alert.

Tollings often were determined by *change ringing*. Ringing of bells according to numerical, not musical schemes, *change ringing*, sounded all possible sequences of all bells. A church bell tower containing six bells, for example, could have 720 strikes to ring all possible changes. Such ringing announced the canonical hours, holidays, danger, celebration, martial success, inauguration, investiture, birth, death, marriage, and excommunication. Rhythm, pitch, timbre, and numbers of strikes were arranged by complicated sequential, sometimes symbolic numberings.

Courtly men and women wore bells. Small tinkling silver bells jingled from men's and women's jeweled girdles, neck strings, cape edges, cloak closures, soft shoe laces, bracelets, rings, and points of hats. Bells were ornaments for decoration and for the delightful pleasure of whimsical sight and sound, a form of synesthesia. Jesters wore bells on their caps. Clerics wore bells on certain vestments of their ecclesiastical garments. Horses jingled bells on their bridles, saddles, and *caparisons*, the ornamental and ceremonial blankets and costume worn with the armored *peytral*, covering the horse's breasts; *crupper*, the armor for the horse's haunches; and *chamfron*, the horse's head armor. Ornamental bells were created with particular pitches to represent a family, a noble house, or a significant monastery, just as people wore distinctive *livery*, the identifying costume and clothing gift of a feudal overlord to all household retainers. Bells' ringing sometimes distinguished subtle levels of rank among those wearing professional uniform.

Dance

Though splendidly entertaining, most medieval dance was not mere frivolous entertainment. *Morris dances*, for example, might be classed today as folk dances partly because everyone performed them, rich and poor, learned and untutored, while ringing, stamp-

ing, and winding their way through marketplaces and noble halls. Their masks and formulaic movements demonstrate their earlier heritage in pagan fertility rites and rituals. Yet other dances such as the *galliard* and *pavan* would now be considered formal dancing or ballroom dancing. These also crossed social boundaries but were particularly cultivated among the wealthy and noble, who were taught dancing from childhood to reflect social prestige.

Dance was excellent exercise. It prepared the body for martial arts. It helped in general poise and demeanor. It demonstrated social rank as well as knowledge of social graces. The 15th-century dance masters Antonio Cornezano and Guglielmo Ebreo (Guglielmo "the Hebrew") listed the six requisites for a good dancer in their treaties on art of dance. The first basic requirement was remembering steps and their sequence correctly, called *memoria*. Dance as a form of music, a significant mathematical and liberal art, required understanding of timing and keeping of good rhythm, called in technic terms *misura*. A proper dancer should be able to express pleasing grace of movement, *aiere*. Moreover a fine dancer needed not only to understand taught steps but to intuit varieties of steps upon basic dance patterns, technically called *diversita di cosa*. The final two requisites connected with gesture, bearing, and a combination of literal and figural social position. A good dancer for purposes of leaps, twirls, pirouettes, and simple avoidance of bumping into neighbors and stepping upon partners' feet needed to know how correctly to estimate the body in space. Technically that was called *compartinmento di terreno*, closely related to the good manners, poise, and posture of *maneria*.

Dance masters were important courtiers responsible for choreography and for cultural ceremony of court. Antonio Cornezano, Domenico da Ferrara (d. 1462), and the Jewish dance master Guglielmo Ebreo taught courtly dancing as well as aesthetic, physical, and political exercises.

DANCE FORMS

morris dance *Morris dances* were popular country sword and stamping dances especially significant in England. Participants usually wore ankle bells and flowing scarves or head wreaths. Ultimately derived from pagan fertility rites and ritual renewals of spring, the morris dance was closely associated with the *maypole*, a tall ceremonial wooden idol decked with leaves, mayflowers, and long streamers that the dancers held and then interwove in circular patterns meant to imitate the course of the Sun. Derived from pre-Christian summer solstice rites celebrating the god of vegetation in a tree, the festivities usually included *rogation processions* and *mumming plays.*

rogation A *rogation* was a Christian ceremonial procession that circumnavigated a bonfire or church grounds or a parish to pray for good crops. The ritual was a survival of pre-Christian fertility rites and Sun charms as well as other maypole rites. The procession followed the direction of the Sun and moved against the Sun, *contra solis*, in reverse, only in times of sadness and mourning.

mumming play *Mumming plays* were masked, mimed, richly choreographed plays performed by "mummers," who preserved ancient agricultural fertility rites of beheading and resurrection. The *mumming* play was popular in England, Ireland, and late in Newfoundland, where it was practiced in two modalities, as a version of the liturgical *mystery play* and as a more popular street theater.

mattachin Associated with *mumming* was a dance called the *mattachin*, a mimed battle dance, often containing a stylized symbolic beheading and resurrection. The related *matassin* was an elaborately costumed dance in which participants were disguised as armored knights or allegorical figures dancing in mock combat. The *buffon* or *buffen* was a well-costumed, sophisticated sword dance related to folk dances and taught with precise instructions as well as musical and dance notation to the noble.

In his remarkable book *Orchesography*, the composer and choreographer Thoinot Arbeau in 1589 described the *buffen* as synonymous with the *mattachin*, a dance precisely choreographed as a fencing contest accompanied by clash of swords and shields, danced to a special tune played in double time. Arbeau's *buffen* steps and arm movements included the *feinte*, with a dancer leaping upon both feet, sword in hand, but without striking, and the *estocade*, in which the dancer drew back his arm and thrust his sword forward to strike his companion's sword. The gesture *taille haute* had the dancer strike at his companion cutting downward from the right hand holding the sword, to the left; contrariwise in *reverse haute* the dancer cut downward from left to right. In *taille basse* the dancer brandished his sword cutting upward from right to left, and in *reverse bas*, from left to right. Arbeau accompanied these instructions on foot positions and arm gestures with delightful illustrative drawings.

moresca A *moresca* (Italian, "Moorish") was a dramatic dance entertainment utilizing miming and costumed sword dances on allegorical and humanistic subjects. The dance form undoubtedly originates in the popular Christian Iberian festival celebrations of *moros y cristianos* (Moors and Christians) first celebrated in the 14th century in remembrance of the defeat of the Muslims in battle. As all the participants were Christians, those representing the Moors would blacken their faces and wear bells attached to their tights to distinguish themselves. The *moresca* emerged as a dance form in 15th-century Italy and was closely related to the *masquerade*, a masked entertainment in which the participants, disguised in fantastical or imaginative costumes, danced, declaimed, and disported for pleasure and political purpose. *Masquerades* were performed outdoors on movable pageant wagons or indoors in a great hall. As did the *morescas*, *masquerades* usually had dance battles between Christians and Saracens and included lascivious skits imitating the manners and dialects of the Moors, such Orlando di Lasso's *Moresche* (1555).

Acrobatic wild man dances or savage dances were common entertainments. The wild man (Latin, *homo sylvestris*, "man of the forest") was depicted as an unkempt, hirsute creature, often brandishing a club and generally symbolizing lust, aggression, and the animality of the human condition. Conversely, he represented simple sylvan life uncorrupted by courtly civilization. *Homo silvestris* was associated with the Christian concept of the wild man as one of *Nebuchadnezzar's children*, crazed people suffering from "congenital madness," melancholy love sickness called *hereos*, other mental disease, or head injuries. These wild people either were rejected as pariahs or celebrated as noble fools by those who observed them. King Nebuchadnezzar of Babylonia (r. 605–561 B.C.E.) was portrayed in medieval Christian literature, art, and dance as the prototypical wild man in one of three conventional ways: as a mad sinner, as an unholy wild man, or as a holy wild man, representing God's triple uses of madness, to punish the damned, to purge sinners, and to prove virtues of saints.

masque   A *masque* was a noble entertainment with a mythological, allegorical, or political subject, combining dancing with music, poetry, mime, acting, costumery, and sets for court participation and performance. These brilliantly, authentically costumed events could be deadly.

John Froissart (d. 1453) in his *Chronicles* depicts France's King Charles VI (r. 1380–1422), surnamed "the Mad," at an incendiary masquerade ball, the *bal des ardents*, the "dance of the flaming ones." Courtiers disguised as wild men, madmen, and madwomen were wearing masks and costumes of grass, straw, and sisal and were accidentally ignited and nearly burned alive by torch sparks from an inquisitive guest's lantern swung near King Charles. He survived thanks to a quick-witted woman who quenched his flames with her skirts.

equestrian dance   The *equestrian dance* or *horse ballet*, known in Italian as *balletto a cavallo* and in French as *danse equestres*, was a mounted extravaganza in which elegantly carisoned horses and exquisitely dressed riders performed intricate geometric, graceful designs, for purposes of spectacle and politics.

ballet de cour   The *ballet de cour*, an early 16th-century dance spectacular, usually with political intent, melded elements of *masquerade*, *triumph*, and *horse ballet* in which dancing, declamation, music, song, and sets were helped by theatrical machines, derricks and cranes carrying on stage mythological and divine creatures as if "from heaven," literally, the "god from the machine," *deus ex machina*.

triumph   A *triumph* imitated Roman warriors' triumphal processions and victorious armies' return to Rome to be feted by the grateful populace. Medieval allegorical figures graced triumphal pageants in life, literature, and art, such as Francesco Petrarch's (d. 1374) popular *Triomfi* and Dante's *Divine Comedy's* *Purgatorio*, canto 29. In painting, sculpture, tapestry, and graphic arts, a spectacular allegorical triumph might portray, for instance, Love riding proudly in her triumphal car then overrun by Chastity, soon to be overtaken by Fame, Time, Death, and Eternity.

ballet comique de la reine Precious dance presentations were common for special holidays and dynastic celebrations. The *ballet comique de la reine* was an early *ballet de cour*, a five-hour spectacle in the two-week celebration of the marriage of Princess Marguerite of Lorraine (b. 1462), one of the first ballets with extent music, which was constantly imitated in the early Renaissance.

DANCE BOOKS

Written collections of dances were valuable instruction books. One such *danserye*, compiled by Tielman Susato in the 16th century, included the popular *pavans, galliards, basse dances*, and *bransles*. A *pavan* was an elegant, stately processional dance performed by couples progressing in a circle or processing down a long hall or outdoor pathway. Popular in Italy, Spain, France, and England, it probably derived from the six basic steps of the *basse dance*. The low dance, the *basse dance*, was a popular 15th-century ceremonial French dance especially important in Burgundian courts. It consisted of elegant "low" gliding and mannered walking movements. These contrasted dramatically with "high" leaps and jumps of the *galliard* with which the pavan routinely alternated. A *galliard* was a leaping dance in moderately fast triple time.

Pierre Attaingnant's (d. 1551) dance book called *Fourteen Galliards, Quatorze Gailliardes*, preserved some of the earliest specimens of the genre, including such steps as the *cinqpas*, five steps executed during six musical beats, also called the *sink-apace*. Another *galliard* step was the *capriolz*, or *capriole*, a rapid, scissorslike step during a leap. Attaignant introduced the tradition of printing music in France. Caprioles also was mentioned as the name of the young ingenuous man who desired to learn dancing in Arbeau's *Orchesography*. Another galliard step was the *saut majeur*, the important leap, a spectacular high jump or elegant leap executed with bravura.

A *bransle* (French *branler*, "to sway") was a popular 15th-century courtly dance in double or triple meter of the "follow the leader" design, a type of *basse dance*. The *Orchesography* lists about two dozen with such descriptive names as *Burgundian, Cassandra, Hay, Official, Scottish, Washerwoman, Maltese, Clog*, and *Horse*.

THE *ORCHESOGRAPHY*

Precious, mannered dances needed to be well taught and well learned. *Thoinot Arbeau* was the pseudonym for Jehan Tabourot, a 69-year-old cleric who adored the art of dance and in 1589 wrote his splendid manual preserving *pavans, basse danses, galliards,* and *bransles* in the delightful format of a dialogue or debate. His instruction book was dedicated to townsmen and -women desiring advice on dance performance, etiquette, and comportment.

To dance was to jump, hop, skip, sway, stamp, tiptoe, and employ the feet, hands, and body in rhythmic movements consisting of leaping, bending, straddling, limping, flexing, rising, twitching, and twirling. Dancing, also called saltation, was pleasant, profitable, and healthful. Proper to the young, it was agreeable to the old, suitable to all. Tragedies, comedies, and pastorals danced in ancient theater were performed on a stage called the orchestra; thus Arbeau entitled his book *Orchesography*, in which he alternated his own narrative voice with the naive, amusing comments of young Capiriol. Arbeau presented dance theory, music, and a brilliant form of notation that dance historians (such as Julia Sutton and Mireille Backer) have translated to modern Labanotation in order to reproduce Arbeau's dances.

Ceremonial movements performed with precision were routine for those willing to train to the level of dance performance required by good breeding, courtesy, and honor. Dancing also helped one find a mate. Better for attracting a spouse than either fencing or tennis, dancing was beautiful; revealed the state of health, and soundness of limb; and, by allowing ritual kissing and touching, ascertained bodily shapeliness and odors. These practical virtues made knowing dancing essential.

DANCE OF LOVE AND DANCE OF DEATH

Metaphorically the *dance of love* united the choreographies of sex, love, and death. *Dance of Love*, referred to as the "Old Dance," was sexual play or foreplay climaxing in intercourse. In Chaucer's *Troilus and Criseyde* the character Pandarus well knew every step in the old dance, making him a good go-between for the lovers. That old dance was erotic, precoital, manipulative exercise, both psychological and physical, that the sex manuals described and the lusty creatures such as Chaucer's Wife of Bath and women of the *fabliaux* exultantly performed.

The 15th-century *Dance of Death* graphically illustrated life's uncertainties and death's inexorable arrival. Old man Death was shown iconographically as a fearsome allegorical figure compelling the unwilling to dance. His sickle or scythe cut down the living. Sometimes as Father Time he held an hourglass whose sands of life ran out. The skeleton Death dragged

In a danse macabre, Death's minions lead a physician with a urine flask and a nobleman. From *La danse macabre des hommes*, Antoine Verard, Paris, 1486.

printers from their presses, physicians from their clinics, revelers from their carousing, and lovers from their dances of love.

The *dance macabre*, also dating to the 15th century, was a vivid depiction of social equality in death. People in strict political hierarchy, from greatest to least, held hands in a circle dance. As *memento mori* (Latin, "remember that you must die"), a remembrance of mortality, the *dance macabre* and the *dance of death* graced literature, art, and personal jewelry. For instance, a bracelet with a meticulously carved ivory or boxwood skull was thought neither morbid nor lugubrious but a reminder in midst of frivolity that life had higher purpose and time's shortness tempered earthly delights.

DANCING MANIA

Dancing mania was the name for an epidemic of mass hysteria that may have been *Saint Vitus' dance*, otherwise known as chorea, a severe central nervous system disorder caused by rheumatic fever. Possibly it was ergotism, a disease caused by fungus in rye bread seeds, producing frenzied bodily movements. There were virulent outbreaks of the epidemic in the Rhine and Mosel regions in Germany, and in 1374 near Liège in Belgium.

According to chronicles, sufferers resorted to graves and deserted places, lying down as if dead, throwing themselves into wells, rolling about in filth, demanding to be beaten, screaming, and foaming at the mouth. Thought demonically possessed, some gathered to celebrate a church festival such as Midsummer Eve and then danced in frenzy until overcome by exhaustion, injury, violence, or death.

As did the *flagellants*, the lay fraternities of self-punishing Christians who flourished in Italy, France, and Germany especially during the *Black Death* (14th to 15th centuries), the sufferers of emotional or psychophysiological diseases whipped and scarified their own bod-

ies as well as those of their fellow believers. They instigated pogroms against the Jews, exhorted pious self-abnegation for salvation, and terrorized towns. The Saint Vitus' dancers attributed their disease to God's wrath at human perfidy.

Aside from the liturgical music accompanying the celebration of the church mass and the divine office and the religious-inspired dance of death and danse macabre, the majority of the music and dance traditions discussed thus far have been secular cultural traditions. Because the dances were profane customs with no obvert Christological signification, the Jews living within Christian Europe had no qualms about participating in and emulating these art forms. Indeed, the example of the dance master Guglielmo Ebreo is but one indication of a shared cultural tradition of music making that cannot adequately be described as "Christian" or "Jewish." The following section explores in greater detail the pious and profane musical and dance traditions of medieval Jews.

JEWISH MUSIC AND DANCE

Medieval Jewish music and dance introduce an intellectual itinerary ranging from early synagogue song, whose ancient melodies and rhythms called *cantillations* Jewish children still learn today in advance of *bar mitzvah* and *bat mitzvah*, to secular music of Sabbaths and weddings. Jewish music shared certain commonalities with Christian and Muslim music. Sometimes Jewish music was imitated and influential; other times Jewish musicians imitated, borrowed, and emended other forms in their own way.

Was music in the Middle Ages thought to be a desecration of Sabbath sanctity? Or was it intrinsic in pious celebration? Who were the professional musicians in the Jewish community? What were their relationships with the rabbis? Were Jewish professional musicians significant in a larger non-Jewish world of medieval court and city? Answers to such questions about medieval Jewish music vary according to country and century. Yet certain patterns of opposition simplify analysis of this vast, disparate, and interesting musical heritage, namely, synagogue versus secular music, Jewish art song versus folk song, and professional entertainers versus amateur music enthusiasts.

A vigorous medieval secular Jewish music tradition existed, with learned rabbis themselves often participating as musicians and dancers. Professional synagogue singers of liturgy, the *chazzanim*, also performed publicly, sometimes as itinerant musicians singing the news from town to city. Jewish musical jesters and jokesters, the *badchonim* and *marshalliks*, and instrumental musicians, the *klezmorim*, as well as ballad singers and romance chanters, the *Spielmänner*, mediated between Jewish and Christian audiences, and sometimes between Jewish and Islamic patrons.

Each culture's qualities intertwined with those of the other. There were Jewish *troubadours* in southern France, Jewish *minnesingers* in Germany, and Jewish *dolce stil novistis* in Italy. Occasionally Jewish performers directed a Christian court's cultural entertainments, such as the aforementioned 15th-century Italian dance master Guglielmo Ebreo, William the Hebrew. For all these medieval musicians, music was a profession honored both within and outside the Jewish community. Music also was a personal expression of piety, even on the Sabbath.

Music in the synagogue is an ancient expression of prayer. Jews as "the people of the book," however, usually are portrayed as reading not singing, closely following text not music. But the Talmud is unequivocally adamant on this musical score. The Bible must be read in public and made understandable to hearers in a musical sweet tune. One who reads the Pentateuch, the five books of Moses, without tune shows disregard for it and the vital value of its laws. In fact, a deep understanding can be achieved only by singing the Torah, and that singing must be in the traditional tunes. Whoever intones the Holy Scriptures in the manner of secular songs abuses the Torah.

Synagogue Music

The traditional cantillation is the musical chanting technique still performed by observant Jews in modern synagogues. But other melodies, sometimes borrowed from secular life, served important mnemonic and inspirational purposes, aesthetically reinforcing the understanding of word. For this singing so significant to sanctity, three separate musical officers existed: the *precentor*; the *chazzan*, or cantor; and the *paytan*.

PRECENTOR

The precentor was the honored amateur, "one of the people" selected as leader of formal communal prayer, biblical singing, and improvisational devotion. The Hebrew title was *mithpallel*, a fascinating use of grammar to define social function. The word contains a reflexive verb meaning "the leading of oneself to pray." The precentor was the leader of the listening self back to the self in the approach to God. Such a man or a woman intercessor had to possess stellar qualities but preeminently a fine, clear, inspirational singing voice.

Rabbi Judah bar Illai of Galilee (second century) enumerated the desiderata for a successful precentor: good pronunciation; knowledge of Jewish law, the *Halakhah;* understanding of folk tradition, the *Haggadah;* memory by heart of all ritual prayer; and respectable reputation. But no quality was so significant as a beautiful voice: a heavenly gift through which people are inspired to devotion.

The precentor's place in the early medieval synagogue was a special platform set slightly *below* the level of the sanctuary floor. Symbolic of this amateur musician's humility with a divine gift of song and reverence for the job to be performed, the precentor sang from below the parishioners, abasing the self while uplifting the spirit of others.

CHAZZAN

In due musical time the job became professional, and so did pride of place. Instead of using the precentor's depressed song box, the cantor, or *chazzan*, sang musical recitation from the raised central stage called the *bimah*. The earlier precentor usually was aided by two assistants as a prompter chorus. The chazzan had the advantage of superior learning. Many of the best were poet-singers and sometimes rabbi-singers. Some used dazzling musical effects and responsorial devices eliciting enthusiastic song from the congregants.

For each special holiday and each day's ritual prayer, the chazzan would sing a special *leitmotif*, a leading musical melody or dominating mode to inspire the parishioners' appropriate mood. These were the *scarbove*, or sacred tunes, joyous and jubilant for festivals, penitential in sound and inciting to atonement for the high holy days. These venerable melodies were called *Mi-sinai* in honor of their supposed origin: Ostensibly God handed down these tunes to Moses at Mount Sinai. The great 14th- to 15th-century German rabbi Yaacov Moelin, known as Maharil (d. 1427), probably created them.

Some Jewish melodies wandered from secular to religious context, from religion to religion, from country to country. Such traveling melodies appearing simultaneously in, say, a Spanish Jewish praise of Zion, a German Catholic hymn to the Virgin, and a Czechoslovakian Bohemian erotic folk song clearly suggest that one borrowed from another.

No one knows for sure which was lender, which was taker. Christians admiringly attended Jewish synagogue services, causing Christian churchmen to rail against Jewish "corruptions" of Christian music. Rabbis warned Jews encountering Christian melodies in marketplaces and concerts to be wary. Even Jewish babies, counsels the aforementioned 13th-century instruction book *Sefer Hasidim* (*The Book of the Pious*, attributed to Judah the Pious Kalonymous [d. 1217]), must not hear Christian lullabies sung by their gentile nursemaids. It would corrupt their thinking.

No matter what the secular source of many Jewish religious melodies, some *chazzanim* insisted upon their right to select effective music for their own important purposes. The *chazzan*'s charge was to intrigue the congregation musically to lead its thoughts to Jewish law. However, some musical techniques were so florid and resounding that they out-shouted the words of God. When, for example, the brilliant 13th-century Spanish poet Judah al-Harizi (d. 1235) visited Mosul in Iraq, he found the *chazzan* there worked up into a frenzied sweat, his parishoners no less boisterously ecstatic, singing a splendid soaring song but with a text full of ridiculous, ignorant errors. When al-Harizi suggested textual corrections, the *chazzan* put the visitor in his place by insisting that intuitive poetry and music of the *chazzan* were far more important than formal prayer.

PAYTAN

In addition to the *precentor* and *chazzan* as music masters of the synagogue, a third artist was the *paytan*. The paytan wrote the *piyyut*, the religious musical poems usually elaborating upon a biblical motif. The *piyyut* was characterized by markedly mannered passion with extravagant puns and such structural virtuosities as alphabetical *acrostics*, ingenious puzzle poems in which the initial letters of horizontal lines make words when read vertically.

Some learned, scholarly poets wrote the *piyyut*, such as the Spaniards Abraham ibn Ezra (d. 1093) and Judah Halevi (d. 1141), men otherwise employed as physicians and translators who volunteered public service with their poetry. Yet the professional *paytan* as a song writer was a moral instructor the Jewish community hired to lure hearers by words and music to the love of God, repentance, or acts of human kindness. While the *paytan* generally was more concerned with facility with word, and the *chazzan* more a celebrant with melody, many a *paytan* was also a *chazzan*, and many a *chazzan* a *paytan*.

Of the three liturgical musical guardians, *precentor*, *chazzan*, and *paytan*, the one most responsible for popular vigor of Jewish melody was the *chazzan*. He not only served a single congregation, but when social and vocal circumstances were best—or worst—traveled. Superior singers were in demand, invited as guest performers in distant Jewish communities during times of relative peace. Conversely, when persecutions and cataclysm made it impossible for a congregation to support a *chazzan*, he would travel among several synagogues singing for his living. This wandering scholar's life had a major compensation in the traveling melodies, the chance hearing of regional, secular, or non-Jewish songs for transmission or for transformation.

Basic holiday melodies demonstrate such medieval musical interdependencies. The rousing Channukah hymn "Rock of Ages" or "Maoz Tzur" would have been equally familiar to a pious sixth-century German Lutheran and a secular soldier, for the melody consists of one theme Martin Luther also used in one of his chorales plus another motif common to the popular battle song "Benzenauer."

Secular Music

FOLK SONG

Such traditional Jewish holiday songs were sung as often in the home or marketplace as in the sanctuary. Their power derived in part from their insistent rhythm, repetitive melodic motifs, easily remembered structure, and apparently inevitable movement from phrase to phrase: the qualities of the best folk songs.

Jewish folk song, as those of all cultures, was the popular oral tradition of rhythmic stanzaic song, authorship unknown and undiscoverable, transmitted person to person by ear, by enthusiasm, and by affection. Of course someone composed the original version of every folk song, but subsequent singing subtly changed and developed that first rhythmic or melodic essay on a perennial subject such as love's perils or work's labors. Particularly fascinating Jewish folk songs are work songs, representing musically a rhythmic physical exertion, the melody usually an aid to the rigors of labor. Jewish sailors' sea chanteys, plowmen's songs, and spinners' songs appear in vernacular languages in both the Ashkenazic or Germanic Jewish world and the Sephardic or Spanish.

Ladino folk songs were a particularly splendid repertory. The texts in the Judeo-Spanish language called Ladino were set to music typical not only of Castile but also of the Eastern countries to which the Spanish Jews were forced in exile after 1492: Egypt, Yemen, Turkey, North Africa, and the Balkans. Love and labor are their most common themes, most particularly love's labors. Some of the most splendid Ladino songs were women's music, such as lovers' laments sung at the spinning wheel in springtime.

Surprisingly many Jewish folk songs (not only in Ladino) also were composed by women and performed by them. Some celebrated homely joys such as clothes, vegetables, hearth, and cradle. Lullabies, such as the medieval German "Raisins and Almonds," "Rosenkes mit Mandeln" are poignant, exquisite, and durable. However, other women's folk songs or "Volklieder" are bitter laments on war, mothers-in-law, widowhood, women's housework, professional trade, and heretical husbands. By turn witty, sarcastic, acerbic, and satiric, these songs are intelligent commentaries on the perils of life and its numerous pretenses.

Women's songs saw behind the world's mask, philosophically exulting in imperfection as well as excellence. The songs merit the keenest study for their subject, which reintroduces to the modern world certain lost details of medieval and Renaissance Jewish culture. Few other sources exist for describing competition between women trades workers, young women's disappointed sexual expectations, the art of handling flirts, and the most effective curses for punishing an unfaithful husband. Women's folk songs also deserve admiring analyses never yet lavished on their astounding rhythms, complex rhyme schemes, and alphabetical acrostics.

ART SONG

Such sophisticated themes and elaborate techniques force us toward another important song form, the art song or court song, which German critics called *Hoflied*. One unequivocal distinction between art song and the anonymous folk song is authorship. Usually we know the art songwriter's name. Second, unlike the amateur folk song creator, the professional art song crafter often self-consciously created a new

style or imitated a musical fashion of the wider Christian or Islamic culture. Third, a wealthy or noble patron usually employed the art songwriter to serve the court by directing music to politics, as in writing political satires or in composing songs for formal feasts and court entertainments.

Jewish troubadours such as Joseph Ezobi, Abraham Bedersi, and Isaac Ben Abraham Gorni flourished in 11th- and 12th-century southern France. Not great but decent, these Jewish poet-musicians wrote about the same subjects that captivated Christian Provençal troubadours. They celebrated courtly love's inborn suffering, which exalted or devastated the noble lover. As did their Christian colleagues, the Jewish troubadours engaged in poetic tournaments and competitions.

Jewish minnesingers such as Susskind von Trimberg, as did his 12th- and 13th-century German Christian contemporaries, sang about love's introspective philosophical pleasures and love's ennobling consequences for lovers. In Italy among the writers of the joyous science of love expressed in the sweet new style, the *dolce stil novo*, Immanuel of Rome (d. 1330), the "master of love and passion," elicited the praise of the circle around Dante for his lusty, loud, laughing songs.

These Jewish musicians practiced magnificently the fashionable techniques their patrons and their times demanded. Though their best work was indistinguishable from the best of their Christian or Muslim colleagues, the Jewish poet-musicians added to their art a chauvinistic vigor. Maintaining that the true origin, in fact, the cultural discovery, of music was traceable to Old Testament Hebrews, the Jewish *troubadours*, minnesingers, and *stil novistis* insisted that they perfected a sweet new courtly style in order to reassert their own ancient heritage. This might have been a deeply principled justification for art. Or it might have been public rationalization to counteract rabbinic complaints that the stylish, secular, sometimes scurrilous songs were inappropriate use of Jewish musical talent.

Art songsters also served as propagandists and political-performers. To the modern eye and ear medieval musical politicization is astonishing. Before printing and the speed media, musicians effectively transmitted political information. A poet-singer employed by an emperor might sing a biting sarcastic song letter to a pope about a land quarrel. The pope's musician would compose a vitriolic counterattack, contemptuous in both verse and melody.

Important political commitments might be announced to the assembled court by song. Disputes would be musically mediated. Messages were transmitted via music. So also were flattery, scorn, complaints, laments, eulogies, and elegies. A powerful poet-propagandist could influence his noble patron's reputation as dramatically as could his battle-winning general.

For good reason the best diplomat-musicians earned high salary. Some poet-singers ruefully complained in begging songs about ungrateful, stingy patrons who paid more with praise than with purse. Susskind von Trimberg, singing in a rich ermin-trimmed robe, bemoaned in a begging poem, a *Bitte Spruch*, his insufficient reward for services rendered, threatening to retire and live "like an old Jew," growing a long gray beard, wearing a long coat, his head under a long pointed hat. That headgear, of course, was the infamous *Judenhut* required of Jews as identifying garment in addition to the Jewish badge, the *rouelle*.

TOWN SONG

Midway between qualities of the court's art song and the people's folk song was the town song. Seemingly artless, though carefully constructed, rhythmically commanding, and melodically inventive, town songs were middle-class levelers of the excesses of each. Neither descending too far to low vulgarity nor soaring too high in preciosity, this middling music, often of notable beauty, was often referred to in the early Renaissance as *Gesellschaftslieder*, the merchantmen's and townspeople's art form.

The town song was commissioned for entertainment, and, as so much bourgeois art, edification. Lyrics wrought with wit and humor, the town song's muse neither flitted nor soared but stood proudly, firmly, buxomly on the ground. That town muse was a lively woman, not the high-born, self-concerned, unattainable, slim beauty celebrated by the troubadours and minnesingers, but an accessible, warm, responsive woman whose physical attentions to the poet-musician would inspire his creativity. She usually was also a good wife. Fifteenth-century Wolflin von Lecham wrote 36 songs, whose words and polyphonic music are dedicated to his beloved wife, Barbara.

How was this great variety of Jewish secular music performed? Where? When? By whom? What did the rabbis say? Good clues to answers are the awesomely vast records of two major Jewish celebrations: the Sabbath and the wedding. Sabbath sanctity in the Middle Ages was stimulated by music. Music was specifically encouraged for reasons of celebration and entertainment. Importance of celebratory music is suggested even in its negative, in Talmudic and rabbinic complaints *against* music on the Sabbath. But almost every prohibition placed in historical context becomes understandable not as hatred of music itself but as response to political or philosophical crisis. Virtually every ban on Sabbath music follows a specific period of persecution or pogrom making rejoicing unseemly, mourning more appropriate. Or a Sabbath music ban follows an event reminiscent of the destruction of the Second Temple, making communal lamentation rather than musical enthusiasm the dominant mode.

Each prohibition had its positive that initiated the negative. There would be no reason to ban frivolous music unless there had been frivolous music to ban. Professional musicians called *Klezmorim* played in 12th-century Eastern synagogues, for example, to accompany hymns, to dedicate a tabernacle, or to consecrate a torah. In many western European cities *Klezmer* ensembles and bands played in homes and public places on the Sabbath, though not in a synagogue. Often their concerts were restricted to special holidays or weddings. Some cities had their own Jewish musician's guilds, and in several of these women musicians were prominent.

Some *Klezmorim* members played for *Christian* celebrations, as public processions, parties, and fairs. An indication of the popularity of such Jewish bands are the heavy taxes local authorities levied on their incomes. Numerous *Klezmorim* graced the courts of kings, caliphs, and popes. Some medieval communities that themselves forbade Jewish *Klezmer* music from Sabbath playing nevertheless invited Christian musicians to do the musical Sabbath honors. In many parts of Europe, Sabbaths sounded gloriously.

The week's only workless day, seventh day required entertainment to complement contemplation. One of the most important music makers catching the popular fancy was the *Spielmann*, the singer of marvelous tales. Performing for pay as well as for food and drink in private homes or social gathering places, the Spielmann would sing long, fashionable stories transforming their original Christian or Islamic character and situation to suit the Jewish audience. For Sabbath entertainments, Judaized Arthurian romances were in vogue for several centuries in western Europe.

Far and away the most beloved knightly romance was Elijah Levita's Bahur's (d.1549) Yiddish poem of courtly adventures, the *Bove Bukh*. First written in Judeo-German in 1507, it was performed orally and then printed and reprinted frequently through the centuries. Its fantastical exaggerations in later versions, then called the *Bove-Masse*, became the pun and exemplar of *Buba-Meise*, old wives' tales, outlandishly delightful and unbelievable.

Elijah Levita's Bahur's *Bove* is an astonishing Yiddish redaction of the Italian version of the English *Sir Bevis of Hampton* tale. In the Italian poetic form *ottava rima*, called in Yiddish *raym in akht-gezets*, Elijah masterfully coerced the Yiddish language to fit the Italian style, in a literary tour de force with a difficult rhyme scheme.

Content is even more improbable than manner. In his bizarre courtly adventures, the noble young knight Sir Bove was joined by his beautiful noble wife, Druzane. These adventurous lovers glow with Yiddish expressions: Saying *shalom* at castle gates, and *mazel tov* after battle victories, they publicly celebrate their twin sons' ritual circumcisions with a *brit* feast. A superb example of the *insular* literary tradition, discussed in chapter 9 on literature, this hilarious romance was commissioned by women. The minstrel (*Spielmann*) Elijah said in his preface, "I, as a servant of all good women of honor and good breeding, publish this book for women at their request so they might pleasantly pass the time on Sabbaths and festivals."

Spielmanner Sabbath entertainments begin and end with formulaic piety. The *Bove Bukh* starts off with "Let God be eternally praised and let him strengthen me to translate this book." The work concludes with a hope for the Messiah's rebuilding the Temple in Jerusalem. But between these Judaic formulae are secular oftentimes scandalous adventures, as in *Bove*, the tangles of intrigue, mistaken identities, rich pomp and ceremony, magical swords, enchanted horses, and even a dog-man named *Plekun*.

The Arthurian Round Table spins quickly on the Jewish pivot point supporting it. Rhythm of action was determined by the music. The narrator employs song to cue the audience to two simultaneous actions, for instance, when the hero Sir Bove rides off on one of his heroic adventures, the narrator will sing a song. The episodes were of length convenient to chanting or singing, interrupted by pauses for refreshment.

If in some Spielmanners' songs the morals for Sabbath's edification were subordinate to the entertainment, the stories neither always pure nor simple, in others there predominated a refined, contemplative, literary sobriety. Sung story was the medium, ethics the message.

WEDDING MUSIC

Certainly music was significant in Sabbath celebration and entertainment but it was *essential* to the Jewish wedding. Singers, dancers, and instrumentalists were amateur or professional, depending on the wealth of the betrothed pair. The great rabbi Maharil counseled those contemplating marriage, "If you live in an area where restrictions are placed on wedding music, then move!"

A local wedding might be traditional but a musical wedding was necessary. Musical harmonies of a marriage celebration would portend the future harmony of married life. To banish music was to invite death. The very stern, antimusical Babylonian rabbi Huna found to his dismay that when he angrily banished musical frivolity and gaiety, he banned all music from his community. Thereafter all commerce and all transport stopped. With no music to sound the hours, rhythmically lighten the labors, advertise the produce, lullabye the children, or whistle away fear, all joy was banished and life effectively stopped. When Rabbi Huna rescinded his prohibition, human harmonies were reintegrated with the music of the celestial spheres.

Such acoustical reflection, such concern with heavenly overtones and earthly undertones, was not idle analogy. A philosophical belief based on medieval scientific ideas caused even the most staid and pious to celebrate rhythmically at weddings. Any Jewish marriage theoretically promised survival of Judaism. Traditions of the past would be transmitted to the future by the consecrated pair's fertility.

Music in many ways accompanied this rite of passage. Wedding music was thought to awaken favorable guardian spirits and to ward off evil ones. Jaunty, beautiful rhythms might please the beneficent spirits. Loud sounds might scare away the baneful. Suddenly in the midst of a wedding reception's joyous hilarity, a Klezmer would sound a startling discordant note or sing a wailing lament to assure listening mischief makers that the bride and groom were not too happy. To shock the wedding guests, cymbals would clang to stimulate mindfulness that for Jews tragedy was perpetual companion to joy. For the same spiritual purposes another common intrusion in wedding music was the shattering of a glass or a dashing to the ground of a metal or porcelain platter as ringing reminder of the potency of the other world.

A second important purpose of marriage music was the earthly imitation of the perfect heavenly harmonies of star music. Thereby the couple could be integrated into God's total harmonious universe. Jewish astronomers, mathematicians, and scientific translators, as their Arabic and Christian colleagues, emphasized similarities among three musical spheres: (1) the rhythmic periodicities of planets, (2) the mathematics of music theory and the physics of acoustics, and (3) human bodily rhythms, such as pulse.

Rabbi Saadya Gaon (d. 942) wrote a book on the eight rhythmic musical modes and their influence on the human soul. Levi ben Gerson in the 14th century wrote an influential treatise, "Musical Harmonic Numbers" (*De numeris harmonicis*), demonstrating the interrelationships among rhythms in the heavens, in human bodies, and in musical instruments. Judah ben

Isaac's Hebrew translation of a Latin music theory text even included the famous *Guido's hand*, the device utilizing human fingers and joints for teaching music students the order of notes in the hexachord. For these theorists, human instrumental or vocal music was the least perfect echo of the splendid melodies of universe and Earth. But humankind's paltry, earthly music nevertheless allied the person with the creator and with God's will.

At weddings, practical application of such theory required music for stimulating a mood of rejoicing and exuberant expression of that happiness. Other nuptial music stimulated the bride and groom's erotic impulses, to assure their consummate coupling. Horns, lutes, cymbals, and bells would sound sexually arousing music of the *shivaree*. Still played at Jewish weddings today as so-called wedding marches, the earlier shivaree accompanied the couple to their bed chamber. Wagner's wedding march from his opera *Lohengrin* is a shivaree, likewise Mendelssohn's wedding march.

Directing dancing at weddings were professional dance masters who worked not only in their own Jewish communities but sometimes for noble Christian courts. Guglielmo Ebreo was one of those who bridged the two cultures. Numerous sober, circumspect medieval rabbis and Talmud students would dance, sing, and cavort at weddings. Pious men would sing special songs praising the bride. A popular song began: "Hail precious one! Beautiful without powders, rouge, or hair dye!" A rabbi such as Judah bar Ilai would vigorously dance in front of a bride, rhythmically waving before her a palm or myrtle branch, an ancient fertility symbol. The venerable sage Rabbi Acha would sway and dance, lifting the bride to his shoulders. When his dismayed disciples asked whether this was entirely decorous behavior for them to imitate, he said, "Certainly. So long as you can withhold yourself from base thoughts."

While some rabbis were paid, others volunteered to rejoice at weddings, having recompense in their participation in a Jewish sacrament. However, a special class of professional musical merrymakers called the *Badchanim* performed at weddings. The *Badchan* was a singing jester, story chanter, comedian, sometimes juggler or mime. But he was usually reasonably learned. His jokes customarily were sprinkled with biblical and Talmudic puns, allowing particular pleasure in humor for the more educated wedding guests. A successful *Badchan* composed extemporaneously, creating on the spot new songs for the particular interests of bride and groom or the qualities of the guests. A common people's diplomat, the *Badchan* was a peacemaker, reconciling at a wedding those guests otherwise in enmity. In Germany the *Badchan* was called the *Marshallik*, a secular master of ceremonies, intelligent jokester, and trained musician. Another wedding entertainer was the *Leitzim*, perhaps identical to the *Bodchan* and *Marshallik*, a comedian–folk song performer, specializing less in word than in movement, juggling, and dancing.

Medieval and Renaissance Jewish weddings, then, as the medieval Sabbaths, resounded with joyous music. Melody and rhythm entertained and instructed. Amateur revelers and professional *Badchanim* alike transmitted in practice certain traditional ideas appreciated by Jewish theorists. Human rhythms were related to the divine. Wedding guests drunk with rhythm and wine achieved a salutary recreation. But the more thoughtful heard with the inner ear a series of heavenly harmonics: the overtones of God's love and the undertones of mankind's hope.

Such exalted purposes of secular music of course were also the synagogue's expectations of music. Amazingly similar ideas pervaded the marketplace and the Jewish home, was music and musicians graced the Sabbath and family festivals. A common concern for educational pleasure and delight in instruction animated medieval Jewish musicians, the precentor, chazzan, troubadour, Minnesinger, Spielmann; writers of folk song, court song, town song; and mathematical-astronomical music theorists.

In the surrounding Christian and Islamic cultures Jewish musicians were both givers and borrowers of melody, subject, and performance techniques. Jewish musicians achieved such reputation for excellence that they became symbols of sophisticated art. The nobleman wanting to demonstrate his court as the finest hired as arbiter of court culture a Jewish master of court ceremonies. Certain Jewish musicians complemented political importance with cultural power.

The Jewish Dance Master

One of the most significant 15th-century political-musical positions was that of the court dancing master. Guglielmo Ebreo, William the Hebrew, the revered 15th-century Italian dance master, wrote a treatise entitled *Trattato dell'arte del ball di Guglielmo Ebreo* (*Treatise of the Art of Dance by Guglielmo Ebreo*), whose richly decorated, beautifully bound manuscripts exist today in Florence, Siena, Modina, Rome, Paris, and New York City. Their number and quality suggest an international concern for dance as well as an appreciation of Guglielmo Ebreo's eminence, a fame corroborated by panegyric poems praising him.

Medieval and Renaissance dance was not a craft for professional performers as much as an art cultivated from early childhood for well-born amateur practitioners trained to be graceful participants and discerning spectators. Dance served three cultural necessities: social entertainment, physical exercise, and cultivation of moral control.

As a daily courtly banquet art form, dance was political entertainment. Carefully choreographed processions, group dances, and solo performances all reasserted the primacy of the

Miriam and her maidens sing and dance in preparation for Passover. Manuscript page from the *Golden Haggadah*, 1320, Add. 27210, f.15 recto.

most honored, the "lead couple," and the venerable "presence" of the leader or the lord or lady before whom all ceremonially bowed. Dance was a ritual ostentatious display of costume, jewels, and physique plus fashionable foreign manners and steps acquired by the well tutored and well traveled.

This courtly entertainment was nearly infallible test of nobility. Since very young children were taught dancing many hours per week, the difficulty of steps and requirements for grace incrementally increasing with age, an adult's dancing poorly or clumsily called into question his upbringing and social class. While an imposter might slip through security with forged papers, or a nouveau riche poser might affect a speech as if to the manor born, nevertheless, bad dancing would shout them out as frauds.

Dancing as liberal art and virtuous science, as Guglielmo Ebreo called it, required a physical exercise harmonizing intellect with body. Guglielmo stated his famous six requisites for a good dancer. First was measure, *misura*: the musical ability in timing, rhythm, and proportion, particularly to the accompaniment of musical instruments. One of Guglielmo's tests for a fine dancer was the ability to keep time when several separate instruments each played in a different rhythm.

Second requirement was memory, *memoria*, the ability to remember the correct sequence of steps and movement accurately. In very complex court dances this required prodigious concentration. Third was *partire del terreno*, the ability to estimate and apportion appropriate space for revolutions, leaps, and twirls.

Guglielmo's fourth and fifth qualities cultivated in daily exercise were *aiere*, general physical facility and lightness of movement, and *maniere*, a perfect integration between motions of the torso and the feet. These culminated in the sixth requisite, *movimento corporeo*, the total balance, posture, poise, and pose that constituted grace.

Dance was a control cultivator, training for the medieval and Renaissance ideal of virtue. The hardest exploits must seem effortless, natural, organic, always having been and forever more to be. Dancing, as Guglielmo Ebreo defined it, was an art for "generous hearts that loved it and for gentle spirits that had a Heaven-sent inclination for it . . . totally superior to those vicious and artless common people" whose "corrupt spirits and depraved minds" debased dance and disparaged its "liberal art" and virtue as "science" (The Letter of Dance. Available online. URL: http://www.pbm.com/~lindahl/lod/vol3/Italian-balli.html).

This 15th-century Jewish dancing master presented a proud theory of the dance along with the music and choreography for the dancers he taught, the noblest, most refined, politi-cally powerful courtiers of his day. Teaching children, coaching adults, arranging choreography of banquet politics, the dance master was a ruler of court ceremony.

Alongside Guglielmo's own dances in one manuscript are two dances composed by the Medici prince Lorenzo the Magnificent (d. 1492). Juxtaposition of work of that noble amateur and the Jewish craft master suggests the triumph of talent over social prejudice. Guglielmo the Jewish dance master, as did the *chazzan*, *troubadour*, *Spielmann*, and *badchan*, enriched both Jewish and Western cultures with music of dazzling variety, intellectual excellence, and audible splendor.

In prayer and at home, medieval Jews had music to obey joyously the command of the Psalms: *Ivdu et Hashem v simcha bo-u lfanav birnana*: "Worship the Lord with gladness. Come before God with song." This religious rationale also informed certain genres of Islamic music, most notably the *sama* tradition of the Sufi mystics. But whereas music formed an integral part of orthodox Christian and Jewish liturgical celebrations, the Islamic tradition was mixed, forever debating the licitness of music and its censure. Independently of these religio-legal discussions, the Islamic world contributed to the global medieval musical tradition via the composition of treatises on musical theory and the transmission of its musical instruments and genres.

ISLAMIC MUSIC AND DANCE

Music in the Islamic world between the eighth and the 16th centuries was a rich blend of Arabic, Syrian, Iraqi, and Persian musical achievements with influences from Byzantine, Christian, and Jewish music. Music theory, musical instruments, composition techniques, performance methods, tonalities, and tastes varied from place to place in the huge geographic space ranging from the Atlas Mountains, the Sahara in Africa, the Arabian Gulf, the Tigris and Euphrates River valleys, the Mediterranean, and the Iberian Peninsula. Islamic music assimilated music of local cultures. Music of Islam's Arabs, Persians, and Turks, however, had distinctive characteristics while sharing an Islamic central core of opposing ideas.

Islamic music is rooted in the music of the tribes of the Arab peninsula. Bedouins sang caravan songs called *huda*, which developed in the Hijaz into a more elegant, secular song called *nasb*, which was sung on joyful occasions such as weddings. In the Umayyad and Abbasid periods, nomadic Arabic music was transformed by contact with the music of Syria, Mesopotamia, Byzantium, and Persia. Poem lyrics still were sung in Arabic, and the Quran was chanted according to traditional rhythmic norms called *tajwid*. But the caliphs, as patrons of wealthy sophisticated courts, encouraged foreign entertainments, learning, and the splendors of the countries and cultures they conquered.

Music as *Halal* or *Haram*

Music was discussed and debated in legal, theological, and mystic writings. One Islamic school of thought, based in Medina, was dominated by thinkers who cultivated music as an art and encouraged music as a science that was permitted, *halal*. Scholars of the rival Islamic tradition censured the theory and performance of music as forbidden, *haram*. Central to both groups was the concept of how music was heard, *sama* as blessed inspiration or as a lure to commit sin. Sufi mystics, for instance, made music integral to prayer, and Sufi music and dance were methods for attaining religious ecstasy. The Iranian

mystic and religious scholars Abu l-Qasim al-Qushayri (d. 1074) and Abu Hamid al-Ghazali (d. 1111), among others, defended music in Islam as a mystical necessity for religious ecstasy. Other religious theorists, such as the Abbasid religious scholar and ascetic Abdallah ibn Abi Dunya (d. 894) and Hanbali theologian Ahmad ibn Taymiyya (d. 1328), censured music as a frivolous distraction from piety and seductive deflection from concentrating on Allah's perfection. Ibn Taymiyya in particular was concerned that music and dance in Islam were barely disguised survivals of pre-Islamic paganism. In the face of such accusations, al-Ghazali and others established norms of propriety and conditions of listening, distinguishing, for instance, between those who listen to music for purely personal pleasure (*sama al-nafs*) and those who listen "according to their heart or spirit." Still other scholars such as Abu Nasr al-Farabi (870–950) wrote treatises on the physics of sound and the emotional effects of sound and rhythm on the human mind. Ibn Khaldun (1332–1406), philosopher and historian, used music as the test for a civilization's health.

Music Theory

Musical theorists from the eighth through the 11th century wrote influential books on performance practice. Al-Khalil ibn Ahmad (d. 791) in his book on musical techniques, *Kitab al-nagham* (*The Book of Melody*), analyzed music and textual meter, rhythm, and prosody, uniting Indian, Arabic, and Persian concepts. Al-Hasan ibn Ahmad and Ibn al-Tahhan of the late 10th and early 11th centuries, respectively, wrote treatises on vocal technique.

Ibrahim al-Mawsili (742–804) and Ishaq Ibn Ibrahim Al-Mawsili (767–850) Ibrahim al-Mawsili and his son, Ishaq ibn Ibrahim al-Mawsili, founded the classical Arabic language school for singing. Ibrahim was said to have composed 900 melodies of his own. Abu l-Farj al-Isfahani mentions in his *Kitab al-aghani* that the son, Ishaq, was the most skilled and accomplished musician in the art of singing of his time. He was also a master of music composition and is credited with having finalized a codification system of eight melodic modes and eight rhythmic cycles and with having developed a definition of lute fretting independently of the ancient Greek theorists.

Ishaq's performance art was superb, his tunes exotic, his rhythms harmonious, and his manner unequaled by any predecessor or successor. Ishaq also was a great composer and writer. He wrote the *Great Book of Songs* (*Kitab al-aghani al-kabir*) and treatises on melody and rhythm. He also wrote about dancing and gait, and about the women singers of the Hijaz, Basta, and Kufa.

Tunes were considered proprietary. A slave woman named Dumon, who belonged to Ishaq, reported that she was the one slave woman successful in striking an intimate sexual relationship with Ishaq and one night tricked him and stole one of his tunes. Poems, songs, and melodies had monetary value. The elite of Baghdad exchanged tunes of songs much as they exchanged other types of gifts such as precious antiques. Song gifts suggest that melodies were written down and recorded during the Abbasid period.

Bayt al-Hikmah

The ninth-century Abbasid caliph al-Mamun, founded a cultural center, library, and translation institute called the House of Wisdom, Bayt al-Hikmah, in Baghdad. There scholars such as translated into Arabic important classical Greek musical works that introduced into Islamic culture the philosophical, mathematical, and musical ideas of Pythagorus and his followers, of Plato, of Aristotle, and of Plotinus. Greek musical treatises were translated into Arabic sometimes directly from the Greek but more often through Syriac translations of the Greek originals made by Nestorian Christians. Among the important Greek treatises in Arabic were Aristotle's *De Anima* (*On the Soul*) and the *Problemata* (*Problems*), Aristides' *De Musica* (*On Music*), Aristoxenus's *Harmonica*, Ptolemy's *Harmonica*, Euclid's *Canon*, Nichomachus's *Enchiridion* (*Manual*), and Cleonides' *Introductio Harmonico* (*Introduction to Harmony*).

These texts dealt only in part with musical performance and emphasized music as intellectual discipline and as mathematical science. Likewise, in the Latin West music was one of the four disciplines of the university *quadrivium*, along with geometry, arithmetic, and astronomy. From the Greeks a comprehensive, rich musical nomenclature was translated into Arabic.

Abu Yusuf Yaqub al-Kindi (d. c. 866)

The philosopher Abu Yusuf Yaqub al-Kindi studied the Greek musical past and the contemporary Islamic present and combined information about both in his treatises. Al-Kindi wrote a book about the lute, *al-ud*, the stringed instrument known as the "prince of enchantment," *amir al-tarab*, from which the modern guitar is derived. The lute was a favorite instrument of composers, professional instrumentalists, and amateur performers. Al-Kindi discussed the science of sound. He described musical intervals. He analyzed musical composition. He elaborated on the diatonic *ud* fretting popular in the ninth century and added a fifth string to the four-stringed *ud* to expand the pitch range to two octaves. He also theorized about the psychology of music, commenting upon its effect upon the soul and the emotions and its therapeutic value.

Al-Kindi lauded the *ud* as part of God's great macrocosmological plan in which the four strings of the earthly *ud* represented the four seasons, the four elements of which the universe is made, the four humors of the human body, and the four points on the compass. Musical effects of the *ud* were consonant with heavenly harmonies of planets and constellations.

Among those influenced by al-Kindi were the 10th-century Brethren of Purity, Ikhwan al-Safa, to whom are attributed a musical text that follows al-Kindi in emphasizing cosmology and numerology. The text is found in their compendium of *Epistles* (*Rasail*) in the section dealing with mathematics.

Abu l Faraj al-Isfahani (897–967) Abu l Faraj al-Isfahani was mentioned earlier as the author of the prodigious 24-volume *Book of Songs, Kitab al-aghani al-kabir*. Isfahani listed musical virtuosi and the music they performed. He described classical modes with song lyrics to express moods and passions. Each mode was indicated by the names of the fingers and the frets used when playing the *ud*. His songs expressed praise, complaint, lament, and love and were used in work, ritual, healing, wedding ceremonies, and funerals. Al-Isfahani also described music's importance to preserving history and story, since it was composed and performed in the service of panegyric, politics, art, and entertainment. He noted programmatic music's mimetic power to represent the natural world in galloping hoofbeats, singing birds, and babbling brooks, and the world of men in clashing of weapons.

In his songbook *Kitab al-Aghani*, al-Isfahani related stories of singers who by vocal power could induce fits of ecstasy and other somatic experiences in their audience members. A particular singer stood on a bridge and sang so magnificently that soon people of all ages and social classes gathered around to hear him. People feared that the bridge might collapse under the weight of those enraptured by his exquisite sounds. Some music fans would throw themselves into the river Euphrates in a frenzy of elation and ecstasy.

Even the dignified chief judge (*qadi*) of Baghdad, Ahmed ibn Abi Daud (d. 854), who had disdained singing and singers, was transformed from skeptic to passionate admirer after listening to a particular singer. The judge had traveled with the caliph al-Mamun in the mounted entourage of Prince al-Mutasim to Syria and while riding heard such a magnificent voice of a musician that the judge was transfixed and unconsciously dropped the whip from his hand. The caliph offered the judge an encore of that very moving song if the judge would retract his condemnatory comments against singing. The judge was so grateful to be emotionally moved by song he never again ridiculed singing.

Abu Nasr al-Farabi (870–950) Abu Nasr al-Farabi wrote an astonishingly comprehensive book that he called *The Grand Treatise on Music, Kitab al-musiqa al-kabir*, that united music theory with practice. He discussed sound as science, consonance, dissonance, harmony, rhythm, intervals, tetrachords, octave species, melodic structure, vocal style, and musical instruments. Al-Farabi also considered music composition and music's effects on listeners. His own *ud* playing was so rapturous and sensual that he was said to hypnotize his audience. Likewise in the West, the best Celtic bards, troubadours, and trouveres were described as casting spells with their music. Al-Farabi's music could induce his audience to laugh, to cry, or to sleep. The musician created the effects of the "prince of enchantment," *amir al-tarab*, by elaborate lute fretting and two newly introduced intervals. Al-Farabi also described two distinct long-necked fretted lutes called the *tunbur*, each with a different fret system, one Arabian lute with frets that produced quarter-tone intervals, the other lute from Khorasan with intervals based on divisions of the Pythagorean whole tone.

Abd al-Mumin Safi al-Din al-Urmawi (d. 1294) Abd al-Mumin Safi al-Din al-Urmawi is the author of the *Kitab al-adwar* (*The Book of Modes*) by far the most widely diffused and influential musical treatise for centuries and the most translated into Western and Oriental languages. It is here that we find for the first time the division of octaves into 17 steps, and the complete nomenclature and definition of the 12-*maqam* scale system, and use of letters and numbers for the notation of melodies. He was further credited with inventing the arch lute, *mughari*, and the psaltery, the *nuzha*. His work on musical cycles discussed rhythm, pitch, and note divisions of the octave. His discussion of musical meter, melodic modes, and modal intervals included a theoretical scale similar to that of the Khorasani *tunbur* that al-Farabi described. Safi al-Din's seven-tone scale later became influential in Iran and Turkey. As did al-Kindi, Safi al-Din preserved song fragments, which he recorded in a notation system based on the alphabet. Safi al-Din's remarkable talent as a musician and particularly as a lute player was called to the attention of the caliph, al-Mutasim, who invited him into his exclusive circle of boon companions. He composed more than 130 songs in the popular musical genre known as *nawba*, and his disciples extended his music into Egypt, Syria, Iraq, and Persia. Abd al-Qadir al-Maraghi (d. 1432), one of the greatest Persian-langauge writers on music, wrote an extensive commentary on the *Kitab al-adwar* He also authored several treatises about musical form and distinguished Persian from Arabic composition and performance techniques.

Other Theorists Other authors of musical treatises include Abu l-Wafa Muhammad al-Buzjani (d. 998), a mathematician, who wrote about the theory of rhythm. In his *Risalat fil-musiqa wa kashf rumuz kitab al-aghani* (*Epistle on Music and the Melodic Ciphers of the Book of Songs*) Ali ibn Yahya ibn al-Munajjim (d. 912) described a system of eight melodic modes, each with its own diatonic scale, the octave span of Pythagorean half- and whole steps, commonly used in the eighth and ninth centuries. Ahmad ibn Muhammad al-Sarakhsi (d. 1286) developed ideas similar to al-Kindi's and wrote treatises on melodic composition. The philosopher-physician Ibn Sina or Avicenna (d. 1037) included a chapter on music in his encyclopedic *Kitab al-shifa* (*The Book of Remedy*), placing music alongside astronomy and geometry as a mathematical science. He wrote about the phenomena of sound, dissonance, consonance, lute fretting, rhythm, and melodic modes.

Islamic Song and Vocal Artists

Instruments commonly were subordinate to the voice, as instrumental music served as prelude, interlude, and postlude to songs. Virtuosic singers sang solo, a cappella, with no instrumental accompaniment. Or they accompanied themselves with one of a half-dozen common instruments: the short-necked lute, *ud*; the long-necked lute, *tunbur* (tambourine); the psaltery, *mi zafa*; and the *duff*, variant of the tambourine; the percussion stick, *qadib*; and the drum, *tabl*.

Other common musical instruments were the Persian trumpet, Byzantine organ, and a new type of flute called the *shafut* that replaced the old Persian flute. The renowned eighth-century musician Zalzal apparently introduced the new flute to the Abbasid court.

When a singer was accompanied by an instrumentalist, voice was primary, instrument secondary, whether it was the woodwind *nay* or stringed *ud* or *tunbur* or a combination of several *ud* or *nay* and *ud*. However, a good singer was expected to be able to accompany himself or herself with a stringed instrument and be able to play with harmonic, melodic, and rhythmic ornaments.

Singing was a complex intellectual enterprise that required knowledge of pitch, melody, rhyme, rhythm, and Classical Arabic poetic forms. In performance a singer sat, stood, walked, or danced. The excellent singer was assumed to have a broad repertoire of memorized songs—thousands of songs for particular purposes: entertainments, holidays, weddings, births, greetings, deaths, change of seasons, and particular moods of the patron. A great performer also had the ability to improvise and to change the familiar songs melodically and rhythmically.

Both women and men were among the earliest Arabic musicians. Two renowned seventh-century women singers, Azza al-Mayla and the woman known only as Jamila, were appreciated also for their aesthetic sophistication. The learned singer Ubaydallah ibn Surayj (c. 637–726) wrote a treatise on musical theory that listed the qualities of a fine singer. He stated that a singer required accuracy of diction, fine grammar, vocal control, ability to embellish rhythm and melody, proper selection of poetic lyric, and capacity to conjoin melody and text skillfully.

Though Muslims who sang made music indoors and outdoors such as in parks, gardens, and palace courtyards, only a formal indoor concert was called a *majlis*, or music "assembly." At court musicians were required to appear on command or at the prescheduled performance day for a specific musician, the *nawba*.

QIYAN

The *qiyan* (s. *qayna*), educated, musically trained slave women, played a vital role in developing the art of singing and composition, and both the names and the works of many of these singers have survived the centuries, their memory and feats having been preserved in al-Isfahani's *Kitab al-aghani* and in treatises written especially about them. Many introduced foreign musical forms from the lands from which they were taken. Byzantine tunes were used for chanting Arabic verse thanks to talented slave singers. Slave women transferred the art of melody from the Hijaz to Iraq and led Islamic music to an apogee in the Abbasid court. Diplomatic ties and marital links between Muslims and Christians in Spain and across the Pyrenees introduced the *qiyan* to the courts of Europe, establishing a possible vehicle of influence of the Arabic music and poetic traditions on European courtly love poetry and lyric.

Slave women exquisitely sang love songs in taverns to entertain paying patrons, or they performed at court to please the caliph. They were highly prized by the well-to-do to entertain visiting dignitaries. Whether the slave songstresses simply sang for their supper or also provided sexual favors is a subject that modern critics have debated. The *qayna* was a virtuoso singer who had in her repertoire two types of songs, the slow, ornate *sinad* and the fast, exuberant *hazaj*. Her repertoire of songs—some of which were her own lyrical compositions—included love songs, elegies, eulogies, and lamentations expressing nostalgia and loss.

The caliphs purchased the most expensive *qiyan*, who learned Arabic song repertoires and introduced foreign musical styles from their homelands. Caliph al-Amin (r. 809–813) purchased the distinguished slave Bazl (because the singers were slaves, the literary texts only preserve their first name) for the astronomical amount of 20 million dirhams.

Slave owners trained their slave women in the arts of singing in their own courts or gave them over to the singing celebrities of the time. Ibrahim al-Mawsili taught his slave women—who were for sale—all the rules of singing in order to boost their price to more than double their original worth.

Muhammad ibn Abu Uyayna, the Abbasid governor of Rayy, Iran (r. 754–775), said that he had fallen in love with a slave woman called Aman but her master kept raising her price. Then he entrusted her to Ibrahim al-Mawsili and his son, Ishaq al-Mawsili, to train her in singing, and the more she perfected melody and song, the more her master raised her price. Abu Uyayna recognized that al-Mawsili had elevated his "diabolical art" to increase the slave's value. His singing and now hers captivated both the heart and the ear with ecstasy.

The bond maiden Sharya first was purchased for 300 dinars but after she was trained in singing for one year, Ishaq al-Mawsili bought her back for 3,000 dinars. He declared that she was worth much more.

Renowned eighth-century slave women singers of the Abbasids included Bazl, Muttayam, and Dananir. All had exquisite voices, talent as poets, and skill with musical instruments. The ninth-century Iraqi polyglot al-Jahiz devoted an entire treatise to the subject of Arabic female singers, *Risalat al-qiyan* (*The Epistle on Singing-girls*).

Bazl Bazl whose name means "gift," was originally from Medina and, according to Abu al-Faraj, was attractive in appearance, clever, and accomplished in instrumental music. Jafar ibn Musa al-Hadi originally had bought her then later sold her to Caliph al-Amin for the astronomical price of 20 million dihrams. Bazl was remarkably competent in "each and every amiable thing" and was the greatest singer of her time both in the quality of her work and in the number of songs she could perform. She composed a book on singing that included 12,000 tunes that she taught to her master, Ali ibn Hisham (Farmer 134). She was said to have been able to sing 30,000 different tunes.

Muttayam al-Hashimiyya Bazl taught other slave women the art of singing. Muttayam ("Enslaving") was one of her disciples. Mut-

tayam excelled both in singing and in composing. The author of the *Kitab al-aghani* related that the illustrious Ishaq al-Mawsili stole one of Muttayam's songs and attributed it to himself. He offered this tune to Ali ibn Hisham for a high price, which he refused to pay since the tune was composed by his own slave. Ishaq admitted his ruse but retorted saying that people would more likely believe him. Muttayam's artistic talent was ranked third after Ishaq and Ulaya and before the great Abd Allah al-Rabeey.

Dananir Dananir ("Wealth") was said to be one of the most beautiful and witty women of her time, a singer and revered poetry reciter. Bazl was her teacher. Dananir was said to have composed a book (*Kitab mujarrid al-aghani, Book of Choice Songs*) on singing and songs. Both women performers were influenced by the great singing masters such as Fulayh ibn Abi l-Awra al-Makki (eighth century), Ibrahim al-Mawsili, Ishaq ibn Ibrahim al-Mawsili, Abul-Qasim Ismail ibn Jami, a rival and friend of Ibrahim al-Mawsili, and other luminaries.

A man from Medina owned the singer Dananir. He gave her a superb education and musical training. When the minister of Caliph Harun al-Rashid (r. 786–809) first saw her, he was deeply impressed by her charm and purchased her. The caliph heard Dananir sing and became infatuated with her melody and beauty. He showered her with precious gifts and money and soon everyone in Baghdad was discussing al-Rashid's attraction to the magnificent slave woman. Al-Rashid's wife, Zubayda, was not pleased. As the story from the *Thousand and One Nights*, "The Tale of Harun al-Rashid and the slave-girl and the Imam Abu Yasuf" reveals, the caliph had been willing to divorce his own wife in exchange for this slave girl. But after all had heard Dananir sing, no one blamed al-Rashid for his admiration (*The Thousand and One Nights* [Burton transl.] Available online. URL: http://www.wollamshram.ca/1001/vol_4).

Qalam Not all of the *qiyan* were Arab women. Qalam, a 10th-century songstress in the Umayyad court of Spain, was a young Christian woman of Basque or Navarese origin. She was captured by Muslim troops during military campaign and sold into slavery. Qalam, whose name in Arabic means "pen," was taken by ship from Spain to Medina, where she was trained in the time-honored traditions of Arabic language, poetry, music, song, and dance. She rose to fame as a songstress and lute player. Qalam returned to the Iberian Peninsula, where she became one of the most popular attractions at the Umayyad court of Córdoba.

Patronage and Court Music

Abbasid Caliph al-Mahdi (r. 775–785) and Caliph al-Amin were knowledgeable music patrons. They had in their courts the best instrumentalists and singers that money could buy. They often had their children educated by the best musical masters. The Abbasid prince Ibrahim ibn al Mahdi (d. 839), son of the caliph al-Mahdi became a fierce rival of Ishaq al-Mawsili. The young prince was acknowledged in his day as having "a voice of tremendous power" and "the most proficient of mankind in the art of notes" (Farmer, 120–121).

Caliphs patronized erudite performers who wrote treatises about music as well as taught music and performed it, such Ibrahim al-Mahdi and Ishaq al-Mawsili. Theirs and several other texts preserve the names and reputations of Abbasid court musicians, such as the renowned *ud* (lute) virtuoso named Zalzal, who died in 791.

COURT MUSICIANS

Arabic musical history and the history of court music in particular would be impossible without the encyclopedic *Kitab al-aghani* written by Abu l-Faraj al-Isfahani at the personal behest of Caliph Harun al-Rashid. Thanks to al-Isfahani we know that at sophisticated Islamic courts professional musicians entertained and taught music. According to evidence in his *Book of Songs*, the court musician was required to be the close companion of the ruler, earning high honor and generous pay. The musician was expected to be educated in all arts and crafts, and as the perfect companion or *nadim*, he should know literature, poetry, prosody, grammar, history, stories, the Quran, Hadith, law, astrology, medicine, cooking, horse breeding, backgammon, chess, clowning, and magic. Musicians also were to have the refined qualities, but not necessarily the birth pedigree, of a gentleman, correct in behavior and elegant in manners. Ibrahim al-Mawsili as court musician received the munificent regular monthly salary of 10,000 silver dirhams, plus monetary bonuses for excellence. Singing for the caliphs was highly lucrative. Ibrahim's annual income was 24 million dirhams, counting bonuses routinely added to his salary for singing.

The caliph who enjoyed a singer's song invited the singer to name his or her price in money or amnesty or appointment of a friend to a high-ranking post. One tale relates that Caliph Musa ibn al-Mahdi al-Hadi (r. 785–786) asked Ibrahim al-Mawsili to chant light erotic poetry, and this so delighted the caliph that he asked Ibrahim to name his price. The poet requested that the caliph appoint a friend named Marwan as governor of Medina. The stunned caliph instructed his treasurer to provide as alternative whatever Ibrahim cared to take from the private treasury, namely, 50,000 dinars.

COMPETITIONS

A fine performance generated repetitions of the same song, and sometimes singers competed for the audience's appreciation of musical excellence. Approval went beyond praise to money. For one especially wonderful courtly performance, Ibrahim al-Mawsili was rewarded with 150,000 dinars, an extraordinarily generous gift.

Musical competitions and debates were common. Musical battles pitted musical rivals against one another. A professional male court singer and teacher, for instance, might battle against the professional female singer who was an esteemed slave musician. One day when Bazl was singing at the court of Caliph al-Mamun, Ishaq al-Mawsili found fault with one of her tunes. She was silent for an hour. Then she sang three other tunes, one after another. When she finished she demanded that Ishaq identify the three tunes. He could not. Therefore she addressed herself directly to Caliph al-Mamun and said: "Allah is my witness. The three tunes were the compositions of his father [Ibrahim al-Mawsili]. I learned them directly from his mouth. If Ishaq does not recognize his own father's melodies, however could he identify the tunes of others?" Ishaq was taken aback and could not say a single word. Bazl won that singing debate (*The Thousand and One Nights* [Burton transl.]. Available online. URL: http://www.wollamshram.ca/1001/vol_4).

DANCE

The *Kitab al-aghani* provides delicious anecdotes about singing, dancing, and ceremony. Abu l-Muhanna Makhariq (d.c. 845) was the slave of a famous songstress, Atika bint Shuhda who gave him lessons in music. His talent earned him the attention of the Abbasid court where Ibrahim al-Mawsili took him on as a pupil. One day, Makhariq and al-Mawsili were invited to the mansion of Caliph al-Amin. There the rooms were magnificently decorated with candles. Large numbers of beautifully costumed slave women were chanting in rhythm to the sound of trumpets. Everyone in the room was dressed in elaborate horse costume. Al-

Amin himself galloped in the midst of his bevy of galloping horses. The wild equestrian party went on through the night until early morning.

Singing accompanied by dancing had specific rules and standards. Ishaq al-Mawsili wrote his *Great Book of Songs* on singing and dancing. The prolific writer, traveler, and historian Abu l-Hasan Ali al-Masudi (d. 956) also wrote about dancing compatible with specific melodies as well as depicting the qualities of a good dancer.

Music by Region

PERSIAN MUSIC

The fifth-century historian Herodotus remarked that the Persians excelled in the adoption and adaptation of foreign cultural forms. Persian culture triumphed by adoption and adaptation by the Arabs, Turks, and Mongols who militarily conquered Persia's soldiers and overran their cities. Ancient Persia's musical vestiges persevered into the Middle Ages by references of the historians Herodotus, Xenophon, and Athenaeus, who described music in the Achaemenid empire that flourished between the sixth and fourth centuries, the Parthian dynasty that ruled between the fourth and second centuries, and then the Sassanian empire that ruled from the third to the seventh century. Arabs conquered the Persian empire in 642 and directly ruled the region between the seventh and 10th centuries. Writing in Arabic, the Persians al-Kindi, al-Farabi, Ibn Sina, and Safi al-Din described the music of Iran. Persian history and music then were influenced by Turkish and Mongolian conquests between the 11th and 15th centuries and subsequently by the Safavids, who ruled during the 16th century.

Important Persian music texts derive from the Sassanian court, which accorded high honor

to music and musicians. The emperor Chosroes II, called Xosro Parviz (r. 590–628), invited many musicians to his court. Famous among these was Barbod, the performer, composer, and music theorist who was said to have invented the original form of the *dastgah* system, which contained seven modal structures; the royal modes named after Chosroes, the *Xosrovani*; plus 30 derivative modes, called *lahn*; and 360 melodies called *dastan*. These have wonderfully evocative names, even though the music has not survived the centuries: the vengeance of Iraj, *kin-e Iraj*; the throne of Ardesir, *taxt-e Ardesir*; the sovereign's garden, *baq-e Sahryar*; the seven treasures, *haft ganj*; the green spring, *sabz bahar*; and Moon over the mountains, *mah abar kuhan*.

Instruments in Persian Music   The classical Persian musical ensemble included five instruments that played melodies, and a pair or trio of rhythm instruments. Melody makers were the *sehtar, ney, kamanche,* and *santur.* Rhythm keepers were percussion instruments called *tombak, zarb,* and *douf.*

The *sehtar* had four strings (though its Persian name means "three strings," probably referring to a prior form of the instrument). It was a pear-shaped wooden stringed instrument with small holes that allowed sound projection. Because of its delicate, intimate sound, it was the preferred melodic instrument of the Sufi mystics.

The *ney* was a cross between a flute and a recorder. It was played as a recorder pointing downward, with six finger holes and one thumbhole. But, as with a flute, the player blew across the open end. The *ney* was used also in Arabic music and Balkan folk music.

The *kamanche* was a form of spiked fiddle and probably is the ancestor of most European and Asian stringed instruments. It is comparable to the Arabic *rebab*, or in the West, the *rebek*. The *kamanche* was related to the hackbrett in northern Europe, the cymbalum in eastern Europe, the *santouri* in Greece, the *yang chin* in China, and the dulcimer in Britain. The classical Persian *kamanche* had a round wooden soundbox, with a spike on the bottom to support the instrument. It was held vertically and bowed horizontally.

The *santur* was a trapezoid-shaped hammered zither. It is a wooden box with strings stretched across bridges arranged in courses and is played by striking the strings with two light wooden hammers. A *santur* often had four strings per note, and the instrument could play three octaves: bass, middle, and treble.

The *tombak* was a goblet-shaped drum with the narrow end open and the wide end covered by a skin glued to the wooden frame. To play it the musician struck the skin surface with his fingers and achieved different sounds by careful placement of the strike. The fingers hitting the center of the drum produced a deep booming sound (*tom*), while hitting the rim made a high pitched sound (*bak*). The *zarb* was the larger version of the *tombak.*

The *douf* (or *daff*) was a framed drum with metal rings inside, which added a jingling effect to the percussive sound. The *douf* was thus capable of producing intricate rhythmic effects. It is depicted in many Persian miniatures.

OTTOMAN TURKISH MUSIC

Islamic music also assimilated changes introduced by Ottoman Turks who conquered Syria, Palestine, Iraq, the coasts of Arabia, and much of North Africa after 1517. Turkish music itself had already absorbed musical styles and content from Central Asia, Anatolia, Persia, Syria, and Iraq. While these multiple musical influences were heard in major cities such as Aleppo, Damascus, and Cairo, older-style Arab music persisted in the small towns and desert communities of the Syrian Bedouins and North African Berbers.

Ottoman musicians belonged to professional guilds called *tawaif*. In Egypt male instrumentalists were called *alatiyyah* and may have played primarily for male audiences. Women musicians, called "learned women," *awalim*, may have performed primarily for other women. If so, the 16th-century sexual separation contrasted with the earlier medieval musical power of the learned slave songstresses, the *qiyan*, who performed for men and women.

Common Arabic and Turkish instruments that professional musicians played in the cities included the lute or *ud*; the zither, the *qanun*; and the flute, the *nay*. Early forms of the *samai*, known in Turkish as the *saz semai*, and the *bashraf*, also called *pesrev*, were used in the Turkish courts and in Sufi music.

SUFI DANCE AND MUSIC

Music, poetry, and dance intertwined to play an intrinsic part in Sufi spirituality. Sufi *dhikr* consisted of special rhythmic chants, repetitions, and breathing techniques that created a heightened state of spiritual excitement and enlightenment. Often the *dhikr* ritual was accompanied by listening to music (*sama*), and special genres of music were performed, such as the *ghazal* and the *qawwali*, which developed in India.

Mevlevi Whirling Dervishes in Turkey Known in the Western world as Whirling Dervishes, the 13th-century Mevlevis were a mystical Islamic order established in Konya, Turkey. The Mevlevis cultivated instrumental, vocal, and dance forms. Their music spread into parts of Syria, Iraq, and North Africa, although it should be noted that the religious orthodoxy considered dance to be an especially deviant form of behavior. The Hanbali theologian Ibn Taymiyya devoted an entire treatise to the evils of dance. He and likeminded others accused the Sufi ecstatic dancers of demonic

Mevlana Jalaluddin Rumi, founder of the Order of the Dancing Dervishes, expressing his love for the young disciple Husam al-Din Chelebi. From Tardjome-i-Thevakib (*A translation of the stars of the legends*), *by the Mevlevi Derwish Aflaki.* The Pierpont Morgan Library/Art Resource, NY.

or pagan shamanist influences (introduced by the Mongols who had conquered Baghdad in 1258) and charged that the ecstatic experience induced by such dancing was becoming an end in itself, and thus a distraction from God and the *Sharia*.

Ibn Arabi (d. 1240) The revered Sufi thinker and poet Muhy al-Din Ibn Arabi, who was born in southeastern Islamic Spain in 1165, left al-Andalus as a young man and traveled in the Mediterranean. He used musical modes that evoked particular emotional states and integrated them with texts to heighten their emotional effect. Ibn Arabi's *Interpreter of Desires, Taryuman al-Ashwaq*, translated into Castilian as *El interprete de los deseos*, was an ecstatic composition that was said to be particularly inspirational in a Sufi musical session, *sama*.

Rumi (d. 1273) The Sufi poet Mawlana Jalaluddin Rumi was born in Balkh, Afghanistan; traveled through eastern Iran; made the pilgrimage to Mecca; studied in Syria; and then established himself in Konya, a center of Islamic mysticism. Fluent in Arabic, Persian, and Turkish, Rumi created poetry that influenced Persian and Turkish literature and music that inspired Sufi music in India. Rumi's greatest work, the *Maznavi-ye-manavi (Spiritual Couplets)*, was so praised that some called it the [Persian Quran]. The 14th-century Persian poet Muhammad Shamsuddin Hafiz (1325–90) followed the musical tradition of Rumi.

Sufi poetry, which often was recited with music, celebrated the mystic's overwhelming yearning for God and the divine. This Persian poetry of rapture described the passion of the mystic toward God as if it were an erotic-spiritual love affair between a man and a woman. Rumi's Ode "You've Become a Lover, O Heart" was an imaginary dialogue expressing the mystic's yearning for union with the beloved:

> This heart-seeing eye was a teardrop and
> became an ocean; its ocean is saying
> "May there be blessings for your ocean!"

> O hidden lover, may that Beloved become
> your companion! O seeker of loftiness,
> may there be blessings for your
> exaltedness!

> (Dar-al-Masnavi. Available online. URL:
> http://www.dar-al-masnavi.org.)

MUSLIM SPAIN

For the more than 700 years between 713 and 1492, Muslims in the Iberian Peninsula heard and performed the music of Islam while also influencing and being influenced by music of Christian western Europe and music of Judaism. The wealth and splendor of the courts of Seville, Granada, and Córdoba inspired new musical forms in al-Andalus. All three musical idioms affected one other in mathematical musical theory, in technical nomenclature, in rhythm, in song forms, in performance techniques, and in musical instruments.

Likewise during the Crusades of the 11th through 13th centuries, Islamic music met Western Latin music and both traditions were enriched. The 13th-century Spanish king Alfonso X, the Wise, el Sabio (d. 1284), commissioned the magnificent manuscript song book *Songs of Saint Mary, Cantigas de Santa Maria*, elegantly decorated with miniatures depicting musicians, including Moors, playing the lute, psaltery, and double-reed shawm.

The foremost influence on the musical tradition of Islamic Spain stems from the Arab East, particularly in the works of Ishaq al-Mawsili. Ziryab (d. 850), a freed slave musician who was forced under polemical circumstances to move from Baghdad to Córdoba, is credited with introducing this tradition into al-Andalus, where he became a respected singer, *ud* player, and music teacher in the Umayyad court.

Ziryab had been a pupil of Ishaq al-Mawsili at the court of Baghdad during the reign of Harun al-Rashid. His extraordinary talent and charismatic personality so captivated the caliph that he was prepared to name Ziryab master of music, to the detriment of Ishaq. The rivalry between the two musicians came to a head when caliph Harun invited Ziryab to perform using his teacher Ishaq al-Mawsili's *ud* (lute). When Ziryab refused, saying he preferred to play his own *ud*, al-Mawsili informed him that he would not tolerate such a rival at court. Implying that

From Madinat al-Zahra, Spain, 986, is this ivory pyxis of Prince al-Mughira showing three musicians. Erich Lessing/Art Resource, NY.

songs, usually *muwashshaha* or *zajal*, sung in faster meter. As discussed in the previous chapter, *muwashshaha* and *zajal* are genres of Arabic stanzaic poetry, the former composed in Classical Arabic and the latter in the vernacular, that are indigenous to al-Andalus and are meant to be sung or recited with musical accompaniment. Ziryab was said to have memorized a staggering 10,000 songs. He had a repertoire of 24 *nawbat* alone, each of which was a composite of vocal and instrumental pieces in a certain melodic mode. Muslims expelled from Iberia in the late 15th century took *nawba* tradition with them to North Africa. This composition technique presented romantic subject matter in a new style with strophic texts with refrains. The genre thrived in North Africa and the Levant and was especially cultivated in Aleppo, Syria.

It is interesting to note that Western names of many instruments seem derived from Arabic nomenclature, such as the lute from *al-ud*; the nakers, or kettledrums, from *naqqarat*; the rebec from *rabab*; the organ from *urghun*; the guitar from *qitara*; and the anafil, the natural trumpet, from *al-nafir*.

the upstart musician weight suffer an "accident" for which Ishaq would not be held responsible, Ziryab took the "hint" and fled westward to al-Andalus. Ziryab's influence on Andalusian music is seen in the performance of musical concerts, *nawbat* (s. *nawba*), in which the sequencing of individual musical pieces in a *majlis* is determined in order to maximize their aesthetic appeal. The word *nawba* means "turn" and thus also referred to the sequencing of musicians, that is, assigning them specific days or hours of the day to perform at the court and designating the order of their performance at a musical concert. With regard to the sequencing of the *nawba*, the ideal order was to begin with slow rhythmic vocal pieces and end with upbeat

READING

Christian Music and Dance

CHURCH MUSIC

Reese 1940 and 1959, Sadie 1980, Seay 1975, Wangermee 1968: music in the Middle Ages, in general; Bukofzer 1942, Heninger 1974, Hollander 1961, Spitzer 1963: music theory and world order; Sadie 1980, Seay 1975: chant forms.

MUSICAL MODES AND NOTATIONS

Cosman 1996, Sadie 1980, Seay 1975: Guido's hand.

SECULAR MUSIC

Cosman 1978: Machaut; Cosman 1976 and 1978, Siraisi 1975: music and medicine; Cosman 1976 and 1981: feast, hunting, and sexual music; Cosman 1966, 1976 and 1981: music and ceremony; Cosman 1966: music and manners; Goldin 1973 and 1974: troubadours, *trouvères*, minnesingers; Hatto and Taylor 1958: Neidhart von Reuental.

MUSICAL INSTRUMENTS

Brown 1965: instrumental music; Cosman 1996, Sachs 1940, Winternitz 1971: development of musical instruments; Winternitz 1971 and 1979: musical instruments in art; Heninger 1961, Morley 1952, Spitzer 1963: harmony, practical and theoretical.

DANCE

Brainard 1980 and 1998, Cosman 1976 and 1996, Crane 1968, Wilson 1992: dance in the Middle Ages, in general; Bainard 1998, Sparti 1993: dance master; Brainard 1980 and 1998: music for dance; Doob 1974: Nebuchadnezzar's children; Arbeau 1967, Brainard 1998: Thoinot Arbeau's *Orchesography*; Meydenbach 1492: *Der Toten Dantz*.

Jewish Music and Dance

SYNAGOGUE MUSIC

Idelsohn 1967: general history of Jewish music; Idelsohn 1967: music in the synagogue and the roles of chazzan, precentor, and paytan.

SECULAR MUSIC

Cosman 1981, Idelsohn 1967: holiday and festival music; Cosman 1976, 1981, and 2000, Metzger and Metzger 1982: Jewish troubadours, minnesingers, Immanuel of Rome, and the *dolce stil novisti*; Baron 1967, Cosman 1981, Idelsohn 1967: *Gesellschaftslieder, Klezmorim*; Lacy 1996: Elijah Bahur's *Bove Bukh*; Roth 2002: *Spielmanner* Sabbath entertainments; Altmann 1961, Idelsohn 1967: Saadya Gaon on the musical modes and their influence on the human soul; B Goldstein 1974 and 1977, Idelsohn 1967: Levi ben Gerson's treatise *Musical Harmonic Numbers*; Baron 1967, Roth 2002: Judah ben Isaac; Cosman 1981, Idelsohn 1967: Guglielmo Ebreo and wedding entertainers; Winternitz 1979: musical instruments.

THE JEWISH DANCE MASTER

Cosman 1981: Guglielmo Ebreo. Arbeau Thoinot 1967, Cosman 1981: the dance master.

Islamic Music and Dance

MUSIC AS *HALAL* OR *HARAM*

D'Erlanger 1930, al-Faruqi 1981, Farmer 1967 and 1986, O Wright, 1986; Mountain 2003, Poche 1996, Sawa 1982, Shiloah 1993, 1994 and 1995, Touma 1996: music, in general; Racy 1983: Arab music history.

MUSIC THEORY

Al-Freih n.d., Neubauer 1965, Sawa 1982 and 1989: song in the Abassid courts; Farmer 1925, 1929–30, 1930, and 1940, Shiloah 1963 and 1979, Werner and Sonne 1941 and 1942–43, Wright 1978: music theory and theorists; Nallino 1999: al-Isfahani; Farmer 1929, Gray 2001, Jolivet, and Rashed 1999, al-Kindi 1974: al-Kindi; Sourdel 1999: Bayt al-Hikma; Farmer 1929, Gray 2001, al-Kindi 1974, Robson 1938, Sawa 1989: musical instruments.

ISLAMIC SONG AND VOCAL ARTISTS

Boase 1999, Farmer 1929, Al-Freih, al-Jahiz 1980, Pellat 1988, Sawa 1989, Shiloah 1963: singing slave women; Farmer 1929, Gray, al-Kindi 1974, Robson 1938, Sawa 1989, Shiloah 1995: musical instruments.

PATRONAGE AND COURT MUSIC

Al-Freih n.d., Neubauer 1965, Sawa 1982 and 1989: song in the Abassid courts; During 1988, 1989, 1992, and 1999, al-Ghazzali 1901, Ibn al-Jawzi 1948, Ibn Taymiyya 1905, Pouzet 1983: *sama*; Al-Freih n.d., Sawa 1989, Shiloah 1962: dance in the Abbasid courts; McGee 1982, Menocal 1981 and 1987: Islamic influences on medieval European dances.

MUSIC BY REGION

Farmer 1929, Gray 2001, al-Kindi 1974, Robson 1938, Sawa 1989, Shiloah 1993 and 1999: musical instruments; Gray 2001: classical Persian music; Kersten 2004, Mjost 2004: mystical Persian music; Racy 1983: Arab music; Guettat 1980: music in the Maghrib; Imamuddin 1959, Menocal 1981 and 1987, Monroe 1994, Poché 1995, Shiloah 1991, Wright 1994: music in Muslim Spain; Reynolds 2004: Ziryab.

11

HOLIDAYS
AND FESTIVALS

To understand a people, study its celebrations. Few aspects of a culture reveal so much so quickly. Better than the history of the adventures of important leaders or of battles fought and won, holidays preserve what the people think beautiful, sacred, and important; what the culture considers dangerous and forbidden. Holidays also set patterns for major rites of daily life and influence their customary sounds, sights, odors, tastes, and textures. Celebrations and holidays unite the elders of the culture with the youngest, the most nobly born with the lowest classes. The laity and religious celebrate the same festivals at church, synagogue, and mosque.

In medieval Christian, Jewish, and Muslim societies holidays and festivals fulfilled the same functions: They constituted a form of divine worship, a means of remembering and praising God. They enabled the community symbolically and liturgically to recall and relive the defining moments of its sacred history. Festivals and holidays allowed their observers to celebrate belonging to a community of believers and marked clear boundaries between the community and outsiders.

Holidays as diversions and distractions to those struggling with life put markers on the road of time, allowing things past to be remembered. In measuring time, celebrations gave hope for things future. Holidays were life's balancers, life's rhythm makers. Festivity and celebration provided recreation, reward, hope, and order. Feasts and festivals dramatized sacred ideas and demonstrated the holy as perceived in acts of daily life.

CHRISTIAN HOLIDAYS AND FESTIVALS

Many Christian holiday ceremonies and ritual objects were built upon Jewish feasts, pre-Christian fertility rites, Roman calendar customs, and folk rituals that clever doctors of the church such as Saint Augustine of Hippo (d. 430) and Pope Gregory the Great (d. 604) emended for new pious Christian purpose. Ceremonial fires at June's Midsummer Eve honoring Saint John the Baptist, for instance, originated in the pagan summer solstice bonfires called the *beltane fires* celebrating the Druidic god Bel.

While holiday details differed with country, century, and class of celebrant, certain basic patterns were routine. In folk theatricals called *mummings* or *mumming plays*, an actor playing Saint George fought a Midsummer Eve dragon. This traditional dragon among royalty and wealthy townsmen was a magnificent machine with mechanical wings, bellowing smoke, an expensive marvel of engineering. With equal holiday gusto a poor blacksmith playing Saint George fought a homespun dragon-shaped kite a shepherd boy held from behind with sticks and strings. The Hobby Horse similarly was a beloved feature in folk rituals and pageantry. The hobby horse in country ceremonies was a rustic man riding a broomstick with a painted wooden horse head with bell and rough rope for bridle. In courtly festivity the hobby horse trotted under expensively embroidered *caparison* blankets, with jewel-encrusted reins on a horse head with eyes of precious stones and a mane of woven gold.

Likewise, during November's honoring of Saint Catherine, patron saint of lawyers, wheelwrights, carpenters, rope makers, lace makers, spinners, and women students, people ate delectable wheel-shaped Saint Catherine cakes, rich with sugar, eggs, and caraway seeds. *Cathern cakes* sometimes were triangular, representing the spikes on the wheel of her martyrdom. Local London bakeshops' traditional Cathern cakes probably were less spectacular than *Cathern cakes* baked in noble kitchens, but all alluded to Saint Catherine's wheel and were eaten on her feast day with similar ceremony. Young or old, royalty or craftsman, city mayor or country villager followed customary patterns for celebrating holidays.

Local traditions such as Cathern cakes must take second place to the festivals and traditions that united the whole of Christendom and gave it its distinct identity. The liturgical calendar of Christian feasts was arranged according to the events of the life of Christ, from his birth to his Passion, death, Resurrection, ascension, and joyful expectation of his second coming. Most of the great holy days were fixed in the Christian calendar in the third and fourth centuries, taking definitive form by the 11th century. In chronological order they consist of the Advent season, whose major feasts included *Christmas, the Feast of the Circumcision*, and the *Epiphany*; the Lenten season, whose major feasts include *Ash Wednesday, Palm Sunday, Holy Week*, and the greatest feast of all, *Easter*; the *Feast of the Ascension*; the *Feast of the Pentecost*; the *Feast of the Holy Trinity*; and the *Feast of Corpus Christi*. Over the centuries the need clearly to distinguish orthodox Christianity from other rival beliefs, together with the increasing Marian piety of the 12th and 13th centuries, led to the addition of various Marian festivals to the liturgical calendar, the most important of them the *Nativity of the Virgin, Presentation of the Virgin in the Temple, Annunciation, Dormition of the Virgin, Seven Sorrows of the Virgin, Seven Joys of the Virgin*, and *Feast of the Assumption*. The Christian calendar also contained a prodigious number of saints' days, some of which were universal, honoring the apostles, the early martyrs, and doctors of the church. Others corresponded to pre-Christian spring, summer, autumn, and winter festivals, while still others celebrated the life and heroic death of local personalities. A brief description of each holiday's meaning is given in the following. (*See* chapter 5 on philosophy and religion for the larger theological and philosophical contexts for these ceremonies.)

Calendar of Christian Festivals

ADVENT

Advent, the Christian ecclesiastical season in preparation for the nativity of Christ, began to be observed in the late fifth-century Gallic Church when Bishop Perpetuus of Tours (d. 490) ordered that a fast be held on three days of every week from the Feast of Saint Martin (November 11) to Christmas. Originally this preparatory period was called Quadragesima Sancti Martini (Forty Days' Fast of Saint Martin's). The idea of a penitential fast quickly caught on and spread to different countries, including Spain, Germany, and England, albeit with each starting the fast from a different date. In England, for instance, it coincided with the Feast of Saint Catherine on November 25, while in Scotland it began on the Sunday nearest Saint Andrew's Day (November 30), and the four successive Sundays preceding Christmas.

Interestingly, the original penitential character of Advent as observed in [Gaul, England, Wales, Ireland, and Scotland with their tradition of fasting] was absent in Rome, where the season was one of festive joy. When the Frankish Church accepted the Roman liturgy in the eighth century, a compromise was reached between the longer nine-week solemn observance of the former and the shorter, more festive character of the latter. Medieval Advent was shortened to four weeks in keeping with the practice of Rome but was characterized by a blend of liturgical solemnity and joy, purple vestments, silent organ, partial fasting, and other signs of penitential observance. The Advent fast was not as severe as that of Lent and generally prohibited meat, fowl, butter, and cheese. Fish, an ancient symbol of Christ, and other species of seafood were allowed, as were eggs. The season of Advent does not figure in the Byzantine calendar; however, since the eighth century the Eastern Church has observed a preparatory fasting period, the Quadragesima of Saint Philip (*Tessaranthemeron Philippou*), which begins on November 15, the Feast of the apostle Saint Philip, and lasts until Christmas.

Up until the sixth century the Advent season heralded the incarnation, the coming of Christ in his mortal birth. In the 12th century it marked the "threefold advent of Christ": his past coming in Bethlehem, his present coming through grace in the symbolic representation of the soul's preparation for Christ's arrival, and his future *second coming*. The *second coming* represented Christ's apocalyptic return to Earth in glory to judge the living and the dead at the world's end. This event, portended in the liturgy of *Advent*, stimulated popular belief in the emergence of Antichrist figures. It also was called *Parousia* (Greek, "presence" or "arrival"). The Antichrist was Jesus Christ's chief antagonist in theology, literature, and drama, appearing on Earth before Christ's second coming and the end of the world. A lawless, self-deified maker of mock-miracles, the Antichrist caused apostasy and mass defections from the true church. Christ would destroy the Antichrist.

CHRISTMAS

Medieval Christmas lasted 12 full days, beginning on *Christmas Eve* and ending on *Twelfth Night*. Some calendars counted the days from *Christmas Day* to *Twelfth Day* (January 5) or *Epiphany* on January 6. The triadic celebration of Christ's baptism as Son of God, the journey of the Magi prophesying Christ's kingship, and the miracle at the wedding of Cana, which demonstrated his miraculous power and mystically symbolized Christ's wedding to the church. Three masses, at night, day, and dawn, symbolized Christ's trinal birth. Eternally he was Son of God the Father. Humanly he was

Son from the womb of Mary. Mystically, he lived in the faithful Christian soul.

Many of the holiday's merrymaking festivities derived from the Roman winter festival of Saturnalia. Remarkably, the date for Christmas, December 25, was not based on historical evidence of Jesus's birth but rather replaced the pagan festival *natalis solis invicti*, the birth of the Sun god Mithras, at winter solstice. The intention was to encourage the worshipers of Mithras to abandon their beliefs in a "false" Sun god and to worship the one who is "light of the world" and the true "Sun of justice." The Christian feast honoring Christ's birth was celebrated on December 25 from about the time of the fourth-century Philocalian calendar.

Christmas Symbols and Customs   The *crib* of the infant Jesus was one of the earliest Christian symbols. From late antiquity, churches were decorated with the manger and other motifs from the Bethlehem story. Likewise, Christian families decorated the walls of their homes with representations of Christ's birth as depicted in the Gospels. Saint Francis of Assisi is said to have initiated the custom of building a Bethlehem scene outside the church. According to his hagiographer the Franciscan friar Thomas of Celano (d. c. 1270), the first nativity scene was mounted at his behest in Greccio, Italy, on Christmas Eve 1223. The manger was made of wood and lined with fresh hay and was placed between a live ox and an ass. A crowd of people gathered with Saint Francis before the manger bearing candles and torches to illuminate the night and to welcome the newborn Christ with songs of praise. A solemn Mass was sung, during which Francis sang a carol and then delivered a sermon. Thus Francis's wish that Greccio "become a new Bethlehem" was made reality. From Italy the custom of building a "Bethlehem" in front of churches and in private homes spread to France, Spain, Portugal, and Germany.

The special reverence for the ox and the ass may be traced to apocryphal lore, but the custom expanded to include treating all animals with particular kindness on Christmas Eve and all the 12 holy nights of the Christmas season. Saint Francis urged farmers to give their animals extra hay and grain and implored the people in general to throw grain and corn of the streets so that the wild birds could feast during this blessed period. In some countries saluting animals at Christmas was so important that none could eat until animals first were fed. Throughout medieval Europe animals were fed extra portions of their regular foods, and Christmas bird feeders were stacked high with bird seeds for winter. Christian thanks to those animals who were the infant Jesus's first friends at the time of his need at the original Christmas were extended to all beasts so that they, too, could "rejoice" in the Messiah through their enjoyment of greater comfort.

When Saint Francis sang a Christmas carol at the first Bethlehem scene in Greccio, he was following a tradition from the fifth century when Christmas became an official feast day of the church and special songs were composed for the occasion. Between 400 and 1200 Christmas songs were really hymns, solemn canticles that emphasized the supernatural aspects of the Incarnation. After 1200 the songs acquired a more joyful character and generally accentuated the human elements of Christ's nativity. These joyful songs are called carols, a word derived from the Greek *choraulein* (*choros*, "dance"; *aulein*, to "play the flute"), referring to a dance accompanied by the playing of flutes. Such dancing, usually done in ring form, was very popular in ancient times among the Greeks and Romans, who spread it to the peoples in their empires. Spanish altar boys danced before the altar during mass on Christmas Day to the accompaniment of music and castanets as the congregants sang carols. English choirboys danced in the aisles of the church after morning prayers on Christmas, while the French performed "shepherd dances" in church to celebrate the occasion.

Franciscan and Dominican mystics such as Saint Francis, John Tauler (d. 1366), and Henry Suso (d. 1361) composed beautiful and tender carols that aimed to stir the emotions and heighten devotion to the infant Jesus. The Franciscan Saint Bonaventure (d. 1274) composed the beautiful "Adestes fideles" ("Oh Come, All Ye Faithful") as a poem, which was set to music in the early modern period.

In addition to song and dance, Christians celebrated the nativity of Jesus by performing plays that reenacted the events surrounding his birth. Plays derived from the Christmas *tropes* included the *Paradise Play*, which began to be performed in the 11th century. The *Paradise Play* was a mystery play that dramatized the story of Adam and Eve's expulsion from paradise. Paradise was represented by a single object, a fir tree with apples and wafers representing the Eucharist hanging from their branches. The play does not end with the tragedy of the expulsion but with the promise of Redemption through the savior and the Incarnation. The custom of the Christmas tree most probably derives from this play. Although the Paradise Play was suppressed in the 15th century because of the impious excesses of the laity, Christians began to keep a fir tree decorated with apples, known as the "paradise tree," in their homes. The custom was particularly solemnized in Byzantine homes since the Eastern Church regards Adam and Eve as saints.

Another important Christmas play was the *Play of Three Shepherds*. Customarily part of the Christmas *antiphonal* liturgy, the three shepherds sang: "Let us go and see what has been promised. Let us draw close to the manger." Two midwives stopped the shepherds. The women asked: "Whom do you seek in the manger, o Shepherds? Tell us!" The original Latin question was *Quem quaeritis in prosepe, pastores, dicite.* The shepherds replied, "The savior, the infant Lord, as the angel told us." The midwives then reported, "Here is the little one the prophet Isaiah spoke of long ago. Go now, and announce that he is born." The shepherds bowed, worshipped the mother Mary and the child in the manger, and triumphantly cried, "*Alleluia! Alleluia!* We know the truth of the prophecy, *alleluia!*"

After the shepherds left to tell the good news at the conclusion of the *Play of Three Shepherds*, bells rang wildly. Hand bells and church bells rang 12 strokes followed by another 12, three rings, then another three. These bells were called the *Virgin's welcome* or the *devil's death knell.* Christmas bells ringing news of the birth of the holy child brought Christmas night revelries to their end.

Food and drink were also important in the celebration of the Christmas days. *Wassail,* from the Old Saxon *was haile,* meaning "your health," was a Christmas beverage particular to the English. It was made of ale, roasted apples, eggs, sugar, nutmeg, cloves, and ginger and was drunk while hot. By extension the word *wassailing* was applied to any kind of Christmas revels accompanied by drinking. *Wassailing* activities were repeated in clusters of three, honoring Christ's past, present, and future coming. *Wassailing with the Milly* was the singing of wassail songs and carols while parading a large box called the *Milly box* containing a statue of the Virgin and Child. As singers passed from table to table or house to house, every guest gave a gift to the Milly, My Lady the Virgin, of coins, fruits, even precious jewels, later distributed to the needy. Giving to the Milly assured good luck. Another Christmas drink that enjoyed widespread popularity was *posset,* a sumptuous beverage uniting milk, ale, egg, and nutmeg. In the Latin countries spiced wine was the choice Christmas beverage while Germans and other northerners favored beer.

Elaborate gold and enamel-painted table fountains spouted wines, liquors, and aromatic waters from animal-head finials or architectural terminals such as in this silver-gilt and translucent enamel French fountain of the late 14th century. Courtly and humorous scenes adorn the panels. (France, late 14th century. The Cleveland Museum of Art. Gift of J. H. Wade.)

The array of baked goods associated with Christmas harkens back to its calendrical association with pre-Christian fertility rites. Across Europe people traditionally gave thanks to the old gods for the gift of bread and prayed for a bountiful harvest the next year by making special wheat or bread offerings, decorating their homes with wheat, and baking special breads and cakes. Christians adapted this tradition to the Christian season, baking such delectable traditional foods as *frumenty,* a sweet wheat dish made with boiled milk, eggs, honey, and spices. The Irish, English, Scots, and Welsh baked circular cakes flavored with caraway seeds for each member of the family. German and French Christmas cakes were topped with a likeness of the Christ child made of sugar, and the Greeks adorned theirs cakes with a crucifix. In Spain, Portugal, and Italy the Arabo-Islamic influence is clearly present in the tradition of pastries made of almonds and almond paste, such as *turrón*, the almond paste candy related to the Arabic *halwa*, and *dulce de almendra* (almond sweet), made of almonds, sugar, egg whites, and flour.

The menu and timing of the main Christmas meal varied from country to country, but the prominence of meat was universal, given its prohibition during the Advent period. Among royal and upper-class families of western Europe a boar's head was the central dish, taken to the banquet table in a procession with magnificent pomp. Other delectable meat could be venison, lamb, or beef. Those preferring fowl chose from goose, capon, or swan. Humbler families contented themselves with pigeon, chicken, or rabbit. The Christmas turkey became traditional in the early modern period when the Spaniards introduced the bird into Europe from the Americas circa 1530.

Since Christmas was a 12-day celebration, it ended in January on *Twelfth Night*. Between Christmas and Twelfth Night one somber note was sounded in the observance of *Childermas*, another name for the Christian *Feast of the Holy Innocents*, celebrated December 28. It commemorated the massacre of the children of Bethlehem two years old and younger by Herod the Great in his attempt to destroy the infant Jesus. The Feast of the Holy Innocents was also the official holiday for all choirboys and schoolboys. In the 11th century, the *Feast of the Boy Bishop* was established on December 28. A boy would be chosen from among the choir members to dress up as a bishop or patron saint. He would preside over a mock-devotional service and deliver a sermon.

EPIPHANY AND TWELFTH NIGHT

January's *Twelfth Night*, which ended the 12-day festivity of Christmas, was celebrated on January 5. Four days earlier, on the eighth day after *Christmas*, January 1, Christians celebrated the *Feast of the Circumcision*, a tradition begun in the church of Gaul in the sixth century, whence it spread to Spain, the Frankish Kingdom, and Rome in the eighth and ninth centuries. According to Matthew 2:21, Jesus was circumcised in the Jewish tradition, as a ritual sign of covenant between man and God. In the 15th century devotions to the sacred name of Jesus begun to be celebrated jointly with the Feast of the Circumcision, owing to the ancient custom by which Jewish boys also received their names at their circumcision.

The solemnity of the Feast of the Circumcision, observed with fasting and a reverent Mass, coexisted uneasily with the Bacchic secular New Year also observed on January 1. Irreverence formed part of the Twelfth Night revelries in the celebration of the *Feast of Fools (festum fatuourum)*, a church or town holiday celebrating hierarchies of church and world inverted. Clerks and priests wore masks and monstrous visages during the divine office. They danced in the choir dressed as women or minstrels, sang lascivious songs, played dice at the altar, ran about wildly in the church and throughout town making indecent gestures. Insignificant officials of cathedrals assumed the titles of bishop and cardinal, ceremonials were parodied, and revered people and sacred liturgy were mocked. Although the canons of order were reaffirmed at the end of the festival, it was suppressed in the late 15th century. The *Feast of Fools* had "carnivelesque" similarities to *April Fool's Day* and the *Feast of Asses*.

On *Twelfth Night* multiple celebrations honored the arrival of the three Magi carrying gifts to the Christ child, whose birth signified the true meaning of *Christmas. Twelfth Night* also was called *Epiphany Eve*. Epiphany (Greek, "shining forth" = manifestation) was the Christian feast on January 6, creating a triple celebration of Jesus Christ's manifestation of divine powers. First was Christ's *baptism* (Mark 1), which marked him as the Son of God. Later one of the *seven sacraments*, *baptism* signified spiritual purification realized by immersion in water or sprinking of holy water via an *aspergill*, before the ritual celebration of Christ in the *Eucharist*. Second, the journey of the three Magi to Bethlehem (Matthew 2) manifested Christ as the prophesied king. Third, the miracle at the wedding of Cana (John 20) demonstrated Jesus Christ's prerogative to perform miracles. In the Greek Church *Epiphany* also was called *Feast of the Theophania* (the "shining forth of God").

The celebration of the Feast of the Epiphany predates the celebration of Christmas in the church liturgy, introduced in third-century in Egypt and fourth-century Byzantium, where it originally commemorated the birth of Christ and his baptism. When the Latin Church fixed December 25 as the birth of Christ in the late fourth to fifth century, Epiphany began to be associated primarily with the *Adoration of the Magi*. The Eastern Church also adopted December 25 as the date of Christ's birth according to the flesh and of the Adoration of the Magi and observed Epiphany as Christ's spiritual birth through baptism in the river Jordan, and as the manifestation of his miracles at the Wedding of Cana.

There are a number of ancient liturgical customs associated with the Epiphany and particularly with the Adoration of the Magi. One custom, which began in the early Church of Alexandria, is the *proclamation of feasts*, in which the official date of Easter is calculated and publicly announced. The practice spread to the Latin Church in the sixth century. Another early practice of Eastern origin is the *blessing of the water* to commemorate Christ's baptism in the Jordan. It was customary to bless the baptismal water of all churches on that day, and in Eastern churches, the nearest or most important river is also blessed, the most famous of which is the river Nile in Egypt. After the blessing of the water in the church some of it would be distributed to the congregants in small flasks to be kept at home. This practice became widespread in the Latin Church in the 15th century.

FEAST OF THE THREE KINGS

At least since the 12th century when Archbishop Hildebert of Tours (d. 1133) referred to the Magi as "saints," the Latin Church has venerated the three Magi or kings who gave the infant Jesus gifts of gold, frankincense, and myrrh. From this time onward in the Western Church Epiphany became known popularly as the *Feast of the Three Kings*. Veneration of Saints Gaspar, Melchior, and Baltasar increased in the 13th century when Emperor Frederick Barbarossa obtained the relics of the kings from the archbishop of Milan and transferred them to Cologne in Germany, where a pilgrimage and major devotions were instituted.

The festivities of the three kings also included the performance of mystery plays. The most popular play in medieval Western Christendom was the *Office of the Star*, a pageant of the Magi's visit on the Feast of the Epiphany. This play originated in 11th-century France as a part of the liturgical service in church and soon spread into all European countries. In due time the solemn play was transformed into a boisterous affair, with the introduction of the figure of King Herod, who appeared as a raging lunatic, creating havoc by wildly waving about a wooden spear and beating clergy and laity alike.

Because of these excesses the *Office of the Star* was removed from the liturgical service, and in the 14th century it was replaced by another Epiphany play, the *Feast of the Star*, which was performed partly outside the church and partly inside, independently of the mass or the liturgical office. The first such play was held under the direction of the Franciscan friars in Milan, who ensured that the event would retain its devotional character. Wearing crowns and sumptuous vestments, the "Three Kings" appeared on horseback with a large retinue, bearing golden cups filled with myrrh, incense, and gold. They rode in state through the streets of the city to the church of Saint Eustorgius, where they dismounted, entered the church in solemn procession, and offered their gifts at the Christmas crib. Again, the custom quickly spread throughout western Europe, becoming especially popular in Germany, France, Spain, and Portugal.

An indispensable ingredient in the domestic festivities throughout Europe was the large, squat circular cake in French called "kings' cake," *gateau des rois* or *galette des rois*, also known as the *twelfth cake* or the *Dreikönig-skuchen*. Two kings' cakes allowed selection, respectively, of *king and queen of the bean*, who discovered the favor that for townsmen was a large, dried bean, but in elegant kitchens a precious gold or porcelain bean baked into the served portion. Alternatively, a single large kings' cake would be baked, hiding inside a bean for the king and a pea for the queen.

In England, once the "king" and "queen" were chosen, the festivities would continue outside in a nearby orchard or forest as the "monarchs" superintended *wassailing the trees*. In this ceremony country folk bundled up in cloaks and coats would gather around the largest, oldest tree, the one bearing most fruit during the year, and 12 wassailers rhythmically danced, chanted, and stamped, shouting, *Wassail*, shaking noisemakers and bells. Wassailers cheered the trees with tankards filled with *lamb's wool* (a cider, wine, or beer heated with sugar, nutmeg, and ginger, with roasted apples floating on the surface) and poured libations on the tree. This amusing, noisy ritual was to ensure plentiful fruits, bountiful harvest, a folk charm for encouraging trees to bear copiously and slumbering tree spirits to awaken at spring. Alternatively, people might gather around a live tree in a public hall or an apple-tree sculpture made of papier-mâché, metal, or edible marzipan.

Other *Twelfth Night* customs included the performance of short contest plays. A strong Saint George fought a powerful evil knight, biblical plays and allegories depicted battles between good and evil, and the three kings following a marvelous star outwitted wicked King Herod.

Twelfth Night celebrations imaginatively melded old classical Roman and Indo-European customs with Christian biblical and apocryphal lore surrounding the birth of Christ and the arrival of the three kings from the East. The three Magi carrying gifts to the infant Jesus, outwitting King Herod, presented in the poor stable first a gift of gold, honoring kingship; a gift of spice and frankincense suitable for a god; and the herb myrrh, portending mortality. *Twelfth Day, Epiphany*, celebrated the joyous revelation that a king of kings was born, symbolizing hope, light after darkness, death of winter, birth of Sun, death and resurrection of the Son, and after sorrow, joy.

PRE-LENTEN SEASON

Liturgical preparations for the Christian paschal feast of Easter, the day of Christ's resurrection, occur in a series of five periods, each acquiring a progressively more penitential and severe character. The five periods in chronological order are: (1) the *Season of pre-Lent*, from *Septuagesima Sunday* to *Ash Wednesday*; (2) *Ash Wednesday* (the official beginning of the Lenten season) to *Passion Sunday*; (3) *Passion Week*; (4) the first four days of *Holy Week* from

Palm Sunday to Wednesday; and (5) the *Sacred Triduum* (*Holy Thursday, Good Friday,* and *Holy Saturday*). These last three days are the culmination of penitential fervor as all observances focus solely on the commemoration and reenactment of the Lord's passion, which conclude with the Easter vigil.

The Pre-Lenten season takes place over the course of the three Sundays preceding Lent, which are called Septuagesima ("70th"), Sexagesima ("60th"), and Quinquagesima ("50th"), and was observed in the Byzantine Church as an optional fast of devotion from the fourth century. The practice was introduced into the Roman Church in the sixth century; from there it spread throughout the churches of Western Christendom.

Pre-Lenten masses are suitably somber and penitential: The priests wear the liturgical purple vestments, the joyful hymns "Gloria" and the "Te Deum" are excluded from the liturgy of the mass and the divine office, respectively, and no flowers are placed on the altar.

Clergy and laity observed the optional fast in a progressive manner. In the Byzantine Church abstention from meat began on Septuagesima Sunday. On the following Quinquagesima Sunday, people stopped eating eggs, butter, milk, and cheese.

One of the most moving customs in the Latin Church was the ritual "Farewell to Alleluia." On the Saturday before Septuagesima Sunday, this hymn named after the Hebrew exclamation of joyful praise of the Lord was officially discontinued in all liturgical services, not reintroduced until the solemn Easter vigil on the midnight before Easter Sunday. In the Middle Ages the *deposito* ("discontinuance") of the "Alleluia" assumed a more elaborate ritualized character. The "Alleluia" was bidden farewell with great emotion as though departing from a beloved friend. Thus numerous "Alleluias" were inserted into pre-*deposito* celebrations and special odes such as the "Alleluia, dulce carmen" ("Alleluia, Song of Gladness") were composed in France and elsewhere especially for the occasion.

To increase popular fervor for the "Alleluia" hymn French churches began the custom in the 11th century of celebrating a quasi-liturgical "burial of the Alleluia" on the Saturday before Septuagesima Sunday, in which choirboys officiated and the laity actively participated. Choirboys would carry a small coffin in procession down the aisle of the church mourning and moaning until they reached the cloister, where they sprinkled the coffin with incense and holy oil and buried it. Afterward, a small straw figure bearing the gold-embossed word *Alleluia* was buried in the church courtyard.

Carnival The name *Carnival* derives from the *Dominica carnivala* (Carnival Sunday), from the Latin *carnem levare* or *carnelevarium,* which means the "withdrawal" or "removal" of meat from all meals. This was the optional fast that many clergy and laity undertook on the Quinquagesima Sunday, Monday, and Tuesday preceding Ash Wednesday. For most people, however, Carnival was a time of festive merrymaking and above all fabulous feasting to ensure that every ounce of meat, bread, eggs, cheese, milk, and other fatty products was entirely consumed before the onset of the Lenten fast. Anything not consumed would be burned, a practice reminiscent of the Jewish custom of assiduously removing all leavened products from the home in preparation for Passover.

Many countries developed special foods for Carnival and especially for Tuesday, known mainly as "Fat Tuesday" from the French, *Mardi Gras,* or *Shrove Tuesday* among the British. Especially prominent are pastries made of butter, eggs, milk, and fat. The English and French prepare pancakes and crepes. Celebrations also included games, plays, masquerading, and general festivities. Dramas were performed in marketplaces and courts, such as the *Fastnachtspiel* in German-speaking areas. In England *mumming plays* incorporated Indo-European fertility and sword dances, such as the *moresca, mattachin,* and *morris dance,* whereas in the Latin countries Roman Saturnalia influences were seen in the custom of masquerading. In 15th-century Rome the pope himself instituted the Carnival pageant in Rome.

THE SEASON OF LENT

Lent was the spring season's 40-day Christian fast beginning on *Ash Wednesday* and concluding on Easter eve, commemorating Moses's, Elijah's, and Christ's 40-day fast in the wilderness. The tradition of fasting 40 days was adopted universally in the church between the third and fourth centuries and the season came to be known as the *Quadragesima* ("40th" in the Latin Church, its equivalent *Tessarakosta* in the Byzantine Church. In all Romance language countries the word for Lent is derived from the Latin term *Quadragesima,* for instance, *Cuaresma* in Spanish. The English word *Lent* derives from the Anglo-Saxon *Lengten-tide,* a reference to springtime, when the days grow longer. In Germany the period was referred to as *Fastenzeit,* meaning "fasting time."

As noted, the Lenten season is characterized by fasting from all meat and meat by-products, including milk, butter, and eggs. In addition, on Fridays and certain other days, an even more "rigorous" fast called the *jejunium* was imposed; it consisted of consuming only one meal a day and drinking only water at other times. This strict fast was relaxed after the ninth century to permit eating bread and water at other meals.

Within the liturgy of the Church Lent is the holiest of all seasons, a blessed time of enhanced penitential devotion, severe fasting, and prayer in preparation for the great feast of Easter. The solemnity of the season was manifested in church liturgy with the wearing of purple vestments and draping of the altar in purple cloth; discontinuance of the celebratory hymns the "Alleluia," "Gloria," and "Te Deum" in all seasonal masses and offices; silencing of church organs; and prohibition of weddings and other joyous celebrations. From the earliest days of the church, the *jejunium* fast, additional prayer services, ritual expulsion from the community, and other penitential exercises were imposed upon those who had committed grave public sins and crimes. Lent was also the season to prepare catechumens and new converts for their acceptance into the church via baptism. During their period of instruction in the Christian faith catechumens were frequently subjected to questions about their knowledge and understanding of what they had been taught. A public scrutiny (*scrutinia*) was held, in which the bishop determined whether the catechumen had truly renounced all his or her sins, and witnesses were produced to testify for or against the sincerity of the person's motives for baptism or conversion.

From Ash Wednesday to Passion Week
The name *Ash Wednesday* dates to the papacy of Urban II (d. 1099), who coined the term in Latin, *Feria quarta cinerum.* Previously the day was called simply the "beginning of the fast" (*initium jejunii*). During the celebratory mass priests anoint the foreheads of the congregants with blessed ashes in the form of a cross while reciting the biblical verse *Memento homo quia pulvis es et in pulverem reverteris* ("Remember, man, that thou art dust, and to dust thou shalt return") (Genesis 3:19). The use of ashes as a sign of penance and sorrow is a Jewish tradition attested in the Old Testament (cf. Jonas 3:5–9 and Jeremias 6:26 and 25:34), as well as in the New Testament in Matthew 11:21. Ash Wednesday is not observed in the Eastern Church. Lent officially begins on the Monday before Wednesday and is called Clean Monday

because the house must be completely cleansed of all meat and meat products beforehand.

In addition to the obligatory general fast, those who committed grave sins causing public scandal had to begin their period of "public penance" on Ash Wednesday. Such sinners would confess their sins to a priest beforehand and then be taken before the bishop outside the cathedral. Barefoot and dressed in humble sackcloth regardless of their social condition, the sinners stood with heads bowed in ritual humiliation as the bishop personally meted out penitential punishments and exercises according to the nature and gravity of the sin. The penitents then entered the church behind the bishop and together they sang penitential psalms, were sprinkled with holy water, and received a special sackcloth to wear. They were then led out of the church and were forbidden to enter at any time before the reinitiation ceremony of Holy Thursday. During this period the penitents were in "quarantine," physically and spiritually cut off from the church and from Christian society. Prohibited from residing with other Christians, most sought refuge in monasteries, where they went barefoot and were banned from cutting their hair or bathing.

The Lenten season is divided into various periods. *Judica Sunday* (Latin, *Iudica*, "Pass judgment on me") was the first Sunday in Lent, named for the opening words of the Latin mass of Psalm 42: "Judge me, sentence me, O God!" Medieval celebrants delighted in *Laetare Sunday* (Latin, *laetor*, to "exult"). This fourth Sunday in Lent was named from the opening words of the Mass, "Rejoice with Jerusalem." It was celebrated with a relaxing of the Lenten penitential observances. Flowers were allowed on the altar, organ music could be played during mass, and the liturgical purple was replaced by rose-colored vestments. In England the day was called *Mothering Sunday* for the custom of allowing novices to return home to the "mother" church where they had been baptized and lay flowers on the altar. Children would also give flowers to their own mothers.

Passion Sunday was the fifth Sunday in Lent, beginning *Passion Tide*, the two final weeks of Lent, and ending in *Holy Saturday*. Crucifixes, sculptures, and images in the church were draped in purple as a sign of mourning. *Palm Sunday* was the Sunday before *Easter* and *Holy Week*, commemorating Christ's exultant entry into Jerusalem, just one week before his Resurrection. In the liturgy the Passion according to Matthew (26:36–27:54) was sung in its entirety in place of the usual gospel reading of the mass. Three clergy would perform the readings in contrasting voices: The tenor represented Matthew, the voice of the narrator; the high tenor chanted the role of the individuals and crowds; and the bass intoned the words of Christ. Penitents in procession carried palm fronds that symbolized Christ's victory and represented his protection. Substitutions for palm fronds such as the Irish yew plant or the Mediterranean olive branch were used in countries where that plant was not autochthonous. The plants chosen were usually traditional symbols of immortality; both the evergreen yew and the olive tree lived for centuries and since ancient times had been planted at cemeteries.

Holy Week *Holy Week* was the calendrical week preceding *Easter*, devoted to celebrating and reenacting Christ's Passion with prayers, drama, and liturgy. Particular solemn events on *Good Friday*, a day of fasting, penitence, and abstinence, marked the only day of the liturgical year that mass was not celebrated. All events of Holy Week anticipated commemoration of Christ's Resurrection. The colors in the church, ecclesiastical vestments, music, and drama such as the "Quem quaerities trope" were essentials of the spectacular season beginning nine weeks before *Easter Sunday* (on *Sep-*

tuagesima) and ending eight weeks after Easter Sunday on *Trinity Sunday*.

Spy Wednesday was the Wednesday before *Good Friday* commemorating Judas Iscariot's betrayal of Jesus Christ (Matthew 26:14). The Christian holiday of *Easter* was closely connected to the Jewish festival called *Pesach* or *Passover*, celebrating the biblical Exodus from Egypt commemorated with a *seder*, an order of service in which a Jewish *Haggadah* was read and *matzoh*, the unleavened bread; bitter herbs; and *charoset*, the savory remembrance of mortar used for building the pyramids, were served as symbolic foods. This *Passover seder* was Christ's *Last Supper* in Jerusalem with his twelve apostles foreshadowing his betrayal. In consecrating the bread and wine, Jesus initiated the first *communion*, a first *Eucharist*, eating the spiritual food of souls. "Whoever eats my flesh and drinks my blood abides in me and I in him" (John 6:56). This Last Supper liturgically was commemorated during the *Triduum Sacrum* (Latin, "three sacred days"), *Maundy Thursday*, *Good Friday*, and *Holy Saturday*, the last three days of *Holy Week* dedicated to Christ's *Passion* and death.

Sacred Triduum: Maundy Thursday, Good Friday, and Holy Saturday *Maundy Thursday* was named either after Jesus Christ's *mandatum novum* (Latin, "new commandment"), the first words of the ceremony for washing the feet, or after the *maund*, the *alms basket* used to distribute food to the poor. Bells were silent after mass on that day until the "*Alleluia,*" during the vigil of Easter evening on *Holy Saturday*. Another name for *Maundy Thursday* was *Green Thursday* (Latin *dies viridium*, "green day") because penitents who had made Confession on Ash Wednesday were to carry green branches signifying reception into full *communion*, the rite of spiritual union between a Christian and Christ.

Also on *Maundy Thursday* the liturgical *stripping of the altars* took place. The priests dressed in liturgical purple removed the linen, candles, decorations, and veils from every altar and tabernacle except the repository shrine where the host was kept. The bare altar symbolized the denuded Christ, who was stripped of his garments before being sacrificed. It was at this time that the altars ceremonially were washed clean with holy water and wine, giving rise in Britain to the name *Sheer Thursday* (Anglo-Saxon *skere* or *sheer*, "clean" or "free from guilt"). On this day people confessed their sins and requested and received *absolution*, a priest's or bishop's conferring of formal forgiveness of sins by Christ's grace to the penitent. *Absolution* also was a service of prayers for a dead person's soul. Sinners completing the "public penance" were formally reconciled with the church by the bishop, who invited them into the church and absolved them of their sins and crimes after the Mass of Reconciliation. They were now able to resume their normal life, to bathe, and to cut their hair in preparation for the Easter celebration.

Good Friday has been known since early Church history as the day of bitterness and fasting. Its official Latin name is *Feria sexta in Parasceve*, a term ultimately derived from the word *Paraskeue*, which Greek-speaking Jews used to designate preparing for the Sabbath. The early church also employed the term *Pasch* from the Hebrew *pesach*, or Passover, to refer to both Good Friday and Easter Sunday, the former the "Pasch of Crucifixion" (*pascha staurosimon*) and the latter the "Pasch of Resurrection" (*pascha anastasimon*). As noted, Good Friday is the only day of the liturgical year in which Mass is not said. Instead, the *Synaxis*, or prayer with mass, is celebrated. Priests silently prostrate themselves before the altar, portions of the Bible are read, the Passion According to Saint John is solemnly chanted, and prayers are said on behalf of the community.

The highlight of the ceremony is the *adoration of the cross*. The presiding priest unveils the cross singing, "Behold the wood of the Cross, on which hung the Salvation of the world!" The kneeling choir and congregants respond, "Come, let us adore!" The priest then takes the cross and places it on a pillow on the floor before the altar; then all the priests approach the cross, genuflect three times, and kiss the feet of the image. The laity are then invited to do the same.

Crusaders returning from Jerusalem introduced into Europe the extraliturgical tradition of the *Holy Sepulcher*, a devotion particular to the Church of Jerusalem consisting of a vigil before the location of Christ's tomb that lasted from Good Friday until the beginning of the Easter services. Across Europe the crucifix, or the blessed sacrament, or sometimes both, were taken out of the church and paraded in a solemn procession to a shrine called the sepulcher. There the officiating priest deposited them in a tabernacle shaped like a tomb, and the faithful held vigil there throughout Good Friday and Holy Saturday. In the Byzantine Church priests or elders of the parish solemnly carried a cloth bearing an icon of the dead Christ to the shrine of the Sepulcher, where it was placed on a table and venerated by the people.

People in the Latin countries held Good Friday processions in which images of the crucified Christ and the sorrowful Virgin were taken out of the church and carried solemnly through the street on a raised platform. Those who carried the images and the laypeople who walked in procession behind them donned simple penitential robes or sackcloth and covered their heads with a hood as a sign of humility. The penitents walked through the streets in silence carrying candles. In the 13th to 15th centuries zealous flagellants inflicted terrible wounds on themselves on Good Friday and throughout the Lenten period.

Good Friday was also observed with special foods and extreme forms of fasting. In many countries people only ate bread and water. The Irish practiced the "black fast," in which they consumed nothing but tea or water all day. Meals were mostly consumed in silence and standing. It was a widespread popular tradition from Greece to the British Isles to mark the bread dough with a sign of the cross before baking it. In England the tradition of baking "hot cross buns" was introduced in the 14th century in Saint Albans Abbey so that these smaller bread portions could be more easily distributed to the poor.

Holy Saturday (*Sabbatum sanctum*) was the vigil day before Easter Sunday, commemorating Christ's resting in the tomb, anticipating *Resurrection*. Holy Saturday also was called *Easter eve*. No liturgical services were held during the daylight hours of this day until the beginning of the Easter vigil. Catechumens about to be baptized or converted would gather at the church, where the priest would perform the rite of exorcism from the powers of evil. The priest touched their ears and nostrils to symbolize the opening of the spirit to the words and grace of God. Each catechumen turned to face the west and pointed the forefinger to the direction of the sunset and uttered the words "I renounce thee, Satan, with all thy pomps and all thy works." She or he then faced eastward and made the same gesture and pronounced the words "To Thee I dedicate myself, Jesus Christ, eternal and uncreated Light." Each catechumen then recited the Creed and then retired to spend the last night before baptism in silence and prayer.

EASTER

Easter Sunday was the most solemn celebration of the Christian liturgical year. This feast commemorating Christ's *Resurrection* on the third day after his *crucifixion* honored Christ's rising from the dead, observed by the three Marys and the 12 apostles (Mark 14:50). *Easter Sunday* is rightfully called the "peak of all feasts" and the "queen of all solemnities." For the majority of the nations of Western and Eastern Christendom the festival name derives from the Greek and Latin term *pascha*, which in turn is from the Hebrew *pesach*. The English word *Easter* and the German *Ostern* derive from a Norse name (*Eostur, Eastur, Ostara,* or *Ostar*) that referred to the entire season of spring or a feast of the rising Sun. It was the English scholar and ecclesiast the Venerable Bede (d. 725) who attributed the name Easter to a pagan goddess of the dawn and of spring, *Eostre*. Most scholars now agree that the saint misinterpreted the name of the season for the name of a goddess.

At least since the fourth century, Easter celebrations have begun after sunset on Holy Saturday with the lighting of candles symbolizing the triumph of Jesus, the "uncreated and eternal light," over the darkness of sin, death, and the powers of evil. Churches and homes alike were illuminated with candles and torches turning the night into day, according to contemporary descriptions. The faithful would congregate in churches to spend the night in prayer and celebrate the Eastern vigil. The service began with the lighting of the paschal candle, which was accompanied by the jubilant singing of Easter songs. A prayer service was held, passages of the Bible were read, and everyone recited psalms. Just before midnight the priests approached the baptismal font, consecrated the water, and proceeded to baptize the catechumens. After the ceremony the new Christians were given sandals and white robes, which they wore for the remainder of Easter Week. The sacred host or cross was raised from the sepulcher in a ritual called the *elevatio*, or "raising." In solemn procession the clergy would carry the host or the cross back to the church and restore it to its place on the main altar.

Saint Patrick, the founder of the church in Ireland, is credited with instituting the tradition of lighting bonfires outside the church on Holy Saturday night as a substitute for the ancient Druid practice of lighting spring bonfires. The church approved this custom since it allowed the Christianization of surviving Indo-European spring rites common throughout Europe.

Mass on Easter Sunday was a jubilant celebration. The mournful purple liturgical vestments were replaced with white, the symbol of purity, or gold in the Byzantium tradition. Altar decorations were restored, including lilies and other flowers. The "Alleluia," "Gloria," and "Te Deum" hymns and organ music were restored to the liturgy. Congregants remained standing throughout the mass and were not allowed to kneel as a sign of the risen Lord. After mass, the doors of the church opened wide and the people sang the hymn "Surrexit Deus" (God Is Risen), and the church bells rang.

Many Easter popular customs beautifully combined Christian beliefs with Indo-European fertility concepts. Eggs were an ancient symbol of spring. The Persians, for instance, would exchange gifts of painted eggs at the spring equinox. Christians retained the symbol of the egg, seeing in it a representation of the tomb from which Jesus emerged to new life at the Resurrection. *Pace egging* was the ritual by which mummers and other entertainers performed short dramas and then begged for coins and pace eggs for their labors. *Pace* meant *Pasch*, from the same Hebrew word as the Jewish holiday of *Passover*, or *Pesach*. Pace eggs were hardboiled eggs decorated with flower and vegetable dyes, borders of lace, embroidery, and tiny glass jewels. Elaborate pace eggs were painted with each guest's family designs and coats of arms. Pace egging also was a form of egg rolling, through wickets, in particular formulaic designs, without breaking the shells.

Throughout Europe from the British Isles to Scandinavia and from the Iberian Peninsula to France, Italy, and central Europe pig or wild boar has been the favored meal to celebrate

Easter Sunday. Pre-Christian Indo-European peoples considered the pig and the wild boar to be a sign of prosperity and good luck and would consume the flesh of these animals at weddings and festivals and on other joyous occasions. In Spain eating roasted pig or boar assumed the added role of culturally distinguishing Christians from Jews and Muslims, whose religion prohibited the eating of these animals. Whether pork, boar, or lamb, the main meat dish was usually arranged on a bed of green leafy vegetables on a platter surrounded by boiled, colored Easter eggs. Easter tables overflowed with all the foods forbidden during the Lenten season: meats, sausages, cheese and other dairy products, and breads and pastries made of butter and eggs. Tables would be decorated with garlands, flowers, and plants. Easter breads would be baked with Christian symbols such as the cross, the letters *JC* or the paschal lamb.

A festive Easter custom of pre-Christian origin in Britain was the *morris dance. Morris dancers* performed stamping steps with jingling bells and holly wreaths on their heads and carried tall straight canes with flowing scarves. Accompanied by cymbals, pipes, and tabor drums, morris dancers stamped and jumped high in the air, performing traditional spring fertility rituals. Insistent tapping steps and bell ringings originally were thought to awaken slumbering field spirits. Leaping was a reminder to allow grain to grow high, flocks to multiply, and people to prosper.

Elegantly clothed and seated at the high table, the hostess, beneath a richly decorated baldachin canopy, greets the entertainers who regale the guests with music and mummery. Sword-carrying musicians play a variety of fifes, flutes, recorders, shawms, drums, and stringed instruments. Bird-masked, armed entertainers mime and act a play. Most mumming preserved ancient fertility rites, including beheadings and resurrections, as in morris dances. The lead mummer carries a baton or torch and faces the ermine-collared surveyor of ceremonies, who directs the feast, alternating courses with entertainments. From Hans Burgkmair, *Der Weisskunig*, late 15th century. Courtesy of the Metropolitan Museum of Art, New York. Gift of Anne and Carl Stein, 1961.

LOW SUNDAY AND JUBILATE SUNDAY

The first Sunday after Easter was called *Low Sunday* or *Quasimodo Sunday*, the name derived from the opening words of the introit of the mass, *quasi modo geniti*, "as if in the manner of a newborn." *Jubilate Sunday* was the third Sunday after Easter, so named from the words of the mass *jubilate deo omnis terra*, "All the Earth, rejoice in the Lord," from Psalm 100, or from the *introit*, Psalm 66, an ornate, antiphonal first chant of the mass.

FEAST OF THE ASCENSION

The *Feast of the Ascension* commemorated Christ's final triumphal appearance on Earth before leaving his astonished apostles at Bethany, outside Jerusalem, and ascending from Mount Olivet into heaven (Luke 24). In the liturgy, *Ascension* has been celebrated on the sixth Sunday after Easter in both the Roman and the Eastern Churches since the fourth century. The solemn mass emphasizes the divine mystery of the ascension rather than the historical event, noting that Christ ascended into heaven so that Christians could share in his divinity. The celebrations included a liturgical procession outside the church and up to a hill, reenacting Christ's leading his apostles "out toward Bethany" (Luke 24:50). In the Byzantine Church, the priest delivered his sermon from atop the mountain. In the 10th and 11th centuries the procession became more elaborate with the addition of theatrical elements. In Germany, for instance, these rudimentary *Ascension plays* consisted of the priest's lifting up a cross on a hill when the words *Assumptus est en coelum* ("He ascended into heaven") were psalmodized. Thirteenth-century representations took place inside the church, with the crucifix raised up to the ceiling, as the congregants stretched up their arms and sang hymns. In Bavarian churches a platform was installed in the center of the church and the image of the risen Christ would be raised aloft. Choirboys wearing white dresses and wings represented angels who descended from heaven to meet Christ and accompany him on his celestial journey.

FEAST OF THE PENTECOST

Christian *Pentecost*, the seventh Sunday after Easter, celebrated the descent of the Holy Ghost in the form of tongues of fire to the apostles (cf. Acts 2:1–4). Also called *Whitsunday* or *White Sunday*, this day required white liturgical vestments, baptismal garments, and church hangings. In Judaism *Pentecost* (Greek, "50th day") was the *Feast of Weeks*, *Shevuot*,

the 50th day after the Jewish *Passover*, or *Pesach*, commemorating both the gift of the divine law to Moses on Mount Sinai and the first fruits of harvest. It was customary in late antiquity and the early Middle Ages to imitate the Jewish custom of referring to Pentecost as the entire 50-day season. For Christians, this meant the entire period from Easter Sunday to Pentecost Sunday. Liturgical vestments are red, the color of the love of the Holy Spirit and the color of the tongues of fire. It is also a day of fasting and penitence to atone for any sins or excesses committed during the Easter season.

On the basis of the gospel account of Jesus's baptism (Luke 3:21–22), the dove was a symbol of the Holy Spirit in ecclesiastical and popular culture. Church liturgy for the Feast of Pentecost dramatized the descent of the Holy Ghost. At the sequence in the mass in which the priest sang the hymn "Venite Sancte Spiritus" (Come, Holy Spirit) the choirboys would make a sound "as of a violent, blowing wind" (Acts 2:2) by hissing, humming, rattling their benches, or blowing a trumpet. A disk decorated with an image of a dove surrounded by golden rays would then descend from the "Holy Ghost hole" in the ceiling as the choir sung. When the "dove" settled, flowers would be dropped on those present to symbolize the gifts of the Holy Spirit. In the cathedrals of France live white doves or pigeons were used in the ceremony.

TRINITY SUNDAY

Trinity Sunday honored the Holy Trinity, the central Christian mystery of God's unity and three persons, the one God existing in the Father, Son, and Holy Spirit. The early church did not celebrate Trinity Sunday, since every day of the liturgical year technically praised the mystery of the Trinity. The fixing of *Trinity Sunday* as the first Sunday after Pentecost originated in the Frankish Kingdom in the ninth century under the impetus of the abbot Alcuin (d. 804). The church of France, Germany, England, and the Netherlands quickly adopted the custom of celebrating Trinity Sunday, albeit on various dates. The official date was definitively established in 1334 by Pope John XXII. In England it was associated with Saint Thomas à Becket, consecrated in the year 1162 on that day. The Byzantine Church does not observe Trinity Sunday; the first Sunday after Pentecost is the *Feast of All Saints*.

THE FEAST OF *CORPUS CHRISTI*

Until the 14th century the church did not have a feast day devoted to the veneration of the Eucharist, the body of Christ. Maundy Thursday commemorated the institution of the first communion at the Lord's supper, but the mournful character of the tridium precluded the joyful celebration of the Eucharist. Pope Urban IV (1261–65) established the holiday in 1264 as the Thursday following Pentecost week. The feast day is intimately associated with the mystic piety of a Belgian nun, Saint Juliana (d. 1258), who received visions of the full Moon in a brilliant light except for one part of its disk, which remained dark. In one of the visions Christ appeared to her and explained its meaning, saying that the Moon represented the liturgical year and the black spot indicated the absence of a feast dedicated exclusively to the Eucharist. The bishop of Liàge and the canon lawyers of church, who included the man who would be become Pope Urban IV, supported her cause. The Dominican theologian Saint Thomas composed hymns in praise of the *Corpus Christi* (the body of Christ). *Corpus Christi* was celebrated almost from the very beginning with solemn processions in which the blessed sacrament was taken out of the church after mass and carried through the streets. Mystery plays and Corpus Christi dances formed part of the celebrations in Spain, France, Portugal, Italy, Belgium, Germany, and elsewhere.

MARIAN FEASTS

Doctrinal differences emerging in the early churches and the increasing devotion to the Virgin from the 12th century explain the establishment of numerous feast days venerating the Virgin Mary. The *Presentation of Christ in the Temple* was the Christian feast celebrated on February 2, coinciding with the *Purification Feast* or *Candlemas*. Following Jewish tradition (as depicted in Leviticus 12), the *Purification Feast* was a sacrifice of two turtle doves and two young pigeons for ritual purification of the new mother. The *Feast of the Purification* (Luke 2:22) purified Christ's mother, Mary, and commemorated the consecration of Christ at the Temple in Jerusalem. This day also coincided with *Candlemas*, a holiday noted for its ritual processions with lighted candles.

Other important holidays celebrating aspects of the Virgin Mary's life were the *Nativity of the Virgin*, celebrated from the seventh century on September 8. The *Annunciation of the Blessed Virgin Mary*, which commemorated the archangel Gabriel's announcement to Mary that she would bear the living God as Christ child, was observed on March 25 from the seventh century. Mary's death or *Dormition of the Virgin*, is discussed in chapter 5 on philosophy and religion. A particularly emotional feast was the *Feast of the Seven Sorrows*, observed on the Friday after Passion Sunday. It commemorates the painful events of her life, and especially her witnessing of the Passion of her son. The beautiful poem "Stabat Mater Dolorosa" (The Sorrowful Mother Stood) was composed for the occasion by a Franciscan friar in the early 14th century. Shrines with images of the sorrowful Virgin were installed in churches throughout Europe and became the object of profound veneration.

SAINT VALENTINE'S DAY

At least three saints named Valentine had deeds or deaths on February 14 in the second and third centuries. Somehow their names were linked to love, along with the names of Cupid and Venus, classical goddess of love, mother of the winged blind boy Cupid, who mischievously shot arrows caused people to fall in love at first sight. Saint Valentine's Day was a popular wedding day, thought in nature to be the time birds selected mates, imitated by western European people by celebrating a natural season for love.

Decorating a Saint Valentine's Day hall required love lanterns; vegetable candle holders made from hollowed out turnips, firm vegetables, or fruits; with a face cut through the skin, piercing to the now-empty center. A thick candle set inside was lighted, resembling modern Halloween jack-o-lanterns. Soft, gentle valentine lights accompanied sensual fragrances from rosemary, basil, marjoram, yarrow, and bay leaves crushed and floating on rosewater in small bowls and incense burners swinging with the fresh sweet smell of laurel and pine.

Guests wore love tokens. A small gold or silver pin worn on a chain or over the heart was called a *love knot*. An infinity sign, shaped like the number 8 resting on its side, the love knot represented perfection of affection without beginning and without end, and when made of gold, the metal never tarnishing, never dying, it signified eternal love. Women made love knots with their braided hair as their bridal coiffure, promising eternal love. Another jewelry love emblem was the *crowned A*. Worn on the chest or as metal clasp for a cloak, the letter *A* with a royal crown stood for the famous Latin tribute to Love, *amor vincit omnia*, "love conquers all," either the emotion called love or Cupid, the blind god of love, king of human love. Chaucer's proud Prioress in the *Canterbury Tales* wore a crowned *A* on her garments.

A lover wore a red heart cut from fabric or a jewelry heart celebrating love, the god of love, or its saint, Valentine. Popular love music was called the *chivaree*. The melodies and rhythms were designed to lift the spirits and create the mood for love. Some Valentine melodies imitated songs of birds, and others used stirring horn melodies with a strong beat, with rapidly increasing intensity of sounds and crescendos to arouse listeners to a thrill of pleasure and sexual excitement.

Valentine's Day foods of love included meats, fish, birds, eggs, vegetables, fruits, spices, and wines thought to be aphrodisiacs, stimulating affection. Peacock was served roasted, then refeathered, with camphor and cotton in its mouth set ablaze, making the ardent bird appear to breathe fire. Roasted partridge and stewed quail also quickened erotic emotions. At least one feast dish was made of eggs, and not simply chicken eggs. Other birds' eggs sensual to eat were those of geese, pheasant, quail, and sparrow. Seedy fruits were important foods of love, especially figs and pomegranates; apples, associated with sexual love since the biblical Garden of Eden; and sweet pears, favorite of the goddess Venus. Delicate red and purple cakes called *plum shuttles* were long finger-length oval cakes made with purple plums, currants, and caraway seeds. Resembling shuttles that weavers used to guide threads through warp and weft of cloth, the cakes signified weaving love into the fabric of life. Small heart-shaped cakes made with cherries, plums, or pomegranates indicated heartfelt feelings.

Fascinating combinations of pagan and Christian lore were preserved in Valentine's Day love divinations to answer such questions as "Who is my true love?" Divination used common objects that, studied "correctly," revealed answers. Divining by hemp seed revealed identity of a future husband or wife. A player holding a bag of hemp seed threw seeds over the left shoulder to fall either on flat ground or into a trough of water. The seed pattern foretold the beloved's name or profession. A pattern resembling a house promised a wealthy suitor; a crown implied power and nobility. Another Valentine divination used the yarrow plant, whose vigor or death portended faithfulness or faithlessness in love. Fading, wilting yarrow indicted wavering, waning love, and withered or dead leaves spelled love's doom.

APRIL FOOLS' DAY

April in various countries began with the celebration of *All Fools' Day*. The April world was upside down. Things were not what they seemed. All Fools' Day was a splendid celebration of the ridiculous. Instead of a lord or lady presiding at high table, the chair of honor was reserved for a jester, the Lord of Misrule. Dressed in fool's costume called "motley," he wore a long, floppy, pointed hat with bells at its tip and carried a scepter topped with a small head, also wearing a belled fool's cap. Servitors performed their jobs backward. Least important tables were served first, the high table last. Bows were not made toward people but from them. People wrote notes in mirror writing starting at the right side of the page with letters moving left. Festivities took place in reverse order.

All Fools' Day sometimes shared activities with the January church holiday called the *Feast of Fools*. In churches, monasteries, and schools, students controlled teachers and the young ruled the old. Among the choirboys a "boy bishop" was chosen to preside over a mock mass and deliver a sermon.

The Lord of Misrule, leading the day, also was associated with a *Feast of Asses* and *Balaam's ass*. A celebration of the *Feast of Asses*, *Festum asinorum*, was particularly popular in the French towns of Rouen and Beauvais. Short plays depicted the adventures of the biblical prophet Balaam and his wondrous donkey. For a hefty fee, an evil king asked Balaam to prophesy and curse the children of Israel. Instead, Balaam blessed them. Later, when he foolishly disregarded certain instructions God gave him, his ass obeyed them. Balaam's ass became protector of the prophet, the rider directed by his mount. Balaam's ass wisely counseled the foolish prophet who would not hear.

Other asses taught and preached on *All Fools' Day*. Interspersed among excellent feast foods and entertainments, asinine, ridiculous tales were read or acted out from a brilliantly funny 12th-century satire called the *Mirror of Fools* (*Speculum stultorum*). The late 12th-century

A jester dressed in motley blows his horn.   From a woodcut by Albrecht Dürer in Sebastian Brant, *Stultifera Navis*, Basel Johann Bergmann, 1497.

Benedictine monk Nigel Wireker wrote it about a university student at Salerno and Paris, the donkey named Brunellus the Ass, who founds a monastic order. He left farmwork because he was annoyed that his tail was too short. In his donkey world, cattle talked, turtles flew, oxen were harnessed behind their carts, donkeys gave lute concerts, and bold rabbits threatened fearful lions. The *Mirror of Fools* was written as a scathing criticism of the rival Cistercian Order and an allegory for the Christian sinner based on the words of Saint Paul in Corinthian 1:18–25): "Has not God made foolish the wisdom of the world?"

Sense in all this nonsense was *All Fools' Day's* reminder to merrymakers that though rules are uncomfortable to follow, disorder is disastrous. Conditions may seem difficult, but the world turned upside down would be even worse. After the amusements of *All Fools' Day*, people willingly turned their attentions forward and dealt with the restraints of life right side up.

MAYDAY

Mayday customs, costumes, decorations, dances, and delectable green foods signaled change of season. Many Mayday rituals were remembrances of pre-Christian ritual to seduce spring to return to the world. Dancers stamped the ground to reawaken it; shrill May horns and whistles and tinkling May bells alerted sleeping spirits of fields and forests to the new season. The *maypole* was at the center of revelry. Its strong, tall wooden shaft crowned with garlands of leaves and flowers resembled a giant tree. The *maypole* idol had long pendant streamers held by dancers who interwove them in circular patterns meant to imitate the course of the Sun. Derived from Indo-European summer solstice rites celebrating the god of vegetation in a tree, the festivities usually included *morris dances*, *mumming plays*, and *rogation processions*. Near it, the *queen of the May* was crowned.

Around it, she led circle dances and maypole contest games to identify the tallest, strongest, swiftest, prettiest, bravest, smallest, loudest, and best. Mayday festivities in a country often began before dawn. *Collecting the May* was the ceremony for young men and women going to the forest and fields to collect evergreen boughs and meadow flowers. These were woven into the wreaths and decorations for the hall, guests, and maypoles. *Going-a-Maying* was the name of the early woodland party.

Rogation days celebrated on certain Sundays during the Advent and Lenten seasons were days for Christian ceremonial processions circumnavigating the church precinct, parish, or a bonfire, to pray for good crops, protection against plague, sufficient rainfall, or other needs of the community. In times of severe drought Jews and Muslims were known also to participate in the ceremonies of Spain and Portugal. The ritual was derived from Celtic and other Indo-European fertility sun charms and *maypole* rites. The procession followed the direction of the Sun and moved against the Sun, *contra solis*, in reverse, only during times of mourning.

While on most holidays, participating in games was more important than winning games, on *Mayday*, competition and superlative performance were the purpose. In ancient Celtic spring rites, the gods were thought to listen most to requests from those already blessed with superlative abilities. The best therefore petitioned for all. Therefore the queen of the May directed games determining the fastest race, longest leap, farthest throw of a ball, longest-held note, most skillful hoop roll, most accurate ring toss, best guess of number of beans in a barrel, and finest archer. Celebrants played such games as backgammon, chess, and billiards. *Nine man's morris*, also called *merrils* or *merrelles*, was a popular pastime in Spain, France, the Scandinavian countries, Germany, and the British Isles. An illustration of the game appears in *The Book of Games* (*Los Libros de acedrex dados e tablos*) produced in the late 13th century under the auspices of King Alfonso X (1221–84) of Spain, where the game was popular among Muslims, Jews, and Christians.

Noblemen or shepherds played indoors or out- on a small well-carved board or roughly cut grass or dirt court. In the basic nine man's morris pattern, each player had nine counters, identifiable by color or shape, made of ivory or wood, carved and enameled, or simply crude sticks or stones. Counters were called *morrells*, another name for the game itself. The object was to get three morrells in a straight row. The player making such a line had the privilege of taking any one morrell from his opponent. The player collecting the most morrells won the game. When played outdoors on a life-size board with people as the counters, the movements of the players resembled a morris dance, possibly the origin of the game's name, *nine man's morris*.

MIDSUMMER EVE: THE FEAST OF SAINT JOHN THE BAPTIST

Midsummer Eve on June 24 has been celebrated as the beginning of summertime since Neolithic times among the peoples of Europe and North Africa. It commemorated the summer solstice, when the Sun seemed to stand still, the year's days were longest, and nights shortest. Midsummer festivities honored the Earth's awakening from winter's sleep, resembling the Mayday festival. Midsummer ceremonies often used divination, as magic and plant remedies were thought to be especially powerful and efficacious on that night. The vast majority of nations celebrated the summer solstice with bonfires, often accompanied by singing, dancing, or leaping.

Two feast days dedicated to Saint John the Baptist, the precursor of Jesus Christ, are among the earliest festivals of both the Eastern and the Roman Church. The *Decollation* ("Beheading") *of Saint John the Baptist* was fixed on August 29. The most important festival is the *Feast of the Nativity of Saint John the Baptist*, which was established as June 24, based on suggestions in the Gospels that the precursor was born six months before the savior. The Feast of Saint John the Baptist is one of the few saints' days that commemorate the birth rather than the death of the saint, and it is one of the very few to be endowed with the highest qualification of a *solemn* festival, meaning that it is observed as usual even if it falls on a Sunday. The liturgical honors accorded to this saint reflect his unique theological role in heralding the coming of Christ, and his proximity to Christ as his earthly cousin. This proximity to Christ is emphasized in the liturgy for Saint John's Day as well. As the festival of Christmas has, *Saint John's Day* has three masses, the first in the middle of the night on *Saint John's Eve* to symbolize his role as precursor. The second is celebrated at daybreak to symbolize his preaching and baptism, and the third is held at the hour of terce to honor his sanctity.

Popular celebrations of Saint John's Day dating from the seventh century demonstrate the ease with which Christians magnificently and merrily mixed customs of ancient Indo-European and Nordic Sun worship with medieval Christian lore. This often meant simply adding the name *Saint John* to a pre-Christian custom. In various parts of western Europe, a particular counting game was played with Saint John's bread or carob, named for the legend that while Saint John fasted alone in the desert, he kept himself alive and healthy by eating locust seedpods, his bread of life.

To a question beginning with "How many?" the answer was obtained by biting into and eating Saint John's bread, carefully removing the seeds, and counting them. The long, brown, delectably sweet seedpods from the locust tree produced flat seeds so regular in shape, size, and weight that the carob seed was a measure for precious metals and jewels. The weight of 24-carat gold or the size of a four-carat diamond originally was determined by Saint John's bread, the carob seed. Carats derived from carobs.

As in valentine divinations with yarrow, for testing whether love would endure, each guest was given a fragrant, leafy branch of the plant Saint John's Wort. If leaves did not wilt by the feast's end, love was durable. If Saint John's wort taken home overnight remained fresh in the morning, love would be vigorous and long lasting. Drooping, dying, or dead, Saint John's wort predicted a short, bleak romance. Christianity as the new belief retained what was useful in the old to make it serve the new. Pope Gregory and Saint Augustine agreed that what people enjoyed in their earlier faith could be turned to Christian advantage. Medieval physicians and churchmen often encouraged people to look for Saint John's fern as an excellent medication to change mood. Saint John's fern was thought to allow total escape from unpleasantness by providing tranquility and invisibility!

Most Midsummer entertainment revolved around building bonfires, which were believed to ward off evil spirits. In its origins the word *bonfire* referred to fires fueled by animal bones, which were thought to ward of evil spirits. Under pressure from the ecclesiastical authorities bonfires were usually lit in the open air with lighted logs, the wood considered a less "pagan" and more seemly material for combustion. In the Iberian Peninsula under the influence of the Muslim population, who also joined in the festivities, fireworks as well as bonfires lit up the night. Fire was also a feature of Midsummer Eve rogation ceremonies. People entering a midsummer festival space walked in procession toward a central pyre, which they then circled clockwise, imitating the path of the Sun, rising in the east and setting in the west. Men and boys jumped over the flame, and cattle and other livestock were driven over or near the fire to keep them free from disease.

FEAST OF SAINT JAMES THE GREAT

A popular summer liturgical festival celebrated throughout Europe was the *Feast of Saint James the Great*, observed on July 24. James, his brother John, and Peter are depicted in the Synoptic Gospels as the apostles closest to Jesus. Jesus called James and his brother "Sons of Thunder' (*Boanergas*) (Mark 3:17) because of their fiery zeal for his cause. James was the first of the apostles to be martyred. Pious apocryphal legend held that James had preached the Gospel in the Iberian Peninsula, and after his execution in 44 C.E. by King Herod, his followers transported his body to Galicia in northern Spain for burial. Centuries later his body was "rediscovered" and a shrine was built for his relics circa 900 in the Galician city of Compostela. The kings of Castile claimed the saint as their personal patron in their battles to defeat the Muslims of Spain. The saint was said to have miraculously intervened in battles clad as a warrior, riding a white horse in midair, and brandishing a sword with which he personally slew the Muslim enemy. Saint James appeared in official church iconography as the "Moorslayer," *Santiago Matamoros*, including on the facade of churches dedicated to him.

By the 12th century, the Shrine of Saint James of Compostela had become one of the Latin Church's most important shrines, on par with Rome and Jerusalem. The pilgrimage to Santiago exceeded those to Rome and Jerusalem during difficult times when access to the Holy Land was hindered by the crusader wars or by the schisms affecting the papacy. Major pilgrimage routes were established from Germany, the British Isles, and France to Galicia, drawing thousands of pilgrims every year from these lands as well as Italy, the Netherlands, and the Scandinavian countries. All the Saint James pilgrims wore a distinctive uniform consisting of a short cloak, cape, and a hat and carried a pouch for receiving alms. Pilgrims decorated their costumes with scallop shells, a symbol of Saint James and a reference to one his most famous miracles.

Those unable to make the pilgrimage in time for the feast day celebrated by building a grotto made of scallop shells (or oyster shells in their absence). Children would ask passers-by for alms to honor the saint. In France and Spain images of the saint were taken out in procession and bread was distributed to the poor. Eating scallops or oysters on that day was believed to gain good luck. Saint James's pastries, such as the Spanish *tarta de Santiago*, bore the emblem of the scallop shell or the red dagger-pointed cross, the emblem of the military religious Order of Saint James, founded in Spain in the 11th century.

LAMMAS DAY

August was bread time, especially *Lammas Day*, from Anglo-Saxon ("loaf mass"), marked by a church celebration blessing grains and breads and offering thanks to God for the good harvest. Bakers gave lessons in geometry by baking round breads, square breads, ovals, rectangles, trapezoids, and figure eights. The rainbow's colors were mixed with delicious fragrances in red rose-petal bread, golden orange saffron bread, yellow lemon bread, green parsley bread, blue thistle bread, indigo plum bread, and purple violet bread. Whimsical animal breads represented monkeys, elephants, and dragons. Architectural bread sculptures depicted castles and multidecked warships. Special molded breads depicted Eve in the Garden of Eden or Roman noblemen or kings of foreign lands. Celestial breads were stars, Sun, and Moon,

and almost every bake shop or street vendor sold pretzels, some salty, some sweet with raisins, and glazed with honey. The pretzel was a popular double-baked bread shaped in imitation of a young scholar's arms crossed on his chest in prayer.

Lammas lands were fields growing grains and crops usually fenced to keep animals out so that they would not trample or eat the harvest. On Lammas Day, however, the gates of certain fields were open and sheep and other animals were allowed to graze these Lammas Lands with free pasturage. Lammas feasts were held in townhouse, country cottage, and noble castle, with breads important for feast decorations and the menu. Tremendous bread and pastry subtleties were paraded through the hall: a bread castle, for instance, raised on a platform in the middle of the room, its colors and turrets admired until feast's end, when it was eaten. Courses were served on bread or the courses themselves consisted of types of bread, such as currant buns, shortbread, gingerbread, cucumber bread, and plum bread.

FEAST OF THE TRANSFIGURATION

In the *transfiguration* as narrated in the Gospels (Matthew 17, Mark 9, and Luke 9), Christ manifested his divinity to his disciples Peter, John, and James during his lifetime, by appearing shining to them. Accompanied by Moses and Elijah, Jesus Christ appeared with God's voice announcing, "This is my Son." Accounts variously placed this event on Mount Tabor, Mount Hermon, or the Mount of Olives. Representations of transfiguration, showing Christ's face as radiantly transformed and his clothing brilliant white, were especially common in art of the Eastern Church, where the *transfiguration* was celebrated as a feast, beginning in the sixth century. August 6 was not designated as the *Feast of the Transfiguration* in the Western Church until the 15th century.

MICHAELMAS

September 29 was celebrated in the Latin Church as the feast-day of Saints Michael, Gabriel, and Raphael the Archangels. Saint Michael's exploits as a warrior leading the heavenly armies appeared in the Bible. Apocalypse 12:7 describes a "great battle in heaven" in which "Michael and his angels fought with the dragon." Saint Michael has four missions or "offices": to lead the war against Satan, to rescue the souls of the faithful from the devil, to champion God's people as the patron saint of many military orders, and to carry souls before God at the last judgment. Saint Michael's feats also included the miraculous apparitions on mountaintops to intervene in war or fight plague. He also used his supernatural powers to create springs from rock and to endow bodies of water with medicinal curative powers. The church bestowed special honors upon Saint Michael. Churches, chapels, and monasteries located on mountaintops near the sea were named after him, such as the magnificent Mont Saint-Michel in France. In Egypt he is the patron saint of the river Nile, and in Greece and other areas of Europe he is the patron saint of thermal baths and hot springs.

In England the fall season was called *Michaelmas*. People who pay rent for house or land four times a year call the autumn quarter the Michaelmas rent. Schools and universities named their autumn term Michaelmas. Even the September Moon or harvest Moon was called the Michaelmas Moon. The pleasures of Michaelmas often included a glove, goose, and ginger.

Every September a gigantic glove suspended from a pole on the roof of an important town building represented the Michaelmas Fair. Merchants traveled from miles away and from foreign countries packing beautiful fabrics, glassware, jewelry, and wines, and local craftsmen carried saddles, swords, and fireplace tongs.

Weavers displayed tapestries, potters purveyed pitchers and platters, and farmers carted wheels of cheese and fresh vegetables. Michaelmas Fairs attracted so many thousands of people that the Pie Powder Courts held trials for those breaking market laws. The glove implied that the king, local nobleman, or town mayor gave permission for the market to welcome all sellers and buyers. The glove was symbolic of promise and contract. The king pledged to allow the fair and to provide the place and the money to announce it. The merchants and fair managers swore to give a percentage of the profits to either the nobleman or the king or a worthy charity. The English king John in 1211 granted the town of Sturbridge its charter for a fair to help support a hospital for lepers. The glove also symbolized open-handedess and generosity.

Michaelmas feast menus traditionally featured roast goose. A particularly skillful cook would skin, stuff, cook, and then refeather the bird to look as if it were alive. Carried to table with great ceremony on a platter decorated with autumn fruit and flowers, the goose was carved with special flourish, the neck reserved for the most honored guest.

Ginger accompanied feast dishes. Alternating with simpler foods were ginger ale, ginger beer, ginger wine, gingerbread, ginger snaps, and ginger cake. Michaelmas fish was baked with ginger. A fine ginger dessert called chardwardon was made with large succulent wardon pears, sugar, cinnamon, nutmeg, and, of course, ginger. Ginger caramels served with curls of ginger root shavings concluded the feast. Medieval physicians usually considered ginger a healing herb good for stomach and chest illnesses and protection against infection. Just as Saint Michael was a guardian and healer, so the ginger plant with similar qualities was remembered when he was. Ginger was its most plentiful best in Europe in September. A legend concerned a rich 12th-century merchant with a huge boatload of ginger carried from the East to sell at an English Michaelmas Fair. He refused to pay a nasty new high tax to the town; instead, he broke open his crates; hired jugglers, trumpeters, minstrels, and puppeteers to entertain; and gave away ginger free to anyone who asked. Everyone did. Each gift was plenty for a year's worth of delicacies. Supposedly, then, Michaelmas was so full of ginger, vim, and vigor that the September feast was spiced with ginger ever after.

HALLOWEEN AND THE FEAST OF ALL SAINTS

Celebrating Halloween in October represented the end of the year in the ancient Celtic calendar. October's end was also called summer's end, *Samhain*, in Gaelic. This festival allowed one last opportunity for outdoor bonfires and for games comparable to those at Mayday and June's Midsummer. The holiday signaled entrance to winter. October was the month ghosts, spirits, witches, and supernatural beings were thought most powerful and most lonely. Supernatural beings of course were important in traditional in Christian beliefs about October. Halloween was the evening before *All Hallows'* or *All Saints' Day*, when the ghosts of those departed were most likely to appear to their loved ones and plead for their intercession. The Christian holiday *All Saints' Day* was fixed on November 1 in the eighth century by Pope Gregory III (731–741) to honor all the Christian saints. The next day, November 2, was *All Souls' Day*, when prayers were offered for all the dead whose souls were waiting in purgatory. Halloween festivities combined beautifully the customs of pre-Christian Samhain with Christian Hallows.

Ruling the high table was a guest disguised as King Crispin, dressed magnificently in regal robes, crowned and flourishing a scepter, wearing a heavy chain around his neck attached to which was a large medallion with the design of one huge boot. King Crispin or Saint Crispin was the patron saint of the cordwainers, the boot makers or shoemakers who worked with cordwain, or Cordovan leather from Spain. Since Saint Crispin's Day was a few days before Halloween, the two were often combined. Halloween divinations were common and resembled the Valentine's Day divinations with hemp seed, yarrow, eringoes, and pillow faces, as well as the Midsummer divinations with diviner eggs, destiny cakes, and flowers removed petal by petal. One divination on Halloween was so common that the holiday itself was called Nutcrack Night: If a man and woman ready to be married placed whole walnuts or hazelnuts in the glowing embers of a fire, the heated nuts would burst their shells. Nuts that crackled loudly portended hope. Nuts that burned and withered suggested a human love that would briefly flame but soon parish. Other love divinations included apple paring; a whole apple was peeled with a small knife and the long spiral of apple skin thrown over the shoulder would land in a shape resembling the initial letter of the beloved's name. Apple bobbing was a frolic to which divination was added. Every apple bobbed for was given the name of a desired mate. The bobber who succeeded in biting the apple on the first try would thrive with the love of that name. If the apple was caught on the second bite, love would exist only briefly. Success on the third chance meant hate, not love.

SAINT CATHERINE'S DAY

November was the time to celebrate the Feast of Saint Catherine of Alexandria, virgin and martyr. Saint Catherine was a fourth-century noblewoman who single-handedly confronted the emperor Maximinus to reprimand him for persecuting Christians and to instruct him in the true faith. Maximinus sent his most erudite philosophers and scholars to debate with her, but each one ended up converting to Christianity. Catherine was imprisoned and sentenced to death. She was to be martyred on the wheel, but it shattered at her touch. Instead, she was beheaded. *Catherine wheels* were symbols of the death of this most famous of women saints, Saint Catherine of Alexandria. The wheel symbolized her death. In popular festivities jugglers made wheels of fire. Acrobats wearing silver ankle bands turned cartwheels, also known as Catherine wheels. Round chandeliers, round windows, and wheel-shaped pins on costumes honored Saint Catherine, patron saint of lawyers, wheelwrights, rope makers, carpenters, lace makers, spinners, unmarried women, and women students.

French unmarried women and girls would visit local images of Saint Catherine in their churches on her feast day to pray for a husband. The unfortunate girl who had reached 25 years old but was still unmarried was called a "Catherinette." Catherinettes wore special "Saint Catherine's bonnets" of yellow and green, the colors of faith and wisdom. During the Black Plague that ravaged Europe between 1346 and 1349, Saint Catherine was one of the saintly *fourteen holy helpers* invoked in rogation processions.

A Typical Fabulous Feast

The fabulous feast formed a fundamental part of any major secular or religious celebration. Customarily, townsmen and noble people as well as country folk participated in calendar festivities as lavishly as time and wealth allowed. Each person filed into the banquet hall dressed in best clothes. Rich and wealthier townspeople wore velvets, silks, jewels, and brocades. Costumed young servants directed them to their tables. The most noble guests or the host sat at the *high table*, raised above the others by a plat-

form or dais so as to see and be seen by the other guests. Behind the high table the fancy canopy called a *baldaquin* marked the seat of honor. Everyone sat according to social rank at long tables called *sideboards* arranged along the sides of the hall.

Religious feasts often featured foods that symbolized in some way the festival being honored. Multicourse meat and fowl dishes and rich pastries made of milk, flour, and eggs were *de rigueur* at weddings and harvest festivals, and on joyous liturgical occasions such as Christmas and Easter, and at the Carnival banquets leading up to the 40-day Lenten fast.

WELCOME

The *surveyor of ceremonies* was the feast hall's banquet manager. Carrying a large gold key attached to a heavy chain around his neck, the surveyor welcomed the guests heartily. There followed elaborate ceremonies before exquisitely prepared foods were elegantly served. Medieval feasting was theatrical ceremony. As important as food texture and taste were food coloring and food form. Dishes alternated with entertainments. Food followed instrumental music. Food alternated with singing and juggling. Magic, mime, minstrelsy, dancing, dramatic performance all were interspersed among feast courses.

The surveyor's inauguration of the banquet was followed by *presenting the salt* to the guests at the high table. The *salt* was an extravagant salt container. Often shaped like a ship, called a *nef*, it had practical and symbolic purpose. Salt, as a most valuable spice, signified rank. The most noble sat "above the salt." The other guests sat "below the salt." Remembering this ceremony, modern people identify the place of honor as the seat "above the salt."

The *pantler* then proceeded to the *cutting the upper crust*. The pantler, the noble servant in charge of bread, customarily slung a long,

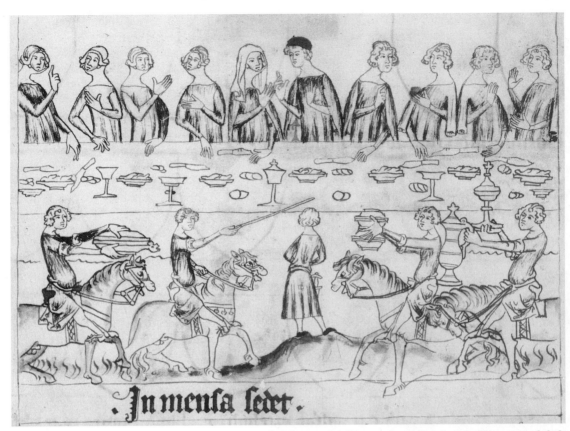

. Jn mensa sedet .

Mounted servitors carry large covered tureens and elaborate drinking and pouring vessels. The covered dish on the left has an animal-shaped mouth; the large hanap held by the cupbearer on the right is surmounted by a cross. On the table, footed drinking vessels and groaning wide-lipped serving platters share space with several knives of special design and small, sliced breads. Wielding the wand of his office is the steward, who directs the food service in the hall. Woodcut by M. Wohlgemuth, from *Der Schatzbehalter*, A Koberger, Nuremberg, 1491. Courtesy of the Metropolitan Museum of Art, New York. Rogers Fund, 1919.

fringed fabric called a *portpayne* on his shoulder. Using the fabric as if it were a presentation tray, he ceremonially carried loaves of bread. The pantler then cut the upper crust; using special knives, he horizontally cut the top from a round, delicately spiced, beautifully colored loaf. This "upper crust" he presented to the most honored guest, who then was called the "upper crust," a phrase used even today for socially important people.

Breads usually were delicately colored: red with rose petal, green with parsley, gold with saffron, violet with plum. From such fragrant loaves the pantler earlier would have fashioned the other guests' platters. Individual metal or porcelain plates also were used. But edible, aromatic, practical bread platters called *trenchers* supported various foods. With sauces and gravies well absorbed, the trenchers made nutritious, delicious bread slices to eat at the meal's end, or they were toasted to eat the next morning at breakfast, floating in wine, then called a *sop*. Bread trenchers were offered to the eager resident dogs or saved as a food gift called *alms*, given to the poor waiting at the castle gate. The *almoner* collected such gifts in a huge bowl called the *alms dish* and distributed them to the needy.

The *laverer* then presented the *aquamanile*, the pitcher holding warmed, spiced, and herbed water for hand washing. The *aquamanile* often was amusingly shaped like a lion, dragon, wolf, or griffin whose mouth was the waterspout. Hand washing served both ceremony and hygiene. On the medieval table spoons and knives were used but no forks. Rather, the portable, practical extensions of the hands, the fingers, were used in elegant finger choreography. Every feaster ate with the fingers to assure that dining pleasure lingered. Finger etiquette determined which fingers were used for picking up meat, fish, fruit, and fowl. Pinky fingers were kept free of any food, used only for conveying spice, such as dried sweet basil, cinnamon, powered mustard, salt, and sugar. Forefinger and thumb in opposition were for conveying meat or flesh. Third finger and thumb in opposition were used for fish. Fourth finger and thumb fetched fowl. Fifth fingers were reserved as spice fingers. Certainly not crude or vulgar, finger eating was as practical as ceremonial.

Next the surveyor directed the *cup bearer* to test the wine. The master of wine bottles and barrels, the *butler* poured the drink. Testing assured the hosts, noble guests, and feasters that wine and cider were pure, safe, and free of poison. The *credence test* was performed by tasting or by dipping into the fluid a credence stone such as the *bezoar stone*. The bezoar changed color in the presence of particular impurities and poisons such as arsenic. Credence testers were well-paid, trusted banquet servitors who sometimes led, short, dangerous lives.

After the clergy or host blessed the food of the feast, then horns, trumpets, cornettes, shaums, drums, and bells played the fanfare signaling service of the first of the 17 courses or 29 or 77 or 127 courses, depending upon the holiday and the wealth and magnificence of the owners of the banquet hall.

MAIN COURSE

Servitors elegantly marched dishes for presentation first to guests at the *high table*. They proceeded to serve guests in descending order of social rank. Variety of tastes, textures, and food types astonish modern audiences. Superbly prepared meats, fish, fowl, vegetables, fruits, and sweets were served for appearance as well as taste and fragrance. Beautiful feathered birds such as partridges, pheasants, and peacocks were roasted, then refeathered, to create the illusion that they were alive. Their claws and beaks gleamed with painted gold. Other illusion foods delighted by surprising, looking as though they were one thing but actually another. *Golden apples*, for instance, were delicately spiced meatballs wrapped in gold-tinted pastry with marzipan green leaves. *Saint John's urcheon* was a whimsical hedgehog sculpture made of chopped meat wrapped in brown carob pastry with edible quills. *Four-and-twenty-blackbird pie* was not filled with cooked birds but rather live, tethered, feathered creatures that when the pie shell was cut burst through it to fly around the hall to amaze and delight the guests.

Subtleties were large, dramatic festival foods made of spun sugar, almond paste, marzipan, or pastry, an edible sculpture of an elephant, lion, or fire-breathing dragon with camphor and cotton in its mouth set ablaze. Some subtleties were crafted to resemble a queen, a warrior, a pope, or symbols such as a pear tree or a unicorn in a fenced garden. Venetians dazzled their banquet guests with sculptures of the highly prized sugar molded into the shape of lions and other animals, a queen riding horseback, popes, King David, Saint Mark, plants, and fruit. Even the plates and serviettes were made of sugar.

FEAST MUSIC

Feast music announced courses and served as entertainment. Musicians walked in procession preceding servitors or played from *musicians' galleries* built high on the walls over the feasters' heads. Festival music cheered, pleased, and aided digestion. Some foods were thought best digested to particular melodies and rhythms, and some feasters because of their physiological temperaments were thought to eat best with music associated with their astrological moods. Therefore the sanguine and hopeful personality had special music, as did the phlegmatic and lethargic, the choleric and excitable, and the melancholic and sadly thoughtful. Banquet food also followed astrological temperaments, with feasters' personalities determining menu and order of food service. The best feasts suited meats, wines, herbs, and spices to the hosts' or honored guests' temperaments.

COOK, CARVER, AND WARNER

The *chief cook* of a noble house or castle customarily held a position under feudal land tenure called *petty sergeanty* granting land in return for personal service to the overlord. The chief cook's symbol of authority was a long-handled tasting spoon swinging like a medallion from a heavy chain. He tested food's quality and excellence by tasting. Often carrying a large feather brush for food painting of elaborate, fanciful dishes needing last-minute decoration, the chief cook had two major duties, protecting health and creating food art. If the banquet hall routinely served large numbers of guests, the chief cook supervised a staff of hundreds of kitchen helpers.

The *carver* was the feast expert who cut meat into portions. Carving etiquette books taught hand motions graceful as a dancer's, with particular foot positions and bows required as accompaniment for flourishings of the knives. Specially bladed and handled knives were held in proper finger positions for specific cuttings. There was a distinct carving vocabulary for each animal carved, as *breaking a deer, unbracing a mallard, winging a partridge,* and *tying a pigeon*.

Another banquet artist was the *warner*. As did the *chief cook*, the *warner* carried a feather paintbrush and a curved knife. The *warner* was a food sculptor who created *subtleties* sometimes paraded through the hall to "warn" guests that an important course was forthcoming. Subtleties were called warners, as were their creators.

BANQUET SERVITORS

Medieval feasts entertained all senses with banquet theater. The *surveyor* was chief actor and stage director, following a carefully crafted script to please an important audience. All other banquet performers had their precise parts with well-practiced entrances and exits. Each wore a costume suitable to social rank and carried an instrument both useful and symbolic of the profession. The following brief alphabetical catalog lists 22 common banquet performers on the dining hall stage. The *almoner* carried the large alms dish for collecting and dispensing food gifts to the poor. The *butler* with large keys to the wine cellar protected and mixed wines. The *carver* carried multiple knives for carving meats at table. The *chief cook*, identified by tasting spoon and painting feather, protected the feasters' health and created food art. The *cup bearer* wore on a chain around his neck a tasting cup for testing wines and drinks for purity and safety. The *dresser* carried tweezers and scissors for arranging food on serving platters. A *juggler* used balls, daggers, and rings for feats of juggling.

A *laverer* carried an *aquamanile*, bowl, and fringed towel for ceremonial and hygienic hand washing. A *magician* used balls, scarves, and boxes for feats of magic. A *master of venerie*, identifiable by his hunting horn, presented game animals as hunt trophies. A masked *mime* performed wordless drama. A *minstrel* played a

Saint and queen, Elizabeth of Hungary smuggled scraps from her own table to feed the poor while her jealous, miserly husband, the king, tried to catch her out and prosecute her for disobedience. When he tried to grab her bowl from her, the food was miraculously transformed into roses. From a hand-colored woodcut, 1470s, South German. Courtesy of the Metropolitan Museum of Art, New York. Harris Brisbane Dick Fund, 1930.

lute to accompany his singing. A *musician* carried a horn or stringed instrument for performing fanfares, music for pleasure, and melodies for digestion.

Pages, young people in household service wearing the house *livery*, directed guests to table, filled drinking cups, helped serve, and participated in hall ceremony. The *pantler* carried a *portpayne* (the bread scarf or shawl) and knives for cutting the upper crust and the edible platters, the *trenchers*. The *patisser* used an icing comb for making and decorating pastry and cakes. A *quistron* wore heavy gloves for turning the spits in kitchen or banquet hall for roasting meats and helped the *rotisser*, who carried long needlelike skewers for preparing and presenting roasted foods. The *saucer* used a stirring spoon for preparing sauces and glazes.

Most *servitors* wore a baldric, a ribbon crossing the chest from shoulder to hip, for identifying rank, house, or holiday, ceremonially serving foods at table. The *surveyor of ceremonies*, wearing a large key, directed all feast festivity. Last, the *warner* carried his painting feather and sculpturing knife for creating *subtleties*. While not every manor house throughout Europe between the 12th and 16th centuries had all these banquet performers, many had most of them. Certain jobs easily were combined. A *butler* might also be *cup bearer*, *pantler*, and *carver*. When a troupe of mimes arrived in town and magicians were in short supply, mimes made marvelous entertainment, their magic in silence.

European Christendom expressed its unique cultural identity through penitential fasting at Lent and on other solemn feast days, and through feasting on foods that often set them apart from their Jewish and Muslim neighbors. The roasted wild boar, baked hams, and pork sausages that graced the tables of medieval Christian homes and castles in Britain, France, Spain, Germany, Italy, and elsewhere, as the maximal symbol of prosperity and joy were

With wind instruments accompanying service, a noble banqueter eats from rectangular trenchers served by the pantler. Wine flagons cool in a footed cumelin. At two long sideboards, 20 feast from round trenchers, using an occasional spoon. Woodcut by M. Wohlgemuth, from *Der Schatzbehalter*, A Koberger, Nuremberg, 1491. Courtesy of the Metropolitan Museum of Art, New York. Rogers Fund, 1919.

rejected and reviled by Jews and Muslims. It was not uncommon to find Jews and Muslims participating in the celebration of certain holidays of a secular nature, such as New Year's Day and Midsummer Eve. Other Christian festivals, however, especially Holy Week and Corpus Christi, were clearly markers of a distinct religious identity and could and did become the occasion for bigoted attacks upon Jews. The following section on Jewish holidays

and festivals gives special attention to weddings, Sabbath, and liturgical festival celebration, the three cultural forms that enabled Diaspora Jews to retain their unique character whether living in Christendom or in Dar al-Islam.

JEWISH WEDDINGS, SABBATHS, AND HOLIDAYS

The *Midrash*, the collection of homilies, legends, and tales explaining Scripture, contains no fewer than four variations of the story of Rabbi Jose and the conceited woman. An exceedingly wealthy woman of ancient Rome asked Rabbi Jose Bar Shalafta, "How long did God take to create the world?" "Six days." She then asked, "And what has God been doing since that time?" Rabbi Jose replied, "The Holy One has been sitting in heaven arranging marriages."

"Indeed!" she said, "I could do that myself. Why, I could marry thousands in a single hour." So she commanded 1,000 male servants to form a single line. Then she created another line with 1,000 female servants. She paired them off. The next day there were chaos and insurrection. New husbands and wives, battered, beaten, and bedraggled, begged her to annul their marriages. They threatened revolt. She was forced to rescind her matrimonial commands. Humbly she reported she had underrated matchmaking's delicacy and difficulty. Other examples of marriages made in heaven also suggest God's direct and benevolent intervention in human affairs, particularly marriage. In some tales, God as master matchmaker of marriages revealed his matrimonial designs in the stars.

King Solomon had proprietary curiosity about one such plan of God's. The king had discovered by astrology that his beautiful daughter was destined to wed the poorest man in the nation. Amiably intending to see just how powerful were God's foreordinations, and with no intended offense to divinity or his daughter, he shut her up in a tower with sheer rock walls, guarded by 70 aged watchmen. No man, poor or rich, could approach her there.

One day a weary, tattered, barefoot young traveler fainting from hunger and cold sought shelter from the wind by sleeping in the skeleton of an ox. A giant bird swooped down and lifted the carcass with its unconscious cargo and deposited it on the tower roof at the princess's door. The next morning she found him, clothed him, and anointed him. Soon they fell in love and she asked him to marry her. Since they had no ink for the marriage contract, the *ketubah*, he wrote it with his own blood, secretly solemnizing their marriage before God. When King Solomon learned of this and learned that his new son-in-law fit the description of the prophecy, he rejoiced, blessing God, who gives wife to man.

The Midrash stories of Rabbi Jose and King Solomon express the medieval ideas animating essential Jewish ceremonies: God cares specifically and directly about his people. Earthly ceremonies merely express God's heavenly plan. Feasts, fasts, and festivals are human reconsecrations of God's ancient covenant with the Jews.

Customs and ceremonies, the *Minhagim*, simultaneously serve four purposes. Ceremony creates a mood for celebrating God's splendors. Second, holidays establish an opportunity for demonstrating piety. Third, observances unite the individual with the current Jewish community and symbolically with the 5,000-year-old heritage. Last, liturgy and ceremony set the Jew apart from others.

Nevertheless, Jewish feasts and festivals such as the wedding, the Sabbath, and the calendrical holidays such as the spring festival of Purim demonstrate astonishing cultural interdependencies. A Jewish ritual wedding headdress is indistinguishable from a pagan Roman fertility wreath. Purim revelries and parodies parallel Christian festive bonfires, bean cakes, masks, and *mummings* of the *Feast of Fools, Twelfth Night*, and *Saint John's Day*. In these Jewish traditional rites of marriage, Sabbath, and Purim, folk tradition and learned heritage magnificently converge.

The Wedding

For the marriage planned in heaven, medieval celebrations on Earth require a formidable number of professional and amateur wedding personnel. Alternatively, weddings can be valid with none at all. As in King Solomon's daughter and her bird-borne lover's marriage, personal pledges of devotion would constitute a legitimate ceremony recognized by Jewish law. Until the 16th century it was not required in Judaism, or in Christianity, to solemnize matrimony in a house of worship. No rabbi, no cantor, no formulaic promises were necessary. A man and woman would simply pledge themselves in marriage to one another before two witnesses, or 10, and exchange a token, such as a loaf of bread, a shoe, or a ring. Such marriage would be perfectly legal.

With such flexible betrothing, however, many an unintentional wedding caused grief to an unsuspecting bride who innocently received a love token given as a humorous prank or in malignant malice. Rabbis often counseled women in their communities to accept no gifts in jest lest they become accidental wives in earnest.

But while not a legal requirement, custom demanded public celebration. So did practical humane consideration. The newly married pair almost invariably were children. Consider the young bride Miriam, daughter of a local Jewish nobleman in Granada, Spain, and the young groom Yehudah, also from a family of wealth and learning, son of a rabbi and physician. Both Miriam and Yehudah were aged 14. They were not particularly young to be marrying, for such was the custom among medieval Jews as well as Christians and Muslims of child marriage arranged by parents for the good of the families or the towns. Life was too short to be wasted too long on childhood.

Miriam's cousin, aged nine, was a widow living with her parents who managed her finances while finding her another suitable husband. Her brother, age 12, waited another year at home before protesting his union with an older woman of 24. In a neighboring house, the wife of a silk merchant was pregnant. If her unborn babe was a girl, she already was legally betrothed to the equally unborn prospective son of the goldsmith. This commitment in utero could be revised, if the infants' sexes were reversed, or, of course, revoked if the sexes were identical.

The usual age of consent was 13 for a boy and 12½ for a girl, sufficient time for refusal before the marriage contract was signed and the union sexually consummated. Parents, loving their children, were not likely to make arbitrary or dangerous alliances. Nor would the professional marriage arranger, the *shadkan*, particularly if she or he valued his or her commission, which usually amounted to 1 to 2 percent of the dowry. The *shadkan* often was a respected rabbi, such as the famous 14th-century Maharil, Rabbi Jacob Levi Molin. As earthly match-maker, he simply expressed in human terms the intentions of God's matrimonial design. Often a *shadkan* was a merchant-traveler meeting at fairs and markets likely mates for townsmen less mobile.

The matchmaker frequently was a woman considered particularly skillful in balancing requirements of personality, family, and community. These arranged marriages worked as well or as poorly as those based on freer choice. A couple such as Miriam and Yehudah had a Talmudically typical two-stage betrothal. Aged 13 last year at their ceremony of engagement, called *erusin*, Yehudah lived in Miriam's father's residence for the year before their actual wedding, called *nissuin*. As was customary, he, but not she, wore a simple gold engagement band. It was a gift from her father. The young people, studying together, riding horseback, playing chess, singing, dancing, and talking, learned fondness and shared instructions of their tutors.

Elsewhere in Europe, the two-stage matrimony of *erusin* and *nissuin* was joined, often taking place the same day, as in 14th-century Germany, one at dawn, preceded by a candlelight procession; the other, in the afternoon. Or both were combined in the same service.

A wealthy bride from a distant community to be married in her husband's town in the Rhineland or Italy arrived in festive horseback procession. She might be met by riders on caparisoned horses. With musicians playing fanfares and marches, the men might engage in mock-tournaments along the way. If she arrived at night by barge on a river or canal, a torchlight procession with musicians, dancers, and jesters signaled her arrival at her future home.

The professional bride preparer combed her hair, making symbolic braids. Emulating the figure eight or love knot, the coiffure portended the endless intertwining of love. The bride preparer perfumed the bride with alluring scents and then dressed her. If the family had household servants, the bride preparer had little else to do but garb the bride in her gown, which was as colorful, rich, and elaborate as wealth allowed. Then the bride preparer cinched her around the waist or hip with a metal-linked bridal belt and crowned her head with a myrtle wreath.

Depending on the town and the century, the bride might cover her gown with a *sargenes*, a white cloak. The groom also wore over his wedding clothes a white *sargenes* with a hooded cowl. Not an assertion of virginal purity, as one might suppose, the *sargenes* was remembrance of the death shroud. All who rejoiced must be mindful of delight's mutability into disaster.

The crowns and head wreaths worn by both groom and bride were made of myrtle leaves or designed to imitate them. Leaves from the myrtle tree sacred to the love goddess Aphrodite in pagan lore were thought in Jewish folklore hospitable to benevolent spirits, the odors driving away evil demons. So myrtle crowns as well as bouquets held above the heads of the wedding party protected them against baleful spirits.

If the bride and groom were not particularly wealthy, the bride preparer would be mistress of marriage etiquette, directing the betrothal reception and supervising her catering staff for the later feast. She would rent to the parents the dishes, nappery, and extra tables and chairs for the guests. She then would act as surveyor of festivities, directing the wedding ceremonies and reception. The bride preparer also would arrange for the payment to the town of a sumptuary tax or ostentation tax, depending on the number of guests and the quality of the wedding festival.

A wedding feast almost always began on Friday. If the festivities were grand, it was not only because the family was lavishly gracious. Because so many guests traveled so far so long so hard to get there, those journeying on road or sea for two weeks had to be entertained for at least a week to justify their voyage. The musicians, the *klezmorim*, played vigorous wedding music throughout the ceremony and stimulated joyous mood not only to entertain but to signal the momentous events, such as the march to the wedding canopy, the *huppah*.

WEDDING RITUAL OBJECTS

Originally the *huppah* was an elaborate bridal pavilion, often, as the Talmud describes it, of crimson silk embroidered with gold. It was a fully enclosed tent for the marriage bed. There in the groom's house the couple would consummate their union in privacy.

Later that *huppah* pavilion was replaced by a long narrow canopy, held above the heads of bride and groom, formed of a thin prayer shawl or *tallit*. Maharil used the long veil attached to his daughter's bridal crown to cover her head and her husband's. Sometimes the *huppah* was a large square cloth, the *sudar* held high by hand. Or it was a canopy held aloft on four poles, the underside painted or embroidered with Moon and stars of the night sky. That four-poster symbolically returned to the original fertility pavilion, the multiple stars intimating the couple's future numerous bright radiant children.

The bridal ring was the second important marriage ritual object. A simple or embellished gold band was placed on the bride's forefinger of the right hand while each pledged future fidelity. Some Italian synagogues lent the couple a huge, elegant, gold, enameled, and filigreed ring, often topped with a golden building or roof, opening to reveal the words *mazel tov*: "May you have good stars and good luck." That building symbolically represented several houses: the couple's future home, or the Temple of Jerusalem, or the local synagogue. Whichever, that communal ring reaffirmed the couple's ritual place, building with their union and their progeny more mansions in God's community.

After the couple's standing beneath the *huppah* and placing the ring, the groom was expected to stamp hard on a glass placed beneath his heel. Among the learned, the groom broke the glass believing it a reminder in the midst of joy of the destruction of the Jerusalem Temple. But in Jewish folk tradition it meant something quite different. That earlier glass was a slender-necked bottle, if the bride was a virgin. If she was a widow or a divorcée, the glass was a wide-necked flask. Filled with wine, the vessel was tossed hard against a particular stone, usually on the north wall of the synagogue. Inscribed on the stone was a six- or eight-pointed star, along with the first words of Jeremiah's statement (7:34) "The voice of mirth and the voice of gladness, the voice of the bridegroom and the voice of the bride."

The broken wine bottle hurled against that stone simultaneously served as bribe and propitiation to evil spirits. The wine symbolically fed their demonic thirst and represented the blood of the virgin bride at the consummation of the marriage. The hurling of the glass and its shattering were, first, a symbolic reference to the breaking of the woman's hymen, and second, aggressive actions against evil powers that might injure the newly married happy pair or interfere with their physical reproductivity. The shattering of the glass, then, was a womb charm.

The fourth and most important wedding ritual object was the marriage contract, the *ketubah*, which guaranteed the woman's dowry rights. A legal document containing exact numbers and inventories of her goods and money, the *ketubah* protected the woman's property, particularly in case of a husband's death or their divorce. The *ketubah* also specifically enumerated the man's financial, social, and sexual obligations. Since this contract was displayed to the wedding guests and was one of the most important legal documents in the household, it usually was gorgeously embellished and illuminated. People of the book showed reverence for words by adorning those they hoped would endure.

MARRIAGE FEAST

At the wedding feast, beautiful foods and wines were served to musical accompaniment. The bride and groom ate food and drank wines thought erotically stimulating, as did the guests. Though varying from country to country, traditional marriage feast fare required at least one egg dish, one spiced and herbed capon or chicken course, and the universal triumvirate of aphrodisiac fruits: fig, pear, and pomegranate. Erotically stimulating courses alternated with instrumental music, dancing, singing, reading of epithalamia or wedding odes, chanting, juggling, moral discourses, drama, mime, and magic. Quiet, pious, staid, scholarly men and women, rabbis and students, venerable matriarchs and patriarchs, all were encouraged to rejoice at weddings and ritually abandon restraints.

Wandering scholars, *bahurim*, and itinerant rabbis claimed a place in wedding revelry, enlivening dancing and singing with new "foreign" steps, songs, or jokes from distant lands. They were welcomed to the feast as a so-called commandment meal, the *seudot*, granting hospitality. Directing these colorful matrimonial festivities was the *bodchan*, the professional comedian-musician, clever master of celebration. The *bodchan* was the merrymaker responsible for sanctifying the wedding by joy.

DIVORCE

As the *ketubah* marriage contract signified the word of union, so breaking the pledge of devotion was possible only by written document of divorce, the *get*. Another legal separation was the conditional divorce. This was especially important for people in professions requiring long travel, such as gem or spice merchants, or in particularly dangerous distant jobs, as the international ship captains.

Consider Tamar, the 12th-century woman who when married only six months said farewell to her husband, a silk merchant, who left on a trading ship bound for India. It was the same route that Maimonides' brother David followed before he drowned in a storm in the Indian Ocean. Tamar's husband vanished without trace; he never returned. That had been 12 years earlier. They were too young, too stubborn, and too sentimental to get a conditional divorce so that after a specific time if he had not returned she could be free to marry again.

No one knew whether he was dead or alive. As he was, she was forever in a limbo state. In Jewish law, she was *agunah*, somewhere between but neither wife nor widow, neither married nor maiden. A woman without womanhood, she had left to her only yearning beyond hope.

Celebrating the Sabbath

Medieval and Renaissance Judaism preeminently was family religion. To celebrate the law the total Jewish community had the synagogue at its center. Nevertheless, after the destruction of the Second Temple in Jerusalem, the focus of Jewish religious celebration became the home. In fact, the tabernacle became the table. The modest household table was altar and ark of the covenant, where ceremonies of sanctity were practiced and ritual objects were not only venerated but used. At no time was this more so than on the Sabbath. Sabbath ceremonial vessels ranged from the prosaic practical to the embellished ornamental.

The Talmud maintains that observing the day of rest is to equal all other Jewish obligations combined. So critical is the Jews' obedience to the commandment to remember the Sabbath day to keep it holy, whosoever forgets the Sabbath invites punishment in the afterlife.

Everyone deserved the Sabbath, not simply the Jews who must obey the commandment to observe: Servants of the Jews must not work on the Sabbath. According to the 12th-century moral, mystical instruction book *The Book of the Pious*, even Jews' pack animals and plow beasts must be relieved of burden and set to graze on the Sabbath. Christian goldsmiths fashioning Jewish ritual objects must not work on Saturday.

Armies in the field must cease hostilities. The 11th-century Jewish prince and army commander in Muslim Spain Samuel ibn Nagrela lit Sabbath lamps in his battlefield tent. This weekly day of rest required by God's command also provided the triple benefits of physical, mental, and moral medicine.

Sabbath observance as a domestic Jewish ritual was especially the intelligent woman's responsibility. No matter what she might learn of Torah or Talmud, no matter what she knew of Jewish law, *Halakah*, she had the privilege and the responsibility of custom and ritual: *minhagim*. Let any man debate theoretical precepts of Halakah. But let every woman express them in ceremonial beauty of *minhagim*.

For in custom and in ceremony are truth and beauty born. To achieve holiness in beauty and beauty in holiness, the concept called *hiddur mitzvah*, the Sabbath celebrant used ritual objects beautifully embellished. The purposes of using exquisite ritual objects, as Profiat Duran insisted, were to enlarge the soul, quicken the heart, and empower the mind.

Primary among the Sabbath necessities was the lamp. The woman must light it, chanting a ritual prayer. The idea of kindling two Sabbath candles commemorating the biblical injunctions to remember and to observe, *zakor* and *shamor*, is a relatively modern 18th-century phenomenon. While candles were known and used in medieval Europe, the lamp of choice was the oil lamp, either table standing or a chandelier. The Ashkenazic (or Germanic) star lamp, the *Judenstern*, was raised during weekdays, lowered by ratchets on Sabbath eve. The Sephardic (or Spanish) and Eastern Sabbath lamp was the whimsically named "pregnant hourglass" suspended by ornamented chains. Lamp lighting officially welcomed the Sabbath.

Other aspects of Sabbath ritual were observed scrupulously. Just as marriages made in heaven had their earthly actuality, so the Sabbath peace and tranquility were foretastes

A 14th-century cast and engraved bronze German Sabbath and festival lamp. The Jewish Museum/Art Resource, NY.

of paradise. The Sabbath meals themselves were prefigurations of the final feast of the righteous at the coming of the Messiah. So what otherwise might be mere kitchen chore was invested with dramatic dignity.

Hand washing served ceremony and good hygiene, for in usual medieval fashion, to assure aesthetic pleasure lingers, all foods were eaten with the fingers. An iron or bronze water pitcher, its mouth its spout, had the blessing for hand washing inscribed on its flank.

The woman arranged for the wine and the wine cups, for the saying of the kiddush blessing, and the baking of the ceremonial twist bread, the *chaleh*, which almost always was braided, either oval or round. As with the ritual unleavened bread, the matzoh at Passover, the woman superintended correct baking, beautiful finishing, and proper choreography of bread service. Symbol superseded mere sustenance.

Since kitchen labor was forbidden so that the Sabbath could be devoted to study rather than cooking, the traditional Sabbath feast food in much of western Europe was a slow-cooking stew that could be prepared the previous day. The *cholent* was an aromatic, savory stew combining in a single pot meat, vegetables, herbs, spices, and dried fruits cooked the day before and slowly mellowed overnight in a still warm oven. Cholent, challeh, fruits, cold fish dishes, cakes, and wines were conventional western European Sabbath fare.

Sabbath spices, as foods, served more than mere aesthetic pleasure. They were presented in a decorative spice box. Aromatic herbs, crushed and burned for their pleasant fragrance, called *mugmar*, common in Jewish homes during Roman times, had their substitute in myrtle and flowers both in Sabbath spice box and in sprigs on the table. The special spirit inspiring the celebrant of the Sabbath is, according to the Talmud, an extra soul inhabiting the body. It mystically rests on the myrtle and herbs and is breathed in with the aroma. A simpler rationalistic interpretation of the special Sabbath quality and the effect of its spices are increased spirituality and heightened peace of mind.

Another reason justifies the use of spices such as myrtle on Sabbath eve. Myrtle stimulates erotic emotion. An important aphrodisiac in pagan lore, the myrtle transferred to Judaism was thought especially effective for strengthening sexuality on Friday night. The Mishnah also suggested eating aphrodisiac garlic as sexual stimulus on Friday evenings. The wife's right to sex and the husband's obligation to provide it were specifically written into the marriage contract. In fact, a man's denial of his sexual responsibilities was one of the three acceptable reasons for a wife to initiate a divorce. The other two were cruelty and encroachment on personal liberty.

As with all good things, even on Sabbath eve, there were a time for going out and a time for going in. A husband and wife must not sexually join during her menstrual period. Abstinence, after all, stimulated desire. After menstruation, she must take a ritual bath, immersing herself in a *mikvah*. Some medieval women routinely preferred to bathe each Sabbath eve before joining their husbands in bed.

Reminding her of these Sabbath responsibilities, a rich medieval woman might own a splendid nielloed silver and gold coffer resembling a jewel box, a typical bridal gift, *sivlonah*. The customary design had front panels depicting the woman's three major symbolic rites or mitzvahs: *chaleh* baking, *mikvah* bathing, and candle lighting. These three obligations the Mishnah says are so important that forgetfulness of them could cause a woman to die in childbirth.

Typical Sabbath boxes had clock dials on the cover to help the woman keep her house in perfect order and her mind tranquil on the Sabbath. On a splendid box currently in the Hebrew Museum in Jerusalem there are eight dials, each with an inscription reading, sheets, tablecloths, towels, shirts, undergarments, handkerchiefs, underwear, and aprons. The dials would allow the woman to set them to reflect her exact inventories in her locked linen cabinets. On Sabbath eve, all keys were taken from the locks, placed in the coffer, and locked in, and one golden key to the key chest worn around the mistresses' neck. This would assure that no servant would steal when she was away at synagogue on the Sabbath. A beautiful, practical device, it symbolized her spiritual responsibility for the home tabernacle.

After the synagogue service conduced by rabbi and cantor, Sabbath contemplation was complemented by quiet entertainments, or exuberant story sung by the professional tale chanter, such as the German *Spielmann* wending his lyrics through Arthurian romance and fantastical heroic epic.

At twilight the beautiful ceremony called *havdalah* signaled the outgoing of the Sabbath, requiring blessings over lights and spices. The light usually was a braided candle of wax threads of two colors (customarily blue and white) intertwining. The candle represented the week's one sacred day and six profane days interanimated. The aromatic spices comforted and refreshed the mind lamenting loss of Sabbath spirituality because of return to the workaday world. But the spices also promised after another week the regaining of Sabbath peace. To followers of the mystic rabbi Rashi, havdalah spices were the myrtle leaf vehicle for the departing "extra soul" of a Sabbath. In fact, the spice box even today is called *hadas*, the Hebrew word for "myrtle." The glory of spirituality, as of other consuming passions, is its renewability.

Calendar of Jewish Festivals

Beginning with *Rosh Hashanah*, literally the "head of the year," followed by *Yom Kippur*, the sacred Day of Atonement, followed by *Sukkot*, the harvest festival, through *Chanukah*, the celebration of lights, the Jewish ritual calendar contains monthly observances commemorating both biblical and historical events.

The medieval Jewish calendar was lunar, not solar; therefore dates for holidays and festivals followed the monthly phases of the Moon. Unlike the Christian solar calendar, which primarily adhered to fixed dates for celebrating church festivals, such as Christmas on December 25, Jewish lunar reckonings make every calendrical celebration a movable feast.

Lunar reckonings of time's passage describe 12 months for each ordinary year. Ten days shorter than the solar year of the Christian world, the lunar calendar has been adjusted every few years by an additional 29-day month of *Adar*, the second *Adar*, *Adar Sheni*, making a

383-day leap year. The day after the sighting of the new Moon is called *Rosh Chodesh*, the "head of the month."

Hebrew names for the months are *Nissan, Iyyar, Sivan, Tammuz, Av, Elul, Tishri, Cheshvan, Kislev, Teveth, Shevat, Adar.* Five months have 30 days (Tishri, Shevat, Nissan, Sivan, Av), and the remaining five have 29 days to make a total of 354 days plus eight hours, 48 minutes, and 36 seconds. This short year requires the leap year readjustments to enable the lunar calendar to adhere to the biblical injunction to celebrate Passover and spring festivals within springtime and harvest celebrations such as Sukkot in the bountiful autumn.

ROSH HASHANAH

Rosh Hashanah falls on the first and second days of Tishri, the seventh month in the Jewish calendar. The name *Rosh Hashanah* is not attested in the Bible. Leviticus 23:24–25 institutes the observance of the feast under the names of *Yom Zikkaron* ("Day of Remembrance") and *Yom Teruah* ("The Day of the Sounding of the Shofar"). As the biblical names indicate, the feast day is one of introspection, of remembering the wrongdoings one may have committed toward God or one's fellows, and pledging to start anew with acts of restitution, prayer, and piety. The two days of Rosh Hashanah are the beginning of the so-called 10 Days of Awe (*Yamim Noraim*), which begin on 1 Tishri and culminate in the 10th day, Yom Kippur, the Day of Repentance.

If the Sabbath was celebrated mainly in the home, Rosh Hashanah was observed primarily in the synagogue. The blowing of the *shofar*, a horn's ram that sounds like a trumpet blast, in the synagogue was essential for the observance of Rosh Hashanah. According to Leviticus, the shofar must be blown a total of 100 times over the two-day festival. Medieval Jews would spend most of the days of Rosh Hashanah in

On Yom Kippur, as on Rosh Hashanah, the shofar is sounded and reminiscent of the Akedah. From German manuscript, early 14th century, Bodleian Library, Oxford.

the synagogue praying and listening to the sounding of the shofar blasts.

FAST OF GEDALIA

On the third day of the month of Tishri immediately after Rosh Hashanah, Jews observe the Fast of Gedalia. The origin of the fast lies in 2 Kings 25ff. and the Book of Jeremiah 40–41, which recount the political assassination of Gedalia, son of Ahikam, by a fellow Jew, Yishmael. After the Babylonians destroyed the First Temple of Jerusalem in 582 B.C.E., they appointed Gedalia king of Judea. Yishmael, a member of the royal house of David, was bent on restoring Jewish autonomy and probably resented Gedalia's appointment both because he was willing to collaborate with Babylonian rule and because he did not belong to the Davidic line. Whatever Yishmael's motivations, he murdered Gedalia and his followers, ending Jewish settlement in Judea. Jews remember this political murder as a grave sin and a tragedy since it occurred during the sacred Days of Awe and dealt the final blow to the Jewish monarchy. The Fast of Gedalia lasts from sunrise to sunset as a sign of mourning.

TEN DAYS OF AWE

The Ten Days of Awe (*Yamim Noraim*), which extend from Rosh Hashanah to Yom Kippur, are days of somber reflection. According to Jewish belief, God only forgives the sins committed against him; he does not forgive the wrongdoings that humans commit against one another. Lest these deeds be inscribed as well in the "Book of Life" on the Day of Atonement, Jews spend the days before Yom Kippur making amends to anyone whom they have hurt, for any vows that they have broken before the End of Days.

YOM KIPPUR

The Ten Days of Awe culminate in *Yom Kippur*, the Day of Atonement, a solemn feast day spent in fasting and prayer to beg God's forgiveness for sins committed and to make amends to one's fellows for any wrongdoings. The observance begins the day before as each family prepares a special banquet that much be eaten prior to sunset. During the meal each person asks and receives forgiveness from whomever he or she has wronged during the year. With this accomplished, a strict and complete fast officially begins at sunset and lasts until after nightfall on the following day. Not only are all food and drink prohibited, but people must also refrain from bathing, anointing the body with perfume or oils, or wearing leather shoes and must abstain from sexual relations.

At sunset it is customary to gather in the synagogue to recite the prayer "Kol Nidre" (All the Vows) from a special prayer book called the *Machzor*. The prayer is recited three times to signal the official beginning of the Yom Kippur feast. It may seem ironic to note that in the "Kol Nidre" prayer Jews ask God to annul all vows that they will make in the next year. The prayer is in fact a reminder of the solemn duty to honor all vows even if made under duress.

During times of persecution, when Jews were forced to convert to Christianity or Islam or were tried by the Inquisition, the "Kol Nidre" comforted those who felt bound to honor their conversion.

Another significant and special part of the Yom Kippur liturgy is the confession of the sins of the community. The confession is a two-part communal prayer: The first part, the "Ashmanu," is a brief list of sins of a general, moral nature, for instance, "We have been treasonable; we have been aggressive; we have been slanderous." The second confession, called the "Al Chet," is a longer and more specific list asking forgiveness of various sins, for instance, "For the sin we sinned before you by acting callously." These prayers conclude with a general confession asking forgiveness for breaching any of the positive commands or the negative commands, whether knowingly or unknowingly. It is interesting to note that most of the sins belong to the category of the "sins of the mouth" (*lashon ha-ra*), such as slander, lying, offensive speech, scoffing, and giving false testimony.

Most people spend the entire day at the synagogue praying. The ark of the tabernacle, which holds the Torah scrolls, is kept open throughout the festival. Yom Kippur concludes with the recitation of a lengthy prayer called "Neila." The congregation must recite the entire prayer standing before the open ark, and it should be intoned using a tone of desperation in recognition of the final opportunity to repent all sins before the Book of Life is "closed."

SUKKOT

The somberness and sobriety of Yom Kippur give way a mere five days later to the joyful celebration of the seven-day Festival of Sukkot on 15 Tishri, which is mandated in Leviticus 23:34. The unabashed ritualized joyfulness of the holiday is noted in the liturgical literature, where it is often referred to as *Zman Simchateinu* "the season of our rejoicing." During the seven days of the festival, Jews leave the comfort of their homes and live in temporary dwellings or booths, the meaning of the word *sukkot*. The holiday has a dual significance as a harvest festival and as a commemoration of a biblical event.

It recalls the 40-forty year period of wandering in the desert when the Israelites lived in temporary shelters. The booth must be made of two and a half walls and be large enough to eat and sleep in, in order to fulfill the command of "dwelling." The roof must be a material covering called *sekhakh* (lit. "covering") made of anything that grows from the ground and is cut specifically for the holiday. Typically the *sekhakh* is made of tree branches, corn stalks, or bamboo reeds and must be put on last.

Another key element of the Sukkot observance is the *Arba minim*, or "four species," of plants with which Jews are to "rejoice before the Lord," in keeping the Leviticus 23:40: "On the first day, you will take for yourselves a fruit of a beautiful tree, palm branches, twigs of a braided tree and brook willows, and you will rejoice before the Lord your God for seven days." The four plants are a citron, a palm branch, two willow branches, and three myrtle branches. The latter three are bound together and collectively are called a *luvav* ("palm branch"), while the citron, a citrus fruit, is held separately. Holding all four species in one hand, the celebrants recite a blessing and wave the species in all six directions, north, south, east, west, up, and down, symbolizing that God is everywhere. On each of the seven days of Sukkot, celebrants parade in procession around the *bimah*, the pedestal in the center of the synagogue where the Torah ark is positioned, and recite a prayer in which the words *Hosha na* ("Save us!") are repeated. The procession around the bimah recalls the ancient processions the people of Israel made around the sacred Temple in Jerusalem. On the seventh day the people circumambulate around the *bimah* seven times.

SIMCHAT TORAH

After the booths are dismantled and the period of Sukkot officially ends, the joyfulness of occasion continues for two days more with the celebration of Shmenei Atzeret and Simchat Torah, respectively. According to Leviticus 23:34, on the eighth day (the day after the seven-day observance of Sukkot), God commanded the Jews "to make a holy convocation" for the Lord. This "holy convocation" is Shmeini Atzeret, the literal meaning of which is "the assembly of the eighth day." Rabbinic literature explains that the Lord has enjoyed the presence of the Jews in his house so much during the previous seven days of Sukkot that he invites them to stay one day longer.

The following day is the festival of Simchat Torah ("Rejoicing in the Torah"), a joyful celebration that marks the end of the annual cycle of Torah readings in the synagogue. On Simchat Torah the last portion of the Torah, Deuteronomy 34, is read aloud and this is followed immediately by the reading of the first portion, Genesis 1, as a reminder that the Torah is a never-ending cycle. As a sign of their jubilee and in gratitude for the gift of Torah, the rabbi removes the Torah from the ark and the people parade with it in procession around the synagogue, singing and dancing to exhibit the happiness of the occasion. The scrolls are passed along, permitting as many people as possible the honor of carrying them, and *aliyas* ("blessings") are recited over them.

Abundant wine drinking is an essential element of the celebration.

CHANUKAH

Chanukah is the Festival of the Rededication of the Temple, also known as the Festival of

Lights for the eight days during which candles are lit at home and in the synagogue as part of the celebration. Chanukah is a postbiblical festival instituted in the text Shabbat 21b of the Babylonian Talmud (and the apocryphal Book of Maccabees), which stipulates that the feast begins on the 25th of Kislev and is to be observed with *Hallel* ("prayers of praise") and thanksgiving.

Chanukah traces its roots to the reign of Alexander the Great and his benign policy of allowing the peoples conquered to continue practicing their own religion and traditions and to maintain a degree of political autonomy. This laissez-faire attitude actually encouraged the Jews, as well as the Egyptians, Syrians, Iranians, and other subjects of the Greek Empire, to adopt Hellenist customs rather than cling to their own traditions. Under the reign of Antiochus IV, however, this live-and-let-live situation deteriorated as the king ordered the persecution of his Jewish subjects: A Hellenistic priest was appointed to control the Temple and the blasphemous sacrifice of pigs was carried out on its altar. Those who protested were murdered and the Jews were finally prohibited from practicing their religion. The ensuing Hasmonean Revolt led by Mattathias and his son, Judah the Maccabee, succeeded in defeating the Greeks and wresting the control of the Temple from the Hellenized Jews.

Legend has it that there was very little purified oil left to light the *menorah* ("candelabrum") needed to rededicate the Temple because most of it had been polluted by the Greeks in the course of performing their own religious rituals. Miraculously, the remaining oil, which should have been enough to burn throughout only one whole night, kept burning continuously for eight days, giving the Jewish priests time to prepare a fresh batch of ritually pure oil. Chanukah celebrates the memory of this glorious miracle with the burning of the menorah candles.

On the first day only one candle is lit, on the second day two candles are lit, and so on, progressively until the eighth day, when all eight are lit because, according to Shabbat 21b of the Babylonian Talmud, "We increase in sanctity but do not reduce." The menorah candelabrum has nine candle holders, one for each of the eight candles, plus one more of a slightly different height, which is called the *shammus* ("servant"). The procedure for lighting the candles is highly regimented: On the first night those present recite three blessings: *l'hadlik neir* (a general prayer over candles), *she-asah nisim* (a prayer thanking God for performing the original miracle), and *she-hekhianu* (a general prayer thanking God for being alive to celebrate this day). When the blessings are completed, a candle is lit and placed on the far right. Then the shammus candle is lit and placed in its holder. On each successive night another candle is added to the menorah from right to left; however, the candles themselves are lit from left to right. Moreover, the third blessing, the *she-hekhianu*, is only recited on the first night.

Hymns of praise are sung during the ceremonial lighting whose lyrics commemorate the miraculous events. One such hymn, dating to the 13th century, beseeches God, the "rocky fortress of my salvation" to "restore my House of Prayer" from the "blaspheming foe." Besides the lighting of the candles, the significance of oil is seen in the foods prepared for the occasion. Fried food requiring abundant oil takes pride of place.

TU BSHVAT

Tu Bshvat literally means "the 15th of the month of Shevat," the date more commonly known as the New Year for Trees. Tu Bshvat is not named as a festival in the Bible, but rather as a reminder of the tithes due to God. According to Leviticus 19:23–25, when a tree is planted, its fruit "shall be treated as forbidden and not eaten." In the fourth year all the fruit must be sanctified and offered to God, and finally in the fifth year the fruit may be consumed as normal. There is no liturgy as such that accompanies this day, but Jews would normally observe it by eating a new fruit from one of the permitted trees.

PURIM

Purim, the *Festival of Lots*, falls on the 14th and 15th of the month of Adar and is the outrageously joyful celebration of Jewish delivery from certain massacre by the Babylonian king, as a result of the ingenuity of the heroine Esther. Reading from the Book of Esther is essential to the celebration, however, as later detailed discussion will indicate, the feast is complex and filled with carnivalesque events.

PESACH

Pesach, the Jewish "Passover," is the major festival of Judaism and celebrates the miraculous delivery of the Jewish people from slavery in Egypt. The festival begins on the 15th of the month of Nissan and lasts for seven days. The name *pesach*, or "Passover," refers to the angel of the Lord who "passed over" the houses of the Jews and slew only the first sons of all the houses of the Egyptians, including pharoah's own heir. (*Pesach* also alluded to the "sacrificial offering" of the lamb that was made on this date in the Jerusalem Temple.) The festival is often referred to as the "Feast of Unleavened Bread" in recollection of the biblical command that "for seven days you shall eat unleavened bread" (Exodus 12:16).

Preparations for the festival usually begin the evening before with the complete removal of all leavened substances (*chametz*), meaning wheat, oats, spelt, rye, and barley, from the home. As will be recalled from the biblical narrative, in their hasty Exodus from Egypt, God commanded the Jews to "remove all leaven" from their homes and to take with them only the unleavened bread called *matzoh*, which is made of flour and water and cooked very quickly. Accordingly, medieval Jews removed all *chametz* products from their homes, although interesting differences arose between the Ashkenazic and Sephardic communities over the permissible ingredients for making matzoh. Sephardic Jews used *kitniyot* (literally, "bits") of non-*chametz* products such as chick peas, lentils, rice, or sesame seeds, which they ground to make bread. Ashkenazic Jews followed a stricter interpretation of the command and prohibited the use of the *kitniyot*, since they were being used as *chametz*.

Food assumes a prominent role in the celebration of Pesach. The first night of the holiday Jewish families have a special meal called the *seder* (meaning "order"), which must be consumed in a ritual order and whose ingredients are filled with symbolic meaning. So extensive is the accompanying liturgy for the ritual that it is recounted in a special prayerbook called the *Haggadah*, which narrates the story of the Exodus and explains the meaning of the symbols used in its observance. Medieval Passover Haggadahs were richly illuminated with biblical scenes.

The seder begins with a *kaddesh*, a "sanctification," of the wine that is drunk in honor of the holiday. The head of the family pronounces the blessing, everyone drinks, and a second cup is poured. Next is the *urekatz*, the ritual "washing of hands," in preparation for eating the first of the requisite food items, the *karpas*. The *karpas* is a common dark green vegetable, most often parsley, which is dipped in saltwater and eaten. The karpas symbolizes the humble origins of the Jews and the saltwater symbolizes the tears shed while in slavery.

After this, the celebrants begin to consume the matzoh bread. Altogether there should be three matzohs on the seder table. A piece from the middle bread is broken off in a ritual called *yachatz* ("breaking") and is set aside for later, while the remainder is replaced on the table. The participation of children is important in the seder ritual, and often it will be a child who is given charge of setting the broken matzoh piece aside or even hiding it.

In Ashkenazic homes the youngest child in the family takes center stage in the next ritual, the *maggid*, the "retelling of the story," of the Exodus and the first Pesach. The child asks four questions, each of which begins with the words *Mah nisthanah* ("What is different?"). In Sephardic homes the entire family will recite the questions in unison. The order of the questions also differs in the Ashkenazic and Sephardic traditions. In the former, the four questions are "Why eat matzoh?" "Why eat *maror* [bitter herbs]?" "Why dip the green vegetables twice?" and "Why recline at the dining table?" Sephardis switch the order, asking why dip twice, why eat matzoh, why eat maror, and why recline.

At the end of the maggid a blessing is pronounced over the second cup of wine and it is drunk. Among Sephardic Jews it was tradition to reenact a Passover play at this point. The person presiding over the meal would get up, leave the table, go to another room, and return with a walking stick and the *afikomen*, the piece of matzoh removed earlier, in a sack over his shoulder. The children would ask him, "Where are you coming from?" to which he would reply, "From Egypt," and he would go on to tell them the story of the Exodus. Then the children asked him, "Where are you going?" and he replied, "To Egypt!" The Ashkenazic do not perform this reenactment.

The maggid is followed by another ritual washing of the hands, called *rachtzah*, which is done while reciting a blessing in preparation for eating the matzoh. Before the matzoh is eaten, a special blessing especially for grain products, called the *ha-motzi*, is said over the bread. Another blessing is recited over the matzoh and each person eats a piece.

Next, a blessing is said over the *maror*, or bitter herbs, and a portion of them are eaten. In fact, there are two types of bitter herbs, the maror proper, usually horseradish or a bitter lettuce, and the *chazaret*, which is eaten later in the ritual. The maror is dipped in a pasty substance (the second of the ritual "dippings") usually made of wine, cooked apples, nuts, and cinnamon. The bitter herbs recall the bitterness of slavery and the paste, called *charoset*, symbolizes the mortar that the Jews used when forced to build the pharoahs' tombs in Egypt. The other bitter herbs, the *chazaret*, are eaten next, together with another piece of the matzoh bread, which together are called *korech*.

The symbolic foods are placed on a special large plate called the seder platter. Again there are noteworthy differences between Sephardic and Ashkenazic practices. Seder platters of the Sephardic Jews of Spain and Portugal were much larger than their Ashkenazic counterparts and richly decorated in the Arabic style of ceramics. Sephardic platters are larger because the Sephardim would place all six symbolic foods plus the three matzoh breads on it, while the Ashkenazis use a separate plate for the three matzoh, which in turn will have two dividers preventing the breads from touching each other.

Spanish Jews endowed the symbolic foods with kabbalistic meanings and arranged them on the platter to resemble the cabalistic "tree of life." For the Sephardim, each of the symbolic foods and the plate mystically represent the 10 *sefirot*, or attributes of the divine godhead. Thus, the three matzoh, the most important of the ritual foods, symbolize the first three *sefirot* of the godhead, *Keter* ("Crown") *Hokmah* ("Wisdom") and *Binah* ("Understanding"), and are placed at the top of the platter. Below them on the left side of the "Kabbalistic tree" are the roasted egg (*beitzah*), which symbolizes *Gevurah* ("divine judgment"), and in parallel placement on the right side is the shank bone (*zeroah*) corresponding to *Hesed* ("grace"). The maror are placed in the center of the tree and stand for *Tiferet* ("beauty"). Below to the left of the maror is the other green vegetable, *karpas*, which symbolizes *Hod* ("majesty"), while to the right is the charoset dip, which corresponds to *Netzah* ("eternity"). At the bottom of the seder platter lies the chazeret, the other bitter herb, which symbolizes *Yesod* ("foundation"). The seder platter symbolizes the *Shekinah*, representing God's kingdom or presence.

Once this symbolic meal is completed, the family moves on to the main course of the dinner, the *shulkhan oreh*. Here there are no specific requirements, except the avoidance of all leavened substances. Sephardic Jews tended to prefer lamb for the main meat dish, while Ashkenazic Jews ate beef or chicken. After dinner was finished the piece of matzoh bread set aside earlier was recovered for the dessert, or *afikomen*. Again, the children might be asked to find the bread and each person would eat a tiny bit. After this, a third cup of wine was poured and a special blessing, the *birkat ha-mazon* ("grace after the meal"), was recited, and the wine drunk. A fourth cup of wine was poured for everyone, with one extra cup for the prophet Elijah, the traditional herald of the Messiah, who is supposed to visit each home to do this. *Hallel*, or hymns of praise, were sung and a blessing was said over the last cup of wine, which everyone proceeded to drink. The Passover seder officially ended with a simple but moving closing statement, the *Nitzah*, proclaiming the end of the meal and expressing the messianic desire that next year Pesach could be celebrated in Jerusalem, meaning that the Messiah would have come.

In preparation for Elijah's "arrival" Jews would usually leave the front door open during the seder. In the Middle Ages, leaving the door open served a more practical, if pathetic purpose of assuring suspicious Christians that the Jews were not desecrating the eucharistic host or using the blood of Christian babies to make the matzoh bread. Previous chapters have noted the tragic consequences of the Christian paranoia that the Jews stole eucharistic hosts and defiled them to make their matzoh bread.

LAG BOMER

In Leviticus 23:15 the Jews were commanded to undertake the *Lag Bomer*, or "Counting of the Omer," the counting of the days between from Passover to Shavuot. In the days of the Jerusalem Temple, an *omer* a unit of measure of barley was cut and taken to the Temple as an offering. Every night from the second night of Passover to Shavuot, Jews would say a ritual blessing and count the unit of measure. Symbolically the ritual is a reminder of the connection between Passover, the commemoration of the Exodus from Egypt, and Shavuot, which celebrates the occasion when God first gave the Torah to Moses. A certain controversy surrounded when the Counting of the Omer should begin, because the word *pesach* is not mentioned in Scripture, but rather *Shabbat*, meaning "Sabbath." While the majority of opinion agreed that the Shabbat mentioned referred to the first day of Passover, which is Sabbath in the sense that no work is allowed, the Karaite sect held the view that Shabbat referred to the first Sabbath day during Passover.

SHAVUOT

The Counting of the Omer culminates in the festival of *Shavuot* (Heb. "weeks"), another of the major Jewish holy days, which falls on the fifth or sixth of the month of the month of Sivan. Shavuot, also called Pentecost, is observed on the 50th day after Passover, and as with the Counting of the Omer, Jews were likewise commanded to count the days from Passover to Shavuot (cf. Lev.21:15–16, 21). As Sukkot has, Shavuot has an agricultural symbolism linked to the ancient Temple, corresponding to the time when the first fruits were harvested and taken to the Temple as an offering of thanksgiving. But historically it celebrates the initial giving of the Torah to Moses on Mount Sinah and is thus also known as *Hag Matan Torateinu* ("Festival of the Giving of Our Torah"). Traditionally the rabbis have insisted on the term *giving*, as opposed to *receiving*, the Torah, because each day Jews "receive" the Torah when they pray; however, it was only "given" for the first time once.

Passover and Shavuot are connected spiritually, because while the Exodus freed the people of Israel from their corporeal bondage, the gift of the Torah liberated them from their spiritual bondage to sin, idolatry, and mortality. No work is allowed on Shevuot and most people would observe it by staying awake the entire night and reading and studying Torah. Traditionally one of the meals eaten on Shavuot would be a dairy meal, which some believe is a symbol of the promise to Israel of a land "flowing with milk and honey." The liturgical reading for the day is taken from the Book of Ruth.

TISHA BAV

Joy turns into mourning with the observance of *Tisha BAv*, literally, the ninth day of the month of Av, since, according to the Book of Kings 2:25, Jeremiah 52, Zechariah 7, as well as the Talmud, the worst calamities afflicting the Jews occurred during this month: The Persian king Nebuzaradan burned the Temple, the Romans destroyed the Second Temple, and the city of Jerusalem was destroyed. The same degree of severe fasting is observed on this day as on Yom Kippur with the total abstention from all food; drink, including water; and sex; refraining from

bathing and anointing the body with oil or perfume; and not wearing leather shoes. People may also adopt the ritualized gestures of mourning, refraining from smiling, laughing, or engaging in idle conversation.

A solemn liturgy is observed in the synagogue, featuring readings from Lamentations and the recitation of mourning prayers. The Torah ark is draped in a black cover. From the Middle Ages, Jewish observers began to associate the distant tragedies of the destruction of the Temple and the city of Jerusalem with the more contemporary tragedies of massacres, pogroms, and forced conversions.

Most holiday celebrations, as with the Jewish wedding, Passover, and the Sabbath, portray God's direct intervention in human affairs. The interventionist hand of God is joyfully recalled in the festival of Purim.

PURIM

Intriguingly, the Book of Esther is the only biblical book in which the name of God is not mentioned. The Purim feast and festival represent, as do the wedding and Sabbath, ingenious psychological ploys for making discipline endurable and desirable. Purim celebration also demonstrates marvelous cultural interdependencies among Christians, Muslims, and Jews, while also retaining vestiges of classical paganism.

The story is familiar: the Persian and Median king Ahasuerus angrily dismissed his wife Vashti and welcomed as queen the Jewish beauty Hadassah, or Esther, niece of the learned Mordecai. Together they overcame the wicked Prime Minister Haman's attempt to exterminate the Jews.

The Book of Esther is one of the last scrolls, a *megillah* of the third part of the Bible, called the *Hagiography* or *Ketubim*, the "Writings." Numerous elaborations upon this dramatically complete tale appear in the Apocrypha, the

Talmud, and the Midrash. The Megillah reading in the synagogue is musically presented by traditional cantillations, the joyous Megillah mode tempered by the sadder Lamentations mode. Medieval and Renaissance listeners created responses that have become traditional, many of them still sounding in Jewish temples worldwide.

First was the erasure of the tyrant Haman's name. Each time the cantor or chazzan read the name *Haman*, the audience was obligated to eliminate it. Each congregant might write the name *Haman* on one of two flat, hand-held stones and vigorously rub them together to "rub out" the name. Or each celebrant would write the hated name on the sole of the shoe and stamp and scrape at each mention of the name. The more staid wrote the word several times on a slip of paper or vellum and literally rubbed it out with an abrasive. The most common eliminator of the spoken word was cacophony by sounding a loud raucous percussion instrument, the *grogger*.

The *grogger*, a ratchet rattle particularly common in 13th-century France and Germany, was a combination of two primitive noisemakers: the "bull roarer" (an object on a string whirled around the head to make a whining sound) plus the "scraper" (a notched or ridged stick or washboard rubbed by a flat stick, creating a grating sound). The grogger has its Christian equivalent in the *crazelle* used at Mardi Gras and on Saint John's Day. In another form, lepers shook or sounded a grogger, to warn people of their approach to prevent exposure to the disease and possible contamination.

The second Purim ritual was the beating or burning of Haman in effigy. A straw figure set up in a marketplace either would be attacked by men on horseback, tilting at it with lances or swords, or placed in the synagogue courtyard or nearby, set afire, and burned until consumed. The congregants' chanting and moving in a circle followed the course of the Sun in its daily rotation. That ritual is identical to the originally pagan but later Christian bonfire rogations on Midsummer Eve or Saint John's Day. The 13th-century Italian Jewish satirist Kalonymous ben Kalonymous described the merry making around a Haman puppet set high on a stage, amid shouts of vengeance and blowing of trumpets, the custom called *ira*, Italian for "fury" and "vengeance."

Guiding festivities for the Purim carnival was the Purim king or the Purim rabbi, a young man selected to parody the habits of a venerable synagogue leader or Talmudic scholar. The Purim king delivered a mock-sermon, using language and poetic meters of Scripture in celebration of something banal such as wine. Comparable to the boy bishop or the Lord of Misrule in the Christian *Twelfth Night* (after Christmas) and *Feast of Fools*, the Jewish Purim rabbi was the intelligent fool whose socially permitted abandonment of restraint and once-yearly profanation of the sacred reaffirmed social discipline.

Similarly, the masks and masquerades, the mimes and mummeries dramatizing part of the Esther story allowed a cathartic excess, a pleasurable release from the bonds of decorum. Soon such freedom became a fear of chaos. Then it stimulated yearning for familiar restriction. Once again, the Christian *Feast of Fools*, *Twelfth Night*, and Lenten Carnival achieved similar purpose with play.

The *Purimspiele*, a drama specifically written for the Purim festival, utilized such ingenious psychological manipulation. Well known in Germany by the 15th century (though scripts apparently were not published until the 17th century), the *Purimspiele* doubtless was a phenomenon far older. Its first performers were the wedding jesters, the *bodhanim*, delivering monologue parodies of important community figures and burlesque impersonations of holy luminaries. Some early *Purimspiele* were allegorical morality plays: dialogues between personified abstractions as Good and Evil, Summer and Winter, the Learned and the Ignoramus. Others dramatized the Esther-Haman hatred or similar triumphs over political tyrants, such as David's overcoming Goliath, or Joseph's outwitting his treacherous brothers.

Common folk and students, the *bachurim*, were the major actors of the *Purimspiele*, integrating professional jesters, jugglers, and musicians in the festivities. They also borrowed stock characters from secular popular drama. Later *Purimspiele* routinely had such characters as the Loudmouth Shrew or the Charlatan Physician, emended from the popular *commedia dell'arte*. One character constant to most *Purimspiele* was named called *Montrish* or *Smart Alec*, a pompous fool. Players moved from town square to marketplace or house to court or performed in the communal dance hall. They collected money for themselves and for charity. *Purimspiele*'s humor, bawdry, and revelry were essentials of the Purim feast.

The Book of Esther expressly commands Purim days of feasting and gladness, of sending "portions" one to another; and of gifts to the poor (19:22). Three separate culinary pleasures were inherent in this biblical stricture: the making of the Purim banquets (*sedurot*), the sending of food portions to friends (*mishloah monot*), and the giving of food gifts (or money) as charity. In his hilarious parody of 13th-century Italian Purim practices, Kalonymous ben Kalonymous lists no fewer than 24 meat and pastry dishes, so respected by tradition even then that the recipes are said to have been translated down from the supreme chef to Moses at Mount Sinai.

Four of these historical cookery symbols have persevered for pleasing Purim palates among the Ashkenazic Jews today. The most familiar is the triangular, poppy-seed filled pastry *Hamantaschen*, originally called in German *Mohn* (poppyseed) *Taschen* (pockets or pouches). Similarity in sound to the hated Haman's name, plus the assumption that he wore a three-cornered Persian hat, probably caused the name change from *Mohntaschen*, "poppy pockets," to *Hamantaschen*.

A second popular feast dish is kreplah, pastry triangles filled with savory chopped meat. Supposedly kreplah with its beaten meat is eaten on those days when emotional "beating" or flogging is required, as on the Day of Atonement, Yom Kippur; on Hoshanna Rabba, when willow branches are beaten; and on Purim, when Haman's effigy is flogged. A variation upon triangular kreplah is *verenikes*, a round pastry filled with chopped liver, mashed vegetables, or a grain beaten from its plant, as *kasha*.

Queen Esther's abstemious food while in the Persian harem was commemorated by *Nahit*, *Bub*, or *Babbelech*, a vegetarian dish of salted, herbed, and spiced beans in their pods or chick peas. A fourth medieval Purim feast specialty was the bean cake. A huge cake was baked with a large bean or amulet or small sculptured favor hidden within. Whoever found the portion with the favor had the "luck" for the year, and the appointment as Purim king or Purim rabbi for the duration of the festival.

Remarkably similar to the Christian *Twelfth Night cake* or *king's cake*, in which the bean assigned the position of power to the boy bishop or King of Misrule, both Jewish fortune cakes served ceremonial purposes of reaffirming discipline after intentional unyoking from restraints. Purim encouraged hilarity and riotous behavior usually with intellectual weapons of verbal swords and stilettos meant to wound, not to kill.

Purim foods and festivities with their associated folk themes appealed alike to the more and the less educated. For the most learned scholars, Purim offered an excuse for the most scandalously ingenious Jewish satirical writing of the Middle Ages and Renaissance. The Purim parody is a particular form of satire playfully, or viciously, ridiculing the original text it imitates plus the human subject it is meant to mock. One of the earliest Purim parodies is 12th-century Menachem ben Aaron's *Hymn to the Night of Purim*. In style it is wicked parody of a religious Passover hymn. Its subject celebrates wine drinking and drunkenness and particular leaders who enjoy wine overmuch.

To appreciate these glorious medieval parodies, it is useful to acquire a new vocabulary not customarily taught in institutions of higher learning. For instance: One ought to know not only the language and rhythms of the Talmud for reading Kalonymous ben Kalonymous's *Masseket Purim*, which it parodies, but the language of bars, distilleries, and all-night feasting halls where one might meet a glutton who, fishing for a choice piece of meat, doffs his clothes to dive naked into a giant bowl of soup. Linguistically dazzling, these parodies bristle with puns and brilliant imitations of learned pomposities and of holy word. Their satire on human foibles and vices ranks among the finest condemnations of the miser, the idler, the drunk, the whore, and the hypocrite.

A culture secure in its own discipline will dare to mock its own sacred text and laugh at its own people. Certainly, exaggerations of personal debauchery are not to be read as fact. The distinguished 14th-century scientist and astronomer Levi ben Gershon wrote the *Megillat satarim*, a mock-biblical book of the prophet named Bottle. A humorously ingenious swipe at pretentiousness and at abstinence, it partly burlesques language of rabbinic exhortations to rejoice at Purim and simultaneously describes gross, illogical results of unrestrained revelry. The Purim parodies' gargantuan exaggerations extend the limits of decorum. They are great solemnizations of gullet and gut. They are as hilarious as the classical Roman *Trimalchio's Feast* satire and the Renaissance crudities of Rabelais.

Mirth and roistering characterize many medieval Purim documents. Essentially the holiday revivifies two concepts: First, tyranny can be fought and must be vanquished. Second, no matter how intense the anti-Semitism or impossible the circumstance, Jews ultimately will triumph and celebrate with relief their deliverance.

Belief in God's saving power demonstrated in the original biblical Purim was translated to personal signification in nearly 20 medieval and Renaissance special Purims. Local town, city, family, or even individual escapes from persecution annually were celebrated by name and form as "a Purim." The Purim of Shiraz celebrated 13th-century Persian Jews' relief from forced conversion to Islam. The Purim of Castile commemorated the downfall of a Haman-like Jew baiter in 14th-century Spain. The Purim of Zaragoza commemorated a 15th-century miraculous release from a potential political disaster.

Knowledge that Purim could be used as an outlet of protest against contemporary Jewish persecution led some European Christian rulers to ban Jews from celebrating it, or at least from burning the effigy of Hamam, fearing it to be a closeted attack on Christianity or Christians. Such fears had their basis in fifth-century events when Syrian Purim celebrants taunted a Christian boy, accidentally causing his death. As a result, the emperor Theodosius II (401–450) included the prohibition of the burning of Hamam effigies in the Theodosian Code issued in 438.

Likewise, there were the Purim of the Poisoned Sword, Purim of the Bombs, Purim of *Fatmilk*. All of these second or special Purims were holidays on the date pertinent to the event but shared with the biblical Purim of Esther the same pastimes, the reading of a commemorative *megillah*, the dispensing of charity to the poor, and traditional feasting and festivity.

Purim's spiritual lesson dramatically generalized to personal life of a human being or a city. The inherent message was that God's hand directly guides his people's destiny. God directly rescues his people from the destroyers' hands.

The customs and ceremonies of Purim, the Sabbath, and marriage vivify three important interdependencies: First, God directly participates in human affairs, God to man, God to woman. Second, surprising interchanges occurred among classical, Judaic, and Christian ritual forms, if not philosophies, such as marriage crowns and aromatic spices, bonfires, and masquerading fools. Many Christian holidays, such as Lent and Pentecost, were transformed versions of their Jewish predecessors. We shall also see in the next section that the celebrations of Muslim festivals, such as Ashura and Ramadan, find their precedent in Jewish parallels and share many of the same features. Third, Jewish folklore and learned tradition merged, as in the shattered wedding glass, both a decorous reminder of the Temple's destruction and a bridal fertility charm for guarding by good spirits and avoidance of evil influences. Feasts and ceremonies of Jewish marriage, Sabbath, and Purim validate studying a culture by tasting its food and testing its festivals.

ISLAMIC HOLIDAYS AND FESTIVALS

An Islamic feast or festival was called an *id*. Two major canonical festivals in the Islamic calendar are the Feast of the Sacrifice, the *Id al-Adha* or *Id al-Qurban*, and the Feast of Breaking the Fast, the *Id al-Fitr*. Of the two canonical holidays, the Feast of the Sacrifice, which ends the ritual celebrations of the hajj pilgrimage, is considered the greater feast day, hence its alternative name *al-Id al-Kabir* ("The Great Feast"), while the Feast of Breaking the Fast, which closes the month-long fast of Ramadan, is referred to as the Minor Feast (*al-Id al-Saghir*). Both shared customs and rites.

The celebration of both festivals is a solemn communal obligation, requiring the performance of the communal prayer called *The Prayer of the Two Festivals, Salat al-Idayn*. These communal prayers were held according to particular time schedules, and special donations and gifts of charity, *zakat*, were obligatory. The Prayer of the Two Festivals was led by an *imam* and was obligatory for Muslims living in a city large enough for a communal mosque, a *jami* mosque. The prayer took place in the morning between sunrise and noon. The typical Friday prayer took place after noon.

The customary Friday prayer was preceded by a first call to prayer, the *adhan*, followed by a second call to prayer, the *iqana*. Yet the Prayer of the Two Festivals was preceded by a simple invitation to prayer, a liturgical formula repeated only once: "Come to public prayer," *al-salat jami atan*. In the customary Friday prayer, the sermon, or *khutba*, preceded the prayer itself. In the Prayer of the Two Festivals, however, the *khutba* followed the prayer. The prayer itself was much simpler and shorter in form than the Friday prayer, consisting of only two *rakas*, or cycles of prayer formulas and prostrations. The *imam* and the congregation would begin the prayers by uttering many more *takbirs* (the ritual formula *Allah akbar*, or "God is great") than in the normal prayers.

On the Festival of Breaking the Fast, *id al-fitr*, the *khutba* included a set of instructions concerning the charity or alms, the *zakat*, for that festival. On the Festival of Sacrificing, the *id al-adha*, the *khutba* described the regulations for sacrifice. The local mosque was a routine site for regular Friday prayers. Yet the Prayer for the Festivals took place in the antecourtyard of the mosque, the open-air *musalla*. In the city of Mecca, however the Prayer for the Festivals took place in the Mosque of the Prophet.

In addition to the two canonical *ids*, medieval Muslims observed many voluntary festivals in the belief that the special prayers, rituals, fasts, and charitable acts that they performed on these days would merit a divine reward. The sermons of popular preachers, Sufi mystics, and the theologians who wrote treatises on the virtues (*fadail*) connected these festivals to the practices of Muhammad and promised that those who observed them would have their sins forgiven and be spared from the torments of the grave.

Ibn Iyas (d. 1525), the Egyptian historian, wrote a chronicle of Cairo during the reign of the Mamluks in which he listed the ceremonies of the Prophet's birthday, the cutting of the Cairo dike to free the Nile to flow, the beginning and end of Ramadan, and the departure and welcome of the pilgrimage caravan. Special occasions for celebration included the welcoming of a foreign ambassador and the birth of a son to the ruler. At these festivals the merchants and shopkeepers festooned the city with lights and the ruler processed in pomp and circumstance.

Certain religious judges, such as the ultraconservative Andalusian Maliki judge al-Turtushi (d. 1126) or the equally conservative Hanbali judge of Damascus Ibn Taymiyya (d. 1328), denounced these popular practices as *bida*, or innovations that departed from or contradicted with the legitimate (*sunni*) practices of Muhammad and the early Muslim community, and tried to have them banned.

Pilgrimage

The Quran commanded that the pilgrimage to Mecca, *hajj*, was a duty: "It is the duty of all men to come to the House a pilgrim, if he is able to make his way there." (Q 3:97) Though it was possible to make pilgrimage at any time of the year, the prescribed time was the month of Dhul-Hijja, the 12th month of the Muslim calendar. Every Muslim of sound mind and body was expected to make the hajj at least once in a lifetime. Those too poor or too young were excused, as were women without a husband or guardian. People on pilgrimage were never alone for long. Most pilgrims traveled in large caravans by land or sea. By the time of the Mamluks the most favored pilgrimage starting points were Cairo and Damascus. Pilgrims from the Maghrib went by sea or land to Cairo, met Egyptians traveling there, and then by land traveled in camel caravans across the Sinai desert, then through western Arabia to the holy cities. The caravans were organized by, protected by, and led in the name of the ruler of Egypt. The journey from Cairo to Mecca took between 30 and 40 days. Pilgrims from Anatolia, Iran, Iraq, and Syria met in Damascus and traveled for 30 to 40 days. Pilgrims from West Africa crossed the Sudan, then the Red Sea, and traveled from southern Iraq and the Gulf ports across central Arabia to Mecca. Depending on one's point of departure, the entire journey could take months, and accordingly many pilgrims combined travel in search of knowledge and business with the fulfillment of the religious duty.

The great 14th-century traveler Ibn Battuta expressed the exhilaration of the pilgrimage: "Of all the wondrous doings of Allah the most high he created in the hearts of men an instinctive desire to seek these sublime sanctuaries, a yearning to present themselves at these illustrious sites, and has imbued each man's heart with such love for the holy places that once one enters them they seize the whole heart and once one leaves them one suffers grief of separation." (cited in Hourani, 151)

On the approach to Mecca the pilgrim would wash to purify himself symbolically and put on a white garment symbolizing a funeral shroud called the *ihram*, customarily made of one single cloth. Women would wear either a white or a black cloak covering them from head to foot and not don any jewelry. In an act of consecration, the pilgrim said: "Here am I, O my God; here am I. No partner hast Thou; here am I. Verily the praise and the grace are Thine, and the empire." With these words pilgrims consecrated themselves in mind, body, and soul to God and pledged to refrain from any wrongdoing.

Once in Mecca the pilgrim entered the sacred area, the *haram*. By the 12th century the cluster of symbolic sites for pious visitation included the well of Zamzam that the angel Gabriel opened to save Hagar and her son, Ishmael. Nearby was the stone that preserved the patriarch Ibraham's footprint, known as the *maqam Ibrahim*. The most important building in the *haram* was the Kaaba with the holy Black Stone situated in one of its walls. The pilgrim circumambulated the rectangular Kaaba building seven times and touched or kissed the Black Stone. There were also particular places associated with *imams* of the four legal schools, the *madhhabs*.

An essential ritual of the pilgrimage was to leave the city of Mecca and go toward the hill of Arafa and stand there on the plain for a prescribed time, during which a special *khutba* ("sermon"), which emphasized repentance in preparation for the Day of Judgment, was preached. On the return to Mecca, the pilgrim stopped at Mina to throw seven stones at a pillar representing the devil. Then he sacrificed an animal. At that same time throughout the Islamic world families celebrated the Sacrificial Feast, *Id al-Adha*. For the Meccan pilgrim, the *hajj* was done. The pilgrim removed his white symbolic garment, the *ihram*, and resumed the clothes and the cares of the world, inevitably changed by this profound experience of collective piety. The pilgrim returning home also acquired a higher social status, manifested in the honorific title *Hajji* if a man and "Hajjiyya" if a woman.

FEAST OF THE SACRIFICE, *ID AL-ADHA*

On the 10th day of the month of Dhu l-Hijja, the month of the hajj, Muslims celebrate the

This 1577 miniature shows Muslim pilgrims before the Kaaba in Mecca. Bildarchiv Preussischer Kulturbesitz/Art Resource, NY.

Sacrificial Feast, *Id al-Adha*, which was also named *Id al-Nahr* and *Id al-Qurban*. On this day pilgrims made their sacrificial offerings in the valley of Mina near Mecca, sacrifice there a survival of a pre-Islamic practice maintained in Islam as part of the Prophet's *sunna*. This sacrificial feast commemorated Ibraham's (Abraham's) incomplete sacrifice of his son, Ishmael, in Muslim tradition (Isaac in the Jewish-Christian traditions). During the sacrifice ritual the participants must pronounce various prayer formulas: the *Basmala* ("In the name of God, the merciful, the compassionate") and the *Salat ala al-Nabi* ("God grant blessings and salvation to the prophet Muhammad"). They should then face the direction of Mecca and say the prayer formulas "God is great," "In the name of God, the merciful, the compassionate," and again "God is great," before beseeching God graciously to accept the sacrifice.

Muslims not traveling and wealthy enough to own an animal were assumed, though not absolutely required, to sacrifice a sheep for their own personal piety. One Muslim would sacrifice a cow or camel for as many as 10 faithful Muslims. The animal was required to be perfect: not blind, lame, skinny, or defective in ears or tail. The sacrificed animal flesh would be distributed to the poor or rich, but one-third was to be reserved for charity, *sadaqa*.

The sacrifice physically took place directly on the Festival of Sacrifice or the first or second day thereafter. The location was either the *musalla* of the mosque or a special slaughter site called a *manhar*.

PILGRIMAGE CEREMONIES

Ceremonies surrounding the yearly *hajj* to Mecca were celebrated in all Muslim countries. In addition to the Festival of the Sacrifice that coincided with the *hajj* sacrifices, Muslims celebrated three other customs: the welcoming of the pilgrim caravans, the parading of the *kiswa*, and the procession of the carriage called the *mahmal*. The *kiswa* was the fabric covering for the sacred stone of the Kaaba. The caliph in Egypt sent the *kiswa* with the pilgrim caravan after it had been ritually paraded through the streets of Cairo and Fustat before being carried to Mecca. From the 13th century on, an empty, highly decorated cart or carriage was drawn by the camel leading the caravan to Mecca. It may have contained a prayer book that was displayed to the populace after the return of the caravan from the *hajj*. For an Islamic ruler, the sending of the *mahmal*, as providing the *kiswa*, became an important statement of political independence.

Ramadan

Ramadan was the month that the Quran began to be revealed to Muhammad. All Muslims older than 10 years old were required to fast, to refrain from all food and drink, sexual intercourse, and smoking, from daylight to nightfall. These physical abstentions and hardships were a necessary precursor to the internal fast of repenting one's sins and pledging to abstain from sinful thoughts, words, or deeds. No one was excluded except those too physically weak, the mentally unfit, the heavy laborer, the warrior, and the long-distance traveler. The intention of the fast was for the pious person to draw nearer to God and to unite with other Muslims in recalling what distinguished them from other communities, namely, the revelation of the "Glorious Quran" and the blessing of the prophet Muhammad, the last, or "seal," of the prophets. In addition to maintaining the fast, the pious Muslim might spend the greater part of the day or evening praying in the mosque, reciting or listening to quranic recitation, engaging in religious studies, or listening to sermons and pious stories (*qisas*) about Muhammad and the other prophets. Each day at sunset, Muslims would break their fast in a custom called *iftar*, usually consisting of a few dates and juice followed by a larger, more festive meal. At the end of the month the entire community celebrated the holiday for Breaking the Fast, *Id al-Fitr*.

NIGHT OF THE DIVINE DECREE, THE *LAYLAT AL-QADR*

The Night of the Divine Decree, the *Laylat al-Qadr*, was celebrated on the 27th day of Ramadan and celebrated the night that Allah began to dictate the Quran to Muhammad. On this night the heavenly gates were thought to be opened and prayer especially efficacious. The Quran itself fosters this belief, saying "The Night of Prayer is better than a Thousand nights." (Q 97:3) The most pious in certain Islamic groups believed that the Quran was revealed sometime during the last 10 days of Ramadan and therefore practiced a retreat from the world, known as *itikaf*, in a mosque. The faithful gathered in the mosques at night and kept vigil, reciting the Quran in its entirety.

FESTIVAL OF BREAKING THE FAST, *ID AL-FITR*

The Festival of Breaking the Fast was celebrated on the first day of the month of Shawwal, which follows Ramadan. Two requirements were attending the Prayer of the Festivals and paying alms, *zakat al-fitr*, the latter of which must be paid before the commencement of the communal prayer. Charity consisted of food for the needy and the poor; however, many celebrants also bestowed culinary gifts on family and friends. These ritual gifts consisted of particular amounts of wheat, dates, raisins, or barley.

Popular custom added festivities and costumes. People were expected to wear clean new clothes and pay visits to the homes of relatives, friends, and patrons, as well as the graves of loved ones in the cemeteries. Clothing gifts were so common, especially in Egypt, where the caliph distributed elaborate costumes and robes of honor to members of his court and bureaucracy, that the holiday was popularly known as the *Festival Gala of Costumes, Id al-hulal*.

The route to the *musalla* of the mosque for the Festival of Breaking the Fast was required to be one way only, with the return to follow a different itinerary. The learned ascribed the one-way routing as promoting distribution of the largest amount of *zakat* to the hands of individual needy people. Yet the purpose might well have had a mystical or allegorical interpretation as well. The walk to the *musalla* provided the opportunity for the faithful to dispose of their sins before reaching the sacred service. Taking a new route home from the service prevented the pious from reencountering their old sins.

Supererogatory Festivals

THE PROPHET'S BIRTHDAY, *MAWLID AL-NABI*

The birthday of the Prophet, *mawlid al-Nabi*, was observed on the 12th day of the month of Rabi al-Awwal (the third month of the Muslim calendar) and was celebrated with prayers and ritual recitations. Writing in the 12th century, the Tunisian traveler Ibn Jubayr mentions that the official celebrations took place in Mecca, where the pious would visit the house where Muhammad was born and pray there in the hope of receiving divine blessings (*baraka*). In 14th-century Cairo, the official Mawlid al-Nabi celebration took place in the courtyard of the Citadel palace. A tall tower was constructed to give the Mamluk prince the seat of honor. On the eve of the Prophet's birthday after the evening prayer, the people gathered briefly in the palace courtyard bearing torches and candles as a symbol of Muhammad's sanctity. They returned the following day to attend the sermons and listen to the poetry and songs played in honor of the Prophet of Islam.

The Fatimid Shiites gave the holiday a great impetus as the sanctification of the Holy Family was the foundational myth of their legitimacy as descendants of the Prophet through his successor, Ali, and his wife, Fatima, the Prophet's daughter. Thus in Fatimid Egypt three other birthdays also were celebrated: the *mawlids* of Ali and Fatima and the *mawlid* of the current living *Imam*. Later the birthdays of Hasan and Husayn were added and were celebrated with elaborate ceremonials and rites. Birthdays were opportunities for the Fatimid caliph to reaffirm his legitimacy before his people, as he sat in splendor, veiled, on a balcony of his palace. Three canonical preachers (*khutaba*) of the Cairo mosques each delivered a sermon in which, in addition to extolling the blessings and virtues of the Prophet, they extolled those of the ruler, comparing him to Muhammad. The recitation of a special genre of panegyric, also called a *mawlid* or *mawlidiyyat*, formed an important part of the celebration.

Sufis also celebrated the *mawlids* of their saints in which the "birth" being commemorated was in reality the saint's death, the day he or she was "reborn" in God, a custom also observed in Christian saints' festivals. In the Middle Ages as well as today, the birthdays of Muhammad and the other Islamic prophets and local saints were popular festivals. The Sufis added their mystical practices to these birthday celebrations. A particular Sufi ritual invocation of the names of God, called *dhikr*, became extremely popular as the general public attended and participated in these practices. In Egypt celebrations of saints' birthdays included those of women saints such as *al-Sayyida Zaynab* (the daughter of Ali ibn Abi Talib) and *al-Sayyida*

Nafisa (d. 824, also a descendent of the Prophet through Ali ibn Abi Talib), as well as that of *Ahmad al-Badawi*, the renowned 12th-century founder of the Badawi Sufi order. Conservative *qadis* such as Ibn Taymiyya, referred to earlier, denounced these practices as a reprehensible imitation of the Christian cult of saints. On the other hand, many *qadis* of al-Andalus, North Africa, Egypt, and elsewhere, while recognizing that the *Mawlid al-Nabi* was an innovation (*bida*), justified and encouraged its celebration in part to deter Muslims from participating in the celebration of Christmas. To this end, children were particularly encouraged to celebrate the prophet's birthday by donning new clothes, and bringing candles to school as gifts for their teachers.

NIGHT OF ASCENSION, *LAYLAT AL-MIRAJ*

The Night of the Ascension, *Laylat al-Miraj*, commemorated the night Muhammad ascended to heaven and returned to Earth. It was celebrated on the 27th day of Rajab, the seventh month of the Muslim calendar. Some Islamic traditions associated the Night of the Ascension with Muhammad's night journey from Mecca to Jerusalem, the *isra*. According to the legend, one night Muhammad was sleeping in Mecca when the angel Jibrail (Gabriel) took him to a winged creature called al-Buraq and transported him across to sky to "the farthest mosque," which most sources identify as Jerusalem. From there he ascended the ladder into the seven heavens, where he encountered and conversed with the previous prophets, including Ibrahim, Moses, and Jesus, before going before the seat of God. During this encounter God commands that Muslims pray five times a day. That event was celebrated with prayers and recitations of the details of Muhammad's famous night journey on the winged al-Buraq to the holy city.

NIGHT OF FORGIVENESS, *LAYLAT AL-BARAA*

The Night of Forgiveness or the Night of Quittance, the *Laylat al-Baraa*, was celebrated on the 15th day of the month of Shaban, the eighth month of the Muslim calendar. That holiday commemorated the time that God descended to the lowest of the seven heavens and summoned human beings to request his forgiveness of their sins. On that night the tree of life was shaken. On each leaf of the tree the name of a living being was inscribed. When the tree was shaken, certain leaves fell to the ground. On those leaves were the names of those who would die in the forthcoming year. Muslims spend the night in prayer and sometimes fasting in the belief that their prayers and supplications will surely be answered and sins forgiven.

Shiite Festivals

The Shiite conviction that Muhammad explicitly appointed Ali to succeed him as caliph, that Ali and his heirs were also divinely favored, and that the holy family was victim of a terrible injustice at the hands of the Umayyads gave rise to the creation of a number of feasts commemorating these events.

ASHURA

Ashura, the 10th day of the first month of the Islamic calendar, Muharram, was a fascinating optional fast day that Shiites observed as the anniversary of the death of the martyr Husayn at Karbala in southern Iraq. Shiites considered it a day of mourning and made pilgrimages to Karbala. On that day they also performed passion plays called *taziya* vividly representing the deaths of their martyrs.

In Egypt during the reign of the Shii Fatimids, Ashura was celebrated with elaborate banquets featuring the traditional mourning foods made of lentils. Many ritual prayers accompanied the feasts. In its origins Ashura coincided with the 10th of the Jewish month of Tishri, the Day of Atonement, which the Jews of Arabia celebrated. Muhammad and his community also observed this day as a day of repentance and fasting from sunrise to sunset. When the Prophet's relations with the Jews worsened, he ordered the obligatory fast to be moved to the month of Ramadan in order to distinguish it from Jewish practice.

In the Sunni world fasting the day of Ashura, and most often the first 10 days of the month, became a "commendable" act deserving of spiritual rewards and blessings. Islamic lore was filled with the tales of the blessings that occurred on this day in sacred history: Noah's ark landed on this day, Abraham was saved from the fire, Adam and Eve received God's forgiveness. Thus for the Sunnis, perhaps to distinguish themselves from the Shia, the celebration of Ashura acquired a joyous character with the promise that sincere acts of repentance, fasting, prayer, and charity would be generously rewarded, as surely as God had saved the scriptural prophets from peril.

FESTIVAL OF GHADIR KHUMM

Ghadir Khumm is the name of a pool located at Khumm, a valley between Mecca and Medina. When the prophet Muhammad was on his way back to Medina from his farewell pilgrimage to Mecca, he stopped at this site and pronounced a speech before his community. Taking Ali by the hand, he asked the people whether it was true that he was closer to them (*awla*) than they were to themselves, to which they enthusiastically replied, "It is so, O Apostle of God!" He then said, "He of whom I am the patron [*mawla-hu*], Ali is his patron." This event is acknowledged in both canonical Sunni and Shiite sources, although the sects interpret its meaning differently. According to Shiite interpretations, Muhammad's pronouncement merely made public one of the divine secrets that God revealed to him during his heavenly journey (*miraj*), making Ali's succession a divine decree. The Sunnis, however, maintain that in this speech Muhammad merely intended to show his public support for Ali in the aftermath of a minor dispute. The Fatimid Shiites and subsequent Shiite dynasties celebrated the day of Ghadir Khumm, the 18th of Dhu l-Hijja, as a solemn feast.

Christian Celebrations

Many medieval Arabs were Christians and of course celebrated all the Christian festivals. But many Muslims living in Egypt, Syria, al-Andalus, and other countries with significant Christian populations also celebrated Christian festivals such as Christmas and Easter and observed secular holidays like New Year's Day. In Baghdad particular patron saints' days were popular. In Cairo Muslims and Christians celebrated Palm Sunday, *Shaanin*, along the Nile, as well as Easter and Christmas.

Egyptians often celebrated the Christian feast of Epiphany, called in Arabic *The Festival of Diving, Id al-Ghitas*. Epiphany was called *Id al-Ghitas* because Christians wearing their crosses and carrying high their candles often would dive into the Nile. Many Andalusian Muslims celebrated Christmas, preparing special foods, buying new clothes, and sharing meals and exchanging presents with their Christian neighbors. Depending upon the country and the century, caliphs and *qadis* condemned popular celebrations that united Christians and Muslims just as they lamented the tendency of Muslims to celebrate Jewish holidays. Nevertheless particular caliphs, particularly in Egypt, built facilities to observe such festivities, such as a caliph's riverside pleasure house, called a *manazir*.

Secular Festivals and Rites of Passage

INVESTITURE OF THE RULER, *BAYA*

According to ancient Arabian custom, the *baya* was a hand clasp between prominent members of a community and a new leader, a ritual that conferred on the latter communal allegiance and obedience. The practice continued in the Islamic period, as the early community formally recognized its the first caliph, Abu Bakr, through the gesture of the *baya*. When a new caliph assumed the throne, the *baya*, now an official ceremony of investiture, served to present the ruler to his people. Hafsid Tunisia had a two-part ceremony consisting of the government officials' pledge of allegiance to the new ruler and then a presentation of the ruler to the people of the capital city.

NEW YEAR'S DAY

In Islamic Egypt New Year's Day was celebrated three times. First was the Persian New Year called *Nawruz*, which was also celebrated in al-Andalus, the Maghrib, and elsewhere. The second was the Coptic New Year, which was celebrated in August, coinciding with the annual flood period of the Nile. The third new year was the beginning of the Muslim year, the first of Muharram, the date commemorated as the day of the Hijra, or "migration," of the Prophet and his community from Mecca to Medina, thus inaugurating the creation of the Islamic *umma*. The Persian and Coptic New Years were times of celebration, in contrast to the more reserved, pious observances of the Muslim New Year.

While piety was important, the celebrations of the Muslim New Year were occasions for magnificent processions in which the caliph was followed by thousands of mounted soldiers all wearing extravagant expensive costumes and caparisons for their animals, and ostentatious displays of wealth and magnificence. In Egypt, for instance, the trees, the shops, and the streets were decorated in Cairo and Fustat to demonstrate the religious and political might of the caliph.

FLOODING OF THE NILE, *WAFA AL-NIL*

The flooding of the Nile was also a holiday called *Wafa al-Nil*. Celebrated in ancient Egypt, the flooding of the Nile River led to fertility of the land and abundance of crops and wealth. The level of the Nile was registered by a calibrated Nilometer. One was established in pre-Islamic times on Roda Island in the center of the Nile. A dam was built at the mouth of the canal at Cairo. Every year that the flood waters were appropriately powerful, it burst, and the breaking of the dam signaled that flood waters would sweep into the canal and irrigate all adjacent land. Islamic celebrations of the flooding of the Nile utilized pre-Islamic rites probably going back to pharoanic times. The caliph's visits to the Nilometer and to the dam were pagan fertility rites. Muslim prayers and recitations of the Quran were part of the festivities.

BIRTH OF A CHILD

Two family holidays were associated with the birth of a child. The sacrifice on the seventh day after a child's birth, called *aqiqa*, might involve a sacrifice of two rams if the child was a boy and one ram if the child was a girl. This was the only time other than the *Id al-Fitr* that Muslims were required to perform a sacrifice. Customarily, the child's hair was shaved on that day.

The second family festival pertaining to children was circumcision, *khitan* or *tahara*. Ritual circumcision often was communal. When a ruler's sons were circumcised, several hundred other boys also would submit to the ritual operation of removing the foreskin of the boy's penis.

READING

Christian Holidays and Festivals

Cosman 1976, Huizinga 1971: role of celebration in culture; Cosman 1976 and 1981, Hanawalt and Reyerson 1994, Harrowven 1980, Post 2001: medieval holidays.

CALENDAR OF CHRISTIAN FESTIVALS

Cosman 1976 and 1981, Cross and Livingstone 1977, Post 2001, Weiser 1958; Wybrew 1997: Orthodox celebrations; Post 2001, Wybrew 1997: Orthodox Marian celebrations; Boss 1999, Boyer 2000, English 1998, Johansson 1998, Preston 1982: Marian feasts; Dunn and Davidson 2000, Fletcher 1984, Williams and Stones 1992, Stone 1927: Feast of Saint James the great; Bynum and Freedman 2000, Gordon and Marshall 2000, Schmitt 1998: Feast of All Saints, belief in ghosts; Skal 2002: history of Halloween.

A TYPICAL FABULOUS FEAST

Cosman 1976 and 1981, Henisch 1976, Strong 1973: fabulous feasting; Furnivall 1969, Hartley 1954, Henisch 1976, Ladurie 1971, Robson 1980, Russell 1868, Tannahill 1988, Wright 1862: food in festival.

Jewish Weddings, Sabbaths, and Holidays

Goldin 1955, Herford 1978: Talmud Midrash Rabba; Baron 1967, Cosman 1976 and 1981, Metzger and Metzger 1982, Marcus 1938: holidays and festivals.

THE WEDDING

Cosman 1976, Feldman 1987: betrothal and marriage; Baron 1967, Marcus 1934: professional matchmakers; Cosman 1976, Feldman 1987, Metzger and Metzger 1982, Roth 2002: wedding etiquette, clothing, and ceremonial objects; Cosman 1976: feasting; Biale 1984, Feldman 1987: Jewish marriage and Jewish divorce; Goitein 1973: conditional divorce in merchants' families; Biale 1984: the *agunah*.

CELEBRATING THE SABBATH

Grossman 1995, Gutmann 1968, Kanos 1969, Kedourie 1979, Narkiss 1979, Metzger and Metzger 1982, Roth and Narkiss 1971, Wigoder 1972: Jewish ceremonial articles; Baron 1967, Mansoor 1991, Yerushalmi 1971: Sabbath instructions in the *Book of the Pious*; Baron 1967, Schirmann 1951: armies and Sabbath observance; Greenberg 1978: the *Judenstern*; Gutmann 1968, Kanos 1969, Roth and Narkiss 1971, Wigoder 1972: Sabbath candles and lamps; Abrahams 1969, Baron 1967, Metzger and Metzger 1982: Sabbath rituals; Cosman 1976 and 1981: Sabbath food; Cosman 1981: Sabbath sex; Narkiss 1958: Sabbath boxes; Roth 2002: Havdalah rituals.

CALENDAR OF JEWISH FESTIVALS

Baron 1967, Mansoor 1991: Jewish ritual calendar; Glazer 2004: food and ritual; Baron 1967, Mansoor 1991, Mindal 1961: Rosh Hashanah; Agnon 1948, Baron 1967, Mansoor 1991, Mindal 1981: Ten Days of Awe, Sukkot, Simchat Torah; Baron 1967, Mansoor 1991, Mindal, 1961: Chanukah, Tu Bshvat; Baron 1967, Mansoor 1991, Mindal 1961, Culi 1978: Passover Haggadah; Culi 1978, Diaz-Mas 1992: Sephardic-Ashkenazic differences; Abrahams 1969, Caspi 1995, Kanos 1969, Mansoor 1991, Marcus 1938: medieval versions of the Book of Esther and Purim rituals; Narkiss 1969, Sed-Rajna 1987: Book of Esther; Grossman 1995, Gutmann 1968, Kanos 1969, Metzger and Metzger 1982: *grogger*; Baron 1967, Marcus 1938: Purim parodies; Abrahams 1969, Baron 1967: special Purims celebrating local escapes from persecution.

Islamic Holidays and Festivals

PILGRIMAGE AND RAMADAN

Westermarck 1926: Islamic liturgical calendar; Ahsan 1987, Bousquet 1949, Goldziher 1966, Gulevich 2004, Hourani 1991, Hughes 1895, Kuban 1974, Lane 1963, Macdonald 1965, Sakr 1999, Sanders 1982: festival and holiday observances; Ghazi 1996, Goitein 1968: Ramadan; Gulevich 2004, Steward and Strathern 2005: festivals and identity; Goitein 1968, Wagtendonck 1968: religious fasting.

SUPEREROGATORY RITUALS

Gulevich 2004, Memon 1973, Sakr 1999, Usmani 2002: ritual celebrations; Knappert 1985, Smith 1984, Westermarck 1973: saints and hagiography; Plessner 1999: Laylat al-Baraa; Kaptein 1993: Muhammad's birthday festival; Fierro 1995, Hawting 1994: Ashura in Sunni Islam; Wagtendonck 1968: religious fasting.

SHIITE FESTIVALS

Momen 1985, Tabataba'i 1975, Nasr 1988: Shiite Islamic practices, general; Ahsan 1987, Gulevich 2004, Steward and Strathern 2005: festivals and identity; Kaptein: Fatimid Mawlid festivals; Vecchia Valieri 1999: Ghadir Khumm; Ayoub 1978, Hawting 1994: Ashura and *taziyeh* plays; Knappert 1985: saints and hagiography.

CHRISTIAN CELEBRATIONS

Bousquet 1949, de la Granja 1970, Goldziher 1966, Hourani 1991, Hughes 1895, Kuban 1974, Lane 1963, Macdonald 1965, Memon 1976, Westermarck 1973.

SECULAR FESTIVALS, RITES OF PASSAGE

Ahsan 1987, Gulevich 2004, Hourani 1991, Steward and Strathern 2005, Westermarck 1973; Bousquet 1949, Goldziher 1966, Hourani 1991, Hughes 1895, Kuban 1974, Lane 1963, Macdonald 1965, Sakr 1999, Sanders 1982: *khitan, tahara, Chronicle of Ibn Iyas.*

12

CLOTHING,
COSTUME,
AND TEXTILES

Clothing and costume identified from afar those whose power originated in the altar, sword, and ledger. In the Middle Ages uniform costume was used to identify members of a nation, tribe, profession, guild, social class, religion, philosophy, or political idea. Uniform costume provided triple visual identification. Clothing self-identified the person wearing a garment volitionally with pride or involuntarily with loathing. For wearer and observer the uniform allowed instant recognition of others from the same group to allow for allegiance or avoidance. For leaders clothes reliably enforced hierarchical order. The priestly class, whether Christian clergy, Jewish rabbis, or Muslim ulema (religious scholars and functionaries), wore clothing to distinguish themselves from laypeople. The clothing and accoutrements of warriors distinguished them clearly from civilians. Rulers and aristocrats reserved for themselves certain clothing and regalia. And secular laypeople wore clothing suitable for their daily activities, for their profession or craft, for their celebrations and ceremonies, and for symbolic social purposes.

Christians, Muslims, and Jews created sumptuary laws to restrict freedoms in clothing and costume and to enforce visible, quick identifying devices. Jews legislated among Jews to distinguish themselves from the gentiles and to avoid ostentation that called dangerous attention to their wealth. Christians legislated for Christians to avoid the sin of pride and to reinforce social hierarchies. Christians and Muslims created sumptuary laws governing clothing of the "infidels" living among them, at certain times and places requiring distinctive livery. Under the cross Jews and Muslims wore clothing differentiators, with Jews, for instance, required by civil and ecclesiastical laws to wear the Jewish hat, the *Judenhut*, and the Jewish badge, the *rouelle*. Under the crescent, Jews and Christians as non-Muslims wore identifying garb and hats. Islamic law in Mamluk Egypt obligated Jews to wear yellow outer garments, Christians to wear blue, and Samaritans red.

CHRISTIAN CLOTHING

Religious Vestments

VESTMENTS AND CANON LAW

Vestments were ecclesiastical garments men and women afflicted with the Christian Church wore for ceremonial occasions, including robes, gowns, capes, and hats. Colors, shapes, designs, and ornaments of ecclesiastical garments were not whimsical, arbitrary, or individualistic, but strictly controlled by tradition and canon law: a vast compilation of laws and regulations made or adopted by the ecclesiastical authorities in order to govern every aspect of the organization of the church and the lives of its members. The laws so decreed concerned the tenets of faith, the status and administration of the seven sacraments, ecclesiastical government, holy orders, clerical discipline, laws on marriage, and ecclesiastical garments. The sources of canon law ultimately originated with God, the divine law revealed in the Old and New Testaments, particularly in the person of Jesus Christ, whose words and deeds were interpreted by Christians as having abrogated many aspects of the "old laws" governing the Jewish community. In addition to the biblical Gospels and the apostolic letters, canon law was compiled from early papal letters, decretals and decrees of important bishops, and judgments of church councils. Not until the ninth century were steps taken to centralize and unify canon law, albeit through the initiative of individual members of the church. The most significant private initiative was undertaken by the 12th-century Italian canon lawyer, jurist, and churchman Gratian, who collected, selected, and ordered about 4,000 texts by subject, recognizing and resolving contradictions. Although as a private initiative *Gratian's Decree, Decretum Gratiani,* or *Concordantia discordantanium canonum* (Concordance of Discordant Canons) (1140) does not have official status in the church, its scientific method served as the model for later decretal compilations and pronouncements by church councils. Pope Innocent III's (1198–1216) *Compilatio tertia* (Third Compilation), the first official and systematic compilation of canon law, relies heavily upon Gratian's *Decretum*. Succeeding popes continued to make canon law based upon additions to Gratian's work, for instance, Pope Gregory IX (1227–41) in his *Extravagantes* and the *Novo compilatio decretalium* (*The New Compilation of Decretals*), Pope Boniface VIII (1294–1303), and Pope John XXII (1316–34). Mention must also be made of the canons promulgated in ecumenical councils, such as Council of Vienna (1311–12) and the Council of Trent (1545–63).

Throughout western Europe Christians entering churches for prayer and praise of God encountered the same colors for the visual and theological identification of the festival season or particular day. Liturgical colors for vestments, banners, altar frontals, and other fabric decorations of the church and clergy were carefully prescribed as follows: White, the symbol of purity and holiness, was required for the Christmas and Easter seasons (except Good Friday), Corpus Christi, Ascension, Trinity Sunday, and feasts of angels, virgins, and unmartyred saints. Gold, also representing holiness and purity, might be used as an alternative color in the Western Church on the aforementioned occasions and was particularly favored in the Eastern Byzantine Church. Red, the symbol of fire and blood, was the primary color for Pentecost (in memory of the tongues of fire that descended upon the apostles), Palm Sunday, Good Friday, Holy Cross Day, and other feasts of the cross and martyred saints' days. Green, the symbol of hope, was the guiding color for Epiphany and the days between the Monday after Trinity Sunday and the beginning of Advent. Purple, the symbol of penance, was the principal decoration for Advent and Lent. Blue was the color for almost all feasts pertinent to the Virgin Mary. Black, the symbol of death and mourning, was the dominant color for funerals, All Souls' Day, and requiem masses. Monastic orders, orders of the friars, and lay confraternities often distinguished one another by the colors of their habits. For instance, Benedictine monks and Dominican friars wore black, and Carmelite friars wore white to distinguish themselves from the Franciscan friars, who wore gray.

GLOSSARY OF RELIGIOUS VESTMENTS

alb   The *alb* vestment was an ankle-length tunic, a shirtlike garment, with round neck and narrow sleeves, made of white linen, sometimes embroidered. Originally secular clothing, it became exclusively liturgical for a priest or deacon. Often the *alb* was decorated in front and back by an *orphrey*, an embroidered panel usually of a vertical rectangular shape, often jeweled and bordered with precious fringe and lace, depicting holy scenes, symbols, or saints and their attributes.

baldrics   Some ecclesiastical figures were required to wear *baldrics*. A baldric was a fabric or the leather band worn diagonally across the chest and back, anchored at one shoulder, tied or buckled at the opposite hip. For ceremonial occasions, knights, monarchs, and ecclesiastics sported them, encrusted with jewels, mottos, emblems, medals, and appliqué.

barrette A *barrette* was a round felt or wool hat, sometimes as small as a skullcap, resembling the *yarmulka* worn by observant religious Jewish men.

cardinal's hat A *cardinal's hat* was almost always red, wide brimmed, originally secular, tied by a cord beneath the chin, and slung on the back when off the head. This flamboyant hat when not worn was carried in ceremonial processions. After a cardinal's death, his hat was hung above his tomb. Pope Innocent IV in 1245 declared red the color for cardinals. Cardinal rank was defined by the number of tassels terminating the hat cords.

chasuble Over the *alb* was the *chasuble* (Latin, *casula*, "little house"), the outermost liturgical vestment, its color depending on the church season or feast being celebrated. Worn during ecclesiastical processions and while elevating the Eucharist, the chasuble usually was ornamented with a cross on the back or with an embroidered band called an *orphrey* on both front and back. The chasuble was associated symbolically with Christ's crucifixion garment and exemplified the all-encompassing virtue of Christian charity.

cilice The *cilice* was a penitential hair shirt, the traditional sack of sackcloth and ashes (Matthew 11:21). Public penitents wore the cilice from Ash Wednesday until reconciled with the church on Maundy Thursday. Monks, hermits, and pious lay folk wore a cilice during Lent, as intentional suffering in imitation of Christ, *imitatio christi*. Would-be saints for their sins wore a cilice as a daily garment, suffering penance of perpetual itch and pain.

cingulum A priest wore a *cingulum*, a white girdle or colored rope to belt the alb when dressing for mass. The belt was symbol of priestly celibacy. *Zond* was another name for the priest's white *cingulum*.

dalmatic A *dalmatic* was a formal, knee-length over-tunic worn by kings at coronations, and by ecclesiastics, especially deacons, during mass. The vestment often was made of silk and designed with an embroidered border that decorated wide flaring sleeves, the wide neck, and openings. A jewel-studded belt encircled the wearer's waist. The *tunicle* was an ecclesiastical vestment shaped like a small tunic and similar to a *dalmatic*, often worn over the *alb* at celebrations of the Eucharist.

lappet A *lappet* was a pair of flat lace ribbons or pendant fabric strips usually worn in pairs and attached to a *miter*, cap, crown, or clerical headdress. An infula was a *lappet* or ribbon on a bishop's *miter*.

maniple On the middle of the arm, a priest wore a *maniple*, an embroidered linen or silk scarf customarily worn on the left arm or hand. The ecclesiastical *glove* resembled the layman's utilitarian hand cover and protector, an important article of fashion from the 12th century on. Popular fabrics were cotton, silk, velvet, or soft animal skins, such as deer, dog, buck, chicken, sheep, beaver, and doe. Rings usually were worn on or over gloves. In the 13th and 14th centuries glove cuffs were deep, buttoned, slashed, dagged, and sometimes ornamented with bells and jewels.

miter A bishop was distinguished by a *miter*, a tall, deeply cleft hat or headdress. From the front, the *miter* resembled a pointed arch. From the side, it resembled the two horns of Moses, though sometimes positioned on the head with arch visible from the sides and horns of Moses frontal. Moses's mythical horns, familiar from Michelangelo's magnificent depiction, were culmination of an earlier tradition depicting Jews as horned, an image traceable to fourth-century Saint Jerome's mistaken confusion of the Hebrew word *qeren*, meaning "scintillating with rays of light" (Exodus 34:29), with the Latin *cornuta*, meaning "horned." Horns as symbols of honor in ancient, barbarian, and Anglo-Saxon arts, particularly when worn on warrior's helmets, degenerated later into emblems of infamy, demonic attributes of Satan and of Jews. The 12th-century Christian theologians Robert Paululus and Petrus Cantor associated Moses's horns and the horns of the bishop's *miter* with the Old and New Testaments. Or according to William Durandus (d. 1296), bishop of Mende (Norbonne), the horns on the miter were signs of God's resplendent brightness and truth. The miter was made of linen or satin fabric, often embroidered and bejeweled. Permission to wear a *miter* also was granted to abbots and abbesses of important monasteries.

pall   A *pall*, originally a full cloak worn by a philosopher, became a popular ecclesiastical vestment, often worn by an archbishop. An altar cloth, a Eucharistic chalice cover, and a coffin shroud at a funeral were also called a *pall*. The *cope* was originally a secular, hooded rain cape. It was a semicircular armless and hood-less ecclesiastical cape or cloak worn over the *alb* by priests and bishops. Made from silk, brocade, or embroidered fabric, it was fastened by a brooch called a morse (Latin *modere*, "to bite"), a clasp or fastening for a cape or cloak, usually wrought in gold or silver and set with stones. The *cope* often was ornamented with an *orphrey* and an imitation hood.

scapular   A particularly important symbolic garment was the *scapular* (Latin, *scapulae*, "shoulder blades"). It was a narrow cloak or stole and was an essential part of most monastic habits, the technical name for ecclesiastical garments. The Benedictine Rule institutional-ized the use of the scapular. Symbolically the scapular represented the yoke of Jesus Christ, and thus it was sometimes also referred to as the *jugum Christi* (Latin, "Christ's yoke").

surplice   The *surplice* (Latin, *super* + *pellicia*, "over-fur-coat") was a loose-fitting cloak, usually white and ankle-length, worn by clerics and choir singers from the 13th century onward. A ceremonial garment crossing the boundaries between ecclesiastical and royal was the *pluvial*, a floor-length, open-fronted mantle, worn as a ceremonial ecclesiastical vestment and as coronation regalia for nobility.

tiara   Only the pope wore a *tiara*, a triple-tiered or triple-crowned headdress. When the pope was not wearing his tiara, it was carried in front of him during important though non-liturgical functions. The coronets symbolized the Trinity or the three estates of the church, Rome, Christendom, and spiritual sovereignty, in which each had rights and responsibilities and the church's ideas and judgments were supreme.

tonsure   The *tonsure* was a distinctive clerical haircut for men. It was achieved by shaving all or part of the head. Different monastic orders favored shaving the front from ear to ear or creating a bald circle on the crown of the head.

MONASTIC VESTMENTS

Members of the Carmelite Order of friars wore white habits and scapulars and were known familiarly as the White Friars. White Monks, members of the Cistercian Order, wore a habit made of white or undyed fabric. Living under strict interpretation of the Benedictine Rule, the Cistercians were founded in 1098 by Robert, abbot of Molesme. In 1200 Saint Bernard of Clairvaux dedicated his Bernardine Cistercian monks to spiritual mysticism. The Cistercian habit was white or gray under a black scapular.

A Black Friar was a member of the Dominicans Order, founded by Saint Dominic of Guzman in the 13th century, so named because of the black-hooded habit worn by regulation. The Black Monks of the Order of the Benedictines, founded in the sixth century by Benedictine of Nursia, usually wore a black habit in accordance with the Benedictine Rule; however, it became obligatory from the 13th century onward.

The Gray Friars or minorites or friars minor were Franciscans, followers of Saint Francis of Assisi and his 13th-century mendicant order, whose habit was a gray or brown robe or cloak belted with a rope.

The Carthusians, whose order was founded in the 11th century by Saint Bruno, were purely contemplative hermit monks, bound by vows of silence and strict vegetarianism. Their habit was pure white, consisting of a cowl and gown. The Donates, from the Latin, meaning "gifts," were lay brothers who wore the same habit as the monastic house to which they belonged. Carthusian Donates wore a white cowl and gown.

Secular Clothing

MARRIAGE CLOTHES AND MOURNING GARB

Marriage clothing almost never was white. Both the man and the woman wore as flamboyant and colorful clothes as wealth and whimsy permitted. Though matrimony was one of the seven sacraments, with the double purpose of uniting man and woman for procreation and preservation of the species and for comfort, companionship, and satisfaction, it nevertheless did not have to be celebrated in a church until the 16th-century Council of Trent required that marriage be sanctified by the clergy. The essential religious properties of marriage were unity and indissolubility. However, clandestine marriage permitted an essentially private, non–liturgically blessed union that nevertheless was recognized by civil law and canon law.

Though child marriage was common, theologians and exponents of canon law, such as the great jurist Gratian, insisted on marriage by consent. Each of the partners had to agree to the matrimonial union. The usual age for a boy was 12 and for a girl age 13. Since the wedding ceremony was a public celebration even before it was sanctified in a church, the wealthiest families provided sumptuous marriage garb and even the lowest peasant wore "best" clothing for the momentous occasion.

Though the church's color for mourning and requiem masses was black, black was not a universal European color for medieval mourning garb.

FASHIONABLE HATS AND HEADGEAR

Men and women wore fashionable hats and veils. Young and old, rich and poor, laborer and scholar, all wore hats in summer and winter. Headgear often proclaimed a social, cultural, religious, or moral message to the observer by means of the hat style, fabric, and distinctive method of presentation. Wealthy or noble Christian women in 15th-century France and Burgundy wore the stylish pointed, conical *hennin* headdress, whose mild to extravagant height ascended according to the woman's social rank. English, French, and Burgundian women wore a forehead ornament called a *frontlet* when exaggeratedly high, wide foreheads were fashionable. Consisting of a small pendant loop of velvet, silk, or precious metal attached to the edge of an undercap, such as the *calotte* worn beneath the tall pointed *hennin*, the frontlet often indicated rank or wealth. A gold loop suggested substantial yearly income. Another woman's hat was the *caul*, an elaborate headdress consisting of silken sheaths covering strands of hair or braids. Over the cover was a netting of reticulated gold or silver cord embellished with pearls, beads, jewels, spangles, sequins, or bells. Or a woman might wear a

At her bridal feast, the slender bride, seated regally beneath a red canopied baldachin, allows her long golden hair to cascade down her back, cinched above by her elaborate gold-and-red headdress, called a crowned atour. Her hat's two "horns" are stylistically related to the single-horn hats, or hennins, fashionable in 15th-century Europe, that her two gentlewomen wear. With pendent diaphanous veils called lambrequins, hennins enabled a small woman to appear tall and a noblewoman effectively to assert power. The latter's hat usually was the tallest spire in a procession, emulating the Gothic cathedral's vault and vertical skyward thrust toward God in heaven. A carver serves the women at the high table whole birds. Servants enter the dining hall from the kitchen to serve guests seated at the long table, the sideboard. Musicians standing in an overhead gallery play fanfares on long trumpets to announce the progression of courses in the feast, to entertain, and to aid digestion. A blue-robed surveyor of ceremonies presides over the feast service, standing near a tall Gothic wooden aumbry displaying silver and gold pitchers and platters. A white-pawed hound majestically prances on the decorated tile floor. The servitors, shod in long pointed poulaines, wear cinch-waisted buttock-hugging tunics called pourpoints whose extravagantly exaggerated shoulders and sleeves are extended by cylindrical pads called mahoîtres. Fifteenth-century noble costume complemented the exquisite physiques both women and men cultivated by exercise and diet.   From *Histoire de Renaud de Montauban*, France, 1468–70. Courtesy of Bibliothèque de l'Arsenal, Paris, Manuscript 5073.

chaplet, a head wreath, usually a garland of real or artificial leaves or flowers. A chaplet also was a circlet with gems or a twisted cloth or padded roll holding a veil on the head.

Men and women in Spain and Italy wore the graceful tripartite headdress hood the *chaperone*, consisting of a *roundlet*, a stuffed fabric circlet covered by a turban called a *garget*, which was folded lengths of fabric fulsomely wound around the head and culminating in a *liripipe*, the long fabric tail of the hat worn wound around the neck or swung over the shoulder, often ornamented with bells, fringe, or decorative precious stones. As did the height of the *hennin*, the length of the *liripipe* signified hierarchical rank.

Shown here is a chaperone, a graceful headdress for a man, popular between the 12th and 16th centuries, consisting of a turban wound upon a roundlet and a long garget. Isabella Stewart Gardener Museum, Boston.

Hats served multiple practical purposes. In the cold north, a hat conserved bodily warmth. Hatless, a woman or a man was obligated to wear heavier gowns, coats, cloaks, and capes, but a cotton or silk hood or hat enabled the wearer to achieve comfort with fewer and lighter garments on the body. Likewise, with the head covered, one could travel lighter and better in a carriage or cart, on horseback, or on foot. Hats also served both men and women to maintain their hairstyles in place. A hat, then as now, could cover multiple sins of hair gone wild. Even more important was the hat's role in asserting importance and power. A person in a position of authority wore the hat signifying dignity, respect, and control. The more powerful the person, the more attention accorded to the headdress, which ideally should both flatter the face and transmit appropriate social ideas to onlookers. Men and women wearing ceremonial headgear with veils that trailed down the back appeared regal and patrician when facing the audience; when they turned aside or around, the back view confirmed magnificence.

Hoods and hats also were worn in bed at night. No matter how fine the building construction or cozily curtained the bed, in the days before central heating, drafts were inevitable in almost all seasons. Therefore men and women wore lightweight silk or cotton nightcaps in summer and heavier silk or wool in winter. Bed hats also prevented hair from being messed as one turned on pillows. Another reason for hats in bed was to protect the bed linens if one colored the hair. Blacks, browns, reds, and other dyes were important cosmetics that as temporary or semipermanent colorings could stain pillow covers and sheets. For neatness of head and bed, it was customary for hair to be hatted.

Outdoors or inside, another reason for wearing a beautiful hat or hood, particularly one decorated with precious metal ornaments or encrusted with jewels, was that valuable headgear provided portable property immediately convertible to cash when necessary. Medieval Jews wore elaborate hoods, hats, and headgear not merely for fashion or ostentation but for informal banking, if attacked by robbers on the highway or pirates on the sea, or when unexpectedly requiring ready cash while traveling without the luxury of advance credit or promissory notes.

Sumptuary Laws

Sumptuary laws were rigorously enforced rules and regulations promulgated by civic or religious authorities to govern clothing, as well as food, entertainment, and all articles and actions of ostentatious display. Certain furs, fabrics, silks, and taffetas could be worn only by particular classes, nationalities, and professions. Certain colors also were restricted. Royal purple was meant for nobility. Red was the favored color for physicians. In the 14th century prostitutes could be fined or jailed for wearing fur-lined hoods, which were allowed only for noblewomen. Specific colors were reserved for special classes. Among the constitutions produced by the Fourth Lateran Council presided over by Pope Innocent III in 1215 was the legislation requiring that Jews and Muslims be distinguished from Christians by the character of their dress. In practice this meant that when Jews ventured outside the ghetto they had to wear distinctive badges, specifically identifiable capes, coats, and hats, such as the nefarious yellow pointed *Judenhut.*

Fur sumptuary laws allocated particular animal skins to specific social ranks. Common city whores who wore the fur hoods of noble ladies forfeited their garb before being clapped into jail. Lining, edging, and cloak furs included squirrel, fox, marten, beaver, and white imitation ermine called *laitice.* Only royalty and members of the court were permitted to wear garments made of *gris vair,* budge, and ermine as either exterior furs or cape and cloak linings.

Wearing a sumptuously brocaded robe with huge pendent sleeves lined with ermine, and a headdress that partially covers her lavishly braided hair, a noblewoman presents her children to their royal grandfather. Crowned and seated on a throne beneath a fringed baldachin upheld by stout columns, the monarch greets his family while his counselor gesticulates at his side. Children's costumes emulated adults' clothes. Sumptuary laws regulated by profession or class who could wear which fabric, fur, color, or style. From Hans Burgkmair, Der Weisskunig, late 15th century. Courtesy of the Metropolitan Museum of Art, New York. Gift of Anne and Carl Stein, 1961.

Beaver, otter, hare, and fox graced the garments of the lower nobility and middle classes. Common people used lamb, wool, goat, and sheepskin.

In the late Middle Ages English statutes regulated the ornateness of dress and limited extremes in the shortness of doublets and the extravagant length of long coats. Since the purpose was to regulate overindulgence in luxury and extravagance in dress, food, drink, and lifestyles, statutes marked class distinctions clearly and attempted to prevent any person from assuming the appearance of a superior class.

CLOTHING AND THE BONFIRE OF THE VANITIES

The sumptuous and ostentatious clothing of royalty and the aristocracy became an obvious target of preachers and spiritual reformers. Between the 13th and 15th centuries, at the very moment when the most flamboyant items of clothing became fashionable within the church and the European courts, a veritable counterculture exalting religious poverty and the humble apostolic life emerged. The "lives of the saints" composed in these centuries abounded with stories of wealthy lay men and women who, as did Saint Francis and Saint Clará of Assisi (d. 1253), renounced their wealth, social position, vanities of the world, symbolized by luxurious clothing and jewelry. Lay movements such as the Beguines and the Beguards and the Franciscan and Dominican tertiaries demonstrated their rejection of worldly wealth and their adoption of the ascetic apostolic life by draping themselves in simple dark clothing and wearing hairshirts and pebbles in their shoes as acts of penance.

Charismatic preachers such as the Franciscan friar Bernardino of Siena (1380–1444) wandered throughout western Europe preaching poverty and staging spectacular "bonfires of the vanities." After a sermon was delivered to the multitudes in an outdoor square, the throngs would push forward, throwing their wigs, cosmetics, sumptuous clothes, jewelry, as well as other frivolous or dangerous items—such as playing cards, dice, and amulets—onto the pyre. As an eyewitness wrote after attending one such bonfire in Santa Croce:

> You never saw more beautiful flames, going way up into the air to the spite of the enemy of God, the Devil, and to the glory and praise and honor and reverence of our Lord Jesus Christ, supreme God. . . . I can't begin to describe, it seemed like thunder, and the tears shed out of piety, what great devotion. Amen. (Mormondo, 1999, p. 107)

The anonymous eyewitness attests that for the Franciscans, the Dominicans, and the lay voluntary poverty movements, the rejection of fashionable clothing was a sign of Christian piety and humility, the visible symbol for all to see of a life dedicated solely and exclusively to praising God. Thus even within different sectors of Christian society, clothing not only identified social status and profession, it also revealed religious affiliation and established clear boundaries between the spiritually humble and pious and the worldly and vain.

Finally, in spite of the sumptuary laws requiring marking distinctions in Christian, Jewish, and Muslim garb, many items of clothing were cross-cultural. Indeed, it could be argued that Lateran IV's decree that Christians, Jews, and Muslims be clearly distinguishable through their clothing needed to be imposed precisely *because* the three peoples wore similar clothing. (*See* the glossary of clothing items at the end of this chapter, which further demonstrates the adoption and adaptation of some Muslim clothing and headwear by both Jews and Christians.)

JEWISH COSTUMES AND CLOTHING

The reverence for light, reverence for sign, and reverence for the written word that animated Jewish art applied as well to the wearable art of costume. While medieval Jewish costume mistakenly is thought somber, monochromatic, and usually black, the authentic manuscript, commercial, and legal evidence demonstrates costume and clothing of spectacular colors, flamboyant styles, and varieties of fabric. Between the ninth and 16th centuries Jewish costume exemplified the celebration of light through a stunning spectrum of color. Medieval Jewish and Muslim traders precisely identified minute differences among fabric pigments, shades, and hues. Words for different shades and hues of red and yellow, for instance, alluded to specific local flowers; to precious gems; to the spices of turmeric, saffron, and pepper; to the fruits quince, pomegranate, and apricot; and to the feathers of grouse and peacock. Exquisitely colorfully garbed medieval Jews as represented in the Cairo *geniza* documents seem to have been "color intoxicated."

Signs and symbols adorned clothing of the wealthy and the poor. Jews ornamented their clothes with decorative traditional silver, gold, base metal, and jewels. They wore embroidered amulets, such as the *kameah*, to assure good luck, and the symbolic upraised open hand against the evil eye, to prevent malevolence. Muslims also followed the custom of wearing protective amulets and as well as the upraised hand, called the hand of Fatima. Jews wore certain signs and symbols of self-distinction, while others were imposed as identifiers to distinguish them from Christians and Muslims. In Muslim lands laws prescribed Jewish robe colors, usually yellows, and hat styles. In Christian Europe Jews by law wore the *Jewish badge* and the *Jew's hat*, the *Judenhut*.

Jewish respect for word had a surprising corollary in costume that ideally signified the wearer's spiritual condition. Hebrew Scripture gave reasons for dressing carefully and well. Costume aided a Jew's praising God and demonstrating piety. As owning a Bible, a *menorah* light, and a *mezzuzah*, marking the doorposts of the home as site for ritual observance and prayer, Jewish daily garments had spiritual import. The Talmud (Yevamot 63b) said: The glory of God is Mankind. The glory of Mankind is clothes.

COSTUME AS MORAL STATEMENT

Such Talmudic sentences seem shockingly worldly. What power resides in costume to make it equal the best of creation? How is costume mankind's image? How can clothing represent the intrinsic, invisible self? Fashion, associated in medieval Christian thought with dangerous vainglory and pernicious pride, took such precedence in medieval Jewish life that the marriage contract, the *ketubah*, usually listed the sums the new husband was required to expend on his wife's clothing. For Jews living under Muslim law, garments were substantial percentages of dowries, representing up to half the wealth the woman took to her marriage.

Costumes entered Jewish wills. While valuable garments were passed down through generations as heirlooms, some wills also transmitted the philosophy of dressing well. Just as a Jewish last will and testament transferred material goods to the family, an *ethical will* transmitted best advice and counsel. Jacob ben Asher (d. 1343) wrote in his ethical will that the true purpose for studying law is to know personally how to pursue the right and avoid the wrong, which included respectful care and clothing of the body. "A man's toil in the concerns of his body is to preserve the soul." In a 14th-century Spanish ethical will, a father specifically implored his sons; "Accustom yourselves, your wives, and your children always to wear clean and beautiful clothes so that both God and man may honor you."

Even the great sage Rabbi Akiba (d. c. 135) honored his beloved wife with radiant clothing and a gold crown. He started to study Torah at the late age of 40 and by the age of 53 became an honored teacher to multitudes thanks to his generous wife, Rachel, who supported the family while Rabbi Akiba studied. According to the ethical code *The Sayings of the Fathers, Pirke Avot*, Rabbi Akiba honored Rachel's graciousness by praising her and giving her precious garments to wear, including golden sandals for her feet and for her hair a golden tiara in the shape of the walled city of Jerusalem. As Rabbi Akiba told his disciples, "Many were the trials she suffered for my sake, that I might study Torah." Rachel's costume gift was visible, public signifier of her acquired dignity, inherent merit, and good name. Rabbi Simeon, also cited in the *Pirke Avot*, celebrated four crowns, the traditional three diadems, the crown of Torah, the crown of the priesthood, and the crown of kingship, and excelling them all, the crown of a good name.

Clothing to differentiate people by appearance was thought part of God's divine plan: If God had not distinguished men's taste, they would have envied one another. Had God not distinguished appearances, then women of Israel would not recognize their husbands and men could not recognize their wives.

The Jewish attitude toward clothing and fascination with beautiful costume may be explained partly on the basis of biblical and Talmudic teachings and partly as a result of internally- and externally-imposed sumptuary laws: When God created animals he endowed them with copious fur to protect them against the elements. Yet when God created human beings, he made the human body naked with only minimal hair. Jews praise God for creating the body by treating it with the gratitude, piety, and dignity that bespeak its holiness.

Hence Jews must cover the holiness of the body and protect it against both the natural perils of the sun, wind, rain, snow, and ice, and the human-made perils of fire, dirt, glass, malice, and accidents. Not any garment will do, however. Jews show their obedience to God by observing the law against *shatnez*—the mixing of fabrics. As it is written in the Torah, "You shall not wear combined fibers, wool and linen together." (Deut. 22:11). The Torah also states that men's and women's clothing must be clearly defined and describes cross-dressing as an "abomination": "Male garb shall not be on a woman, and a man shall not wear a feminine garment, for anyone who does so is an abomination of the Almighty" (Deut. 2:5).

Apart from these restrictions, splendorous dressing is a means of expressing gratitude for God's handiwork. It is a sign of the use of the God-given intellect by which humanity imitated God. Moreover, beautiful clothes are difficult to create and expensive to buy, and keeping them fit for wear is difficult. Special occasions such as the Sabbath, holidays, and weddings require a special wardrobe. God delights in seeing his creatures use their rationality, creativity, and ingenuity in creating beautiful clothes to wear as they remember, praise, and worship him. He appreciates art in praise. Clothing choice and fabrication are art forms, *hiddur mitzvah*, the art of holiness and the holiness of art.

Clothing serves not only to protect the body and to give thanks for God's creation. Wearing clean attractive clothes also demonstrates respect for other people. People judge one another by their clothing. As the Talmud says, "At home you know the name, abroad the costume" (Talmud B. Shabbat 145b). Relatives and neighbors who know one another can ignore outward appearances. But the person traveling abroad causes an impression by the clothes he or she wears. Clothing intimates character. When Joshua appeared unkempt before the angel of the Lord, the angel ordered him to remove his filthy clothes. He then said to Joshua, "See, I have taken away your sin and I will put rich garments on you" (Zech. 3:4). Hence the choice clothing, its care, and carriage of the wearer subtly demonstrate inherent disposition and intrinsic attributes of the wearer. And upon death, the soul is separated from its physical garment and re-clothed in the pure, clean, spiritual garments of the Rabbinical Mantle, or spiritual body, *Haluka d'Rabbanan*. This is the true meaning of the "fine clothes" to which the angel referred when speaking to Joshua—the raiment of spiritual energy that those being led into paradise will wear.

Last but not least, fine clothing showed one's respect for God and for other people. But the tendency toward superfluous luxury had to be tempered with reason, with compassion, and with sumptuary laws. Sumptuary laws were more or less rigorously enforced rules and regulations governing clothing, food, entertainment, and articles of ostentatious display. Sumptuary legislation limited clothing design, fabrics, furs, colors, expense, and flamboyance. Sumptuary laws promulgated by Jews within Jewish communities, such as the laws of the Italian city of Forli, were intended to protect individuals from immorality of excess and to prevent the Jewish community from stimulating envy among non-Jews.

Costume as Cultural and Social Statement

Costume demonstrated the extravagant plenitude of medieval urban civilization, contemporary Mediterranean documents reveal a cornucopia of fabric names and textile vocabulary intimating the multiplicities of luxury. Twelve different types of silk were distinguished among more than 60 distinct classes of fabrics listed in the Cairo *geniza* documents, the storehouse of a Jewish synagogue that preserved such Jewish historical treasures as inventories for trousseaus, marriage, and divorce; business ledgers and ships' manifests; personal diaries and works of literature; sacred book fragments and profane texts. Commercial notices dated between the seventh and 13th centuries identify 183 Arabic and Persian names for discrete fabrics.

Made from these multiple materials were varied styles and qualities of robes, coats, capes, shawls, caftans, tunics, leggings, tights, stockings, and shoes, and great profusions of hats and veils of various vogues, sizes, purposes, ornamentation, and materials worn by both men and women. Copious headgear names enrich medieval commercial vocabulary. More than half of the named garments in trousseau lists from the Cairo *geniza* are of headgear and veils, such as the woman's *mindil, bukhnuq, isaba maila, khimar, khirqa, miqnaa,* and *tarha*. Scholarly men also wore the *tarha* and *taylasan*.

Clothing was a symbol of wealth and the physical expression of it. Clothes were also portable property readily convertible to cash when traveling. In sites far from banks and credit, precious fabric items that could be easily folded, packed, and transported could be sold and transferred far more easily than real estate. Costumes, and tapestries, could be used to pay ransoms. Valuable costumes became cherished family heirlooms, displayed at holidays, worn for honorific occasions, and protected by legal documents when transferred at wedding by dowry and at death by will. Ceremonial items of attire, especially among Jews in Muslim lands, were ritually bestowed or received as robes of honor.

Sumptuary Laws Demarcated Social Status and Religious Affiliation

Christians and Muslims created sumptuary laws for the double purpose of demarcating social status and distinguishing religious affiliation both within their respective communities and with respect to members of other religions.

Humble clothing was the essential outward sign of the lay, friar, and monastic orders of voluntary, apostolic poverty that flourished in late medieval Christian Europe. Jews wore their own traditional ceremonial garb such as the *tallit* for prayer, for Jewish festivals, and for life's rites of passage such as weddings. In all cases, for wearer and observer, clothing allowed instant recognition of others from the same group to allow for association or avoidance. Anxious to differentiate insiders from outsiders clearly, Christian and Muslim authorities imposed sumptuary laws that readily identified the outsiders living among them.

While Jews obeyed dress codes of both their Christian and Muslim leaders, they had their own sumptuary laws that controlled flamboyance and ostentation in households, in community celebration, and in details of daily life. Rigorously enforced sumptuary rules and regulations governed clothing, food, entertainment, and articles of public display. Laws determined which furs, fabrics, silks, designs, and jewels could be worn; which were prohibited; when and where a person was free of sumptuary legislation; and how and when a person would be punished for violating the strictures. Remarkably, the city itself benefited from the fines for broken laws of Jewish self-government. In Italy in 1416 the Jews at Forli, for example, created the law requiring that no Jewish man or woman wear a cloak or hood of sable, ermine, or mixed furs, or of fabric colored red or violet. A fur-lined hood or cloak was acceptable so long as the fur was hidden, with no fur displayed on the outer covering. Women's fur-lined hoods and cloaks were permissible if worn indoors but not in public unless cloaks were covered with an overcape or garment completely hiding the fur. Any hoods or coats lined with fur must be designed and crafted to hide the precious pelts.

Moreover, no woman was permitted to wear a necklace or a gold hairnet on her head unless she covered it with a veil. Newly married brides might wear golden hair nets, however, but only for the 30 days after the wedding. Thereafter they, too, must veil their glittering hair cover.

Monetary fines for transgressing these laws on clothing and ornamentation were 10 silver coins or their value paid to the treasury of the city for each offense. Men were responsible for their wives' infractions of these rules. Anyone refusing to obey clothing ordinances was refused admittance to the prayer *minyan* and forbidden to read the Torah.

Similarly, in Valladolid in 1432, a synod of Castilian Jews promulgated the rule that no woman unless unmarried or a bride in the first year of her marriage could wear a gold brooch or one made of pearls, or a string of pearls on her forehead. Likewise, women were forbidden to wear dresses with trains on the ground beyond a precise measured length, nor fringed Moorish garments, nor coats with high collars, nor red fabrics. No son of Israel aged 15 or older could wear any cloak of gold thread, olive-colored material or silk, or any cloak trimmed with gold or olive material or silk, or a cloak bearing rich trimmings of olive color or gold cloth.

These prohibitions did not include clothes worn at the time of festivity, at the reception of a lord or a lady, at balls, or on similar social occasions. Jewish lawmakers, recognizing the diverse clothing customs among Jewish communities and consequent impossibility of fair and reasonable universal laws, authorized each community to make local sumptuary ordinances as they saw fit, the stricter the better.

Why did Jews create sumptuary laws? The Forli prelude to the 1416 regulations stated the intentions directly and typically: "We make the following decree to present ourselves modestly and humbly before the Lord our God, and to avoid arousing envy among the Gentiles." (cited in Finkelstein [1964] 292). Though heretofore accustomed to highly colored garb, no Forli Jews, from inception of the decree in 1416 until the year 1426, were permitted to make a hooded cloak called a *foderato-cinto* unless its color was black. If open-sleeved, there was to be no silk lining showing. Any Jews already owning a *foderato-cinto* made in colored fabric, not black, could continue to wear the cloak until it wore out, provided that the sleeves were not open and the cloak was worn closed both front and back.

CHRISTIAN SUMPTUARY LAWS REGULATING JEWS

The same Pope Innocent III who supported King John of England during the debate over the *Magna Carta* announced in 1215 at the *Fourth Lateran Council* his two important goals, recovery of the Holy Land and reformation of Catholic life. As noted, this reform required Jews to wear distinctive dress. The council's 68th canon stated that in some church provinces a difference in dress distinguished Jews and Saracens from Christians, but in others there was great confusion and Jews could not be distinguished. Therefore at times it happened "through error that Christian men have relations with Jewish and Saracen women. And Jews and Saracens have relations with Christian women." To prevent uncertainty and to forestall future pretexts and excuses for "such accursed intercourse," the pope decreed that Jews and Saracens of both sexes in every Christian land at all times should be distinguished in the eyes of the public from other peoples by character of their dress. The pope thought this particularly correct for Jews because Moses in Numbers 15:37–41 imposed upon Jews a law of distinct dress.

Amusing confusions between Jews and the Christian clergy led to revisions of prohibited and required garments. The Council of Albi, for instance, had required Jews to wear round capes. But in 1254 the council forbade round capes to Jews because customarily Christian clergymen wore round capes and people greeted the caped clergy with appropriate deference and respect. Jews wearing round capes were so often mistaken for Christian clergy that they inappropriately garnered approval rightfully reserved only for Christian holy men. Henceforth, Jews were forbidden to wear round capes.

In 1396 Jews under the jurisdiction of King John of Aragon were required to wear a *gramalla*, a long outer gown or cloak or other garment reaching to the toes, and a yellow badge affixed to the breast. Majorcan Jews also wore a *gramalla* with a funnel-shaped cowl attached to the hood. The city of Cologne in 1404 required Jews to wear garments conforming to a minutely precise dress code. All sleeves on coats and jackets could not exceed half an *elle* in width. Collars on jackets and cloaks could not be wider than one finger's width. No fur could show at either neck or hem. Lace was permitted on sleeves only. Sleeve cuffs could not exceed the length of the hand. Coats were required to be fringed and reach the calves. Cloaks could not be opened on both sides and could not be floor length but rather hemmed to within a hand's width from the ground.

Men over the age of 13 were required to wear hoods as long as one *elle*, and a shoulder collar one and a half *elles* but not wider than one-eighth of the length. For both men and women, silk shoes were forbidden indoors and out. No child over the age of three could wear "open" clothing. A girl could not wear hair ribbons worth more than six *gulden* or of a width wider than two fingers. On nonfestival days, women were not permitted to wear more than one ring on each hand nor any ring valued at more than three *gulden* and could not wear gold belts nor a belt wider than two fingers. However, on festivals they were permitted to wear belts up to the value of two silver marks and two rings valued at six *gulden*.

In Valladolid in 1412 all Jews were required to wear long robes over their clothing down to their feet. They were not permitted to wear cloaks. In all cities, towns, and places they were required to wear distinctive red badges. However, the ruler King Juan of Castile (d. 1454) recognized that these distinctive clothes might put the Jews in danger while traveling. Therefore on the road the clothing restrictions were suspended and customary garments allowed. Nevertheless, all Jewish and Muslim women of the kingdom and its dominion were required to wear long, floor-length mantles with hoods. Anyone acting contrary to the rule would forfeit all the clothes on the body down to the undergarments. Within 10 days of the signing of the law, no Jew or Moor was permitted to wear a suit made of cloth costing more than 30 *maravedis.*

Punishment for a first offense was forfeiture of apparel down to the level of the shirt. For a second offense, the perpetrator would lose all clothing, to nakedness, and receive 100 lashes of the whip. A third violation of the sumptuary law would result in forfeiture of all personal property to the royal treasury. At the king's pleasure, however, Jews could fabricate new clothing out of old clothes they currently possessed.

Moreover, Jews and Moors were not to shave their beards or have them shaved with either razors or scissors, nor trim or cut their hair, but to wear them long and natural. Any acting contrary to this law would receive 100 lashes plus pay a fine of 100 *maravedis* for each transgression.

The Jewish Badge Beginning with Pope Innocent's *Fourth Lateran Council* in 1215, Jews were required throughout western Europe to wear an identifying badge. Fashions varied according to city and date. Usually the Jewish badge was round, often yellow, resembled the letter *O*, and was worn on the chest. So common was this circle that it was called by its French name *rouelle*, worn by men, women, and children, usually stipulated as required from age seven on.

The Jewish badge was a good fund-raiser for municipalities. In some towns and cities Jews were required to purchase the badge, sometimes in multiples, because badges had to be worn on both front and back of a coat or on both cloak and hat. Elsewhere, Jews could buy their way out of the necessity to wear the badge, thereby exchanging money for the degrading nuisance of wearing the badge. The most valuable municipal use of the badge was in collecting fines for violation of the law. In some cities, definitive fines were established, posted, and enforced. Elsewhere fines depended upon the graciousness or viciousness of the prosecuting authority. In Barcelona in 1313, the penalty for not wearing the badge was either a fine or 20 strokes of the whip. Understandably, medieval Jews considered the badge, whatever its shape, the badge of infamy.

Informers who reported Jews who violated clothing statutes were rewarded with money, sometimes an equivalent of the value of the Jew's costume, and or with the Jew's clothing itself. In 1314 at Perpignan where Jews were required to wear a cape with a badge of contrasting color of cotton or silk worn on the middle of the chest, offenders forfeited their clothing and the informer received one-third of its value.

The ring-shaped badge that originated in France was first described in 1208. In 15th-century Grenoble, a badge with two colors was required to be worn by men on the chest and by women on the head. At Valence Jewish women wore their badge on their clothing. In Spain Pope Honorius III imposed a yellow badge upon all Jews in the year 1219. In 1313 Jews in Barcelona were required to wear yellow or red badges. In 1315 Ismail I, the Nasrid king of Granada (r. 1314–25) imposed a Jewish badge as a distinguishing mark to prevent confusion with Muslims. When Enrique II ascended the throne as king of Castile in 1368 he vigorously enforced badge laws. In Aragon Pope Benedict XIII in 1415 imposed a red and yellow badge men wore on the breast and women on the forehead.

Portuguese Jews customarily wore a red badge with six points resembling a Jewish star of David, a *mogen David*. Italian Jews in the year 1222, under Holy Roman Emperor Frederick II, wore a blue badge shaped like the Greek letter *T*, whereas Jews in the Papal States wore a yellow patch if male and two blue stripes if female. Jews wore a star in Verona in 1433. At Palermo, Sicily, in 1488, red cloth cut to the size of a ducat coin Jews wore on the left side of garments at the level of the heart.

From the year 1218 English Jews residing in the kingdom of Henry III wore a badge resembling two "tables of the law," the *tabula*, consisting of two broad strips of white linen or parchment. In 1275 a statute required every Jew over age seven to wear a badge in the form of two tables made of yellow cloth, specifically six fingers long and three fingers wide. German Jews customarily wore their *Jewish hats* but as of 1434 the Council of Augsburg required a yellow badge on the breast. The *Jewish badge* and *Jewish hat* converged amusingly in Switzerland, where at Schaffhausen in 1435 each Jew wore a badge shaped like a *Jew's hat*.

Jewish Hats and the *Judenhut* Local ordinances on the *Jewish hat* were enforceable on authority of Pope Innocent III's canon law in 1215 as well as preceding council decrees. Papal interest in Jewish costume began prior to the ninth century. Describing Jewish fur-trimmed hoods and cloaks, a ninth-century writer reported that Pope Nicolas was strongly opposed to Arsenius, bishop of Orta, because of his effort to introduce Jewish fur garments into fashion, the *Judaicae peluciae*. The pope threatened to exclude Bishop Arsenius from the Palatine procession unless he vowed to discard the clothes of "the superstitious race" and agreed to walk in the procession wearing only the priestly hat called the *fillet*. The bishop who admired the Jewish fur-trimmed hood succumbed to papal sartorial authority.

Certain exclusively Jewish hats derived from canon law. In 1257 the pope required Jewish women to wear the veil with two blue stripes called the *oralia*. That veil rule was reconfirmed as law by the Council of Ravenna in 1311, and by the Council of Cologne in 1442. As did the *oralia*, the Jewish *cornalia* and the German *sendelbindel* or *riese* consisted of a pointed stiff veil or headdress, like the *hennin*, resembling a horn or steeple. Sometimes the hat having two peaks, a double-horned hat, was comparable to the *atour*. Another hat popular as synagogue gear in 14th- to 16th-century Germany was the *Viereckiger schleier*, a cap covering head and hair, featuring two stiffly starched square wings of white linen. Sometimes also required by law to be decorated with two blue stripes, as was the *oralia*, the *Viereckiger schleier* also was called the *square veil*.

For men, the *Judenhut* probably was the most common identifier of Jews in medieval art. Resembling an inverted martini glass, variations in shapes of Jew's hats from country to country and century to century nevertheless retained the basic pointed cone. The Jew's hat originally may have been a pointed cap similar to the Persian *kalansuwa* that in Muslim countries was required identifier for both Christians and Jews. The Jewish hat resembled the later tall pointed headdress called the dunce cap, named after the Scholastic philosopher Duns Scotus, and often was surmounted by a round knob at the pinnacle. Colored yellow, red, or white, the Jew's hat was mandatory costume. In the 13th-century German code of law, the *Schwabenspiegel*, Jews were required to wear the *Judenhut*, and that

Men and women wear typical 16th-century Dutch clothes, including the chaperones, collared capes, and Jews' hats—even in this feast for King Herod, where the head of St. John the Baptist is presented to Herodias. From a woodcut by Leyden, 16th century, Netherlands. Courtesy of the Metropolitan Museum of Art, New York. Harris Brisbane Dick Fund, 1925.

prescription was confirmed in the 14th-century *Sachsenspiegel* code.

In 13th-century Poland at Gnesen, as well as at Breslau, at Strasbourg, and in all of Austria, Jews were required to continue wearing the traditional pointed hat called in these laws the *pileus cornutus*. In Portugal King Alfonso IV (r. 1325–57) required Jews to wear a yellow hat or hood. In 15th-century Nuremberg, Jews wore a red *Judenhut* and later a *barrette*. Jews who disobeyed hat edicts and were caught wearing hats of current Christian fashions were punished with stiff fines.

Unlike the *Jewish badge*, considered a mark of infamy and degradation, Jews themselves celebrated the *Jewish hat* in manuscript art and in Jewish heraldry. In the coats of arms of Jewish families, the *canting arms*, alluding to the name of the family, for the names of Judden or Judei of Westphalia used three gold *Jewish hats* placed in triangular formation within a shield surrounded by Hebrew letters.

JEWISH CEREMONIAL GARMENTS

The *Tallit* Worn over the head and shoulders, the *tallit* in the Middle Ages, as well as today, was a prayer shawl worn by Jews during worship. Fringes called *ziziyyot* on the borders of the tallit were symbolic reminders to the wearer of the duty to observe all 613 commandments of the Torah. Numbers 15:3–41 established the wearing of those fringe reminders: "Speak to the children of Israel and direct them to make a tassel on the corners of their garments throughout their generations and to put on it a twined blue cord."

Ziziyyot fringes are biblical, though the *tallit* to which they are attached is not. Each *tallit* fringe is composed of four threads passing through a hole, doubled, twisted, and knotted at the four corners of the *tallit*. Jews wishing to wear fringes daily created a special garment called the *arba kanfot*, "the four corners," an undergarment worn under simple work tunic or extravagant ceremonial attire.

Though the *tallit* usually covered head and shoulders, sometimes it enwrapped the whole body, like a large shawl or ceremonial blanket. During wedding ceremonies, particularly in France, the *tallit* was used as a wedding canopy, a *chuppah*, spanning the head of both bride and groom during the marriage ceremony, simultaneously symbolizing their temporal home and their place in God's universe.

Not all observant Jews wore the *tallit* at prayer at all times. Medieval manuscript depictions of the pious in communal prayer sometimes show worshipers and rabbis wearing the *tallit*, sometimes only rabbis wear it, and yet other times no one at all wears a *tallit*. For major holidays, however, medieval Jews wrapped themselves in the *tallit*, sometimes worn only over the shoulders, sometimes covering the head, usually with the fringed end thrown over one shoulder. By the 14th century, it was customary to have a richly embroidered band of design or inscription on that part of the *tallit* covering the wearer's forehead, therefore ritualistically a crown, called an *atara*. Generally woven of silk, cotton, or wool, the *tallit* usually had stripes woven across the width, near the edges, grayish brown in the 13th century, later red, black, or blue.

Sabbath Clothes The dress code for synagogue consisted primarily of clean garments and "good" clothes as opposed to work clothes. Women and men wore overcoats and capes whose extravagant fur linings and brocade cuffs and collars carefully were hidden during those periods when sumptuary laws were strictly enforced and flamboyantly displayed otherwise. Women's Sabbath hats for synagogue varied according to local fashion. Scarves and veils were customary in Muslim lands. In western Europe women wore hats called the *oralia, cornalia, sendelbindel,* and *viereckiger schleier* with two blue stripes. The remarkable plethora of hat styles merits longer lists and explanations, later. Men in western Europe wore to synagogue the customary hats of their era and city, such as the *chaperone* with *liripipe* or the *barrette*.

Jewish badges and the *Jewish hat* sometimes were worn to synagogue, other times not, depending on whether in a particular time and place the sumptuary laws were vigorously enforced, rigorously obeyed, politely ignored, or individuals or the total community bought the privilege of freedom from wearing the distinguishing items by paying copiously for independence.

Wedding Clothes Neither bride nor groom wore white. Wedding garb was as elegant, graceful, colorful, and stylistically varied as local fashion, individual wealth, and taste allowed. Jewish moralists and Jewish sumptuary laws railed against the dangers of extravagance at weddings, warning Jews that ostentation leads to notice, envy, and social reprisals.

Customarily the groom wore his most magnificent Sabbath clothes as his wedding garb. So did the bride. She, however, usually sported a marriage belt fashioned from silver, gold, or brocaded fabric with elaborate metal or jeweled clasps. Some wedding belts were valuable engagement gifts, called *sivlonoth*, exchanged by bride and groom or as gift from parents. A 15th-century bride in the Rhineland received a gold-studded belt from her fiancé and a silver belt from her mother. She also wore a *kurse*, a cape-like short jacket, and a garland on her hair.

Pistachio green was a favorite color among medieval Jewish grooms in the Muslim Mediterranean, symbolic of fertility and of the Garden of Eden. Often both bride and groom dressed according to the current fashion of parti-colored clothes, *mi-parti*, in which two colors, symbolic or whimsical, were used for fabricating left half versus right half of a gown, left leg versus right leg of tights, left side versus right side of a hat. Medieval Jews, as did Christians, selected particular color combinations, or specifically avoided them, because of their association with family coats of arms and heraldic devices. The Jewish couple wishing to celebrate connection with a noble house selected those house colors for *mi-parti* clothing and for festive decoration.

In Muslim countries, medieval Jewish brides customarily wore veils. Veiling for modesty was not so common as veiling for historical tradition, imitating the biblical matriarch

Rebecca, who covered her eyes before she met her groom. In both the East and West, women lavished attention on the bride's hair beneath the veil. Often a professional bride preparer would be hired to create a magnificent hair design. (*See* chapter 11, Holidays and Festivals.) For the poor bride as well as the rich, pre–wedding-ceremony rituals usually began with hairstyling. The bride preparer, the bride's matrons of honor, and her bridesmaids combed the bride's hair, fashioned symbolic braids, such as forming a figure eight to imply endless continuity of love, or clever, whimsical designs. They would cover her hair with a garland, fillet, or crown before placing the bridal veil on and accompany this ritual with songs, dancing, and games. In some wedding ceremonies, for all or part the groom alone or both the bride and groom wore over their flamboyant wedding garb a floor-length white linen high-necked coat called a *sargenes*. The *sargenes* or *kittel* was the Talmudically sanctioned garment pious Jews wore during the New Year celebration of the High Holy Days and especially on the day of atonement, *Yom Kippur*. The leader of the Passover *seder* also would celebrate wearing the *sargenes*.

Brit Clothes The same moralists and promulgators of sumptuary laws who castigated extravagant weddings also lambasted Jews for attracting invidious attention during the *brit milah*, the circumcision ceremony eight days after a baby boy's birth. Similar flamboyance marked the parents' and guests' costumes at *brit* celebrations as at weddings and, according to the sumptuary legislators, might incite envy and anger among non-Jews.

Mourning Garb Medieval Jews apparently did not wear black for mourning the dead except in those times and places where they wore black routinely. In the 14th and 15th centuries, the darker, more restrictive, more pernicious the laws against Jewish life, the greater the tendency toward wearing black clothing. When Queen Maria of Aragon (d. 1456) attempted to force all Jews to wear black, her intentions were less sartorial then ecclesiastical. Furious that the Aragonese Jews refused to convert to Christianity, the queen ordered black clothing for them as symbolic of their dark, hard, stubborn, unrepentant hearts.

FASHIONABLE HATS AND HEADGEAR

In addition to Jewish hats by prescription, Jews wore the same fashionable hats and veils that were popular among the Christians of almost every European and Mediterranean country. Men and women wore them, young and old, rich and poor, laborer and scholar, in summer and winter. Jewish men and women followed local Christian and Muslim fashions in hat style, fabric, and distinctive method of presentation. When wealthy or noble Christian women in 15th-century France and Burgundy were wearing the stylish pointed, conical *hennin* headdress, whose mild to extravagant heights ascended according to the woman's social rank, so Jewish women adorned their heads with *hennin*-like hats made from stiffened silk or velvet with a veil flowing from the pinnacle. Jewish texts call the *hennin* the *cornalia* or *sendelbindel*. Similarly, when both men and women in Spain and Italy wore the graceful headdress hood, the *chaperone*, so did the local Jews. The tripartite chaperone consisted of a *roundlet*, a stuffed fabric circlet covered by a turban called a *garget*, which was folded lengths of fabric fulsomely wound around the head and culminating in a *liripipe*, the lavishly long fabric tail of the hat worn wound around the neck or swung over the shoulder, often ornamented with bells, fringe, or decorative precious stones. As with the height of the *hennin*, the length of the *liripipe* often signified hierarchical rank.

Although modern observant religious Jewish men routinely wear a *yarmulka*, a skullcap when indoors and outside, this head covering is not prescribed in the Bible. It may well be a custom acquired during the Babylonian exile and adapted and adopted by Oriental Jews. Western European Jews in the Middle Ages sometimes covered their heads in synagogue, sometimes not. French Jews did not use a head cover in the 12th century, nor later in France and Germany in the 13th century. Fourteenth- and 15th-century representations of worshipping Jews routinely show their heads covered in synagogue, with the styles varying city to city, sometimes a small cap, or *coif* also called a *cale*, or a hood such as a *capuchon*.

Outside the synagogue Jewish men and women wore hats as varied and flamboyant as wealth, social class, and courage allowed. Medieval Jews seem to have worn headgear as frequently or uncommonly as their neighbors living under jurisdiction of crescent or cross. The variety of Jewish hats and headgear surpasses the plenitude of overgarments and shoes represented in manuscript art, sculpture, the decorative arts, literature, and the commercial documents from the Cairo *geniza*.

Just as men and women in northern climates customarily covered their heads for warmth, so people in temperate and hot desert climates covered their heads for Sun protection. The number of veils and head shawls listed in the Cairo *geniza* documents demonstrates astonishing prevalence of headgear in various colors, designs, and styles for draping not only around and over the head and neck but the face. The yellow tripartite face veils called the *talthinas* were very popular among women in the 12th- and 13th-century Mediterranean. Judges in law courts also wore the *talthina*. Face veils offered protection against Sun, wind, and sand; when the appropriate section removed for indoor use, the veil served to signal dignity and station.

MUSLIM CLOTHING AND TEXTILES

As with the Christian and Jewish communities, dress and accessories were markers of identity and social status among Muslims. Clothing quickly distinguished men from women, rich from poor, nomads from city dwellers, Muslims from non-Muslims. Descendants of the Prophet wore green turbans. A turban with 12 folds indicated allegiance to the 12th Shiite imam. Muslim mystics were so identified by their distinctive coarse woolen cloak called a *suf* that they came to be called Sufis.

Though fashions varied from country to country and from century to century, two basic clothing traditions were distinguished in medieval Islam. In Arabia and the Mediterranean, people wore loose flowing robes made of lengths of cloth draped like togas on the body or sewn together with relatively little tailoring. In Iran and Central Asia, people wore close fitting garments outlining the shape of the body and limbs. Trousers and shirts were cut from lengths of cloth, carefully tailored, and sewn together. In certain periods styles merged and flowing robes were worn in Iran and tailored garments in Egypt.

Men wore the turban called the "crown of the Arabs." Women sometimes wore veils in public. At some times and places veiling was the fashion or the custom, the *urf*, but not a religious duty as part of *Sharia*. There was surprising variety in the way veils were used and what they signified: what part of the face, hair, or neck was covered, what was revealed; what social class the wearer belonged to, whether she was married or virgin, slave or free born. Likewise, there were wide variations in the age when a girl donned a veil, and what purpose the headdress promoted: modesty, decoration, celebration, or mourning. In some countries men, such as the Tuareg and the Almoravid Berbers of North Africa, wore veils. There women did not.

Head covers for men and women in northern climates provided warmth and head covers in temperate and hot desert climates provided protection against the Sun. A large number of veils and head shawls were listed in documents of the Cairo *geniza*. Veils and headgear were worn in various colors, designs, and styles for draping around and over the head and neck, and across and around the face. Yellow tripartite face veils called the *talthinas* were very popular among Muslim and Jewish Mediterranean women in the 12th and 13th centuries. Judges in law courts also wore the *talthina*. Face veils offered protection against Sun, wind, and sand. Veils were worn indoors as well as out, and with the appropriate section of the veil removed for indoor use. The veil served to signal dignity and station.

Clothing Styles

FROM BEDOUIN AUSTERITY TO UMAYYAD SPLENDOR

Clothing in the time of the prophet Muhammad retained the simplicity that characterized the vestments of pre-Islamic Arabia. Two common garments were the *zeira*, a long, flowing garment fastened with a belt, and the *izar*, also called *azr* or *mizar*, a large, versatile unisex sheetlike wrap that could be worn as a loincloth, mantle, or waist cloth. Generally speaking the complete wardrobe of men and women consisted of an undergarment or *izar*; a body shirt (*qamis*); a long dress, gown, or tunic, generically known as a *thawb*; a mantle or cloak as outerwear; and a head cover. Footwear was simple as well, usually sandals (*nal*). Under the

influence of Persia, Arab men and women also adopted the *sirwal*, a type of pantaloon or long billowing trousers. An outer garment popular in Syria was the *jubba*, a woolen tunic with narrow sleeves.

Modesty and austerity were the guiding principles of dress during the Prophet's lifetime. Many hadiths attest to his urging modesty for men and women in public. Muhammad is said to have forbidden seven things: silver vessels, gold rings, garments of silk, garments of brocade (*dibaj*), the *kassi* (a striped Egyptian fabric made of silk), garments of satin, and tanned hides. He expressed a preference for the simple *izar* over the more decorative black *khamisa* cloak with its richly embroidered borders. The Prophet's penchant for modesty in seen in the following anecdote: He once received as a gift a robe made of fine silk, wore it, even prayed in it, then suddenly threw it off as loathsome, saying that the God-fearing should not wear silk in this world but that they would be adorned with in paradise (N. Stillman, "Libas," *Encyclopedia of Islam*, 1999, 732a). Muhammad is most often associated with wearing a green wide-bordered woolen cloak of Yemeni design called a *burda*. Hadiths depicting Muhammad draping his *burda* over his family or bestowing a *burda* as a gift to his favorite poet would be immortalized in poetry and legend.

In addition to covering the body, clothing had important social uses. Clothes were customarily given as gifts to show one's appreciation or esteem. Despite his own austerity, Muhammad is said to have bestowed valuable items of clothing on his followers as a sign of favor—a custom that would be taken to unimaginable heights under the Abbasids and the Fatimids. Clothing formed a major component of women's dowries. Clothes could be used as currency in lieu of cash in order to purchase basic or luxury items or to pay the prescribed *zakat* (alms tax). Garments were important items of war booty.

RITUAL CLOTHING

The ritual purity required for prayer, quranic and Hadith recitation, and performance of the greater and the lesser pilgrimages (hajj and *umra*, respectively) applied not only to the body but also to one's clothing. While no particular item of attire was prescribed for ritual performances by law, a devout Muslim should ideally wear clean clothing and sprinkle the body with musk when going to the mosque or engaging in prayer. She or he should remove shoes from the feet when praying as a sign of humility and to protect oneself and God's house from the impurities on the soles of the shoe.

Even in later periods from the Umayyad dynasty onward when luxurious and opulent fashion became the order of the day and the measure of social status, wealth, and refinement, a pilgrim on the hajj to Mecca was required by law scrupulously to observe the ritual *ihram* ("consecration"). As noted in chapter 11's description of the Muslim hajj, after performing the special ablutions, all men regardless of their rank wore two seamless white garments—white, the color of purity—the *izar* cloth wrapped around the loins and the *rida* cloak draped over the upper body. Men's heads must be bare—the bare head was the ultimate sign of humility—and the feet dressed only in simple sandals or backless shoes. While no particular garb was prescribed for the woman pilgrim, she was expected to wear plain, modest attire such as a long sleeved, full-length tunic; to cover her hair and breast with a veil; and to use no perfume.

Pilgrims of all classes and distinctions usually wore amulets hanging from or sewn into their clothing in order to assure divine protection while traveling. In fact, the wearing of amulets was a long and venerated custom throughout Mesopotamia, the Mediterranean, and North Africa retained from pre-Islamic times. In the Islamic period, however, amulets, whether made of shells, stone, cloth, or other materials, typically had verses of the Quran, litanies to God or the prophet Muhammad inscribed upon them. Caliphs and the nobility, elegant urban men and women, traders and merchants, soldiers, rural people, pregnant women, and even the savviest religious scholars wore amulets for protection from the evil eye, while traveling or going off to battle.

Menstruating women wore a special garment in imitation of the custom of the Prophet's wives. While there was no official mourning garb, one was expected to wear one's oldest and worst clothing as a sign of mourning. The law did prescribe that the dead be buried in a seamless white shroud and some pilgrims chose to be buried in their *ihram* garment. Islam prohibited women in mourning to wear dyed clothing. Conversely, new and brightly dyed clothing was associated with joyful celebrations, be they marriage, the birth of children, the circumcision of baby boys, or religious festivals such as Feast of the Breaking of the Fast (*Id al-Fitr*), which ends the month-long Ramadan fast; the celebration of the Prophet's birthday, first endorsed in the 10th century by the Shiite Fatimids.

CLOTHING COLOR AND RELIGIOUS IDEOLOGY

The second Abbasid caliph, Abu Jafar al-Mansur (r. 754–775), is said to have instituted the color black as the symbol of the Abbasid dynasty and the color to be worn at official ceremonies. The Shiite Fatimids chose green as their official color in remembrance of certain hadiths stating that it was the Prophet's favorite color and the color of his famous *burda* cloak with which he had draped Ali, Fatimid, and their sons, Hassan and Husayn. Green was also the color of the *sharifs*, persons, Sunni or Shiite, who derived their nobility (*shurf*) from their descent from the Prophet's family. Indeed, during the reign of the Abbasid caliph al-Mamun (r. 813–833), green was briefly imposed as the official state color in order to vindicate their claims of descent from the Prophet.

Among the Shiites it became customary to wear black as a sign of mourning during the observance of Ashura, in commemoration of the 10th day of the month of Muharram when the Prophet's grandson, Husayn, was murdered by the Umayyad ruler Muawiyya in 661. In Umayyad Spain and elsewhere in the Sunni world, however, Muslims showed their rejection of Shiism by joyfully celebrating Ashura as a great festival of divine forgiveness by spending generously on the household, donning one's finest attire, and giving gifts of expensive new clothing and delicious food.

UMAYYAD *TIRAZ* AND SUMPTUARY LAWS

The establishment of the Umayyad caliphate and the transfer of the Islamic capital out of Bedouin Arabia to urbane Damascus provoked indelible changes in culture, fashion, and overall sense of aesthetics. Umayyad legitimacy, power, nobility, and ideology were now to be manifested in the use of clothing and luxurious fabrics, institutionalized by the establishment of *tiraz* factories for fabricating embroidered garments (discussed later).

In the Arabia of the early Islamic period Arab clothing was clearly distinguishable from the attire worn by non-Arab Jews, Persians, and others. Under the Umayyads, however, the urbane taste for fine clothing was shared by Muslim, Jews, and Christians alike, provoking the caliphs to introduce unprecedented sumptuary laws (*ghiyar*, literally, "laws of distinction"). The *Ahl al-Dhimma*, the Jews, Christians, and Zoroastrians, were forbidden to wear Arabo-Islamic headgear such as the turban (*imama*) and the *taylasan* head wrap. They also were required to wear distinctive belts called *mintaq* or *zunnar*, around their tunics.

While the sumptuary laws seemed to have been enforced under the Abbasids as well, the information obtained in the Cairo *geniza* records clearly indicates that they were not applied in Fatimid and Ayyubid Egypt (10th to mid-13th centuries). Jewish, Coptic, and Muslim women wore the same attire and there was no specification of difference in the fabrics or colors that could be used. All dressed in the same fashionable *tiraz* embroidered garments such as the *bukhnuq*, *isaba maila*, *khimar*, and *khirqa*, and all covered their heads and faces with the *miqnaa*, *mindil*, *tarha*, and other styles of veils, shawls, and scarves. The Mamluks appear to have enforced the sumptuary laws more vigorously than their Ayyubid and Fatimid predecessors.

ABBASID REFINEMENT AND GOOD MANNERS

The aesthetics of artistic refinement, good manners, and impeccable taste that was the subject of much of the *adab* (belles-lettres) literature of the Abbasid golden age was paralleled in the new attention accorded clothing and costumes. Gone were the last vestiges of the modesty and simplicity that were the leitmotifs of proper dress in the time of Muhammad and the first generation. Under the influence of the tasteful Persian secretarial class, the Abbasid nobility and the bourgeoisie who imitated them now draped themselves in intricately decorated silks and satins, made possible in large part by the introduction and production of new embroidered fabrics and garments, collectively known as *tiraz* (*see* under textiles).

When the Abbasids seized power from the Umayyads in 749–750, they came riding in on horseback bearing black embroidered banners. Black was the color of Abbasid robes of state.

Abbasid caliphs such as Harun al-Rashid wore elegant caftans made of Tustari silk imported from Persia, distinguished by their gold and silver brocade (*tiraz*) and sleeves that buttoned in the front. Caliphs and nobles wore on their heads the *kalansuwa*, the high conical hat fashioned out of a wicker or wooden frame and covered with colorful silk, another Persian import.

Clothing and dress did not escape the attention of the writers of *adab* (belles-letters). One Abbasid man of letters, al-Washsha (d. 936), has left a vivid record of the fashionable outfits of the bourgeoisie. His *Kitab al-muwashsha wal-zarf wa l-zurafa* (*The Book on Elegance and Elegant People*) is a veritable "how-to" of fine dress: The fashionable man should outfit himself with several layers of clothing, starting with an undershirt (*ghilala*) over which he wore a heavier lined shirt (*qamis mubattan*), both made of the finest linen from Egypt or Persia. Over his *qamis* he should wear a *jubba*, a long tunic made of the finest silk, linen, or *mulham*, a novel combination of silk and wool. In public the man of honor donned his *rida*, the cloak hallmarking his honor and rank, and covered his head with a turban with its silk *taylasan* draped about it. The man of good taste should be clean, his body perfumed—but not his clothing, as was the custom of slaves—his clothing, spotless and of harmonious colors. His shoes or sandals must be of fine leather, and sporting a shoe of a different color on each foot was particularly popular.

Al-Washsha described the elegant woman as wearing as her undergarments a smoky gray colored *ghilala* shirt and gray or white *sirwal* pantaloons. She avoided white outerwear at all costs—white was the color of masculinity. Her long colorful dress should have wide sleeves and a round collar fastened by a drawstring. Only an outer wrap (*rida*) made in Rosetta in Egypt or Tabaristan in Iran was good enough to cover her body. She covered her head with a *mijar*, preferably black, and draped her face with a veil (*miqnaa*).

FATIMID COURTLY SPLENDOR

Clothing took pride of place in creating the unrivaled splendor, pomp, and ceremony that characterized the Fatimid dynasty. As the descendants of the Prophet through his son-in-law, Ali, and his daughter, Fatima, through splendorous clothing and adornments they visibly indicated their noble rank. Every official, every member of the court received a sumptuous wardrobe of ceremonial clothing fashioned out of the finest silk, linen, and brocade. The preferred color for their ceremonial robes was white ornamented with gilded and silver threaded embroidery, symbols of the divine light that illuminated from them. Shiite lore claims that the divine light that God cast upon Muhammad, Ali, Husayn, and his successors also dwelt within the Fatimid rulers. Each member of the imperial retinue wore a precious turbaned headdress (*imama*), but none equaled the majesty of the caliph's headgear, known as the "noble crown" (*al-taj al-sharif*). The noble

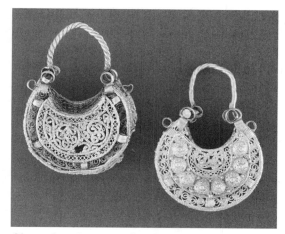

Shown here is a pair of 11th-century golden earrings.   HIP/Art Resource, NY.

crown consisted of an enormous jewel-bedecked turban (*shashiyya*) around which was an enormous *mandil* wrapped in a way unique to the caliph and centered on the caliphal crown was an enormous solitary jewel (*yatima*).

WOMEN'S WEAR: MECCAN GARMENTS AND PERFUME

The 14th-century world traveler Ibn Battuta described Meccan men and women as very elegant and clean in their dress. Most wore white garments that looked fresh and snowy. Meccans used a great deal of perfume and kohl. They also freely used toothpicks of green arak wood. Meccan women were extraordinarily beautiful, pious, and modest. They made such great use of perfume that they preferred to go to bed hungry in order to buy perfume with the price of their food. They visited the mosque every Thursday night, wearing their finest clothes. The whole sanctuary was saturated with the smell of their perfume. When a perfumed woman left the mosque the odor of her perfume clung to the place long after she was gone.

TURKISH WOMEN'S CLOTHING

Ibn Battuta described the opulent clothing of 14th-century Turkish women, who were so revered by their husbands that they seemed to hold more a dignified position than the men. Near Qiram Ibn Battuta saw the Turkish princess, wife of the *amir*, traveling in a wagon covered with rich blue woolen cloth, with the windows and doors of the tent open, accompanied by four maidens, exquisitely beautiful and richly dressed, and followed by more wagons with women in her entourage. When they arrived at the *amir*'s camp, 30 maidens carried the train of the princess's gown, which had loops that lifted the train off the ground to enable her to walk with elegant stateliness. The *amir* arose to greet her and she sat beside him and poured a beverage into a cup for him, which she presented as she knelt before him. They then ate together, and the *amir* then gave her a ceremonial robe before she withdrew to her quarters.

Likewise Ibn Battuta observed that a wife of a merchant or common man would travel in a horse-drawn wagon attended by three or four maidens to carry her train and wear on her head a conical headdress encrusted with pearls and topped by peacock feathers. Since the windows of the tent were open her face was visible, for Turkish women did not veil themselves. If a woman was accompanied by her husband, his dress might mark him as her servant for he wore only a sheep's wool cloak and a matching high cap.

SUF AND *KHIRQA*, THE GARB OF THE MYSTICS

Before going on to speak of the magnificent tradition of textile fabrication introduced by the Umayyads, a final word must be given to the attire of the Sufi mystics and ascetics. Some four centuries before the voluntary poverty movement emerged in 12th-century Christian Europe, Muslim ascetics, scandalized by the opulence and vanity of the Umayyads and the Abbasids, began showing their yearning for the austerity, humility, and simplicity of the Prophet's generation by clothing themselves in sober garments made of wool (*suf*). Of course wool, as the cheapest and most available fabric, had always been worn by the urban poor, rural dwellers, and Bedouins. But the ascetics and after them the Sufi mystics would make the poor woolen garb their garment of glory, in imitation of a famous saying by Muhammad that "my poverty is my pride."

Hagiographic dictionaries make frequent mention of the clothing as a sign of the renunciation of the world. One 12th-century Andalusian account tells of the jurist Abu l-Rabi Sulayman al-Jazuli, who was "a powerful and influential emir of his country. . . . He resigned from his position, no longer mounted a horse or carried a sword, and dressed in complete humility in the poorest rags" (Meier, 1999, p. 435). A 14th-century hagiographic notice of the renounced Sufi judge and preacher Ibn Abbad of Ronda depicts him perfectly imitating the prophet Muhammad's custom and wearing his favorite color, green:

> His greatest enjoyment from the mundane world was perfume and much frankincense. He undertook the matter of serving himself by himself, for he did not marry and he did not have a maid. At home he wore rags and tatters but if he went out would cover them over with a green or a white burnoose. (Ibn Qunfud, 1965, p. 79)

Thus while caliphs, the aristocracy, and the bourgeoisie glorified their status and wealth by draping themselves in stunning embroidered attired, the ascetics and Sufis wrapped themselves in woolen mantles and rags of poverty and humility.

Textiles and Colors

Fabrics and cloths were so important to the history of Islam that the culture itself has been described as draped, as in the scholar Golombek's title *The Draped Universe of Islam*. Textiles protected people from the Sun and provided warmth in winter. They covered and defined spaces. A single space could have multiple functions depending upon the way textiles were spread or hung. Rugs were spread on floors. Curtains and other hangings adorned walls. Strung on a cord or wire across a room, a curtain separated space for functions as if by walls. While furniture in western Europe usually elevated people above the floor on sturdy materials such as wood, furniture in the Islamic world indicates that human actions were best performed on the floor with the help of fabrics.

Portable fabric storage sacks functioned in place of trunks, seat cushions and back bolsters in place of chairs. Tablecloths might be spread on the floor for meals. Diners sat on the floor and served themselves from communal trays perched on a low stand. After dinner ended, the tablecloths were removed. Rugs, blankets, and bedspreads then could be placed on the floor for sleeping. Carpets were so admired for their warmth, softness underfoot, and beauty that stone mosaic pavements sometimes imitated carpets. In the early Umayyad palace of Khirbat al-Mafjar near Jericho, the beautiful mosaic in the *diwan* had *tesserae*, or tiles, set to imitate a carpet with fringe.

Textiles were important to all social classes. Nomads used fabrics for clothing, furnishing, carrying of goods, storage, and shelter. Tents were sturdy portable houses with rigid supports sustaining a cloth cover. Two basic tent types in the Muslim world were the Middle Eastern tent and the Central Asian tent. The typical Middle Eastern tent had poles supporting a fabric covering secured by ropes. The typical Central Asian tent was a self-supporting wooden lattice covered with felts. Within either type of tent, space was partitioned into men's and women's zones by textile hangings. Nomad tents used for royalty increased the size, splendor of fabrics, and opulence of floor coverings and fabric furnishings. The great Mongol conqueror Timur or Tamerlane (d. 1405) erected tent cities for his court.

THE SACRED *KISWA* OF THE KAABA

Textiles were important from the earliest days of Islam. A holy veil called the *kiswa* covered the Kaaba in Mecca. The veil draped over the holy Black Stone of the Kaaba, a venerated black meteorite thought to belong to the original pre-Islamic structure, had political as well as religious import. Rulers fought for the right to supply the veil, because it was an honor and sign of their sovereignty. The *kiswa* fabric could be any one of several colors, including white, green, or red. (Nowadays the Kaaba is veiled in black cloth with bands of inscriptions from the Quran woven in gold.)

In Muhammad's time each new *kiswa* was draped on top of the previous one. During the caliphate of Umar (r. 634–644), the Kaaba was threatened by collapse from the weight of all the coverings draped over it. The *kiswa* veil probably symbolized a sacred tent. A parallel could be found in Jewish tradition, for the Israelites made a beautiful tent for the Ark of the Covenant (cf. 2 Samuel 6:17), where it was said that God himself dwelled.

Luxurious textiles are well known from legal documents in seventh-century Arabia. The Quran and the hadith referred to sumptuous materials and their decoration. The Quran described voluptuous silks adorning the virtuous in paradise: The garments of the virtuous will be made of silk (suras 22:23 and 35:33). The virtuous will recline on carpets lined with rich brocade (sura 55:54). Because silk was associated with paradise, most schools of Islamic law prohibited men on Earth from wearing silken garments next to the skin. Some legal theorists permitted textiles of silk mixed with another fiber, such as the hybrid *mulham*, while others allowed silk cushions, prayer mats, and silk outer garments, so long as another fabric intervened between the silk and the skin.

Decorated fabrics were associated with Hadith traditions from the Prophet's life. One story in the Burkhari collection described Muhammad as surprised when his wife Aisha hung a curtain decorated with figures of animals and birds. The Prophet exclaimed that those who imitated God's creative acts will be severely punished on judgment day. Aisha took down the curtain and cut it up to make it into cushion covers. That pleased the Prophet. Some scholars interpreted this as proof that figural decorations were dangerous and caused idolatry. Other scholars viewed this as proof that elegant fabrics existed in Muhammad's household and whatever Muhammad did was worthy of imitation.

Moreover, the Prophet himself used the cosmetic kohl to decorate and protect the eyes. When the 14th-century traveler Ibn Battuta visited Upper Egypt, hoping to cross the Hijaz, he stayed at the monastery of Dayr at-Tin, which housed illustrious relics of the Prophet— a fragment of his wooden basin and the pencil he used to apply the cosmetic kohl. There also was the awl the Prophet used for sewing his sandals.

MUHAMMED'S CLOAK, THE *BURDA ODE*

Many legends surround the cloak (*burda*) that the prophet Muhammad wore. In the rebuilding of the Kaaba textiles were related to honor. Workmen had removed the venerated Black Stone from its place during reconstruction work. When ready to reinstate it the workmen erupted in a quarrel over who should have the honor of repositioning the sacred relic. The laborers decided to honor the first passerby. Fortunately Muhammad arrived, gently placed the stone in his cloak, and gave one corner each to the head of each tribe to carry the sacred stone.

The Quran relates that one morning the Prophet wore his black cloak while he went walking and encountered his daughter, Fatima; his son-in-law, Ali; and his grandsons, Hassan and Husayn. He took them all under his *burda*, hugged them, and said, "People of the House, God only desires to put away from you abomination and to cleanse you" (Sura 33:32). The Shiites customarily interpreted this incident as demonstrating the right of the Prophet's family to lead the Muslim community.

In another tradition the Prophet gave his *burda* to his follower, the seventh-century poet Kab ibn Zuhayr, as a reward for a poem he wrote. The Umayyad caliph Muawiya I (r. 661–680) bought that cloak from the poet's son, kept it in the treasury of the Abbasid caliphs in Baghdad, and only lost it when the Mongols conquered the city in 1258. Some scholars claimed that Muhammad's *burda* was burned, others that it was saved, but it eventually reappeared as a relic in the treasury of the Ottoman sultans in Istanbul.

The holy garment was immortalized in a poem composed by the 13th-century Egyptian poet Sharaf al-Din al-Busiri after he was miraculously cured of fatal illness when the Prophet appeared to him and draped the *burda* over the poet's shoulders, as once he had for the poet Kab ibn Zuhayr. The ode to Muhammad's *burda* was a renowned poem in Arabic. The ode was thought to convey the cloak's blessing (*baraka*) to all who heard it.

WOOL, LINEN, COTTON, AND SILK FABRICS

Four major textiles used in the Islamic world were wool, linen, silk, and cotton. Each had its own history, source, and production techniques. Wool apparently was native to the Mediterranean, as was linen. Cotton and silk were imported from Asia. Wool was one of the most versatile and important fabrics to Muslim economies. Shorn from sheep, goats, and camels, the sheared fleece was cleaned, carded, combed, then spun into long threads and thereafter woven into fabrics. Nomads, farmers, and town dwellers used almost all parts of a sheep. Wool was shorn from the animal's undercoat. Its skin made leather for shoes and book bindings. Its flesh was eaten, its milk churned into cheese, and its excrement use to fertilize crops.

Linen was far stronger than wool though more difficult to prepare and harder to color with dye. Fabricated from the flax plant, flax stalks were dried, fermented in warm water, then pounded, combed, and spun into threads. Great amounts of water were required for linen

production. Since linen fibers rotated naturally to the left they were usually spun counterclockwise, producing an S twist. This became characteristic of Egyptian fibers. Elsewhere, fibers were spun with a clockwise or Z twist. In the fifth century before the Common Era, the Greek historian Heroditus already had noted the unusual quality of Egyptian spinning, and Egypt was a major center of linen production. Linen also was produced in Syria, Mesopotamia, Sicily, North Africa, and Spain.

Cotton was a plant fiber harvested then spun. Native to India, cotton was introduced as early as the first century in Central Asia and cultivated in large oases near rivers. Cotton was grown in Mesopotamia under the Persian Sassanians (third to seventh centuries) and became a major manufacture in the Mediterranean after the Muslim conquest. Iraq, Syria, Palestine, and Yemen were important Muslim cotton-producing centers. Cotton usually was glazed or starched to produce a smooth surface for decoration.

Silk was produced by silkworms' spinning cocoons that when unraveled released a fine filament that was twisted with other filaments to create a thread, and then woven. Mulberry trees provided the silkworms' food. Silk production, sericulture, thrived where mulberry trees were cultivated. The secret of silk culture was smuggled from China to Central Asia, India, and then Persia. Silkworms were cultivated in Persia under the Sassanians and in northern Syria as early as the sixth century. The Byzantine emperor Justine I (r. 527–565) was said to have induced two itinerant monks to hide silkworm eggs and mulberry seeds in their hollow walking canes in order to smuggle these essentials for silk production from Central Asia to his capital city of Constantinople.

Soon silk manufacturing in the Byzantine Empire was a state monopoly, as earlier it had been in China. Syria evolved as its major center of production. When the Muslims conquered Syria in the seventh century, they increased silk production and silk profits. Silk was introduced to Spain by the ninth century and to Sicily by the late 11th or early 12th century.

Significant commodities in international trade, silk thread, silk cloth, silk textiles, and silk finished goods were among the most important exports from the Muslim world. Silks were shipped overland along the silk routes through Central Asia, Iran, and the Fertile Crescent to the Mediterranean. In the 14th century weavers of the Italian city of Lucca gained sufficient skill and excellence to break the Islamic monopoly on silk production.

EGYPTIAN COLORED LINEN, ELEGANT TURBANS, FABRIC SHOPS

Egyptian colored linen was so highly valued that the Persian poet and traveler Nasr-i Khus-raw (d. c. 1078), who visited the fabric manufac-turing town of Tennis, meticulously described in his *Safarnama* linen woven in the royal work-shops that was so precious that it was not to be sold to anyone. Even kings could not buy it. The king of Fars tried to buy one suit of cloth-ing of the special Egyptian material and sent 20,000 dinars to Tennis through his agents, who remained there for several years but returned home empty-handed. Nasr-i Khusraw himself observed the extravagant turban woven for the caliph that was estimated to be worth 4,000 dinars. So elegant and refined was cloth making in Egypt, and so great the moral author-ity of the caliph, that fabric sellers, as did others who dealt in precious commodities, money-lenders, and jewelers, did not have to lock their shops. They merely lowered a net across the front to indicate the workday was done. No one dared tamper with anything.

MULHAM, HYBRIDS, AND DYES

Fabric combinations were important in Muslim trade. A diaphanous fabric called *mulham* or half-silk combined raw silk with cotton. Egyp-tian linens often had wool or silk bands woven into the fabric. Mesopotamian cottons usually were embroidered in brightly colored silk. Woolen rugs sometimes were knotted on cotton for extra strength. An annual cloth market in Jiddah, situated the port of Mecca, encouraged trading of Egyptian linen for Indian cotton.

Dyes were associated with their regions of origin. Most dyes were derived from indige-nous, natural substances, though imported when necessary. Saffron from crocuses pro-vided yellow. The herb madder created red. Vibrant reds were derived from the insect ker-mes, cochineal, and lac. Indigo leaves created a bright blue dye. Minerals such as copper pro-vided verdigris, green. Gold and silver were wrapped in filaments with silk.

Chemical mordants made the colors fast. Alkali fixed the color of golden saffron. Sumac and gall nuts were used for both dyes and mor-dants. Bleaches, niter, and quicklime degreased wool, and starches helped finish the fabrics and glaze them. Fullers earth made wool soft and cleaned it.

WEAVING LOOMS

"Horizontal" and "vertical" looms were com-monly used in the Muslim world. Nomadic tribes preferred horizontal looms because they were easily collapsible and portable, although they created relatively narrow woven strips. Large fabrics were created by sewing multiple strips side by side. Vertical looms were used in towns and cities. Excellence of fabric was deter-mined by fiber, thread thickness, and weaving techniques. The sturdiest fabrics, meant for tents and transport bags, customarily were woven of wool and goat hair. Veils and shawls and rich fabrics often combined silk and cash-mere, the hair from the underbelly of the Kash-mir goat. Carpets were woven from wool and silk, knotted into a woven substratum. An early wool carpet discovered in the ruins of Fustat (Egypt) had six colors, and a medallion with a stylized sharp-clawed four-legged animal and was woven with Z-spun warp and weft. Though in Egypt S spinning was traditional, the old carpet might have been imported.

Felt was created by matting wool fibers by pressure, heat, and moisture. Felting was important for making camel blankets and tents. In Central Asia, even before fabrics were spun and woven, felting was a major fabric technique.

IKAT AND FABRIC MOSAIC

Stripes and checks in woven fabrics were created by coloring individual threads with dye before weaving them. *Ikat* was a common technique in the Islamic world, in which the warp and sometimes weft threads were tie-died to create patterns when woven. Popular in Indonesia, central Asia, and Yemen, it originated in India. Spectacular cotton fabrics were made at Sanaa, capital of Yemen, in the ninth and 10th centuries. Cotton warps were dyed blue and brown before weaving and then woven with natural cotton wefts, creating a typical variegated stripe. Yemeni *ikats* often were decorated with embroidery or painted with gold with inscriptions blessing the owner.

Mosaic pattern decorations were created during weaving of tapestry by using discontinuous wefts that were woven around a few warps to create a small area of many colors. Bands and medallions with animals, birds, and inscriptions were woven and added to plain linen fabrics. Compound weaves utilized two or more sets of warps and wefts simultaneously. Compound weaves allowed complex figural patterns to be produced in several colors. Fabrics from Egyptian graves such as Akhmim in Upper Egypt preserved Greek and Coptic names, implying they were made for the Christian market. Others with Arabic inscriptions also were excavated. Other decorations were added after weaving. Throughout the entire piece of fabric or only on sections of the fabric, parts of the design were covered with black to prevent the dye from penetrating into that part, as in the batik or resist-dye technique. Then other designs were painted or block printed on the fabric. Embroidery or sewing in various colored threads on the finished fabric or appliqué embellished pieces of textile that were sewn in patches, forming elaborate patterns.

KHILA

Manufacturing and trading textiles were significant to Islamic economy and Islamic art. Large numbers of people were employed to create in textiles those items that in the West graced households and public places fabricated of wood and other sturdy materials. Specialized textile manufacturing took place in royal cities for the production of tribute and honor garments called *khila*. Textiles were diplomatic gifts. Robes of honor, *khila*, were rewards for high officials and court favorites. Yearly gifts as well as celebratory gifts of fabric garments were common.

Other manufactures of textile art were sold in the *suqs* and exported by caravan and ship to a world glad to pay for Islamic fabrics that could be crafted into European costume styles or for finished goods in cushions, bolsters, carpets, blankets, curtains, embroidered wall coverings, tapestries, tents, horse blankets, and other items for practical purposes and ostentatious display. Wealth bought specific colors, weavings, embroideries, and fabulous silks.

Moreover, the caliphs, and from 1250 onward the Mamluk sultans, had the privilege of providing a new *kiswa*, the ornamental cloth or veil covering the *Kaaba* at Mecca. The fabrication of the *kiswa* provided opportunity for employing numerous fabric makers and decorators at the court textile factory.

TIRAZ

The Umayyad caliphs who reigned between 661 and 750 established large palace weaving factories called *Dar al-tiraz* (House of Embroidery). *Tiraz*, from the Persian and Arabic words meaning "inscription," were bands of linen or other cloth embroidered with inscriptions. *Tiraz* was reserved for royal purposes. The most common type of *tiraz* embroidery was the long band inscribed with a ruler's name, and often the place and date of manufacture. Fabrics were made in state workshops for distribution by the ruler to his court. Apparently the caliph provided cloth for clothes for both summer and winter garments. The *tiraz* system expanded under the Abbasids, who established factories in Central Asia, Mesopotamia, and Egypt in order to clothe their enormous retinues.

Some embroideries were in silk on cotton; others on *mulham*, the combination of cotton and silk; or on linen. Large numbers of people were involved in every aspect of making *tiraz*, from the creation of the raw materials from which thread was spun to weaving of cloth, design and fabrication of cloth into garments, then cleaning, storing, and bestowing of *tiraz* garments upon those selected.

The estate of the caliph Harun al-Rashid (d. 809) consisted of 8,000 coats, 400 lined with sable or other fur, 400 lined with figured cloth; 10,000 shirts and tunics; 10,000 caftans, 2,000 trousers; 4,000 turbans; 1,000 hooded cloaks; 1,000 outer capes; and 5,000 kerchiefs. Other furnishings made of fabric included 1,000 Armenian carpets, 4,000 draperies, 5,000 cushions, 5,000 pillows, 1,500 silk pile carpets, 100 silk spreads, 1,000 silk cushions, 300 carpets from Maysan, 1,000 carpets from Drabjird, 1,000 brocade cushions, 1,000 cushions made of striped silk, 1,000 pure silk drapes, 300 brocade drapes, 500 carpets, 1,000 cushions from Tabaristan, 1,000 small bolsters, and 1,000 pillows. Since Islamic law required burial in a plain white shroud, Muslims were buried in their white pilgrimage garment and gave gifts of white honor garments.

Baghdad was famous for its fabric factories that created *tiraz* and *mulhams* richly decorated with embroideries and inscriptions. Rows of medallions with animals flanking stylized trees or plants were common decorations in the Baghdad fabrics.

Spain, Syria, and the province of Fars in Iran had important textile industries. Spain produced magnificent woven silks. Palmettes and scrolling vines were signature decorations on Spanish silks, as were eagles, animals, and human figures. The "lion strangler" was a common motif.

COPTIC CLOTH

Islamic fabric workers utilized techniques derived from the Copts, who flourished in the fabric trades in Egypt and created exquisite fabrics woven in silk, wool, or wool combined with linen. Coptic fabrics used bold colors such as deep aqua, citrus green, and tomato red. Designs included palmettes, running animals, human figures, mystical symbols, and magical devices. Woven in multiple bands of fabric then joined, the Coptic textiles continued to flourish in Egypt under the Shiite Fatimids who ruled between 909 and 1171.

ANATOLIAN CARPETS, EGYPTIAN SILK, SPANISH SILK

Anatolia, particularly from the 13th century onward, was significant for creating Islamic pile carpets. These became popular in Europe and were a major export. Fabric production was a major source of income in 14th-century Mamluk Egypt and Syria. Particularly notable were Egyptian silks with Chinese designs such as the large lotus blossom. During the reign of Sultan al-Malik al-Nasir Muhammad (r. 1293–

Shown here is a fifth-century Coptic cloth depicting a man with a club offering food to a tiger. Borromeo/Art Resource, NY.

wool of the Kashmir goat. *Taffeta* is from *taf-ton*, the Persian verb meaning "to spin." A rich satin was and is called *atlas*.

An amazingly well-preserved fabric dating from the eighth or ninth century was excavated from a tomb at Moshchevaya Valka in the northern Caucasus Mountains. Apparently a prince's robe, it was emerald green with long sleeves. The garment wrapped around the body and was fastened with golden buckles. It was decorated with rows of medallions depicting in yellow the *simurgh*, the mythical lion-headed bird from the Persian *Book of Kings*, *Shah-Nameh*, that nurtured the heroic white-haired Zal in her nest. Facings and bindings of the robe were made of silk. Many precious fabrics constructed this burial clothing for a remote ruler in a remote land on part of the Silk Road connecting China and central Asia to Byzantium and the West. Opulent silks were imported into Syria for murals at the Umayyad palace of Khirbat al-Mafjar. The study of Islamic textiles reveals Islam's wealth, power, cultures, technology, and diffusion.

TEXTILES AND PROFESSOR MUHYI AL-DIN

The *Rihla* of Ibn Battuta records the prevalence of textiles in polite 14th-century Islamic society, with its rich tents, carpets, cushions, embroidered fabrics, embellished cloaks, honor clothes, and clothing gifts. One day Ibn Battuta decided to visit a distinguished theologian in the town of Birgi named Muhyi al-Din. Ibn Battuta went to his madrasa and found him just arriving, mounted on a spirited mule and wearing gold-embroidered garments, surrounded by his slaves, servants, and students. Ibn Battuta later visited the professor in his garden, which had a stream of water flowing through a white marble basin rimmed with enameled tiles. There the professor looked like a king seated on his raised seat covered with embroidered cloths, his students and slaves beside

1340) silk woven with a particular form of flame-shaped lotus blossoms along with inscriptions proved to be popular commission.

From the 13th century onward many fabric workers employed a new type of embroidery. It was characterized by inscriptions, interlaced grids, S curves, and half-palmettes stylized in wedge shapes. Decorative motifs in 14th-century Islamic Spain almost always were variations on geometric interlaces and radial star designs.

Arabic and Persian words that described Islamic fabrics, weaving techniques, and important cities in the cloth trades still are used today. *Damask* derives from Damascus. *Muslin* was from Mosul in Iraq. *Organdy* is from the place-name *Urgench* in Central Asia. Mohair was from the Arabic word *mukhayyir*, meaning "choice" or "select." *Cashmere* derives from the him. The professor announced Ibn Battuta's arrival to the sultan of Birgi, living at his summer home nearby, who sent the traveler the gift of a tent called a *kurgan* consisting of a dome of wood lathes covered with felt, the upper part open to admit light and air.

The sultan offered food and hospitality for many days and then an extended visit to his city palace, where they sat in the sultan's opulent audience hall with daises covered with carpets, on one the sultan's cushion. But the sultan sat down with Ibn Battuta and the professor on the carpets, the Quran readers nearby. During the 14-day stay at the palace the sultan showed Ibn Battuta a hard black stone that had fallen from the sky, an asteroid, and gave him lavish gifts of food, fruit, candies, candles, 100 pieces of gold, 1,000 dirhems, a complete set of new garments, and a Greek slave named Michael.

The sultan also sent a robe and money gift to each of the traveler's companions. After leaving the sultan, Ibn Battuta visited the ancient Greek town of Ephesus, where he visited the cathedral mosque that formerly had been a church. There he bought a Greek slave woman for 40 dinars.

A GLOSSARY OF CHRISTIAN, JEWISH, AND MUSLIM HAT STYLES AND CLOTHING

Hats and Headwear

almuce—a cloth or fur hood worn by secular Jewish and Christian men and women, sometimes with pendant bands draped over the wearer's chest. In Christian vestments the *almuce* also was called an *amict*.

atara—a crown, or the embroided strip on a Jewish *tallit* which when worn over the head hung down the forehead.

atour—a two-horned hat. A bifurcated, cylindrical, or parallel cone-shaped hair net or hat popular among 15th-century Jewish and Christian women. The hat resembled or covered upswept hair shaped like conical horns. The *atour* was constructed as if two *hennins*, one worn above each ear.

barbette—a linen head band or veil passing over the chin or just under it, essentially hiding chin and neck. Older Christian and Jewish women and sometimes widows wore the *barbette* with a *coverchief*, a fabric headdress piled or wound, sometimes fastened beneath the chin and crowned with a standing starched band. A *barbette* also could form a *wimple*, a face-framing linen or silk headband, enveloping the forehead, chin, sides of face, and neck.

beguin—a head covering for Christian men, women, and children named after the 12th-century semimonastic women's religious movement called the Beguines, consisting of a three-piece cap. Made of fine linen for the wealthy, the same style beguin was made from coarser cloth for common people.

berrette a cannelatto—fashionable in Mantua and Lombardy among Christians and Jews, this brimless hat had a layered crown with felt piping around its bottom edge.

biretta—originally a soft skullcap, it developed into a fashionable headdress for professors, physicians, churchmen, and businessmen, consisting of a fine fabric hat built over a rigid elevated hat framework consisting of three or four joined panels topped by a pom-pom.

bonnet—like the Christian *beguin*, a three-piece head covering tied with strings under the chin. In 15th-century France, the common style was the "sugar loaf bonnet," a particularly high-crowned cap primarily worn by men over bobbed hair.

bukhnuq—a woman's veil or head shawl popular in the Muslim Mediterranean.

cale—a linen skullcap that Jewish and sometimes Christian men fastened under the chin and wore under a hat. Without the chin strap, it was called a *coif*.

calotte—a 13th-century flat skullcap made of leather, velvet, wool, or cotton, worn by Jews and Christians.

cappuccio a foggia—often though not exclusively worn by Jewish physicians, it was a compound hat composed of a wide fillet with a long *liripipe* slung over one shoulder or wrapped around as a shawl covering both shoulders.

capuchon—a hooded cape sometimes long, sometimes short, worn both by secular Jewish men and women as well as Christian churchmen. Later pointed hood became the *chaperone* turban with an extravagantly pendant tail called a *liripipe*.

caul—an elaborate headdress worn by Jews and Christians consisting of silken sheaths concealing strands or braids of hair covered by a netting of reticulated gold or silver cord further embellished with pearls, beads, jewels, spangles, sequins, or bells.

chape—a *capuchon* hood worn by Jews and Christians as rain protection or as a disguise for a reveler against identification.

chapeau—either an ordinary hat worn by Jews and Christians or a heraldic cap of dignity worn by rulers, made of crimson velvet and bordered with ermine.

chaperone—of tripartite construction, a popular hat among Christians and Jews consisting of a *roundlet*, a stuffed circlet over which long folds of turban called a *garget* were wound, concluding in the *liripipe*, the exceedingly long tail draped over the wearer's shoulder. In 14th-century Spain, one fashionable chaperone style was a relatively short hood whose closed end called the *peal* was drawn from the back of the head to the top to form a crest.

chaplet—a head wreath, usually a garland of leaves or flowers; or a circlet encrusted with gems; or a twisted cloth or padded roll holding a veil on the head, worn by Christians and Jews.

circlet—a headdress holding back the hair, consisting of a narrow band of precious metal, silken braid, flowers, or a bejeweled fabric that a Jewish or Christian man or woman wore encircling the forehead between eyebrows and hairline.

coif—a close-fitting cap worn by Jews made of linen worn beneath a helmet or hood. It was essentially a *cale* without its chin strap.

cornalia—worn by Jewish women, a pointed stiff veil or headdress resembling a horn, a *hennin*. Sometimes it was a doubled-horned hat, the *atour*. The *hennin* evolved from the simpler *oralia* that in Germany was called the *flieder* or *riese*.

coverchief—a Jewish fabric headdress piled or wound over the head, sometimes fastened beneath the chin, and crowned with a standing starched band. The more exuberant coverchiefs weighed as much as 10 pounds.

crespinette—a variant of the Jewish *caul* headress.

diadem—a Jewish crown or ornamental headband, symbolizing honor, royalty, or dignity. Often it was a metal or fabric fillet, either simple or adorned with jewels, circling the head, worn low on the forehead.

escoffion—a women's headdress of a silk or gold thread trellis net, worn by Christians and Jews. Sometimes it was an elaborate velvet or satin reticulated cap covered with a bejeweled gold net.

escoffion a sella—resembling an upside-down saddle, this headdress popular in northern Europe and Italy was attributed to Flemish, French, or "foreign" influence, as in, respectively, *escoffion alla fiamminga, alla francese,* or *alla di la.*

estrain—straw hat popular among Jews and Christians.

fillet—a Jewish and Christian women's stiff linen encircling band worn low about the forehead, plain, embroidered, or bejeweled. Alternatively a hat worn by Christian priests.

flieder—a variant on the fashionable *cornalia,* widely used, but especially favored by German Jews for secular and synagogue events.

fret—a women's headdress, worn by Jews and Christians, made of gold or silver trelliswork or netting, reticulated, jeweled, and spangled.

frontlet—a forehead ornament worn by Christian and Jewish women to accentuate the width of the head, consisting of a small pendant loop of velvet, silk, or precious metal attached to the edge of the under cap, usually worn as a mark of social rank or wealth. A gold loop particularly suggested nobility and wealth.

A frontlet ornament was worn by women when exaggeratedly high, wide foreheads were fashionable. Consisting of a small pendent loop of velvet, silk, or precious metal attached to the edge of the under cap, the calotte worn beneath the hennin, often to indicate rank or wealth. A gold look suggested a substantial yearly income. The young lady of fashion shown here is wearing a frontlet.   Isabella Stewart Gardener Museum, Boston.

galile—popular in England, this diamond-shaped headdress worn by Christian and Jewish women entirely concealed the hair, and usually was worn with a *wimple* and *gorget.*

garget—that part of the chaperone consisting of folded lengths of fabric wound around the head.

godron—a tall, frilled, pleated collar of starched muslin, a ruff worn by both Jewish and Christian men and women in the early Renaissance, often so high it was virtually a head cover.

gorget—a linen neck cover worn by Jews and Christians.

guimp—a *wimple*, a light veil, surrounding a women's face, popular among Jews and Christians.

gularon—the part of the *chaperone* hat covering the shoulders, worn by Jews and Christians.

headrail—a Jewish oblong linen or cotton headdress usually with a chinstrap held in place by a fillet or a crown.

hennin—a pointed conical headdress worn by Christian and Jewish women, popular in late medieval France and Burgundy, usually made of stiffened silk or velvet with a veil following from the pinnacle, the veil called a *lambrequin*. Originally it was taken to France by Isabel of Bavaria in the 14th century. Its extravagant height was regulated by sumptuary laws.

horned headdress—a variant of the Jewish *atour*.

huve—a projecting headdress with many folds worn by Christian and Jewish women, it was anchored to the side of the head by long pins and *bodkins*.

isaba maila—woman's veil or head shawl popular in the Muslim Mediterranean, as evidenced by frequent appearances in women's trousseau lists in the Cairo *geniza*, worn by Muslim and Jewish women alike.

Jew's hat, Judenhut—a conical pointed hat, usually yellow in color, that adult male Jews were required to wear in public in Christian Europe. The *Judenhut* was officially imposed by Pope Innocent III at the Fourth Lateran Council in 1215.

kalansuwa—a peaked Persian hat worn by Jews, Christians, and Muslims, crafted of particular colors and adorned with two special button-shaped emblems or badges. When sumptuary laws were enforced in Muslim countries, the *kalansuwa* was often worn only by non-Muslims.

khimar—a woman's veil or head shawl popular in the Muslim Mediterranean, worn by Muslim and Jewish women alike.

khirqa—a woman's veil or headdress appearing often in trousseau lists in the Muslim Mediterranean, worn by Muslim and Jewish women alike. Alternatively, the cloak garment worn by Sufi mystics.

lambrequin—a veil or scarf worn by Christian women, attached to the pinnacle of the *hennin* or to a knight's helmet as a token of love.

liripipe—the extravagantly long fabric tail of a *chaperone* hood worn wrapped around the head or neck or swung over the shoulder and ornamented with bells, fringe, or decoratively set semiprecious stones. Its length often signified social rank among Christians and Jews.

maajirs—a woman's hat popular in the Muslim Mediterranean, worn by Muslim and Jewish women alike.

marfors—a long narrow veil covering a woman's head, pendant to her shoulders.

mazzochio a cianbella—a huge turban topped by a tall, wide crown, the folded fabric making a wide, flexibly limp, and elaborately draped hat, worn by Italian Jews.

mentonniere—a type of Jewish headgear, essentially a chin piece, sometimes made of braided brocade or piping, and attached to a *coverchief*.

mindil—a woman's veil or headdress popular in the Muslim Mediterranean, worn by Muslim and Jewish women alike.

miqnaa—a woman's headdress appearing in trousseau lists in Muslim Mediterranean towns, worn by Muslim and Jewish women alike.

oralia—a Jewish woman's headdress veil with two blue stripes, required by 13th-century law and later superseded by the extravagant, horned *cornalia*.

orle—a narrow heraldic band that bordered a Christian woman's headdress or a knight's helmet. Often part of a *chaplet*, the orle represented the wearer's identifying colors and often was parti-colored, *mi-parti*.

pileus cornutus—a tall conical hat worn by the Jews, a *Judenhut*.

reticule—a hairnet or hair cover resembling a net, usually adorned with jewels, sequins, and precious-metal braiding. Particularly popular among Jews in Italy, France, and England, reticules customarily were worn alone over hair though often beneath a veil or hat.

riese—a pointed veiled hat, comparable to the *hennin*, fashionable among German-Jewish women.

roundlet—a stuffed fabric circlet or a crownless underhat worn by Christians and Jews either alone or covered by the turban folds of the *chaperone*, usually ending in a long *liripipe*.

saffa—a small, embroidered women's bonnet trimmed with coins, worn by Syrian women.

shal—an Arab woman's woolen shawl.

snood—a net hair covering usually ornamented with pearls, jewels, and small designs in precious metal, similar to the *caul, tressour,* and *reticule* favored by Jews.

tajira—a large embroidered shawl worn by Jewish and Muslim women in the Muslim Mediterranean.

takiya—a common unisex skullcap worn by Muslims either alone or under a headdress.

talthima—yellow tripartite face veil worn by Jewish and Muslim women and by Islamic judges in the Muslim Mediterranean.

tantur—a high, conical cap worn by Sufis; alternatively, a woman's headdress.

tarha—a veil Jewish and Muslim women wore and, likewise, the covering scholarly men wore in the Muslim Mediterranean countries.

taylasan—in Muslim-ruled lands, a popular face veil of Persian origin worn by women and men, a special favorite of scholars.

touret de nez—a fabric attachment to a hood, fitting over the upper part of the face, often including a small transparent pane for visibility, to protect the nose and eyes against northern cold, common among French and Burgundian Christians.

tressour—a fabric girding and decoration for tresses, or an elaborate jeweled headdress or *caul*, sometimes resembling the Jewish *reticule*.

truffeau—false hair fringes added to natural hair, as well as struts used to create bouffant hairstyles, popular among Jews and Christians.

Jewelry imitations of such hairstyles also were called *truffeau*.

viereckiger Schleier—an Ashkenazic Jewish woman's synagogue hat, customarily worn to synagogue and at home during the Sabbath. Closely covering the head and hair, it featured two stiffly starched square and pointed wings of white linen. In certain cities it was required by law to have two blue stripes.

wimple—a linen or silk headband that framed the face, enveloping the forehead, chin, sides of face, and neck, often worn with a *caul*; worn by Jewish women and Christian laywomen and nuns.

Fashionable Garments

aba—a unisex coat, shoulder mantle worn by peninsular and Eastern Mediterranean Arabs.

antari—a short to knee-length lined vest worn by Egyptian and eastern Mediterranean Arab women.

arisard—a mantel or plaid cloak worn by Scottish women, hooded, and ankle length, cinched or draped at the waist.

balandras—a 12th-century hooded rain cape, opening either at the front or side, worn by Christian women.

blanchet—a woman's long outer garment, a form of doublet, usually white, lined, and fur trimmed. Also, the name of a low-grade inferior wool fabric comparable to russet, used for clothing by the poor.

bliaut—a long overgown used by both Christian and Jewish men and women, often richly ornamented. The women's version was closely fitted at the bustline with long wide sleeves and slits to the sides to allow easy mounting of horses. Men wore a bliaut under chain male armor.

branc—a woman's smock common to Jews and Christians.

broigne—a man's rugged leather or linen vest or *jerkin* strengthened by a metal or bone framework, particularly popular in the 12th century as a protective garment before the *hauberk* superseded it.

brusttuch—a wide fabric stole worn by Jews and Christians, draped to fall loosely over the chest, usually jeweled and decorated with pearls, cradling the hands as if a muff.

burda—a heavy woolen wrap worn by Arabian and Egyptian men.

burnose—a woolen hooded cloak of North African origin.

byrrus—a heavy woolen, cowled cloak popular among Christians and Jews.

caban—a fitted cloak with wide sleeves probably derived from the Arabic *gaba*, introduced from the East to Europe through Venice in the 14th century. Its sleeves were open under the armpit.

caftan—a long-sleeved, unbelted outer garment of Persian origin made of wool, brocade, silk, or velvet, usually between knee length and floor length.

capa—a short, silk-lined, hooded cape worn by 11th through 13th-century men and women.

carcaille—an extravagantly flared collar of a *pourpoint* or *houppelande*, riding right up to the wearer's ears.

chamarre—a long, wide, fur-lined, braided, and decorated coat derived in the late 15th century from the sheepskin *samarra* of Spanish shepherds.

chemise (camise, kamise)—a shirtlike undergarment most commonly made of linen, originally unisex but increasingly worn only by Muslim, Christian, and Jewish women, and derived from the Arabic *qamis*.

cloak—from the French word for "bell," *cloche*, a bell-shaped outer cape.

cope or Cape—originally a circular, hooded rain cape, it was adopted in the 13th through 14th centuries as an ecclesiastical vestment worn over an *alb* by priests and bishops. The secular cope generally was designed from silk, brocade, or embroidered fabric and was fastened at the neck by a brooch and often ornamented with an *orphrey* and an imitation hood. A variant was used by monks on special occasions.

cote—a tunic that Christian and Jewish women wore in the 12th to 15th centuries, with long narrow sleeves, tight fitting bodices, sometimes buttoned down the front or back, usually culminating in a full skirt. Tunics often were *mi-parti*.

cotehardie—a long, close-fitting overgarment worn by Christian and Jewish men and women, held at the hip by a girdle or belt, usually tight-sleeved, embellished with buttons from elbow to pinky finger. Its high neck sometimes was secured with a drawstring. A *cotehardie* frequently was *mi-parti* with two colors alternating on the garment as well as the wearer's hose, as one leg green, one leg red; one shoulder green, the alternate hip green; the other shoulder and sleeve red, their opposing hip also red. Customarily *cotehardie* and tights were worn with *poulaines*.

Emperor Maximilian I, 1518, wearing the Order of the Golden Fleece over a richly brocaded cloak trimmed with pearls. This large woodcut is based on a portrait that Dürer drew of Maximilian from life in June 1518. HIP/Art Resource, NY.

cotelette—a German popular sleeveless, open-sided overdress worn by Christians and Jews without a belt by young girls and married women, comparable to a *sargenes*.

cotteron—a short, standard, utilitarian peasant smock ranging in length according to climate and season from a short minidress to a long commodious floor-length garment.

cyclas—a short, capelike cloak worn by men and women crafted of the rich silk manufactured in the Cyclades. At the coronation of England's King Henry III, guests and citizens of London wore the *cyclas*. An alternative term is *ciclatoun*, which ultimately derived from the Persian *sakarlat*, via the Arabic *siqlatun* or *siqala*.

dogaline—an aristocratic Venetian fashion for men and women consisting of a long brocade or velvet robe with wide, flaring sleeves reaching down to the knee. Lined and bordered with fur, the sleeve's lower edges were fastened to the shoulder to reveal the undergown sleeve.

doublet—a short, fitted, quilted "doubled" or lined garment worn beneath armor and in civilian clothes customarily embellished with trimmings and edgings, usually worn with *hose* or *chausses* (lightweight colored or striped leggings knitted or woven of linen, cotton, silk, or wool originally covering only foot and leg but later rising up the trunk when short robes became fashionable, the forerunners of modern tights).

epitoga—a wide, unbelted robe with bell sleeves sometimes worn as an academic gown and often called an *epomine hood*.

fichets—slits in the side of a surcoat, allowing the hands to pass through.

flugel—long, open, ground trailing sleeves for 15th-century German garments, usually edged with fur or brocade.

frock—a long, hooded gown, often girdled at the waist with rope.

gabardine—a loose-fitting smock or frock, commonly made of a coarse-grained fabric, and worn by men, women, and children.

gardecorps—a unisex, loose, flowing hooded garment, sometimes worn over a *surcoat*, often sleeveless or with wide short sleeves. It virtually replaced the *surcoat* in the 14th century.

garnache—a warm overrobe or *supertunic* similar to a *tabard*, with short capelike sleeves, usually fur-lined and falling to the elbows.

giornea—a very popular tunic worn by Italian Christian and Jewish men and women, sometimes short and thigh level worn with tights, sometimes just above the knee, and sometimes midleg in length. Often sleeveless, the *giornea* allowed elegance of style and color of the undergarment, especially with elaborate sleeves, to show to advantage. The *giornea* was worn over a shirt with sleeves of contrasting color or over a *justaucorps* with sleeves tight fitting at the wrist and billowing toward the shoulder. The *giornea* was worn free or belted at the waist or hip.

gippon—a padded, quilted short tunic, tight fitting and buttoned to breeches, trousers ranging in length from ankle to short trunks.

gonelle—a hooded cloak opening at the front or a long tunic worn by knights.

gramalla—a long outer garment reaching from the neck to toes. In the 14th century, King John I of Aragon (1350–96) required all Jews under his jurisdiction to wear it in addition to the Jewish badge and a special hood.

great coat—a short, loose fitting, full-sleeved outer garment for men decorated with gold and elaborate stones, also called a *paletot*.

habara—a dark, silk enveloping wrap worn by Muslim women.

haincelin—a short *huppelande* with embroidered sleeves, named after the fool or jester of King Charles VI of France (1380–1422), whose name was Haincelin Coq.

herigaute—a type of long shawl, similar to the *housse* or *gardecorps*, open at the side.

houpelande—a popular 14th- and 15th-century voluminous robe or gown worn by both Jewish and Christian men and women. It was full and richly ornate in fabric, belted at waist or hip, with exceedingly long, usually fur-lined, funnel-shaped sleeves and a funnel-shaped collar called a *carcaille*. The sleeves and the collar often both had *dagging*, ornamental cuff edging, with borders shaped as leaves, tongues, or scallops.

housse—a short mantle of coarse cloth worn by rural women to cover the head and body; also spelled *houce*.

huque (haik, huke)—a long or short flowing robe often edged with fur or embroidered with precious stones, mostly worn by Christians and Jews.

izar—a large enveloping body wrap worn by Arab men and women.

jacket—a man's close fitting, upper-body garment derived from the *jack*, which was a quilted, padded military sleeveless doublet often armored with small, intertwined metal leaves.

jerkin—a padded *jacket* derived from an earlier *cotehardie*, worn by Jews and Christians.

Jewish badge—a device to distinguish Jews and thereby ostracize them. Taking many shapes and colors, in the Papal States, a yellow fabric patch for men, yellow and blue striped patch for women; a yellow or red circle in Barcelona; in Rome, a parti-colored circle, yellow and red, worn on men's breasts and women's foreheads; a blue insigne shaped like the Greek letter *tau*, in Sicily and Naples. The Verona Jewish badge was a yellow star. In Spain a coin-sized red cloth was worn over the heart. Elsewhere the badge was shaped as a tablet or star. Shaped as the letter *O*, it was called *rouelle* or *rowel*. The badge was worn in addition to or as a substitute for the *Jew's hat* or *Judenhut*.

jillaya—a Muslim woman's embroidered wedding costume or a man's wedding caftan.

journade—an elaborate parade cloak, worn by Jews and Christians, consisting of a flowing cape with wide, slit sleeves.

jubba—a unisex outer garment of Arab origin.

jube—a silk or wool overshirt with elbow length sleeves decorated with needlework or braid.

jupe—a loose fitting jacket derived from the Arabic *juba*, "short jacket."

jupon—a close-fitting tunic or doublet, especially worn by knights, also derived from the Arabic *juba*.

kagoule—a peasant's short, hooded cape of cloth or fur.

karry—a black-hooded cloak, traditional in the British Isles and central Europe.

khalwatiyya—a variety of *aba* popular in Syria.

khirqa—a woman's cloak appearing often in trousseau lists of Jewish and Muslim women in the Muslim Mediterranean. Among Sufi mystics the *khirqa* was the patched woolen cloak placed around the mystical novice at the moment of his investiture into a Sufi order, which symbolized the spiritual bond between the disciple and master.

kirtle—a long tunic worn by Christian and Jewish men and women, sometimes an undergarment, usually an outer garment or coat often made of velvet, silk, taffeta, or satin, with elaborate trimming and close-fitting sleeves buttoned hand to elbow.

kittel—another term for the *sargenes*, a white linen overgarment with voluminous sleeves; also the name of the lace collar worn by Jewish men to attend the synagogue.

kubran—a unisex jacket with long, wide sleeves worn by Syrian men.

libas—unisex trousers or underpants popular in Arabia, Iraq, Egypt, and Syria.

livery—contractually or customarily guaranteed clothing given by feudal overlords to household retainers. The livery was made using heraldic colors and emblems and with different fabrics and furs to identify social rank. A professional uniform identified members of craft guilds and professions, such as the red livery required for Jewish physicians.

mahoître—cylindrical pads for extending shoulder width on men's garments such as the *gippon* and the extravagantly wide *pourpoint*, the wide shoulders were complemented by a tightly cinched waist.

mandilion—a *tabard*, an open-sleeved, hip-length garment usually with heraldic emblems worn either by civilians or by knights over their armor.

manteline—a short parade mantle, often hooded and elaborately decorated, worn by Jews and Christians.

mantle—a semicircular or rectangular cloak clasped at the neck or shoulder with a fibula and sometimes embroidered and bordered with braid or fur.

maphorion—a long great cloak or cape.

milhafa—a large, enveloping wrap worn by eastern Mediterranean women.

paletot—a short greatcoat.

paltoch—a short, fitted doublet laced to hose or to a *chausse*, the prototype of tights.

peasecod-bellied doublet—worn by men with *hose* or with *chausse*, an extravagantly wide and padded doublet with a wooden or bone armature shaping the front section covering the genitals, called the *codpiece*.

pelicon—a woman's *overtunic*, fur-lined, fabricated of silk, wool, or other fine textile, usually knee length and unbelted, sometimes adorned with a hip girdle and pouch.

pelisse—a popular, full-length, long-sleeved, fur-lined cloak worn by both men and women, comparable to the pelicon.

plastron—a protective metal armor breastplate worn by both warriors and fencers, and an adornment for women's garments laced to the bodice.

pluvial—a floor-lengthed, open-fronted mantle worn as a ceremonial garment and for the nobility, coronation regalia.

pourpoint—a man's short ceremonial coat popular in France from the 13th through 15th centuries. The coat had extravagantly wide shoulders padded with *mahoitres* and a tightly cinched waistline, fine for displaying a magnificent physique, and worn with long pointed shoes, *poulaines*.

qamis/a—a unisex shirtlike tunic worn by Arabs and adopted in the West as the *chemise*.

rheno—a 12th-century hoodless, short cloak lined with sable, ermine, or other expensive fur. Favored by the Angevin nobility, it was imitated by courtiers.

robe—all the elements of a costume from the undergarments to the outer cloaks, the smallest lacings, major fabrics, and fur components. Some classes of robes included *robe deguisee*, the richly ornamented, daring, new fashions; *robe de commune*, the ordinary daily wear; *robe gironnee* or a *plis gironnees*, the pleated, full-folded garb, belted at the waistline; and *robe longue*, an academic gown or physician's gown.

roc—a woman's overgarment, comparable to a man's overtunic.

roquet—a short, hooded, smocklike wool cape worn by commoners and young boys, particularly those serving as pages in noble households.

sarbal—a sleeveless cloak or gown.

sargenes—in Muslim lands, a white linen overgarment with voluminous sleeves, lace collar usually worn with a matching cap and girdle belt, worn by Jews. Customarily worn at the synagogue during the High Holy Days, particularly *Yom Kippur*, the *sargenes* was often worn by bridegrooms as well as by the leader of the seder at Passover. The *sargenes* was also called *kittel* or a *sukenis*.

sirwal, shalwar—loose unisex trousers or pantaloons of Persian origin.

socq—a flaring, regal ceremonial cloak fastened at the right shoulder, worn for coronations and important ceremonies, worn by Christians and Jews.

sorquenie—a woman's tunic tightly fitted at the bustline, flowing freely down to the hemline, worn by Christians, Jews, and Muslims.

sottana—A 12th- and 13th-century Italian solid color or striped undergown for a *tunic*, worn by both men and women.

stomacher—a vest worn over armor covering the chest worn by Christians and Jews. A woman's stomacher was an ornamental breast covering beneath lacings of a bodice.

sukenis—a woman's tunic worn by Christians and Jews.

supertunic—a circular, full-sleeved overgarment, often belted at the waist, worn by Christians and Jews.

surcoat—a knee- to floor-length overgarment, with side slits for horseback riding, usually sleeveless or half-sleeved though sometimes with long tight sleeves, worn by Christians and Jews.

surtout—from the French word meaning "over everything," an outer cloak, coat, or cape worn over all other garments by Christians and Jews.

tabard—a short-sleeved or sleeveless short coat, usually open at the sides, and worn over a shirt or a *justaucorps*. Knights wore tabards with armorial devices emblazoned on front, back, and sleeves. Special colors identified the wearer's social group. In 1360 all Jews of Rome with the exception of physicians were required to wear a red tabard.

thawb—the basic, full-length tunic worn by men and women throughout the Muslim Middle East.

tiraz livery—under Islam, *tiraz* (from the Persian word meaning "embroidery") fabrics were spun and woven in state workshops. The caliph then distribted cloth or complete garments to his court for an official uniform for the summer and another for the winter. Likewise, in the Christian West, both Jews and Christians received contractually or customarily guaranteed costume and clothing gifts from feudal overlords given to household retainers. The livery was constructed to identify heraldic colors and emblems. Subtle distinctions among fabric and fur indicated social rank. A professional uniform identified members of craft guilds and professions, such as the required red livery of Jewish physicians.

tunic—a shirtlike garment worn by men and women, usually with round neck and narrow sleeves. Of knee or ankle length, it was simple or elaborate according to social class. The tunic or *cote* usually was worn beneath a *supertunic* or mantle.

Shoes

babush—Middle Eastern slippers made of soft leather.

brodequin—a light boot, probably derived from the closed Roman shoe called the *caliga*, worn inside heavier boots. For ostentation, the wealthy had them fashioned from rich ornamented stitched silk or velvet.

campagus—a popular Byzantine low boot worn through the Carolingian period. It was fitted above the ankles and laced over the instep.

cordovan—soft, fine-grained goat skin leather from Córdova, Spain, supple and strong, used for making shoes as well as articles of clothing, wall covering, and jewel boxes. Córdovan often was painted, gilded, or embroidered.

cracowes—Polish shoes popular at the Cracow court, having outlandishly long-pointed toes that required anchoring by thongs or chains at the knee, or even the waistline. Fashionable in the French and Burgundian courts, where they were called *poulaines*.

duck bill shoes—exaggeratedly wide-toed leather shoes popular in the 15th century, dramatically contrasting with *poulaines*.

eschapins—light, flat shoes, ornamentally slashed or pierced on top.

galliochios—Gaulish shoes, wooden-soled shoes with leather straps protecting fine undershoes from rough stone pavement, mud, and water.

gillie—a shoe made of rawhide, tongueless and laced with a thong.

hose—cotton, wool, or leather stockings, sometimes fitted with a thin leather sole, making shoes unnecessary. As garments became shorter, hose became longer or higher, covering from the waistline to the toes. Hose traditionally was worn with a *doublet*.

houseaux—tall, thick-soled leather boots ranging in height from beneath the knee to midthigh. They often had an open toe or heel.

khuff—short boots or leather outer socks worn in Arabia and the eastern Mediterranean.

markub—pointed men's shoes of Moroccan origin made of thick red leather.

patten—a thick-soled, high-heeled shoe popular among Christians and Jews in Spain, Italy, and France, usually made of decorated leather or velvet and worn over a slipper. When fitted with a blade, it was an ice skate.

pedule—a northern European rawhide boot worn by both men and women, sometimes laced to breeches.

pigaches—fashionable 11th- and 12th-century shoes with long, upturned, pointed toes, similar to a classical shoe called the *calceus rependus.* They were a prototype of the extravagant *poulaines.*

poulaines—from the French meaning "Polish," shoes with extravagantly long and pointed toes, fashionable in 14th- and 15th-century France and Burgundy; also called *cracowes, poulaines* affected the gait, dance, and etiquette of the wearer. Toe points sometimes were long enough to curve upward to reach the wearer's knees or belt. Following Polish fashion, *poulaines* were derived from the earlier *pigaches.*

sabaton—a broad-toed boot or shoe, and if made of metal, part of armor.

Such were the magnificent varieties, shapes, colors, and names of clothing of medieval Christian, Jewish, and Muslim men, women and children.

READING

Christian Clothing

GENERAL

Brooke 1963 and 1964, Colthrop 1931, Davenport 1948, Enlart 1916, Kohler 1963, Laver 1952: history of costume, in general.

RELIGIOUS VESTMENTS

Cosman 1996, Cross and Livingstone 1977: church vestments; Mellinkoff 1970: the horned Moses; Cross and Livingstone 1977, *see* chapter 5: orders of friars and monks.

SECULAR CLOTHING

Rubens 1973: hairstyles; Evans 1951: jewelry; Brooke 1963 and 1964, Cosman, 1996, Davenport 1948, Husband and Hayward 1975, Kohler 1963, Metzger and Metzger 1982, Platt 1979, Stillman 1972 and 1995: clothing styles; Boissonade 1964, Cosman 1976 and 1996, Coulton 1960, Evans 1969, Neckham 1966, Quennell and Quennell 1948, Strong 1973: clothes in daily life; Dale 1932, Goitein 1973, Power and Postan 1933, Power 1941, Stillman 1972, 1995: merchants' records as a source for information about clothing.

ASUMPTUARY LAWS

Baldwin 1926, Cosman 1976, Reilly 1992 and 1993: sumptuary laws; Baer 1961, Finkelstein 1964, Grayzel 1933, Reilly 1992, Roth 1946 and 1949, Rubens 1973: Jewish insignia; Grayzel 1933: dress restrictions imposed by various church councils; Little 1978, Walker Bynum 1987 and 1992: spiritual poverty, women: Mormondo 1999: Bernardino of Siena.

Jewish Clothing and Costume

GENERAL

Y Stillman 1972 and 1995: colorful clothing as described in traders' letters in the Cairo *geniza; Talmud* (Yevamot 63b), Cosman 1976, Metzger and Metzger 1982, Rubens 1973: spiritual importance of clothing.

COSTUME AS MORAL STATEMENT

Y Stillman 1995: clothing as dowry; Abrahams 1969, Mansoor 1991, Metzger and Metzger 1982: advice for dressing in ethical wills; Goldin 1995: Rabbi Akiba's wife; Herford 1978: Rabbi Simeon's four crowns; Goldin 1995, Talmud B. Shabbat 145b: the Talmud on what clothes can teach; Rubens 1973, Roth 1946 and 1959: sumptuary laws in the Italian city of Forli.

COSTUME AS CULTURAL AND SOCIAL STATEMENT

Baron 1967, Cosman 1976, Metzger and Metzger 1982: sumptuary laws to identify and subjugate Jews; Goitein 1973, N Stillman 1970, Y Stillman 1972: descriptions of textiles, fabrics, and clothing in the Cairo *geniza* documents.

SUMPTUARY LAWS

Kedouris 1979, Metzger and Metzger 1982, N Roth 2002, Rubens 1973: Jewish badges and the Jewish hat; Finkelstein 1964, Metzger and Metzger 1982, Rubens 1973: sumptuary laws imposed from inside the Jewish community; Baer 1961, Grayzel 1933, Reilly 1992, Roth 1959, Rubens 1973: sumptuary laws imposed from outside the Jewish community; Rubens 1973, Roth 1946, 1959: sumptuary laws in Forli; Grayzel 1933: dress restrictions under various church councils; Rubens 1973: proscriptions on Jewish and Muslim hairstyles.

JEWISH CEREMONIAL GARMENTS

Metzger and Metzger 1982: tallit designs; Cosman 1996, Rubens 1973: Sabbath and wedding clothing in Muslim lands; Cosman 1996, Rubens 1973: Sabbath and wedding clothing in western Europe; Metzger and Metzger 1982, Rubens 1973: changing fashions for mourning.

JEWISH FASHIONABLE HATS AND HEADGEAR

Cosman 1996 and 2000, Rubens 1973: various fashionable headgear; Goitein 1973, Y Stillman 1972: headgear depicted in the Cairo *Geniza* documents; Metzger and Metzger 1982: yarmulke.

Muslim Clothing and Textiles

GENERAL

Blair and Bloom 1994, Metzger and Metzger 1982, Rubens 1973, Y Stillman 1995: the cultural meanings of clothing; Y Stillman 1999: Umayyad, Abbasid, Fatimid, and Mamluk clothing, Muslim sumptuary laws.

CLOTHING STYLES

Sharon 1983: Abbasids; Y Stillman 1995 and 1999: Umayyad, Abbasid, Fatimid, and Mamluk clothing, Muslim sumptuary laws; Guthrie 2001: medieval women; Gibb 1958, Morgan 2001: Ibn Battuta; Y Stillman 1972, 1995 and 1999: women's fashionable garments; Behrens Abou Seif 1999, Frenkel 1999, Ibn Arabi, 1990, Michon 1999, Qustantini 1965, Y Stillman 1995 and 1999: Sufi *khirqa* and *suf*; Behrens Abou Seif 1999, Stillman 1999: ritual and religious ideology; Sharon 1983: Abbasids; Sanders 1994: Fatimid ritual; Stetkevych 2002: Umayyad ritual; Steensgard 1999: religious attitudes toward silk; Budge 1959, Dols 1992: amulets and clothing.

TEXTILES AND COLOR

Atil 1981, Beckwith 1959, Britton 1938, Lamm 1937, May 1957, Sergeant 1972: textiles and rugs; Goitein 1967, 1971 and 1971, N Stillman 1970, Y Stillman 1972 and 1995: descriptions of textiles, fabrics, and clothing in the Cairo *Geniza* documents; Blair and Bloom 1994: the *Burda Ode*; Thackston 1986: Nasir-i Khosraw on the manufacture and sale of linen; Atil 1981, Beckwith 1959, Blair and Bloom 1994, Britton 1938, Sergeant 1972, Whelan 1982: textile techniques; Atil 1981: textiles in the Mamluk courts; Beckwith 1959: Coptic textiles; Lamm 1937: cotton textiles; May 1957: silk textiles in Spain; Sergeant 1972, Whelan 1982: textile motifs; Gibb 1958, Morgan 2001: Ibn Battuta; Y Stillman 1972 and 1995: fashionable garments.

BIBLIOGRAPHY

Aarne, Antti. *Types of the Folktale. A Classification and Bibliography.* Edited by Stith Thompson. Helsinki: Suomalainen Tiedeaktemia, 1961.

Abbot, Nabia. *Two Queens of Baghdad: Mother and Wife of Harun al-Rashid.* Chicago: University of Chicago Press, 1946.

Aberth, John. *From the Brink of the Apocalypse: Confronting Famine, War, Plague, and Death in the Later Middle Ages.* New York: Routledge, 2000.

Abrahams, Israel. *Jewish Life in the Middle Ages.* 2d ed. New York: Meridian Books, Jewish Publication Society of America, 1961. Reprint, New York: Kegan Paul, Int., 2007.

Abrahams, M. A. Israel. "The Spanish-Jewish Poets (I)." In *Chapters on Jewish Literature.* Available online. URL: http://www.authorama.com/chapters-on-jewish-literature-10.html.

Abrams, A. "Women Traders in Medieval London." *Economic Journal* 26 (1916): 276–285.

Abu-Haidar, J. A. *Hispano-Arabic Literature and the Early Provencal Lyrics.* Richmond, Surrey, U.K.: Curzon Press, 2001.

Abulafia, Anna Sapir. *Christians and Jews in Dispute.* Aldershot, U.K., and Brookfield, Vt.: Ashgate, 1998.

Abulafia, David. *Commerce and Conquest in the Mediterranean, 1100–1500.* Aldershot, U.K., and Brookfield, Vt.: Variorum, 1993.

———. "The King and the Jews—the Jews in the Ruler's Service." In *The Jews of Europe in the Middle Ages,* edited by Christoph Cluse, 43–53. Turnhout, Belgium: Brepols, 2004.

Abu Ma'shar. *On Historical Astrology: The Book of Religions and Dynasties.* Vol. 33–34, *Islamic Philosophy, Theology, and Science.* Translated and edited by Charles Burnette and Keiji Yamamoto. Leiden, The Netherlands: E. J. Brill, 2000.

Abun-Nasr, J. M. *A History of the Maghrib in the Islamic Period.* Cambridge: Cambridge University Press, 1987.

Acland, James H. *Medieval Structure: The Gothic Vault.* Toronto: University of Toronto Press, 1972.

Adams, Robert M. *Land behind Baghdad.* Chicago and London: University of Chicago Press, 1965.

Addas, Claude. "Andalusi Mysticism and the Rise of Ibn 'Arabi." In *The Legacy of Muslim Spain,* edited by Salma K. Jayyusi, 909–933. Leiden, The Netherlands: E. J. Brill, 1994.

———. *Ibn 'Arabi ou la quête du soufre rouge* (Ibn al-'Arabi and the quest for red sulphur). Paris: Gallimard, 1989. Translated by P. Kingsley as *Quest for Red Sulphur: The Life of Ibn 'Arabi.* Cambridge: Islamic Texts Society, 1993.

Adler, Elkan. *Jewish Travellers in the Middle Ages.* New York: Dover, 1987.

Adler, Marcus N., ed. and trans. *The Itinerary of R. Benjamin of Tudela.* London, 1907. Reprint, New York: Philipp Feldheim, 1964.

Agajanian, Shakeh. "The Uses of Animals, Manafi Al-Hayawan." *Natural History* 67 (December 1958).

Ahmad, Maqbul. *India and the Neighbouring Territories as Described by the Sharif al-Idrisi.* Leiden, The Netherlands: E. J. Brill, 1960.

Ahmad, Nafis. *Muslim Contribution to Geography.* Lahore: M. Ashraf, 1947.

Ahmed, Leila. *Women and Gender in Islam.* New Haven, Conn.: Yale University Press, 1992.

Ahmed, Muhammad S., et al. *Herb Drugs and Herbalists in the Middle East.* Tokyo: Institute for the Study of Languages and Cultures of Asia and Africa, 1979.

Ahsan, M. M. *Muslim Festivals*. Vero Beach, Fla.: Rourke Enterprises, 1987.

———. *Social Life under the Abbasids*. Harlow, U.K.: Longman, 1979.

Alexander, Paul J. *The Patriarch Nicephorus of Constantinople: Ecclesiastical Policy and Image Worship in the Byzantine Empire*. Oxford: Clarendon Press, 1958.

———. "Religious Persecution and Resistance in the Byzantine Empire of the Eighth and Ninth Centuries: Methods and Justifications." *Speculum* 52 (1977).

Ali, Ahmed. *Al Qur'an*. Princeton, N.J.: Princeton University Press, 1988.

Ali, Ahmed, trans. *The Quran*. Introduction by Jaroslav Pelikan. New York: Quality Paperback Book Club, 1992.

Allan, James W., and K. A. C. Creswell. *A Short Account of Early Muslim Architecture*. Cairo: American University Press, 1989.

Allen, Roger. *The Arabic Literary Heritage*. Cambridge: Cambridge University Press, 1998.

———. *An Introduction to Arabic Literature*. Cambridge: Cambridge University Press, 2000.

Allmand, Christopher, *The Hundred Years War: England and France at War, c. 1300–c. 1450*. Cambridge and New York: Cambridge University Press, 1988.

Altmann, Alexander. "Saadya Gaon's *Book of Doctrines and Beliefs*." In *Three Jewish Philosophers*, edited by Lewy et al. New York: World Publishing, 1961.

Alvilda Petroff, Elizabeth. *Body and Soul: Essays on Medieval Women and Mysticism*. Oxford: Oxford University Press, 1994.

Alvilda Petroff, Elizabeth, ed. *Medieval Women's Visionary Literature*. New York: Oxford University Press, 1986.

Ambroise. *The Crusade of Richard the Lionheart*. Translated by Merton Jerome Hubert. New York: Columbia Press, 1941.

Amt, Emilie. *Women's Lives in Medieval Europe: A Sourcebook*. New York: Routledge, 1993.

Ancelet-Hustache, Jeanne. *Master Eckhart and the Rhineland Mystics*. Translated by Hilda Graef. New York: Harper, 1957.

Anderson, F. J. *An Illustrated History of the Herbals*. New York: Columbia University Press, 1977.

Anderson, J. N. L. *Law Reform in the Muslim World*. London, 1976.

Anderson, M., and B. Williams. *Old English Handbook*. Boston: Houghton Mifflin, 1935.

Anderson, Roger Charles. *Oared Fighting Ships*. London: P. Marshall, 1962.

Anderson, Trevor, "Dental Treatment in Medieval England." *British Dental Journal* 197 (2004): 419–425.

Andrae, Tor. *Mohammed: The Man and His Faith*. New York: Harper, 1960.

Andreas Capellanus. *De Amore: On the Art of Courtly Love (c. 1190)*. Translated by J. J. Parry. New York: Columbia University Press, 1941.

Andrew, Malcolm, and Ronald Waldron, eds. *The Poems of the Pearl Manuscript*. Berkeley and Los Angeles: University of California Press, 1978.

Angold, M. "Administration of the Empire of Nicaea." *Byzantinische Forschungen* 19 (1993): 127–138.

———. *A Byzantine Government in Exile: Government and Society under the Laskarids of Nicaea (1204–1261)*. London: University Press Oxford, 1975.

———. *The Byzantine Empire 1025–1204: A Political History*. London and New York: Longman, 1984.

Antonius, George. *The Arab Awakening*. New York: Capricorn, 1965.

Arano, Luisa Cogliati. *Medieval Health Handbook, Tacuinum Sanitatis*. Translated by Adele Westbrook and Oscar Ratti. New York: George Braziller, 1976.

Arazi, A., and H. Ben-Shammay. "Risala." *Encyclopaedia of Islam*. 2d ed. Vol. 8. Leiden, The Netherlands: E. J. Brill, 1999, 532–543.

Arbeau, Thoinot. *Orchesography*. Translated by Mary Stewart Evans. New York, 1948. Reprint with corrections, a new introduction, and notes by Julia Sutton, and representative steps and dances in Labanotation by Mireille Backer. New York: Dover Publications, 1967.

Arberry, Arthur J. *Classical Persian Literature*. Richmond, Surrey: Curzon Press, 1994.

———. *Omar Khayyam: A New Version Based upon Recent Discoveries*. London: Murray, 1952.

———. *Scheherazade. Tales from the Thousand and One Nights*. New York: New American Library, 1955.

Arenson, Sarah. "Ships and Shipbuilding, Red Sea and Persian Gulf." In *Dictionary of the Middle Ages*, edited by Joseph R. Strayer. New York: Scribners, 1982–89.

Ariès, Philippe, and Georges Duby, eds. *From Pagan Rome to Byzantium*. Cambridge, Mass.: Harvard University Press, 1987.

Armstong, A. H., ed. *The Cambridge History of Later Greek and Early Medieval Philosophy*. Cambridge: Cambridge University Press, 1967.

Armstrong, Karen. *Islam: A Short History*. New York: Modern Library, 2000.

———. *Jerusalem: One City, Three Faiths*. New York: Ballantine Books, 1997.

———. *Muhammad: A Biography of the Prophet*. San Francisco: HarperSanFrancisco, 1992.

Armstrong, Regis J. J., Wayne Hellmann, and William J. Short, eds. *Francis of Assisi: Early Documents*. Vol. 1, *The Saint*. Hyde Park, N.Y.: New City Press, 1999.

Arnold, Benjamin. *German Knighthood, 1050–1300*. Oxford: Clarendon Press, 1985.

Arnold, Thomas W. *Painting in Islam: A Study of the Place of Pictorial Art in Islam*. Oxford: Clarendon, 1928.

Arnold, Thomas W., and A. Grohmann. *The Islamic Book*. London: Pegasus Press, 1929.

Arnold, Thomas W., and Alfred Guillaume. "Geography and Commerce." In *The Legacy of Islam*, 2d ed., edited by J. Schacht and C. E. Bosworth. Oxford: The Clarendon Press, 1974.

Ar-Rusafi de Valencia. *Poemas*. Madrid: Hiperion, 1980.

Arthur, Marylin B. "Early Greece: The Origins of the Western Attitude toward Women." *Arethusa* 6 (Spring 1973).

Asher, A., ed. *The Itinerary of R. Benjamin of Tudela*. London: A. Asher, 1840–41.

Asher, Catherine. *Architecture of Mughal India*. Cambridge and New York: Cambridge University Press, 1992.

Ashley, Kathleen, and Pamela Sheingorn, eds. *Sainte Anne in Late Medieval Society*. Athens and London: University of Georgia Press, 1990.

Ashmand, J. M. *Ptolemy's Tetrabiblos*. 1917. Republished, Mokelumne Hill, Ca.: Health Research, 1969.

Ashtiany, Julia, T. M. Johnstone, J. D. Latham, and R. B. Serjeant, eds. *Abbasid Belles-Lettres*. Vol. 3, (*Cambridge History of Arabic Literature*) Cambridge: Cambridge University Press, 1990.

Ashtor, Eliyahu. *A Social and Economic History of the Near East in the Middle Ages*. Berkeley: University of California Press, 1976.

———. *The Jews and the Mediterranean Economy, 10th–15th Centuries*. London: Variorum Reprints, 1983.

———. *The Jews of Moslem Spain*. 2 vols. Philadelphia: Jewish Publication Society of America, 1973.

Asín, Jaime Oliver. "En torno a los orígenes de Castilla." *Al-Andalus* 38 (1973): 319–391.

Asín Palacios, Miguel. *Shadilies y alumbrados*. Madrid: Ediciones Hiperión, 1990.

Atil, Esin. *Art of the Arab World*. Washington, D.C.: Freer Gallery of Art, 1975.

———. "Mamluk Art." In *Dictionary of the Middle Ages*, edited by Joseph R. Strayer. 12 vols. New York: Scribner, 1982–89.

———. *Renaissance of Islam: Art of the Mamluks*. Washington, D.C.: Smithsonian Institution Press, 1981.

———. "Textiles and Rugs." In *Renaissance of Islam: Art of the Mamluks*. Washington, D.C.: Smithsonian Institution Press, 1981.

———, ed. *Islamic Art and Patronage: Treasures from Kuwait*. New York: Rizzoli, 1990.

Atiya, A. S. *Crusade, Commerce, and Culture*. Oxford: Oxford University Press, 1962.

———. *The Crusade in the Later Middle Ages*. London: Methuen, 1938.

Augustine, Saint. *City of God*. Edited by David Knowles. New York: Penguin, 1972.

Augustine of Hippo. *The City of God against the Pagans*. Translated by R. W. Dyson. *Cambridge Texts in the History of Political Thought*. Cambridge: Cambridge University Press, 1998.

Austin, R. W. J. *Sufis of Andalusia*. London: George Allen & Unwin, 1971.

Austin, Thomas, ed. *Two Fifteenth Century Cookery Books*. London: Trubner, 1888.

Averroës (Ibn Rushd). *El libro de las generalidades de la medicina [Kitâb al-Kulliyat fil-tibb]*. Al-Andalus: Textos y Estudios. Translated by María de la Concepción Vázquez de Benito and Camilo Álvarez de Morales. Madrid: Trotta, 2003.

———. *On the Harmony of Religion and Philosophy.* London: International Commission for the Translation of Great Works, 1926.

d'Avray, David L. *The Preaching of the Friars: Sermons Diffused from Paris before 1300,* Oxford: Clarendon Press, 1985.

Awadain, M. Reda, "A Recent Look and Study of Some Papers of al-Zahrawi's Book '*al-Tasrif*.'" Available online. URL : http://www.islamset.com/isc/zahrawi/awadain.html#awaid1#awaid1.

Ayalon, David. *Mamluk Military Society.* London: Variorum Reprints, 1979.

———. "Preliminary Remarks on the Mamluk Military Institution in Islam." In *War, Technology, and Society in the Middle East,* edited by V. J. Parry and M. E. Yapp. New York: Oxford University Press, 1975.

Ayoub, Mahmoud. *Redemptive Suffering in Islam: A Study of the Devotional Aspects of 'Ashura in Twelver Shi'ism.* The Hague: Mouton, 1978.

———. *The Qur'an and Its Interpreters,* 2 vols. New York: State University of New York Press, 1982 and 1992.

Ayrton, Michael. *Giovanni Pisano, Sculptor.* New York: Weybright and Talley, 1969.

al-Azmeh, A., ed. *Islamic Law: Social and Historical Contexts.* London: Routledge, 1988.

Azmi, Mohammad Mustafa. *Studies in Early Hadith Literature.* Indianapolis: American Trust Publications, 1978.

Babcock, William S., ed. *The Ethics of St. Augustine.* Atlanta, Ga.: Scholars Press, 1991.

Bacharach, Jere L. *A Middle East Studies Handbook.* Seattle: University of Washington Press, 1984.

Bachrach, Bernard S. *Early Carolingian Warfare: Prelude to Empire.* Philadelphia: University of Pennsylvania Press, 2001.

———. *Early Medieval Jewish Policy in Western Europe.* Minneapolis: University of Minnesota Press, 1977.

———. *Jews in Barbarian Europe.* Lawrence Kans.: Coronado Press, 1977.

Bacou, Roseline, and Maurice Serullaz. *Great Drawings of the Louvre Museum.* New York: George Braziller, 1968.

Baer, Eva. *The Human Figure in Islamic Art: Inheritances and Islamic Transformations.* Costa Mesa, Calif.: Mazda Publishers, 2004.

Baer, Yitzhak. *A History of the Jews in Christian Spain.* New York: Jewish Publication Society of America, 2002.

———. *The Jews of Christian Spain.* 2 vols. Philadelphia: Jewish Publication Society of America, 1961.

Bagrow, Leo. *The History of Cartography.* 2d ed. Cambridge, Mass.: MIT Press, 1985.

Bailey, D. S. *Sexual Relations in Christian Thought.* New York: Harper, 1959.

Baird, Forrest E., and Walter Kaufmann. *Medieval Philosophy,* 2d ed. Vol. 2. Philosophic Classics. Upper Saddle River, N.J.: Prentice Hall, 1997.

Baker, P. S., ed. *Beowulf: Basic Readings.* New York: Garland Press, 1995.

Baldick, J. *Mystical Islam: An Introduction to Sufism.* London: I. B. Taurus, 1989.

Baldini, Umberto. *The Brancacci Chapel.* New York: Harry N. Abrams, 1991.

Baldwin, F. E. *Sumptuary Legislation and Personal Regulation in England.* Baltimore, Md.: Johns Hopkins Press, 1926.

Banckes, R. *Banckes's Herbal.* Edited by S. Larkey and T. Pyles. New York: New York Botanical Garden, 1941.

Barber, Elizabeth. *Women's Work: The First 20,000 Years.* New York: W. W. Norton, 1994.

Barber, Richard, and Juliet Barker. *Tournaments, Jousts, Chivalry, and Pageants in the Middle Ages.* New York: Weidenfeld & Nicolson, 1989.

Bareket, Elinoar. "Radhanites." In *Jewish Civilization: An Encyclopedia,* edited by Norman Roth, 558–561. London and New York: Routledge, 2002.

Barnett, R. D. *Catalogue of the Jewish Museum of London.* London: Jewish Museum, Harvey Miller, and New York Graphic Society, 1974.

Baron, Salo Wittmeyer. *A Social and Religious History of the Jews.* 2d ed. New York: Columbia University Press and Philadelphia: Jewish Publication Society of America. 1967. Vols. 3–8, *High Middle Ages, 500–1200.* Vols. 9–13, *Later Middle Ages 1200–1650.*

Baron, Salo Wittmeyer, et al. *Economic History of the Jews.* Jerusalem: Keter Publishing House Jerusalem, c. 1975.

Barratt, Alexandra. *Women's Writing in Middle English*. London, New York, 1992.

Barron, Caroline M. *The Medieval Guildhall of London*. London: Corporation of London, 1974.

Barstow, Anne. "Joan of Arc and Female Mysticism." *Journal of Feminist Studies in Religion* 1 (Fall 1985): 29–42.

Bartlett, Robert. *England under the Norman and Angevin Kings, 1075–1225*. Oxford: Clarendon Press, 2000.

———. *Making of Europe: Conquest, Colonization and Cultural Change, 950–1350*. Princeton, N.J.: Princeton University Press, 1993.

Bartusis, M. *The Late Byzantine Army: Arms and Society, 1204–1453*. Philadelphia: University of Pennyslvania Press, 1992.

Bass, George F. *A History of Seafaring Based on Underwater Archaeology*. New York: Walker, 1972.

Bass, George F., and Fredrick H. Van Doorninck. Yassi Ada 1: *A Seventh-Century Byzantine Shipwreck*. College Station, Texas: A&M University Press, 1982.

Bassiouni, M. Cherif. *Introduction to Islam*. Chicago: Rand McNally, 1988.

Bates, Michael L. "Islamic Numismatics." *Middle East Studies Association Bulletin* 12–13 (1978–79).

———. "Mints and Money, Islamic." In *Dictionary of the Middle Ages*, edited by Joseph R. Strayer. 12 vols. New York: Scribner, 1982–89.

Bateson, Mary. "Origin and Early History of Double Monasteries." *Transactions of the Royal Historical Society* n.s. 13 (1899): 137–198.

Baumgarten, Elisheva. *Mothers and Children: Jewish Family Life in Medieval Europe*, Princeton, N.J.: Princeton University Press, 2004.

Beardwood, Alice. *Alien Merchants in England, 1355–77*. Monographs of the Mediaeval Academy. Cambridge, Mass.: Mediaeval Academy, 1931.

Beckwith, John. "Coptic Textiles." *Ciba Review* 12 (1959).

———. *Early Medieval Art: Carolingian, Ottonian, Romanesque*. London: Thames & Hudson, 1985.

Bede. *Historia Ecclesiastica Gentis Anglorum*. Edited and translated by T. Miller. London: Early English Text Society, 1890–91.

Beedell, Suzanne. *Windmills*. New York: Scribner, 1979.

Beer, F. *Woman and Mystical Experience in the Middle Ages*. Woodbridge, U.K.: Boydell Press, 1992.

Beeston, A. F. L., T. M. Johnstone, R. B. Serjeant, and G. R. Smith, eds. *Arabic Literature to the end of the Umayyad Period*. Cambridge: Cambridge University Press, 1983.

Behrens-Abouseif, Doris. *Beauty in Arabic Culture*. Princeton, N.J.: Markus Wiener, 1999.

———. *Fath Allah and Abu Zakariyya: Physicians under the Mamluks*. Cairo: Institut français d'archéologie orientale, 1987.

———. "The Image of the Physician in Arab Biographies of the Post-Classical Age." *Der Islam* 66 (1989): 331–343.

———. *Islamic Architecture of Cairo, An Introduction*. Leiden: E. J. Brill, 1989.

Beinart, H. *Conversos On Trial: The Inquisition*, in Ciudad Real. Jerusalem: Magnes Press, Hebrew University, 1981.

Bell, J. N. *Love Theory in Later Hanbalite Islam*. Albany: State University of New York Press, 1979.

Bell, Rudolph M. *Holy Anorexia*. Chicago: University of Chicago Press, 1987.

Bellitto, Christopher M. *The General Councils: A History of the Twenty-One General Councils from Nicaea to Vatican II*. New York: Paulist Press, 2002.

Belting, Hans. *Likeness and Presence: The Image before the Era of Art*. Chicago: University of Chicago Press, 1994.

Ben-Amos, Dan, "Jewish Folk Literature." *Oral Tradition* 14, no. 1 (1999): 140–274.

Benbassa, Esther. *The Jews of France: A History from Antiquity to the Present*. Translated by M. B. DeBevoise. Princeton, N.J.: Princeton University Press, 2001.

Benisch, A., trans. *Travels of Rabbi Petachia*. London: Trubner, 1856.

Benjamín, Sandra. *The World of Benjamín of Tudela: A Medieval Mediterranean Travelogue*. Vancouver, British Columbia: Fairleigh Dickinson University Press, 1995.

Bennett, H. S. *The Pastons and Their England*. Cambridge: Cambridge University Press, 1951.

Bennett, Josephine Waters. *Rediscovery of Sir John Mandeville*. New York: Modern Language Association, 1954.

Ben Sahl de Sevilla. *Poemas*. Madrid: Hiperión, Ediciones 1983.

Benson, Larry D., and Theodor M. Andersson, eds. *The Literary Context of Chaucer's Fabliaux*. Indianapolis and New York: Bobbs-Merrill, 1971.

Berechiah ha-Nakdan. *Fables of a Jewish Aesop*. Translated by Moses Hadas with an introduction by W. T. H. Jackson. Boston: Godine/Nonpareil, 1967.

Berger, David. *From Crusades to Blood Libels to Expulsions: Some New Approaches to Medieval Antisemitism*. New York: Touro College Graduate School of Jewish Studies, 1997.

Berkey, Jonathan P. *The Formation of Islam: Religion and Society in the Near East, 600–1800*. Cambridge: Cambridge University Press, 2002.

Berman, Harold J. *Law and Revolution: The Formation of the Western Legal Tradition*. Cambridge, Mass.: Harvard University Press, 1983.

Bernard of Clairvaux. *Homilies in Praise of the Blessed Virgin Mary*. 18A. Translated by Marie-Bernard Said. 1979. Reprint, Kalamazoo, Mich.: Cistercian Publications, 1993.

———. *The Letters of St. Bernard*. Translated by B. Scott James. Chicago: H. Regneny, 1963.

———. *Selected Works*. Classics of Western Spirituality 55. Translated by Gillian R. Evans. New York: Paulist Press, 1987.

Bernardi, Paola. *Carthusian Monastery of Pavia*. Rome: Istituto Geografico de Agostini, 1986.

Bernavi, Eli, ed. *A Historical Atlas of the Jewish People*. New York: Knopf, Schocken Books, 1992.

Bernhard, Marianne. *Monasteries: A Hundred Jewels of European Architecture*. Munich: IP-Verlagsgesellschaft, 1999.

Bernhardt, Karl A., and Graeme Davis. *The Word Order of Old High German*. Vol. 19, *Studies in German Language and Literature*. Lewiston N.Y.: Edwin Mellen Press, 1997.

Biale, Rachel. *Women and Jewish Law: An Exploration of Women's Issues in Halakhic Sources*. New York: Schocken Books, 1984.

Bickerdyke, John. *The Curiosities of Ale and Beer*. An Entertaining History 1889. Reprint, London: Spring Books, 1965.

Bieler, Ludwig. *The Irish Penitentials*. Dublin: Dublin Institute for Advanced Studies, 1963.

Biller, Peter, and A. J. Minnis, eds., *Handling Sin: Confession in the Middle Ages*. Woodbridge, Suffolk: York Medieval Press, 1998.

Biller, Peter, and Barrie Dobson. *The Medieval Church: Universities, Heresy, and the Religious Life: Essays in Honour of Gordon Leff*. Rochester, N.Y.: Boydell, 1999.

Birge, John K. *The Bektashi Order of Dervishes*. London: Luzac & Co., 1937.

Biringuccio, Vannoccio. *Pirotechnia*. Edited by M. T. Gnudi and C. S. Smith. Cambridge, Mass.: MIT Press, 1966.

Bisheh, Ghazi. "From Castellum to Palatium: Umayyad Mosaic Pavements from Qasr al-Hallabat in Jordan." *Muqarnas* 10 (1993): 49–56.

Bisson, Thomas N. "Unheroed Pasts: History and Commemoration in South Frankland before the Albigensian Crusades." *Speculum* 65 (1990): 281–308.

Blades, W. *The Life and Typography of William Caxton*. London, 1863.

Blair, Claude. *The James A. De Rothschild Collection at Waddesdon Manor, Arms, Armour and Base-Metal Work*. London: National Trust, 1974.

Blair, Sheila S., and Jonathon M. Bloom. *The Art and Architecture of Islam 1250–1800*. New Haven, Conn.: Yale University Press (Pelican History of Art), 1994.

Blakney, Raymond Bernard. *Meister Eckhart*. New York: Harper & Row, 1941.

Bland, Kalman P. *The Artless Jew: Medieval and Modern Affirmations and Denials of the Visual*. Princeton, N.J.: Princeton University Press, 2001.

Blau, Joseph Leon, and Jean Thenaud. *The Christian Interpretation of the Cabala in the Renaissance*. Port Washington, N.Y.: Kennikat Press Rpt. 1965, 1944.

Bloch, Howard. *Medieval Misogyny and the Invention of Western Romantic Love*. Chicago: University of Chicago Press, 1991.

Bloom, Harold. *Genius: A Mosaic of 100 Exemplary Creative Minds*. New York: Warner Books, 2002.

Bloom, Jonathan. *The Minaret Symbol of Islam*. Oxford: Oxford University Press, 1989.

Bloom, Jonathan, and Shelia Blair. *Islamic Arts*. London: Phaidon, 1997.

Bloom, Jonathan M. *Paper before Print: The History and Impact of Paper in the Islamic World*. New Haven, Conn.: Yale University Press, 2001.

Blum, Richard, and Alexander Golitzin. *Sacred Athlete: On the Mystical Experience and Dionisios, Its Westerworld Fountainhead.* Lanham, Md.: Rowman and Littlefield, 1991.

Blumenthal, Uta-Renate. *The Investiture Controversy: Church and Monarchy from the Ninth to the Twelfth Century.* Philadelphia: University of Philadelphia Press, 1988.

Blunt, W., and S. Raphael. *The Illustrated Herbal.* New York: Thames & Hudson and London: Frances Lincoln, 1979.

Boase, T. S. R. *Death in the Middle Ages: Mortality Judgement, and Remembrance* New York: McGraw-Hill, 1972.

Boccaccio, Giovanni. *The Decameron.* Oxford: Oxford University Press, 1999.

Bogin, Meg. *The Women Troubadours.* New York: Norton, 1976.

Boissonade, P. *Life and Work in Medieval Europe: The Evolution of Medieval Economy from the Fifth to the Fifteenth Centuries.* Translated by Eileen Power. New York: Dover, 1964.

Boke of Nurture. Rhode, 15th century. Published as *The Babees Book & Manners and Meals in Olden Time.* London: Roxburghe Club, 1867, 1868.

Bolton, Brenda. "Mulieres Sanctae." In *Women in Medieval Society,* edited by Susan M. Stuard. Philadelphia: University of Pennsylvania Press, 1976.

Bonaventure. *The Soul's Journey into God.* Classics of Western Spirituality. 5. Translated by Ewert Cousins. New York: Paulist Press, 1978.

Bonner, Michael, Mone Ener, and Amy Singer. *Poverty and Charity in Middle Eastern Contexts.* Albany: State University of New York Press, 2003.

Bonvesin de la Riva. *De Magnalibus urbis Mediolani.* Milan: 1288.

Boorde, Andrew. *A Dyetary of Helth.* Edited by F. J. Furnivall. London: Trubner, 1870.

Boorstin, Daniel J. "The Realms of Pride and Awe." In *Circa 1492,* edited by Jay A. Levenson. Washington, D.C.: National Gallery of Art, New Haven, Conn.: Yale University Press, 1991.

Bornstein, Daniel, and Roberto Rusconi. *Women and Religion in Medieval and Renaissance Italy.* Translated by M. Schneider. Chicago: University of Chicago Press, 1996.

Bornstein, Diane, ed. *Ideals for Women in the Works of Christine de Pizan.* Detroit, Mich.: Michigan Consortium for Medieval and Early Modern Studies, 1981.

Borroff, Marie, ed. and trans. *Sir Gawain and the Green Knight.* New York: W. W. Norton, 1967.

Bos, Gerrit. "The Miswak, an Aspect of Dental Care in Islam." *Medical History* 37 (1993): 68–79.

Bos, Gerrit, ed. and trans. *Qusta Ibn Luqa's Medical Regime for the Pilgrims to Mecca: The Risala Fi Tadbir Safar al-Hajj.* Leiden and New York: E. J. Brill, 1992.

Bosley, Richard N., and Martin Tweedale. *Basic Issues in Medieval Philosophy: Selected Readings Presenting the Interactive Discourses among the Major Figures.* Peterborough, Ont., Canada: Broadview Press, 1997.

Boss, Sarah Jane. *Empress and Handmaiden: On Nature and Gender in the Cult of the Virgin Mary.* London: Cassell, 2000.

Boswell, John Eastburn. *Christianity, Social Tolerance, and Homosexuality: Gay People in Western Europe from the Beginning of the Christian Era to the 14th Century.* Chicago: University of Chicago Press, 1982.

———. *Same-Sex Unions in Premodern Europe.* New York: Random House, 1994.

Bosworth, C. Edmund, and M. E. J. Richardson, eds. *A Commentary on the Qur'an Prepared by Richard Bell.* 2 vols. Manchester: Manchester University Press, 1991.

Bosworth, C. Edmund, and D. Sourdel. "Ghulam." *Encyclopaedia of Islam,* 2d ed. Vol. 2. Leiden, The Netherlands: E. J. Brill, 1999, 1,079–1,091.

Bosworth, Clifford E. *Cambridge History of Iran.* Edited by J. A. Boyle. Cambridge: Cambridge University Press, 1968.

———. *The Ghaznavids: Their Empire in Afghanistan and Eastern Iran, 994–1040.* Edinburgh: Edinburgh University Press, 1963.

———. "Ghurids." *Encyclopedia of Islam.* New ed. Leiden: E. J. Brill, 1978.

———. *The Islamic Dynasties.* Edinburgh: Edinburgh University Press, 1967.

———. *The Medieval History of Iran, Afghanistan, and Central Asia.* London: Variorum Reprints, 1977.

———. *The Medieval Islamic Underworld.* Edinburgh: Edinburgh University Press, 1976.

Botticini, Maristella, and Zvi Eckstein. "From Farmers to Merchants: A Human Capital Interpretation of Jewish Economic History." Manuscript, May 2004. Available online. URL: http://people.bu.edu/maristel.

Boulton, D'Arcy Jonathan D. *The Knights of the Crown: The Monarchical Orders of Knighthood in Later Medieval Europe, 1325–1520.* Rochester, N.Y.: Boydell, 2000.

Bousquet, Georges Henri. *Les grandes pratiques rituelles de l'Islam.* Paris: Presses Universitaires de France, 1949.

Bowie, Theodore. *The Sketchbook of Villard de Honnecourt.* Bloomington: Indiana University Press, 1959.

Boxer, Charles R. *Four Centuries of Portuguese Expansion, 1415–1825.* Berkeley: University of California Press, 1969.

Brainard, Ingrid. "Arena, Antonius de," "Cornazano, Antonio," "Dancing Master," "Domenico da Piacenza," and "Guglielmo Ebreo da Pesaro." In *International Encyclopedia of Dance.* New York: Oxford University Press, 1998.

———. "Dance §III: Middle Ages and Early Renaissance." In *The New Grove Dictionary of Music and Musicians,* edited by Stanley Sadie and John Tyrrell. London: Oxford University Press, 1980.

———. "Music for Dance: Western Music before 1520." In *The International Encyclopedia of Dance.* New York: Oxford University Press, 1998.

Branca, Vittore, ed. *Mercanti scrittori.* Milan: Rusconi, 1986.

Brandenburg, D. *Islamic Miniature Painting in Medical Manuscripts.* Basel, Switzerland: Editiones Roche, 1982.

Brandl, A., and O. Zippel. *Middle English Literature.* New York: Chelsea Publishing, 1947.

Braudel, Fernand. *Capitalism and the Material Life.* 1400–1800. Translated by M. Kochas. New York: Harper Colophon, 1973.

———. *The Mediterranean and the Mediterranean World in the Age of Phillip II.* New York: Harper & Row, 1972.

Braun, Hugh. *An Introduction to English Medieval Architecture.* New York: Faber, 1968.

Bredero, Adriaan H. *Bernard of Clairvaux between Cult and History.* Grand Rapids, Mich.: Wm. B. Eerdmans, 1997.

Breger, Jennifer. (1993). "The Role of Jewish Women in Hebrew Printing." *A Bookman's Weekly* 91, no. 13: 1,320–1,329.

Brenner, Reuven, and Nicholas M. Kiefer. "The Economics of the Diaspora: Discrimination and Occupational Structure." *Economic Development and Cultural Change* 29 (April 1981): 517–534.

Brentano, Robert. *Rome before Avignon: A Social History of Thirteenth-Century Rome.* Berkeley: University of California Press, 1991.

Brett, Gerard. *Dinner Is Served: A History of Dining in England.* London: Hart-Davis, 1968.

Bridenthal, Renate, and Claudia Koonz. *Becoming Visible: Women in European History.* Boston: Houghton Mifflin, 1974.

Briffault, Robert. *The Troubadours.* Bloomington: Indiana University Press, 1965.

Brinner, William A. "The Karaites of Christendom—the Karaites of Islam." In *The Islamic World: Essays in Honor of Bernard Lewis.* Princeton, N.J.: Princeton University Press, 1989.

British Museum Cottonian Manuscript Claudius D II. c. 1450.

British Museum Harleian Manuscript 279. 1420.

British Museum Harleian Manuscript 4016. 1450.

Britton, Nancy P. *A Study of Some Early Islamic Textiles in the Museum of Fine Arts.* Boston: Boston Museum of Fine Arts, 1938.

Broadhurst, R. J. C. *Travels of Ibn Jubayr.* London: Routledge, 1952.

Brody, Heinrich, ed. *Selected Poems of Jehudah Halevi.* Philadelphia: The Jewish Publication of America, 1974.

Brody, Robert. *The Geonim of Babylonia and the Shaping of Medieval Jewish Culture.* New Haven, Conn.: Yale University Press, 1998.

Brogger, A. W., and Haakon Shetelig. *The Viking Ships: Their Ancestry and Evolution.* Translated by Katherine John. London and Oslo: C. Hurst, 1971.

Brooke, George J., ed. *Jewish Ways of Reading the Bible.* New York: Oxford University Press, 2002.

Brooke, Iris. *English Costume of the Early Middle Ages, 10th through 13th Centuries.* London: A. and C. Black, 1964.

———. *English Costume of the Early Middle Ages, 14th and 15th Centuries.* London: A. and C. Black, 1963.

Broome, Michael. *A Handbook of Islamic Coins*. London: B. A. Seaby, 1985.

Brown, H. M. *Instrumental Music Printed before 1600*. Cambridge, Mass.: Harvard University Press, 1965.

Brown, Joseph E., and Ann Ensign Brown. *Harness the Wind: The Story of Windmills*. New York: Dodd-Mead, 1977.

Brown, Peter. *Augustine of Hippo: A Biography*. Berkeley: University of California Press, 1967.

———. *Authority and the Sacred: Aspects of the Christianization of the Roman World*. Cambridge and New York: Cambridge University Press, 1995.

———. *The Cult of the Saints: Its Rise and Function in Latin Christianity*, Chicago: University of Chicago Press, 1981.

———. "A Dark-Age Crisis: Aspects of the Iconoclastic Controversy," *The English Historical Review* 88 (1973).

Brown, R. Allen. *English Castles*. 3rd ed. London: Batsford, 1976.

Brown, S., and J. O'Sullivan. *The Register of Eudes of Rouen*. New York: Columbia University Press, 1964.

Browne, Edward Granville. *Arabian Medicine*. 1921. Reprint, Westport, Conn.: Hyperion Press, 1983.

Browning, Oscar. *Guelphs and Ghibellines*. A Short History of Medieval Italy from 1250–1409, Rome: s.n., 1974, 1894.

Bryce, J. *The Holy Roman Empire*. New ed. New York: Macmillan, 1968.

Bucher, Francois. *The Pamplona Bibles*. New Haven, Conn.: Yale University Press, 1970.

Bukofzer, M. "Speculative Thinking in Medieval Music." *Speculum* 17 (1942).

Bull, Marcus. *Knightly Piety and the Lay Response to the First Crusade: The Limousin and Gascony, c. 970–c. 1130*. Oxford: Clarendon Press, 1993.

Bulliet, R. W. *The Camel and the Wheel*. Cambridge, Mass.: Harvard University Press, 1975.

Bullough, V. *History of Prostitution*. New York: University Books, 1964.

Bundy, Mildred. *Insular, Anglo-Saxon and Early Anglo-Norman Manuscript Art at Corpus Christi College, Cambridge: An Illustrated Catalogue*. Kalamazoo: Western Michigan University Press, 1998.

Burchardt, Titus. *Alchemy, Science of the Cosmos, Science of the Soul*. Cambridge: Quinta Essentia, 1995.

———. *Sacred Art in East and West: Its Principles and Methods*. London: Perennial Books, 1967.

Burgel, C. *Secular and Religious Features of Medieval Arabic Medicine*. In *Asian Medical Systems: A Comparative Study*, edited by Charles Leslie. Berkeley: University of California Press, 1976.

Burgess, Glyn S. *The Lais of Marie de France: Text and Context*. Athens: University of Georgia Press, 1987.

Burke, John. *Life in the Castle in Medieval England*. New York: British Heritage, 1983.

Burnett, Charles. "Arabic into Latin: The Reception of Arabic Philosophy into Western Europe." In *The Cambridge Companion to Arabic Philosophy*, edited by Peter Adamson and Richard C. Taylor, 370–404. Cambridge: Cambridge University Press, 1994.

———. "The Translating Activity in Medieval Spain." In *The Legacy of Muslim Spain*, edited by Salma K. Jayyusi, 1,036–1,062. Leiden, The Netherlands: E. J. Brill, 1994.

Burnley, David. *The History of the English Language: A Sourcebook*. New York: Longman, 2000.

Burns, Robert I. *Islam under the Crusaders, Colonial Survival in the Thirteenth-Century Kingdom of Valencia*. Princeton, N.J.: Princeton University Press 1973.

———. *Muslims, Christians, and Jews in the Crusader Kingdom of Valencia*. Cambridge: Cambridge University Press, 1984.

Burrell, David. *Knowing the Unknowable God: Ibn-Sina, Maimonides, and Aquinas*. Notre Dame, Ind.: University of Notre Dame Press, 1986.

Butler, W. F. T. *The Lombard Communes: A History of the Republics of North Italy*. New York: Charles Scribner's Sons, 1906 and Westport, Conn.: Greenwood Press, Publishers, 1969.

Cahen, Claude. "Dhimma." In *Encyclopaedia of Islam*, 2d ed. Vol. 2. Leiden, The Netherlands: E. J. Brill, 1999, 231.

———. "Djizya." *Encyclopaedia of Islam*, 2d ed. Vol. 2. Leiden, The Netherlands: E. J. Brill, 1999, 559.

———. "Iktâ," *Encyclopaedia of Islam*, 2d ed. Vol. 3. Leiden, The Netherlands: E. J. Brill, 1999, 1,088–1,091.

———. "Réflexions sur le Waqf Ancien." *Studia Islamica* 14 (1961): 37–56.

Cahill, Thomas. *The Gifts of the Jews: How a Tribe of Desert Nomads Changed the Way Everyone Thinks and Feels.* New York: Nan A. Talese Doubleday, 1998.

Calendar of letter-books of the city of London: D: 1309–1314, 'Folios ci–cx,' (1902): 218–238. Available online. URL: http://www.british-history.ac.uk/report.asp?compid=33083.

Callahan, Gene. *Economics for Real People.* Auburn, Ala.: Ludwig von Mises Institute, 2002.

Cambridge Economic History. Vols. 1 and 2. Cambridge: Cambridge University Press, 1941, 1952.

Cameron, Averil. *Christianity and the Rhetoric of Empire: The Development of Christian Discourse.* Vol. 55. Sather Classical Lectures. Berkeley: University of California Press, 1991, pp. xix, 262.

Campbell, Anna. *The Black Death and Men of Learning.* New York: Columbia University Press, 1931.

Campbell, Bruce M. S., ed., *Before the Black Death: Studies in the "Crisis" of the Early Fourteenth Century.* Manchester and New York, 1991.

Campbell, D. *Arabian Medicine and Its Influence on the Middle Ages.* Amsterdam: Philo Press, 1974.

Campion, Nicholas, "The Concept of Destiny in Islamic Astrology and Its Impact on European Medieval Thought." *ARAM, The Journal for Syro-Mesopotamian Culture* 1, no. 2 (summer 1989): 281–289.

Canard, Marius. "Ibn Fadlan." *The Encyclopedia of Islam,* edited by B. Lewis, et al. 10 vols. Leiden: E. J. Brill, 1960.

Cantor, Norman F. *In the Wake of the Plague: The Black Death and the World It Made.* New York and London: Free Press, 2001.

Cantor, Norman. *Medieval History: The Life and Death of a Civilization.* New York: HarperPerennial, 1994, 1963.

Cantor, Norman F., and Michael S. Werthman, eds. *Medieval Society, 400–1450. The Structure of European History.* Vol. 2. New York: Thomas Y. Cromwell, 1967.

Capp, W. H., and W. M. Wright, eds. *Silent Fire: An Invitation to Western Mysticism.* New York: Harper Forum Books, 1978.

Carboni, Stefano, and David Whitehouse. *Glass of the Sultans.* New York: Metropolitan Museum of Art, 2001.

Carbonneau, Thomas E., ed. *Lex Mercatoria and Arbitration.* Dobbs Ferry, N.Y.: Transnational Juris, 1990.

Cardan, Jerome. *Metacoscopia.* Edited by Thomas Jolly. Paris, 1658.

Cardano, Girolamo. *De vita propria liber.* Translated by J. Stoner as *The Book of Life.* 1930. Reprint, New York: The New York Review of Books, 2002.

———. *Libelli duo Apologia astrologia* (1544).

Cardinale, H. E. *Orders of Knighthood, Awards and the Holy See.* Gerrards Cross, Buckinghamshire: Van Duren, 1983, 1985.

Carey, Hilary M. *Courting Disaster: Astrology at the English Court and University in the Later Middle Ages.* New York: St. Martin's Press, 1992.

Carmi, T., ed. *Penguin Book of Hebrew Verse.* 1981. Reprint, London: Penguin, 2006.

Carmichael, Ann G., and Richard Ratzan. *Medicine: A Treasury of Art and Literature.* New York: Beaux Arts, 1991.

Carolus Clusius. *Rariorum Plantarum Historia.* Antwerp: Moretus, 1601.

Cartellieri, Otto. *The Court of Burgundy.* New York: Knopf, 1929.

Carus-Wilson, Eleanora. "An Industrial Revolution of the 13th Century." *Economic History Review* 11 (1941): 39–60.

Carus-Wilson, Eleanora M. *Medieval Merchant Adventurers.* 2d ed. London: Methuen, 1967.

Caspi, M. M. *Oral Tradition and Hispanic Literature.* New York: Garland, 1995.

Casson, Lionel. *Illustrated History of Ships and Boats.* New York: Doubleday, 1964.

Castaño, Javier, et al. *The Jews of Europe in the Middle Ages.* Ostfildern: Hatje Cantz, 2005.

Castro, Americo. *Espana en su historia: cristianos, moros y judios.* Buenos Aires: Editorial Losada, 1948.

———. *The Structure of Spanish History.* Princeton, N.J.: Princeton University Press, 1954.

Catherine of Siena. *The Dialogue,* Classics of Western Spirituality 17, translated by Suzanne Noffke. New York: Paulist Press, 1980.

Caussin de Perceval. *Essai sur L'histoire des Arabes.* (avant l'islamisme). Gratz: Akademische Druck-u. Verlagsanstalt, 1967.

Cave, Roy C., and Herbert H. Coulson. *A Source Book for Medieval Economic History*. New York: Biblo and Tannen, 1965.

Cawley, A. C., and J. J. Anderson, eds. *Pearl, Cleanness, Patience, Sir Gawain and the Green Knight*. New York: E. P. Dutton, 1976.

Cervantes. *Don Quixote*. Translated by J. M. Cohen. New York: Penguin, 1950.

Chadwick, D. *Social Life in the Days of Piers Plowman*. New York: Russell & Russell, 1969.

Chadwick, Henry. *Augustine*. Oxford: Past Masters Series, Oxford University Press, 1986.

Chamberlain, Michael. *Knowledge and Social Practice in Medieval Damascus, 1190–1350*. Cambridge: Cambridge University Press, 2002.

Charanis, P. *Social, Economic and Political Life in the Byzantine Empire*. Vol. 4. London: Variorum Reprints, 1973.

Charles, R. H. *Eschatology: The Doctrine of a Future Life in Israel, Judaism, and Christianity*. New York: Schocken Books, 1963.

Chase, Steven, ed. *Angelic Spirituality: Medieval Perspectives on the Ways of Angels*, Classics of Western Spirituality. New York: Paulist Press, 2002.

Chaucer, Geoffrey. *The Complete Poetry and Prose of Geoffrey Chaucer*. Edited by John H. Fisher. New York: Holt, Rinehart & Winston, 1977.

Chazan, Robert. *Daggers of Faith: Thirteenth-Century Christian Missionizing and Jewish Response*. Berkeley: University of California Press, 1989.

———. *European Jewry and the First Crusade*. Berkeley: University of California Press, c. 1987.

———. *God, Humanity, and History: The Hebrew First Crusade Narrative*. Berkeley and London: University of California Press, 2000.

Chazelle, C., and Burton Van Name Edwards. *The Study of the Bible in the Carolingian Era*. Turnhout, Brepols: 2003.

Chejne, Anwar. *Muslim Spain: Its History and Culture*. Minneapolis: University of Minnesota Press, 1974.

Chelkowski, Peter, Priscilla Soucek, and Richard Ettinghausen. *Mirror of the Invisible World: Tales from the Khamseh of Nizami*. New York: Metropolitan Museum of Art, 1975.

Chenery, Thomas, and Francis Steingass, trans. *The Assemblies of Al-Hariri*. London: Oriental Translation Fund, 1867–1898.

Chenu, Marie-Dominique. *Nature, Man, and Society in the Twelfth Century: Essays on New Theological Perspectives in the Latin West*, Medieval Academy Reprints for Teaching. Toronto: University of Toronto Press, 1998.

———. *Toward Understanding St. Thomas*. Chicago: Regnery, 1964.

Chernus, Ira. *Mysticism in Rabbinic Judaism*. Berlin and New York: Walter de Gruyter, 1982.

Chittick, W. *Imaginal Worlds: Ibn al-'Arabi and the Problem of Religious Diversity*. Albany: State University of New York Press, 1994.

Chodkiewicz, M. *Seal of the Saints—Prophethood and Sainthood in the Doctrine of Ibn 'Arabi*. Translated by L. Sherrard. Cambridge: Islamic Texts Society, 1993.

Cholakian, P., and B. Cholakian. *The Early French Novella*. Albany: State University of New York Press, 1974.

Choniates, Nicetas. *O City of Byzantium: Annals of Niketas Choniates*. Translated Harry I. Magoulias. Detroit: Wayne State University Press, 1984.

Chorley, Patrick. "The Cloth Exports of Flanders and Northern France during the Thirteenth Century: A Luxury Trade?" *Economic History Review*, 2d ser. 40 (1987): 349–379.

Chretien de Troyes. *Arthurian Romances*. Translated by W. W. Comfort. New York: Dutton, 1975.

Christiansen, Eric. *The Northern Crusades: The Baltic and the Catholic Frontier 1100–1525*. Minneapolis: University of Minnesota, 1980.

Christine de Pizan. *Ballades, Rondeaux and Virelais*. Edited by Kenneth Varty. Leicester, U.K.: Leicester University Press, 1965.

———. *The Book of Fayttes of Arms and of Chyvalrye*. Translated and printed by William Caxton from the French by Christine de Pizan, edited by A. T. P. Byles. London: Oxford University Press, 1932, 1937.

———. *The Book of the Duke of True Lovers*. Translated by Alice Kemp-Welch; ballads, translated by Lawrence Binyon and Eric D. Maclagen. New York: Cooper Square, 1966 (1908).

———. *The Book of the Three Virtues or the Treasury of the City of Ladies*. Translated by Charity Cannon Willard and Madeleine Pelner Cosman. Published as *Medieval Woman's Mirror of Honor:*

Christine de Pizan's Treasury of the City of Ladies. New York: Persea Books, 1989.

Cipolla, Carlo. *Before the Industrial Revolution.* New York: Norton, 1976.

———. *Fontana Economic History of Europe.* Vol. 1, *The Middle Ages.* Glasgow: Collins/Fontana Books, 1972.

———. *Money, Prices and Civilization in the Mediterranean World.* Princeton, N.J.: Princeton University Press, 1956.

———. *Public Health and the Medical Profession in the Renaissance.* Cambridge and London: Cambridge University Press, 1976.

Clark, Alice. *The Working Life of Women in the 17th Century.* London, Routledge, 1919.

Clarke, M. V. *The Medieval City State.* 1926. Reprint, Cambridge: Speculum Historiale, 1966.

Clune, G. *The Medieval (sic) Gild System.* Dublin: Browne and Nolan, Ltd. 1908: Reprint, 1963.

Cluse, Christoph, ed. *The Jews of Europe in the Middle Ages (Tenth to Fifteenth Centuries).* Turnhout: Brepols, 2004.

Coakley, John. "Gender and the Authority of Friars: The Significance of Holy Women for Thirteenth-Century Franciscans and Dominicans." *Church History* 60 (December 1991): 445–460.

Cockayne, O., ed. *Leechdoms, Wortcunning and Starcraft Early England* (Chronicles and Memorials of Britain and Ireland during the Middle Ages). 1864. Reprint, Millwood, N.Y.: Kraus Reprint, 1965.

Cockerell, Sydney. *Old Testament Miniatures.* New York: George Braziller, 1975.

Cocles, Barthelemy. *Physiognomonia.* Strasbourg, 1533.

Cohen, Gerson D. "The Hebrew Crusade Chronicles and the Ashkenazic Tradition." In *Minhah le-Nahum: Biblical and Other Studies in Honor of Nahum M. Sarna,* edited by Michael Fishbane and Marc Brettler, 36–53. Sheffield: Sheffield Academic Press, 1999.

Cohen, Jeffrey Jerome. *Of Giants: Sex, Monsters, and the Middle Ages.* Minneapolis: University of Minnesota Press, 1999.

Cohen, Jeremy. *The Friars and the Jews: The Evolution of Medieval Anti-Judaism.* Ithaca, N.Y.: Cornell University Press, 1982.

———. "The Hebrew chronicles of the first crusade in their Christian cultural context." In *Juden und Christen zur Zeit der Kreuzzuge,* edited by Alfred Haverkamp (1999): 17–34.

———. *Living Letters of the Law: Ideas of the Jew in Medieval Christianity.* Berkeley: University of California Press, 1999.

———. "The Nasi of Narbonne: A Problem in Medieval Historiography," *AJS Review* 2 (1977): 45–76.

———. *Sanctifying the Name of God: Jewish Martyrs and Jewish Memories of the First Crusade.* Philadelphia: University of Pennsylvania Press, 2006.

Cohen, Mark R. *Under Crescent and Cross: The Jews in the Middle Ages.* Princeton, N.J.: Princeton University Press, 1994.

Collins, Roger. *Early Medieval Spain: Unity in Diversity, 400–1000.* New York: St. Martin's Press, 1983.

Colthrop, D. C. *English Costume.* Vol 3. London, 1931.

Colvin, John. *Lions of Judah.* London: Quartet Books, 1997.

Comnena, Anna, *Alexiad.* Translated by E. R. A. Sewter. Baltimore: Penguin Books 1969.

Conant, Kenneth J. *Carolingian and Romanesque Architecture: 800–1200.* New Haven, Conn.: Yale University Press, 1992.

Conde Lucanor y otros cuentos medievales. Barcelona: Bruguera, 1970.

Conrad L. I., M. Neve, V. Nutton, R. Porter, and A. Wear. *The Western Medical Tradition. 800 BC to AD 1800.* Cambridge: Cambridge University Press, 1995.

Conrad, Lawrence J. "The Social Structure of Medicine in Medieval Islam." *Bulletin of the Society for the Social History of Medicine* 37 (1985): 11–15.

Consitt, Frances. *The London Weavers' Company.* Vol. 1. Oxford: Clarendon Press, 1933.

Constable, Giles. *Monastic Tithes: Their Origins to the 12th Century.* New York: Cambridge University Press, 1964.

———. *Monks, Hermits, and Crusaders in Medieval Europe.* London: Variorum Reprints, 1988.

Constable, Olivia Remie. *Housing the Stranger in the Mediterranean World: Lodging, Trade and Travel in*

Late Antiquity and the Middle Ages. Cambridge: Cambridge University Press, 2003.

Constable, Olivia Remie, ed. *Medieval Iberia: Readings from Christian, Muslim and Jewish Sources*. Philadelphia: University of Pennsylvania Press, 1997.

Constantinides, C. N. *Higher Education in Byzantium in the Thirteenth and Early Fourteenth Centuries (1204–ca.1310)*. Nicosia: Cyprus Research Center, 1982.

Cook, Albert S. *A Literary Middle English Reader*. Boston: Ginn, 1943.

Cook, David. *Understanding Jihad*. Berkeley: University of California Press, 2005.

Cook, Michael A. *Early Muslim Dogma*. Cambridge: Cambridge University Press, 1981.

Cook, Michael, *Commanding Right and Forbidding Wrong in Islamic Thought*. Cambridge: Cambridge University Press, 2000.

Cook, William R. *Francis of Assisi: The Way of Poverty and Humility*. Dover, Del.: Michael Glazier, and Collegeville, Minn.: Liturgical Press, 1989.

Coon, Lynda L. *Sacred Fictions: Holy Women and Hagiography in Late Antiquity*. Philadelphia: University of Pennsylvania Press, 1997.

Cooper, Geoffrey, and Christopher Worthan. *The Summoning of Everyman*. Melbourne: Melbourne University Press, 1984.

Cooper, J. *Commentary on the Qur'an*. Vol. 1. Oxford, Oxford University Press, 1987.

Copinger, W. A. *The Law of Copyright in Works of Literature and Art*. London, 1870.

Copleston, Frederick. *A History of Philosophy*. Vol. II: *Medieval Philosophy: From Augustine to Duns Scotus*. Westminster, Md.: The Newman Press, 1950.

———. *A History of Philosophy*. Vol. III: *Late Medieval and Renaissance Philosophy*. Westminster, Md.: The Newman Press, 1953.

Corbin, Henry. "Nasir-i Khusrau and Iranian Ismailism." In *The Cambridge History of Iran*, edited by R. N. Frye. Vol. 4, *The Period from the Arab Invasion to the Saljuqs*. Cambridge: Cambridge University Press, 1975.

Corfis, Ivy A., and Michael Wolfe, eds. *The Medieval City under Siege*. Woodbridge, Suffolk, and Rochester, N.Y.: Boydell Press, 1995; reprint, 1999.

Cosman, Madeleine Pelner. "A Chicken for Chaucer's Kitchen: Medieval London's Market Laws and Larcenies." In *Fabulous Feasts, Medieval Cookery and Ceremony*. New York: George Braziller, 1976–2002.

———. "Criminalization of Women and Trials of Witches." A review of *Women's Secrets: Pseudo-Albertus Magnus' De Secretis Mulieum*, by Helen Rodnite Lemay. *Journal of the History of Medicine and Allied Sciences*, March 1994.

———. *The Education of the Hero in Arthurian Romance*. Chapel Hill: University of North Carolina Press, 1966 and Oxford: University Press, 1967.

———. *Fabulous Feasts: Medieval Cookery and Ceremony*. New York: George Braziller, 1976.

———. "A Feast for Aesculapius: Historical Diets for Asthma and Sexual Pleasure." *Annual Review of Nutrition* 3 (1983): 1–33.

———. *Letterbook of Marvelous Beasts: An Alliterative Alphabet of Marvelous Animals*. Tenafly, N.J.: Bard Hall Press, 1988.

———. "Machaut's Medical Musical World." In *Machaut's World: Science and Art in the 14th Century*, edited by M. P. Cosman and D. Chandler. New York: New York Academy of Sciences, 1978.

———. "Maimonides Treatise on Asthma," *Phi Lambda Kappa Medical Quarterly*. Fall, 1987.

———. "Malpractice and Peer Review in Medieval England." *Transactions of the American Academy of Ophthalmology and Otolaryngology* 80 (May–June, 1975): 293–297.

———. "Medical and Scientific Gold." A review of *The Occult Sciences in the Renaissance*, by Wayne Shumaker. *Journal of the History of Medicine* 36 (1981): 93–94.

———. "Medical Fees, Fines, and Forfeits in Medieval England." *Man and Medicine* (1975): 133–158.

———. "Medical Sexuality and Social Context." A review of Audrey Eccles' *Obstetrics and Gynaecology in Tudor and Stuart England*, in *Journal of the American Medical Association* 249, no. 10 (1983): 1,361.

———. *The Medieval Baker's Daughter / La Hija de la Panadera Medieval*. Tenafly, N.J.: Bard Hall Press, 1984.

———. "Medieval Cookery and Feasting." In *Dictionary of the Middle Ages*, edited by American Council of Learned Societies. New York: Charles Scribner's Sons, 1982–87.

———. "The Medieval Food of Love." *Phi Lambda Kappa Medical Quarterly*. Spring, 1986.

———. "Medieval Gynecological Health." A review of *Medieval Woman's Guide to Health: The First English Gynecological Handbook*, by Beryl Rowland *Journal of the American Medical Association* 247, no. 3 (1982): 357.

———. "The Medieval Health Handbook." *The Quarterly Review of Biology* 52, no. 1 (1977).

———. *Medieval Holidays and Festivals: A Calendar of Celebrations*. New York: Charles Scribner's Sons, 1981.

———. "Medical Herbs of Health." In *Dictionary of the Middle Ages*, edited by American Council of Learned Societies. New York: Charles Scribner's Sons, 1982–87.

———. "Medieval Medical Malpractice: The Dicta and Dockets." *Bulletin of the New York Academy of Medicine* 49, no. 1 (1973): 22–47.

———. "Medieval Medical Malpractice and Chaucer's Physician" *New York State Journal of Medicine* 72. no. 19 (1972): 2,439–2,444.

———. "Medieval Medical Nutrition." *Journal of Food and Nutrition* 42, no. 3 (1986): 100–104.

———. "The Medieval Medical Third Party: Compulsory Consultation and Malpractice Insurance." *Annals of Plastic Surgery* 8, no. 2 (1982): 152–162.

———. *Medieval Wordbook*. New York: Facts On File, 1996.

———. "Music and Manners Make the Man." In *The Education of the Hero in Arthurian Romance*. Chapel Hill: University of North Carolina Press, 1966 and Oxford: Oxford University Press, 1967.

———. "Pharmacology and the Pharmacopeia." In *Dictionary of the Middle Ages*, edited by American Council of Learned Societies. New York: Charles Scribner's Sons, 1982–87.

———. "Sex, Smut, Sin, and Spirit." In *Fabulous Feasts: Medieval Cookery and Ceremony*. New York: George Braziller, 1976–2002.

———. "Surgical Malpractice in the Renaissance and Today." *Annals of Plastic Surgery* (1986).

———. *Women at Work in Medieval Europe*. New York: Facts On File, 2000.

Cosman, Madeleine Pelner, and Rabbi Jack Bemporad. *A Passover Haggadah*. With illustrations by Tobi Kahn. Tenafly, N.J.: Chavurah Beth Sholem, Bard Hall Press, 1996.

Cosman, Madeleine Pelner, and Bruce Chandler, eds. *Machaut's World: Science and Art in the 14th Century*. New York: New York Academy of Sciences, 1978.

Cosman, Madeleine Pelner, and Louis Pelner. "Dr. Elias Sabot and King Henry IV." *New York State Journal of Medicine* 69, no. 18 (1969): 2,482–2,490.

Cosman, Madeleine Pelner, and Charity Cannon Willard, eds. *Medieval Woman's Mirror of Honor: Christine De Pizan's Treasury of the City of Ladies*. New York: Persea Books, 1989.

Cothren, Michael W. *Picturing the Celestial City: The Medieval Stained Glass of Beauvais Cathedral*. Princeton, N.J.: Princeton University Press, 2006.

Coudert, Allison. *Alchemy: The Philosopher's Stone*. Boulder, Colo.: Shambala, 1980.

Coulson, N. J. *A History of Islamic Law*. Edinburgh: Edinburgh University Press, 1964.

Coulson, Noel J. "Bayt al-Mal." *Encyclopaedia of Islam*, 2d ed. Vol. 1. Leiden, The Netherlands: E. J. Brill, 1999, 1,141–1,149.

———. *A History of Islamic Law*. Oxford: Clarendon Press, 1964.

Coulton, G. G. *Medieval Faith and Symbolism*. New York: Harper, 1958.

———. *Medieval Panorama: The English Scene from Conquest to Reformation*. Cleveland, Ohio: World Publishing, 1962.

———. *The Medieval Scene*. Cambridge: Cambridge University Press, 1961.

———. *Medieval Village, Manor and Monastery*. New York: Harper, 1960.

———. *Ten Medieval Studies*. Boston: Beacon Press, 1959.

Cowdrey, H. E. J. *The Cluniacs and the Gregorian Reform*, 1977.

Cox, H. *The Feast of Fools*. Cambridge, Mass.: Harvard University Press, 1969.

Crane, Frederick. *Materials for the Study of the Fifteenth-Century Basse Danse*. Brooklyn, N.Y.: Institute of Medieval Music, 1968.

Crawford, Anne, ed. *Letters of Medieval Women.* Stroud, Gloucestershire: Sutton, 2002.

Crescentius, Petrus. *In Commodu Ruralium or Opus Ruralium Commodorum.* Speyer: Peter Drach, 1490.

Creswell, K. A. C. *Early Muslim Architecture.* Vol. 1, 2d ed. and Vol. 2. Oxford: Oxford University Press, 1969, 1940.

———. *The Muslim Architecture of Egypt.* Oxford: Oxford University Press, 1959.

Crombie, A. C. *Medieval and Early Modern Science.* Cambridge, Mass.: Harvard University Press, 1967.

Crone, Patricia. *Meccan Trade and the Rise of Islam.* Princeton, N.J.: Princeton University Press, 1987.

———. *Slaves on Horses: The Evolution of the Islamic Polity.* Cambridge: Cambridge University Press, 1980.

Cross, F. L., and E. A. Livingstone, eds. *Oxford Dictionary of the Christian Church.* Oxford: Oxford University Press, 1977.

Cross, Richard. *Duns Scotus.* Oxford: Oxford University Press, 1999.

Crotch, W. J. B. *Prologues and Epilogues of William Caxton.* London: Oxford University Press, 1928.

Cuno, James. *Glory and Prosperity: Harvard's Islamic Metalwork Collection on Display for the First Time at Sackler Museum from Vases to Armor, Objects Reflect the High Status of the Art Form.* Cambridge, Mass.: Arthur M. Sackler Museum, Harvard University Art Museums, 2002.

Curran, S. Terrie. *English from Caedmon to Chaucer: The Literary Development of English.* Prospect Heights, Ill.: Waveland Press, 2002.

Curry, Walter Clyde. *Chaucer and the Medieval Sciences.* New York: Barnes & Noble, 1960.

Cutler, A. H., and H. E. Cutler. *The Jew as Ally of the Muslim.* Notre Dame, Ind.: University of Notre Dame Press, 1986.

Dale, M. K. "The London Silk Women of the 15th Century." *Economic History Review* 4 (1932–34): 324–335.

Daniel, Norman. *Heroes and Saracens: An Interpretation of the Chansons de Geste.* Edinburgh: Edinburgh University Press, 1984.

Dante, Alighieri. *The Divine Comedy: The Inferno, the Purgatorio, and the Paradiso.* Translated by John Ciardi. New York: New American Library, 2003.

Davenport, Millia. *The Book of Costume.* Vol. 1. New York: Crown, 1948.

Davidson, Herbert A. *Proofs for Eternity, Creation and the Existence of God in Medieval Islamic and Jewish Philosophy.* New York: Oxford University Press, 1987.

Davies, Brian, and Brian Leftow, eds. *The Cambridge Companion to Anselm.* Cambridge: Cambridge University Press, 2004.

Davies, R. T., ed. *Medieval English Lyrics: A Critical Anthology.* Evanston, Ill.: Northwestern University Press, 1964.

Davis, Norman, ed. *Paston Letters and Papers of the Fifteenth Century.* Oxford and New York: Oxford University Press, 2004.

Davis, Robert C. *Christian Slaves, Muslim Masters: White Slavery in the Mediterranean, the Barbary Coast, and Italy, 1500–1800.* New York: Palgrave Macmillan, 2003.

Dawidowicz, Lucy. *The Golden Tradition: Jewish Life and Thought in Eastern Europe.* New York: Holt, Rinehart, 1967.

Dawood, C. N. J., ed. and trans. *Tales from the Thousand and One Nights.* London: Penguin Classics, 1973.

Dawson, Christopher. *Medieval Essays.* New York: Sheed & Ford, 1959.

Day, Gerald W. *Genoa's Response to Byzantium, 1155–1204: Commercial Expansion and Factionalism in a Medieval City.* Urbana: University of Illinois Press, c. 1988.

Dean, Ruth, and M. Dominica Legge, eds. *The Rule of Saint Benedict, a Norman Prose Version.* Oxford: Blackwell, 1964.

Della Porta, Giovanni Baptista. *Magiae naturalis libri viginti* (1589). Amsterdam: Apud Eliezam Weyerstratem, 1664.

Denholm-Young, N. "The Merchants of Cahors." *Medievalia et Humanistica* IV (1946): 34–44.

Dennis, G. T. *Three Byzantiae Military Treatises.* Washington D.C.: Dumbarton Oaks, 1985.

Denny, Fred. *An Introduction to Islam.* 2d ed. Upper Saddle River, N.J.: Prentice-Hall, 1994.

Dennys, Rodney. *The Heraldic Imagination.* New York: Clarkson N. Potter, 1975.

Derman, M. U. *Letters in Gold: Ottoman Calligraphy from the Sakip Sabanci Collection, Istanbul.* New York: The Metropolitan Museum of Art, 1998.

Derry, T. K., and Trevor I. Williams. *Short History of Technology*. 1956. Reprint New York: Dover, 1993.

Detolnay, Charles. *Hieronymus Bosch*. New York: Raynal, 1966.

Devlin, Dennis. "Feminine Lay Piety in the High Middle Ages: The Beguines." *Medieval Religious Women*. Vol. 1, *Distant Echoes*, edited by John A. Nichols and Lillian Thomas Shank. Kalamazoo, Mich.: Cistercian, 1984.

DeWeese, Devin. *Islamization and Native Religion in the Golden Horde: Baba Tükles and Conversion to Islam in Historical and Epic Tradition*. University Park: Pennsylvania State University Press, 1994.

Dewey, H. W. "Agriculture and Nutrition." In *Dictionary of the Middle Ages*, edited by Joseph R. Strayer. 12 vols. New York: Scribner, 1982–89.

Dewulf, Maurice. *Philosophy and Civilization in the Middle Ages*. New York: Dover, 1953.

Dibdin, A. *Typographical Antiquities of the History of Printing in Great Britain*. London, 1810–19.

Dickie, James. "Allah and Eternity: Mosques, Madrasas and Tombs." In *Architecture of the Islamic World, Its History and Social Meaning*, edited by George Michell. London: Thames and Hudson, 1984.

D'Indagine, Jean. *Chiromance*. Lyons, 1549.

Dingwall, Eric John. *The Girdle of Chastity: A Medico-Historical Study*. 1926. Reprint, New York and London: Routledge, 1959.

Dionysius the Areopagite. *Dionysius the Areopagite: The Divine Names and Mystical Theology*. Translated by C. E. Rolt. London: Society for the Propagation of Christian Knowledge, 1920.

Dioscorides. *The Greek Herbal*. Edited by R. T. Gunther. New York: Hafner, 1959.

Dixon, Philip. *Barbarian Europe: The Making of the Past*. New York: Elsevier Phaidon, 1976.

Dobin, Joel C. *The Astrological Secrets of the Hebrew Sages: To Rule Both Day and Night*. New York: Inner Traditions International, 1983.

———. *Kabbalistic Astrology: The Sacred Tradition of the Hebrew Sages*. Rochester, N.Y.: Inner Traditions International, 1999.

———. *To Rule Both Day and Night: Astrology in the Bible, Midrash, and Talmud*. New York: Inner Traditions International, 1977.

Dobson, R. B. *Clifford's Tower and The Jews of Medieval York*. London: English Heritage, 1995.

Dobson, Richard Barrie. *The Peasants' Revolt of 1381*. London: Macmillan, 1983.

Dodd, W. G. *Courtly Love in Chaucer and Gower*. 1913. Reprint, Gloucester, Mass.: Peter Smith, 1959.

Dodds, Jerrilynn D., ed. *Al-Andalus: The Art of Islamic Spain*. New York: Metropolitan Museum of Art, 1992.

Dols, Michael W. *The Black Death in the Middle East*. Princeton, N.J.: Princeton University Press, 1977.

———. "Famine in the Islamic World." In *Dictionary of the Middle Ages*, edited by Joseph R. Strayer. 12 vols. New York: Scribner, 1982–89.

———. "Herbs, Middle Eastern." In *Dictionary of the Middle Ages*, edited by Joseph R. Strayer. 12 vols. New York: Scribner, 1982–89.

———. *Majnun: The Madman in Medieval Islamic Society*. Oxford: Clarendon Press, 1992.

———. *Medieval Islamic Medicine*. Berkeley: University of California Press, 1984.

———. "The Origins of the Islamic Hospital: Myth and Reality." *Bulletin of the History of Medicine* 62 (1987): 367–390.

Dols, Michael W., and Adil S. Gamal. *Medieval Islamic Medicine: Ibn Ridwan's Treatise 'On the Prevention of Bodily Ills in Egypt.'* Berkeley: University of California Press, 1984.

Donner, F. M. *The Early Islamic Conquests*. Princeton, N.J.: Princeton University Press, 1981.

Doob, Penelope. *Nebuchadnezzar's Children: Conventions of Madness in Middle English Literature*. New Haven, Conn.: Yale University Press, 1974.

Dorff, Rabbi Elliott, "The Use of All Wines." *YD* 123, no. 1 (1985): 1–24. Available online. URL: http:www.rabbinicalassembly.org/teshuvot/docs/19861990/dorff_wines_pdf.

Douglas, David. *William the Conqueror: The Norman Impact upon England*. Berkeley: University of California Press, 1964.

Douglas, Elmer H. *The Mystical Teachings of al-Shadhali*. Albany: State University of New York Press, 1993.

Douglas, Mary. *Leviticus as Literature*. Cambridge: Oxford University Press, 2000.

———. *Purity and Danger: An Analysis of the Concept of Purity and Taboo*. London: Routledge, 2002.

Downing, T. E., and M. Gibson, eds. *Irrigation's Impact on Society*. Tucson: University of Arizona Press, 1974.

Drew, Katherine Fischer. *The Burgundian Code*. Philadelphia: University of Pennsylvania Press, 1977.

———. *The Lombard Laws*. Philadelphia: University of Pennsylvania Press, 1978.

Drogin, Marc. *Medieval Calligraphy: Its History and Technique*. New York: Dover, 1989.

Dronke, Peter. *A History of Twelfth-Century Philosophy*. Cambridge and New York: Cambridge University Press, 1988.

———. *Medieval Latin and the Rise of the European Love Lyric*. Oxford: Oxford University Press, 1968.

———. *Women Writers of the Middle Ages*. New York: Cambridge University Press, 1984.

———. *Women Writers of the Middle Ages: A Critical Study of Texts from Perpetua (+203) to Marguerite Porete (+1310)*. Cambridge and New York: Cambridge University Press, 1974.

Drory, Rina. *Models and Contacts: Arabic Literature and Its Impact on Medieval Jewish Culture*. Leiden: E. J. Brill, 2000.

Drummond, J. C., and Wilbraham, A. *The Englishman's Food*. London: Jonathan Cape, 1940.

Dryden, A., ed. *The Art of Hunting*. Northhampton, 1908.

Dryden, John. "Preface to Fables Ancient and Modern." In *Poems and Fables of John Dryden*. Edited by James Kingsley. London: Oxford University Press, 1962.

Ducas. "Decline and Fall of Byzantium to the Ottoman Turks." An Annotated Translation of "Historia Turco-Byzantina" by Harry J. Magoulias. Detroit: Wayne State University Press, 1975.

Duckett, Eleanor Shipley. *Alfred the Great: The King and His England*. Chicago: University of Chicago Press, 1956.

———. *Carolingian Portraits: A Study in the 9th Century*. Ann Arbor: University of Michigan Press, 1969.

Duckett, Eleanor Shipley, ed. *Women and Their Letters in the Early Middle Ages*. Northhampton, Mass.: Smith College, 1964.

Dunam, Marcel, ed. *Larousse Encyclopedia of Ancient and Medieval History*. Paris and Middlesex: Paul Hamlyn, 1972.

Dundes, Alan, ed. *The Blood Libel Legend: A Casebook in Anti-Semitic Folklore*. Madison: University of Wisconsin Press, 1991.

Dunlop D. M. et al. "Bimaristan." *Encyclopaedia of Islam*, 2d ed. Vol. 1. Leiden, The Netherlands: E. J. Brill, 1999, 1,222–1,226.

Dunlop, Douglas. *The History of the Jewish Khazars*. Princeton, N.J.: Princeton University Press, 1954.

Dunn, Alastair. *The Peasants' Revolt: England's Failed Revolution of 1381*. Cambridge and New York: Cambridge University Press, 2004.

Dunn, Maryjane, and Linda Kay Davidson. *The Pilgrimage to Compostela in the Middle Ages: A Book of Essays*. London: Routledge, 1996, reprint 2000.

Dunn, Ross E. *The Adventures of Ibn Battuta—A Muslim Traveler of the 14th Century*. 1989. Reprint, Berkeley: University of California, 2005.

Duns Scotus, John. *Opera Philosophica*. St. Bonaventure, N.Y.: The Franciscan Institute, 1997.

During, J. *Musique et extase. L'audition spirituelle dans la tradition soufie*. Paris: Institut Français de Recherche en Iran, 1988.

———. *Musique et mystique dans les traditions de l'Iran*, Paris: Institut Français de Recherche en Iran, 1989.

———. "What is Sufi Music?" In *The Legacy of Mediaeval Persian Sufism*, edited by L. Lewisohn, New York, 1992.

Dyas, Dee, Valerie Edden, and Roger Ellis, eds. *Approaching Medieval English Anchoritic and Mystical Texts*. Rochester, N.Y.: D. S. Brewer, 2005.

Dyer, Christopher. *Standards of Living in the Later Middle Ages*. Cambridge: Cambridge University Press, 1989.

E. N. Adler Collection of the Jewish Theological Seminary Library in New York City. (ENA 2939, f.16, India Book 176)

Ebertshaüser, Caroline. *Mary: Art, Culture, and Religion through the Ages*. New York: Herder & Herder, 1998.

Eccles, Audrey. *Obstetrics and Gynecology in Tudor and Stuart England*. Kent, Ohio: Kent State University Press, 1982.

Eckenstein, Lina. *Woman under Monasticism*. New York: Russell & Russell, 1963.

Egbert, Virginia Wylie. *On the Bridges of Medieval Paris: A Record of Early Fourteenth-Century Life*. Princeton, N.J.: Princeton University Press, 1974.

EI2 See under *Encyclopaedia of Islam.*

Eickelman, Dale F., and James Piscatori, eds. *Muslim Travellers: Pilgrimage, Migration and the Religious Imagination.* Berkeley: University of California Press, 1990.

Eidelberg, Shlomo. *Medieval Ashkenazic History: Studies on German Jewry in the Middle Ages.* Brooklyn, N.Y.: Sepher-Hermon Press, c. 1999–2001.

Einbinder, Susan L. *Beautiful Death: Jewish Poetry and Martyrdom in Medieval France.* Princeton, N.J.: Princeton University Press, 2002.

Einhard. *The Life of Charlemagne.* Ann Arbor: University of Michigan Press, 1960.

Eire, Carlos M. N. *From Madrid to Purgatory: The Art and Craft of Dying in Sixteenth-Century Spain.* Cambridge: Cambridge University Press, 1995.

Elgood, Cyril. *A Medical History of Persia and the Eastern Caliphate from the Earliest Times to the Year A.D. 1932.* 1951. Reprint, with additions and corrections by G. van Heusden, Amsterdam: APA-Philo Press, 1979.

Elgood, Robert, ed. *Islamic Arms and Armour.* London: Scholar's Press, 1979.

Elliott, Dyan. *Spiritual Marriage: Sexual Abstinence in Medieval Wedlock.* Princeton, N.J.: Princeton University Press, 1993.

Elwell-Sutton, L. P. *The Persian Meters.* Cambridge: Cambridge University Press, 1976.

———. "The 'Ruba'i' in Early Persian Literature." In *The Cambridge History of Iran.* Vol. 4, *The Period from the Arab Invasion to the Saljuqs,* edited by R. N. Frye. Cambridge: Cambridge University Press, 1975.

Emmerson, Richard K., and Bernard McGinn, eds. *The Apocalypse in the Middle Ages.* Ithaca, N.Y.: Cornell University Press, 1992.

Encyclopaedia Judaica. Jerusalem: Keter Press, 1971.

Encyclopaedia of Islam. 2d ed. Leiden, E. J. Brill and London: Luzac, 1954–seriatim.

Encyclopaedia of Islam, 2d ed. General Editors P. J. Bearman, Th. Bianquis, C. E. Bosworth, E. van Donzel and W. P. Heinrichs et al. CD-Rom Version. Leiden, The Netherlands: E. J. Brill, 1999.

English, Edward. *Enterprise and Liability in Sienese Banking 1230–1350.* Cambridge, Mass.: Medieval Academy of America, 1988.

Enlart, C. *Le Costume.* Paris, 1916.

Entwistle, W. *The Spanish Language.* London: Faber and Faber, 1936.

Epstein, Marc Michael. *Dreams of Subversion in Medieval Jewish Art and Literature.* University Park: Pennsylvania State University Press, 1997.

Equestrian Bride. London, British Library, M.S. Harley 5686, Folio 27 Verso.

Erdmann, Carl, and Goffart, Walter. *The Origin of the Idea of Crusade.* Princeton, N.J.: Princeton University Press, 1977.

d'Erlanger, R. *La musique arabe.* Paris: Librairie Orientaliste Paul Geuthner, 1930–59.

Ernst, Carl W. "Mystical Language and the Teaching Context in the Early Sufi Lexicons." In *Mysticism and Language,* edited by Steven T. Katz, 181–200. Oxford: Oxford University Press, 1992.

———. *Sufism: An Essential Introduction to the Philosophy and Practice of the Mystical Tradition of Islam.* Boston and London: Shambhala, 1997.

Ersch, J. S., and J. G. Gruber. *Allgemeine Encyclopädie der Wissenschaften und Künste in alphabetischer Folge.* Leipzig: F. U. Gleditsh, 1813–1850.

Esack, Farid. *The Qur'an: A User's Guide.* Oxford: Oneworld Press, 2005.

Esfandiary, Hossein-Ali Nouri, ed. *The Rubaiyat of Omar Khayyam.* Illustrated by Hossein Behzad Miniatur. 1949. Reprint, Nishikigoi, Japan: Shumposha Printing Co., 1971.

Esmond Cleary, A. S. *The Ending of Roman Britain.* London: Batsford, 1989.

Ettinghausen, Richard. Forward to *Monuments of Civilization: Islam,* edited by Umberto Scerrato. New York: Grosset & Dunlap, 1976.

———. *Islamic Art in the Metropolitan Museum of Art.* New York: Metropolitan Museum of Art, 1972.

Ettinghausen, Richard, and Oleg Grabar. *The Art and Architecture of Islam: 650–1250.* 2d ed. New Haven, Conn.: Yale University Press (Pelican History of Art), 1992.

Evans, Helen, and William Wixom. *The Glory of Byzantium: Art and Culture in the Middle Byzantium Era, 843–1261.* New York: Metropolitan Museum of Art, 1997.

Evans, Joan. *A History of Jewelry: 1100 through 1870.* 1951. Reprint, New York: Dover, 1990.

———. *Life in Medieval France.* Oxford: Oxford University Press. 3d ed., London: Phaidon, 1969.

Ewert, A. *The French Language.* 1943. Reprint, London: Faber & Faber, 1969.

Fadel, Mohammad. "Two Women, One Man: Knowledge, Power, and Gender in Medieval Sunni Legal Thought." *International Journal of Middle Eastern Studies* 29, no. 2 (May 1997): 185–204.

Fahd, Toufic. "Ibn Wahshiyya." *Encyclopedia of Islam,* 2d ed. Vol. 3, 963–965. Leiden, The Netherlands: E. J. Brill, 1999.

———. *La divination arabe: Etudes religieuses sociologiques et folkloriques sur le milieu natif de l'Islam.* Leiden, The Netherlands: E. J. Brill, 1966.

Fahmy, Aly Mohamed. *Muslim Naval Organization in the Eastern Mediterranean from the 7th to the 10th Century.* 2d ed. Cairo: National Publication & Printing House, 1966a.

———. *Muslim Sea-Power in the Eastern Mediterranean from the 7th to the 10th Century.* Cairo: National Publication & Printing House, 1966b.

Fairbairn, James. *Heraldic Crests.* New York: Dover, 1993.

Fakhry, M. *A History of Islamic Philosophy.* 2d ed. New York: Columbia University Press, 1983.

Fakhry, Majid. *A History of Islamic Philosophy,* 3rd ed. New York: Columbia University Press, 2004.

Fares, Bishr. *Essai sur l'esprit de la decoration islamique.* Cairo: Institute Francias d'archeologie Orientale, 1952.

Farhad, Daftary. *The Ismailis: Their History and Doctrines.* Cambridge: Cambridge University Press, 1990.

The *Farhi Bible* from the Sassoon Collection (Paris Bibliotheque Nationale MS 30).

Farmer, H. G. *The Arabian Influence on Musical Theory.* London, Luzac and Co., 1925.

———. "Greek Theorists of Music in Arabic Translation." *Isis* xiii (1929–30): 325–333.

———. *A History of Arabian Music to the Thirteenth Century.* 1929. Reprint, London: Luzac, 1967.

———. "Meccan Musical Instruments." *Journal of the Royal Asiatic Society* (1929): 489–505.

———. *The Sources of Arabian Music.* Leiden, The Netherlands: E. J. Brill, 1965.

———. *Studies in Oriental Music.* Frankfurt: Institut für Arabisch-Islamischen Wissenschaften, 1986.

Farrar, Clarissa, and Austin Evans. *Bibliography of English Translations from Medieval Sources.* New York: Columbia University Press, 1964.

al-Faruqi, L. I. *An Annotated Glossary of Arabic Musical Terms.* Westport, Conn.: Greenwood, 1981.

Fedorov-Davydov, German A. *The Silk Road and the Cities of the Golden Horde.* English editor, Jeannine Davis-Kimball, English translator, Aleksandr Naymark. Berkeley, Calif.: Zinat Press, 2001.

Feldman, Aharon. *The River, the Kettle, and the Bird: A Torah Guide to Successful Marriage.* New York: C.S.B., 1987.

Fenton, Paul B. "A Mystical Treatise on Perfection, Providence, and Prophecy from the Jewish Sufi Circle." In *The Jews of Medieval Islam: Community, Society, and Identity,* edited by Daniel Frank. Leiden and New York: E. J. Brill, 1995.

Ferrante, Joan M. *To the Glory of Her Sex: Women's Roles in the Composition of Medieval Texts.* Bloomington: Indiana University Press, 1997.

———. *Women as Image in Medieval Literature.* New York, Columbia University Press, 1975.

Ferrante, Joan M., and George Economou, eds. *In Pursuit of Perfection: Courtly Love in Medieval Literature.* Port Washington, N.Y.: Kennikat Press, 1975.

Ffoulkes, Charles. *The Armorer and His Craft.* New York: Dover, 1988.

———. *The Gun Founders of England.* Cambridge: Cambridge University Press, 1937.

Fichtenau, Heinrich. *The Carolingian Empire.* Toronto: University of Toronto Press, 1978.

Field, Richard S. *Fifteenth Century Woodcuts and Metal Cuts from the National Gallery of Art Washington D.C.* Washington: National Gallery of Art, 1965.

Fierro Bello, María Isabel. "The Celebration of 'Ashura' in Sunni Islam." *The Arabist* 1 (1995): 193–208.

Finkelstein, Louis. *Jewish Self-Government in the Middle Ages.* 1924. Reprint, New York: Jewish Theological Seminary of America, 1964.

Fishbane, Michael, ed. *The Midrashic Imagination: Jewish Exegesis, Thought, and History.* Albany: State University of New York Press, 1993.

Fishbane, Michael. *Biblical Myth and Rabbinic Mythmaking.* New York: Oxford University Press, 2005.

Fitchen, John. *The Construction of Gothic Cathedrals: A Study of Medieval Vault Erection.* Chicago: University of Chicago Press, 1997.

Fitzgerald, Edward, trans. *Rubaiyat of Omar Khayyam.* Illustrated by Elihu Vedder. Boston: Houghton Mifflin, 1884.

Fletcher, Richard. *Moorish Spain.* Berkeley: University of California Press, 1992.

———. *The Quest for El Cid.* Oxford: Oxford University Press, 1989, 1991.

Fletcher, Richard A. *Saint James's Catapult: The Life and Times of Diego Gelmírez of Santiago de Compostela.* Oxford: Oxford University Press, 1984.

Fontaine, Jacques. "The Practice of Christian Life: The Birth of the Laity:" In *Christian Spirituality I: Origins to the Twelfth Century,* edited by Bernard McGinn, et al. New York: Crossroad, 1989, 453–491.

Forbes, T. R. *The Midwife and the Witch.* New Haven, Conn.: Yale University Press, 1966.

Forster, Robert, and Orest Ranum. *Biology of Man in History.* Baltimore: Johns Hopkins University Press, 1975.

Foucher of Chartres. *The First Crusade: The Chronicle of Fulcher of Chartres and Other Source Materials.* Edited, with an introduction by Edward Peters. Philadelphia, University of Pennsylvania Press, 1971.

Fourquin, Guy. *The Anatomy of Popular Rebellion in the Middle Ages.* Amsterdam and New York: North-Holland, 1978.

Fox, J., and R. Wood. *A Concise History of the French Language.* Oxford: Blackwell, 1968.

France, John, and William G. Zajac, eds. *The Crusades and Their Sources: Essays Presented to Bernard Hamilton.* Aldershot, U.K.: Ashgate Press, 1998.

Francis of Assisi and Clare. *The Complete Works.* Classics of Western Spirituality. 35. Translated by Regis Armstrong and Ignatius C. Brady. New York: Paulist Press, 1982.

Frank, Daniel, ed. *The Jews of Medieval Islam: Community, Society, and Identity.* Leiden and New York: E. J. Brill, 1995.

Fraser, J. T. *Of Time, Passion, and Knowledge.* New York: Braziller, 1975.

———. *The Voices of Time.* New York: Braziller, 1966.

Fraser, Lady Antonia. *The Warrior Queens.* New York: Alfred A. Knopf, 1989.

Freeman, M. *Herbs for the Medieval Household.* New York: Metropolitan Museum of Art, 1943.

———. *The Unicorn Tapestries.* New York: Metropolitan Museum of Art, 1976.

Freeman-Grenville, G.S.P. *The Muslim and Christian Calendars.* London: Rex Collings, 1977.

Freese, Stanley. *Windmills and Mill Wrighting.* Cambridge: Cambridge University Press, 1957.

Fregosi, Paul. *Jihad.* New York: Prometheus Books, 1998.

al-Freih, Seham Abd El-Wahhab. *Bond Maidens and Poetry in the Abbassid Age.* Ph.D. diss., University of Kuwait.

Frenkel, Y. "Suf." *Encyclopaedia of Islam,* 2d ed. Vol. 9. Leiden, The Netherlands: E. J. Brill, 1999, 764–765.

Frick, Fay Arrieh. "Sources for Decorative Motifs on Islamic Ceramics." *Muqarnas* 10 (1993): 231–240.

Friedenberg, Daniel. *Medieval Jewish Seals from Europe.* Detroit, Mich.: Wayne State University Press, 1987.

Friedenwald, Harry. "Jewish Doctoresses in the Middle Ages." In *The Jews and Medicine.* New York: Ktav, 1967.

———. *Jewish Luminaries in Medical History.* New York: Ktav, 1967.

———. *The Jews and Medicine.* 2 vols. New York: Ktav, 1967.

———. "Moses Maimonides the Physician." In *The Jews and Medicine* (1): 193–216. New York: Ktav, 1967.

Friedlander, M., ed. and trans. *Maimonides' The Guide for the Perplexed.* New York: Dover, 1956.

Friedman, John Block. *The Monstrous Races in Medieval Art and Thought.* Syracuse, N.Y.: Syracuse University Press, 2000.

Frigosi, Paul. *Jihad in the West: Muslim Conquests from the 7th through the 21st Centuries.* Amherst, N.Y.: Prometheus Books, 1998.

Frishman, Martin, and Hasan-Uddin Khan, eds. *The Mosque: History, Architectural Development and Regional Diversity.* London: Thames and Hudson, 1994.

Frojmovic, Eva. *Imagining the Self, Imagining the Other: Visual Representation and Jewish-Christian Dynamics in the Middle Ages and Early Modern Period.* Leiden, The Netherlands, and Boston: E. J. Brill, 2002.

Fuks, L. *The Oldest Known Literary Documents of Yiddish Literature* (ca. 1382). Leiden, The Netherlands: E. J. Brill, 1957.

Fulk, R. D., ed. *Interpretations of Beowulf: A Critical Anthology*. Bloomington and Indianapolis: Indiana University Press, 1991.

Fulton, Rachel. *From Judgment to Passion: Devotion to Christ and the Virgin Mary, 800–1200*. New York: Columbia University Press, 2002.

Furman, Daniel C. *A Retrial of Tristan's Morality, Scholia*. New York: Institute for Medieval and Renaissance Studies, 1974.

Furnivall, F. J. *Early English Meals and Manners*. 1868. Reprint, Detroit: Singing Tree, 1969.

Gabrieli, Francesco. *Arab Historians of the Crusades*. Translated by E. J. Costell. Berkeley and Los Angeles: University of California Press, 1969, 1978, 1984.

Galen. *On the Natural Faculties*. Translated by Arthur John Brock. Cambridge, Mass.: Harvard University Press, 1969.

Gambero, Luigi. *Mary in the Middle Ages: The Blessed Virgin Mary in the Thought of Medieval Latin Theologians*. Fort Collins, Colo.: Ignatius Press, 2005.

Gampel, B. *The Last Jews on Iberian Soil. Navarrese Jewry, 1497 to 1498*. Berkeley: University of California Press, 1989.

Gandz, Solomon. *Studies in Hebrew Astronomy and Mathematics*. New York: Ktav Publishing House, 1970.

Ganshof, E. L. *Feudalism*. Translated by Philip Grierson. New York: Harper Torchbooks, 1964.

García Gómez, Emilio. *Cinco Poetas Musulmanes*. Buenos Aires: Espasa-Calpa Argentina, 1945.

García de Valdeavellano, Luís. *El Mercado en León y Castilla durante la edad media*, 2d revised ed. Sevilla: Secretariado de Publicaciones de la Universidad, D. L., 1975.

———. *Orígenes de la burguesía en la España medieval*. 1969. Reprint, Madrid: Espasa-Calpe, 1983.

Gardiner, Eileen. *Visions of Heaven and Hell before Dante*. Ithaca, N.Y.: Cornell University Press, 1998.

Garten der Gesundheit or *Hortus Sanitatis*. Munich: Peter Schoeffer, 1485.

Gaston Phebus. *The Art of Hunting with Hawks*. Reprinted as *Hunting Book of Gaston Phebus: Paris, Bibliotheque Nationale, MS FR. 616*, edited by Marcel Thomas. London: Harvey Miller Publishers, 1998.

Geipel, John. *Mame Loshn: The Making of Yiddish*. New York: Riverrun Press, 1982.

Geoffrey de Villehardouin. *The Conquest of Constantinople*. Translated by M. R. B. Shaw. Harmondsworth, U.K.: Penguin, 1963.

Gerard, J. *The Herbal or General History of Plants*. 1597, 1633. Reprint, New York: Dover, 1975.

Gerber, Jane S. *Jews of Spain: A History of the Sephardic Experience*. New York: Free Press, 1992.

Gerhardt, Mia. *The Art of Story Telling: A Literary Study of the Thousand and One Nights*. Leiden: E. J. Brill, 1963.

Gertrude the Great of Helfta. *Spiritual Exercises*, translated by Gertrude Jaron Lewis and Jack Lewis. Cistercian Fathers Series, 49. Kalamazoo, Mich.: Cistercian Publications, 1989.

Al-Ghazali, Abu Hamid. "Emotional Religion in Islam as Affected by Music and Singing." Translated by D. B. Macdonald. *Journal of the Royal Asiatic Society* (1901): 195–252, 705–748 and (1902): 1–28, 195–252.

Ghazi, Suhaib Hamid. *Ramadan*. New York: Holiday House, 1996.

Gian-Francesco Pico. *De rerum praenotion* (1506).

Gibb, H. A. R. "Islamic biographical literature." In *Historians of the Middle East*, edited by B. Lewis and P. M. Holt. London: Oxford University Press, 1962.

———. *Mohammedanism*. New York: Oxford University Press, Galaxy, 1962.

Gibb, H. A. R., trans. *Travels of Ibn Battuta: 1325–1354*. Vols. 1–2. London and New York: Routledge, 1958.

Gibb, H. A. R., and H. Bowen. *Islamic Society and the West*. London: Oxford University Press, 1950–57.

Gies, Joseph, and Frances Gies. *Life in a Medieval Castle*. New York: Harper & Row, 1974.

———. *Life in a Medieval City*. 1969. Reprint, New York: Harper, 1981.

Gil, Moshe. "The Radhanite Merchants and the Land of Radhan." *Journal of Economic and Social History of the Orient* 17:3 (1976): 299–332.

Gille, B. *The Engineers of the Renaissance*. Cambridge, Mass.: M.I.T. Press, 1966.

Gilman, Stephen. *The Spain of Fernando de Rojas*. The Intellectual and Social Landscape of *La Celestina*. Princeton, N.J.: Princeton University Press, 1972.

Gilson, Etienne. *History of Christian Philosophy in the Middle Ages*. New York: Random House, 1995.

———. *Reason and Revelation in the Middle Ages*. New York: Scribner, 1950.

———. *Thomism: The Philosophy of Thomas Aquinas*. Translated by L. K. Shook and A. Mauer. Toronto: Pontifical Institute of Medieval Studies, 2002.

Gimaret, D. "Mu'tazila." *Encyclopaedia of Islam*, 2d ed. Vol. 7. Leiden, The Netherlands: E. J. Brill, 1999, 783–793.

Gimpel, Jean. *The Cathedral Builders*. New York: Grove Press, 1961.

———. *The Medieval Machine: The Industrial Revolution of the Middle Ages*. New York: Henry Holt, 1976 and Barnes & Noble, 2003.

Gitlitz, David M. and Linda Kay Davidson. *A Drizzle of Honey: The Life and Recipes of Spain's Secret Jews*. New York: St. Martin's Griffin, 2000.

Glaeser, Edward L., H. Kallal, J. Sheinkman, and A. Shleifer. "Growth in Cities." *Journal of Political Economy* 100 (1992): 1,126–1,152.

Gleichgross. *De re militari hebraeorum* (1690).

Glick, Thomas F. *Irrigation and Society in Medieval Valencia*. Cambridge, Mass.: Harvard University Press, 1970.

———. *Islamic and Christian Spain in the Early Middle Ages*. Princeton, N.J.: Princeton University Press, 1979.

Gneuss, Helmut. *Language and History in Early England*. Aldershot, U.K., and Brookfield, Vt.: Variorum, 1996.

Gnudi, Martha Teach, and Cyril Stanley Smith. *The Pirotechnia of Vannoccio Biringuccio*. Cambridge Mass.: MIT Press, 1966.

Gnudi, Martha Teach, and Jerome Pierce Webster. *Gaspare Tagliacozzi, Surgeon of Bologna. Surgical Correction of Bodily Defects by Grafting, De Curtorum Chirurgia per Insitionem*. Los Angeles: Leitlin & Ver Brugge, 1976.

———. *The Life and Times of Gaspare Tagliacozzi Surgeon of Bologna, 1545–1599: Surgical Correction of Bodily Defects by Grafting, De Curtorum Chirurgia per Insitionem*. New York: Reichner, 1950.

Godard, Andre. *The Art of Iran*. New York: Fredrick A. Praeger, 1965.

Godfrey, J. "The Double Monastery in Early English History." *AJ* 79 (1974): 19–32.

Goitein, Samuel D. "Formal Friendship in the Medieval Near East." *Proceedings of the American Philosophical Society* 115 (1971): 484–489.

———. "From the Mediterranean to India." *Speculum* 29 (1954).

———. *Letters of Medieval Jewish Traders*. Princeton, N.J.: Princeton University Press, 1973.

———. *A Mediterranean Society: The Jewish Communities of the Arab World as Portrayed in the Documents of the Cairo Geniza*. Vols. 1 and 2. Berkeley and Los Angeles: University of California Press, 1967, 1971.

———. *Studies in Islamic History and Institutions*. Leiden, The Netherlands: E. J. Brill, 1966.

Goitein, Schlomo D. *A Mediterranean Society: The Jewish Communities of the Arab World as Portrayed in the Documents of the Cairo Geniza*. Vols. 1–5. Los Angeles: University of California Press, 1967, 1971, 1978, 1983, 1988.

Golden, Peter B. "Ghazi." In *Dictionary of the Middle Ages*, edited by Joseph R. Strayer. 12 vols. New York: Scribner, 1982–89.

Goldin, Frederick. *German and Italian Lyrics of the Middle Ages*. New York: Anchor Doubleday, 1973.

———. *Lyrics of the Troubadours and Trouveres*. New York: Anchor Doubleday, 1974.

Goldin, Judah. *The Fathers According to Rabbi Nathan*. New Haven, Conn.: Yale University Press, 1955.

Goldman, Berthold. "Introduction I." In *Lex Mercatoria and Arbitration*, edited by Thomas E. Carbonneau, xv–xix. Dobbs Ferry, N.Y.: Transnational Juris Publications, 1990.

———. "Lex Mercatoria," *Forum Internationale* 3 (1986): 1–24.

Goldscheider, Ludwig. *Michelangelo: Paintings, Sculptures, Architecture*. New York: Phaidon, 1963.

Goldstein, Bernard R. "The Arabic Version of Ptolemy's Planetary Hypotheses." *Proceedings of the American Philosophical Society*, N.S. 57 (1967).

———. *The Astronomical Tables of Levi Ben Gerson*. New Haven, Conn.: Archon Books, 1974.

———. "Levi Ben Gerson: On Instrumental Errors and the Transversal Scale." *Journal of The History of Astronomy* 8 (1977).

———. "The Role of Science in the Jewish Community in Fourteenth Century France." In *Machaut's World: Science and Art in the 14th Century*, edited by M. P. Cosman and D. Chandler. New York: New York Academy of Sciences, 1978.

Goldstein, David. *The Ashkenazi Haggadah: A Hebrew manuscript of the mid-15th Century from the Collections of the British Library written and illuminated by Joel Ben Simeon*. London: Thames and Hudson, 1985.

———. *The Jewish Poets of Spain, 900–1250*. Harmondsworth, U.K.: The Penguin Classics, 1971.

Goldstein, Thomas. *Dawn of Modern Science: From the Arabs to Leonardo De Vinci*. Boston: Houghton Mifflin, 1980.

Goldziher, Ignaz. *Introduction to Islamic Theology and Law*. Translated by Andras and Ruth Hamori. Introduction by Bernard Lewis. Princeton, N.J.: Princeton University Press, 1981.

———. "Uber die Benennung der Ichwan al-Safa." *Der Islam* X (1910).

———. "Veneration of Saints in Islam." *Muslim Studies* 2 (1966).

Golombek, Liza. "The Function of Decoration in Islamic Architecture." In *Theories and Principles of Design in the Architecture of Islamic Societies*, edited by Margaret Bentley Sevcenko. Cambridge: Aga Khan Program for Islamic Architecture, 1988.

Golombek, Liza, and Donald Wilber. *The Timurid Architecture of Iran and Turan*. Princeton, N.J.: Princeton University Press, 1988.

Goodman, L. E. "al-Razi, Abu Bakr Muhammad b. Zakariyya." *Encyclopaedia of Islam*, 2d ed., Vol. 8. Leiden, The Netherlands: E. J. Brill, 1999, 474–477.

Goodman, Len E. *The Case of the Animals versus Man before the King of the Jinn*. Boston: Twayne, 1978.

Goodrich, Michael E. *Lives and Miracles of The Saints: Studies In Medieval Latin Hagiography*. Aldershot, U.K., and Burlington, Vt.: Ashgate Variorum, 2005.

Goodwin, Godfrey. *A History of Ottoman Architecture*. London: Thames and Hudson, 1971.

Goody, Jack. *Islam in Europe*. Cambridge: Polity Press, 2004.

Gordon, Bruce, and Peter Marshall. *The Place of the Dead: Death and Remembrance in Late Medieval and Early Modern Europe*. Cambridge: Cambridge University Press, 2000.

Gottfried von Strassburg. *Tristan*. Translated and with an introduction by A. T. Hatto. New York: Penguin, 1960.

Gottheil, Richard, and Meyer Kayserling. "Hasdai Ibn Shaprut." *Jewish Encyclopedia*. Available online. URL: http://www.Jewish Encyclopedia.com.

Grabar, Oleg. *Early Islamic Art, 650–1100*. Aldershot, U.K., and Burlington, Vt.: Ashgate/Variorum, 2005.

———. *The Formation of Islamic Art*. 2d ed. New Haven, Conn.: Yale University Press, 1987.

———. *The Great Mosque of Isfahan*. New York: New York University Press, 1990.

———. *Islamic Visual Culture, 1100–1800*. Aldershot, U.K., and Burlington, Vt.: Ashgate/Variorum, 2006.

———. *The Mediation of Ornament*. Princeton, N.J.: Princeton University Press, 1992.

———. *Muqarnas: An Annual on Islamic Art and Architecture*. Leiden, The Netherlands: E. J. Brill, 1988.

———. "Patronage in Islamic Art in Kuwait." In *Islamic Art and Patronage: Treasures from Kuwait*, edited by Esin Atil. New York: Rizzoli, 1990.

———. *Studies in Medieval Islamic Art*. London: Variorum Reprints, 1976.

———. "The Umayyad Dome of the Rock in Jerusalem." *Ars Orientalis* 3 (1959): 34–62.

Graetz, H. *History of the Jews*. 2 vols. Philadelphia: Jewish Publication Society, 1893.

Graham, W. A. *Divine Word and Prophetic Word in Early Islam*. The Hague: Walter De Gruyter, 1977.

de la Granja, Fernando. "Fiestas cristianas en Al-Ándalus." *Al-Ándalus* 34 (1970): 1–53 and idem, 35 (1970): 119–142.

Grant, Edward. *Planets, Stars, and Orbs: The Medieval Cosmos, 1200–1687*. Cambridge: Cambridge University Press, 1996.

Grape, W. *The Bayeux Tapestry*. Munich and New York: Prestel, 1994.

Graves, Robert, and Omar Ali-Shah. *The Rubaiyyat of Omar Khayyam: A New Translation with Critical Commentaries*. London: Cassell, 1967.

Gray, Basil. *Treasures of Asia: Persian Painting*. New York: Rizzoli, 1977.

Gray, Simon. "Classical Persian Music" (2000). Available online. URL: http://www.star-one.org. uk/music/permus1.htm.

Grayzel, Solomon, ed. *The Church and the Jews in the Thirteenth Century.* Vol. 1, 2d ed., Vol. 2. New York: Hermon Press, 1966; New York: Jewish Theological Seminary in America and Detroit: Wayne State University Press, 1989.

Green, Monica H. *The Trotula, a Medieval Compendium of Women's Medicine.* Philadelphia: University of Pennsylvania Press, 2001.

Green, Otis H. *Spain and the Western Tradition.* Madison: University of Wisconsin Press, 1966.

Greenberg, Susan. *The History and Art of the Sabbath Lamp.* Master's thesis, Institute for Medieval and Renaissance Studies, City College of City University of New York, 1978.

Greenstein, E. L. "Medieval Bible Commentaries." In *Back to the Sources,* edited by B. W. Holtz. New York: Summit Books, 1984.

Gregg, Joan. *Devils, Women and Jews: Reflections of the Other in Medieval Sermon Stories.* Albany: State University of New York Press, 1997.

Gregory Bishop of Tours. *History of the Franks.* Selections translated with notes by Ernest Brehaut. New York: W. W. Norton, 1969.

Greif, Avner. "Reputation and Coalitions in Medieval Trade: Evidence on the Maghribi Traders." *Journal of Economic History* 49, no. 4 (December 1989): 857–882.

Grete Herball. London: Peter Treveris, 1526.

Grillot de Givry, Emile. *Illustrated Anthology of Sorcery, Magic and Alchemy.* New York: Causeway, 1973.

———. *A Pictorial Anthology of Witchcraft, Magic, and Alchemy.* Translated by J. Courtenay Locke. Chicago and New York: University Books, 1958 and New York: Dover, 1971.

Griovot, Denis, and George Zarnecki. *Gislebertus: Sculptor of Autun.* New York: Orion Press, 1961.

Gross, C. *The Gild Merchant.* 1890. Reprint, Oxford: Clarendon Press, 1964.

———. *Guild Merchant, II,* 214 (in French), and Davies: History of Southampton, pp 139 ff. (English), trans and ed. E. P. Cheyney, University of Pennsylvania. Dept. of History: *Translations and Reprints from the Original Sources of European history,* published for the Dept. of History of the University of Pennsylvania. Philadelphia: University of Pennsylvania Press [1897]. Vol. II, No. 1, pp. 12–17.

Grossman, Avraham. *Pious and Rebellious: Jewish Women in Medieval Europe.* Waltham, Mass.: Brandeis University Press, 2004.

Grossman, Grace Cohen. *Jewish Art.* New York: Beaux Arts Editions, 1995.

Grubb, Nancy. *Angels in Art.* New York: Artrabas Publishers, 1995.

Gruenwald, Ithamar. *Apocalyptic and Merkavah Mysticism.* Leiden, The Netherlands: E. J. Brill, 1980.

Grunebaum, Gustave Von. *Medieval Islam: A Study in Cultural Orientation.* Chicago: University of Chicago Press, 1953.

———. "The Sacred Character of Islamic Cities." In *Mélange Taha Hussain,* edited by A. R. Badawi, 25–37. Cairo: al-Maaref, 1962.

Guettat, M. *La musique classique du Maghreb.* Paris: Sindbad, 1980.

Guggenhein, Yacov. "Jewish Community and Territorial Organization in Medieval Europe." In *The Jews of Europe in the Middle Ages,* edited by Christoph Cluse, 71–91. Turnhout: Brepols, 2004.

Guillaume, Bernard. *Les papes d'Avignon.* Paris: Editions du Cerf, 1998.

Guillaume de Lorris and Jean de Meun. *The Romance of the Rose.* Translated by Harry W. Robbins. New York: E. P. Dutton, 1962.

Gulevich, Tanya. *Understanding Islam and Muslim Traditions: An Introduction to the Religious Practices, Celebrations, Festivals, Observances, Beliefs, Folklore, Customs, and Calendar System of the World's Muslim Communities.* Detroit, Mich.: Omnigraphics, 2004.

Gunther, R. W. T. *Early Science in Oxford.* 1925. Reprint, London: Dawsons, 1967.

Gutas, Dimitri, *Greek Thought, Arabic Culture.* London, and New York: Routledge, 1998.

Guthrie, S. *Arab Women in the Middle Ages: Private Lives and Public Roles.* London: Saqi, 2001.

Gutmann, Joseph. *Jewish Ceremonial Art.* New York: Thomas Yoseloff, 1968.

———. "When the Kingdom Comes: Messianic Themes in Medieval Jewish Art." *Art Journal* 27 (1967–68): 168–175.

Gysin, Frederic. *Swiss Medieval Tapestries.* London: Batsford, 1947.

Habermann, Abraham. *Sefer Gezerot Ashkenaz ve-Zarfat.* Jerusalem: Ofir, 1971.

Habig, Marion A., ed. *St. Francis of Assisi: Writings and Early Biographies, English Omnibus of Sources for the Life of St. Francis.* Chicago: Franciscan Herald Press, 1983.

Hackwood, Frederick W. *Inns, Ales, and Drinking Customs of Old England.* London: T. Fisher Unwin, 1909.

Hadas, Moses. *Berechiah haNakdan, Fables of a Jewish Aesop.* New York: Columbia, University Press, 1967.

Haddad, Sami I. *History of Arab Medicine.* Beirut: Oriental Hospital, 1975.

Haddawy, Hussain, trans. *The Arabian Nights.* London and New York: W. W. Norton, 1990.

Haldane, D. "The Fire-Ship of Al-Salih Ayyub and the Muslim Use of 'Greek Fire'." In *The Circle of War in the Middle Ages: Essays on Medieval Military and Naval History*, edited by Donald J. Kagay and L. J. Andrew Villalon. Woodbridge, Suffolk, U.K.: Boydell Press, 1999.

Ha-Levi, Eleazar. "Jewish Heraldry." Proceedings from the Caidan Heraldic Symposium and Scribe's Conclave. July 8–9, 1989. 2 vols. Los Angeles, California: Known World Heraldic Symposia.

———. "Jewish Naming Convention in Angevin England." *Society for Creative Anachronism.* Available online. URL: http://www.sca.org/heraldry/laurel/names/jewish.html.

Halivni, David Weiss. *Peshat and Derash: Plain and Applied Meaning in Rabbinic Exegesis.* New York: Oxford University Press, 1998.

Hall, Bert S. "Giovanni de Dondi and Guido da Vigevano: Notes Towards a Typology of Medieval Technological Writing." In *Machaut's World: Science and Art in the Fourteenth Century*, edited by Madeleine P. Cosman and Bruce Chandler. New York: New York Academy of Sciences, 1978.

Hallam, Elizabeth. *The Plantagenet Chronicles.* New York: Barnes & Noble, 2000.

Hallaq, Wael B. *Ibn Taymiyya against the Greek Logicians.* Oxford: Clarendon Press, 1993.

———. *The Origins and Evolution of Islamic Law.* Cambridge: Cambridge University Press, 2005.

Halsall, Paul. "Internet Medieval Sourcebook: Islam." Available online. URL: http://www.fordham.edu/halsall/sbook1d.html.

Hamarneh, Sami Khalaf. *Health Sciences in Early Islam: Collected Papers.* Edited by Munawar A. Anees. 2 vols. Blanco, Tex.: Zahra, 1983–84.

Hamilton, George. "Trotula." *Modern Philology* 4 (1906): 377–380.

Hamilton, Michelle M. "Poetry and Desire: Sexual and Cultural Temptation in the Hebrew Maqama Tradition." In *Wine, Women and Song: Hebrew and Arabic Literature of Medieval Iberia*, edited by Michelle M. Hamilton, Sarah J. Portnoy, and David A. Wacks, 59–73. Newark, Del.: Junn de la Cuesta, 2004.

Hamori, Andras. "Arabic Poetry." In *Dictionary of the Middle Ages*, edited by Joseph R. Strayer. 12 vols. New York: Scribner, 1982–89.

———. "Arabic Prose." In *Dictionary of the Middle Ages*, edited by Joseph R. Strayer. 12 vols. New York: Scribner, 1982–89.

Hanawalt, Barbara. "The Female Felon in Fourteenth Century England." In *Women in Medieval Society*, edited by Susan Stuard. Philadelphia: University of Pennsylvania Press, 1976.

———. *The Ties That Bound: Peasant Families in Medieval England.* Oxford: Oxford University Press, 1989.

———. *Women and Work in Pre-Industrial Europe.* Bloomington: Indiana University Press, 1986.

Hanawalt, Barbara and Kathryn Reyerson, *City and Spectacle in Medieval Europe.* Minneapolis: University of Minnesota Press, 1994.

Haraszti-Takacs, Marianne. "Fifteenth-Century Painted Furniture with Scenes from the Esther Story." *Jewish Art* 15 (1989): 14–25.

Harington, Sir John. *Schoole of Salerne.* In *Elizabeth-Jacobean Drama*, edited by G. Blakemore. London: A&C Black, 1987.

Harksen, Sibylle. *La Femme au Moyen-Age.* Leipzig, Edition Leipzig: 1974; translated as *Women in the Middle Ages.* New York and London: Abner Schram, 1975.

Harpur, James. *Secrets of the Middle Ages.* New York: Konecky, 1995.

Harris, A. S., and L. Nochlin. *Women Artists: 1550–1950.* New York: Los Angeles County Museum of Art, Knopf, 1976.

Harris, Cyril. *Illustrated Dictionary of Historic Architecture.* New York: Dover, 1983.

Harrison, Robert. *Gallic Salt.* Berkeley: University of California Press, 1974.

Harrowven, Jean, *The Origins of Festivals and Feasts.* London: Kaye & Ward, 1980.

Harte, Negley B., and Kenneth G. Ponting, eds. *Cloth and Clothing in Medieval Europe: Essays in Memory of Professor E. M. Carus-Wilson.* Pasold Studies in Textile History No. 2. London: Heinemann Educational Books, 1983.

Harte, Negley B., ed. *The New Draperies in the Low Countries and England, 1300–1800.* Pasold Studies in Textile History. Vol. 10. Oxford and New York: Maney Publishing, 1997.

Hartel, Herbert. *Along the Ancient Silk Routes: Central Asian Art.* New York: Metropolitan Museum of Art, 1982.

Harthan, John. *The Book of Hours.* New York: Park Lane, 1977.

Hartley, Dorothy. *Food in England.* London: Macdonald, 1954.

———. *Water in England.* London: Macdonald, 1964.

Hartley, Dorothy, and M. Elliot. *The Life and Work of the People of England.* New York: G. P. Putnam's Sons, 1931.

Harvey, Alan. *Economic Expansion in the Byzantine Empire 900–1200.* Cambridge: Cambridge University Press, 2003.

Harvey, J. *English Medieval Architects, a Biographical Dictionary Down to 1550.* 2d ed. Gloucester: Alan Sutton, 1984.

———. *The Master Builders: Architecture in the Middle Ages.* New York: McGraw-Hill, 1971.

Harvey, L. P. *Islamic Spain, 1250 to 1500.* Chicago: University of Chicago Press, 1990.

Hary, Benjamin H., John L. Hayes, and Fred Astren, eds. *Judaism and Islam Boundaries, Communication and Interaction: Essays in Honor of William M. Brinner.* Leiden, The Netherlands and Boston: E. J. Brill, 2000.

Hasan, Hadi. *A History of Persian Navigation.* London: Methuen, 1928.

Hasan, Z. M. *Hunting as Practised in Arab Countries of the Middle Ages.* Cairo: Government Press, 1937.

Hashmi, Sohail. "Interpreting the Islamic Ethics of War and Peace." In *Islamic Political Ethics: Civil Society, Pluralism, and Conflict,* edited by Sohail Hashmi. Princeton, N.J.: Princeton University Press, 2001.

Haskins, Charles Homer. *The Renaissance of the Twelfth Century.* Cambridge, Mass.: Harvard University Press, 1927.

———. *The Rise of Universities.* Ithaca, N.Y.: Cornell University Press, 1972.

al-Hassan, Ahmad Y., and Donald R. Hill. *Islamic Technology: An Illustrated History.* Cambridge: Cambridge University Press, 1986.

Hatto, A. T., and R. J. Taylor. *Songs of Neidhart von Reuental.* Manchester: University of Manchester Press, 1958.

Haverkamp, Alfred. "The Jews of Europe in the Middle Ages: By Way of Introduction." In *The Jews of Europe in the Middle Ages,* edited by Christoph Cluse, 1–15. Turnhout: Brepols, 2004.

Hawting, G. R. *The Development of Islamic Ritual.* Vol. 26, *The Formation of the Classical Islamic World.* London: Ashgate, 1994.

———. *The First Dynasty of Islam: The Umayyad Caliphate A.D. 661–750.* London: Routledge, 1986.

Hays, H. R. *The Dangerous Sex: The Myth of Feminine Evil.* New York: G. P. Putnam's Sons, 1964.

Hayward, Jane, and Walter Cahn. *Radiance and Reflection: Medieval Art from the Raymond Pitcairn Collection.* New York: Metropolitan Museum of Art, 1982.

Head, Thomas, ed. *Medieval Hagiography: An Anthology.* New York: Garland Publishing, Inc., 2000.

Head, Thomas, and Richard Landes, eds. *The Peace of God: Social Violence and Religious Response in France around the Year 1000.* Ithaca, N.Y.: Cornell University Press, 1992.

Heath, Peter. *The Thirsty Sword: Sirat 'Antar and the Arabic Popular Epic.* Salt Lake City: University of Utah Press, 1996.

Hecker, Joel. *Mystical Bodies, Mystical Meals: Eating and Embodiment in Medieval Kabbalah.* Detroit, Mich.: Wayne State University Press, 2005.

Heer, Friedrich. *The Medieval World.* Translated by Janet Sondheimer. New York: Mentor, George Weidenfeld, 1962.

Heffernan, Thomas J. *Sacred Biography: Saints and Their Biographers in the Middle Ages.* New York: Oxford University Press, 1988.

Hellman, Robert, and Richard O'Gorman. *Fabliaux: Ribald Tales from the Old French.* London: A. Barker, 1965.

Helm, Barbara Lois. "Rabi'ah As Mystic, Muslim, and Woman." *The Annual Review of Women in World Religions* 3 (1994): 1–87.

Henderson, A. *History of Ancient and Modern Wines.* London, 1824.

Hendy, M. F. *Studies in the Byzantine Monetary Economy c. 300–1450.* Cambridge: Cambridge University Press, 1985.

Heninger, S. K. *Touches of Sweet Harmony.* San Marino, Calif.: Huntington Library, 1974.

Henisch, B. A. *Fast and Feast: Food in Medieval Society.* University Park: Pennsylvania State University Press, 1976.

Henricus Ranzovius, *Tractatus astrologicus* (1602).

Henry, Francoise. *The Book of Kells.* New York: Knopf, 1974.

Henry, Patrick. "What was the Iconoclastic Controversy About?" *Church History* 45 (1976): 21–25.

Henry, Sondra, and Emily Taitz. *Written Out of History: A Hidden Legacy of Jewish Women Revealed through Their Writings and Letters.* New York: Block Publishing, 1978.

Herbarius. Mainz: Peter Schoeffer, 1484.

Herford, R. Travers. *Pirke Aboth, the Ethics of the Talmud: Sayings of the Fathers.* New York: Schocken, 1978.

Herlihy, David. "Land, Family, and Women in Continental Europe, 701–1200." In *Women in Medieval Society,* edited by Susan Mosher Stuard. Philadelphia: University of Pennsylvania, 1976.

———. "Life Expectancies of Medieval Women." In *The Role of Women in the Middle Ages,* edited by Rosemarie Morewedge. Albany: State University of New York Press, 1975.

———. *Medieval and Renaissance Pistoia.* New Haven, Conn.: Yale University Press, 1967.

———. *Medieval Households.* Cambridge, Mass.: Harvard University Press, 1985.

———. *Opera Muliebria: Women and Work in Medieval Europe.* New York: McGraw Hill, 1990.

———. *Women in Medieval Society.* Houston: University of St. Thomas, 1971.

Herlihy, David, Robert S. Lopez, and V. Slessarev. *Economy, Society, and Government in Medieval Italy.* Kent, Ohio: Kent State University Press, 1969.

Herlihy, David, Harry A. Miskimin, and A. L. Udovitch. *The Medieval City.* New Haven, Conn. and London: Yale University Press, 1977.

Herrad of Landsberg. *Hortus Deliciarum, the Garden of Delights.* Edited by Aristide Caratzas. New York: Caratzas Brothers, 1977.

Herrin, Judith. *The Formation of Christendom.* New ed. London: Weidenfeld & Nicholson, 2001.

Herrlinger, R. *History of Medical Illustration.* Translated by G. Gulton-Smith. New York: Editions Medicina Rara, 1970.

Herzog, Marvin, et al., ed. *YIVO: The Language and Culture Atlas of Ashkenazic Jewry.* 3 vols. Tubingen: Max Niemeyer Verlag, 1992–2000.

Heschel, Abraham J. *Maimonides: A Biography.* Translated by J. Neugroschel. New York: Farrar, Straus & Giroux, 1982.

Heschel, Susannah. *On Being a Jewish Feminist.* New York: Schocken Books, 1983.

Higgs Strickland, Debra. *Saracens, Demons, & Jews: Making Monsters in Medieval Art.* Princeton, N.J. and Oxford: Princeton University Press, 2003.

Higham, R., and P. Barker. *Timber Castles.* London: Batsford, 1992.

Hildegard of Bingen. *Scivias.* Classics of Western Spirituality 67, translated by Columba Hart and Jane Bishop. New York: Paulist Press, 1990.

Hill, Donald R. *Islamic Science and Engineering.* Edinburgh: Edinburgh University Press, 1993.

———. *Studies in Medieval Islamic Technology.* Aldershot, UK: Ashgate, 1998.

———. "Trebuchets." *Viator* 4 (1973): 99–114.

Hillenbrand, R. *Islamic Art and Architecture.* (The World of Art). London: Thames & Hudson, 1998.

Hillenbrand, Robert. *Islamic Architecture: Form, Function and Meaning.* Edinburgh: Edinburgh University Press, 1994.

Hillgarth, J. N. *Christianity and Paganism, 350–750: The Conversion of Western Europe.* Philadelphia: University of Pennsylvania Press, 1986.

———. The Spanish Kingdoms, 1250–1516. 2 vols. Oxford: Oxford University Press, 1976–78.

Hills, Richard L. *Power from Wind: A History of Windmill Technology.* Cambridge: Cambridge University Press, 1994.

Himes, N. E. *Medical History of Contraception.* Baltimore: Williams & Wilkins, 1936.

Hitti, Philip. *The Arabs.* Chicago: Henry Regnery, 1967.

Hitti, Philip K., and Richard W. Bulliet. *An Arab-Syrian Gentleman and Warrior in the Period of the Crusades, Written by Usamah ibn Munqidh.* New York: Columbia University Press, 2000.

Hoag, John D. *Islamic Architecture.* New York: Harry N. Abrams, 1977.

Hodges, Richard. *Dark Age Economics: The Origins of Towns and Trade, AD 500–1000.* 2d ed. London: Duckworth, 1989.

Hodgson, M. G. S. "Duruz." In *The Encyclopaedia of Islam,* 2d ed. Leiden: E. J. Brill, 1968.

———. *The Order of Assassins: The Struggle of the Early Nazari Ismailis against the Islamic World.* The Hague: Mouton, 1955.

Hole, Christina. *English Shrines and Sanctuaries.* London: B. T. Batsford, 1954.

Hollander, J. *The Untuning of the Sky.* Princeton, N.J.: Princeton University Press, 1961.

Holloway, Julia B., Constance S. Wright, and Joan Bechtold. *Equally in God's Image: Women in the Middle Ages.* New York: Peter Lang, 1990.

Hollywood, Amy M. *The Soul as Virgin Wife: Mechthild of Magdeburg, Marguerite Porete, and Meister Eckhart.* Studies in Spirituality and Theology. Vol. 1. Notre Dame: University of Notre Dame Press, 1995.

Holmes, Urban T. *A Critical Bibliography of French Literature.* Vol. 1, *The Medieval Period.* Edited by David Clark Cabeen. Syracuse, N.Y.: Syracuse University Press, 1947–68.

Holmes, Urban Tigner. *Daily Living in the Twelfth Century, Based on the Observations of Alexander Neckam in London and Paris.* Madison: University of Wisconsin Press, 1952.

Holt, C. *Magna Carta.* Cambridge: Cambridge University Press, 1965.

Holt, Richard. *The Mills of Medieval England.* Oxford and New York: Basil Blackwell, 1988.

Holum, Kenneth G. *Theodosian Empresses: Women and Imperial Dominion in Late Antiquity.* Berkeley: University of California Press, 1982.

Homerin, T. Emil. *From Arab Poet to Muslim Saint: Ibn al-Farid, His Verse, and His Shrine.* Columbia, S.C.: University of South Carolina Press, 1994.

Hoover, Herbert Clark, and Lou Henry Hoover, trans. *Georgius Agricola De Re Metallica.* New York: Dover, 1950.

Hopkins, Andrea. *Most Wise and Valiant Ladies: Remarkable Lives of Women in the Middle Ages.* London: Welcome Rain, 1997.

Horovitz, Josef. *Islamic Culture,* Vols. 4 and 5. Jerusalem: Hebrew University of Jerusalem, 1930, 1931.

———. "The Origins of 'The Arabian Nights.'" *Islamic Culture* 1 (1927): 36–57.

Hortus Sanitatis. Lubeck: Steffen Arndes, 1492.

Hourani, Albert. *Arabic Thought in the Liberal Age: 1798–1939.* Cambridge University Press, Cambridge, 1993.

———. *A History of the Arab Peoples.* Cambridge, Mass.: Harvard University Press, 1991.

Hourani, Albert, and S. M. Stern, eds. *The Islamic City.* Oxford: Oxford University Press, 1970.

Hourani, George F. *Arab Seafaring.* Princeton, N.J.: Princeton University Press, 1951.

———. "The Early Growth of the Secular Sciences in Andalucia." *Studia Islamica* 32 (1970).

———. *Reason and Tradition in Islamic Ethics.* Cambridge: Cambridge University Press, 1985.

Hourihane, Colum. *Objects, Images, and the Word: Art in the Service of the Liturgy.* Princeton, N.J.: Princeton University Press, 2003.

Housley, Norman. *The Italian Crusades: The Papal-Angevin Alliance and the Crusades against Christian Lay Powers, 1254–1343.* 1982. Reprint, Oxford: Oxford University Press, 1999.

Housley, Norman, ed. *Documents on the Later Crusades, 1274–1580.* New York: St Martin's Press, 1996.

Hovannisian, Richard, and Georges Sabagh, eds. *Religion and Culture in Medieval Islam.* New York: Cambridge University Press, 1999.

Howell, Martha. *Women, Production, and Patriarchy in Late Medieval Cities.* Chicago: University of Chicago Press, 1986.

Huart, C. L., and A. Grohmann. "Kaghad, Kaghid (Paper)." *Encyclopaedia of Islam,* 2d ed. Vol. 4.

Leiden, The Netherlands: E. J. Brill, 1999, 419–420.

Hubert, Gene, and Gene Porcher. *Europe of the Invasions*. New York: George Braziller, 1968.

Huff, Toby E. *The Rise of Early Modern Science: Islam, China, and the West*. Cambridge: Cambridge University Press, 1993.

Hughes, Aaron. *The Texture of the Divine*. Indianapolis: Indiana University Press, 2004.

Hughes, Muriel. *Women Healers in Medieval Life and Literature*. New York: Oxford University Press, 1943.

Hughes, Thomas P. *Dictionary of Islam*. London: W. H. Allen, 1895.

Huizinga, Johan. *Homo Ludens*. Boston: Beacon Press, 1971.

———. *The Waning of the Middle Ages*. Mineola, N.Y.: Dover, 1999.

Hülsmann, Jörg Guido. *Nicholas Oresme and the First Monetary Treatise*. Ludwig von Mises Institute, 2004.

Humble, Richard. *The Fall of Saxon England*. New York: Barnes & Noble, 1992.

Humphreys, R. S. "The Emergence of the Mamluk Army." *Studia Islamica* 65 (1977): 67–99; 66 (1977): 147–182.

———. "Women as Patrons of Religious Architecture in Ayyubid Damascus." *Muqarnas* 11 (1994): 35–54.

Humphreys, R. Stephen. "Mamluk." In *Dictionary of the Middle Ages*, edited by Joseph R. Strayer. 12 vols. New York: Scribner, 1982–89.

Hunter, G. L. *The Practical Book of Tapestries*. Philadelphia: J. P. Lippincott, 1925.

Husband, Timothy, and Jane Hayward. *The Secular Spirit: Life and Art at the End of the Middle Ages*. New York: Metropolitan Museum of Art, 1975.

Husik, Isaac. *A History of Medieval Jewish Philosophy*. New York: Atheneum, 1974.

Hussey, J. M. *The Cambridge Medieval History. Vol. 4, The Byzantine Empire. Part I, Byzantium and Its Neighbors*. Cambridge: Cambridge University Press, 1966.

Hyams, Edward. *Dionysius: A Social History of the Wine Vine*. New York: Macmillan, 1965.

———. *The Grapevine in England*. London: The Bodley Head, 1965.

Ibn Al-'Arabi. *The Bezels of Wisdom*, translated by R. W. J. Austin. New York: Paulist Press, 1980.

Ibn Anas, Malik. *Al-Muwatta of Imam Malik Ibn Anas: The First Formulation of Islamic Law*. The Islamic-Classical Library Series, translated by Aisha Abdurrahman Bewley. London: Kegan Paul, 1989.

Ibn Battuta. *Travels, A.D. 1325–1354*. Translated by H. A. R. Gibb. Edited by C. Defremery and B. R. Sanguinetti. Cambridge: Cambridge University Press, 1958, 1962, 1971.

Ibn Fadlan. *Voyage chez les Bulgares de la Volga*. Translated by Marius Canard. Paris: Sindboat, 1988.

Ibn Hawqal. *Kitab surat al-ard* [Oriental Geography]. Edited by J. H. Kramers. Leiden: E. J. Brill, 1938.

Ibn Hisnam. *The Life of Muhammad*. Lahore: Oxford University Press, 1970.

Ibn Ishaq, Hunayn. *The Book of the Ten Treatises on the Eye Ascribed to Hunain ibn Ishaq (809–977 A.D.). The Earliest Existing Systematic Textbook on Ophthalmology*. Translated and edited by Max Meyerhof. Cairo: Government Press, 1928.

Ibn al-Jawzi. "*Talbis Iblis*, translated by D. S. Margoliouth as The Devil's Delusion." *Islamic Culture* (1935–48): 9–22.

"Ibn Jubayr, Muhammad ibn Ahmad." *Oxford Dictionary of Islam*. Edited by John L. Esposito. Oxford: Oxford University Press, 2003.

Ibn Khaldun. *The Muqaddimah: An Introduction to History*. Princeton, N.J.: Princeton University Press, 1967.

Ibn Munqidh, Usamah. *Memoirs of Arab-Syrian Gentleman*. Translated by P. H. Hitti. Princeton, N.J.: Princeton University Press, 1929.

Ibn al-Nadim. *al-Fihrist*. Translated by Bayard Dodge. Cambridge: The Bodley Head Columbia University Press, 1970.

Ibn Nagrela, Samuel. *Jewish Prince in Moslem Spain: Selected Poems of Samuel Ibn Nagrela*. Introduction and translation by Leon J. Weinberger. University of Ala.: The University of Alabama Press, 1973.

Ibn Qalanisi. *The Damascus Chronicle of the Crusades*. Trans. H. A. R. Gibbs. Mineola, N.Y.: Dover, N.J.: 2002.

Ibn Qunfud. *Uns al-faqir wa'izz al-haqir*. Edited by Mohammed El Fasi and Adolphe Faure. Rabat, Morocco: Editions techniques nord-africaines, 1965.

Ibn Shahriyar, Buzurg. *The Marvels of India.* Translated by L. Marcel. Devic Book of the New York: L. MacVeigh Dial Press, 1929.

Ibn Sina (Avicenna). *Avicenna's Tract on Cardiac Drugs and Essays on Arab Cardiotherapy.* Edited by Hakeem Abdul Hameed. Karachi, Pakistan: Hamdard Foundation Press, 1983.

———. *The Canon of Medicine.* Abjad Book Designers & Builders, 1999.

———. *The General Principles of Avicenna's Canon of Medicine.* Translated by Mazhar H. Shah. Karachi, Pakistan: Naveed Clinic, 1966.

Ibn Taymiyya. "Fi 'l-sama' wa 'l-raqs wa 'l-surakh (On Music and Dance)." In *Rasa'il (Letters).* Edited, translated, and commented by J. Michot. Cairo, 1905, 278–315.

———. *al-Jawab al-sahih li-man baddala din al-masah (The Correct Answer to the One Who Changed the Religion of the Messiah),* In *A Muslim Theologian's Response to Christianity.* Translated by T. F. Michel. Delmar, N.Y.: Caravan Books, 1984.

Ibn Tufayl. *Hayy Ibn Yaqzan.* Translated by Lenn Evan Goodman. New York: Twain, 1972.

Ibn Zabara, Joseph ben Meir. *Libre d'ensenyaments delectables: Sèfer Xaaixuïm.* Translated by Ignasi González-Llubera. Barcelona: Editorial Alpha, 1931.

Idel, Moshe, and Bernard McGinn, eds. *Mystical Union in Judaism, Christianity and Islam: An Ecumenical Dialogue.* New York: Continuum, 1996.

Idelsohn, A. Z. *Jewish Music: Its Historical Development.* New York: Schocken Books, 1967.

Imamuddin, S. M. "Music in Muslim Spain." *Islamic Culture* 33 (1959): 147–150.

Irwin, Robert. *Islamic Art in Context: Art, Architecture and the Literary World.* New York: Harry N. Abrams, 1997.

Jackson, W. T. H. *The Literature of the Middle Ages.* New York: Columbia University Press, 1960.

Jackson-Stops, Gervase. *The Treasure Houses of Britain: 500 Hundred Years of Private Patronage and Art Collecting.* Washington, D.C.: National Gallery of Art and New Haven, Conn.: Yale University Press, 1985.

Jacobs, Jane. *The Death and Life of Great American Cities.* New York: Vintage, 1961.

———. *The Economy of Cities.* New York: Vintage, 1969.

———. *The Nature of Economies.* New York: Modern Library, 2000.

———. *Systems of Survival.* New York: Vintage, 2002.

Jacobs, Joseph, ed. *The Jews of Angevin England: Documents and Records from Latin and Hebrew Sources.* London: David Nutt, Publisher, 1893.

Jadon, Samira. "The Physicians of Syria during the Reign of Salah al-Din 570–589 A.H./1174–1193 A.D." *Journal of the History of Medicine and Allied Sciences* 25 (1970): 323–340.

al-Jāhiz. *Risālat al-qiyān. (The Epistle on Singing-Girls by Jāhiz).* Edited and translated by A. F. L. Beeston. Warminster, U.K.: Aris & Phillips, 1980.

Jakob Schonheintz. *Apoligia astrologia* (1502).

Jakobovits, I. *Jewish Medical Ethics.* New York: Bloch, 1959.

Jal, Auguste. *Archéologie Navale.* Paris: Arthus Bertrand, 1840.

Janeway, Elizabeth. *Man's World, Woman's Place.* New York: Morrow, 1971.

Jarry, Madeleine. *World Tapestry.* New York: G. P. Putman's Sons, 1969.

al-Jawziyya, Ibn Qayyim. *Medicine of The Prophet.* Translated by Penelope Johnstone. Cambridge: Islamic Texts Society, 1998.

Jenkinson, Hilary. *The Later Court Hands in England from the 15th through the 17th Century.* New York: Frederick Ungar, 1969.

Jewish Encyclopedia [especially articles by Morris Jastrow, Jr.; J. Frederic McCurdy; Richard Gottheil; Kausmamn Cohler; Francis L. Cohen; and Herman Rosenthal; and Joseph Jacobs and M. Seligsohn]. Available online. URL: http://www.jewishencyclopedia.com.

The Jews and the Crusaders: the Hebrew Chronicles of the First and Second Crusades, trans. and ed. Shlomo Eidelberg. Madison: University of Wisconsin Press, 1977.

Johansson, Ann-Katrin A., ed. *The Feasts of the Blessed Virgin Mary.* Stockholm: Almquist & Wiksell Int'l., 1998.

John of Damascus, *On the Divine Images: Three Apologies against Those Who Attack the Divine Images,* 1.16. Translated by David Anderson, Crestwood, N.Y.: St. Vladimir's Seminary Press, 1980.

Johnson, C., and H. Jenkinson. *English Court Hand A.D. 1066 to 1500 Illustrated Chiefly from the Public Records.* 2 volumes. Oxford: Clarendon Press, 1915.

Johnson, Penelope. *Equal in Monastic Profession: Religious Women in Medieval France.* Chicago: University of Chicago Press, 1991.

Johnston, R. C., and D. D. Owen. *Fabliaux.* Oxford: Blackwell, 1957.

Jolivet, J., and R. Rashed. "al-Kindi, Abu Yusuf Yakub b. Ishak." *Encyclopaedia of Islam*, 2d ed. Vol. 5. Leiden, The Netherlands: E. J. Brill, 1999, 122–123.

Jomier, J. "al-Azhar." *Encyclopaedia of Islam*, 2d ed. Vol. 1, Leiden, The Netherlands: E. J. Brill, 1999, 813–821.

Jones, Linda G. "The Boundaries of Sin and Communal Identity: Muslim and Christian Preaching and the Transmission of Cultural Identity." Ph.D. Thesis (unpublished). University of California at Santa Barbara, 2004.

Jones, Michael. *The End of Roman Britain.* Ithaca, N.Y.: Cornell University Press, 1996.

Jones, W. R., "Pious Endowments in Medieval Christianity and Islam." *Diogenes* 109 (1980): 23–36.

Jordan, William C. *The Great Famine: Northern Europe in the Early Fourteenth Century.* Princeton, N.J.: Princeton University Press, 1996.

———. *Women and Credit in Pre-Industrial and Developing Societies.* Philadelphia: University of Pennsylvania Press, 1993.

Jost, Jean E. *Ten Middle English Arthurian Romances: A Reference Guide.* Boston: G. K. Hall, 1986.

Jost, Marie. "Ravishing Sufi Music and Poetry." Available online. URL: http://www.worldmusiccentral.org/article.php?story=20040709212852341. Accessed July 10, 2004.

Julian of Norwich. *Showings.* Classics of Western Spirituality 1, translated by Edmund Colledge & James Walsh. 1978. Reprint, New York: Paulist Press, reprint, 2005.

Juynboll, G. H. A. *Muslim Tradition.* New York: Cambridge University Press, 1983.

Kaegi, Walter E. *Army, Society and Religion in Byzantium.* London: Variorum Reprints, 1982.

———. *Some Thoughts on Byzantine Military Strategy.* Brookline, Mass.: Hellenic College Press, 1983.

Kagan, Donald, Steven Ozment, and Frank M. Turner. *The Western Heritage.* 5th ed. Upper Saddle River, N.J.: Prentice Hall, 2006.

'Ali ibn 'Isa al-Kahhal. *Memorandum Book of a Tenth-Century Oculist for the Use of Modern Ophthalmologists.* Translated by Casey A. Wood. Chicago: Northwestern University Press, 1936. Reprinted. Birmingham, Ala.: The Classics of Ophthalmology Library, 1985.

Kahn, Deborah. *Canterbury Cathedral and Its Romanesque Sculpture.* Austin: University of Texas Press, 1991.

Kamen, Henry. *The Spanish Inquisition.* New Haven, Conn.: Yale University Press, 1997.

Kamm, M. W. *Old Time Herbs for Northern Gardens.* New York: Little Brown/Dover, 1971.

Kanos, Abram. *Jewish Ceremonial Art and Religious Observance.* New York: Harry N. Abrams, 1969.

Kantorowitz, Ernst H. *The King's Two Bodies: A Study in Medieval Political Theology.* Princeton, N.J.: Princeton University Press, 1957.

Kaptein, N. J. G., *Muhammad's Birthday Festival: Early History in the Central Muslim Lands and Development in the Muslim West until the 10th/16th Century.* Leiden, The Netherlands: E. J. Brill, 1993.

Karamustafa, Ahmet T. *God's Unruly Friends: Dervish Groups in the Islamic Later Middle Period, 1200–1550.* Salt Lake City: University of Utah Press, 1994.

Katz, Jacob. *Tradition and Crisis: Jewish Society at the End of the Middle Ages.* New York: Schocken Books, 1971.

Katz, Solomon. *The Jews in the Visigothic and Frankish Kingdoms of Spain and Gaul.* 1937. Reprint, The Medieval Academy of America, 1970.

Katzenellenbogen, A. *Allegories of the Virtues and Vices in Medieval Art.* London: Warburg Institute, 1939. Reprint, New York: W. W. Norton, 1964.

Kealey, Edward J. *Harvesting the Air: Windmill Pioneers in the 12th Century England.* Berkeley: University of California Press, 1987.

Keck, David. *Angels and Angelology in the Middle Ages.* Oxford: Oxford University Press, 1998.

Kedar, B. Z. *Crusade and Mission: European Approaches toward the Muslims.* Princeton, N.J.: Princeton University Press, 1984.

Kedar, Benjamin. *Merchants in Crisis: Genoese and Venetian Men of Affairs and the 14th-Century Depression.* New Haven, Conn.: Yale University Press, 1976.

Keddie, N., and B. Baron, eds. *Women in Middle Eastern History.* New Haven, Conn.: Yale University Press, 1991.

Kedourie, Elie. *The Jewish World: History and Culture of the Jewish People.* New York: Harry N. Abrams, 1979.

Keen, Maurice. *Chivalry.* New Haven, Conn.: Yale University Press, 1986.

Keen, Maurice, ed. *Medieval Warfare: A History.* Oxford: Oxford University Press, 1999.

Kelley, David H. "Who Descends from King David?" *Toledot: The Journal of Jewish Genealogy* 1 no. 3 (1977–78): 3–5.

Kelly, Amy. *Eleanor of Aquitaine and the Four Kings.* New York: Vintage Books, 1957.

Kelly, H. A. "Clandestine Marriage and Chaucer's Troilus." *Viator* 4 (1973): 435 ff.

Kennedy, E. S. "A Survey of Islamic Astronomical Tables." *Transactions of the American Philosophical Society.* New Series 46, no. 2 (1956): 123–177.

Kennedy, H. *The Early Abbasid Caliphate.* London: Croom Helm, 1981.

———. *Muslim Spain and Portugal: A Political History of al-Andalus.* London: New York: Longman, 1996.

———. *The Prophet and the Age of the Caliphates.* London: Longman, 1986.

Kennedy, Hugh. *The Early Abbasid Caliphate.* London: Croom Helm, 1981.

———. *The Prophet and the Age of the Caliphates.* London: Longman, 1986.

Kennedy, Phillip F., ed. *On Fiction and Adab in Medieval Arabic Literature.* Wiesbaden: Harrassowitz, 2005.

Kenny, Anthony, ed. *The Oxford Illustrated History of Philosophy.* Oxford: Oxford University Press, 1991.

Kenton, Warren. *Astrology, the Celestial Mirror.* New York: Avon, 1974.

Kenyon, John R. *Medieval Fortifications.* Leicester: Leicester University Press, 1990.

Kermode, Frank, ed. *English Pastoral Poetry.* New York: W. W. Norton, 1972.

Kern, Fritz. *Kingship and Law in the Middle Ages [Gottesgnadentum und Widerstandsrecht im früheren Mittelalter].* Edited and translated by S. B. Chrimes.

Studies in Mediaeval History 4. 1939. Reprint, Westport, Conn.: Greenwood Press, 1985.

Kersten, Carool. "Rambles: Review of Persian Mystical Music." Available online. URL: http://www.rambles.net/jooya_persmys03.html. Accessed February 14, 2004.

Khaddouri, Majid and H. J. Liebeseney, eds. *Law in the Middle East.* Vol. 1. Washington: The Middle East Institute, 1955.

Khadra Jayyusi, Salma, ed. *The Legacy of Muslim Spain.* Edited by Leiden and New York: E. J. Brill, 1992.

Khan, Gabriel Mandel. *Arabic Script: Styles, Variants, and Calligraphic Adaptations.* New York: Abbeville Press, 2001.

Khatibi, Abdelkebir, and Mohammed Sijelmassi. *The Splendor of Islamic Calligraphy.* Paris: Thames & Hudson, 1994.

Khoury, Nuha N. N. "The Dome of the Rock, the Ka'ba, and Ghumdan: Arab Myths and Umayyad Monuments." In *Muqarnas 10: An Annual on Islamic Art and Architecture*, edited by Margaret B. Sevcenko. Leiden, The Netherlands: E. J. Brill, 1993.

———. "The Meaning of the Great Mosque of Cordoba in the Tenth Century." In *Muqarnas 13: An Annual on the Visual Culture of the Islamic World*, edited by Gülru Necipoglu. Leiden, The Netherlands: E. J. Brill, 1996.

———. "The Mihrab Image: Commemorative Themes in Medieval Islamic Architecture." In *Muqarnas 9: An Annual on Islamic Art and Architecture*, edited by Oleg Grabar. Leiden, The Netherlands: E. J. Brill, 1992.

Kidson, Peter. *The Medieval World.* New York: McGraw-Hill, 1967.

Kieckhefer, Richard. *Magic in the Middle Ages.* Cambridge: Cambridge University Press, 2000.

———. *Repression and Heresy in Medieval Germany.* Philadelphia: University of Pennsylvania Press, 1979.

———. *Unquiet Souls: Fourteenth-Century Saints and Their Religious Milieu.* Chicago: University of Chicago Press, 1984.

Kimble, George H. T. *Geography in the Middle Ages.* New York: Russell & Russell, 1968.

Kinder, Terryl N., and Michael Downey. *Cistercian Europe: Architecture of Contemplation.* Grand Rapids, Mich.: William B. Eerdmans, 2002.

al-Kindī. *Mukhtaṣr al-mūsīqī fī ta'līf al-nagham wa-san 'at al- 'ūd* [Summary on music with reference to the composition of melodies and lute making]. French translation by A. Shiloah. "Un ancien traiti sur le "ūd d'Abū Yūsuf al-Kindī." *Israel Oriental Studies* 4 (1974): 179–205.

Kinnamos, John. *Deeds of John and Manuel Comnenus.* Translated by Charles M. Brand. New York, Columbia University Press, 1976.

Kirschner, Julius, and Suzanne Wemple, eds. *Women of the Medieval World.* Oxford: Basil Blackwell, 1985.

Kisch, Bruno Z. *Scales and Weights.* New Haven, Conn.: Yale University Press, 1965.

Kister, M. J. *Society and Religion from Jahiliyya to Islam.* Hampshire: Variorum Reprints, 1990.

Klein, H. Arthur. *Graphic Worlds of Peter Bruegel the Elder.* New York: Dover, 1963.

Klingender, Francis. *Animals in Art and Thought to the End of the Middle Ages.* Cambridge, Mass.: MIT Press, 1971.

Klocker, Harry R. *William of Ockham and the Divine Freedom.* Milwaukee, Wis.: Marquette University Press, 1992.

Klossowski De Rola, Stanislas. *Alchemy: The Secret Art.* New York: Bounty Books, 1974.

Knapp, Gottfried. *Angels, Archangels, and All the Company of Heaven.* New York: Prestel Publishing, 1999.

Knappert, Jan. *Islamic Legends: Histories of the Heroes, Saints and Prophets of Islam.* Leiden, The Netherlands: E. J. Brill, 1985.

Knight, Stan. *Historical Scripts: From Classical Times to the Renaissance.* 2d rev. ed. Oak Knoll Books, 1998.

Knowles, D. *The English Mystical Tradition.* London: Burns & Oates, 1961.

Knowles, D., C. L. Brooke, and Vera C. M. London. *The Heads of Religious Houses: England and Wells 940–1216.* Cambridge: Cambridge University Press, 1972.

Knysh, Alexander. "'Orthodoxy' and 'Heresy' in Medieval Islam: An Essay and Reassessment." *The Muslim World* 83 (January 1993): 48–67.

Kobler, Franz, ed. *Letters of Jews throughout the Ages.* London: London East and West Library, 1953.

Koch, H. W. *Medieval Warfare.* London: Bison Books, 1982.

———. W. *Medieval Warfare.* London: Dorset Press, 1978.

Kohler, Carl. *A History of Costume.* New York: Dover, 1963.

Kops, Lothar, and F. S. Bodenheimer. *The Natural History Section from a 9th Century "Book of Useful Knowledge."* Paris: Académie internationale d'histoire des sciences, 1949.

Kramer, Heinrich, and Jacob Sprenger. *Malleus Maleficarum (The hammer of witches).* Translated by M. Summers. 1928. Reprint, New York: Dover, 1971.

Kramer, S. *The English Craft Gilds*, Kirchner, Ont.: Batoche, 2000.

Kren, Thomas, and Scot McKendrick. *The Renaissance: The Triumph of Flemish Manuscript Painting in Europe.* Los Angeles: The J. Paul Getty Museum, 2003.

Kretzmann, Norman, Anthony Kenny, Jan Pinborg, and Eleonore Stump. *The Cambridge History of Later Medieval Philosophy: From the Rediscovery of Aristotle to the Disintegration of Scholasticism, 1100–1600.* Cambridge and New York: Cambridge University Press, 1982.

Kreutz, Barbara M. "Mediterranean Contributions to the Medieval Mariner's Compass." *Technology and Culture* 14 (1973).

———. "Ships and Ship Building, Mediterranean." In *Dictionary of the Middle Ages*, edited by Joseph R. Strayer. 12 vols. New York: Scribner, 1982–89.

———. "Ships, Shipping, and the Implications of Change in the Early Medieval Mediterranean." *Viator* 7 (1976).

Kuban, Dogan. *Muslim Religious Architecture.* Leiden: E. J. Brill, 1974.

Kuchenmeisterey. Augsburg: Johann Froschauer, 1507.

La Lumia. *Gli Ebrei Siciliani.* Palermo, 1870.

Lacy, Norris J. *New Arthurian Encyclopedia.* New York and London: Garland, 1996.

Ladurie, Emmanuel Le Roy. *Montaillou: The Promised Land of Error.* New York: George Braziller, 1978.

———. *Times of Feast, Times of Famine: A History of Climate since the Year 1000.* Garden City, N.Y.: Doubleday, 1971.

Lagorio, Valerie M. "The Medieval Continental Women Mystics: An Introduction." *An Introduction to the Medieval Mystics of Europe*, edited by

Paul E. Szarmach. Albany: State University of New York Press, 1984.

Laiou, A. E. "The Byzantine Economy in the Mediterranean Trade System: Thirteenth–Fifteenth Centuries." *Dumbarton Oaks Papers* 34–35, 1980–81, 177–223, in Laiou, A. E. ed., *Gender, Society and Economic Life in Byzantium.* Vol. 7. London: Variorum Reprints, 1992.

———. *Gender, society and economic life in Byzantium.* Vol. 7. London: Variorum Reprints, 1992.

Laistner, M. L. W. *The Intellectual Heritage of the Early Middle Ages.* Ithaca, N.Y.: Cornell University Press, 1957.

Lambton, Ann K. S. *State and Government in Medieval Islam.* Oxford: Oxford University Press, 1965.

Lamm, Carl J. *Cotton in Medieval Textiles of the Near East.* Paris: Librairie Orientaliste Paul Geuthnev, 1937.

———. *Das Glas Von Samarra.* Berlin: D. Reimer, 1928.

Lane, Edward. *Arabian Society in the Middle Ages.* London, Curzon Press: 1987 reprint of 1883 edition, edited by Stanley Lane-Poole. London: Chatto Windus.

Lane, Edward W. *The Manners and Customs of the Modern Egyptians.* London: J. M. Dent, 1836; New York: E. P. Dutton, 1923.

Lane, Frederic. *Andrea Barbarigo, Merchant of Venice 1419–1449.* 1944. Reprint, Baltimore: Johns Hopkins University Press, 1967.

———. "The Mediterranean Spice Trade: Its Revival in the Sixteenth Century." *The American Historical Review* 45 (1940): 581–590.

———. "Pepper Prices before Da Gama." *The Journal of Economic History* 28 (1968): 590–597.

Lane, Frederic C. *Venetian Ships and Ship Builders of the Renaissance.* Baltimore: Johns Hopkins University Press, 1934.

———. *Venice and History.* Baltimore: Johns Hopkins University Press, 1966.

———. "Venture Accounting in Medieval Business Management." *Bulletin of the Business Historical Society* 19 (1945): 161–172.

Lane, Frederic C., and J. C. Riemersma, eds. *Enterprise and Secular Change.* London: Allen Unwin, 1952.

Langermann, Tzvi, ed. *The Jews and Science in the Middles Ages.* Aldershot, U.K.: Ashgate, 1999.

Lansing, Carol. *The Florentine Magnates: Lineage and Faction in a Medieval Commune.* Princeton, N.J.: Princeton University Press, 1992.

———. *Power & Purity: Cathar Heresy in Medieval Italy.* Oxford: Oxford University Press, 1998.

Lapidus, Ira M. *A History of Islamic Societies.* Cambridge: Cambridge University Press, 1988.

———. *Muslim Cities in the Later Middle Ages.* Cambridge, Mass.: Harvard University Press, 1984.

Laslett, P., and R. Wald. *Household and Family in Past Time.* Cambridge: Cambridge University Press, 1972.

Lassner, J. *The Shaping of Abbasid Rule.* Princeton, N.J.: Princeton University Press, 1980.

———. *The Topography of Baghdad in the Early Middle Ages.* Detroit: Wayne State University Press, 1970.

Latham, J. D., and W. F. Paterson. *Saracen Archery.* London: Holland Press, 1970.

Laurie, S. S. *The Rise and Early Constitution of Universities with a Survey of Mediaeval Education.* New York: D. Appleton and Company, 1902.

Laver, J. *Clothes.* London: Burke, 1952.

Lea, H. C. *History of Sacerdotal Celibacy in the Christian Church.* London: Watts, 1932.

Leaf, W. and Purcell, S. *Heraldic Symbols: Islamic Insignia and Western Heraldry.* London. Victoria and Albert Museum, 1986.

Leclerq, Jean. *The Love of Learning and the Desire for God: A Study of Monastic Culture.* New York: Fordham University Press, 1982.

Leclercq, Jean, François Vandenbroucke, and Louis Boyer. *The Spirituality of the Middle Ages.* Vol. 2, *A History of Christian Spirituality.* New York: Seabury Press, 1968.

Lecomte, L. "Ibn Kutayba, Abu Muhammad 'Abd Allah." *Encyclopaedia of Islam,* 2d ed. Vol. 3, Leiden, The Netherlands: E. J. Brill, 1999, 844–847.

Leedy, Walter. *Fan Vaulting: A Study of Form, Technology and Meaning.* Santa Monica, Calif.: Arts & Architecture Press, 1980.

Leff, Gordon. *Heresy, Philosophy and Religion in the Medieval West.* Aldershot, U.K.: Ashgate, 2002.

———. *Medieval Thought: St. Augustine to Ockham.* Harmondsworth, U.K.: Penguin Books, 1958.

———. *Paris and Oxford Universities in the Thirteenth and Fourteenth Centuries: An Institutional and Intel-

lectual History. Huntington, N.Y.: R. E. Krieger, 1975, 1968.

———. *The Relation of Heterodoxy to Dissent c. 1250–c. 1450.* Manchester, U.K.: Manchester University Press, 1999.

Leggett, W. *Ancient and Medieval Dyes.* Brooklyn, N.Y.: Chemical Publishing, 1944.

Le Goff, Jacques. *The Birth of Purgatory.* 1986. Reprint, Chicago: University of Chicago Press, 1991.

———. *Medieval Callings.* Translated by Lydia Cochrane. Chicago: University of Chicago Press, 1987.

———. *Time, Work, and Culture in the Middle Ages.* Translated by Arthur Goldhammer. Chicago: University of Chicago Press, 1980.

———. *Your Money or Your Life: La Bourse et la vie.* Translated by Patricia Ranum. New York: Zone Books, 1988.

Lehner, Ernest, and Johanna Lehner. *Picture Book of Devils, Demons, and Witchcraft.* New York: Dover, 1971.

Lehrs, Max. *Late Gothic Engravings of Germany and the Netherlands.* New York: Dover, 1969.

Leibell, Jane Frances, Sister. *Anglo-Saxon Education of Women: From Hilda to Hildegarde.* New York: Burt Franklin, 1971.

Leiser, Gary. "Medical Education in Islamic Lands from the Seventh to the Fourteenth Century." *Journal of the History of Medicine and Allied Sciences* 38 (1983): 48–75.

Lejard, Andre. *French Tapestry.* Paris: Les Editions du Chêne, 1947.

Lemay, Helen Rodnite. *Women's Secrets: A Translation of Pseudo-Albertus Magnus' De Secretis Mulieum with Commentaries.* Binghampton, N.Y.: SUNY Press, 1992.

Lemay, Richard. *Abu Ma'shar and Latin Aristotelianism in the 12th Century.* Beirut: American University of Beirut, 1962.

———. "Arabic Numerals." In *Dictionary of the Middle Ages,* edited by Joseph R. Strayer. 12 vols. New York: Scribner, 1982–89.

———. "The Hispanic Origin of Our Present Numeral Forms." *Viator* 8 (1977).

Leon, Vicki. *Uppity Women of Medieval Times.* Berkeley, Calif.: Conari Press, 1997.

Leonard, Jonathan. *Early Japan.* New York: Time-Life Books, 1968.

Lerner, Robert E. *The Heresy of the Free Spirit in the Later Middle Ages.* Notre Dame, Ind.: University Press, 1972.

Lescott, Michel. *Physionomie.* Paris, 1540.

Le Strange, Guy, trans. *Nasir–i Khusrau's Book of Travels, Safarnama, Diary of a Journey through Syria and Palestine.* London: Palestine Pilgrims' Text Society, 1893.

Letters and Papers of the Reign of Henry VIII, vi, 427.

Levanon, Yosef. *The Jewish Travellers in the Twelfth Century.* Lanham, Md.: University Press of America, 1980.

Levenson, Jay A. *Circa 1492: Art in the Age of Exploration.* Washington, D.C.: National Gallery of Art and New Haven, Conn.: Yale University Press, 1991.

Levey, Martin. *Early Arabic Pharmacology: An Introduction Based on Ancient and Medieval Sources.* Leiden, The Netherlands: E. J. Brill, 1973.

———. *The Medical Formulary or Aqrabadhin of Al-Kindi.* Madison: University of Wisconsin Press, 1966.

Levi-Provençal, E., and Emilio García Gómez, *El tratado de Ibn Abdun,* Madrid: Moneda y Crédito, 1948.

Lewis, Archibald R. *Naval Power and Trade in the Mediterranean, 500–1100.* New York: Johnson Reprint, 1970.

Lewis, Archibald, and Timothy Runyan. *European Naval and Maritime History, 300–1500.* Bloomington: Indiana University Press, 1985.

Lewis, Bernard. *The Arabs in History.* New York: Harper, 1960.

———. "The Assassins." In *Dictionary of the Middle Ages,* edited by Joseph R. Strayer. 12 vols. New York: Scribner, 1982–89.

———. *The Assassins: A Radical Sect in Islam.* New York: Basic Books, 2002.

———. *The Crisis of Islam.* New York: Modern Library, 2003.

———. "The Fatimids and the Route to India." *Revue de la Faculté des Sciences Economiques de l'Université d'Istanbul* 11 (1949–50).

———. *Islam and the West.* New York: Oxford University Press, 1993.

———. *The Jews of Islam.* Princeton, N.J.: Princeton University Press, 1984, 1987

———. *The Muslim Discovery of Europe.* New York: W. W. Norton, 2001.

———. *The World of Islam*. London: Thames and Hudson, 1976.

Lewis, Bernard, and P. M. Holt, eds. *Historians of the Middle East*. London: Oxford University Press, 1962.

Lewis, C. S. *The Allegory of Love*. New York: Oxford University Press, 1958.

Lewis, G. R. *The Stannaries: A Study of the English Tin Miner*. Mass.: Boston and New York: Houghton, Mifflin and Co., 1924.

Lewy, Hans, Alexander Altmann, and Isaak Heinemann. *Three Jewish Philosophers*. New York: World, 1961.

Leyerle, J., ed. "Marriage in the Middle Ages." *Viator* 4 (1973): 413–501.

Lilley, S. *Man, Machines, and History*. 2d ed. London: Lawrence & Wishart, 1965.

Lindberg, David C., and Numbers, Ronald L. *God and Nature: Historical Essays on the Encounter between Christianity and Science*. Berkeley: University of California Press, 1986.

Lipton, Sara. *Images of Intolerance: The Representation of Jews and Judaism in the Bible moralisée*. Berkeley: University of California Press, 1999.

Little, Lester K. *Religious Poverty and the Profit Economy in Medieval Europe*. Ithaca, N.Y.: Cornell University Press, 1978.

Lloyd, H. Alan, "Giovanni de Dondi's Horological Masterpiece, 1364." *La Clessidra* xvii nos. 9–11 (1961).

Lochrie, Karma. *Covert Operations: The Medieval Uses of Secrecy*. Philadelphia: University of Pennsylvania Press, 1999.

Loeb, Isidor. "Reflections sur les Juifs." In *Review des Etudes Juives* XXVIII.

Lokkegaard, Frede. *Islamic Taxation in the Classic Period*. Copenhagen: Branner & Korch, 1950.

London Guildhall, 11 Richard II. A.D. 1388. Letter-Book H. fol. ccxxvi. (Latin).

London Guildhall, 47 Edward III. A.D. 1373. Letter-Book G. fol. cciv. (Norman French).

London Guildhall, 48 Edward III. A.D. 1374. Letter-Book G. fol. cccxviii. (Latin).

London Guildhall, 8 Edward II. A.D. 1314. Letter-Book D. fol. clxv. (Latin).

London Guildhall, Letter-Book H. fol. CCCIV. (Norman French).

Long, Pamela O. *Science and Technology in Medieval Society*. New York: New York Academy of Sciences, 1985.

Longnon, Jean, and Raymond Cazelles. *The Tres Riches Heures of Jean, Duke of Berry*. New York: George Braziller, 1969.

Loomis, Roger S. *Arthurian Literature in the Middle Ages*. Oxford: Clarendon Press, 1959.

———. *Arthurian Tradition and Chretien de Troyes*. New York: Columbia University Press, 1949.

Loomis, Roger S., and Rudolph Willard. *Medieval English Verse and Prose*. New York: Appleton Century Crofts, 1948.

Lopez, Robert S. *The Commercial Revolution of the Middle Ages*. Englewood Cliffs, N.J.: Prentice Hall, 1971.

———. *The Commercial Revolution of the Middle Ages, 950–1350*. Cambridge and New York: Cambridge University Press, 1998, 1976.

———. "European Merchants in The Medieval Indies." *Journal of Economic History* 3 (1943).

Lopez, Robert S., and H. A. Miskimin. "The Economic Depression of the Renaissance." *The Economic History Review*, 2d Series, vol. 4. Oxford: Basil Blackwell, 1962.

Lopez, Robert, and Irving Raymond. *Medieval Trade in the Mediterranean World*. New York: Columbia University Press, 1968.

López-Baralt, Luce. *Islam in Spanish Literature: From the Middle Ages to the Present*, translated by A. Hurley. Leiden, The Netherlands: E. J. Brill, 1992.

———. *San Juan de la Cruz y el Islam*. México: Colegio de México, 1985.

———. *The Sufi Trobar Clus and Spanish Mysticism: A Shared Symbolism*. Translated by A. Hurley. Leiden, The Netherlands: E. J. Brill, 2000.

Lovejoy, Arthur O. *The Great Chain of Being: A Study of the History of an Idea*. Cambridge, Mass.: Harvard University Press, 1936.

de Lubac, Henry. *Medieval Exegesis: The Four Sense of Scripture*: Vol. 1. Grand Rapids, Mich.: Wm. B. Erdmans Publishing Co., 1998.

Luca Bellanti. *Liber de astrologica veritate*. Florence, Italy: n.p., 1498.

Lucas, Angela M. *Women in the Middle Ages*. New York: St. Martin's Press, 1983.

Luck, George. *Arcana mundi: Magic and the Occult in the Greek and Roman Worlds*. Baltimore, Md.: Johns Hopkins University Press, 1985.

Luquiens, Frederick Bliss. *The Song of Roland*. New York: Macmillan, 1952.

Luttrell, Anthony. *Latin Greece, the Hospitallers, and the Crusades, 1291–1440*. London: Variorum Reprints, 1982.

Luzzatto, Gino. *An Economic History of Italy from the Fall of the Roman Empire to the Beginning of the 16th Century*. Translated by Philip Jones. London: Routledge and Kegan Paul, 1961.

Lyons, Albert, and Joseph Petrucelli. *Medicine: An Illustrated History*. New York: Harry N. Abrams, 1977.

Maalouf, Amin. *The Crusades through Arab Eyes*. Translated by Jan Rothschild. New York: Schocken Books, 1985.

Al-Ma'arri, Abu l-'Ala Ahmad. Available online. URL: http://www.humanistictexts.org/al_ma%27arri.htm.

Macaulay, David. *Castle*. New York: Houghton Mifflin/Walter Lorraine Books, 1977.

MacCana, Proinsias. *Celtic Mythology*. London: Hamlyn, 1970.

Macdonald, Duncan B. *The Religious Attitude and Life in Islam*. Beirut: Khayats, 1965.

MacDougall, Elizabeth, and Richard Ertinghausen, eds. *The Islamic Garden*. Washington, D.C.: Dumbarton Oaks, 1976.

Mackay, Angus. *Spain in the Middle Ages: From Frontier to Empire, 1000–1500*. New York: St. Martin's Press, 1977.

Mackeen, A. M. Mohamed. "The Rise of al-Shadhili (d. 656/1258)." *Journal of the American Oriental Society* 91, no. 4 (October–December, 1971): 477–486.

Mackenney, R. *Tradesmen and Traders: The World of the Guilds in Venice and Europe*. London: Barnes & Noble, 1987.

MacKinney, Loren. *Medical Illustrations in Medieval Manuscripts*. Berkeley: University of California Press, 1965.

Madelung, Wilferd. "Isma'iliyya." *The Encyclopaedia of Islam*. 2d ed. Vol. 4. Leiden, The Netherlands: E. J. Brill, 1994, 198–206.

———. *Religious Schools and Sects in Medieval Islam*. London: Variorum, 1985.

Madelung, Wilferd, and Walker, Paul E. *The Advent of the Fatimids: A Contemporary Shi'i Witness: An English Translation of Ibn al-Haytham's Kitab al-Munazarat*. London: I. B. Tauris, 2000.

Maguire, E., and Henry Maguire. *Other Icons: Art and Power in Byzantine Secular Culture*. Princeton, N.J.: Princeton University Press, 2006.

Maguire, Henry. *The Icons of their Bodies: Saints and their Images in Byzantium*. Princeton, N.J.: Princeton University Press, 2000.

Mahdi, Muhsin. *Ibn Khaldûn's "Philosophy of History."* Chicago: University of Chicago Press, 1957. Reprint, 1971.

Maimonides (Moses ben Maimon). *The Book of Women*. Book IV, *The Code of Maimonides*. New Haven, Conn.: Yale University Press, 1972.

———. *The Commandments (Sefer ha-Mitzvoth)*. Translated by Charles B. Chavel. 2 vols. London, Soncino Press, 1967. *The Commandments*: Sefer, ha-Mitzvoth of Maimonides.

———. *Commentary on the Mishah*: Avodah Zarah 1.3. Edited by Y. Kafih. Jerusalem, 1965, 2:225, no. 10.

———. *The Guide of the Perplexed (Moreh Nevukhim)*. Translated by Shlomo Pines. Chicago: University of Chicago Press, 1963.

———. *The Guide of the Perplexed*. Translated by Chaim Rabin. Indianapolis, Ind.: Hackett, 1995.

———. *The Guide for the Perplexed*. Translated by M. Friedlander. 1904. Reprint, New York: Dover 1956.

———. *A Maimonides Reader*. New York: Behrman House, 1972.

———. *Treatise on Asthma* or *Sefer Hakazerith*. Edited by S. Muntner. Jerusalem: Rubin Mass and Philadelphia: Lippincott, 1963.

Majano, Guido. *The Healing Hand*. Cambridge, Mass.: Harvard University Press, 1975.

Makdisi, G. *Religion, Law and Learning in Classical Islam*. 1991.

———. *The Rise of Colleges: Institutions of Learning in Islam and the West*. Edinburgh: Edinburgh University Press, 1981.

———. "The Topography of Eleventh Century Baghdad." *Arabica* 6 (1959): 178–197, 281–309.

Makowski, Z. S. *Analysis, Design and Construction of Braced Barrel Vaults*. London: Routledge, 1986.

Male, Emile. *Art and Artists of the Middle Ages*. Redding Ridge, Conn.: Black Swan, 1987.

———. *Chartres*. Notre Dame de New York: Harper & Row, 1983.

Male, Emile, and Harry Bober. *Religious Art in France: The Late Middle Ages: A Study of Medieval Iconography and Its Sources*. Princeton, N.J.: Princeton University Press, 1987.

Male, Emile, and Dora Nussey. *The Gothic Image: Religious Art in France of the Thirteenth Century*. New York: Harper & Row, 1972.

Malino, F. *The Sephardic Jews in Bordeaux*. 1978.

Mallett, Michael E. *The Florentine Galleys in the Fifteenth Century*. Oxford: Clarendon Press, 1967.

Malory, Sir Thomas. *Le Morte D'Arthur*. New York: Harrison House, 1985.

Malter, H. *Saadia Gaon, His Life and Works*. 1921. Reprint, New York: Hermon Press, 1969.

Malti-Douglas, Fedwa. *Studies in Arabic Literature, Supplements to the Journal of Arabic Literature*, 11. Leiden, The Netherlands: E. J. Brill, 1985.

Manahem Mansoor. *Sign, Symbol, Script: Origins of Written Communication and the Birth of the Alphabet*. Princeton, N.J.: Films for the Humanities and Sciences, 1996.

Manchester, William. *A World Lit Only by Fire: The Medieval Mind and the Renaissance Portrait of an Age*. Boston: Little, Brown, 1992.

Manion, Margaret, and Vera Vines. *Medieval and Renaissance Illuminated Manuscripts in Australian Collections*. Melbourne: Thames and Hudson, 1984.

Mann, Jacob. *The Jews in Egypt and in Palestine under the Fatimid Caliphs*. 1922. Reprint, New York: Ktav Pub. House, 1970.

———. *The Responsa of the Babylonian Geonim as a Source of Jewish History*. 1919. Reprint, New York: Arno Press, 1973.

Mann, Vivian B. "Art and Material Culture of Judaism—Medieval and Modern Times." *Encyclopedia of Judaism*. General Editors Jacob Neusner, Alan J. Avery-Peck, and William Scott Green. Vol. 1. E. J. Brill Online, 2006. URL: http://www.brillonline.nl/public/art-material-culture.html#.

———, Thomas F. Glick, and Jerrilynn D. Doods, eds. *Convivencia-Jews, Muslims, and Christians in Medieval Spain*. New York: George Braziller, 1992.

Mansoor, Menahem, trans. *Bahya ben Joseph Ibn Pakuda: The Book of Direction to the Duties of the Heart*. London: Routledge and Kegan Paul, 1973.

Mansoor, Menahem. *Jewish History and Thought*. Hoboken, N.J.: KTAV, 1991.

———. *The Thanksgiving Hymns*. Leiden: E. J. Brill, 1965.

Manuel II Palaeologus, Emperor of the East, 1350–1425, The Letters of Manuel II Palaeologus: Text, Translation, and Notes. Washington: Dumbarton Oaks Center for Byzantine Studies, Trustees for Harvard University; Locust Valley, N.Y., distributed by J. J. Augustin, 1977.

Marcus, I. G. "History, Story and Collective Memory: Narrativity in Early Ashkenazic Culture." *Prooftexts* 10 (1990): 365–388.

Marcus, Ivan G. *Piety and Society: The Jewish Pietists of Medieval Germany*. Leiden: E. J. Brill, 1981.

Marcus, Jacob R. *The Jew in the Medieval World: A Source Book 315–1791*. New York: Jewish Publications Society, 1938.

Margoliouth, D. S. *The Table Talk of a Mesopotamian Judge*. London: Royal Asiatic Society, 1922.

Margolis, Max L., and Alexander Marx. *A History of the Jewish People*. Philadelphia: The Jewish Publication Society of America, 1927.

Margotta, Roberto. *The Story of Medicine*. New York: Golden Press, 1967.

Marie de France. *Lais*. Edited and Translated by Robert Hanning and Joan Ferrante. New York: Baker Books, 1978.

———. *Medieval Fables*. Translated by Jeanette Beer. New York: Dodd-Mead, 1983.

Markel, Howard. *Quarantine*. Baltimore: Johns Hopkins University Press, 1999.

———. *When Germs Travel*. New York: Pantheon Books/Alfred A. Knopf, 2002.

Marks, Claude. *Pilgrims, Heretics, and Lovers*. New York: Macmillan, 1975.

Markus, R. M. *The Jew in the Medieval World: A Source Book, 315–1791*. Cincinnati: Sinai Press, 1938.

Marshall, Richard K. *The Local Merchants of Prato: Small Entrepreneurs in the Late Medieval Economy*. The Johns Hopkins University Studies in Historical and Political Science, 117th Series, number 1. Baltimore: Johns Hopkins University Press, 1999.

Marsilio Ficino. *De vita coelitus comparanda* (1489).

Martin, Christopher. *The Philosophy of Thomas Aquinas: Introductory Readings*. London: Routledge Kegan & Paul, 1988.

Martin, F. R. *The Miniature Painting and Painters of Persia, India, and Turkey, from the 8th to the 18th Century*. 1912. Reprint, London: Holland Press, 1968.

Martin, R. C, M. R. Woodward, and D. S. Atmaja, eds. *Defenders of Reason in Islam: Mu'tazilism from Medieval School to Modern Symbol*. Oxford: Oneworld Publications, 1997.

Martinez de Toledo, Alfonso. *Arcipreste de Talavera o Corbacho*. Madrid: Castalia 1970.

Marx, Alexander. "The Correspondence between the Rabbis of Southern France and Maimonides about Astrology." *Hebrew Union College Annual* 3 (1926): 311–358.

Massignon, Louis. *Al-Hallâj: Mystic and Martyr*. Translated, edited, and abridged by Herbert Mason. Princeton, N.J.: Bollingen, 1994.

Massing, Jean Michel. "Observations and Beliefs: The World of the Catalan Atlas." In *Circa 1492*, edited by Jay A. Levenson. Washington: National Gallery of Art and New Haven, Conn.: Yale University Press. 1991.

Mastnak, Tomaå. *Crusading Peace: Christendom, the Muslim World, and Western Political Order*. Berkeley and Los Angeles: University of California Press, 2002.

Matarusso, Pauline, ed. *The Cistercian World: Monastic Writings of the 12th Century*. New York: Penguin Books, 1993.

Mate, Mavis E. *Daughters, Wives, and Widows after the Black Death: Women in Sussex* 1350–1535. Rochester, N.Y.: Boydel, 1998.

Matt, Daniel Chanan. *Zohar: The Book of Enlightenment*. New York: Paulist Press, 1983.

Matter, E. Ann. *The Voice of My Beloved: The Song of Songs in Western Medieval Christianity*. Philadelphia: University of Pennsylvania, 1990.

Matthews, Gareth B. *The Augustinian Tradition*. Berkeley and Los Angeles: University of California Press, 1999.

May, Florence L. *Silk Textiles of Spain: 8th to 15th Century*. New York: The Hispanic Society of America, 1957.

May, Larry. *The Morality of War: Classical and Contemporary Readings*. Upper Saddle River, N.J.: Pearson Education, 2006.

Mayer, L. A. *Saracenic Heraldry*. Oxford: Oxford University Press, 1933. Reprint, 1999.

McAuliffe, Jane Dammen, Barry Walfish, and Joseph Goering. *With Reverence for the Word: Medieval Scriptural Exegesis in Judaism, Christianity, and Islam*. New York: Oxford University Press, 2002.

McDonnell, Ernest W. *The Beguines and Beghards in Medieval Culture*. New Brunswick, N.J.: Rutgers University Press, 1969.

McGaha, Michael. *The Creation of Kabbalah: Jewish Mysticism in Medieval Spain*. In Press.

———. "Naming the Nameless, Numbering the Infinite: Some Common Threads in Spanish Sufism, Kabbalah, and Catholic Mysticism." *Yearbook of Comparative and General Literature* 45/46 (1997–98): 37–53.

McGee, Timothy. "Eastern Influences in Medieval European Dances." In *Cross-Cultural Perspectives on Music*, edited by Robert Falck and Timothy Rice. Toronto: University of Toronto Press, 1982.

McGinn, Bernard. *The Presence of God: A History of Western Christian Mysticism*. Vol. 1, *The Foundations of Mysticism: Origins to the Fifth Century*. New York: Crossroad Publishing, 1991; Vol. 2, *The Growth of Mysticism: 500 to 1200 A.D.* New York: Crossroad Publishing, 1996; Vol. 3, *The Flowering of Mysticism: Men and Women in the New Mysticism, 1200–1350*. New York: Crossroad Publishing, 1998.

McGinn, Bernard, ed. *Meister Eckhart and the Beguine Mystics*. New York: Continuum, 1994.

McGinn, Bernard et al., eds. *Christian Spirituality I: Origins to the Twelfth Century*. New York: Crossroad, 1989.

McKendry, Maxine. *Seven Centuries Cookbook*. New York: McGraw-Hill, 1973.

McKitterick, Rosamond. *Carolingian Culture*. Cambridge: Cambridge University Press, 1993.

———. *The Carolingians and the Written Word*, Cambridge and New York: Cambridge University Press, 1989.

McLaren, Angus. *A History of Contraception from Antiquity to the Present Day*. London: Blackwell, 1990.

McNeill, John Thomas. *The Celtic Penitentials and Their Influence on Continental Christianity.* Paris: Édourad Champion, 1923.

McNeill, T. *Castles.* London: English Heritage/Batsford, 1992.

McNeill, William H. *Plagues and Peoples.* New York: Anchor/Doubleday, 1976.

Meier, Fritz. "Tahir al-Safadi's Forgotten Work on Western Saints of the 6th–12th Century." In *Essays on Islamic Piety and Mysticism,* edited by Fritz Meier. Leiden, The Netherlands: E. J. Brill, 1999, 423–503.

Meisami, Julie Scott. "Symbolic Structure in a Poem by Nasir-i Khusrau." *Iran* 31 (1993).

Meiss, Millard. *The Belles Heures of Jean, Duke of Berry.* New York: George Braziller, 1974.

———. *The Great Age of Fresco.* New York: George Braziller, 1970.

Meister Eckhart, *The Essential Sermons, Commentaries, Treatises, and Defense.* Classics of Western Spirituality, 28. Edited by Edmund Colledge and Bernard McGinn. New York: Paulist Press, 1981.

Melchert, Christopher. *The Formation of the Four Sunni Schools of Law, 9th–10th Centuries C.E.* Studies in Islamic Law and Society, vol. 4. Leiden, The Netherlands: E. J. Brill, 1997.

Melikoff, I. "Ghazi." *Encyclopaedia of Islam,* 2d ed., vol. 2: 1,043–1,045. Leiden, The Netherlands: E. J. Brill, 1999.

Mellinkoff, Ruth. *The Horned Moses in Medieval Art and Thought.* Berkeley: University of California Press, 1970.

Memon, Muhammad Umar. *Ibn Taimiya's Struggle Against Popular Religion: With An Annotated Translation of His Kitab iqtida' as-sirat al-mustaqim mukhalafat ashab al-jahl.* The Hague: Mouton, 1976.

Le Menagier de Paris. (*The Goodman of Paris*). Translated by E. Power. London: Routledge, 1928.

Menendez Pidal, Ramon. *The Spaniards in Their History.* London: Hollis and Carter, 1950.

Menninger, K. *Number Words and Number Symbols.* Translated by P. Broneer. Cambridge, Mass.: MIT Press, 1969.

Menocal, Maria Rosa. *The Arabic Role in Medieval Literary History: A Forgotten Heritage.* Philadelphia: University of Pennsylvania Press, 1987.

———. "Close Encounters in Medieval Provence: Spain's Role in the Birth of Troubadour Poetry." *Hispanic Review* 49, no. 1, Williams Memorial Issue (winter 1981): 43–64.

———. *The Ornament of the World: How Muslims, Jews, and Christians Created a Culture of Tolerance in Medieval Spain.* Boston: Little, Brown, 2002.

Menocal, Maria Rosa, Raymond P. Scheindlin, and Michael Sells, eds. *The Literature of Al-Andalus.* Cambridge and New York: Cambridge University Press, 2000.

Mercier, Louis. *La chasse et les sports chez les arabes.* Paris: M. Riviere, 1927.

Mercier, Raymond, ed. *Studies in the Transmission of Medieval Mathematical Astronomy.* Aldershot, U.K.: Ashgate, 2004.

Merwin, W. S., trans. *Poem of the Cid.* New York: Meridian, 1959.

Metlitzki, Dorothee. *The Matter of Araby in Medieval England.* New Haven, Conn., and London: Yale University Press, 1977.

Metzger, Therese, and Mendel Metzger. *Jewish Life in the Middle Ages—Illuminated Hebrew Manuscripts of the Thirteenth to the Sixteenth Centuries.* Fribourg, N.Y.: Alpine Fine Arts, 1982.

Meydenbach, Jacob. *Der Toten Dantz.* Mainz, 1492.

Meyendorff, John. *Byzantine Theology: Historical Trends and Doctrinal Themes.* New York: Fordham University Press, 1979.

———. "Society and Culture in the Fourteenth Century: Religious Problems." In *Byzantine Hesychasm: Historical, Theological and Social Problems.* Vol. 8. London: Variorum Reprints, 1974.

Meyerhof Max, ed. and trans. *Un glossaire de matière médicale composé par Maimonide.* Cairo, 1940.

———. "Ibn al-Nafis, 'Ala' al-Din Abu 'l-Ala 'Ali." *Encyclopaedia of Islam,* 2d ed., Vol. 3: 897–898. Leiden, The Netherlands: E. J. Brill, 1999.

———. *Studies in Medieval Arabic Medicine: Theory and Practice.* Edited by Penelope Johnstone. London: Variorum Reprints, 1984.

———. "Thirty-three Clinical Observations by Rhazes, from the *al-Hawi*." *Isis* 23 (1935): 321–356.

Meyerson, Mark D., and Edward D. English, eds. *Christians, Muslims, and Jews in Medieval and Early Modern Spain: Interaction and Cultural Change.* Notre Dame, Ind.: University of Notre Dame Press, 1999.

Meyerson, Mark D., Daniel Theiry, and Oren Falk, eds. *"A Great Effusion of Blood": Interpreting Medi-*

eval Violence. Toronto: University of Toronto Press, 2004.

Michelet, Jules. Satanism and Witchcraft: A Study in Medieval Superstition. New York: The Citadel Press, 1939.

Michell, George. Architecture of the Islamic World, Its History and Social Meaning. London: Thames and Hudson, 1984.

Michon, J. L., "Khirka." Encyclopaedia of Islam, 2d ed., Vol. 5: 17–18. Leiden, The Netherlands: E. J. Brill, 1999.

Millas Vallicrosa, J. M. Literature hebraicoespanola. Barcelona: Labor, 1968.

Miller, Konrad. Mappae arabicae. Vols. I–II. 1926–1931, Reprint, as University of Frankfurt Islamic Geography Series, Frankfurt University of Chicago, 1994.

Miller, Thomas, ed. The Old English Version of Bede's Ecclesiastical History of the English People. 4 vols. Early English Text Society, o.s., nos. 95, 96, 110, 111. 1890–1898. Reprint, Millwood, N.Y.: Kraus Reprint, 1978–88.

Milman, H. H., The History of the Jews. London: Ward, Lock, & Co., 1829.

Minne-Saeve, Viviane, and Hervbe Kergall. Romanesque and Gothic France: Art and Architecture. New York: Harry N. Abrams, 2000.

Mises, Ludwig von. Human Action: A Treatise on Economics. 4th rev. ed. Irvington-on Hudson, N.Y.: The Foundation for Economic Education, 1996.

———. The Ultimate Foundation of Economic Science. New York: Van Nostrand, 1962.

Miskimin, H. A. The Economy of Early Renaissance Europe. Englewood Cliffs, N.J.: Prentice Hall, 1969.

Miskimin, Harry A., David Herlihy, and A. L. Udovitch, eds. The Medieval City. New Haven, Conn.: Yale University Press, 1977.

Mitchell, G. Frank. Treasures of Early Irish Art: 1500 B.C. to 1500 A.D. New York: Metropolitan Museum of Art, 1977.

Mitchell, Otis C. Two German Crowns: Monarchy and Empire in Medieval Germany. Bristol, Ind.: Wyndham Hall Press, 1985.

Mitchiner, Michael. Oriental Coins and Their Values: The World of Islam. London: Hawkins, 1977.

Mladen, Leo Mucha. "Bartolus the Man." In Mauchaut's World: Science and Art in the Fourteenth Century, edited by Madeleine P. Cosman and Bruce Chandler. New York: New York Academy of Sciences, 1978.

Modarressi, Tabata'i, H. Crisis and Consolidation in the Formative Period of Shi'ite Islam. Princeton, N.J.: Darwin Press, 1993.

———. An Introduction to Shi'i Law: A Bibliographical Study. London and Ithaca, N.Y.: Cornell University Press, 1984.

Modder, Montagu Frank. The Jew in the Literature of England. New York: Meridian Books, 1960.

Mollat, G. The Popes in Avignon 1307–1378. London: Thomas Nelson, 1963.

Mollat, Michél, and Philippe Wolff. The Popular Revolutions of the Late Middle Ages. London: Allen & Unwin, 1973.

Momen, Moojan. An Intoduction to Shi'i Islam. New Haven, Conn.: Yale University Press, 1985.

Monroe, James T. Hispano-Arabic Poetry: A Student Anthology. Piscataway, N.J.: Gorgias Press LLC, 2004.

———. Islam and Arabs in Spanish Scholarship. Leiden: E. J. Brill, 1970.

———. "Zajal and Muwashshaha: Hispano-Arabic Poetry and the Romance Tradition." In The Legacy of Muslim Spain, edited by Salma K. Jayyusi. Leiden, The Netherlands: E. J. Brill, 1994.

Mooney, Catherine M. "Disentangling Voices: Medieval Women Writers and their Male Interpreters." Lecture at Harvard University, April 1992.

Mooney, Catherine M., ed. Gendered Voices: Medieval Saints and Their Interpreters. Philadelphia: University of Pennsylvania Press, 1999.

Moore, Robert Ian. The Formation of a Persecuting Society: Power and Deviance in Western Europe, 950–1250. Oxford and New York: Blackwell, 1987.

Moreno Fernández, Francisco. Historia social de las lenguas de España. Barcelona: Ariel, 2005.

Moreno, Manuel Gomez. The Golden Age of Spanish Sculpture. Greenwich, N.Y.: New York Graphic Society, 1964.

Morgan, D. O. "Ibn Battuta and the Mongols." Journal of the Royal Asiatic Society 11 (April 2001).

Morley, Thomas. A Plaine and Easy Introduction to Practical Musicke. Edited by R. Harman. 1953. Reprint, New York, W. W. Norton, 1973.

Mormondo, Franco. The Preacher's Demons: Bernardino of Siena and the Social Underworld of Early

Renaissance Italy. Chicago: University of Chicago Press, 1999.

Morris, A. E. J. *A History of Urban Form: Before the Industrial Revolutions.* 2d ed. London: Godwin, 1991.

Morris, Colin. *The Discovery of the Individual 1050–1200.* Toronto: University of Toronto Press, 1987.

———. *The Papal Monarchy: The Western Church from 1050 to 1250.* Oxford: Clarendon Press, 1989.

Morris, Joan. *The Lady Was a Bishop.* New York: Macmillan, 1973.

Morrison, Karl E. "The Gregorian Reform." In *Christian Spirituality I: Origins to the Twelfth Century,* edited by Bernard McGinn et al., 177–194. New York: Crossroad, 1989.

Mottahedeh, Roy. *The Mantle of the Prophet: Religion and Politics in Iran.* London: Oneworld Publications, 1986. Reprint, 2000.

Mountain, Rosemary. *Facets of Islamic Musical Tradition.* Concordia College Muslim Women's Forum. Concordia College, Montreal, Canada, Oct. 5, 2003.

Mueller, Reinhold C. *The Venetian Money Market: Banks, Panics and the Public Debt, 1200–1500. Money and Banking in Medieval and Renaissance Venice.* Vol. 2. Baltimore and London: Johns Hopkins University Press, 1997.

Muendel, John, "The Mountain Men of Casentino during the Late Middle Ages." In *Science and Technology in Medieval Society,* edited by Pamela Long. New York: New York Academy of Sciences, 1985.

Muir, William. *The Life of Muhammad from Original Sources.* Edinburgh: J. Grant, 1923.

———. *The Mamluke or Slave Dynasty of Egypt: 1260–1517 A.D.* London: Smith Elder, 1896.

Mumford, Lewis. *Technics and Civilization.* New York: Harcourt, Brace & World, 1934.

Mundy, J. H., and Peter Riesenberg. *The Medieval Town.* Princeton, N.J.: Van Nostrand, 1958.

Mundy, M. "The Family, Inheritance and Islam." In *Islamic Law: Social and Historical Contexts,* edited by Aziz al-Azmeh. London: Routledge, 1988.

Munro, John. "The 'Industrial Crisis' of the English Textile Towns, 1290–1330." In *Thirteenth-Century England:* VII, edited by Michael Prestwich, Rich-ard Britnell, and Robin Frame. 103–41. Woodbridge, U.K.: Boydell Academic Press, 1999.

———. "The Origins of the English 'New Draperies': The Resurrection of an Old Flemish Industry, 1270–1570." In *The New Draperies in the Low Countries and England, 1300–1800,* edited by Negley B. Harte, 35–127. Pasold Studies in Textile History no. 10. Oxford and New York: Maney Publishing, 1997.

———. "The Symbiosis of Towns and Textiles: Urban Institutions and the Changing Fortunes of Cloth Manufacturing in the Low Countries and England, 1270–1570," *The Journal of Early Modern History: Contacts, Comparisons, Contrasts,* 3, no. 1 (February 1999): 1–74.

———. "Textiles as Articles of Consumption in Flemish Towns, 1330–1575." *Bijdragen tot de geschiedenis,* 81, no. 1–3 (1998): 275–288.

Murk-Jansen, Saskia. *Brides in the Desert: The Spirituality of the Beguines.* Traditions of Christian Spirituality Series. Maryknoll, N.Y.: Orbis Books, 1998.

Musallam, B. *Sex and Society in Islam.* Cambridge: Cambridge University Press, 1983.

Musgrave, Peter. "The Economics of Uncertainty: The Structural Revolution in the Spice Trade, 1480–1640." In *Shipping, Trade, and Commerce,* edited by P. L. Cottrell and D. H. Aldcroft. Leicester: Leicester University Press, 1981.

Nallino, M. "Abu 'l-Faradj al-Isfahani." *Encyclopaedia of Islam,* 2d ed. Vol. 1, 118, Leiden, The Netherlands: E. J. Brill, 1999.

Narkiss, Bezalel. *Hebrew Illuminated Manuscripts.* Jerusalem: Encyclopaedia Judaica, 1969.

———. *Picture History of Jewish Civilization.* New York: Tudor, 1970.

Narkiss, Mordechai. "An Italian Niello Casket of the 15th Century." *Journal of the Warburg and Courtauld Institutes* 21 (1958).

Naser-e Khosraw's Book of Travels (Safarnama). Translated and with an introduction by W. M. Thackston. New York: Persian Heritage Association, Bibliotheca Persica, 1986.

Nasr, Seyyed Hossein. *Islamic Art & Spirituality.* New Delhi and New York: Oxford University Press, 1990.

———. *Science and Civilization in Islam.* Cambridge, Mass.: Harvard University Press, 1968.

———. Shi'ism: Doctrines, Thought, and Spirituality and Expectation of the Millennium: Shi'ism in History. Albany: State University of New York Press, 1988.

Nasr, S. H., and O. Leaman, eds. History of Islamic Philosophy. London: Routledge, 1996.

Necipoglu, G. Architecture, Ceremonial, and Power, The Topkapi Palace in the Fifteenth and Sixteenth Centuries. Cambridge, Mass.: Massachusetts Institute of Technology Press, 1991.

———. "Framing the Gaze in Ottoman, Safavid, and Mughal Palaces. (Topkapi Palace, Istanbul; Safavid Palace, Isfahan; The Red Fort, Delhi)." Ars Orientalis 23 (1993): 303–342.

Neckham, Alexander, and U. T. Holmes, Jr., eds. Daily Living in the 12th Century. Madison: University of Wisconsin Press, 1966.

Needham, Joseph. Science and Civilization in China. Vol. 4. New York: Cambridge University Press, 1971.

Needham, Joseph, W. Ling, and Derek J. DeSolla Price, Heavenly Clockwork: The Great Astronomical Clocks of Medieval China. Cambridge: Cambridge University Press, 1960.

Needham, Joseph, and Nathan Sivin, eds. Science and Civilization in China. Vol. 6, Biology and Biological Technology: Medicine. Cambridge: Cambridge University Press, 1999.

Ne'eman, Yuval, "Astronomy in Sefarad." Wise Observatory, 2005. Available online. URL: http://wise-obs.tau.ac.il/judaism/sefarad.html.

———. "An Evolutionary View of Jewish Humanism." Public address at the 1975 Jewish Educational Convention, Johannesburgh, South Africa.

———. Harmony among the Sciences. Washington, D.C.: ICP, 1976.

Nelli, Rene. L'érotique des troubadours. Toulouse: Privat, 1963.

Nelson, B. N. The Idea of Usury. 2d ed. Chicago: University of Chicago Press, 1969.

———. "Usurer and the Merchant Prince: Italian Businessmen and the Ecclesiastical Law of Restitution." Journal of Economic History 7 (1947): 107–122.

Netanyahu, Benzion. The Origins of the Inquisition in Fifteenth-Century Spain. New York: Random House, 1995.

Netton, I. Muslim Neoplatonists: An Introduction to the Thought of the Brethren of Purity. London: Allen & Unwin, 1982.

Neubauer, Eckhard. Musiker am Hof der fruhen Abbasiden. Dissertation, University of Frankfurt, 1965.

Neuman, Abraham A. The Jews in Spain—Their Social, Political and Cultural Life During the Middle Ages. 2 vols. New York: Octagon Books, 1969.

Neusner, Jacob. Judaism and Christianity in the Age of Constantine: History, Messiah, Israel, and the Initial Confrontation. Chicago: University of Chicago Press, 1987.

———. "New Perspectives on Babylonian Jewry in the Tannaitic Age." In History of the Jews in the Second through Seventh Centuries of the Common Era. Origins of Judaism, edited by Jacob Neusner. Vol. VIII, Part 1, 430–56. New York and London: Garland, 1990.

Newman, A. J., ed. Islamic Medical Wisdom, the Tibb al-a'imma. Translated by Batool Ispahany. London: Muhammadi Trust, 1991.

Newman, Barbara, ed. Voice of the Living Light: Hildegard of Bingen and Her World. Berkeley and Los Angeles: University of California Press, 1998.

Newman, F. X., ed. The Meaning of Courtly Love. Albany, N.Y.: SUNY Press, 1968.

Newton, A. P. Travel and Travellers of the Middle Ages. London: Kegan Paul, Trench, Trubner, 1926.

Newton, William R. "Alchemical Symbolism and Concealment: The Chemical House of Libavius." In The Architecture of Science, edited by Peter Galison and Emily Thompson. Cambridge, Mass.: MIT Press, 2000.

———. "The Philosopher's Egg: Theory and Practice in the Alchemy of Roger Bacon." Micrologus 3 (1995): 75–101.

———. Promethean Ambitions: Alchemy and the Quest to Perfect Nature. Chicago: University of Chicago Press, 2004.

Nicholas, David. The Domestic Life of a Medieval City: Women, Children and the Family in 14th-Century Ghent. Lincoln: University of Nebraska Press, 1985.

———. The Growth of the Medieval City: From Late Antiquity to the Early Fourteenth Century. London and New York: Longman, 1997.

————. *The Later Medieval City, 1300–1500.* London and New York: Longman, 1997.

Nicholas, David N. M. *Town and Countryside; Social, Economic, and Political Pensions in Fourteenth Century Flanders.* Bruges: de Tempel, 1971.

Nicholson, Helen J. *Love, War and the Grail: Templars, Hospitallers and Teutonic Knights in Medieval Epic and Romance.* Leiden, The Netherlands: E. J. Brill, 2004.

Nicholson, Reynold A. *Studies in Islamic Mysticism.* 1921. Reprint, Richmond, U.K.: Curzon Press, 2005.

————. *The Mystics of Islam.* London: Routledge and Kegan Paul, 1966.

Nicol, Antonio T. de. *St. John of the Cross (San Juan de la Cruz): Alchemist of the Soul.* New York: Paragon House, 1989.

Nicol, D. M. "The Byzantine Church and Hellenic Learning in the Fourteenth Century." In *Byzantium: Its Ecclesiastical History and Relations with the Western World.* Vol. 12. London: Variorum Reprints, 1972.

————. *The Last Centuries of Byzantium, 1261–1453.* 2d ed. Cambridge: Cambridge University Press, 1972.

Nicolle, C. David. *Medieval Siege Weapons: Byzantium, the Islamic World, and India A.D. 476–1526.* Oxford: Osprey, 2003.

Nicolle, David. *Medieval Siege Weapons: Western Europe AD 585–1385.* Reprinted, Oxford: Osprey, 2002.

Nicolson, Marjorie. *Science and Imagination.* Ithaca, N.Y.: Cornell University Press, Great Seal Books, 1956.

Nielsen, Hans F. *The Germanic Languages: Origins and Early Dialectal Interrelations.* Tuscaloosa: University of Alabama Press, 1989.

————. *Old English and the Continental Germanic Languages : A Survey of Morphological and Phonological Interrelations.* Innsbruck: Institut für Sprachwissenschaft der Universität Innsbruck, 1985.

Nigg, Walter. *The Heretics.* New York: Knopf, 1962.

Nirenberg, David. *Communities of Violence: Persecution of Minorities in the Middle Ages.* Princeton, N.J.: Princeton University Press, 1998.

Noble, Thomas and Thomas Head, eds. *Soldiers of Christ: Saints and Saints' Lives from Late Antiquity and the Early Middle Ages.* Philadelphia: Pennsylvania State University Press, 1994.

Noonan, J. T., Jr. *Contraception: A History of Its Treatment by Catholic Theologians and Canonists.* Cambridge, Mass.: Harvard University Press, 1966.

————. *The Morality of Abortion: Legal and Historical Perspectives.* Cambridge, Mass.: Harvard University Press, 1970.

Noonan, Thomas S. *The Islamic World, Russia and the Vikings, 750–900: The Numismatic Evidence.* Aldershot, Eng. and Brookfield, Vt.: Ashgate, 1998.

North, John David. *Stars, Minds, and Fate: Essays in Ancient and Medieval Cosmology.* London: Hambledon, 1989.

Norwich, John Julius. *Byzantium.* 3 Vols. London: Viking, 1988–95.

————. *Byzantium. The Decline and Fall.* London: Viking, 1995.

Novak, David. "Maimonides on Judaism and Other Religions": The Samuel H. Goldenson Lecture, February 23, 1997. Hebrew Union College-Jewish Institute of Religion, Cincinnati, Ohio. Available online. URL: http://www.icjs.org/what/njsp/maimonides.html.

Nutting, Anthony. *The Arabs.* New York: Clarkson Potter, 1964.

Nykrog, Per. *Les Fabliaux.* New ed. Geneva: Librairie Droz, 1973.

O'Callaghan, Joseph. *Alfonso X and the Cantigas De Santa Maria: A Poetic Biography. Medieval Mediterranean.* Vol. 16. Leiden, The Netherlands: E. J. Brill, 1998.

O'Donnell, James J. *Augustine, Sinner & Saint: A New Biography.* London: Profile, 2005.

Ogg, Frederic Austin ed. *A Source Book of Medieval History.* New York: American Book Co., 1907.

Oikonomides, N. "Byzantium and the Western Powers in the Thirteenth to Fifteenth Centuries." In *Byzantium and the West c.850–c.1200,* edited by Howard-Johnston, Amsterdam: A. M. Hekkert, 1988.

O'Kane, Bernard. "From Tents to Pavilions: Royal Mobility and Persian Palace Design." *Ars Orientalis* 23 (1993): 249–268.

Oken, Alan. *Pocket Guide to the Tarot.* Freedom, Calif.: Crossing Press, 1996.

Oldenbourg, Zoe. *The Crusades*. London: Phoenix Press, 2003.

Oliver, Prudence. "Islamic Relief Cut Glass: A Suggested Chronology." *Journal of Glass Studies* 3 (1961).

Oman, Sir Charles. *Art of War in the Middle Ages A.D. 378–1515*. Ithaca, N.Y.: Cornell University Press, 1960.

———. *The Great Revolt of 1381*. Oxford: Clarendon Press, 1906.

Origo, Iris. *The Merchant of Prato: Francesco di Marco Datini, 1335–1410*. 1957. Reissue, Boston: David Godine, 1986.

Ormsby, Eric L., ed. *Moses Maimonides and His Time*. Washington, D.C.: Catholic University Press, 1989.

Ostrogorsky, G. *History of the Byzantine State*, 2d ed. New Brunswick N.J.: Rutgers University Press, 1969.

———. *Pour l'histoire de la feodalite byzantine*. Brussels: Editions de l'Institut de philologie et d'histoire orientales et slave, 1954.

O'Sullivan, Daniel E. *Marian Devotion in Thirteenth-Century French Lyric*. Toronto: University of Toronto Press, 2005.

Otto I, Bishop of Freising. *The Deeds of Frederick Barbarossa. By Otto of Freising and his Continuator, Rahewin*. Translated and annotated by Charles Christopher Mierow and Richard Emery. New York: Norton, 1966.

Ouspensky, Leonid. *Theology of the Icon*. New York: SVS Press, 1978.

Ousterhout, Robert G. *Master Builders of Byzantium*. Princeton, N.J.: Princeton University Press, 1999.

Owen, D. R. D. *Evolution of the Grail Legend*. Edinburgh and London: Oliver and Boyd, 1968.

Oxford Dictionary of the Christian Church. Edited by F. L. Cross. 3rd ed. edited by E. A. Livingstone. Oxford: Oxford University Press, 1997.

Oxford University Bodleian Ashmole Manuscript 1439. c. 1450.

Oxford University Bodleian Douce Manuscript 55. c. 1450.

Oxford University Bodleian Laud Manuscript 553. c. 1450.

Pagel, Walter. *Paracelsus: an introduction to philosophical medicine in the era of the Renaissance*. New York: Karger, 1958.

Palmer, R. R., J. C. Colton and L. S. Kramer. *A History of the Modern World*. 9th ed. New York: Knopf, 2002.

Palter, Robert. *Toward Modern Science: Studies in Ancient and Medieval Science*. New York: Farrar, Straus, 1961.

Panofsky, Erwin. *Tomb Sculpture*. New York: Harry N. Abrams, 1964.

Paracelsus. *Astronomica et astrologica opuscula*. Cologne, 1567.

Pardoe, Rosemary, and Darroll Pardoe. *The Female Pope: The Mystery of Pope Joan: The First Complete Documentation of Facts behind the Legend*. New York: Harper Collins, 1988.

Paris, G. "Lancelot du Lac." *Romania 12*, no. 459 (1883).

Parker, J. H., and J. A. S. Parker. *Our English Home: Its Early History and Progress*. Oxford, 1861.

Parkes, James William. *The Conflict of the Church and the Synagogue: A Study in the Origins of Antisemitism*. Cleveland: World Pub. Co., 1961; New York: Athenium, 1981.

Parry, V. J., and M. E. Yapp, eds. *War, Technology and Society in the Middle East*. New York: Oxford University Press, 1975.

Paschos, Emmanuel A. and P. Sotiroudis. *The Schemata of the Stars: Byzantine Astronomy*. River Edge, N.J.: World Scientific, 1998.

The Paston Letters. Edited by James Gairdner. London, 1872–1875, 1896.

The Paston Letters. Edited by Norman Davis. Oxford: Clarendon Press, 1958.

Patai, Raphael. *The Jewish Alchemists*. Princeton, Princeton University Press, 1994.

Patch, H. R. *The Goddess Fortuna in Medieval Literature*. Cambridge, Mass.: Harvard University Press, 1927.

Pavlin, J. "Sunni Kalam and Theological Controversies." In *History of Islamic Philosophy*, edited by S. H. Nasr and O. Leaman, 105–118. London: Routledge, 1996.

Payer, Pierre. *Sex and the Penitentials: The Development of a Sexual Code, 550–1,150*. Toronto: University of Toronto Press, 1984.

Pearson, J. D., ed. *Index Islamicus*. Cambridge: Welteffer; London: Mansell, 1977–93.

Pedersen, J. "Some Aspects of the History of the Madrasa." *Islamic Culture* 3 (1929): 525–537.

Pedersen, J., and G. Makdisi. "Madrasa." *Encyclopaedia of Islam.* 2d ed., Vol. 5. Leiden, The Netherlands: E. J. Brill, 1999, 1,123–1,154.

Pedersen, J., et al. "Masjid." *Encyclopaedia of Islam* 2d ed. Vol 6. Leiden, The Netherlands: E. J. Brill, 1999.

Peers, E. Allison. *The Complete Works of St. Teresa of Jesus.* 3 vols. London: Sheed and Ward, 1972.

Peers, Glenn. *Subtle Bodies: Representing Angels in Byzantium.* Berkeley and Los Angeles: University of California Press, 2002.

Pelikan, Jaroslav. *Mary through the Centuries: Her Place in the History of Culture.* New Haven, Conn.: Yale University Press, 1996.

Pellat, Charles, trans. *Le livre des avares de Gahiz (Kitab al-bukhala).* Paris: Maisonneuve et Larose/UNESCO, 1951.

Pellat, Charles. *The Life and Works of Jahiz.* Translated from the French by D. M. Hawke. London: Routledge & Kegan Paul, 1969.

Perho, I. "The Prophet's Medicine: A Creation of the Muslim Traditionalist Scholar." *Studia Orientiali* 74 (1995).

Peters, Edward, ed. *The First Crusade: The Chronicle of Fulcher of Chartres and Other Source Materials.* Philadelphia: University of Pennsylvania Press, 1971.

Peters, Edward, ed. *Heresy and Authority in Medieval Europe.* Philadelphia: University of Pennsylvania Press, 1980.

Peters, F. E. *Aristotle and the Arabs: The Aristotelian Tradition in Islam.* New York: New York University Press, 1968.

———. *Muhammad and the Origins of Islam.* Albany, N.Y.: State University of New York Press, 1994.

Petersen, Joan M. *Handmaids of the Lord: The Lives of Holy Women.* Cistercian Studies 143. Kalamazoo, Mich.: Cistercian Publications, 1996.

Petit-Dutaillis. *The Feudal Monarchy in France and England, from the Tenth to the Thirteenth Century.* London: Routledge and Kegan Paul, 1949.

Petrosyan, Yuri A., and Oleg F. Akimushkin. *Pages of Perfection: Islamic Paintings and Calligraphy from the Russian Academy of Sciences, Saint Petersburg.* Lugano: Arch Foundation, 1995.

Pevsner, Sir Nikolaus. *Penguin Dictionary of Architecture and Landscape Architecture.* New York: Penguin USA, 2000.

———. *Yorkshire: The West Riding.* Pevsner Buildings of England Series. London: Penguin, 1959.

Pevsner, Sir Nikolaus, John Fleming, and Hugh Honour. *The Penguin Dictionary of Architecture.* 5th ed. London: Penguin Books, 1998.

Pico della Mirandola, Giovanni. *Disputationes adversus astrologiam divinatricem* (1495). Florence: Vallecchi, 1946–52.

Picot, Guillaume, ed. *La Poesie lyrique au moyen age.* Librairie Larousse, 1975.

Pinchart, Alexandre. *Histoire Générale de la Tapisserie.* Paris, 1878–85.

Pinches, J. H. *European Nobility and Heraldry: A Comparative Study of the Titles of Nobility and their Heraldic Exterior Ornaments for each Country, with Historical Notes.* Ramsbury, Wiltshire: Heraldry Today, 1994.

Pipes, Daniel. *Slave Soldiers and Islam.* New Haven, Conn. and London: Yale University Press, 1981.

Pirenne, Henri. *Early Democracies in the Low Countries: Urban Society and Political Conflict in the Middle Ages and the Renaissance.* New York: Harper & Row, 1963.

———. *Medieval Cities: Their Origins and the Revival of Trade.* Translated from the French by Frank D. Halsey. 1925. Reprint, Princeton: Princeton University Press, 1939.

———. *Mohammed and Charlemagne.* 1939. Reprint, New York: W. W. Norton & Company, 2001.

Plant, Richard. *Arabic Coins and How to Read Them.* London: B. A. Seaby, 1973.

Platina. 1475. *De Honesta Voluptate.* Venice: L. De Aguila. Translated by E. B. Andrews as *On Honest Indulgence and Good Health.* St. Louis: Mallinckrodt, 1967.

Platt, Colin. *The Atlas of Medieval Man.* New York: St. Martin's Press, 1979.

———. *The English Medieval Town.* London: Secker and Warburg, 1976.

———. *King Death: The Black Death and Its Aftermath in Late Medieval England.* Toronto: University of Toronto Press, 1996.

———. *Medieval Archaeology in England: A Guide to the Historical Sources.* Isle of Wight: Pinhorns, 1969.

———. *Medieval England: A Social History and Archaeology from the Conquest to 1600 A.D.* London: Routledge, 1996.

———. *Medieval South Hampton, The Port And Trading Company: 1000–1600.* London, Routledge, 1973.

Platts, B. *Origins of Heraldry.* London: Procter Press, 1980.

Plessner, Martin. "Ramadan." *Encyclopaedia of Islam,* 2d ed., Vol. 8. 417–418. Leiden, The Netherlands: E. J. Brill. 1999.

———. "The Natural Sciences and Medicine." In *The Legacy of Islam.* 2d ed., edited by J. Schacht and C. E. Bosworth. Oxford: The Clarendon Press, 1974.

Plucknett, T. F. T. *A Concise History of the Common Law.* 5th ed. Boston: Little, Brown, 1956.

Poché, C. *La musique arabo-andalouse.* Arles: Cité de la musique/Actes Sud, 1995.

———. *Musiques du monde arabe: écoute et découverte.* Paris: Librairie orientaliste Paul Geuthner, 1996.

Poliak. "Classification of Lands in the Islamic Law." *American Journal of Semitic Languages* (1940).

Pontano, Giovanni. *De rebus coelestibus.* Book 13 (1512).

Pope-Hennessy, John. *Italian High Renaissance and Baroque Sculpture.* New York: Phaidon, 1963.

Porète, Marguerite. *The Mirror of Simple Souls.* Classics of Western Spirituality, 79. Translated by Ellen Babinsky. New York: Paulist Press, 1993.

Posner, Raphael, and Israel Ta-Shema. *The Hebrew Book: A Historical Survey.* Jerusalem: Keter, 1975.

Postan, Michael M. *The Medieval Economy and Society.* London: Weidenfeld and Nicolson, 1972.

———. *Medieval Trade and Finance.* Cambridge: Cambridge University Press, 1973.

Potkay, Monica Brzezinski, and Regula Meyer Evitt. *Minding the Body: Women and Literature in the Middle Ages, 800–1500.* London and New York: Twayne, 1997.

Pouzet, L. "Prise de position autour du "sama'" en Orient musulman au VIIe/XIIe siecle." *Studia Islamica,* 57 (1983): 193–234.

Power, Eileen. *Medieval English Nunneries circa 1275 to 1535.* Cambridge: Cambridge University Press, 1922.

———. *Medieval People.* 10th ed. London: Methuen, 1963.

———. *Medieval Women.* Edited by Michael M. Postan. Cambridge: Cambridge University Press, 1975.

———. "Some Women Practitioners of Medicine in the Middle Ages." *Proceedings of the Royal Society of Medicine* 15 (1922): 17–34.

———. *The Wool Trade in English Medieval History.* Oxford: Oxford University Press, 1941.

Power, Eileen, and Michael M. Postan. *Studies in English Trade in the 15th Century.* London: Routledge and Kegan Paul, 1933.

Prawdin, Michael. *The Mongol Empire.* London: Allen and Unwin 1961.

Prawer, Joshua. *The History of the Jews in the Latin Kingdom of Jerusalem.* Oxford, Clarendon Press and New York: Oxford University Press, 1988.

Prendergast, William J. *The Maqamat of Badi Al-Zaman Al-Hamadhani.* London, 1915.

Preston, James J., ed. *Mother Worship and Theme Variations.* Chapel Hill: University of North Carolina Press, 1982.

Preziosi, D. "Introduction: Power, Structure, and Architectural Function." In *The Ottoman City and Its Parts: Urban Structure and Social Order,* (*Subsidia Balcanica, Islamica Et Turcica* 3), edited by I. A. Bierman, R. A. Abou-El-Haj and D. Preziosi. New York: Aristide D. Caratzas, 1991.

Pritchard, V. *English Medieval Graffiti.* Cambridge: Cambridge University Press, 1969.

Prochazka, A. B. *Mosques.* Zurich: Muslim Architecture Research Program, 1986.

Proctor, Robert. *The Printing of Greek in the 15th Century.* London: Oxford University Press, 1900.

Przybilski, Martin. "Traces of Cultural Transfer Between Jews and Christians in German Literature of the High and Late Middle Ages." In *Bulletin des Simon-Dubnow-Instituts* 3 (2001): 85–89.

Putnam, George H. *Books and Their Makers During the Middle Ages.* 1896. Reprinted, New York: Hillary House, 1962.

Quennell, Marjorie, and C. H. B. Quennell. *A History of Everyday Things in England.* London: Batsford, 1948.

Quennell, Peter, trans. *The Book of the Marvels of India by Buzurg ibn Shahriyar.* London: Routledge, 1928.

Rabbat, Nasser. "The Dialogic Dimension in Umayyad Art." *Res: Anthropology and Aesthetics* 43 (spring 2003): 78–94.

————. "The Dome of the Rock Revisited: Some Remarks on al-Wasiti's Accounts." *Muqarnas* 10 (1993): 67–75 (Special Issue: Festschrift for Oleg Grabar).

Rabinowitz, Louis. *Jewish Merchant Adventurers: A Study of the Radanites*. London: Edward Goldston, 1948.

Racy, Ali Jihad, and Jack Logan. "Arab Music." Available online. URL: http://trumpet.sdsu.edu/M151/Arab_Music1.html.

Radding, Charles M., and William W. Clark. *Medieval Architecture, Medieval Learning: Builders and Masters in the Age of Romanesque and Gothic*. New Haven, Conn.: Yale University Press, 1994.

Rafi, Grafman and Myriam Rosen-Ayalon. "The Two Great Syrian Umayyad Mosques: Jerusalem and Damascus." *Muqarnas* 16 (1999):1–15.

Rageb, F. J., and Sally P. Rageb. *Tradition, Transmission, Transformation: Proceedings of Two Conferences on pre-Modern Science Held at the University of Oklahoma*. Leiden, The Netherlands: E. J. Brill, 1996.

Rahman, Fazlur. *Health and Medicine in the Islamic Tradition: Change and Identity*. New York: Crossroad, 1987.

————. *Islam*. 2d ed. Chicago: University of Chicago Press, 1979.

————. *Major Themes of the Qur'an*. Minneapolis: Bibliotheca Islamica, 1980.

Raitt, Jill, ed. *Christian Spirituality II: High Middle Ages and Reformation*. New York: Crossroad, 1987.

Randall, Lilian. *Images in the Margins of Gothic Manuscripts*. Berkeley: University of California Press, 1966.

Raphael, Chaim. *The Sephardi Story—a Celebration of Jewish History*. London: Vallentine Mitchell, 1991.

Rapoport, Yossef. *Marriage, Money and Divorce in Medieval Islamic Society*. Cambridge Studies in Islamic Civilization. Cambridge: University of Oxford, 2005.

Rashdall, Hastings. *The Universities of Europe in the Middle Ages*. 1895. New edition, Oxford: Clarendon Press, 1936.

Ravitzky, Aviezer. "Prohibited Wars in the Jewish Tradition." In *Ethics of War and Peace*, edited by T. Nardin, 115–128. Princeton, N.J.: Princeton University Press, 1996.

Raw, Barbara C. *Trinity and Incarnation in Anglo-Saxon Art and Thought*. Cambridge, Cambridge University Press, 1997.

Raymond of Capua, *De Catharina Senensi virgine de poenitentia S. Dominici* 'AASS April 30: 853–959; English translation: *The Life of Catherine of Siena by Raymond of Capua*, translated by Conleath Kearns. Washington D.C.: Dominicana Publications, 1994.

Rayter, Zenon, *History of Breast Cancer Surgery*. Cambridge: Cambridge University Press, 2003.

al-Razi, Abu Bakr Muhammad b. Zakariyya. *The Spiritual Physick of Rhazes*, translated by A. J. Arberry. London: John Murray, 1950.

————. *Traité sur le calcul dans les reins et dans la vessie*. Translated by P. de Koning. Leiden, The Netherlands: E. J. Brill, 1896.

————. *A Treatise on Smallpox and Measles*. Translated by W. A. Greenhill. London: Sydenham Society, 1848.

Reese, Gustave. *Music in the Middle Ages*. New York: W. W. Norton, 1940.

————. *Music in the Renaissance*. New York: W. W. Norton, 1959.

Reeves, Marjorie. *The Influence of Prophecy in the Later Middle Ages: A Study in Joachimism*. Notre Dame, Ind. and London: University of Notre Dame Press, 1969, 1993.

Regimen Sanitatis. Strassburg: Mathias Hupfuff, 1513.

Reilly, Bernard F. *The Conquest of Christian and Muslim Spain: 1131–1157*. Cambridge, Mass.: Blackwell, 1992.

————. *The Medieval Spains*. Cambridge: Cambridge University Press, 1993, 1994.

Remensnyder, Amy G. *Remembering Kings Past: Monastic Foundation Legends in Medieval Southern France*. Ithaca, N.Y.: Cornell University Press, 1995.

Renard, John. *Islam and the Heroic Image: Themes in Literature and the Visual Arts*. Columbia: University of South Carolina Press, 1993.

Renouard, Yves. *Les hommes d'affaires italiens du Moyen Age*. Edited by Bernard Guillemain. Paris: Colin, 1968.

Reti, Ladislao. *The Unknown Leonardo*. New York: McGraw Hill, 1974.

Reuther, Rosemary. "Misogynism and Virginal Feminism in the Fathers of the Church." In *Religion* and Sexism, edited by Rosemary Ruether. New York: Simon & Schuster, 1974.

Reynolds, Dwight F., "Al-Andalus." Interview on radio program, Afropop Worldwide: "The Musical Legacy of Al-Andalus, Part 1: Europe," Madrid: 2004. Available online. URL: http://www.afropop.org/multi/interview/ID/57/Al-Andalus-Dwight+Reynolds.

Reynolds, Dwight F., et al., eds. Interpreting the Self: Autobiography in the Arabic Literary Tradition. Berkeley and Los Angeles: University of California Press, 2001.

Reynolds, Susan. Fiefs and Vassals: The Medieval Evidence Reinterpreted. 2001.

———. Kingdoms and Communities in Western Europe, 900–1300, 2d. edition. Oxford: Oxford University Press, 1997.

Richards, Donald S., ed. Islam and the Trade of Asia: A Colloquium. Philadelphia: University of Pennsylvania Press, 1970.

Richardson, Henry G. The English Jewry under the Angevin Kings. London: Methuen, 1960.

Riche, Pierre. Education and Culture in the Barbarian West. Columbia: University of South Carolina Press, 1976.

Riches, Samantha J. E., and Sarah Salih, eds. Gender and Holiness. Men, Women and Saints in Late Medieval Europe. London: Routledge, 2002.

Rickard, Peter. A History of the French Language. 2d ed. London and New York: Routledge, 1989. Reprint, 1996.

Riddle, John M. Contraception and Abortion from the Ancient World to the Renaissance. Cambridge, Mass.: Harvard University Press, 1992.

———. Eve's Herbs: A History of Contraception and Abortion in the West. Cambridge, Mass.: Harvard University Press, 1997.

Rietbergen, Peter, Europe: A Cultural History, London: Routledge, 2006.

Rigby, Paul. Original Sin in Augustine's Confessions. Ottawa: University of Ottawa Press, 1987.

Riley, H. T. Memorials of London and London Life. London: Longmans, Green & Co., 1868.

Riley-Smith, Jonathan. The First Crusade and the Idea of Crusading. London: Athlone, 1986.

Rippin, Andrew. Approaches to the History of the Interpretation of the Qur'an. Oxford: Clarendon Press, 1988.

———. "Literary Analysis of Qur'an, Tafsir, and Sira: The Methodologies of John Wansbrough." In Approaches to Islam in Religious Studies, edited by R. C. Martin. Tucson: University of Arizona Press, 1985.

Rispoli, G., C. Serarcangeli, and F. Armellino, "Ancient Herniotomy Surgical Instruments: From Celsus to the Eighteenth Century." Hernia 4, no. 3 (2000): 171–174.

Rivers, Theodore John. Laws of the Alamans and Bavarians. Philadelphia: University of Pennsylvania Press, 1977.

Robbins, Rossell Hope. The Encyclopedia of Witchcraft and Demonology. New York: Bonanza Books, 1959.

Roberson, Barbara Allen. "Averroes, Ibn Rushd." In The Concise Oxford Dictionary of Politics, edited by Iain McLean and Alistair McMillan. Oxford: Oxford University Press, 2003.

Robertson, Durant Waite. The Works of Geoffrey Chaucer. Boston: Houghton Mifflin, 1957.

Robinson, Neal. Discovering the Qur'an: A Contemporary Approach to a Veiled Text. 2d ed. Washington, D.C.: Georgetown University Press, 2003.

Robson, J., trans. and ed., as described by al-Mufadded ibn Salama (9th c.) Ancient Arabian Musical Instruments. Glasgow, The Civic Press, 1938.

Robson, J. R. K. Food, Ecology, and Culture: Readings in the Anthropology of Dietary Practices. New York: Gordon & Breach, 1980.

Rockhill, W. W., ed. and trans. The Journey of William of Rubruck to the Eastern Parts of the World, 1253–55, as Narrated by Himself, with Two Accounts of the Earlier Journey of John of Pian de Carpine. London: Hakluyt Society, 1900.

Roden, Claudia. The Book of Jewish Food: An Odyssey from Samarkand to New York. New York: Knopf, 1996.

Rodinson, M. "Ghida." Encyclopaedia of Islam, 2d ed. Vol. 2. 1,057–1,072. Leiden, The Netherlands: E. J. Brill, 1999.

Rodley, L. Byzantine Art and Architecture: An Introduction. Cambridge: Cambridge University Press, 1994.

Rogers, Michael. The Spread of Islam. New York: Elsevier-Phaidon, 1976.

Roman, Christopher. Domestic Mysticism in Margery Kempe and Dame Julian of Norwich: The

Transformation of Christian Spirituality in the Late Middle Ages. Ceredigion, U.K., and Lewiston, N.Y.: Edwin Mellen Press, 2005.

Roolvink, R. *Historical Atlas of the Muslim Peoples*. Amsterdam: Djambatan, 1957.

Roover, Raymond de. *L'Evolution de la lettre de Change*. Paris: S.E.V.P.E.N., 1953.

———. *Money, Banking, and Credit in Medieval Bruges*. Cambridge, Mass.: Medieval Academy of America, 1948.

———. *The Rise and Decline of the Medici Bank, 1397–1494*. Cambridge, Mass.: Medieval Academy of America, 1963.

Rosenthal, Franz. *Greek Philosophy in the Arab World*. Aldershot, U.K.: Variorum, 1990.

Rosenthal, Franz. *The Herb: Hashish Versus Medieval Muslim Society*. Leiden, The Netherlands: E. J. Brill, 1971.

———. *Science and Medicine in Islam: A Collection of Essays*. London: Variorum Reprints, 1990.

Rosenthal, Monroe, and Isaac Mozeson. *Wars of the Jews: A Military History from Biblical to Modern Times*. New York: Hippocrene Books, 1990.

Ross, David John A. *Illustrated Medieval Alexander Books in Germany and the Netherlands: A Study in Comparative Iconography*. Cambridge: Cambridge University Press, 1971.

Roth, Cecil. *History of the Jews in England*. Oxford: Clarendon Press, 1949.

———. *History of the Jews in Italy*. Philadelphia: Jewish Publication Society of America, 1946.

———. *A History of the Marranos*. New York: Harper & Row, 1932.

———. *The Jews in the Renaissance*. New York: Harper & Row, 1959.

Roth, Cecil, and Bezalel Narkiss. *Jewish Art*. Greenwich, Conn.: New York Graphic Society, 1971.

Roth, Norman. *Conversos, Inquisition, and the Expulsion of the Jews from Spain*. Madison: University of Wisconsin Press, 1995.

———. *Jews, Visigoths, and Muslims in Medieval Spain: Cooperation and Conflict*. Leiden: E. J. Brill, 1994.

Roth, Norman, ed. *Routledge Encyclopedias of the Middle Ages*. Vol. 7, *Medieval Jewish Civilization: An Encyclopedia*. New York: Routledge, 2003.

Rouaze, Isabelle. *Un Atelier de Distillation du Moyen Age*. Paris: Comite travaux historiques scientifiques, 1978.

Rowland, Beryl. "Exhuming Trotula, Sapiens Matrona of Salerno." *Florilegium* 1 (1979): 42–57.

———. *Medieval Woman's Guide to Health: The First English Gynecological Handbook*. Ohio: Kent State University Press, 1981.

Rubens, Alfred. *A History of Jewish Costume*. London: Weidenfeld and Nicolson, 1973.

Rubin, Miri. *Corpus Christi: The Eucharist in Late Medieval Culture*. Cambridge and New York: Cambridge University Press, 1991.

Ruck, E. H. *An Index of Themes and Motifs in Twelfth-Century French Arthurian Poetry*. Cambridge, Mass.: D. S. Brewer, 1991.

Ruderman, David B., and Giuseppe Veltri, eds. *Cultural Intermediaries: Jewish Intellectuals in Early Modern Italy*. Philadelphia: University of Pennsylvania Press, 2004.

Ruelland, Jacques G., Cornellia Fuykschot, and Jeanne Poulin. *Holy War: The History of an Idea*. Ceredigion, U.K. and Lewiston, N.Y.: Edwin Mellen Press, 2007.

Ruether, Rosemary Radford. *Mary: The Feminine Face of the Church*. Philadelphia: Westminster Press, 1977.

Ruiz, Juan, Arcipreste de Hita. *Libro de Buen Amor*. Madrid: Castalia, 1980.

Ruiz, Teofilio F. "Almogavres." In *Dictionary of the Middle Ages*, edited by Joseph R. Strayer. 12 vols. New York: Scribner, 1982–89.

Runciman, Steven. *Byzantine Civilisation*. Cambridge: Edward Arnold, 1966.

———. *The Emperor Romanus Lecapenus and His Reign: A Study of Tenth-Century Byzantium*. Sydney: Cambridge University Press, 1988.

———. *History of the Crusades*. 3 vols. Cambridge: Cambridge University Press, 1954.

———. *The Sicilian Vespers: A History of the Mediterranean World in the Later Thirteenth Century*. Cambridge: Cambridge University Press, 1958.

Runes, Dagobert. *Treasury of Philosophy*. New York: Philosophical Library, 1955.

Russell, Frederick H. *The Just War in the Middle Ages*. Cambridge and New York: Cambridge University Press, 1975.

Russell, Jeffrey Burton. *A History of Medieval Christianity: Prophecy and Order*. New York: Thomas Y. Crowell Company, 1968.

Russell, John. *Boke of Nurture.* In J. J. Furnivall *Early English Meals and Manners.* London: Early English Text Society, N. Trubner & Co., 1868.

Ruusbroec, John. *The Spiritual Espousals and Other Works.* In *The Classics of Western Spirituality.* Edited by James A. Wiseman. New York: Paulist, 1985.

Ryerson, Kathryn. *Business, Banking, and Finance in Medieval Montpellier.* Toronto: Pontifical Institute of Mediaeval Studies, 1985.

Rypka, J. *The Cambridge History of Iran.* Cambridge: Cambridge University Press, 1968.

Saalman, Howard. *Medieval Cities.* New York: George Braziller, 1968.

Sachar, Howard M. *Farewell España: The World of the Sephardim Remembered.* New York: Knopf, 1994.

Sachau, Edward, trans. *Alberuni's India.* Edited by Ainslie Embree. New York: Norton, 1971.

Sachs, C. *The History of Musical Instruments.* Mineola, N.Y.: Dover Publications, 2006.

Sackville-West, Vita. *Saint Joan of Arc.* New York: Literary Guild, 1936.

de Sacy, Silvestre. *Memoire sur la dynastie des Assassins et sur l'origine de leur nom.* 1809.

Sadek, Mahmoud. *The Arabic Materia Medica of Dioscorides.* St Jean-Chrystosome, Canada: Les Editions du Sphinx, 1983.

Sadie, Stanley, and John Tyrrell, eds. *The New Grove Dictionary of Music and Musicians.* London: Oxford University Press, 1980.

Sagi, Avi. "The Punishment of Amalek in Jewish Tradition: Coping with the Moral Problem." *Harvard Theological Review* 87, no. 3 (July 1994): 323–346.

Sahas, Daniel J. *Icon and Logos: Sources in Eighth-Century Iconoclasm.* Toronto: University of Toronto Press, 1986.

Saidi, Ahmad. *Ruba'iyat of Omar Khayyam.* Berkeley: Asian Humanities Press, 1991.

Sakr, Ahmad H. *Feast, Festivities and Holidays.* Lombard, Ill.: Foundation for Islamic Knowledge, 1999.

Saliba, George. "Astrology/Astronomy, Islamic." In *Dictionary of the Middle Ages,* edited by Joseph R. Strayer. 12 vols. New York: Scribner, 1982–89.

———. *A History of Arabic Astronomy: Planetary Theories during the Golden Age of Islam.* New York: New York University Press, 1994.

Salter, Elizabeth, and Derek Pearsall, eds. *Piers Plowman.* Evanston, Ill.: Northwestern University Press, 1969.

Salzman, L. F. *Building in England Down to 1540: A Documentary History.* 1952. Reprint, Oxford University Press, 1992.

Samuel, Edgar. "Was Moyse's Hall, Bury St. Edmunds, a Jew's House?" *The Jewish Historical Society of England Transactions* 25 Miscellanies X, 1977.

Sánchez Sánchez, Manuel Ambrosio. "Vernacular Preaching in Spanish, Portuguese and Catalan." In *The Sermon, Typologie des Sources du Moyen Âge Occidental,* edited by Beverly Mayne Kienzle, 759–858. Turnhout: Brepols, 2000.

Sanders, Paula. "Feasts and Festivals, Islamic." In *Dictionary of the Middle Ages,* edited by Joseph R. Strayer. 12 vols. New York: Scribner, 1982–89.

———. *Ritual, Politics, and the City in Fatimid Cairo.* Albany, N.Y.: Suny Press, 1994.

Sapori, Armando. *The Italian Merchant in the Middle Ages.* Translated by Patricia Anne Kennen. New York: Norton, 1970.

Sarton, George. *A History of Science.* 1952–1959. Reprint, New York: W. W. Norton, 1970.

———. *A History of Science.* New York: John Wiley, 1959.

———. *Introduction to the History of Science.* Baltimore: Williams & Wilkins, 1927, 1931, 1947.

Saunders, J. J. *A History of Medieval Islam.* London: Routledge and Kegan Paul, 1980.

Savage, Ann. *The Anglo Saxon Chronicles.* New York: Barnes & Noble, 1997.

Savage-Smith, Emilie. "Islamic Magical Texts vs. Islamic Magical Artifacts," *Societas Magica Newsletter* 11 (fall 2003): 1–6.

Savage-Smith, Emilie, and Marion B. Smith. *Islamic Geomancy and a Thirteenth-Century Divinatory Device.* Studies in Near Eastern Culture and Society, Malibu, Calif.: Undena Publications, 1980.

Savonarola, Girolamo. *Contra L'astrologia divinatrice* (1497).

Sawa, George Dimitri. "Music, Middle Eastern." In *Dictionary of the Middle Ages,* edited by Joseph R. Strayer. 12 vols. New York: Scribner, 1982–89.

———. *Music Performance Practice in the Early 'Abbasid Era.* Toronto: Pontifical Institute of Mediaeval Studies, 1989.

al-Sawwaf, Mujahid M. "Early Tafsir—A Survey of Qur'anic Commentary up to 150 A.H. "In *Islamic Perspectives*, edited by K. Ahmad and Z. I. Ansari, 135–145. Leicester: Islamic Foundation, 1979.

Sayers, Dorothy L. *Song of Roland.* New York: Viking Press, 1957.

Scanlon, George T., ed. and trans. *Ansari, a Muslim Manual of War, Tafrij al-Kurub fi tadbir al-hurub.* Cairo: The American University at Cairo Press, 1961.

Scerrato, Umberto. *Monuments of Civilization: Islam.* New York: Grosset & Dunlap, 1976.

Schacht, J. "Hiyal." *Encyclopaedia of Islam,* 2d ed. Vol. 3. Leiden, The Netherlands: E. J. Brill, 1999, 510–512.

———. *An Introduction to Islamic Law.* Oxford: Oxford University Press, 1964.

Schaefer, Claude. *The Hours of Etienne Chevalier.* New York: George Braziller, 1971.

Schäfer, Peter. "Jews and Christians in the High Middle Ages: *The Book of the Pious.*" In *The Jews of Europe in the Middle Ages,* edited by Christoph Cluse, 29–41. Turnhout: Brepols, 2004.

Schama, Simon. *A History of Britain: At the Edge of the World, 3500 BC–1603 AD.* New York: Hyperion, 2000.

Scheindlin, Raymond P. *The Gazelle: Medieval Hebrew Poems on God, Israel and the Soul.* New York: Oxford University Press, 1999.

Schevill, Ferdinand. *Medieval and Renaissance Florence.* New York: Harper & Row, 1963.

Schimmel, Annemarie. *As Through a Veil: Mystical Poetry in Islam.* London: Oneworld Publications, 2001.

———. *Islam: An Introduction.* New York: State University of New York Press, 1992.

———. *Mystical Dimensions of Islam.* Chapel Hill: The University of North Carolina Press, 1975.

Schipperges, Heinrich. *The World of Hildegard of Bingen: Her Life, Times, and Visions,* translated by John Cumming. Collegeville, Minn.: The Liturgical Press, 1999.

Schirmann, Jefim. "Samuel Hannagid, the Man, the Soldier, the Politician." *Jewish Social Studies* 9, no. 2 (April 1951): 99–126.

Schirokauer, Conrad. *China's Examination Hell.* New Haven, Conn.: Yale University Press, 1981.

Schmemann, A. "Symbols and Symbolism in the Orthodox Liturgy." In *Orthodox Theology and Diakonia.* Brookline, Mass.: Hellenic College Press, 1981.

Schmidt, Jean-Claude. *Ghosts in the Middle Ages: The Living and the Dead in Medieval Society.* Chicago: University of Chicago Press, 1998.

Schmitt, Miriam, and Linda Kulzer, eds. *Medieval Women Monastics: Wisdom's Wellsprings.* Collegeville, Minn.: Liturgical Press, 1996.

Scholem, Gershom G. *Jewish Gnosticism, Merkabah Mysticism and Talmudic Tradition* New York: The Jewish Theological Seminary of America, 1965.

———. *Kabbalah.* New York: Quadrangle and New American Library, 1974.

———. *Major Trends in Jewish Mysticism.* New York: Schocken Books, 1974.

———. *Zohar: The Book of Splendor.* New York: Schocken Books, 1963.

Schoy, K. "Geography of the Muslims in the Middle Ages." *Geographical Review* 14 (1924).

Schroeder, H. J. *Disciplinary Decrees of the General Councils: Text, Translation and Commentary.* St. Louis, Mo.: B. Herder, 1937.

Scott, Karen. "Catherine of Siena, *Apostola.*" *Church History* 61 (1992): 34–46.

Scott, Mary A. *Elizabethan Translations from the Italian.* Boston: Houghton Mifflin, 1916.

Seay, Albert. *Music in the Medieval World.* 2nd ed. Englewood Cliffs, N.J.: Prentice Hall, 1975.

Sed-Rajna, Gabrielle. *The Hebrew Bible in Medieval Illuminated Manuscripts.* New York: Rizzoli, 1987.

Sells, Michael A. *Early Islamic Mysticism: Sufi, Qur'an, Mi'raj, Poetic and Theological Writings.* New Jersey: Paulist Press, 1996.

Sergeant, R. B. *Islamic Textiles.* Beirut: Librairie du Liban, 1972.

———. *Islamic Textiles: Material for a History up to the Mongol Conquest.* Beirut: Librairie du Liban, 1972.

Setton, Kenneth M. *Catalan Domination of Athens, 1311–1388.* Revised edition. London: Variorum, 1975.

Sevcenko, Margaret Bentley, ed. *Theories and Principles of Design in the Architecture of Islamic Societies.* Cambridge: Aga Khan Program for Islamic Architecture, 1988.

Shahar, Shulamith. *The Fourth Estate: A History of Women in the Middle Ages*. London: Methuen, 1983.

Shapiro, N. R. and J. Wadsworth. *The Comedy of Eros: Medieval French Guides to the Art of Love*. Urbana: University of Illinois Press, 1971.

Sharon, M., *Black Banners from the East*. Leiden: E. J. Brill, 1983.

Shatzmiller, Joseph. *Shylock Reconsidered: Jews, Moneylending, and Medieval Society*. Berkeley: University of California Press, c. 1990.

Shatzmiller, Maya. *Labour in the Medieval Islamic World*. Leiden, The Netherlands: E. J. Brill, 1994.

Shepkaru, Shmuel. "To Die for God: Martyrs' Heaven in Hebrew and Latin Crusade Narratives." *Speculum* 77 no. 2 (2002): 311–341.

Shestack, Alan. *Fifteenth Century Engravings of Northern Europe from the National Gallery of Art Washington D.C.* Washington, D.C.: National Gallery of Art, 1967.

Shiloah, Amnon. *Caractéristiques de l'art vocal arabe au Moyen-Age*. Tel-Aviv: Israel Music Institute, 1963.

———. *The Dimension of Music in Islamic and Jewish Culture*. Aldershot, Eng.: Variorum, 1993.

———. "The Meeting of Christian, Jewish and Muslim Musical Cultures on the Iberian Peninsula (before 1492)." *AcM* 64 (1991): 14–20.

———. *Music in the World of Islam*. Aldershot: Scholar Press, 1995.

———. "Notions d'esthétique dans les traités arabes sur la musique." *Cahiers de musique traditionnelles* 7 (1994): 51–74.

———. "Réflexions sur la danse artistique musulmane au Moyen-Age." *Cahiers de civilisation médiévale* 5 (1962): 463–474.

———. *The Theory of Music in Arabic Writings (c. 900–1900): Descriptive Catalogue of Manuscripts in Libraries of Europe and the U.S.A.* Munich: G. Henle Verlag, 1979.

Shopkow, Leah. *History and Community: Norman Historical Writing in the Eleventh and Twelfth Centuries*. Washington, D.C.: Catholic University of America Press, 1997.

Shoshan, Boaz. "On Costume and Social History in Medieval Islam." In *The Medieval Levant: Studies in Memory of Eliyahu Ashtor (1914–1984)*, edited by B. Z. Kedar and A. L. Udovitch. *Special Issue of Asian and African Studies: Journal of the Israel Oriental Society* 22 (November 1988), 35–51.

Shumaker, Wayne. *The Occult Sciences in the Renaissance: A Study in Intellectual Patterns*. Berkeley: University of California Press, 1972.

Sigerist, Henry. *History of Medicine*. Oxford: Oxford University Press, 1961.

Simkin, Colin. *The Traditional Trade of Asia*. London: Oxford University Press, 1968.

Simon, Norton. *Gothic and Renaissance Sculpture and Works of Art*. New York: Parke-Bernet Galleries, 1971.

Simonsen, D. "Les Marchands juifs appelés 'Radanites.'" *Revue des Etudes Juives* 54 (1907).

Simonsohn, Schlomo. *History of the Jews in the Duchy of Mantua*. New York and Jerusalem: Ktav, 1977.

Singer, Charles. *From Magic to Science*. New York: Dover, 1958.

———. "The Herbal in Antiquity and Its Transmission to Later Ages." *Journal of Hellenic Studies* 47 (1921).

Singman, Geoffrey, and Will McLean. *Daily Life in Chaucer's England*. Westport, Conn.: Greenwood Press, 1995.

Siraisi, Nancy G. *Avicenna in Renaissance Italy: The Canon and Medical Teaching in Italian Universities after 1500*. Princeton, N.J.: Princeton University Press, 1987.

———. *Medieval and Early Renaissance Medicine*. Chicago: Chicago University Press, 1990.

———. "The Music of Pulse in the Writings of Italian Academic Physicians." *Speculum* 50 (1975).

———. *Taddeo Alderotti and His Pupils: Two Generations of Italian Medical Learning*. Princeton, N.J.: Princeton University Press, 1981.

Sirat, Colette. *A History of Jewish Philosophy in the Middle Ages*. Cambridge and New York: Cambridge University Press, 1985.

Skal, David J. *Death Makes a Holiday: A Cultural History of Halloween*. New York: Bloomsbury USA, 2002.

Smail, Daniel Lord. *Imaginary Cartographies: Possession and Identity in Late Medieval Marseille*. Ithaca, N.Y.: Cornell University Press, 2000.

Smail, R. C. *Crusading Warfare (1097–1193)*. Cambridge: Cambridge University Press, 1956.

Smalley, Beryl. *The Study of the Bible in the Middle Ages*. Oxford: Blackwell, 1952.

Smith, Charles E. *Papal Enforcement of Some Medieval Marriage Laws*. University, La.: 1940. Reprint, Port Washington, N.Y.: Kennikat Press, 1972.

Smith, David Eugene, and Louis Charles Karpinski. *The Hindu-Arabic Numerals*. Boston: Ginn, 1911.

Smith, Jacqueline. "Robert of Arbrissel: Procurator Mulierum." In *Medieval Women*, edited by Derek Baker. Oxford: Blackwell, 1978.

Smith, Margaret. "Rabi'a al-Adawiyya al-Qaysiyya." *Encyclopaedia of Islam*, 2d ed. Vol. 8: 354–355. Leiden, The Netherlands: E. J. Brill, 1999.

———. *Rabia the Mystic and Her Fellow-Saints in Islam: Being the Life and Teachings of Rabia al-Adawiyya Al-Qaysiyya of Basra Together with Some Accounts of the Place of the Women Saints in Islam*. Cambridge and New York: Cambridge University Press, 1984.

———. *Readings from the Mystics of Islam*. London: Luzac, 1950.

Smith, Margaret, comp. *The Sufi Path of Love: An Anthology of Sufism*. London: Luzac, 1954.

Smyser, H. M. "Ibn Fadlan's Account of the Rus with Some Commentary and Some Allusions to Beowulf." In *Franciplegius: Medieval and Linguistic Studies in Honor of Francis Peabody Magoun, Jr.*, edited by Jess B. Bessinger, Jr., and Robert P. Creed. New York: New York University Press, 1965.

Snyder, James. *Medieval Art: Painting, Sculpture, Architecture, 4th–14th Century*. New York: Prentice Hall, 1988.

Soloveitchik, Haym. "Religious Law and Change: The Medieval Ashkenazic Example." *AJS Review* 12, No. 2 (autumn, 1987): 205–221.

Soucek, Priscilla, ed. *Content and Context of Visual Arts in the Islamic World*. University Park: Pennsylvania State University Press, 1988.

Soucek, Priscilla P. "Solomon's Throne, Solomon's Bath: Model or Metaphor." *Ars Orientalis* 23 (1993): 109–134.

Souchal, G., and F. Salet. *Masterpieces Of Tapestry*. Paris and New York: Metropolitan Museum of Art, 1973.

Sourdel, D. "Bayt al-'Ilm." *Encyclopaedia of Islam*, 2d ed. Vol. 2: 127. Leiden, The Netherlands: E. J. Brill, 1999.

———. "Bayt al-Hikma." *Encyclopaedia of Islam*, 2d ed. Vol. 2: 126. Leiden, The Netherlands: E. J. Brill, 1999.

Sourdel-Thomine, J. "Hammam." *Encyclopaedia of Islam*, 2d ed. Vol. 3: 139–145. Leiden, The Netherlands: E. J. Brill, 1999.

Southern, R. W. *The Making of the Middle Ages*. New Haven, Conn.: Yale University Press, 1953.

———. *Medieval Humanism*. Oxford: Blackwell, 1970.

———. *Western Views of Islam in the Middle Ages*. Cambridge, Mass.: Harvard University Press, 1980.

Spade, Paul Vincent, ed. *The Cambridge Companion to Ockham*. Cambridge and New York: Cambridge University Press, 1999.

Sparti, Barbara, ed. *Guglielmo Ebreo of Pesaro: On the Practice or Art of Dancing*. Oxford: Oxford University Press, 1993.

Spink, M. S., and G. L. Lewis, *Albucasis on Surgery and Instruments*. London: Wellcome Institute of the History of Medicine, 1974.

Spitzer, L. *Classical and Christian Ideas of World Harmony*. Baltimore: Johns Hopkins University Press, 1963.

Spoto, Donald. *The Reluctant Saint*. New York: Viking, 2002.

Spufford, Peter. *Money and Its Use in Medieval Europe*. Cambridge: Cambridge University Press, 1988.

———. *Power and Profit: The Merchant in Medieval Europe*. London: Thames & Hudson, 2002.

Starr, J. "Jewish Life in Crete under the Rule of Venice." *Proceedings of the American Academy for Jewish Research* 12 (1942).

Steel, A. B. *Richard II*. Cambridge: Cambridge University Press, 1941.

Steenberghen, Fernand van. *Aristotle in the West: The Origins of Latin Aristotelianism*. New York: Humanities Press, 1970.

Steenberghen, Fernand van, editor. *St. Thomas Aquinas and Radical Aristotelianism*. Washington, D.C.: Catholic University of America Press, 1980.

Steffens, Franz. *Lateinische Paleographie*. Berlin and Leipzig: Verlag von Walter De Gruyter, 1929.

Stenton, Frank. *The Bayeux Tapestry*. London: Phaidon Press, 1965.

Stern, S. M. *Studies in Early Isma'ilism*. Leiden, The Netherlands: E. J. Brill, 1983.

Stetkevych, Suzanne Pinckney. *The Poetics of Islamic Legitimacy [electronic resource]: Myth, Gender, and*

Ceremony in the Classical Arabic Ode. Blooming-ton: Indiana University Press, 2002.

Stewart, Pamela J. and Andrew Strathern, eds. *Contesting Rituals: Islam and Practices of Identity-Making.* Durham, N.C.: Carolina Academic Press, 2005.

Stillman, Norman A. *East-West Relations in the Islamic Mediterranean in the Early Eleventh Century: A Study in the Geniza Correspondence of the House of Ibn Awkal.* Ph.D. Diss. Philadelphia: University of Pennsylvania Press, 1970.

———. "The Jew in the Medieval Islamic City." In *The Jews of Medieval Islam: Community, Society, and Identity,* edited by Daniel Frank. Leiden and New York: E. J. Brill, 1995.

Stillman, Norman A. *The Jews of Arab Lands: A History and Source Book.* Philadelphia: Jewish Publication Society of America, 1979.

Stillman, Norman A., and Yedidah Stillman. "Magic and Folklore, Islamic." In *Dictionary of the Middle Ages,* edited by Joseph R. Strayer. 12 vols. New York: Scribner, 1982–89.

Stillman, Yedida Kalfon. "Costume as Cultural Statement: The Esthetics, Economics, and Politics of Islamic Dress." In *The Jews of Medieval Islam: Community, Society, and Identity,* edited by Daniel Frank. Leiden and New York: E. J. Brill, 1995.

———. *Female Attire in Medieval Egypt: According to the Trousseau Lists and Cognate Material from the Cairo Geniza.* Ph.D. Diss. Philadelphia: University of Pennsylvania Press, 1972.

Stillman, Yedida Kalfon, and Norman A. Stillman, eds. *Arab Dress: A Short History from the Dawn of Islam to Modern Times.* In *Themes in Islamic Studies.* Vol. 2. Boston: E. J. Brill, 2000.

Stock, Brian. *Myth and Science in the Twelfth Century: A Study of Bernard Silvester.* Princeton, N.J.: Princeton University Press, 1972.

Stockman, Robert L. *Low German (Platt Düütch): A Brief History of the Low German Language & People.* Alto, Mich.: Low German Press, 1998.

Stoetzer, W. "Rubai (pl. Rubaiyyat.)" *Encyclopaedia of Islam,* 2d ed. Vol. 8. Leiden, The Netherlands: E. J. Brill, 1999, 578–584.

Stone, Brian. *Medieval English Verse.* Baltimore: Penguin, 1964.

Stone, Caroline. "Ibn Fadlan and the Midnight Sun." *Saudi Aramco World,* no. 2 30:2 (March/April 1979).

Stone, George Cameron. *A Glossary of the Construction, Decoration and Use of Arms and Armor.* New York: Jack Brussel, 1961.

Stone, James S. *The Cult of Santiago: Traditions, Myths, and Pilgrimages.* London: D. D. Longmans, Green & Co., 1927.

Stouck, Mary-Ann, ed. *Medieval Saints: A Reader.* Peterborough, Ont.: Broadview Press, 1999.

Strack, H. L., and G. Stemberger. *Introduction to the Talmud and Midrash.* Minneapolis: Fortress Press, 1992.

Strauch, Gabriele L. *Dukus Horant: Wanderer zwischen zwei Welten.* Amsterdam and Atlanta, Ga.: Rodopi, 1990.

Strayer, Joseph R., ed. *Dictionary of the Middle Ages.* 12 vols. New York: Scribner, 1982–89.

Strong, H. A. and Kuno Meyer. *History of the German Language.* London: Le Bas & Lowrey, 1886.

Strong, Roy. *Splendor at Court.* Boston: Houghton Mifflin, 1973.

Summers, Montague. *Reginald Scot's The Discoverie of Witchcraft.* New York: Dover, 1972.

Sumption, Jonathan. *The Hundred Years War. Vol. 1, Trial by Battle.* Philadelphia: University of Pennsylvania Press, 1999.

———. *The Hundred Years War. Vol. 2, Trial by Fire.* Philadelphia: University of Pennsylvania Press, 2001.

———. *Pilgrimage: An Image of Mediaeval Religion.* London: Faber and Faber, 2002.

Sung, Ying-Hsing. *T'ien-Cung K'ai-Wu: Chinese Technology in the 17th Century.* University Park and London: Pennsylvania State University Press, 1966.

Svat, Soucek. *A History of Inner Asia.* Cambridge: Cambridge University Press, 2000.

Swan, Charles, trans. *Gesta Romanorum.* London: George Routledge and Sons, Ltd., 1905.

Swanton, Michael, ed. *The Anglo-Saxon Chronicles.* London: J. M. Dent, 1996.

Szabo, George. *Masterpieces of Italian Drawing in the Robert Lehman Collection.* New York: Hudson Hills Press, 1983.

Tabataba'i, Muhammad Husayn. *Shi'ite Islam* (tr. Seyyed Hossein Nasr), Persian Studies Series. Albany: State University of New York Press, 1975.

Tabbaa, Yasser. "The Muqarnas Dome: Its Origin and Meaning." *Muqarnas 3, Art and Architecture,* edited by Oleg Grabar. Leiden, The Netherlands: E. J. Brill, 1985.

———. *The Transformation of Islamic Art during the Sunni Revival.* Seattle: University of Washington Press, 2001.

Tacuinum Sanitatis, c. 1475. Nine versions: seven in manuscript, two printed: (a) New York: New York Public Library, Spencer Collection MS 65; (b) Liege: University Library; (c) Paris: Bibliotheque Nationale; (d) Rome: Casanatense Library *(Theatrum Sanitatis);* (e) Rouen: Municipal Library MS 3054; (f) Venice: Marciana Library Latin MS 315; (g) Vienna: National Library MSS 5264 & 2396; (h) printed Arabic to Latin, 1531. Strasbourg: Jehan Schott; (i) German, 1533. Strasbourg: Jehan Schott.

Talbot, C. H. "Dame Trot and Her Progeny." *Essays and Studies* 25 (1972): 1–14.

———. *Medicine in Medieval England.* London: Oldbourne History of Science, 1967.

———. "A Medieval Physician's Vade Mecum." *Journal of the History of Medicine and Allied Sciences* (1961).

Talbot, C. H., and Hammond, E. A. *The Medical Practitioners in Medieval England.* London: Wellcome Historical Medical Library, 1965.

Talmage. F. "Apples of Gold: The Inner Meaning of Sacred Texts in Medieval Judaism." In *Jewish Spirituality—From the Bible through the Middle Ages.* Vol. 1, edited by A. Green. London: Routledge & Kegan Paul, 1986.

Tannahill, Reay. *Food in History.* New York: Crown, 1988.

al-Tawhidi, Abu Hayyan. *Kitab al-Imta'wa 'l-mu'anasa.* Edited by Ahmad Amin and Ahmad al-Zayn. Tunis: Dar Bu Salamah, 1988.

Taylor, E. G. R. *The Haven-Finding Art.* New York: Abelard-Schumann, 1956.

———. *Sex in History.* New York: Vanguard Press, 1954.

Taylor, Nathaniel L. "Saint William, King David, and Makhir: A Controversial Medieval Descent." *The American Genealogist* 72 (1997): 203–221.

Tellenbach, Gerd. *Church, State and Christian Society at the Time of the Investiture Contest.* Oxford: Basil Blackwell, 1948. Reprint, Toronto: University of Toronto Press, 1991.

Temko, Allan. *Notre-Dame of Paris: The Biography of a Cathedral.* New York: Viking, 1959.

Tentler, Thomas N. *Sin and Confession on the Eve of the Reformation.* Princeton, N.J.: Princeton University Press, 1977.

Teresa de Jesús. *Obras completas*, edited by Efren de la Madre de Dios. Madrid: BAC, 1954.

Tester, Jim. *A History of Western Astronomy.* New York: Ballentine Books, 1987.

Tetel, M. *Marguerite de Navarre's Heptameron.* Durham, N.C.: Duke University Press, 1973.

Thackston, Wheeler M., ed. and trans. *Naser-e Khosraw's Book of Travels (Safarnama).* New York: Persian Heritage Association, Bibliotheca Persica, 1986.

Thackston, Wheeler M., ed. and trans. *Nasir-i Khusraw's Book of Travels.* Bibliotheca Iranica: Intellectual Traditions Series, No. 6. Costa Mesa, Calif.: Nazda Publishers, 2001.

Theodore the Studite. *On the Holy Icons* 1.7. Translated by Catharine P. Roth. Crestwood, N.Y.: St. Vladimir's Seminary Press, 1981.

Theophilus Protopatharius. *On Divine Arts.* Edited by Cyril Stanley Smith. Chicago: University of Chicago Press, 1963.

Thiebaux, Marcelle. "The Medieval Chase." *Speculum* 42 (1967): 260 ff.

Thomas Aquinas, Saint. *Summa Contra Gentiles. Book One: God.* Translated, with an introduction and notes by Anton C. Pegis. Notre Dame, Ind.: University of Notre Dame Press, 1955. *Book Two: Creation.* Translated, with an introduction and notes by James F. Anderson. Notre Dame, Ind.: University of Notre Dame Press, 1956.

———. *Summa Theologica.* Edited by Timothy McDermott. Notre Dame, Ind.: Thomas More Publishers, 1997.

———. *Summa Theologica.* London: Trubner, 1916.

Thomas, Marcel. *The Grandes Heures of Jean, Duke of Berry.* New York: George Braziller, 1971.

Thompson, Daniel V., trans. *Cennino d'Andrea Cennini's The Craftsman's Handbook.* New Haven, Conn.: Yale University Press, 1933.

Thompson, Daniel. *Materials and Techniques of Medieval Painting.* New York: Dover, 1956.

Thompson, Stith. *Motif-Index of Folk-Literature: A Classification of Narrative Elements in Folktale . . . Medieval Romances . . . Fabliaux.* Bloomington, Ind.

1932–1936; computer file, CD-ROM, Bloomington, Ind.: Indiana University Press, 1989.

Thomson, S. Harrison. *Latin Book Hands of the Later Middle Ages: 1100–1500*. Cambridge: Cambridge University Press, 1969.

Thorndike, Lynn. *A History of Magic and Experimental Science*. New York: Macmillan, 1934.

———. *History of Magic and Experimental Science*. 1929–1958. Vols. 1–5. 1923. Reprint, New York: Columbia University Press, 1964.

———. "Sanitation, Baths, and Street Cleaning in the Middle Ages and Renaissance." *Speculum* 3 (1928), 192–203.

Thrupp, Sylvia, ed. *Change in Medieval Society*. New York: Appleton Century-Crofts, 1964.

Thrupp, Sylvia, ed. *Early Medieval Society*. New York: Appleton Century-Crofts, 1967.

Thrupp, Sylvia, "Medieval Industry, 1000–1500." In *Fontana Economic History of Europe*. Vol. 1, *The Middle Ages*, edited by Carlo Cipolla, London: Collins/Fontana, 1973. 221–273.

———. *The Merchant Class in Medieval London*. Ann Arbor: University of Michigan Press, 1962.

Tibbetts, Gerald R. *Arab Navigation in the Indian Ocean before the Coming of the Portuguese*. London: Royal Asiatic Society of Great Britain and Ireland, 1981.

Tierney, Brian. *The Crisis of Church and State 1050–1300*. Englewood Cliffs, N.J.: Prentice Hall, 1964.

Tietze-Conrat E. *Dwarfs and Jesters in Art*. New York: Phaidon, 1957.

Ting, Joseph S.P., ed. *The Maritime Silk Route: 2000 Years of Trade on the South China Sea*. Hong Kong: Urban Council of Hong Kong, 1996.

Toaff, Ariel. *Love, Work, and Death: Jewish Life in Medieval Umbria*. London: Littman Library of Jewish Civilization, 1996.

Toch, Michael, ed. *Peasants and Jews in Medieval Germany: Studies in Cultural, Social, and Economic History*. Aldershot, Eng.: Ashgate, 2003.

Tolkien, J. R. R., and E. V. Gordon. *Sir Gawain and the Green Knight*. Oxford: Oxford University Press, 1955.

Toney, Anthony. *One Hundred and Fifty Masterpieces of Drawing*. New York: Dover, 1963.

Touma, Habib. *The Music of the Arabs*. Portland, Oreg.: Amadeus Press, 1996.

Tout, T. F. *The Empire and the Papacy, 918–1273*. 8th ed. London: Rivingtons, 1965.

Trackman, Leon E. *The Law Merchant. The Evolution of Commercial Law*. Litteton, Colo.: F. B. Rothman, 1983.

Treadgold, Warren. *A History of the Byzantine State and Society*. Stanford: Stanford University Press, 1997.

Trimingham, J. Spencer. *The Sufi Orders in Islam*. London: Oxford University Press, 1971.

Tritton, A. S. *The Caliphs and their Non-Muslim Subjects: A Critical Study of the Covenant of 'Umar*. London: Oxford University Press, 1930.

———. *Materials on Muslim Education in the Middle Ages*. London: Luzac and Co., 1957.

Trotula of Salerno. *The Diseases of Women*. Translated by Elizabeth Mason-Hohl. Los Angeles: The Ward Richie Press, 1940.

Tschanz, David W. "The Arab Roots of European Medicine." *Aramco World*, 48, no. 3 (May–June 1997).

Tugwell, Simon, ed. *Early Dominicans: Selected Writings*. Classics of Western Spirituality. 33. New York: Paulist Press, 1982.

Turberville, A. S. *Medieval Heresy and the Inquisition*. London: Archon Books, 1964.

Turnbull, Stephen. *The Knight Triumphant: The High Middle Ages, 1314–1485*. London: Cassell, 2001.

Tuttle, Edward. "The Trotula and Old Dame Trot: A Note on the Lady of Salerno." *Bulletin of the History of Medicine* 50 (1976): 61–72.

Twersky, I. *Introduction to the Code of Maimonides (Mishneh Torah)*. New Haven, Conn.: Yale University Press. 1980.

———. *A Maimonides Reader*. New York, 1972.

———. *Rabbi Moses Nahmanides (Ramban): Explorations in his Religious and Literary Virtuosity*. Cambridge, Mass.: Harvard University Press, 1983.

———. *Studies in Jewish Law and Philosophy*. New York: Ktav Publishers, 1982.

Twersky, Isadore and Jay M. Harris, eds. *Studies in Medieval Jewish History and Literature*, 3 vols. Cambridge, Mass.: Harvard University Press, 1979–2000.

Tyan, E. "Djihad." *Encyclopaedia of Islam*, 2nd ed. Vol. 2. Leiden, The Netherlands: E. J. Brill, 1999, 538–539.

Udovitch, Abraham L. "Commercial Techniques in Early Medieval Islam." In *Islam and the Trade of Asia*, edited by Donald S. Richards. Philadelphia: University of Pennsylvania Press, 1970.

———. *Partnership and Profit in Medieval Islam.* Princeton, N.J.: Princeton University Press, 1970.

Udovitch, Abraham L., ed. *The Islamic Middle East, 700–1900: Studies in Economic and Social History.* Princeton, N.J.: Princeton University Press, 1981.

Ullman, Manfred. "Al-Iksir." *Encyclopaedia of Islam,* 2nd ed. Vol. 3. Leiden, The Netherlands: E. J. Brill, 1999, 1,087.

———. "Al-Kimya." *Encyclopaedia of Islam,* 2nd ed. Vol. 5. Leiden, The Netherlands: E. J. Brill, 1999, 110–114.

———. *Islamic Medicine.* Islamic Surveys 11. Edinburgh: Edinburgh University Press, 1978.

Unger, Richard W. *The Ship in the Medieval Economy: 600–1600.* London: Croom Helm, 1980.

———. "Ships and Ship Building, Northern European." In *Dictionary of the Middle Ages,* edited by Joseph R. Strayer. 12 vols. New York: Scribner, 1982–89.

Unger, Richard. "Warships and Cargo Ships in Medieval Europe." *Technology and Culture* 22 (April 1981): 233–252.

Urban, William. *The Baltic Crusade.* 2d ed. Chicago: Lithuanian Research and Studies Center, 1994.

———. *The Livonian Crusade.* 2d ed. Washington, D.C.: University Press of America, 2004.

Urry, William J. *Canterbury, under the Angevin Kings.* London: University of London, Athlone Press, 1967.

Usmani, Mufti Muhammad Taqi. *Islamic Months: Merits and Precepts.* Karachi: Maktabah Ma'riful Quran, 2002.

Vajda, George, et al. "Idjaza." *Encyclopaedia of Islam,* 2d ed. Vol. 3. Leiden, The Netherlands: E. J. Brill, 1999. 1,020–1,021.

Van Weveke, Hans, editor. *Miscellanea Mediaevalia.* Berlin: W. de Gruyter, 1968.

Vann, Theresa M. *Queens, Regents and Potentates: Women of Power.* Dallas, Tex.: Academia, 1993.

Vauchez, André. *The Laity in the Middle Ages: Religious Beliefs and Devotional Practices.* Translated by Margery J. Schneider. Notre Dame, Ind.: University of Notre Dame Press, 1993.

———. *Sainthood in the Later Middle Ages,* translated by Jean Birrell. Cambridge: Cambridge University Press, 1997.

Vecchia Valieri, L. "Ghadir Khumm." *Encyclopaedia of Islam,* 2d ed. Vol. 2. Leiden, The Netherlands: E. J. Brill, 1999. 993–994.

Verbeke, Werner, Ludo Milis, and Jean Goossens, eds. *Medieval Narrative Sources: A Gateway into the Medieval Mind.* Leuven, Belgium: Leuven University Press, 2005.

Vernet, Juan. *La cultura hispanoárabe en Oriente y Occidente.* Barcelona: Ariel, 1978.

Vernet, J. "Natural and Technical Sciences in al-Andalus." In *The Legacy of Muslim Spain,* edited by Salma K. Jayyusi, 937–952. Leiden, The Netherlands: E. J. Brill, 1994.

Vire, F. "Sayd." *Encyclopaedia of Islam,* 2d ed. Vol. 9. Leiden, The Netherlands: E. J. Brill, 1999, 98.

de Vitry, Jacques. *The Exempla of Jacques de Vitry.* Edited by Thomas Frederick Crane. London: Folk Lore Society, 1890.

Vivanco, Laura. *Death in Fifteenth-Century Castile: Ideologies of the Elites.* Series A: Monografías 205. London: Tamesis, 2004.

Vlasto, A. P. *The Entry of the Slavs into Christendom: An Introduction to the Medieval History of the Slavs.* Cambridge: Cambridge University Press, 1970.

Vogt, Ulya G. *Mosques: Grand, courants de l'architecture islamique.* Paris: Editions du Chêne, 1975.

Von Heyking, John. *Augustine and Politics as Longing in the World.* Columbia: University of Missouri Press, 2001.

de Voragine, Jacobus. *The Golden Legend: Readings on the Saints.* Translated by William Granger Ryan. Princeton, N.J.: Princeton University Press, 1993.

———. *Legenda Aurea, The Golden Legend.* Translated by G. Ryan and H. Ripperger. New York: Arno Press, 1969.

Vries, B. W. de. *From Pedlars to Textile Barons: The Economic Development of a Jewish Minority Group in the Netherlands.* Amsterdam and New York: North Holland, 1989.

Waagenaar, Sam. *The Pope's Jews.* LaSalle, Ill.: Open Court, 1974.

de Waal, Esther. *The Way of Simplicity: The Cistercian Tradition.* Traditions of Christian Spirituality Series. Maryknoll, N.Y.: Orbis Books, 1998.

Wack, Mary. *Love Sickness in the Middle Ages: The Viaticum and its Commentaries.* Philadelphia: University of Pennsylvania Press, 1990.

Waddell, Helen. *The Desert Fathers*. Ann Arbor: University of Michigan Press, 1957.

Wafai, M. Zafer, ed. *The Arabian Ophthalmologists*. Compiled from Original Texts by J. Hirschberg, J. Lippert and E. Mittwoch, translated into English by Frederick C. Blodi, Wilfried J. Rademaker, Gisela Rademaker, and Kenneth F. Wildman. Riyadh, Saudi Arabia: King Abdulaziz City for Science and Technology, 1993.

Wagner, A. *Heralds and Heraldry in the Middle Ages*. 2nd ed. London: Oxford University Press, 1956.

Wagtendonck, K. *Fasting in the Koran*. Leiden, The Netherlands: E. J. Brill, 1968.

Wake, C. H. H. "The Changing Pattern of Europe's Pepper and Spice Imports, ca. 1400–1700." *Journal of European Economic History* 8, no. 2 (Fall 1979): 361–403.

al-Wakeel, Yasir. "Muslim Medicine." *Oxford Medical School Gazette*. Oxford: Oxford University Press, 2003.

Wakefield, Walter L. *Heresy, Crusade and Inquisition in Southern France, 1100–1250*. Berkeley: University of California Press, 1974.

Walden, Lord Howard de. *Reminiscences of Henry Angelo*. Philadelphia: Lippincott, 1904.

Walfish, Barry Dov. *Esther in Medieval Garb: Jewish Interpretation of the Book of Esther in the Middle Ages*. Albany: State University of New York Press, 1993.

Walker, Barbara. *The Woman's Encyclopedia of Myths and Secrets*. San Francisco: Harper San Francisco, 1983.

Walker Bynum, Carolyn, and Paul Freedman. *Last Things: Death and the Apocalypse in the Middle Ages*. Philadelphia: University of Pennsylvania Press, 2000.

Walzer, Michael. "War and Peace in the Jewish Tradition." In *Ethics of War and Peace*, edited by T. Nardin, 95–114. Princeton, N.J.: Princeton University Press, 1996.

Walzer, Richard. *Greek into Arabic, Essays on Islamic Philosophy*. Cambridge, Mass.: Harvard University Press, 1962.

Wangermee, Robert. *Flemish Music and Society in the 15th and 16th Centuries*. Translated by Robert Erich Wolf. New York: Praeger, 1968.

Wansbrough, John. *Qur'anic Studies: Sources and Methods of Scriptural Interpretation*. Oxford: Oxford University Press, 1977.

———. *The Sectarian Milieu*. Oxford: Oxford University Press, 1978.

Ward, Benedicta. "Anselm of Canterbury." In *Christian Spirituality I: Origins to the Twelfth Century*, edited by Bernard McGinn et al., 196–205. New York: Crossroad, 1989.

Warner, A. G., and E. Warner, trans. *The Shahnama of Firdausi*. London: K. Paul, Trench, Trubner, 1905–1925.

Warner, Charles Dudley. *Library of The World's Best Literature, Ancient And Modern*. Volume 2. Available online. URL: http://www.ebooksread.com/authors-eng/warner/the-worlds-best-literature-ancient-and-modern-vol-2-887/1-the-worlds-best-literature-ancient-and-modern-vol-2-887.shtml.

Warner, Marina. *All Alone of Her Sex: The Myth and the Cult of the Virgin Mary*. 1976. Reprint, London: Picador, 1985.

Warner, S. *Antiquitates Culinariae* London, 1791. Reprint, London: Nachdruck, 1981.

Waters, D. W. *The Art of Navigation in England in Elizabethan and Stuart Times*. New Haven, Conn.: Yale University Press, 1967.

———. *The Rutters of the Sea: The Sailing Directions of Pierre Garcie*. New Haven, Conn.: Yale University Press, 1967.

Watson, Andrew M. *Agricultural Innovation in the Early Islamic World: The Diffusion of Crops and Farming Techniques, 700–1100*. Cambridge: Cambridge University Press, 1982.

———. "A Medieval Green Revolution: New Crops and Farming Techniques in the Early Islamic World." In *The Islamic Middle East, 700–1900: Studies in Economic and Social History*, ed. Abraham L. Udovitch. Princeton, N.J.: Darwin Press, 1981.

Watt, W. Montgomery. "Ash'ariyya." *Encyclopaedia of Islam*, 2d ed. Vol 1: 696. Leiden, The Netherlands: E. J. Brill, 1999.

———. *The Faith and Practice of Al-Ghazali*. London: George Allen & Unwin. 1953.

———. *The Formative Period of Islamic Thought*. Edinburgh: Edinburgh University Press, 1973.

———. *Muhammad at Mecca*. Oxford: Clarendon Press, 1953; and Albany: State University of New York Press, 1981.

———. *Muhammad at Medina*. Oxford: Clarendon Press, 1956; and New York: Oxford University Press, 1981.

Watt, W. Montgomery, ed. *Bell's Introduction to the Qur'an*. Edinburgh: Edinburgh University Press, 1970.

Weibtraub, Melissa. "Torture, *Pikuakh Nefesh*, and the *Rodef* Defense." *Rabbis for Human Rights—North America*. 2005. Available online. URL: http://www.rhr-na.org/torture/butdoestorture.html.

Weinberger, Leon. *Jewish Prince in Moslem Spain: Selected Poems of Samuel ibn Nagrela*. University: University of Alabama Press, 1973.

Weinberger, M. *Michelangelo, The Sculptor*. New York: Columbia University Press, 1967.

Weiner, A. "A Note on Jewish Doctors in England in the Reign of Henry IV." *The Jewish Quarterly Review*, Vol. 18 (1906).

Weinstein, Donald, and Rudolph M. Bell. *Saints and Society: The Two Worlds of Western Christendom, 1000–1700*. Chicago: University of Chicago Press, 1982.

Weiser, Francis X. *Handbook of Christian Feasts and Customs*. New York: Harcourt, Brace, 1952. Reprint, New York: Harcourt, Brace, 1958.

Weisheipl, James A. *Thomas D'Aquino: His Life, Thought and Work*. Washington, D.C.: Catholic University of America Press, 1974.

Weitzmann, Kurt. *Late Antique an Early Christian Book Illumination*. New York: George Braziller, 1977.

Welch, Stuart Cary. A *King's Book of Kings: The Shah-Nameh of Shah Tahmasp*. New York: Metropolitan Museum of Art, 1972.

———. *Persian Painting: Five Royal Safavid Manuscripts of the Sixteenth Century*. New York: George Braziller, 1976.

Welch, Stuart Cary, and Martin B. Dickson. *The Shah-Nameh*. Cambridge, Mass: Harvard University Press, 1973.

Welch, Stuart Cary, and Anthony Welch. *Arts of the Islamic Book*. Ithaca, N.Y.: Cornell University Press, 1982.

Wensinck, A. J. *The Muslim Creed*. Cambridge: Cambridge University Press, 1982.

Werner E., and I. Sonne. "The Philosophy and Theory of Music in Judeo-Arabic Literature." *Hebrew Union College Annual* 16 (1941): 251–319; 17 (1942–43): 511–572.

West, A. F. *Alcuin and the Rise of the Christian Schools*. New York: Charles Scribner's Sons, 1909.

Westermarck, Edward. *Ritual and Belief in Morocco*. 2 vols. London: Macmillan & Co., Ltd., 1926.

Weston, Jessie L. *From Ritual to Romance*. 1920. Reprint, Princeton, N.J.: Princeton University Press, 1993.

Whelan, Estelle. "Textiles, Islamic." In *Dictionary of the Middle Ages*, edited by Joseph R. Strayer. 12 vols. New York: Scribner, 1982–89.

Whipple, Allen O. *The Role of the Nestorians and Muslims in the History of Medicine*. Princeton, N.J.: Princeton University Press, 1967.

White, Lynn, Jr. "Eilmer of Malmsbury, an Eleventh Century Aviator: A Case Study of Technology Innovation, its Context, and Tradition." *Technology and Culture* 2 (1961): 97–111.

———. "Medical Astrologers and Late Medieval Technology." *Viator* 6 (1975): 296–309.

———. *Medieval Technology and Social Change*. Oxford: Oxford University Press, 1964.

———. "Medieval Uses of Air." *Scientific American* 223, no. 2 (August 1970): 92–100.

White, William Charles. *Chinese Jews: A Compilation of Matters Relating to the Jews of K'ai-feng Fu*. New York: Paragon. Reprint, University of Toronto Press, 1966.

Whitehouse, David. "Glass, Islamic." In *Dictionary of the Middle Ages*, edited by Joseph R. Strayer. New York: Scribner, 1982–89.

Whitehouse, David, and R. Hodges. *Mohammed, Charlemagne and the Origins of Europe*. Ithaca, N.Y.: Cornell University Press, 1983.

Wickham, C. J. *Early Medieval Italy: Central Power and Local Society, 400–1000*. London: Macmillan, 1981.

Wieck, Roger S. *Painted Prayer: The Book of Hours in Medieval and Renaissance Art*. New York: George Braziller, 1997.

Wieck, Roger S., Lawrence R. Poos, and Virginia Reinburg. *Time Sanctified: The Book of Hours in Medieval Art and Life*. New York: George Braziller, 1988.

Wigoder, Geoffrey. *Jewish Art and Civilization*. New York: Walker, 1972.

Wilkinson, J. C. *Water and Tribal Settlement in South-East Arabia*. Oxford: Clarendon Press, 1977.

Willaert, Frank, Herman Braet, Thom Mertens, and Theo Venckelee, eds. *Medieval Memory: Image and Text*. Turnhout: Brepols, 2004.

Willard, Charity Cannon, and Madeleine Pelner Cosman. *A Medieval Woman's Mirror of Honor: The Treasury of the City of Ladies by de Pisan Christine.* Translated by C. Cannon Willard. Tenafly, N.J.: Bard Hall Press, 2001.

William of Rubruck. *The Mission of Friar William of Rubruck: His Journey to the Court of the Great Khan Mongke, 1253–1255.* Translated by Peter Jackson. London: The Hakluyt Society, 1990.

Williams, David. *Deformed Discourse: The Function of the Monster in Mediaeval Thought and Literature.* Montreal and Kingston: McGill Queens University Press, 1999.

Williams, John A. *Al-Tabari. Vol. 1, The Reign of Abu Ja'far al-Mansur A.D. 754–775: The Early 'Abbasi Empire.* Cambridge: Cambridge University Press, 1988.

———. *The History of Al-Tabari.* Vol. 27, *The Abassid Revolution.* Albany: State University of New York Press, 1985.

———. *Islam: The Tradition and Contemporary Orientation of Islam.* New York: George Braziller, 1960.

Williams, John A., ed. *Themes of Islamic Civilization.* Berkeley: University of California Press, 1971.

Williams, John, and Alison Stones, *The 'Codex Calixtinus' and the Shrine of St. James* (Jakobus-Studien 3). Tubingen: Narr, 1992.

Williams, Thomas. *The Cambridge Companion to Duns Scotus.* New York: Cambridge University Press, 2003.

Williman, Daniel. *The Black Death: The Impact of the 14th Century Plague.* Binghamton, N.Y.: SUNY Press, 1982.

Wilson, David R. *The Steps Used in Court Dance in Fifteenth-Century Italy.* Cambridge, Mass.: 1992.

Wilson, Peter Lamborn, and Gholam Reza Aavani. *Forty Poems from the "Divan" by Nâsir-i Khusraw.* Tehran: Imperial Iranian Academy of Philosophy, 1977.

Windeatt, Barry, ed. *English Mystics of the Middle Ages.* New York: Cambridge University Press, 1994.

Winkworth, Margaret. *The Herald of Divine Love.* New York: Paulist Press, 1993.

Winternitz, Emanuel. *Musical Instruments and Their Symbolism in Western Art.* New York: W. W. Norton, 1967 and New Haven, Conn.: Yale University Press, 1979.

———. *Pleasing Eye and Ear Alike.* New York: Metropolitan Museum of Art Bulletin, October, 1971.

Wirszubski, Chaim. *Pico della Mirandola's Encounter with Jewish Mysticism.* Cambridge, Mass.: Harvard University Press, 1988.

Wischnitzer, Rachel. *From Dura to Rembrandt: Studies in the History of Art.* Milwaukee, Wis.; Vienna; Jerusalem: Aldrich; IRSA Verlag; Center for Jewish Art, 1990.

Wittkower, Rudolf. *Bernini.* New York: Phaidon Press, 1967.

Wolf, Kenneth Baxter. *Conquerors and Chroniclers of Early Medieval Spain.* Liverpool: Liverpool University Press, 1990.

Wolfson, Elliot R. *Through a Speculum That Shines: Vision and Imagination in Medieval Jewish Mysticism.* Princeton, N.J.: Princeton University Press, 1994.

Wolohojian, A., trans. *The Romance of Alexander the Great by Pseudo-Callisthenes.* New York: Columbia University Press, 1969.

Wolter, Allan B., OFM. *Duns Scotus: Philosophical Writings.* Indianapolis: Hackett Publishing Company, 1987.

———. *Duns Scotus on the Will and Morality.* Washington, D.C.: The Catholic University of America Press, 1986.

Wood, Margaret. *The English Medieval House.* New York: Harper Colophon Books, 1965.

Woodcock, T., and J. M. Robinson. *Oxford Guide to Heraldry.* Oxford: Oxford University Press, 1988.

Woods, Richard. *Mysticism and Prophecy: The Dominican Tradition.* Maryknoll, N.Y.: Orbis Books, 1998.

Wright, Owen. "Arab Music." In *New Grove Dictionary of Music and Musicians,* edited by Stanley Sadie. London: MacMillan, 1980.

———. *The Modal System of Arab and Persian Music, A.D. 1250–1300.* London Oriental Series, Vol. 28. Oxford: Oxford University Press, 1978.

———. "Music." In *The Legacy of Islam.* 2d ed., edited by Joseph Schacht and C. E. Bosworth. Oxford: Oxford University Press, 1979.

———. "Music in Muslim Spain." In *The Legacy of Muslim Spain,* edited by Salma K. Jayyusi. Leiden, The Netherlands: E. J. Brill, 1994.

Wright, T. *A History of Domestic Manners*. London: Chapman & Hall, 1862.

Wrigley, E. A. *People, Cities, and Wealth: The Transformation of Traditional Society*. Oxford: Blackwell, 1987.

Wybrew, Hugh. *Orthodox Feasts of Christ and Mary: Liturgical Texts with Commentary*. London: SPCK, 1997.

Wynkyn de Worde. *Boke of Kervynge*. In *Early English Meals and Manners*, edited by J. J. Furnivall. London: Early English Text Society, N. Trubner & Co., 1888.

Wynne, Peter. *Apples*. New York: Hawthorn Books, 1975.

Yerushalmi Y. S. *From Spanish Court to Italian Ghetto*. New York: Columbia University Press, 1971.

Young, M. J. L., J. D. Latham, and R. B. Sergeant, eds. *Religion, Learning and Science in the 'Abbasid Period*. The Cambridge History of Arabic Literature. Cambridge: Cambridge University Press, 1990.

Younger, William. *Gods, Men, and Wine*. Cleveland, Ohio: World Publishing, 1966.

Yule, Henry. *Cathay and the Way Thither*. Vol. 2. London: The Hakluyt Society, 1866.

al-Zahrawi. *Albucasis on Surgery and Instruments. A Definitive Edition of the Arabic Text with English Translation and Commentary*, translated and edited by M. S. Spink and G. L. Lewis. Berkeley and Los Angeles: University of California Press, 1973.

Zand, K. H., J. A. Videan, and I. E. Videan, trans. *The Eastern Key: Kitāb al-Ifādah wa-al-i'tibār of Abd al Latif, Al-Baghdad translated into English*. London: George Allen and Unwin, 1964.

Zeitlin, Solomon. *Maimonides, a Biography*. New York: Block Pub., 1955.

Zink, Michel. *La prédication en langue romane avant 1300*. Paris: H. Champion, 1977.

Zohar. *The Book of Enlightenment*. Translated by Daniel Chanan Matt. New York: Paulist Press, 1983.

Zuckerman, Arthur. *A Jewish Princedom in Feudal France 768–900*. New York: Columbia University Press, 1972.

INDEX

NOTE: **Boldface** page numbers indicate extensive treatment of a topic. Page numbers in *italic* indicate illustrations. Page numbers with the suffix *g* refer to glossary entries.

A

Aaron of Baghdad 450
aba 863*g*
abacus 545
abased 287
Abbasid caliphate (Abbasids) 67–70
    farms 231
    Ghazis 299
    and Islamic historiography xi
    Muslim clothing 848–849
    and Mutazila movement 393
    palaces 618–619
    poetry 685–690
    taxation 152
abbots 48
Abd al-Latif 149
Abdun, Muhammad ibn Abd Allah
    ibn 144–145
abortifacients 494, 495
abortion 494–496
Abraham (biblical figure) 388, 389,
    440–441
Abraham ben Meir ibn Ezra 682
Abraham ibn Hasdai 670, 673
absinthe 479
Abubacer 402
Abu Dulama 688
Abu Hanifa 141
Abu Hayyan al-Tawhidi 700
Abu Jafar Abdallah al-Mansur 689

Abu l-Atahiyya, Ismail ibn Qasim ibn
    Qaysan 688–690
Abulcasis 497, 528–530
Abu l-Faraj al-Isfahani 696, 750, 754
Abu l-Hasan Ali al-Masudi 696
Abu Nuwas 688, 690
Abu Said 163
Abu Tayyib Ahmad ibn al-Husayn
    al-Jufi 688
Abu Uyayna, Muhammad ibn
    752–753
achievement 290
acorns, roasted 489
adab literature 698–701
Adam and Eve *328*
    Christian philosophy and religion
        328–329
    and gluttony 137
    and Jewish sensuality 174
Adam de la Halle 646
al-Adawiyya, Rabia 453–454
Adonai 373
Adoptionists 327, 361–362
Adoration of the Magi 334, 770
Advent 765–766
"Adventures of Gushtasp and
    Sarkad" (Firdawsi) 707–708
aeromancy 433
Aesop's Fables 651–653
aesthetics, Islamic 603–604

afarit 462
afterlife 355
age of consent 796
agraffe
    architecture 556
    body armor 273, 275
Agricola, Georgius
    gunpowder in Christian Europe
        279
    mining 510–511
agriculture. *See* farms and farming
agrimony 477–478
Ahmad ibn Ishaq 688
Ahmad ibn Khallikan 697
Ahmad ibn Yahya al-Baladhuri 696
ahwal 457
aillette 273
akehah 440–441
Akhhab, Huyayy ibn 315
Alamans 120
alb 827*g*
alba 640
albarellos 570
Albéric de Pisançon 638
Albertus Magnus
    and Thomas Aquinas 351
    Christian philosophy and religion
        333
Albigensian Crusade 29–30
Albigensians 362–363

Abu Yazid al-Bistami 454–455
alcacería 197
alchemy 463
    Christian 424–430, *426*
    Islamic 537–538
Aldrovandi, Ullises 502–503
aleuroimancy 433
Alexander the Great
    and Chanukah 805
    economy and trade 208–209
    Persian literature 706
Alexander the Great (Nizami
    Ganjawi) 706
Alexandria
    geography 223
    Ibn Battuta 241
    sea trade 214
alexandrine 638
Alexios I Comnenos (Byzantine
    emperor) 101, 658
Alfonsine tables 432–433
Alfonso V (king of Castile) 100
Alfonso VI (king of Castile) 100
Alfonso VI (king of Léon)
    Jewish soldiers 317–318
    and Jews in Christian Iberia 88
Alfonso VIII (king of Léon) 318
Alfonso X el Sabio (king of Castile
    and León) **42,** 657, 661, 664, 758
Alfred the Great (king of England) 99
algebra 545
Alhazen 546
Ali 63–64
Ali ibn Abi Talib 63, **75,** 142,
    406–407
Alive, Son of Awake! (Abubacer) 402
Allah
    and Asharis movement 394
    and Islamic empire 59
    and Islamic mysticism 453
    jihad 292
allegorical writings 341, 654–656
alleluia 717
allidade 505
All Saints' Day 788
All Souls' Day 788
Almagest (Ptolemy) 538, 540
almanacs 432
Almaric of Bena 364
Almogavares
    as slave-soldiers 299–300
    warfare and weapons, Islamic
    299–300

Almohad dynasty 227–228
almonds 474
Almoravids
    coinage in Islamic world 227
    Jews in Lucena 96
almuce 858g
aloe vera 477
al pezzo 200
alphitomancy 433
altar 582
aman 408
Ambrose, Saint 263
ambulatory 559
amir 309, 310
Amos (Jewish prophet) 590
amputation 488
anagorical level of meaning
    (scripture) 341
anal fistula surgery 490
anamorphosis 577
anapestic meter 719
anatomy 528, 529
al-Andalus 67
Andreas Capellanus 636, 646–647
anecdotes, books of 700
anelace 267
angels (in Christian theology)
    342–343
anger 474
Anglo-Norman language 632, 659
Anglo-Saxon architectural style 567,
    567
Anglo-Saxon language 632, 658
animal hearts, in Jewish magic 450
animals
    and art for seder 599
    beasts of prayer, Jewish art and
    600
    in Christian literature 651–653
    and Christmas 767
    hunting music, Christian 724
    and Jewish mysticism 448, 449
    and Sabbath 799
Anna Comnena **56,** 658
annates
    Babylonian Captivity 24
    papal triplicity 26
annihilation, in Islamic mysticism
    457, 458
annulet 288
Annunciation, feast of the 333
ansar 57

Anselm of Canterbury, Saint 117–
    118, 350–351
antari 863g
Antichrist 766
Antidotarium (Nicholas of Salerno)
    491
anti-iconic tradition 589–590
Antiochus IV (Seleucid king) 805
antiphonal calligraphy 573, 575
anti-Semitism
    Jewish merchants 203
    Jewish moneylenders 203, 248
    Polemic in Christian art 588
Aphorisms According to Galen
    (Maimonides) 516
apocalypse
    Christian 343–345
    in Jewish mysticism 448–449
Apocrypha, Christian 346
apoplexy 529–530
apostles 330–331
Apostles' Creed
    Christian philosophy and religion
    330
    church mass 717
apostolic poverty
    Albigensian Crusade 29, 30
    and friars 359
    and William of Ockham 356
appralere 480
apprentices
    guilds 193
    in western Europe 38
April Fools' Day 782–783
apse 556, 559
aquamanile
    Christian architecture 554
    Christian religious art 584
    Jewish art 592
    in medieval European medicine
    478
arabesques 617
    Hispano-Moresque architectural
    style 569
    manuscripts, Christian 571
al-Arabi, Ibn
    and Islamic art 605
    and Islamic mysticism 455–457
    and jihad 295, 296
The Arabian Nights 158
Arabic language 407–409
    Bible translation to 368
    on Iberian Peninsula 661

as sacred language of Quran 391
translations into 68–69
Umayyad caliphate 66
Arabic numerals 545
Aragonese-Catalan languages
661–662
arbalest 270
arbalesters 270
Arbeau, Thoinot 733, 735
arcanum 425, 429
archaeus 429
archangels 342
Archimedes 542
Arcbipoeta 724
architecture
about 552
Christian **554–563**
Anglo-Saxon 567
architects 554–556
Byzantine 567–568
Carolingian 568–569
castle 556–559
church and cathedral 559–561
Gothic 565–566
Hiberno-Saxon 566–567
Hispano-Moresque 569–570
house 562–563
insular 566
monastery 561–562
Norman 569
Romanesque 563–565
styles 563–570
vaults of wood, stone, and
brick 556
Islamic
beauty and aesthetics in 603
Dome of the Rock 613
madrasas 613–614
mosques 609–613
partonage of the arts 607
and wild individualists 608,
609
Jewish 593–595
resources 625–627
architrave 568
arch lute 726
arcrostics 368
Arderne, John 490
d'Arezzo, Guido 720
argentum vivum 429
Arians 361–362
arigot 726–727
arisard 863g

Aristotelianism
and Abu Hamid Muhammd ibn
al-Ghazzali 399–400
and Boethius 349
and John Duns Scotus 354–355
Jewish philosophy and religion
367
in Judaism 374, 375
and Maimonides 378–379
and Thomas Aquinas 351–354
Aristotle
and Averroës 403
and Abraham ibn Daud 375, 376
and al-Farabi 397
and al-Kindi 396
translation of, into Hebrew *366*
on women 119
ark, holy 594
Ark of the Covenant 594
Arles 315
armet 272
armilause 273
armillary sphere 504
arms and armor 266–276. *See also*
heraldry and arms
body armor 273–275
crossbow and arbalest 270
grenade and caltrop 270
head armor 270–273
horse armor 275–276
lance, halberd, mace, morning
star 268–269
longbow, shortbow, javelin
269–270
sword, dagger, and rapier
267–268
women 282–286
Arnold of Lübeck 406
arquebuses 281
arradab 303–304
arranged marriages 796
ars antiqua 719
ars moriendi 649–650
ars nova 719, 725
art (in general)
about 552
of heraldry 286–287
patronage of the arts 552–554
resources 625–627
art, Islamic **603–624**
beauty and aesthetics in 603–604
and Ibn Khaldun's three classes
of patrons 606–608

manuscripts 614, 622–624
patronage of the arts 606–608
religious art 609–617
calligraphy 614–617
Dome of the Rock 613
madrasas 613–614
mosques 609–613
Quran manuscripts 614
secular art 617–624
ceramics, glass, and
metalwork 620–622
painting, manuscript
illumination, and miniatures
622–624
palaces 618–620
styles 617–618
theology and philosophy in
605–606
wild individualists 608–609
art, Jewish **588–602**
anti-iconic tradition v. *Hiddur
Mitzvah* 589–590
beasts of prayer 600–602
buildings 593–595
major themes in 591–593
manuscripts 595–599
commentaries in 596
humor in 597–599
micrographic masorah 596–597
for seder 599–600
artemisia 495
Artemisia abrotanum 477
Arthurian romance
Christian literature 631,
636–638
Jewish literature 666
artisans 35, 36
arts and crafts **563–588**
Byzantine 567–568, 572,
585–586
Cennino Cennini 581
ceramics 579–580
cross and crucifix 584–585
icons 585–586
manuscripts 570–576
Byzantine 572
calligraphy styles 572–575
Hiberno-Saxon 572
insular style 571–572
paper, vellum, and parchment
techniques and works
575–576
metalwork 577–579

arts and crafts (continued)
  mosaics 585
  painting 580–581, 585
  polemic in 587–588
  religious art 582–584
  styles 563–570
    Anglo-Saxon 567
    Byzantine 567–568
    Carolingian 568–569
    Gothic 565–566
    Hiberno-Saxon 566–567
    Hispano-Moresque 569–570
    insular 566
    Norman 569
    Romanesque 563–565
  woodwork 576–577
art song 741–742
ascension 334
Ascension, feast of the 778–779
Ascension plays 779
ascetic communities 4
asceticism
  Islamic mysticism 452
  Jewish mysticism 447
al-Ashari, Abu l-Hasan 393
Asharis 393–395
Ashekenazic Judaism 81–82
  Judaism, restructuring of 77
  and Pesach 807
Ashura 819
Ashura, festival of 161
Ash Wednesday 773, 774
asperge 582
"Assassins" 405–406
assation 429
Assize of Measures 198
assumption 334
asthma 516–520
astrarium 504
astrolabe 505, 541
  in Islamic world 541
  in medieval Europe 505
  in medieval European medicine
    484
  and secular Christian music
    722–723
astrology 523
  Christian 430–433
  in Islamic world 539–540
  and Jewish medicine 521–522
astronomical clock 505
astronomical tables 432–433

astronomy
  Levi Ben Gershon 524–525
  in Islamic world 538–541, 539
astrum 429
Asturian kingdom 17
atara 858g
Athanasian Creed 327
Athanasius, Saint 327, 330
Athanasius of Athena 632
athanor 427
atour 858g
Augustine of Hippo, Saint 118,
    348–349, 633
  and angels 342
  and creation of Christian
    holidays 764, 785
  and doctrine of just war 263
  and doctrine of Original Sin
    328, 329
  and Donatist controversy 363
  and Jews in western Europe 80, 81
  and Manicheans 363
  and Pelagian controversy 363
Augustinian monks 360
aumbry
  castles 558
  monasteries 562
aurefaction 425
autobiographical writing
  Arabic 697–698
  Christian 633
autonomy and self-government
    166–169
Avenpace 401–402
Averroës (Ibn Rushd) 101, 402,
    402–403, 532
Averroists 351, 352
aviation 505–506
Avicenna (Ibn Sina) 698
  and Islamic philosophy 397–399
  and medicine in Islamic world
    530–532
  music theory, Islamic 751
Avignon popes 23–24
awqaf 72
Ayn Jalut, Battle of 73
Ayyubid dynasty 71–73, 310
al-Azhar University 148
azoth 426

B

babush 869g
Babylonian Captivity ix, 23–24

Babylonian Talmud
  and Jews in Byzantine Empire 91
  and Jews in Capetian France 84
Bacon, Roger 513–514
  and Christian magic 424
  gunpowder in Christian Europe
    279
  Ibn Sina 531–532
Badchanim 745
badger 203
Baghdad
  Abbasids 67
  Benjamin of Tudela 255
  sea trade 214
Baghdad Manifesto 71
bagpipes 727
Bahri Mamluk dynasty 71–72
al-Baladhuri, Ahmad ibn Yahya 408
balancing agents 474
balandras 863g
baldaquin 557–558
baldness 477
baldrics 827g
Baldwin of Boulogne 658
al-Balki, Mashar 538
ball-and-chain governors 543
ballet comique de la reine 735
ballet de cour 734
ballista 277–278
Baltic Crusades 30
balustrade 557
bananas 232–233
bankers
  Christian 206
  Jewish 35, 79, 203
banquettes 561
Banu Musa brothers 542, 543
Banu Qurayza Jews 58
baptism
  Christian philosophy and religion
    335
  forced 87, 89, 248
bar (weapon) 289–290
barbarian invasions 5–7, 6
Barbarossa, Ariadeno 216
barbette 858g
Bar Hiyyah, Abraham 523
Barlaam and Josaphat 633
barley soup 491
barrette 828g
barrows 567
Bartolus de Saxoferrato 290
Bashar ibn Burd 689

bas relief 578
al-Basri, Hasan
    and Islamic mysticism 453
    and Qadiriyya movement 392
basse dance 735
bassinet and *camail* 272
basson 727
bastardy 286
baths and bathing *124*, 124–126, *126*
    and Jewish sensuality 173
    palaces, Islamic 618
battering rams 277
battlement 557
baya (investiture of the ruler) 820
Bayeux Tapestry 569
Bazl (Arabian musician)
    and court music, Islamic 755
    music and dance, Islamic 753
beast epic 653
beast fables
    Chrisitan literature 652–653
    literature, Jewish 668–670
    Persian literature 699–700
beast literature
    Arabic 701–702
    Christian 651–653
beasts of prayer 447, 600–602
"beauty mark" 476
Bede, Venerable 632, 657, 777
beffroy 276
beguin 858g
bell, book, and candle 337
belladonna 479
bellarmines 579
Bellifortis (Kyeser) 281
bells
    Christmas 768
    as musical instruments 731–732
bendlet 288
Benedict XIII (pope) 89, 104
Benedictine Order 132, 350
benedictop 265
benedictus 718
Benjamin of Tudela 255–256
Beowulf 635–636, 659
Berechiah Ha Nakdan 666, 668, 682
Bergbarte 268
Bernard, Saint 359
Bernardino of Siena 651
Bernard of Clairvaux 30, 101, 417–418
berrette a cannelatto 858g

bestiary 651–652
Betrothal of the Virgin (Campin) 587
beverages 518–519
bevor 272
Bezalel
    Jewish art 590
    Jewish mysticism 445
bezoar stone 491
Bhaskara 541
Bible
    and allegorical writings 654
    Christian interpretation of 341
    Jewish interpretation of 368–384
        Hasdai ben Abraham Crescas 383–384
        Judah Halevi 372–374
        Abraham ibn Daud 374–376
        Bahya ibn Pakuda 371–372
        Maimonides 376–382
        Nachmanides 382–383
        Rashi 370–371
        Saddya Gaon 368–370
    translation into Arabic 368
bill of exchange 205
bimah 593
bimaristan 533
biographical dictionaries, Arabic 696–697
birds 647, 652
Birds Head Haggadah 600
biretta 858g–859g
Birgitta, Saint 633
Biringuccio, Vannoccio 509–510
    gunpowder in Christian Europe 279
    guns in Christian Europe 280
birth stool 494
birth time mirror 493
al-Biruni, Abu al-Rayhan 696
    and astrology in Islamic world 540
    geography in Islamic world 223
bishops 4–5
al-Bistami 454–455
Black Death (bubonic plague) 41, 103
    and Great Famine 191
    and medieval European medicine 485, 499–503
    Saint Catherine and 789
    and secular Christian music 723
    spices as medicine 202
black magic 460
bladder 488–491

blanchet 863g
blandreths 558
blazon 287
bliaut 274, 363g
blood, in Christian mysticism 422–423
bloodletting 497–499
boar 777–778
Boards of Health 201–202
Boccaccio, Giovanni 103, 631, 638, 642, 664
Bodel, Jean 636, 645
body armor 273–275, *274*
Body of Civil Law 78
body-soul dichotomy 355
Boethius 349–350
    music theory 715
    and secular Christian music 722
Bohras 407
bones, and medieval European medicine 486–488
Boniface VIII (pope) 99
    Babylonian Captivity 23, 24
    and Thomas Aquinas 354
bonnet 859g
Book of Creation 445
Book of Deight (Zabara) 481
The Book of Doctrines and Beliefs (Saddya Gaon) 368–370
The Book of Healing (Ibn Sina) 532
book of hours 575
The Book of Knowledge of Ingenious Mechanical Devices (al-Jazari) 543
The Book of Margery Kempe 633
Book of Medicine for Mansur (al-Razi) 526–528
The Book of Modes (al-Urmawi) 751
The Book of Roger (al-Idrisi) 223–224
The Book of Saint Foy 632
Book of Songs (al-Isfahani) 750, 754
Book of Splendor, the Zohar (Leon) 446
Book of the Pious (Judah the Pious).
    See also Sefer Hasidim
    Hasidism 85
    and Jewish mysticism 447, 448
    and Jewish sensuality 175
    synagogue music 739
Book of Tradition (Daud) 376
Book of Travelers' Provisions (Nasir-I Khusraw) 405
booksellers 226
border security, in Islamic world 222
Boudicca (queen of the Celts) 282

Bovo-Bukh (Elijah Bahur) 673
branc 863*g*
bread
    at feasts 789–791
    Lammas Day 786
   in medieval European medicine
      478, 490
   in medieval Jewish medicine 517
breast cancer 492, 497
Brethren of the Free Spirit 363–365
brigandine 274
brodequin 869*g*
broigne 274, 863*g*
brothers 358
Brothers of Santa Maria de Évora 31
Brown, Peter 49
Bruno, Saint 358
brusttuch 863*g*
bubonic plague. *See* Black Death
buccine 727
buffon/buffen 733
al-Buhturi 686
bukhnuq 859*g*
burda 863*g*
burning at the stake
    Inquisition 33–34
    Jews, persecution of 84
burnose 863*g*
al-Buzjani, Abu l-Wafa Muhammad
  751
byrnie 274
byrrus 863*g*
Byzantine architectural style
  567–568
Byzantine dome 568
Byzantine Empire (Byzantium) ix,
  43–56, *44, 51*
   arts and crafts 567–568, 572,
    585–586
    collapse of 54–55
   Comnenian restoration 52–54
    contraction of 47–48
   economy and trade 186–187
   and emergence of new cultures xi
   golden age of 50–51
   Great Schism 21–22
   Heraclius 45–47
   historiography x
   Iconoclast Controversy 49–50
   incendiary weapons 307
   Jews in 90–91
   Justinian, reign of 43–45
   key personalities of 55–56

manuscripts 572
manuscripts, Christian 572
monks, nuns, and monasteries
  48–49
Normans 51
and Sassanians 60–61
Seljuks 51–52

C

caban 863*g*
cadency 288–289
Caesar of Heisterbach 651
caeseropapism 49
caftan 863*g*
Cahorism 250
Caillet, Guillaume 192
Cair, founding of 70
Cairo
  Ibn Battuta 241
  Nasir-i Khusraw 238
Cairo *geniza* 93
  economy and trade, Jewish 247
  humanism 250
  and Jewish women 170
caladrius bird 652
calcination 429–430
cale 859*g*
calendars
  in Christian magic 432
  of Jewish festivals 801–813
  and Jews in Byzantine Empire 91
Calendula 479
caliphs/caliphate. *See also* Abbasid
  caliphate (Abbasids); Umayyad
  caliphate (Umayyads)
  and court music, Islamic 754
  as Islamic art patrons 606, 607
  landed estates 152–153
  palaces, Islamic 618
  qiyan 752, 753
calligraphy
  Christian 572–575, *574*
  Islamic 544, 614–617, *615*
calms 559
calotte 859*g*
caltrop 270
camail 272, 273
cambium 205
camels 221
camera obscura 525
campagus 869*g*
Campin, Robert 587
cancer 492

Cannon Maior manuscript page *398*
The Cannon of Medicine (Avicenna)
  398
cannons 280–281
canonical hours 357–358
  calligraphy, Christian 575
  church music 718
Canon law
  and Christian religious vestments
    826–827
  and Jewish merchants/
    moneylenders 203
  and Jews 164–165
The Canon of Medicine (Ibn Sina)
  530–531, 537
Cantar del mío Cid 635
Canterbury Cathedral *507,* 559
Canterbury Tales (Chaucer) 122, 132,
  360, 631, 642–643, 669
"Canticle of the Sun" (Francis of
  Assisi) 360
canting arms 290
Canute VI, king of Denmark 657
canzo 640
capa 863*g*
caparisoned horse *275*
capeline 272
capers 489
Capet, Hugh 14, 100
Capetian dynasty
  and France 14
  Jews in 83–84
Capparis spinosa 489
cappuccio a foggia 859*g*
capuchon 859*g*
caput moruum 429
caravan routes 214
caraway seeds 477
carbuncle 289–290
carcaille 863*g*
cardinal's hat 828*g*
cargo ships 216
Carmelite mendicant order 360
Carmina burana 642, 724
Carnival, pre-Lenten 772–773
Carolingian architectural style
  568–569
Carolingian kingdom (Carolingian
  Renaissance) 8–9
  Christian philosophy and religion
    345
  and emergence of new cultures
    xi

Investiture Controversy 19–20
Jewish soldiers 316
Jews in 82–83
Carolingian minuscule script 573
carols 767
carpet pages 572
carpets, Anatolian 856–857
Carpini, Giovanni del Pian del 209
Carthusian monks 358
cartomancy 433
cartouche 289
casque 271
casquetel 272
cassapanca 558
cassones 554, 558
Castilian Civil War 318
Castilian language 661
castles, design of 556–559
Catalan language 661–662
catapults
    Villard de Honnecourt 506
    onager 278
    siege techniques and equipment
        277
    warfare and weapons, Christian
        281
cataracts 537
Cathars 29, 30, 363
Cathay 212, 213
Catherine of Siena, Saint **42,** 422–
    423, 764–765
Catherine's Day, Saint 788–789
catnip 495
caul 859g
cauterization 497
    in Christian magic 432
    and medieval European medicine
        483–484
cautery iron 497
cautery man 431
Caxton, William 575–576
celestial kinematics 505
Celestine III (pope) 30
celibacy 22, 357–358
cellarium 559
Celtic languages 639, 660
cementation 512
Cennini, Cennino 581
cenobitic monasticism 48
censer 583
ceramics
    Christian 579–580
    Islamic 620–621

certosine 577
cesarean section 494
chain mail *271*
chalice 582
chamarre 864g
chamfron 275, 276
chamomile 489
champlevé 564–565, 568, 579
chancel 559
La Chançun de Guillelme 634
chanson de geste 630, 631, 634–636,
    673–674
Le Chanson de Roland 634–635
chant 720
Chanukah 804–805
chape 859g
chapeau 859g
chaperone 859g
chaplet 859g
chapter house 561
charge 287
chargers 570
charkh 307
Charlemagne (emperor of the West)
    42, 99, 660
    and Carolingian kingdom 8–9
    Jewish soldiers 315–316
    in literature 631, 634–635
    universities 39
Charles VI (king of France) 103
Charles VII (king of France) 15
Charles of Anjou 102
chasing 578
chasse 583
chasuble 828g
Chaucer, Geoffrey 631, 638, 639,
    642–644, 647, 653, 664
    on food 132–135
    friars and 360
    on gluttony 137
    language of 659
    and medicine in Islamic world
        525
Chauliac, Guy de 482, 497
chazzan 739
cheese 490
cheidomancy 434
chemise 864g
chemistry 511–513
chestnuts 486
chevron 289–290
child marriage 113–114

children
    Islamic holidays surrounding
        birth 821
    and manuscript art, Jewish 598
China 504–505
chi-rho monogram 582
chiromancy 433
Chirstmas tree 767
chivalry 265–266
choirs 559
cholent 592
choleric 485
"chosen people," Jews as 448
chouchant lion 287
chouzia 307
Chrétien de Troyes 101, 637, 638,
    664
chrism 582
Christianity
    effects on philosophy and
        religion, Jewish 367
    and emergence of new cultures
        xi–xii
    and England 13
    and food 136–138
    growth of 3–5
    in Islamic world 820
    and Jewish mysticism 440, 446
    and medieval Jewish physicians
        515
    and merchants/moneylenders
        204, 249–250
    shared dogmas with
        Mutakallimun 394
    in Spain 16–17
Christians **110–138.** *See also specfic
    headings, e.g.:* economy and trade,
    Christian
    in cities 120–123
    and corporations 118–119
    daily hygiene of 123–126
    duality and hierarchy 110–114
    and feudalism 114–117
    and food 131–138
        Chaucer on 132–135
        morality and 136–138
        social class and sumptuary
            laws 131–132
        unnatural and supernatural
            135–136
    hunting by 126–131
        monkeys, hawks, and dogs
            130–131

Christians *(continued)*
    otter 129–130
      wolf trapping 127–129
    parliaments and estates 119
    persecution of 3–4
    sumptuary laws regulating Jews
      839–842
    and taxation 118–119
    and universities/scholasticism
      117–118
    women 119–120
Christine de Pizan 632, 649, 650,
  655, 664, *665*
Christ in the Temple 334, *334*
Christmas 766–769
Christmas carols 767
Christmas plays 767–768
Christotokos
    Christian philosophy and religion
      331
    and Mary, Mother of God 362
Chroniates, Nicetas 658
chronicles
    Arabic 695–696
    Christian 656–658
    Jewish 681–682
Chronique (Enguerrand de
  Monstrelet) 656–657
chronophysica 484–485
    astrolabe 505
    in medieval Europe 504
    and medieval European medicine
      470, 484–485
    in medieval European medicine
      485
    and secular Christian music 722
Chrysostom, John 361
churches and cathedrals, design of
  559–561
church mass 716–718
church music 714–719
    ars nova 719
    church mass 716–718
    Gregorian chant 718
    music theory and world order
      715–716
    Notre Dame school and *ars
      antiqua* 718–719
ciborium 582
Cicle du Roi 634
El Cid 635
cilice 828*g*
cimier 273

cingulum 828*g*
cinnabar 570
circlet (headdress) 859*g*
the Circumcision, feast of 770
cire perdue 578
Cistercian Order 359, 418–419
cithera 727
cities
    Christians in 120–123
    as Islamic art patrons 607–608
    and Jewish autonomy 167
    Muslims in 149–150
cittern 727
City of God (Augustine) 111, 348
    Christian philosophy and religion
      342
    and Jews in western Europe 80,
      81
civil servants 243
Clarenceux 291
clarion 727
class, social 131–132
clavichord 728
cleidomancy 434
Clement VII (pope) 103
clerestory 560, 563
clergy 265, 357–358
cloak 864*g*
clocks 504–505
    in Islamic world 542
    in medieval Europe 504–505
cloisonné
    Byzantine architectural style 568
    metalwork, Christian 579
    Romanesque architectural style
      564
cloth industry
    Flanders and Christian economy
      and trade 197–198
    guilds 195
clothing, costume, and textiles (in
  general)
    about 826
    fashionable garments, terms for
      863–869
    hats and headwear, terms for
      858–863
    resources 870–872
    shoes, terms for 869–870
clothing, costume, and textiles,
  Christian **826–834**
    religious vestments 826–830
      and canon law 826–827

      monastic orders 829–830
      terms for 827–829
    secular clothing 830–833
    and sumptuary laws 833–834
clothing, costume, and textiles,
  Jewish **834–845**
    cultural and social statement,
      costumes as 837
    moral statement, costumes as
      835–837
    and sumptuary laws 837–845
      ceremonial garments 842–
        844
      Christian regulation 839–842
      hats and headwear 844–845
clothing and costume, Muslim **845–
  851**. *See also* textiles, Muslim
    Abbasid dynasty 848–849
    color and religious ideology
      847–848
    Fatimid dynasty 849–850
    ritual clothing 847
    styles of clothing 846–851
    suf and *khirqa* 850–851
    sumptuary laws 848
    Umayyad dynasty 848
    women's wear 850
cloth of gold 584
Clovis I (king of the Franks) 7
Cluny monks 264, 358–359
Cluny Reform movement 20
coat of arms. *See* heraldry and arms
cobblers 195
Codex Abrogans 663
coffers 578
cogito ergo sum 399
cohobation 512
coif 859*g*
coinage
    and Christian economy and trade
      204–205
    in Islamic world 226–228
    weights and measures, Christian
      200
cointise 273
coitus 535
colchicum/colchicine 487
Colegiata de Santa Julia, Santillana
  del Mar, Spain *556*
colise 288
collegantia contracts 206
college of arms 290–292
collyria 473

colobium 585
colors
    Christian religious art 582
    heraldry and arms 288
    manuscripts, Christian 570, 571
Columbus, Christopher 90, 212
"commanding right and forbidding
    wrong" 140–141
commenda contract 206
Commentary on the Bible (Rashi) 370,
    371
*The Commentary on the Metaphysics of
    Aristotle* (al-Tafsir) 402
Commentary on the Mishnah
    (Maimonides) 377
Commentary on the Torah
    (Nachmanides) 382
commerce
    Jewish economy and trade
        243–245
    in western Europe 35–36
communal life 59
Communion
    Christian philosophy and religion
        335
    church mass 718
Comnenian restoration 52–54
Comneni dynasty 52, 54
compagnia contracts 206
conception time mirror 493
Concordat of Worms 21
The Conditions of Women (Trotula of
    Salerno) 492–493
confession 345
Confessions (Augustine of Hippo)
    348, 633
confirmation 336
Consolation of Philosophy (Boethius)
    349–350
constable 291
Constantine I the Great (emperor of
    Rome) 76, 568
Constantine V (Eastern Roman
    emperor) 49, 50
Constantinople 53–54, *301*
    Byzantine Empire 47
    guns in Christian Europe 280
Constantius II (emperor of Rome) 90
Constitution of Medina 57, 60
Constitutions of Clarendon 14
contraception 494–496
contracts 229
conversos 33, 89–90, 419, 420, 423

cope/cape 864*g*
copper coinage 227, 228
Coptic cloth 856
Córdoba
    coinage in Islamic world 227
    and Umayyads in Spain 66
    Umayyad Spain, Jews in 95
cordovan 869*g*
cordwainers 195
cornalia 859*g*
Cornazano, Antonio 648
cornetto 728
corporations 118–119
Corpus Christi, Feast of 780
Corpus hermeticum (Trismegistus) 428
coscinomancy 434
costumes. *See* clothing, costume, and
    textiles
cote 864*g*
cotehardie 864*g*
cotelette 864*g*
Cotrugli, Benedetto 121, 206
cotteron 864*g*
cotton 853
couching 478
Council of Chalcedon 19
Council of Clermont
    Crusades 26
    First Crusade 27
    Peace of God 264, 265
Council of Constance 24, 25, *25*
Council of Constantinople, First
    18–19
Council of Coyanza 87
Council of Ephesus 362
Council of Meaux 83
Council of Nicaea 4, 18, 327, 329
Council of Toledo 98
Council of Toulouse 83
Council of Trent 336
counts
    and Carolingian kingdom 9
    feudalism 34
    and Merovingian kingdom 7–8
courtly love 636
court music, Islamic 754–755
coverchief 859*g*
cracelle 728–729
cracowes 869*g*
cranial chisel 472
creatio ex nihilo 380
Crécy, Battle of 269
credence testers 491

credo 717
crenellation 557
Crescas, Hasdai ben Abraham
    383–384
crescent 288
crespinette 860*g*
crinet 275
crocus 474, 492
cromorne 729
crop rotation 189
crossbow 270, 307
crosses
    Christianity 584–585
    heraldry and arms 289
crossing 559
cross moline 289
Cross of the Scriptures 567
crucifixion of Jesus 329–331
cruet 582
crupper 276
Crusade, First 101
    Comnenian restoration 52
    Jews, persecution and expulsion
        of 84
    and Jews in Capetian France
        83–84
    Usamah ibn Munqidh 239
    siege techniques and equipment
        276
Crusade, Third 101
    warfare and weapons, Islamic
        308–309
    ziyar 304
Crusade, Fourth 102, 658
    Constantinople, sacking of
        53–54
    Fourth Lateran Council 23
Crusade, Fifth
    Fourth Lateran Council 23
    Muslims perspective of 72
Crusade, Seventh 210
crusader chronicles
    literature, Christian 658
    literature, Jewish 681–682
crusader ethos 263–265
Crusader Kingdom of Jerusalem 52
Crusader States *29*
Crusades 26–32
    Albigensian 29–30, 363
    arradah 304
    Baltic 30
    economy and trade 188
    economy and trade, Jewish 243

Crusades *(continued)*
  and emergence of new cultures xi
  historiography x
  indulgences and 345
  Islamic music 758
  and Jewish massacres 248
  and Jewish merchants/
    moneylenders 203, 248
  Usamah ibn Munqidh 238–239
  Muslims perspective of 72–73
  and Peace of God movement
    264–245
  pirates and corsairs 216
  religious military orders 30–32
"The Cuckoo Song" 642
cucumbers 489, 492
cuirass 273
cuir bouilli 274
cultures, emergence of new xi–xii
culverin 280–281
cupel 512
cupola furnace 512
Cur Deus homo (Anselm of
  Canterbury) 351
curtal 729
Curtana 268
cyclas 864g–865g
Cyprian of Carthage, Saint 361
Cyrene juice 495
Cyril, Saint 50

D

dabbabah 309
dactylic meter 719
dagger 267–268
dagging 580
daily hygiene
  Christians 123–126
  Muslims 150–151
dais 70
dalmatic 828g
Damascus
  coinage in Islamic world 227
  commerce in Ummayad mosque
    225–226
  mosques, design of 612
  swords, Islamic 300
  Umayyad caliphate 64
Damietta
  Ibn Battuta 241
  Muslim women and political
    power 156
Dananir 753

dance (in general)
  about 714
  resources 759–761
dance, Christian 732–737
  books 735
  dance of love and dance of death
    736–737
  dancing mania 737
  forms 733–735
  manuals 648
  Orchesography 735
dance, Islamic
  Muslim Spain 758–759
  Ottoman Turkish music 756–757
  Persian music 755–756
  Sufi dance and music 757–758
dance, Jewish *746*, 746–747
dance macabre 736
dance of death 650
Danelaw language 632, 659
Daniel, book of 449
Dante Alighieri 346, 385, 641, 643,
  655, 655–656, 664. *See also Divine
  Comedy* (Dante)
  Ibn Sina 531
  language of 662
darajah 309
Dar al-Hikma 148
Dar al-Ilm 148
Dar al-Islam 245
Daud, Abraham ibn
  Jewish philosophy and religion
    374–376
  Lucena, Jews in 96
Daudi Bohras 407
David, Abraham ben 172, 378
David, Anan ben 92, 99
da Vigevano, Guido 650
da Vinci, Leonardo 543
dawa
  Abbasids 69
  Fatimid *dawa* 70
  and Nasir-I Khusraw 405
Dawoodi 407
*De Amore libri tres (The Art of Courtly
  Love)* (Andreas Capellanus) 646–
  647
Decalogue 367–368
The Decameron (Giovanni Boccaccio)
  103, 631, 638, 642, 664
Deesis
  Byzantine architectural style 568
  Byzantine arts and crafts 586

Defensor pacis (Marsiglio of Padua)
  24
De Incarnatione verbi (Athanasius) 330
De magnalibus urbis Mediolani (Riva)
  196
demicannon 280
denier 205
derash scriptural interpretation 370,
  440
De re metallica (Agricola) 510, 511
dervishes 459, *460*, 757
  and al-Farabi 397
  Ibn Battuta 241–242
Descartes, René 399
Desclot, Bernat 657
Description of India (al-Biruni) 223
The Description of the World (Marco
  Polo) 210
Deuteronomy 176
devil *435*
devine revelation 404
devine unity 393
De Virtutis Balneorum Puteolanis
  (Pietro da Eboli) 126
devotional literature 631–634
dexter 286
dhikr 453, 459
dhimmis 156
  Jewish law 168
  and Jews in Carolingian
    Renaissance 83
  Jews in Islamic empire 92
  and Jews in Islamic empire 94
  Lucena, Jews in 96
  and *Pact of Umar* 165–166
  Umar caliphate 62
  Umayyad caliphate 66
dhow 216
Dhu al-Himma 692–693
diadem 860g
diapering 576
Diaspora
  economy and trade 188
  Jewish x
  Judaism, restructuring of 76, 77
  warfare and weapons, Jewish
    311–312
diastema 476
Díaz de Vivar, Rodrigo 635. *See also*
  Cid, El.
diet
  and health issues 488–490
  and Jewish medicine 517–520

and medicine in Islamic world 535

and medieval European medicine 470, 480, 485–486, 489

dill 472, 490

dimidation 287

dinanderie
    Hispano-Moresque architectural style 570
    metalwork, Christian 579

dinar, gold 227

Dinis, king of Portugal 662

Diocletian (emperor of Rome) ix, 3–4

Dioscorides 495

dirhams, silver 227

disarmed Jews 319–320

Discalced Carmelite Order 420

disease 235, 529. *See also* Black Death

Disputation of Tortosa 89

distillation 511–513, *512*

divination 433–435, 462

Divine Comedy (Dante) 385, *655*, 655–656, 675
    language of 662
    repentance in 346

divine illumination 455

divine intercession 48

diving gear 281

divorce 171, 798–799

diwans
    and Abbasids 68
    palaces, Islamic 618

Dodecachordon 724

dogaline 865*g*

dogs 130–131

dolce stil nuovo 640, 641

Dome of the Rock 535, 613

Dominic, Saint 360

Dominican Order 102, 351, 360

Donation of Constantine (imperial edict) 19, 20

Donatist controversy
    and Augustine of Hippo 348–349, 363
    and doctrine of just war 263

Donatists 363

Donatus Magnus 363

Dondi, Giovanni da 504

donkeys 221

Don Manuel of Castile 651

Doön de Mayence 634

door, in Jewish mysticism 442

dormitory 561

double-entry bookkeeping 207–208

doublet 865*g*

douf 756

dowry 155

Dragon's blood 429–430

drama and theater
    ascension plays 779
    Christian literature 631, 643–646
    Christmas plays 767–768
    Corpus Christi mystery plays 780
    Epiphany plays 770–771
    during Purim 810–811

dreams 434

dream visions 632

drolleries 598

drugs
    Ibn Sina and testing and use of 530–531
    and medieval European medicine 472–474

Druze 406

duality 110–114

dual papacy 111

duck bill shoes 869*g*

Dukus Horunt 672

dulcimer 729

Duns Scotus, John 354–355

Duties of the Heart (Paquda) 371

duty, and jihad 293

dyes 854

E

eagle
    in Christian magic 428
    heraldry and arms, Jewish 320

earthly reward 384

Easter 776–778
    and pre-Lenten season 771–772
    and proclamation of feasts 770

Easter eggs 777, 778

Easter Sunday 774–775

Eben Bochan (Kalonymous ben Kalonymous) 674

Ebreo, Guglielmo 648, 747

Eckhart, Johannes 417

economy and trade (in general) 250–251
    about 186–189
    resources 256–260

economy and trade, Christian **189–213**
    and Black Death 41
    double-entry bookkeeping 207–208
    early economic theory 208
    fairs 198–199
    farms 189–193
        and Great Famine 191–192
        and Jacquérie Revolt 192
        and Wat Tyler's peasant revolt 192–193
    financial system 203–207
        agents 207
        coinage 204–205
        depositors 207
        exchange contracts 205
        factoring 207
        and Jewish merchants/moneylenders 203–204
        joint ventures 206
        loans 205–206
    guilds 193–195
    and medical law 201–202
    medicines 202–203
    merchant cities 195–198
    merchant courts 198–199
    Nicholas Oresme 208
    spices 202
    and travel 208–213
        Alexander the Great 208–209
        Giovanni del Pian del Carpini 209
        John Mandeville 210–212
        Marco Polo 210
        Francesco de Banduccio Perolotti 212–213
        William of Rubruck 209–210
    weights and measures 199–200

economy and trade, Islamic **213–242**
    farms 230–235
        and famine 234–235
        "green revolution" 231–234
        manuals 234
    and financial system 226–230
        coinage 226–228
        exchange rates 228
        financing 229–230
        money lending 229
    goods, role of 224–225
    merchant cities 225–226
    merchants, role of 224

economy and trade, Islamic
(*continued*)
  overland trade 217–222
    border security 222
    Golden Horde 219
    means of transportation
     221–222
    Saharan trade routes 219–
     221
    and water 221
  pastoralists 230, 231
  sea trade 213–217
    Ibn Battuta in Jeddah
     214–215
    maritime technology 215–
     216
    pirates and corsairs 216–217
    ports and customs 217
  and study of geography 222–224
  travel books 235–242
    Ibn Battuta 240–242
    Nasir-i Khusraw's *Safarnama*
     237–238
    al-Kitab of Ibn Fadlan
     236–237
    Usamah ibn Munqudh
     238–239
    Rihla travel diaries 235–236
    Travels of Ibn Jubayr 239–240
economy and trade, Jewish **242–256**
  commercial decline and fall of
   243–245
  crafts and professions 245–247
  in Dar al-Islam 245
  and humanism 250
  king, in service of 242–243
  moneylending 247–250
  and travel 251–256
    Obadiah of Bertinoro
     254–255
    Perahya ben Joseph 254
    Radhanites 252–254
    Travels of Benjamin of Tudela
     255–256
  virtues of trading 250–251
ecstasy, in Islamic mysticism 455
Edict of Milan
  persecution of Christians 3–4
  warfare and weapons, Christian
   262–263
education and learning 145–149
  Ijaza 148–149
  madrasa 146–148

medieval European medicine 482
  Shiite 148
  universities 39
eduction 482
Edward III (king of England) 131
Edward VI (king of England) 118
eel, stewed 479
eggs
  Easter 777
  in medieval European medicine
   486
Egina, Paolo di 497
Egypt, image of *224*
Eilhart von Oberg 638
Eilmer of Malmsbury 505–506
ein sof 446
Eiximenis, Francesc 649
Eleanor of Aquitaine 636, 637, 640
  and Jewish moneylenders 248
  warfare and weapons, Christian
   284
An Elegant Book on Mangonels (al-
  Zaradkash) 303, 307
elephants 652
elixirs 425, 428–429
Elizabeth I (queen of England) 118
embossing 578
embrasure 557
embroidery 562
"emerald tablet" 427–428
emirates 66
emmenagogue 494, 495
emotions 519
enamel(s)
  Byzantine architectural style 568
  ceramics, Christian 580
  metalwork, Christian 578–579
endura 362–363
engineering 505–508, *507*
England 13–14
  economy and trade, Jewish 246
  Hundred Years' War 15–16
  and Jewish moneylenders
   248–249
  literary languages in 658–659
  Michaelmas 787
English language, translations from
  Arabic to 408
engrafting 483
engraving 577–578
Enguerrand de Monstrelet 656–657
enlightenment, spiritual 451
Enoch, biblical book of 449

entertainment
  guilds 194
  Jewish town song 742–744
  and Jewish town song 743
epaule de mouton 274
Epiphany and Twelfth Night 766,
  769–770
epitoga 865g
equestrian dance 734
ergotism 737
ermine 288
eschapins 869g
eschatology, Christian 343–345
eschaton 343
escoffion 860g
escoffion a sella 860g
espringal 304–305
Essenes 48
estates 119
estrain 860g
etching 577–578
eternal light candelabras 594
ethics
  and jihad 293–296
  and Bahya ibn Paquda 371
  philosophy and religion, Jewish
   366
  and Thomas Aquinas 353
Ethics (Aristotle) *366*
Étienne de Bourbon 651
etiquette, books of 700
Eucharist 329, 330, 716, 718
Eugene III (pope) 27
Eugene IV (pope) 26
Europe, medieval
  influence of, on Muslim art 624
  medicine in **470–503**
    bones 486–488
    cancer therapy 492
    the eye 477–481
    face and physiognomy
     474–477
    general medicine 496–499
    the head 471–474
    kidney and bladder 488–491
    the nose 481–486
    obstetrics and genethlialogy
     492–496
    plague 499–503
  science and technology in
   503–514
    chemistry 511–513
    engineering 505–508

instruction books 513–514
keeping time 504–505
metallurgy 509–511
watermills v. windmills 508–509
Europe, western **3–43**
barbarian invasions 5–7
Black Death in 41
Carolingian kingdom 8–9
Christianity, growth of 3–5
commercial revolution 35–36
England 13–14
feudalism 34–35
France 14–16
Germanic tribes, assimilation of 5
guilds 38–39
historical survey 3–18
historiography x
Holy Roman Empire 9–13
Inquisition 32–34
Jews in 78–90
Capetian France 83–84
Carolingian Renaissance 82–83
Christian Iberia 87–88
converso phenomenon 89–90
in 1492 90
France and Germany: Ashkenaz 81–82
Halachic learning 84
Hasidim 86
Italian Jewish culture 79–80
Italian Peninsula settlements 78–79
Merovingian France and Germany 82
papacy 80–81
persecution and expulsion 84–86
in 13th and 14th centuries 88
key personalities 42–43
Merovingian kingdom 7–8
social and economic developments 34–41
Spain 16–18
towns and cities, growth of 36–38
Treaty of Verdun 9
universities 39–41
Eve-Ave antithesis 331–333
Everyman 645–646

evil
and Augustine of Hippo 348
Jewish philosophy and religion 385–386
and Maimonides 381–382
The Exalted Faith (Daud) 374–376
Excalibur 268
exchange contracts 205, 206
exchange rates 205, 228
excommunication, Christian 337
exegesis and fourfold interpretation 341
exempla
Christian 631–632, 650–651
Jewish 680
Exeter Book 653
Exodus 445, 590
exoteric/esoteric texts 439
experiments 480–481, 514
expulsion, edict of 90
Eye Book (Juliani) 480
eyes 477–481, 537
Ezekiel 441, 449
Ezra Synagogue 93

F
fabliaux 631, 652–654
face and physiognomy
and medieval European medicine 474–477
The Face of Religion (Nasir-I Khusraw) 405
factories 35
factoring 207
Fadlan, Ahmad ibn
al-Kitab of 236–237
Rihla travel diaries 235
faience 579
fairs 198–199, 787
falak 540
Falasifa 387
falconry 647
falcons (cannon) 281
falsafa 395–403
Avicenna 397–399
al-Farabi 397
al-Kindi 396
responses by 401–403
Sunni-Kalam reaction 399–401
famines
Great Famine 191–192
in Islamic world 234–235
fana 454

faqirs 459
al-Farabi, Abu Nasr 397, 750
farms and farming *199, 232*
in Christian Europe 189–193
and Great Famine 191–192
and Jacquérie Revolt 192
and Wat Tyler's peasant revolt 192–193
in Islamic world 230–235
famine 234–235
"green revolution" 231–234
manuals 234
fasting
and Christian mysticism 422
during Lent 773
during Ramadan 160, 816
Fast of Gedalia 802
Fatimid caliphate
Jews in 93–94
Muslim clothing 849–850
overland trade in Islamic world 217
Fatimid *dawa* 70–71
Fat Tuesday 772–773
fatwas
and Islamic mysticism 457
jihad 295
Faust plays 646
feast ceremonials 478
Feast of the Star 771
felix culpa 329
femmes soles 194
fencing 267
Ferdinand II (king of Aragon) 17–18, **42–43**, 90, 243
Ferdinand III (king of Castile) 318
fertility 598
fertilizer 233–234
fess 287, 289
Festival of Breaking the Fast (Id al-Fitr) 817
feudalism
in Byzantine Empire 53
and Christians 114–117
in western Europe 34–36
feudalism tithes 117
feudal lords 36
Fibonacci, Leonardo 545
fichets 865g
fidais 405
fiefdoms 34
figs 489
filigree 578

filioque clause 22
fillet 860g
filoque controversy 327
filtration 512
financial system *204, 228*
    in Christian Europe 203–207
       agents 207
       coinage 204–205
       depositors 207
       exchange contracts 205
       factoring 207
       and Jewish merchants/
         moneylenders 203–204
       joint ventures 206
       loans 205–206
    in Islamic world 226–230
       coinage 226–228
       exchange rates 228
       financing 229–230
       money lending 229
Firdawsi 706–708
fire pots 307
First Crusade. *See* Crusade, First
First Temple period 589–590
fish 517
fitna 295
Five Pillars of Islam 139–140
Flamel, Nicholas 425
flame thrower 308
Flanders 195, 197–198
Flavius Vegetius 650
fleur-de-lis
    heraldry and arms, Christian 289
    heraldry and arms, Islamic 310,
      311
    heraldry and arms, Jewish 320
Fleur et Blanchefleur 639
flieder 860g
Flooding of the Nile (holiday) 821
flugel 865g
flutes 729, 751
fluting 576
flying buttresses
    architects, Christian 554
    Gothic architectural style 565
foie gras 478
Foligno, Gentile da 501
folklore 136
folk song, Jewish 740–741
Fons vitae 458
food and drink
    bone-healing 486–487
    and bubonic plague 501–502

    in Christian Europe
      Chaucer on 132–135
      Christian morality and
        136–138
      social class and sumptuary
        laws 131–132
      unnatural and supernatural
        135–136
    during Christmas 768–769
    Jewish 175–180
      medicine 518
      mystical eating, sensual meals
        178–180
      Pesach 806–808
      Purim 811
      Sabbath 800
      sumptuary laws 177–178
    and medicine in Islamic world 535
    Michaelmas 787–788
    Muslims and 159–161
    symbolism of 422
    Valentine's Day 781
Fools, Feast of 770, 782
footbow
    crossbows, Islamic 307
    siege weapons, Islamic 303, 304
forceps 494
Forer, Conrad 647
forma corporeitatis 355
Forrest, William 483–484
four elements 427
Four Horsemen of the Apocalypse
    344
four humors *485*, 485–486
    and bloodletting 498
    and bubonic plague 501
    Maimonides on 521
    and medicine in Islamic world
      526, 527, *527*, 535
    and medieval European medicine
      472–473
    and secular Christian music 721
Fourth Lateran Council 22–23
    Canon law and Jews 164
    confession and 345–346
    Crusades 28
    and Jews in western Europe 81
frame tale (framed tale) 642
    Arabic 702
    Jewish 670–672
France 14–16
    economy and trade, Jewish 246
    Jewish soldiers in 315–317

    Jews in 81–84
    literary languages in 660
    Saint Catherine's Day 789
francisca 268
Franciscan Order 102, 360
    Giovanni del Pian del Carpini
      209
    John Duns Scotus 354–355
    William of Ockham 356
Francis of Assisi, Saint 102, 360, 634
    Giovanni del Pian del Carpini
      209
    and Christmas 766, 767
    Muslims perspective of Crusades
      72
Francis of Siena 491
frankalmoigne 115
Frankish Church 765
Frankish dynasty 7–8
Frankish *manjaniqs* 305, 306
Frederick I (Holy Roman Emperor)
    10, 657
Frederick II (King of Sicily, Holy
    Roman Emperor) 102, 641, 647
    and Holy Roman Empire 10,
      12–13
    Inquisition 32, 33
    Jewish culture in Italy 80
    universities 39–41
Frederick Barbarossa 101
freedom
    and John Duns Scotus 355
    and Saddya Gaon 369
freehold estate 116–117
free will
    and Asharis movement 394
    and Hasdai ben Abraham Crescas
      383, 384
    and John Duns Scotus 355
    and *Ilm al-Kalam* theology 392
    Jewish philosophy and religion
      374
    and Mutazila movement 393
    and Saddya Gaon 369–370
    and Thomas Aquinas 353
Frequens 24–25
frescoes
    churches and cathedrals 560, 561
    Polemic in Christian art 587–
      588
    Romanesque architectural style
      563
fresco secco 571

fret 860g
friars 359–360
frictation 124
Friesling, Otto von 657
frock 865g
Froissart, Jean 192
frontlet *860*, 860g
fruits 518
frumenti 491
Fuch, Leonhart 487
fuero 87
Fulcher of Chartres 658
funerary books 650
furnaces 427
furniture 563
furs 288

G

gaavah 384
gabardine 865g
Gabriel, Archangel 56, 342
gadrooning 576
Gaimar 659
Galaico-Portuguese language 632,
  662
Galen 473, 526, 527
galile 860g
Galileo Galilei 484–485
galliard 735
galliochios 869g
gamatria 450
gaon 96
Gaonic period 77
gardecorps 865g
Garden of Eden 328, 329
Garden of Paradise 535
gardens 535
garderobe 558
garget 860g
gargoyles 558
Garin de Montglane 634
garlic
  in medieval European medicine
    491
  and mystical eating, Jewish 180
garnache 865g
garter 291
Gaston Phebus (count of Foix) 130
Gates of Holiness 173
Gaul 660
gauntlet 274
"Gayumarth, Shah of Iran"
  (Firdawsi) 706–707

Geber 424
Gelasius I (pope) 19
Gemara
  Judaism, restructuring of 77
  Obadiah of Bertinoro 255
General Medicine (Ibn Rushd) 532
genethlialogy 431, 485–486
  in Islamic world 540
  and medieval European medicine
    476, 493–494
Genghis Khan 73, 219
geniza 93
genouillieres 275
Geoffrey I Villehardouin 658
Geography (Ptolemy) 222
geography, study of 222–224
geomancy 434
geometry 545
geonim
  and Jews in Islamic empire 92,
    93
  Judaism, restructuring of 77
  Lucena, Jews in 96
Germanic tribes 660, 663
  assimilation of 5
  migration to England 13
Germany
  economy and trade, Jewish 246
  Hasidim 86
  Jewish soldiers in 317
  Jews, persecution of 84, 86
  Jews in 81–82
  literary languages in 663–664
Gershom ben Judah 100
Gershon, Levi Ben 524–525
Gertrude the Great 418–419
Gessner, Conrad 647
Gesta Danorum (Saxo the
  Grammarian) 657
Gesundheit 481
Ghadir Khumm 819–820
ghazal 686
Ghazis
  as slave-soldiers 299
  warfare and weapons, Islamic
    299
al-Ghazzali, Abu Hamid Muhammd
  ibn 295, 296, 399–401, 698
ghilan 462
ghilman
  as slave-soldiers 296–297
  warfare and weapons, Islamic
    296–297

Ghiyath ibn Ghawth ibn al-Salt (al-
  Akhtal) 685
ghubar numbers 545
Ghurids
  as slave-soldiers 298–299
  warfare and weapons, Islamic
    298–299
gift giving 47
gigue 729
gillie 869g
giornea 865g
Giotto da Bondone 580
gippon 274, 865g
Girart de Roussillon 660
Glagolitic alphabet 50
glair 570, 571
glass, Islamic 620–622
glassmaking 621
gloria 717
gluttony 137–138
Gnosticism 362, 407
God
  existence of
    Anselm of Canterbury
      350–351
    Brethren of the Free Spirit
      363–364
    Hasdai ben Abraham Crescas
      383
    Abraham ibn Daud 375–376
    John Duns Scotus 354–355
    Maimonides 380
    Bahya ibn Paquda 371
    Saddya Gaon 369
    Thomas Aquinas 351
    William of Ockham 357
  foreknowledge of 374, 392
  hand of 441
  justice of 393
  love of
    and Islamic mysticism 453,
      454
    and Jewish mysticism 448
  and Maimonides 382
  nature of
    Avicenna 398–399
    in Christian mysticism 416,
      417
    Christian philosophy and
      religion 327
    Abraham ibn Daud 375
    Judah Halevi 372
    in Jewish mysticism 440
    Maimonides 380

God (continued)
  omnipotentence of 351
  and punishment 384
  Quran and covenant with 389
  and rewards 384
  seeking union with 416, 417
  soul's quest for 420
Godfrey of Bouillon 27, *187*
godhead
  in Christian mysticism 416, 417
  and Jewish mysticism 446
godron *861g*
gold
  in Christian magic 425, 428
  exchange rates in Islamic world 228
  in medieval European medicine 480
  overland trade in Islamic world 219
gold buckle *567*
gold currencies 205
gold dinar 227, *228*
Golden Bull 10, 12
Golden Horde 219
Golden Legend (de Voragine) 347
golden marigold 479, 480
Golden Rule 386
golem 450–451
gonelle *861g*
González, Fernán 17
Gonzalo de Berceo 632–634
Good Friday 774–776
gorget 272, *272*, *861g*
Gothic neumes 720
Gothic script 573
Gothic style
  architecture 565–566
  painting, Christian 580, 581
Gothic wars 43, 45
Gottfried von Strassburg 638
gourd 492
gout 487
Gower, John 659
grace, Christian concept of 335–336, 353–354
gradual 717
grain
  and Great Famine 191
  Lammas Day 786
gramalla *861g*
Grand Chartreuse *561*

The Grand Treatise on Music (al-Farabi) 750
granulation 578
grapper 303
great chain of being 113–114
great coat *865g*
Great Conduit (London)
  Christian architecture 558
  cities 122
Great Famine
  and Black Death 41
  and Christian economy and trade 191–192
great hall 557
Great Interregnum 12
Great Mosque of Córdoba 609
Great Schism 21–22, 63, 364–365
Greece, ancient 525, 526, 638
Greek fire 215, 307, 308
Greek Orthodox Church 329, 336
"green revolution" 231–234
gregor 729
Gregorian chant 718
Gregorian Reforms
  and clerical celibacy 358
  Great Schism 22
  Investiture Controversy 20
  universities 39
Gregory I (pope)
  and creation of Christian holidays 764, 785
  and emergence of new cultures xi
  on gluttony 137
  and Jews in western Europe 80, 81
Gregory VII (pope) **42,** 100
  and clerical celibacy 358
  Investiture Controversy 20
Gregory IX (pope) 132
Gregory XIII (pope) 432
Gregory the Great (pope) 98
grenade 270
greve 275
Grimm, Jakob 450–451
grisaille 559
grotesquerie
  ceramics, Christian 579
  and manuscript art, Jewish 598
  manuscripts, Christian 571
  Norman architectural style 569
Guibert of Nogent 633

Guide for the Perplexed (Maimonides) 378–381, 516
Guideo Guinizelli of Bologna 641
Guido Cavalcanti of Florence 641
Guido's hand
  Jewish wedding music 745
  music, Christian 720
Guildhall (London) 194
guilds
  and Christian economy and trade 193–195
  Ottoman Turkish music 757
  in western Europe 38–39
Guillaume de Lorris 654
Guillaume le Clerc 652
guilt 345
guimp *861g*
gularon *861g*
gunpowder 279–282
guns 280
Gutenberg, Johannes 544, 575, 663

H

habara *865g*
Hadi, Ali ibn 407
Hadith
  biographical dictionaries 696–697
  and fasting 161
  and Islamic magic 451
  and jihad 292–293, 295–296
  and medicine in Islamic world 533
  and philosophy and religion, Islamic 387
Haggadah
  and art for seder 599
  literature, Jewish 630, 667
  manuscript art, Jewish 597, 598
  and Pesach 806
Hagia Sophia 568
hagiography
  Christian literature 631–634
  monks in Byzantine Empire 48
Hai Gaon 444
haincelin *865g*
hair 476–477
hajj 140, 814–816
al-Hakim
  and Dar al-Hikma 148
  and Druze 406
  and Ismailis 404

Ha Kuzari (Judah Halevi) 681
Halachah 84, 667
halakha 377
halal/haram
   food, Islamic 159
   music, Islamic 748
halberd 268–269
al-Hallaj 455
Hallevi, Judah 682
Halloween 788
al-Hamadhani, Badi al-Zaman
   700–701
Hammer of Witches (Kramer and
   Sprenger) 436, 437
Hanafi school of law 141, 142
Hanbal, Ahmad ibn 141
Hanbali school of law 141, 142
hand, in Jewish mysticism 440–442
"The Hand of God" 441
Hanukkah menorah 591
haram 60
harim 153–154, *154*
al-Hariri, al-Qasim 701
al-Harith, Marhab inb 314–315
al-Harizi, Judah 672
harpsichord 728
Hartmann von Aue 663
Harun al-Rashid 690
Harut 460
Hasan al-Basri 453
al-Hashimiyya, Muttayam 753
hashish 406
Hasidism 86, 447–449
Hastings, Battle of 569
hatchment 290
hats and headwear 844–845
hauberk 274, 275
haut boy 729
Hawe, John 483, 484
hawks 130
al-Haytham, Ibn 605
Hayyan, Jabir ibn 424
Hazar Afsana 642
Hazm, ibn, of Córdova 294–295
head, in medieval European
   medicine 471–474
headaches 472–474
head armor 270–273
headrail 861g
healing music 498–499
health boards 201–202, 500
health passes 500

healthy balance 535
heaulm 271
Hebrew Bible 311, 312, 389
Hebrew language 408
Hedwig glass 621
Heinrich de Glichezare 653
hell *346*
hellebore, black 487
hennin 273, 861g
Henry II (king of England) 101
   and England 14
   and Jewish moneylenders 248
Henry III (Holy Roman Emperor)
   100
Henry IV (German king and Holy
   Roman Emperor) 20–21, **42,** 100
Henry IV (king of England) 515
Henry VI (king of England) 104
Henry VIII (king of England)
   and clerical celibacy 358
   and France 15
   and Statute of Uses 116
Heraclius (Byzantine emperor)
   45–47, **55–56,** 91
heraldry and arms
   Christian 286–292
      achievement, hatchment,
         canting arms, *impresa* 290
      art of heraldry 286–287
      bar, carbuncle, chevron
         289–290
      Bartolus de Saxoferrato 290
      blazon, charge, position 287
      cadency 288–289
      chivalry 266
      college of arms 290–292
      colors, tinctures, metals, furs
         288
      fess, pale, crosses 289
      lion and yale 287–288
   Islamic 309–311
   Jewish 320
herbal eye bath 477
herbarium 559
herbs
   bone-healing 486–487
   and bubonic plague 500
   and medieval European medicine
      472–474, 477–480
heredity 474
heresy
   converso phenomenon 89

Inquisition 32–33
Jews and Christians accused
   of *89*
heretical Christian sects 360–365
   Arians, adoptionists, and
      Nestorians 361–362
   Brethren of the Free Spirit
      363–365
   Donatists and Pelagians 363
   Manicheans, Albigensians, and
      Cathars 362–363
herigaute 865g
The Hermit's Guide (Avenpace) 401
heroic romance
   literature, Islamic 692–694
   literature, Jewish 672–673
hevrot 169
Hiberno-Saxon art
   architecture 566–567
   Christian manuscripts 572
Hiberno-Saxon manuscripts 572
hiddur mitzvah 589–590
   art, Jewish 589
   and manuscript art, Jewish 598
high cross 567
high table
   castles 557
   monasteries 561
al-Hikmah, Bayt 749
Hildebrand 20
Das Hildebrandslied 663
Hildegarde of Bingen 421–422,
   495, 664
Hillell II 91
Hillel of Verona 80
Hippocrates 494–495
hirsutism 477
Hispano-Moresque architectural
   style 569–570
Historia Animalium (Conrad
   Gessner) 647
historiated initials 570
historiography x–xi
history
   about 2–3
   chronology 98–104
   resources 104–108
History of the Muslim Conquests (al-
   Baladhuri) 408
History of the Ottomans (Kritoboulos)
   280
hiyal 542–543

Hohenheim, Theophrastud
 Bombastus 425
holidays and festivals (in general)
 about 764
 resources 821–823
holidays and festivals, Christian
 764–794
 calendar of festivals 765–789
  Advent 765–766
  April Fools' Day 782–783
  Ascension, Feast of the
   778–779
  Catherine's Day, Saint
   788–789
  Christmas 766–769
  Corpus Christi, Feast of 780
  Easter 776–778
  Epiphany and Twelfth Night
   769–770
  Halloween and the Feast of
   All Saints 788
  James the Great, Feast of
   Saint 785–786
  John the Baptist, Feast of
   Saint 784–785
  Lammas Day 786
  Lent 773–776
  Low Sunday and Jubilate
   Sunday 778
  Marian feasts 780
  Mayday 783–784
  Michaelmas 787–788
  Midsummer Eve 784–785
  Pentecost, Feast of the 779
  pre-Lenten season 771–773
  Three Kings, feast of the
   770–771
  Transfiguration, feast of the
   786
  Trinity Sunday 779–780
  Valentine's Day, Saint
   781–782
 typical feast 789–794
  banquet servitors 792–794
  cook, carver, and warner 792
  main course 791–792
  music 792
  welcome 789–791
holidays and festivals, Islamic
 813–821
 Christian celebrations 820
 pilgrimage 814–816
 Ramadan 816–817

 secular festivals and rites of
  passage 820–821
 Shiite festivals 819–820
 supererogatory festivals 817–
  819
holidays and festivals, Jewish 374,
 794–813
 calendar of festivals 801–813
  Chanukah 804–805
  Fast of Gedalia 802
  Lag Bomer 808
  Pesach 806–808
  Purim 806, 809–813
  Rosh Hashanah 802
  Shavuot 808–809
  Simchat Torah 804
  Sukkot 803–804
  Ten Days of Awe 803
  Tisha Bav 809
  Tu Bshvat 805–806
  Yom Kippur 803
 sabbath 799–801
 weddings 795–799
holy child of La Guardia 90
Holy Grail
 in literature 638
 prefiguration and 340
holy orders
 Christian philosophy and religion
  336
 and clergy 357
Holy Roman Empire 9–13, *11*, 20,
 99
Holy Saturday 776
Holy Spirit 327, 328
holy war. *See* jihad
Holy Week 330, 774–775
Honnecourt, Villard de 506–507
 architects, Christian 555
 and perpetual motion machines
  541
Honorius III (pope) 12
horned headdress 861*g*
horologium 505
horoscope
 and astrology in Islamic world
  540
 in Christian magic 430
horse, caparisoned *275*
horse armor 275–276
Horsemen of the Apocalypse 343
hose 869*g*
Hosea (Jewish prophet) 590

hospitals
 ibn Battuta 241
 in Islamic world 533
hot-air turbine 543
houpelande 866*g*
houseaux 869*g*
households 556–557
House of Wisdom
 and emergence of new cultures
  xii
 and medicine in Islamic world
  536
houses, design of 562–563
housse 866*g*
Hrsovitha von Gandersheim 665
Huësslin, Rudolph 647
humanism 250
human nature 401
humility 383
humor, in Jewish manuscript art *597*
humoral theory 526
Hunayn ibn Ishaq 697
Hundred Years' War
 and France 15–16
 gunpowder in Christian Europe
  279–280
 Jacquérie Revolt 192
hunting
 and Christians 126–131, *129*
  monkeys, hawks, and dogs
   130–131
  otter 129–130
  wolf trapping 127–129
 by Jews 175
 music, secular Christian 724
 by Muslims 157–158, *158*
hunting and leisure *158*
hunting manuals 647–648
huppah
 and Jewish magic 450
 and Jewish sensuality 172
huque 866*g*
hurdygurdy 727
Hurufis 404
hurve 861*g*
Hus, Jan 24, 104
Husayn ibn Ali 99, 819
hydromancy 434
hygiene
 in Christian world 123–126
 in Islamic world 150–151
 and medicine in Islamic world
  533

I

iambic meter 719
iatrogenic sequelae 484
Iberian Peninsula. *See also* Spain
    Jews in 87–88
    literary languages in 660–662
Ibn Abd Rabbihi 699
Ibn Abi Usaybia 697
Ibn Abi Zayd al-Qayrawani 142
Ibn al-Adim 697
Ibn al-Arabi 455–457, 691
Ibn Arabi 757–758
Ibn Bakhtisheu 702
Ibn Battuta 240–242
    border security 222
    crossing the desert 221
    and Islamic mysticism 459
    overland trade in Islamic world
      219
    on pilgrimage 814
    Rihla travel diaries 235
    sea trade 214–215
    Somalia 226
Ibn Butlan
    and medicine in Islamic world
      534–535
    and medieval European medicine
      492
Ibn al-Farid 691–692
Ibn al-Haytham 546
Ibn Hayyan 696
Ibn Hazm of Córdoba 699–700
Ibn al-Husayn, al-Muayyad Ahmad
    145
Ibn Iyas 814
Ibn al-Jawzi 700
Khafaja, Abu Ishaq ibn Ibrahim ibn
    Abi l-Fath ibn 691
Ibn Khaldun 461, 606,608, 697
Ibn al-Muqaffaa 669–670, 695
Ibn Musa 542
Ibn al-Nafis 532–533
Ibn al-Qalanisi 696
Ibn Qutayba 699
Ibn Rushd. *See* Averroës
Ibn Sina. *See* Avicenna
Ibn Taymiyya, Ahmad
    halal or haram 748
    and Islamic mysticism 458–459
    on Mawlid al-Nabi celebration
      387
Zaydun, Abu l-Walid Ahmad ibn
    Abdallah Ibn 691

Iconoclast Controversy 99
    Byzantine arts and crafts 586
    in Byzantine Empire 49–50
    Great Schism 21–22
iconography
    beauty and aesthetics in Islamic
      art 604
    Byzantine arts and crafts 585–
      586
iconostatis 568, 586
icons 555, 585–586
Id al-Adha 815–816
Id al-Fitr 817
idiophone 729
idolatry
    Iconoclast Controversy 49
    and sumptuary laws, Jewish 178
al-Idrisi 223–224
IHS cross inscription 584
ijaz 390
Ijaza 148–149
ijtihad 458
ikat 855
ilech 430
iliaster 429
illumination
    manuscripts, Christian 570
    monasteries 562
    Romanesque architectural style
      564
ilm al-falak 538
ilm al-hayah 538
ilm al-kalam theology 391–395
    Asharis 393–395
    Mutazila 392–393
    Qadiriyya 391–392
Imad al-Din al-Isfahani 697
imam(s)
    and Druze 406
    Ismailis and seventh 403
    mosques, design of 613
    and Nizari Ismailis 405
    Sunnis and Shiites 63–64
Immaculate Conception 331
Immanuel of Rome 675, 676, 683
immortality
    in Christian magic 429
    and Abraham ibn Daud 376
impresa 290
The Improvement of the Human Reason
    (Abubacer) 402
imputation 329
incarnation, concept of 326–328

Christian philosophy and religion
    331, 333
    Hiberno-Saxon art 567
incendiary weapons 307–309
The Incoherence of the Incoherence
    (Averroës) 402
Incoherence of the Philosophers (al-
    Ghazzali) 400
incunabula 576
Indian Ocean 214, 224–225
indulgence, excessive 382
indulgences 25, 345–346
infidels 392
infirmary 561
inheritance
    Jewish women 170
    Muslim women 155
inhumation 429–430
inlays 576–577
Innocent III (pope) **42**, 101, 102
    and Albigensian Crusade 29, 363
    and Brethren of the Free Spirit
      364
    canon law and Jews 164
    and clergy 357
    confession and 345–346
    Crusades 28
    Fourth Crusade 27
    Fourth Lateran Council 22–23
    and Holy Roman Empire 12
    and Jews in western Europe 81
    and Major Orders 111
Inquisition 32–34, 90, 102
    converso phenomenon 90
    Fourth Lateran Council 23
    and heretics 361
    persecution of heretical sects 363
    and sumptuary laws, Jewish 178
INRI cross inscription 584–585
al-insan 455–456
instruction books
    Arabic 695
    Christian 632, 646–651, *649*
      ars moriendi 649–650
      art of love 646–647
      dance manuals 648
      exempla 650–651
      hunting manuals 647–648
    Jewish 679–680
    in medieval Europe 513–514
insular style
    in architecture 566
    in manuscripts 571–572

insuration 429–430
intaglio 577–578
intarsia 576
interest rates 247
Interior Castle (Teresa of Ávila) 420
interlacing 566, 571
international trade 213
introit 717
Investiture Controversy 100
    and changing role of papacy
      19–21
    and clerical celibacy 358
Investiture of the Ruler (baya) 820
al-Iqd al-farid (Ibn Abd Rabbihi) 699
iqta 153
Iranian art 617
Iraq 223
iron 280
irrigation 233
Isaac 388–389, 440–441
Isaac ibn Sahula 683
isaba maila 861g
Isabella I (queen of Castile) 17–18,
    42–43, 90
Isaiah di Trani the Elder 79
isa presbeia 19
Ishmael 388–389
ishraq 455
Isidore of Seville 652, 657
Iskandar-Nama 706
Islam. *See also specific headings, e.g.:*
    art, Islamic
    and Christian mysticism 420
    and emergence of new cultures
      xi–xii
    historiography of xi
    and Jewish philosophy and
      religion 367
    jihad and conversion to 293
    meaning of 387
    pilgrimage to Mecca 814–816
    and Polemic in Christian art 588
Islamic civilization x
Islamic empire **56–75,** *65*
    Abbasids 67–70
    Ali ibn Abi Talib, role of 63
    Ayyubids and Mamluks 71–73
    Byzantines v. Sassanians 60–61
    expansion of 61–62
    Fatimid *dawa* 70–71
    Jews in 92–96
      Cairo *geniza* 93
      Fatimids 93–94

Karaite schism 92–93
    Lucena 95–96
    Maimonidean controversy
      96–97
    Mamluk dynasty 94
    Seljuks 94
    Sepharad 94–95
    Umayyad Spain 95
    key personalities 74–75
    Khanate of the Golden Horde
      73
    Ottomans 74
    society and culture 59–60
    Sunnis and Shiites 63–64
    Umar caliphate 61–62
    Umayyad caliphate 64–67, 95
    Uthman ibn Affan, role of 62–63
Islamic Jihad, warfare and weapons
    292–311
Islamic law. *See* sharia
Ismailis 403–407
    Bohras 407
    Druze 406
    Nasir-I Khusraw 404–405
    and Nasir-I Khusraw 404–405
    Nizari Ismailis 405–406
    Nusayriyya Alawis 406–407
isospecificity 443–444
Israel 373
Italy
    economy and trade, Jewish 246
    Jewish soldiers in 315–317
    Jews in 78–80
    literary languages in 662
ittihad 454
Ivan III (czar of Russia) 104
ivy, ground 486, 489
iwans 612, 613
izar 866g
Izz al-Din ibn al-Athir 696

J

jabarut 399–400
jabr 392
jabriyya 392
jacket 275, 866g
Jacob's staff 524
Jacopone da Todi 634
Jacquerie Revolt 192
Jacques Bonhomme 192
Jacques de Longuyon 638
Al-Jahiz 698–699
Jaime I. *See* James I of Aragon

jalba 214
Jamal al-Din ibn al-Wasil 696
James I of Aragon 657–658
James the Great, Feast of Saint
    785–786
Jarir ibn Atiyya ibn al-Khatafa 685
jaseran 275
javelin 269–270
Jawhar al-Katib al-Saqilibi 148
al-Jazari, Ibn al-Razzaz 543
Jean de Meun 649, 654
Jeddah
    Ibn Battuta 214–215
    sea trade 214
Jehovah 373
jerkin 866g
Jerome, Saint *341*
Jerusalem 313–314
    Benjamin of Tudela 255
    Crusades 26
    First Crusade 27
    seige techniques and equipment
      276
    Third Crusade 27
jester *782*
Jesus Christ 415
    and adoptionism 361–362
    angels and 342
    in *The Book of Margery Kempe*
      633
    Byzantine arts and crafts 586
    Byzantine manuscript
      illumination 572
    and Catherine of Siena, Saint
      422–423
    and celibacy 358
    and Christian Golden Rule 386
    church mass 716
    crosses and crucifixes 584–585
    Crucifixion and Resurrection
      329–331
    and *felix culpa* 329
    and Gertrude the Great 419
    holidays and festivals celebrating
      life of 765
    Justinian (Byzantine emperor)
      43, 45
    as Lamb of God 328
    mosaics, Christian 585
    as mother figure 423–424
    painting, Christian 580–581
    in Passion Play 644–645
    and prefiguration 340

and Quran 388, 389
Romanesque architectural style
564
Second Coming of 343, 345
and Teresa of Ávila, Saint 420
and Thomas Aquinas 353
Jeu d'Adam 645
Jeu de Saint-Nicholas (Jean Bodel)
645
Jewish badge 164, 243, 866g
Jews and Judaism **75–98, 161–180**.
See also specfic headings, e.g.: art,
Jewish
architecture of 593–595
Ashkenazi 81–82
autonomy and self-government
166–169
as bankers 35, 203
and Black Death 41
in Byzantine Empire 90–91
in Capetian France 83–84
and Carolingian Renaissance
82–83
and Christian festivals 793–794
in Christian Iberia 87–88
Christian persecution of *85*
chronology 98–104
civilization of ix–x
converso phenomenon 89–90
and Hasdai ben Abraham Crescas
383
and emergence of new cultures
xi
food and religious identity
175–180
Kashrut, laws of 175–177
mystical eating, sensual meals
178–180
sumptuary laws 177–178
in France and Germany 81–82
and Halachic learning 84
and Judah Halevi 372–374
Hasidim 86
historiography of x–xi
hunting by 175
on Iberian Peninsula 661
in Islamic empire 92–96
Cairo *geniza* 93
Fatimids 93–94
Karaite schism 92–93
Lucena 95–96
Maimonidean controversy
96–97

Mamluk dynasty 94
Seljuks 94
Sepharad 94–95
Umayyad Spain 95
in Italy 78–80, *80*
key personalities 97–98
legal status of 163–166
canon law 164–165
Pact of Umar 165–166
servus camere regio 163–164
in Merovingian France and
Germany 82
and moneylending in Islamic
world 229
and optimistic realism 161–163
and papacy 80–81
persecution and expulsion of
84–86
and Polemic in Christian art
587–588
and prefiguration 339–340
restructuring of Judaism 76–78
and restructuring of Judaism
76–78
and Second Crusade 27
and sensuality 172–175
shared dogmas with
Mutakallimun 394
and slavery 172
in 13th and 14th centuries 88
in western Europe 78–90
Capetian France 83–84
Carolingian Renaisance
82–83
Christian Iberia 87–88
converso phenomenon 89–90
in 1492 90
France and Germany:
Ashkenazi Jews 81–82
Halachic learning 84
Hasidim 86
Italian Jewish culture 79–80
Italian Peninsula settlements
78–79
Merovingian France and
Germany 82
papacy 80–81
persecution and expulsion
84–86
in 13th and 14th centuries
88
women 169–171
Jew's hat 861g

jihad 292–296
society and culture in Islamic
world 59
spiritual 160
Umar caliphate 61
al-Jili 456
jillaya 866g
Jiménez de Rada, Rodrigo 657
jinn 461, 462
jizya 169
Joachim of Floris 364
Joan of Arc 104, *282*
Job, biblical book of 449
joculatores 644
Johanna of Flanders 284
John I (king of England) 102
John II. *See* Juan II (king of Castile)
John XI (pope) 19
John XII (pope) 99
John XXI (pope) 480–481
John XXII (pope)
and Christian magic 425
Christian mysticism 417
Trinity Sunday 780
and William of Ockham 356
John Lackland (king of England)
115
John of Damascus, Saint **56**
John of Salisbury 646
John the Baptist, feast of Saint
784–785
John the Evangelist, Saint 343
jordan (urine collector) 496–497
Joseph ben Samuel 162–163
Josephus (Jewish historiographer)
590
journade 866g
Journal for Hermits (Grimm)
450–451
journals 206
journeyman 193
jousts 268
Juan II (king of Castile) 319
Juan de la Cruz, San 420–421
Jubayr, Ahmad ibn 235, 239–240
jubba 866g
jube 866g
Jubilate Sunday 778
Judah al-Harizi 682
Judah Halevi 372–374, 666, 676–
677, 681, 682
Judah the Pious 447
Judaism. *See* Jews and Judaism

Judenhut 165, 861g
Judenmeister 83
Judenstern 591
Juliana, Saint 780
Juliani, Peter 480–481
Julian of Norwich 423–424, 664
al-Junayd 454
jupe 866g
jupon *274*, 866g
Justinian (Byzantine emperor) 43–45, **55**, 78–79
Justinian Code 43

K

Kaaba shrine 58–59
kafirs 392, 393
kagoule 866g
kahana 462
kalam 393, 394, 399
kalansuwa 861g
Kalilah and Dimnah 669–670
Kallir, Eleazar 445
kallot 77
Kalonymous, Judah 175
Kalonymous, Kalonymous Ben 524, 674
Kalonymous, Nathan ben Jehiel 79
Kalonymous, Samuel ben 101
kamanche 756
al-kamil 456
Karaite Judaism 92–93, 99
Karaite schism 92–93
    Jewish philosophy and religion 368–369
    and Jews in Islamic empire 92–93
karry 866g
Kashrut, laws of 175–177
katarchai 540
keep 557
kenning 653
Kentish 659
ketubah 172
khalwatiyya 866g
khamriyyat 687–688
Khamseh (Nizami Ganjawi) 705
Khanate of the Golden Horde 73, 74
Al-Khansa 684–685
kharaj tax 153
Kharijites
    poetry of 685
    Sunnis and Shiites 64

al-Khatib al-Baghdadi 697
Khaybar, Jews of 57–58
Khayyam, Omar
    in Islamic world 545–546
    Persian literature 703, *704*
khila 855
khimar 861g
khirqa 850–851, 861g, 866g
Khordadbeh, ibn 252
Khosrow and Shirin 705
khuff 869g
Khusraw, Nasir-i
    economy and trade, Islamic 237–238
    Rihla travel diaries 235
khutba 227
kidney 488–491
kilij 300–302
al-Kindi, Abu Yusuf Yaqub 396, 749–750
kings' cakes 771
kirtle 866g–867g
kishwarha 222, 223
kiswa 851–852
Kitab al-bukhala (Al-Jahiz) 699
Kitab al-Fawaid (ibn Majid) 214
Kitab al-hawi (Razi, al-) 528, 537
Kitab al-hayawan (Al-Jahiz) 698–699
Kitab al-kulliyyat (Ibn Rushd) 532
al-Kitab of Ibn Fadlan 236–237
Kitab al-aghani (al-Isfahani) 754
kittel 867g
Klappvisier 272
Klezmorim 743
Knight of the Garter 291
knights *317*
    chivalry 265–266
    female 285
    lady 284–286
    swords in Christian Europe 268
    tenure of 114–115
Knights Hospitaller 31
Knights of Aviz 31
Knights of Calatrava 31
Knights of Saint Peter 264
Knights of Santiago 31
Knights Templar 30–31
Knyvet, Alice 284, 285
Koran. *See* Quran
Kosher
    and art for seder 600
    and hunting by Jews 175

koumbarion 215
Kramer, Heinrich 436, 437
Kritoboulos, Michael 280
kubran 867g
Kudrun 636
kufic script 614
kuttrolf 427, 512
The Kuzari (Halevi) 373
Kyeser, Konrad 281
kyrie 717

L

label 288
labyrinths 555
ladies (of manors) 284–286
Ladino folk song 740–741
lady knights 284–286
Lag Bomer 808
lai 631, 639
Lamb of God 328, 343
lambrequin 273, 861g
Lammas Day 786
Lamprecht, Pfaffe 638
lamps, in Jewish mysticism and art 442–443, 591
lances 268–269, 302–303
lancet 560
land contracts 206
landed estates
    feudalism 116–117
    of Muslims 152–153
land grants
    Islamic 153
    pronoia system 53
    thema/theme system 46
land tenure 114–116
Langland, William 656
Langues d'Oc (Occitan language) 632, 660
Langues d'Oïl 660
lappet 828g
Las Navas de Tolosa, Battle of 17
Last Judgment 343
Last Supper *330*
    Christian philosophy and religion 330
    church mass 716
Lateran IV (pope)
    canon law and Jews 165
    and Jews in Italy 79
    and Jews in western Europe 81
Latin language 660, 661
lavabo 583–584

Law of the Staple 200
laxatives 491, 519
Layla and Majnun (Nizami Ganjawi) 693–694, 705
Laylat al-Baraa 819
Laylat al-Miraj 818
Laylat al-Qadr 817
lead (element) 430
lecanomancy 434
ledgers 206
leeks 489
leisure, Muslims and 158–159
Lent 773–776
Leo, Archpresbyter 638
Leo I (pope) 19
Leo III (Byzantine emperor) **56**, 99
Leo III (pope)
    and Carolingian kingdom 8
    Iconoclast Controversy 49
Leon, Moses de 446
Leonardo da Vinci 543
lepers 41
Levi Ben Gershom 812
Levita Bahur, Elijah 666, 673, 743
Leviticus (Old Testament) 176
Lex mercatorius 199
libas 867g
lighting 563
Light of the Lord (Crescas) 383
Limoges enamel 580
limud lekaf zekus 384–386
linen 853, 854
lion
    and Christian magic 428
    heraldry and arms 287–288
    heraldry and arms, Jewish 320
    Jewish art 592
liripipe 861g
litanies 725
literal level of meaning (scripture) 341, 380
literature (in general)
    about 630–631
    resources 708–711
literature, Christian **631–665**
    allegorical writings 654–656
    beast literature 651–653
    chanson de geste 630, 631, 634–636
    chronicles 656–658
    drama and theater 643–646
    fabliaux 653–654
    frame tale 642

hagiography and devotional literature 632–634
instruction books 646–651
    ars moriendi 649–650
    art of love 646–647
    dance manuals 648
    exempla 650–651
    hunting manuals 647–648
    mirrors of princes 646
    women's 648–649
kenning 653
lai 639
literary languages 658–664
    England 658–659
    France 660
    Germany 663–664
    Iberian Peninsula 660–662
    Italy 662
lyric poetry 639–642
    dolce stil nuovo 641
    English love lyrics 642
    minnesingers 641–642
    troubadours 640
    trouvères 641
major writers 664–665
riddle 653
romance 636–639
literature, Islamic **683–708**
    heroic romance 692–694
    mystical poetry 691–692
    Persian literature 703–708
        Firdawsi 706–708
        Omar Khayyam 703, *704*
        Nizami Ganjawi 703–706
    poetic genres 686–688
    poets of Abbasid court 688–690
    pre-Islamic Arabic literary genres 683–686
    prose, Arabic 694–702
        Adab literature 698–701
        autobiographical writing 697–698
        beast literature 701–702
        biographical dictionaries 696–697
        frame tale 702
        historical chronicles 695–696
        instruction books 695
        risala 694–695
        sira and *tarikh* 695–696
    Umayyad Spain 690–691
literature, Jewish **665–683**
    Arthurian romance 666

beast fable 668–670
chanson de geste 673–674
crusader chronicles 681–682
exempla 680
frame tale 670–672
Haggadah and Halachah 630, 667
heroic romance 672–673
instruction books 679–680
major writers 682–683
poems of love and war 676–678
religious poetry 678–679
satire 674–676
secular literature 665–667
works of wisdom 681
liturgy 582
livery 193, 867g
Livonian Knights 32
Llull, Ramon 661–662, 664
loans
    Christian economy and trade 205–206
    financing in Islamic world 229
    and Jewish moneylenders 247, 248
Locke, John 379
Lollard movement 104
Lombard League 10, 12
London, England 122–123
longbow 269–270
looms 854–855
loshon hora 384, 385
"lost wax" process 578
Louis IX (king of France) 14–15
love
    in Christian instruction books 646–647
    courtly 636
love knot 781
love poetry 631
Low Sunday 778
lozenge 289–290
luab 305
Lucena 95–96
Lucifer 342
lusterware 570, 580, 621
lutes 750, 751
Luther, Martin 24

M

maajirs 861g
al-Maarri, Abu l-Ala 695, 700
mabr 155

mace 268–269
Macedonian dynasty 50
machicolation 557
madhhabs 72
madih 688
Madonna and Child (Byzantine) *586*
Madonna lily 477
madrasas 146–148
    Abbasids 69
    design of 613–614
Magi 337
magic
    about 414
    Christian **424–438**
        alchemy 424–430
        astrology 430–433
        magical divination 433–435
        occult sciences 435–438
    and food 136
    Islamic **459–464**
    Jewish **449–451**
    lamps 463
    mirrors 463
    resources 464–467
magic circle/square 432
Magino, Meir *246*
magister judeorum 83
Magna Carta 13–14, 115
magnons 277
mahabba 454
Mahberot (Immanuel of Rome) 675
Mahdi 404
mahoitre 867g
Maimonidean controversy 96–97
Maimonidean rationalists 440
Maimonides **97–98**
    and Arabic language translations
        408
    and Hasdai ben Abraham Crescas
        383
    Jewish Culture in Italy 80
    and Jewish medicine 516–523
    Jewish philosophy and religion
        376–382
    Maimonidean controversy 96–97
    in medieval European medicine
        492
    and medieval Jewish medicine
        515
Majid, Ahmad ibn 214
majolica 579
majoram 473
majuscule script 575

malakut 399–400
Malebisse, Richard 248
al-Malik 227
Malik ibn Anas 141, 142, 461
Maliki school of law 141, 142
Malkhut 446
mallet 472
malpractice 483–484
malwiya 613
Mamluks (Mamluk dynasty) 71–72
    coinage in Islamic world 228
    heraldry and arms, Islamic 310
    in Islamic empire 71–73
    Jews in 94
    mosques, design of 613
    Muslim women and political
        power 156
    slavery, Muslims and 157
    as slave-soldiers 71–72, 297–298
    warfare and weapons, Islamic
        297–298
manaqib 697
Mandeville, John 210–212
mandilion 275, 867g
mandrake 473
Manessische Liederhandschrift 641
mangonels
    onager 278
    siege techniques and equipment
        277
    weaponry, Islamic 300
Manicheans 348, 362–363
maniere 747
maniple 828g
manjaniqs 305–307
Mansi, Paola Anav dei 79
al-Mansur
    palace of 620
    Umayyads in Spain 66–67
manteline 275, 867g
mantle 867g
manuals, farm 234
manuscripts
    Christian *570, 570–576, 571*
        Byzantine 572
        calligraphy styles 572–575
        Hiberno-Saxon 572
        insular style 571–572
        paper, vellum, and parchment
            techniques and works
            575–576
    Gothic architectural style 565
    Islamic 614, 622–624

Jewish 595–599
    commentaries in 596
    humor in 597–599
    Quran 614
    Romanesque architectural style
        564
Manzikert, Battle of 52
maphorion 867g
maqama 457, 672, 700–701
Maqamat (al-Qasim al-Hariri) 701,
    701
maqsura 612
maquette 578
Mardi Gras 772–773
marfors 861g
Margaret of Anjou 284
margaritomancy 434
Margery of Kempe 633
Marian feasts 765, 780
Maria of Pozzuoli 285
Marie de France 631, 639, 652–654,
    659, 668
marifa 454, 456
mariology/mariolatry 331–333
maristan 241
maritime technology 215–216
maritime trade 188
market inspectors 194
markets 193
markub 869g
marlet 286, 288
marquetry 576
marramas 584
marranos 34
marriage(s)
    arranged 796
    Christian philosophy and religion
        336
    and Jewish magic 450
    Muslim women and 154–155
marroni 196
Marshallik 745
Marsiglio of Padua 24
Martel, Charles 8
Martin V (pope) 24–26
Martínez, Ferran 103
Martin of Córdoba, Fray 649
Martorell, Joanot 662
martyrdom 86
martyrological poetry 678–679
Marut 460
Mary, Mother of God 331–335
    Byzantine arts and crafts 586
    Christotokos v. Theotokos 331

Eve-Ave antithesis, mariology
and mariolatry 331–333
Immaculate Conception 331
and Nestorians 362
Seven Joys and Seven Sorrows
333–335
virtues of the Virgin 333
Masaccio, Tommaso 581
maskh 463
masonry, doctorate of 555
masorah, micrographic 596–597
masoretic micrography 442–444
masque 734
masquerades 734
mass 561
Matamoros 587
mathmetics, in Islamic world
545–546
Matilda of Tuscany 21, 283–284
mattachin 733
Matthew (disciple of Jesus) 440
matzoh
and art for seder 599
and Pesach 806
Maud Augusta (queen of England)
282–283
Maundy Thursday 775
Mawlid al-Nabi celebration 817–
818
mawlids 71
al-Mawsili, Ishaq Ibn Ibrahim 748–
749, 752, 753
Maximilian I (Holy Roman
Emperor) 267, 730
Maximinus (emperor of Rome)
788–789
Mayday 783–784
maypole 733
mazzochio a cianbella 861g
measles 528
meat 517
Mecca
and Islamic empire 58–59
and philosophy and religion,
Islamic 387
pilgrimage to 814–816
The Meccan Revelations (al-Arabi) 455
Meccan suras 389–390
mechanical clocks 542
mechanical devices 542–543
Mechtilde of Madgebourg 418
mediators 515
medical fees 490–491

medical law 201–202
medical pharmacopoeia 202
medical texts 527
medical timings 484–485, 498, *498*
medical training 519
medical translations
Arabic to Latin 536–537
Greek to Arabic 536
medicine 470
and Abraham ibn Daud 375
in Islamic world **526–537**
Abu l-Qasim al-Zahrawi
528–530
Galen 526
hospitals 533
Ibn al-Nafis 532–533
Ibn Rushd 532
Ibn Sina 530–532
medical herbs and
medications 534–535
medical translations, Arabic
to Latin 536–537
medical translations, Greek to
Arabic 536
pharmacy and the *saydalani*
535–536
prophetic medicine 533–534
al-Razi 526–528
Jewish contributions to **514–523**
air, breathing, and psyche
519
astrology 521–522
diet, as life pattern 520
diet as life pattern 520
diet therapy 517–519
Maimonides 516–523
natural correlative, doctrine
of 519–520
seizure disorders, diet therapy
for 517–519
Treatise on Asthma 516–523
and Jewish women 170
in medieval Europe **470–503**
bones 486–488
cancer therapy 492
and Christian economy and
trade 202–203
the eye 477–481
face and physiognomy
474–477
Frankish medicine 239
general medicine 496–499
the head 471–474

kidney and bladder 488–491
the nose 481–486
obstetrics and genethlialogy
492–496
plague 499–503
toxicology 491–492
prophetic, in Islamic world
533–534
resources 546–549
medieval world, defining the ix–x
Medina
battle in 314–315
and Christian economy and trade
197
sea trade 214
Medinan period 57
Medinan suras 390
Mediterranean diet 232
Megillat satarum (Levi Ben
Gershom) 812
Meir ben Baruch of Rothenberg,
Rabbi **98**, 103, 668, 679
hunting by Jews 175
Jews, persecution of 86
Meister Eckhart 417
melancholic disposition 485–486
Melissa officinalis 487
memorandum books 206
memoria 747
memory charm cakes 450
Mendicants 361
menorah
and Chanukah 805
Jewish art 591
in Jewish mysticism 442–443
menorah psalm 443
mensural notation 720
mental illness 497
mentonniere 862g
merchant cities *196*
and Christian economy and trade
195–198
in Islamic world 225–226
merchant courts 198–199
merchants
and bubonic plague 500
in Islamic world 224
Jewish 188
weights and measures 200
in western Europe 35, 36, 121
merchant ships 215
merchants of the Staple 200
merchant writing 206

Mercian dialect 658–659
mercury 426, 428, 429
mercy room 561
Merkabah 444–445, 447
merlins 281
merlon 557
Merovingian kingdom 7–8, 82
Die Merseburger Zaubersprüche 663
metal inlay 302
metallurgy
   and Christian magic 427
   in medieval Europe 509–511
metalwork
   Christian 577–579
   glory and prosperity 622
   heraldry and arms 288
   Islamic 620, 622
metaphysics 403
metaposcopy 434
Methodius, Saint 50
Mevlevi Whirling Dervishes 757
Meydenbach, Jacob 650
Michael VII Palaeologus (Byzantine
   emperor) 102
Michaelmas 787–788
Michael of Cesena 356
microcosm
   human body as 499
   man as *522*
   medicine as 527
   music theory 715
micrographic masorah 588, *596*,
   596–597
Middle English 659
Middle High German 632, 639,
   663–664
Midrash 794–795
Midsummer Eve 784–785
mihrabs 298, 610, 612, 613
Milan 195–197
milhafa 867g
military instruction books 650
millefiore glass 621
The Million (Marco Polo) 210
minaret 611–612
minbar 149, 610–613
mindil *862g*
miners 276–277
miniatures
   Islamic 623
   manuscripts, Christian 570, 571
   monasteries 562
mining technology 510–511

ministeriales 641
Minnelieder 641–642
minnesingers 640–642
   Jewish art song 741
   song collections, Christian
   725–726
mints 227
minuscule letters 596
miqnaa 862g
Miracle of the Rod (Campin) 587
miracle plays 645
miraj 623
Mirror of Fools (Speculum stultorum)
   782–783
The Mirror of Simple Souls (Porete)
   417
mirrors of princes 646
misericord 267, 584
Mishler Shualim 665–666, 668
Mishle Sendebar 670–671
Mishnah
   Judaism, restructuring of 76–77
   Obadiah of Bertinoro 254
   philosophy and religion, Jewish
   365–366
Mishneh Torah (Maimonides) *377*,
   377–378
al-Miskawayh 696
misura 747
miter 33, 828g–829g
mithaq 456
mitzvah
   Jewish philosophy and religion
   384, 386
   and Jewish sensuality 172, 173
   and mystical eating, Jewish 180
Model City (al-Farabi) 397
molydomancy 434
monasteries
   Byzantine Empire 48
   design of *561*, 561–562
monastic orders 829–830
monastic vows 337, 339
monetary system
   overland trade in Islamic world
   219
   in western Europe 35–36
moneylending
   Christian 249–250
   economy and trade, Jewish
   247–250
   in Islamic world 229
   in western Europe 35, 36

Mongol invasions
   and farms in Islamic world 234
   Khanate of the Golden Horde
   73
   and miniatures, Islamic 623
Mongols 102
   Giovanni del Pian del Carpini
   209
   manjaniqs 306
   overland trade in Islamic world
   219
   William of Rubruck 209–210
monkeys 130, 651
monks 48–49, 358–360
monochord 729
Monologion (Anselm of Canterbury)
   350
Monophysite Christians 43, 45, 46
monotheism 22, 326–328
monsoons 215
monstrance 566
Mont-Saint-Michel *564*
moral code, Jewish 367
morality
   and John Duns Scotus 355
   food and 136–138
   and Jewish sensuality 173
   and Muslim food 159–160
morality play 645–646
moral law 379
moresca 733–734
Moring, Elizabeth 194–195
moriscos 34
morning star 268–269
morris dance 733, 778
mosaics
   Byzantine architectural style 568
   Christian 585
   houses 562
mosan enamels 564, 578
Moses *597*
   beasts of prayer, Jewish art and
   601
   at Mount Sinai 415, 416, 441
Moses, Chanoch ben **97**
mosques *58*, *610*
   as centers of learning 145–146
   design of 609–613
motets 725
motte 557
Mount Sinai 415, 416, 441, 601
movimento corporeo 747
Mozarab 193

Mozarabic dialect 661
Muawiyya 64
muezzin 611
mughari 751
Muhammad **74–75**, 98
  cloak of 852–853
  Constitution of Medina 60
  divine revelation of 388
  Ghadir Khumm 819–820
  Heraclius (Byzantine emperor)
    45
  and Islamic art 605
  and Islamic empire 56–59
  and Islamic historiography xi
  and Islamic magic 451–452, 460
  and Ismailis 404
  and jihad 295, 296
  manuscript illumination, Islamic
    622–623
  and medicine in Islamic world
    533
  Medina, battle in 314
  mosques, design of 610
  Night of the Ascension 818
  and *Pact of Umar* 165
  and philosophy and religion,
    Islamic 387
  and Quran 388–390
  and Ramadan 816
  Sunnis and Shiites 64
  Umayyad caliphate 65
Muhammadan light 456
al-Muhasibi 454, 697
muhtasib 144–145
Muhyi al-Din 857–858
mules 221, 222
mulham 854
mulk 399–400
mullet 288
mullion bars 560
al-mumin 393
mummers 778
mumming plays 733, 764, 810–811
al-Munajjim, Ali ibn Yahya ibn 751
Munqidh, Usamah ibn 238–239
  manjaniqs 306
  Rihla travel diaries 235, 236
Muntaner, Ramon 658
al-Muqaddasi 223
muqarada 229–230
muqarnas 617–618
al-Muqtadir 619
musattah astrolabe 541

mushrooms 486–487
music (in general)
  about 714
  classes of music 715, 716
  at feasts 792
  healing 498–499
  hunting 648
  in medieval European medicine
    498–499
  resources 759–761
  Valentine's Day 781
music, Christian **714–737**
  church music 714–719
    ars nova 719
    church mass 716–718
    Gregorian chant 718
    music theory and world order
      715–716
    Notre Dame school and *ars
      antiqua* 718–719
  musical instruments 726–732
  musical modes and notations
    719–720
  secular music 721–724
  song collections 724–726
music, Islamic **747–758**. *See also*
dance, Islamic
  competitions 754–755
  halal or *haram* 748
  Islamic song and vocal artists
    751–754
  music by region 755–759
    Muslim Spain 758–759
    Ottoman Turkish music
      756–757
    Persian music 755–756
    Sufi dance and music 757–
      758
  music theory 748–751
  patronage and court music
    754–755
music, Jewish **737–747**
  Jewish dance master 746–747
  secular music 740–746
    art song 741–742
    folk song 740–741
    town song 742–744
    wedding music 744–746
  synagogue music 738–740
musical instruments
  Christian 726–732
  Ottoman Turkish music 757
  in Persian music 756

Musical Theory (Boethius of Rome)
  715
musica mundana 432
musicians' gallery
  castles 557
  monasteries 561
music theory 716
  Christian music 715–716
  Islamic music 748–751
muskets 281
Muslims **138–161**. *See also specfic
  headings, e.g.:* art, Islamic
  and Christian celebrations 820
  and Christian festivals 793–794
  and Christian magic 438
  in cities 149–150
  and Crusades 26, 72–73
  daily hygiene of 150–151
  economy and trade 188
  and education/learning centers
    145–149
    Ijaza 148–149
    madrasa 146–148
    Shiite 148
  and food 159–161
  hunting by 157–158
  and Islamic law 139–145
    "commanding right and
      forbidding wrong" 140–
      141
    Five Pillars of Islam 139–140
    sharia in practice 142–145
    ulema and the schools of law
      141–142
  and Jews in Christian Iberia 88
  landed estates of 152–153
  and leisure 158–159
  and non-Muslims 156
  and public administraton/taxes
    151–152
  royal palaces of 150
  and slavery 157
  Umar caliphate 62
  women 153–156
    in *harim* (harem) 153–154
    and inheritance 155
    and marriage/divorce
      154–155
    and political power 155–156
    and polygamy 155
    and Quran 156
Muspilli 663
mustard 486

Mutakallimun
and *Ilm al-Kalam* theology
391–395
and Maimonides 379, 380
and philosophy and religion,
Islamic 387
al-Mutawakkil 620
Mutazila 392–393
Muti ibn Iyas 688
muwashshaha 690–691
mystery plays 645, 780
mystical eating 178–180
mystical poetry 691–692
mysticism
about 414
Christian **416–424**
Bernard of Clairvaux 417–418
Catherine of Siena, Saint
422–423
Gertrude the Great 418–419
Hildegarde of Bingen
421–422
Islamic influences on 458
Juan de la Cruz, Saint
420–421
Julian of Norwich 423–424
Meister Eckhart 417
Marguerite Porete 417
pseudo-Dionysius 416
Teresa of Ávila, Saint 419–
420
trinal triplicity 339
dervishes 459
Islamic 451, **452–459**
Abbasids 70
Rabia al-Adawiyya 453–454
Ibn al-Arabi 455–457
Hasan al-Basri 453
Abu Yazid al-Bistami 454–455
al-Hallaj 455
al-Junayd 454
al-Muhasibi 454
al-Suhrawardi 455
al-Tirmidhi 453
and Brethren of the Free
Spirit 364
dervishes *460*
Jewish 439–449
Islamic influences on 458
levels of meaning 439–444
trends 444–449
resources 464–467
Sufism 457–459

N

Nachman, Yehuda ben 77
Nachmanides, Moses
Jewish philosophy and religion
382–383
and Jewish sensuality 172, 173
nadim 754
naffata 308
nafs 401
naft 308–309
Nagid, Samuel ha **97**
Nagrela, Samuel ibn 319
Naples 315
Narbonne
Jewish soldiers 316
and Jews in Carolingian
Renaissance 82–83
Nasi, Judah ha 76
nasib 684, 686
al-Nasir 299
Nasir-I Khusraw 404–405
nasism 169
naskh script 615
Nasr i-Khosraw 70
nastaliq script 615
nasturtium 489
Nativity scene 766
natural correlative doctrine 519–520
naturalism 565
natural law 378–379
nature, secrets of 424, 425
nave 559
nawbat
Islamic music 758, 759
music theory, Islamic 751
necessarium
castles 558
churches and cathedrals 559
necromancy 434
Neidhard von Reuental 642, 726
Neoplatonism
and Abu Hamid Muhammd ibn
al-Ghazzali 399–400
and Augustine of Hippo 348
and Avenpace 401
and Avicenna 399
and Islamic mysticism 452, 455
and Ismailis 404
and al-Kindi 396
philosophy and religion, Jewish
366–367
nest of weights 200, *200*
Nestorianism 327, 361–362

neumes 720
nevus 476
New Christians 33
New Testament
and allegorical writings 654
food references 136
New Year's Day 820–821
ney 756
Nibelungenlied 636
Nicene Creed
and changing role of papacy
18–19
Christian philosophy and religion
327, 329–331
Great Schism 22
Nicholas II (pope) 100
Nicholas of Lyra 370, 371
Nicholas of Salerno 491
niello 579
Nigel Wireker 783
Night of Forgiveness (Laylat al-
Baraa) 819
Night of the Ascension (Laylat al-
Miraj) 818
Night of the Divine Decree (Laylat
al-Qadr) 817
Nikiou, Battle of 47
Nile, Flooding of the (holiday) 821
Nineveh, Battle of 45
Nine Worthies 638–639
Nizam al-Mulk 146
Nizami Ganjawi 703–706
Nizari Ismailis 405–406
Njal's Saga 658
nominalism 356, 357
noncombatants 294, 295
Norman architectural style 569
Norman Conquest 100
Normans
and Byzantine Empire 51
coinage in Islamic world 227
Norte Dame, Cathedral of 39
Northumbrian dialect 658
nose surgery 481–486
*Notable Commentaries on the History of
Plants* (Fuch) 487
Notre-Dame Cathedral (Paris,
France) 555, *560*
Notre Dame school 718–719
Novellae 79, 91
nudity 598
nuns 48–49
Nusayriyya Alawis 406–407

O

Obadiah of Bertinoro 254–255
Objections, Hassagot (David) 378
obstetric hoop *493*, 494
obstetrics and genethlialogy 492–496
Occitan language. *See* Langues d'Oc
occult sciences
    and bubonic plague 501
    Christian 435–438
    Christian mysticism 416
    in Islamic magic 463
Ockham's Razor 356–357
octofoil 559
oculus 560
offertory 717
Office of the Star 770
ogee arches 566
Oghuz Turks 236
Old Testament, interpretation of
    339–340
Old English 635, 658
Old French language 659
Old Hall Manuscript 724–725
Old High German 663–664
Old Irish language 639
Old Testament
    and allegorical writings 654
    beasts of prayer, Jewish art and
      601
    Christian philosophy and religion
      333
    food references 135–136
onager 278
onah 172–174
*On Commerce and the Perfect Merchant
    (Dell mercantura et del mercnate
    perfetto)* (Cotrugli) 121, 206
oneiromancy 434
onions 478, 490
On Metaphysics (al-Razi) 381
On Music (Boethius) 722
On Musical Theory (Boethius of
    Rome) 715
On the First Philosophy (al-Kindi) 396
ophthalmic art 479–480
ophthalmic feast ceremonials 478
ophthalmic foods 478–479
optimism
    Jewish philosophy and religion
      384
    and Jews 161–163
    Judaism, restructuring of 77
    and Maimonides 382

opus Dei 561
oral hygiene 123–124
oralia 862g
oral law 76–77
Orchesography (Arbeau) 733, 735
Order of Santiago 31
Order of the Glorious Saint Mary
    285
Order of the Katchet 285
ordo mundi 342
Oresme, Nicholas 208
organistrum 729–730
organ portative 730
Original Sin 137, 328–329, 363
orle 862g
ormolu 579
orthopedic surgery 487–488
orthotics 487–488
ostensory 583
ostiarius 357
otter, hunting of 129–130
Otto I (Holy Roman Emperor) 9
Ottoman Empire (Turkey) 74
    and collapse of Byzantine Empire
      54–55
    manjaniqs 305, 306
    mosques, design of 612, 613
    music, Islamic 756–757
Otto von Friesing 657
overland trade 217–222
    border security 222
    Golden Horde 219
    means of transportation 221–222
    routes 218m
    Saharan trade routes 219–221
    and water 221
Ovid 646

P

Pact of Umar
    and Jews 165–166
    Jews in Islamic empire 92
    Umar caliphate 62
painting
    Christian 580–581, 585
    Islamic 623–624
Paiva, João Soares de 662
Pakuda, Bahya ibn 371–372
palaces
    Islamic 618–620
    Muslim 150
pale 287, 289
Palestinian Jews 91

paletot 867g
pall 829g
pallettes 273–274
palmistry 433
Palm Sunday 774
panpipe 727
Pantocrator 572
papacy ix, 18–26
    Babylonian Captivity 23–24
    Byzantium v. Rome 21–22
    dual 111
    Fourth Lateran Council 22–23
    and Holy Roman Empire 10
    investiture controversy 19–21
    Jews and 80–81
    and Jews in western Europe
      80–81
    papal primacy 18–19
    three popes 24–26
papal primacy
    and changing role of papacy
      18–19
    Fourth Lateran Council 23, 24
    and papal triplicity 25
Papal States 10
papal triplicity 24–26
paper and papermaking
    Christian manuscripts 575–576
    in Islamic world 544
Paquda, Bahya ibn 371–372
Paracelsus 425, 427
paradise 174
Paradise Play 767
parapet 557
parchment
    Christian manuscripts 570
    Islamic manuscripts 614
Paré, Amboise 488
Paris, Matthew 657, 664
Paris, Treaty of 15
Parma, Rolando de 497
parodies 811–812
parokhet 594
partire del terreno 747
partnerships 229
passant lion 287–288
Passion of Christ 580
Passion Play 631, 644–645
Passover 175, 775
Paston, Margaret 284–285
pastoralists 230, 231
pastorella 640
patina 578

Patrick, Saint 777
patten 870*g*
Paul, Saint 329, 330
pavan 735
pax 582–583
paytan 739–740
Peace of God 264–265
peacock, roast 479, 487
peacock's tail 428
peasants
    and Great Famine 191
    Jacquerie Revolt 192
    landed estates 152
    Wat Tyler 192–193
Peasants' Revolt 103
peasecod-bellied doublet 867*g*
Pedro IV. *See* Peter IV of Aragon
pedule 870*g*
Pelagian controversy 363
peles 599
pelican (distillation device) 512
pelicon 867*g*
pelisse 867*g*
penache (feather plume) 273
penance, Christian concept of 336,
    345–346
Pentateuch 595
Pentecost, feast of the 779
Peoples of the Book 165
Perahya ben Joseph 254
perfection, human 401
perizoma 585
Perolotti, Francesco de Banduccio
    212–213
perpetual motion machines 507–508
    in Islamic world 541
    in medieval Europe 507
Perpetuus (bishop of Tours) 765
Perrault, William 646
pershat scriptural interpretation 440
Persia
    crossbows 307
    manjaniqs 306
Persian Gulf 215
Persian language
    translations of Arabic to 408
Persian literature 703–708
    Firdawsi 706–708
    Omar Khayyam 703, *704*
    Nizami Ganjawi 703–706
Persian music 755–756
Persian Samanids 217
perspective, three-dimensional 577

Pesach 806–808
peshat 370
pest houses 500
Peter, Saint
    and celibacy 358
    and changing role of papacy 18,
    19
Peter Abelard 118, 633
Peter IV of Aragon 658
Peter of Abano 722
Peter of Abelard 100
Peter of Maricourt 507–508
Petrarca, Francesco 664
Petrus Alfonsus 651, 653
peytral 275, 276
Phaedo (Plato) 339
pharmacognosy 472
pharmacy 535–536
Phebus, Gaston 647–648
Philip Augustus (king of France)
    101, 102
    economy and trade, Jewish 243
    and France 14
Philippe de Thaon 652
Philip IV the Fair (king of France)
    Babylonian Captivity (of papacy)
    23
    and France 15
Philo of Alexandria 590
"Philosopher of the Arabs" 396
philosopher's gold 430
philosopher's stone 424, 425,
    428–429
philosophical egg 428
philosophy and religion (in general)
    about 326
    resources 409–412
philosophy and religion, Christian
    326–365
    angels 342–343
    apocalypse and eschatology
    343–345
    Apocrypha 346
    clergy and canonical hours
    357–358
    Crucifixion and Resurrection
    329–331
    excommunication 337
    exegesis and fourfold
    interpretation 341
    grace and the seven sacraments
    335–336
    indulgences 345–346

Jewish philosophy and religion
    386
Mary, Mother of God 331–335
    Christotokos v. *Theotokos* 331
    Eve-Ave antithesis, mari-
    ology and mariolatry
    331–333
    Immaculate Conception 331
    Seven Joys and Seven
    Sorrows 333–335
    virtues of the Virgin 333
monks and friars 358–360
monotheism, Trinity, and
    incarnation 326–328
Original Sin 328–329
philosophers 347–357
    Anselm of Canterbury, Saint
    350–351
    Augustine of Hippo, Saint
    348–349
    Boethius 349–350
    John Duns Scotus 354–355
    Thomas Aquinas, Saint
    351–354
    William of Ockham 355–
    357
prefiguration 339–340
purgatory and penance 345–346
saints 346–347
sects, heretical 360–365
    Arians, adoptionists, and
    Nestorians 361–362
    Brethren of the Free Spirit
    363–365
    Donatists and Pelagians 363
    Manicheans, Albigensians,
    and Cathars 362–363
    trinal triplicities in 337–339
philosophy and religion, Islamic
    386–409, 700
    Arabic language and translation
    407–409
    falsafa 395–403
    Avicenna 397–399
    al-Farabi 397
    al-Kindi 396
    Sunni-Kalam reaction
    399–401
    ilm al-kalam theology and the
    Mutakallimun 391–395
    Asharis 393–395
    Mutazila 392–393
    Qadiriyya 391–392

Ismailis 403–407
    Bohras 407
    Druze 406
    Nasir-I Khusraw 404–405
    Nizari Ismailis 405–406
    Nusayriyya Alawis 406–407
    Quran 388–391
philosophy and religion, Jewish
    365–386
    Christian philosophy and religion
        386
    Decalogue 367–368
    philosophers and biblical
        interpreters 368–384
        Hasdai ben Abraham Crescas
            383–384
        Judah Halevi 372–374
        Abraham ibn Daud 374–376
        Bahya ibn Pakuda 371–372
        Maimonides 376–382
        Nachmanides 382–383
        Rashi 370–371
        Saddya Gaon 368–370
    and presuming excellence
        384–386
    Shema 367–368
philosophy of war 262–265
phlebotomy 431, 499
phlegmatic constitution 485
physicians
    and medieval European medicine
        470
    medieval Jewish medicine 515
    spices as medicine 202
physiognomy 434, 475, 476
Physiologus 651, 652
da Piacenza, Domenico 648
Pie Powder Courts 198
Pierre de Beauvais 652
piers 563
Piers Plowman 656
Pietro da Eboli 126
pig 777–778
pigaches 870g
pileus cornutus 862g
pilgrimage
    Crusades 26
    holidays and festivals, Islamic
        814–816
    Ibn Battuta 240
    indulgences and 345
    to Mecca 814–816
    to Santiago 785–786

pillow faces 434
Pippin the Younger 8
pirates 216–217
Pirotechnia (Biringuccio) 509–510
pistols 281
piva 730
piyyut 678, 739–740
plagiarism 211–212
plague. See Black Death
plague treatises 501–502
plainsong 718
Planetary Hypotheses (Ptolemy) 540
planets
    in Christian magic 430–432
    in medieval European medicine
        501
Plantagenet dynasty 14
plastic surgery 481–483
plastron 867g
Plato 339
    and al-Farabi 397
    Jewish art 590
Platonism 348
Play of Three Shepherds 767–768
Plotinus 397
pluvial 867g
pocket books 575
poetry
    Abbasid 688–690
    devotional 633–634
    "inebriated" 421
    and Islamic historiography xi
    literature, Islamic 686–688
    literature, Jewish 676–679
    Persian 457
pogroms 203
poison antidotes
    in medieval European medicine
        491
    and secular Christian music 722,
        723
Poisons and Antidotes (Maimonides)
    516
Poitier, Battle of 192
polemic 587–588
polo 159
Polo, Marco
    economy and trade 189
    economy and trade, Christian
        210
    and Nizari Ismailis 406
polygamy 155
Porete, Marguerite 417

portcullis 557
ports 214
position 287
potent 288
Potent Salad 180
poulaines 275, 870g
pourpoint 867g
poverty, apostolic 356, 359
power of attorney 206
The Practice of Commerce (Perolotti)
    212
Pragmatic Sanction of Bourges 26
prayer
    during Islamic holidays/festivals
        813
    philosophy and religion, Jewish
        367
precentor 738
predestiny
    and Asharis movement 394
    Maimonides on 521
    and Mutazila movement 393
prefiguration, Christian concept of
    339–340
pre-Lenten season 771–773
presuming excellence
    and Christian Golden Rule 386
    and Jewish optimistic realism 162
    Jewish philosophy and religion
        385–386
    philosophy and religion, Jewish
        384–386
printing
    in Islamic world 544
    manuscripts, Christian 575–576
proclamation of feasts 770
procurator 206
Prodigal Son allegorical feast 338
pronioa system 55
prophecy 380–381
prophetic medicine 533–534
Prophet of God 388–389
prophets, in Islamic mysticism 456
Prose Lancelot 638
Proslogion (Anselm of Canterbury)
    350
prostheses 488
Protestant Reformation 24
Protestant theologians 336
Prudentius 654
psalms
    calligraphy, Christian 575
    in Jewish mysticism 443

psalters
    calligraphy, Christian 575
    Romanesque architectural style
        564
pseudepigraphy 446
Pseudo-Albertus Magnus 333,
    436–437
Pseudo-Dionysius 415–417
Psychomachia 654
Ptolemaic astronomy 538
Ptolemy
    and astrology in Islamic world
        539
    geography in Islamic world 222
public administraton, in Islamic
    world 151–152
pulmonary circulation 532–533
pulpit
    Christian religious art 583
    mosques, design of 610
pulse 484, 499, 722
punishment
    Christian philosophy and religion
        345
    and Hasdai ben Abraham Crescas
        384
    Inquisition 33
purgatory 345–346
Purification, Christian Feast of 334
Purim 675–676, 806, 809–813
pursuivants 291
puteus 559
pyromancy 434
pyx 582

Q

qadi
    and Abbasids 68
    Jewish law 168
    marriage/divorce, Muslim 155
    Somalia 226
Qadiriyya 391–392
qadr 392
Qalam 754
al-Qalqashandi 309
qamis/a 868*g*
qanat 233
qasida 684–686, 690
qaws al-ziyar 304–305
qibla
    and Islamic empire 58
    mosques, design of 609, 612, 613
qidr Iraqi 308–309

qiyan
    Islamic vocal artists 752–754
    slavery, Muslims and 157
quarantines 500
quatrefoil
    churches and cathedrals 560
    heraldry and arms, Christian
        289
queens 282–284
Quia emptores 116
quicksilver 429
quistron 558
Quran 99, 387–391, *390*
    and Arabic as sacred language
        391
    and Arabic language 407–408
    and Averroës 403
    beauty and aesthetics in Islamic
        art 603
    and Christian magic 438
    and fasting 161
    halal or haram 159
    hunting 157
    interpretation of 391
    in Islamic, magic 463–464
    and Islamic empire 57
    and Islamic magic 451, 462
    and Islamic mysticism 452, 455
    jihad 292, 294
    manuscripts of 614
    and Muslim eduation 146
    and Mutazila movement 393
    and Ramadan 816
    and sharia 139
    translation into Latin 408
    and wine 160
    women and 156
Quraysh
    and Islamic empire 57
    Sunnis and Shiites 64
Quzman, Abu Bakr Muhammad
    ibn 691

R

Raavad 173
rabbinic Judaism 92–93
rabies 647–648
racket 730
Radhanites 253*m*
    economy and trade 188, 251–
        254
    and Jews in Carolingian
        Renaissance 83

Ramadan 816–817
    and fasting 160
    and philosophy and religion,
        Islamic 387
ramens, metal 494
rapier 267–268
Rashi
    Jewish philosophy and religion
        370–371
    and Jews in Capetian France 84
    Judaism, restructuring of 77
Rashid, Ahmad ibn 235, 236
al-Rashid, Harun **75**
    Islamic music 758
    qiyan 753
rationality 250
Rauschpfief 730
Rav Ashi 77
al-Razi 526–528
    and Maimonides 381
    and medicine in Islamic world
        526–528, 537
al-Razi (Rhazes) 698
realgar 571
Reconquista 84, 90, 345, 587
recorders 726
redemption 292
Red Sea
    Ibn Battuta 215
    economy and trade, Islamic 215
    pirates and corsairs 216
refectory 561
regal 730
Regimen of Health (Maimonides) 516
reincarnation 406
relics 566
religious art
    architects, Christian 555
    Christian 582–584
    Islamic 609–617
        calligraphy 614–617
        Dome of the Rock 613
        madrasas 613–614
        mosques 609–613
        Quran manuscripts 614
reliquary 566
remez scriptural interpretation 440
repentance
    and Asharis movement 394
    Christian philosophy and religion
        345
repoussé 578
responsa 77, 93, 370

resurrection 329–331
rete 505
reticule 862g
Retimo 244–245
Revelation, book of 343–345
revelation scenes 601
rhabdomancy 434–435
rheno 868g
rhinoplasty 482, *482*
Richard I the Lionhearted (king of England) 73, 101, *187*
   and Jewish moneylenders 248–249
   Third Crusade 27
Richard II (king of England) 123
ridda 59
riddles 653
riese 862g
rihla 188, 235–236
Rihla (Jubayr) 240
rimmonim 572
risala 694–695
al-Risala (al-Basri) 142–143, 392
rites of passage 820–821
ritual clothing 847
Riva, Bonvesin de la 196
robe 868g
robots 543
roc 868g
rodef principle 312
rogation 733
Rogation days 783
Rogerius of Apulia 658
Roman Catholic Church
   Babylonian Captivity 23
   Christian philosophy and religion 336
   monarchs **42–43**
romance
   Christian literature 636–639
   Islamic literature 692–694
   Jewish literature 672–673
   and Jewish town song 743
Roman de la Rose 654–655
Roman Empire, Jews in 78
Romanesque architectural style 563–565, *564*
Rome
   Great Schism 21–22
   in romance 638–639
rondels 580
roquet 868g
roses 474

rosette 310, 311
rose windows 560
Rosh Hashanah 802
rotulus 572
roundlet 862g
royal charters 83
rubricators 562
rue 491
Ruiz, Juan 665
Rumi, Mawlana Jalaluddin 758
Rumi tomb *457*
ruqya 462
Russell, John 131
Russian steppes 236–237
"Rustam, Son of Zal" (Firdawsi) 707

S
Saadya Gaon 93, **97**
sabaton 275, 870g
al-Sabbah, Hassan 405
sabbath
   art for seder 599
   celebration of 799–801
   holidays and festivals, Jewish 799–801
   Jewish town song 742–743
   mystical eating, Jewish 179
Sabbath lights 591
Sabbatj 313
sabers
   Christian 267
   Islamic 300, 302
sable 288
Sabot, Elias 515
sackbut 730
sacraments
   and Augustine of Hippo 349
   Fourth Lateran Council 23
   and Thomas Aquinas 354
   and William of Ockham 356–357
Sacrifical Feast (Id al-Adha) 815–816
Sacrosancta 24
Saddya Gaon 368–370
Safarnama (Khusraw) 70, 237–238
saffa 862g
al-Saffah 67
saffron 477
sage 477
Sahagun 193
Saharan trade routes 219–221, *220m*

Sahula, Isaac ibn 669
sahw 454
Saint John's Day 784–785
Saint John's wort 785
Sainte-Maure, Benoît de 638
saints, Christian 346–347
saint's day 347
Saint Vitus' dance 737
sakers 281
Saladin (sultan of Egypt) 73, **75**
   and destruction of Dar al-Hikma 148
   Mamluks 71
   Third Crusade 27
salamanders 652
salat 139–140, 387
Salian Franks 119–120
salient lion 288
sallet 272
salt
   at feasts 789
   in medieval European medicine 478
saltpeter 279
salt tax 197
salvation 329
Salvia sclarea 479
Samarran mosque 612–613
Samawal al-Maghribi 698
sambuca 278
Samuel ben Judah of Marseille 523–524
Samuel ibn Nagrela 95, 677–678, 682
san benito 33–34
Sancho (king of Castile) 17
sanguine 485
sanitary cordons 500
santur 756
sappers 276
al-Sarakhsi, Ahmad ibn Muhammad 751
sarbal 868g
sargenes 868g
Sassanians (Sassanids) 60–61, 76, 91
satire, Jewish 674–676
Saturn 432
savich 491
savory (herb) 475
saw, water-powered 506
sawm 140
Saxo the Grammarian 657
saydalani 535–536

scabbards 300–301
scales 199, 200, *201*
scalpels 494
scapular 829g
Scholasticism 39, 117–118
science and technology 470. *See also*
medicine
   in Islamic world **525–526,
      537–546**
      alchemy, exoteric and esoteric
         537–538
      astrolabe 541
      astronomy and astrology
         538–541
      hiyal 542–543
      mathmetics and ghubar
         numbers 545–546
      perpetual motion machines
         541
      Ptolemaic astronomy 538
      robots, papermaking,
         printing, and windmills
         543–545
      temporal hours, water clocks,
         mechanical clocks 542
   Jewish contributions to **514–
      516, 523–525**
   in medieval Europe **503–514**
      chemistry 511–513
      engineering 505–508
      instruction books 513–514
      keeping time 504–505
      metallurgy 509–511
      watermills v. windmills
         508–509
   resources 547–549
scriptorium
   monasteries 562
   Romanesque architectural style
      564
scriptural interpretation
   Christian philosophy and religion
      341
   and Jewish mysticism 440
   and Maimonides 379–380
scrolls 572
sculpture
   Gothic architectural style
      565–566
   Polemic in Christian art 587
   Romanesque architectural style
      563–564
Seafarer 659

sea trade
   Ibn Battuta in Jeddah 214–215
   Jewish 243
   maritime technology 215–216
   pirates and corsairs 216–217
   ports and customs 217
   Radhanites 251–254
second coming 766
Second Commandment 594
secular art, Islamic 617–624
   ceramics, glass, and metalwork
      620–622
   painting, manuscript
      illumination, and miniatures
      622–624
   palaces 618–620
   styles 617–618
secular clothing, Christian 830–833
secular festivals, in Islanic world
   820–821
secular literature, Jewish 665–667
secular music
   Christian 721–724
   Jewish 740–746
      art song 741–742
      folk song 740–741
      town song 742–744
      wedding music 744–746
seder
   art for 599–600
   Jewish art 592
Sefer ha Cabala (Daud) 95–96
Sefer hasidim 679–680
Sefer ha Wikkuah (Nachmanides)
   383
Sefer shaashuim 671–672
Sefer yetzira 445
sefirot *444*, 445, 446
sehtar 756
seige engines 278–279
seige ladder and tower 276
seizure disorders 517–519
Seljuks 94, 100
   and Byzantine Empire 51–52
   Crusades 26
   First Crusade 27
   and Jews in Islamic empire 94
   land grants 153
   overland trade in Islamic world
      217
   Second Crusade 27
sensuality, Jews and 172–175
sensual meals 178–180

Sephardic Jews 94–95
   and emergence of new cultures
      xii
   and Pesach 807, 808
serfs 186
sergeanty 115
Sergius III (pope) 19
Sermon on the Mount 367
Sermons on the Song of Songs (Bernard
   of Clairvaux) 418
servi camare regis 87
servus camere regio 163–164, 242
seven ages 113
Seven Joys and Seven Sorrows
   333–335
The Seven Princesses (Nizami
   Ganjawi) 705–706
seven sacraments 335–336
sex and sexuality
   and Brethren of the Free Spirit
      364
   in Chaucer 133–135
   hunting songs 648
   and Jewish mysticism 447–448
   music, secular Christian 724
shabakah 309
Al-Shafi 141
Shafi school of law 141, 142
shafut 751
shahadah 139, 387
Shah Nameh 623–624
Shajrat al-Durr (sultana of Egypt)
   156
shal 862g
shalom bayit 385
shamshir 300–302
shape shifting 463–464
Shaprut, Hasdai ibn **97**
   crafts and professions 245
   Umayyad Spain, Jews in 95
sharecroppers 152
sharia (Islamic law) 139–145, 387
   "commanding right and
      forbidding wrong" 140–141
   Five Pillars of Islam 139–140
   sharia in practice 142–145
   ulema and the schools of law
      141–142
sharika 229
Shavuot 808–809
sha wadha 461
shawm 730
shechitah 599–600

sheds 309
Shema 367–368
Shia Islam 63–64, 99
    Abbasids 67
    and Druze 406
    education/learning centers 148
    Fatimid *dawa* 70
    Fatimids 93–94, 387
    festivals 819–820
    Muslim women and inheritance
        155
    and Nasir-I Khusraw 404–405
    and Nusayriyya Alawis 406–407
    and philosophy and religion,
        Islamic 387
    schools of law 142, 143, 145
shields 309, *309*
ships and shipbuilding 216, 281–282
shirkargar 300–302
shivaree
    Jewish wedding music 745
    and secular Christian music 721,
        724
shochets 177
shortbow 269–270
Shrove Tuesday 772–773
shumkaya 518
Sicilian dialect 662
Sicily 244
Siddanta 68–69
siddur 368
sideboards
    castles 557
    monasteries 561
siege weapons
    in Christian Europe 276–279
    Islamic 300, 303–307
Siger of Brabant
    and Averroës 403
    and Thomas Aquinas 351
sight symbolism 479–480
sikka 227
silk
    guilds 194
    in Islamic world 853–854,
        856–857
Silphium 495
silver 205, 227, 228
Simchat Torah 804
simiya 461
Simon of Montfort 29, 640
simony 20, 25
simples 472

sin
    Christian philosophy and religion
        345
    gluttony 137–138
Singspiele 646
sira 695–696
Sirat al-Sultan Baybars 693
Sirat Antar 692
Sirat Banu Hilal 693
Sir Tristrem 638
sirventes 640
sirwal, shalwar 868g
Sisebut (Visigoth king) 98
situla 582
Six Chapters (Nasir-I Khusraw) 405
Sixtus IV (pope) 104
Siyer-i Nebi 623
slaves and slavery
    and Jews 172
    Muslims and 157
    overland trade in Islamic world
        219
    qiyan 752–754
slave-soldiers 296–300
    Almogavares 299–300
    Ghazis 299
    ghilman 296–297
    Ghurids 298–299
    Mamluks 71, 297–298
sloth (as deadly sin) *339*
smallpox 528
snood 862g
socaage 115–116
social class 131–132
societas terrae 206
society. *See also* Christians; Jews;
    Muslims
    about 110
    resources 180–184
socq 868g
soldiers, Jewish 313–319, *318*
    classical armies 313
    France and Italy 315–317
    Germany 317
    Jerusalem and the Temple
        313–314
    Medina, battle in 314–315
    Spain 317–319
    thema/theme system 46
    12-century warrior tribes 319
"soldiers of Christ" 26
solidi 193
Solomon (king of Israel) 438

Solomon ibn Gabriol (Avicebron)
    682
Solomon's Temple 590
Somalia 226
song collections, Christian 724–726
*The Song of Roland. See Le Chanson
    de Roland*
Song of Songs (Old Testament) 333,
    418, 419, 421
Soranus 495
sorcery 90, 438
sorquenie 868g
sottana 868g
soul
    and Avicenna 399
    in Christian magic 428
    in Christian mysticism 415, 416
    and Abraham ibn Daud 375, 376
    and Druze 406
    and John Duns Scotus 355
    and Islamic mysticism 457–458
    Jewish philosophy and religion
        374
    and Maimonides 382
    in medieval European medicine
        479
Spain
    Easter meal 778
    economy and trade, Jewish 246
    Jewish soldiers in 317–319
    music, Islamic 758–759, *759*
    in western Europe 16–18
spalling 565
spangenhelm 271
Spanish Inquisition. *See* Inquisition
speaking in tongues 415
speculum matricis 494
spells 435, 462
spices *203*
    and Christian economy and trade
        202
    as medicine in Islamic world 534
Spielmanner Sabbath entertainments
    743
spires 565
spiritual autobiography 633
Spiritual Exercises (Gertrude the
    Great) 419
spiritual life 371–372
spiritual quests 415
spiritual tranquility 533
spondaic meter 719
Sprenger, Jacob 436, 437

Spy Wednesday 775
squash
    in Islamic medicine 535
    in medieval European medicine
        491, 492
    and mystical eating, Jewish 180
Stabat Mater Dolorosa 634
stable table 557
stained glass
    churches and cathedrals 559–
        560
    Gothic architectural style 565
standards 199–200
stanjant lion 288
staple 200
states (Islamic mysticism) 457, 458
stations (Islamic mysticism) 457,
    458
Statute of Laborers 192
Statute of Uses 116
steeple tower 559
stichomancy 435
stomacher 868*g*
strapwork 579
strategos 46
strawberry, wild 479
Subh al-Asha (al-Qalqashandi) 309
sublimation
    in Christian magic 428
    science and technology in
        medieval Europe 512
suf 850–851
sufaf 609
suffering, in Christian mysticism
    422, 423
Sufis and Sufism
    Abbasids 70
    and Abu Hamid Muhammd ibn
        al-Ghazzali 399–401
    and Christian mysticism 420,
        421
    dance, Islamic 757–758
    and fasting 161
    halal or *haram* 748
    and Islamic art 605–606
    and Islamic mysticism 451–455,
        457–459
    and jihad 296
    Mawlid al-Nabi celebration 387
    music, Islamic 757–758
    mysticism 457–459
    and philosophy and religion,
        Islamic 387

sugar
    crops in Islamic world 232
    in medieval European medicine
        489
al-Suhrawardi 455
suhur 160
sukenis 868*g*
Sukkot 803–804
sulfur 428–429
"Sumer is ycumenn in" 642
Summa theologiae (Aquinas) 353, 354
    gluttony and lust 134
    and Jewish merchants/
        moneylenders 204
sumptuary laws
    Christian 833–834
    and Christian social class 131–
        132
    Christians regulating Jews
        839–842
    Jewish 177–178, 837–845
    and Muslim clothing 848
    and *Pact of Umar* 166
sunburn 476
sunna 387
Sunni Islam 63–64
    Abbasids 67, 69
    and Asharis movement 393–394
    Ashura 819
    falsafa 399–401
    Ghadir Khumm 820
    Muslim women and inheritance
        155
    and Nasir-I Khusraw 405
    and Quran 388–391
    schools of law 142, 143
    and Shiites 63–64
supererogatory festivals 817–819
supertunic 868*g*
suras 389–390
surcoat 868*g*
surgery
    and Jewish women 170
    and medicine in Islamic world
        529
    in medieval European medicine
        497
    and secular Christian music 721
surgical instruments 471–472, 481,
    494
surplice 829*g*
surtout 868*g*
Susskind von Trimburg 642

Su Sung 504–505
Sutton Hoo ship burial 567, *567*
sutures 529
swords
    in Christian Europe 267–268
    Islamic 300–302
symbolism
    Abbasids 68
    crosses and crucifixes 584–585
    Jewish art 591–592
    sight 479–480
    typological 339–340
synagogues
    building art, Jewish 593–595
    Italy 78–80
    and Jewish autonomy 167, *167*
    music in 738–740

T

tabard 275, 868*g*–869*g*
al-Tabari, Muhammad ibn Jarir 68,
    696
table
    and art for seder 599
    Jewish mystical eating 179
The Tables of Heaith (Ibn Butlan)
    534–535
taboos 435
Tacitus, Gaius Cornelius
    on feudalism 114
    on women 119
tactus eruditis 499, *499*
tactus eruditus 499
tafsir 391
Tafsir (Saddya Gaon) 368
Tagelied 642
Tagliacozzi, Gaspare 482–483
tajira 862*g*
takiya 862*g*
takkanot 167–169
talavera 579
talim 405
taliq script 615
talismans 461, 462
tallage 117
Talmud
    Babylonian 84, 91
    Jewish art 591–592
    Judaism, restructuring of 76–77
    and Maimonides 378
    philosophy and religion, Jewish
        365
    and Sabbath 799

talthima 862g
tambourine 731
tamgas 310
Tammam ibn Ghalib (al-Farazdaq) 685
tansy 495
tannur 862g
tanzil 406
tapestries
 houses 562–563
 Norman architectural style 569
tarawih 160
tarha 862g
tarikh 696
tariqa 459
tarot cards 433
"Tartar slaves" 543
Tasrif (al-Zahrawi) 528–530
tawaif 757
tawakkul 453–454
tawil 391
 and Druze 406
 and Ismailis 404
Tawq al-hammama (Ibn Hazm of Córdoba) 699–700
taxes and taxation 118–119
 and Christians 118–119
 in Islamic governments 151–152
 and Jewish moneylenders 248–249
 Muslims and 151–152
taylasan 862g
tebah 593
technology
 metallurgy 509–510
 mining 510–511
teeth 123–124
tefillin 371
tempera 571
templon 568
temporal hours 542
Ten Commandments
 and John Duns Scotus 355
 philosophy and religion, Jewish 367–368
 and Sermon on the Mount 367
Ten Days of Awe 803
tenson 640
Teresa of Ávila, Saint 419–420
tessellated pavement 562
tesserae 568
"testing the cure" 484
Teutonic Knights 31–32

textiles (in general). *See* clothing, costume, and textiles
textiles, Muslim 851–858
 carpets, Anatolian 856–857
 Coptic cloth 856
 cotton 853
 dyes 854
 hybrids 854
 ikat and fabric mosaic 855
 khila 855
 kiswa 851–852
 linen 853, 854
 Muhammed's cloak 852–853
 Muhyi al-Din 857–858
 mulham 854
 silk 853–854, 856–857
 tiraz 856
 weaving looms 854–855
 wool 853
thawb 869g
theater. *See* drama and theater
theme system 46, 54, 55
Theodora (empress of Byzantine) 43, 45, **55**
Theodoricos de Campo 716
Theodosian Code
 Canon law and Jews 164
 Jews in Byzantine Empire 90–91
 and Jews in Italy 78
Theodosius (emperor of Rome) ix, 4
Theodosius II (Eastern Roman Emperor) 164
Theology (Plotinus) 397
theosophy 445–446
Theotokos
 Byzantine architectural style 568
 Christian philosophy and religion 331
 and Mary, Mother of God 362
theriac 472, 501–503
theurgy 445
thewe 194–195
Third Crusade. *See* Crusade, Third
Thirteen Principles of Faith (Maimonides) 377
Thomas à Becket, Saint 14, 780
Thomas Aquinas, Saint 102, 351–354, *352*
 and angels 342
 and fourfold interpretation 341
 on gluttony and lust 134
 and Jewish merchants/ moneylenders 204
 and sacraments 335

Thomas of Britain 637–638, 659
Thomas of Celano 633, 634, 766
The Thousand and One Nights
 and frame tale 642, 702
 influence of 630
 in Islamic, magic 463
 and Islamic magic 462
 qiyan 753
Three Kings, Feast of the 770–771
thuluth script 615
tiara 829g
Tiferet 446
tigerware 579
tile, encaustic 562
time and timekeeping
 and Averroës 403
 in medieval Europe 504–505
 in medieval European medicine 484–485
time mirror 493
tinctures 288, 427
tiraceros 193
tiraz 856
tiraz livery 869g
al-Tirmidhi 453
Tisha Bav 809
toad 428
Toledot Yeshu 98
tombak 756
tonsure 829g
toothache 497
Torah
 Jewish art 592
 and Jewish mysticism 445
 laws on warfare, Jewish 312
 and Maimonides 379
 and Nachmanides 382
 philosophy and religion, Jewish 365
Torquemada, Thomas de 33
tortoise (defense mechanism) 276–277
Der Toten Tanz (Jacob Meydenbach) 650
touret de nez 862g
towns and cities, growth of 36–38, 37
town song 742–744
toxicology 491–492
traction machines 487, 488
trade. *See under* economy and trade
trade fairs 197
trade routes 252–254

Transfiguration, feast of the 786
transi tombs 650
translations
    from Arabic 407–409
    and medicine in Islamic world
        536–537
transom 560
transportation, means of 221–222
transubstantiation
    Christian philosophy and religion
        335, 336
    church mass 716
    Fourth Lateran Council 23
trapping 127, 129
Trastamara Wars 103
travel narratives 188
Travels of Benjamin of Tudela
    255–256
Travels of Ibn Jubayr 239–240
Travels of Sir John Mandeville
    (Mandeville) 210–212
The Treasury of Mysteries (Nizami
    Ganjawi) 705
The Treatise (Oresme) 208
Treatise on Asthma (Maimonides)
    516–523
Treatise on Poisons (William of Amara)
    722
*Treatise on the Truth of the Catholic
    Faith against Unbelievers* (Aquinas)
    354
Trebizond Empire 54
trebuchet 277, 278
tree, in Jewish mysticism 443–444
Tree of Knowledge 328, 329, 340
trencher table 561–562
trepan 471–472
tressour 862g
tribrachic meter 719
Trier (Spanish Christian Priscillian)
    361
trinal triplicities 337–339
Trinity 326–328
    and Brethren of the Free Spirit
        364
    Byzantine architectural style 568
    Christian philosophy and religion
        326
    and Thomas Aquinas 353
Trinity Sunday 779–780
triptych 577
triquetra 327–328
Trismegistus, Hermes 427–428

triumph (dance) 734
trobaritz 640
trochaic mode 719
tropers 725
tropes 631
tropological level of meaning
    (scripture) 341
Trotula of Salerno 492–493, 495
troubadours 640
    Jewish art song 741
    song collections, Christian 725
trouvères 641, 725
Troyes, Treaty of 15
truffeau 862g–863g
trumba marina 731
trumpet 731, *731*
Tu Bshvat 805–806
tunbur 750
tunic 274, 869g
Turkey. *See* Ottoman Empire
Turkish Bulghars
    ibn Fadlan 236, 237
    al-Kitab of Ibn Fadlan 236, 237
    overland trade in Islamic world
        217
Turkish language 408
Turmeda, Fray Anselmo (Abdallah
    Turjuman) 698
turtles (defense mechanism) 277
al-Tusi, Abu Jafar 143, 145
Twelfth Night 766, 769–770
Twelve Apostles 330
Twelve Equals 634
twice-told Eve *332*
Two Sicilies, Kingdom of the 12
tympans 505

U

Ucles, Battle of 88
udhri poetry 686, *687*
al-Ukhaydir, valley of 221
ulema 63, 141–142
Ulrich von Zatzikhoven 638
Umar caliphate 61–62
Umar ibn al-Khattab **75,** 151
Umayyad caliphate (Umayyads)
    64–67, 95
    clothing 848
    coinage in Islamic world 227
    incendiary weapons, Islamic 308
    Jews in Islamic empire 92
    mosques *225,* 225–226, 612
    and *Pact of Umar* 166

palaces, Islamic 618
poetry 685–686, 690–691
Sunnis and Shiites 64
Abu l-Qasim al-Zahrawi 528
Umayyad Spain 66–67
    Jews in 95
    literature, Islamic 690–691
umma
    Heraclius (Byzantine emperor)
        45
    Umar caliphate 61
uncial majuscule 573
Unitarians 406
universal intellect, manifestations
    of 404
universals, theory of 356
universe
    and Abu Hamid Muhammd ibn
        al-Ghazzali 399–400
    and al-Farabi 397
    Maimonides on 521
    Mutakallimun 394–395
universities *40*
    and Christians 117–118
    in western Europe 39–41
University of Bologna 39
University of Constantinople 39
"upper crust" 790
Urban II (pope) **42,** 101
    Christian philosophy and religion
        345
    Crusades 26
    First Crusade 27
    Peace of God 264, 265
Urban IV (pope) 780
Urban VI (pope) 422
urinalysis *496,* 496–497
al-Urmawi, Abd al-Mumin Safi al-
    Din 751
Usama Ibn Munqidh 698
The Uses of Animals (Ibn Bakhtisheu)
    701–702
ushr 152, 153
Uthman ibn Affan 62–63
Uyun al-akhbar (Ibn Qutayba) 699

V

vaginal dilaters 494
vair 288
Valentine's Day, Saint 781–782
Valley of the Dry Bones 441
vamplate 303
van Eyck, Jan 581

vaults 556
vegetables
    in medieval European medicine 492
    and medieval Jewish medicine 517
vellum
    Christian manuscripts 575–576
    manuscripts, Christian 570
Venice *211*
Verdun, Treaty of 9
vestments 826–830
vices 555
viereckiger schleier 863g
Vigevano, Guido da 278–279, 650
Viiola odorita 477
Viking funeral 236, 237
Vikings 13
Vincent Ferrer, Saint 89
vinegar 487
violence
    and famines in Islamic world 234–235
    and Jewish moneylenders 248–249
    and Maimonides 381–382
violet, sweet 486
viols 726
Virgil *655*, 655–656
Virgin Mary *335*
    churches and cathedrals 560
    and Eve-Ave antithesis 333
    and *felix culpa* 329
    painting, Christian 580
    and Quran 388
virtues, theological 339
virtues of the Virgin 333
Visigothic script 573
Visigoths
    Jews in Christian Iberia 87
    and Spain 16
visions
    and Christian mysticism 419–423
    and Islamic mysticism 456–457
Visitation of Our Lady, Feast of 333–334
vita activa 357
vita contemplativa 357
Vitry, Jacques de 651, 658
Vitry, Philippe de 719
vocal artists 751–754
volvelle 484
Voragine, Jacobus de 347, 633
Vulgar Latin 660

W

Wace 659
wahdat al-wujud 457
wainscot 562
wakil 217
Walcher hanging position 530
Walshe, Ann 652
Walther von der Vogelweide 642
Walworthe, John 123
Wanderer 659
al-Wansharishi, Ahmad 143
waqf 152
warfare and weapons (generally)
    about 262
    resources 320–323
warfare and weapons, Christian **262–292**
    arms and armor 266–276
        body armor 273–275
        crossbow and arbalest 270
        grenade and caltrop 270
        head armor 270–273
        horse armor 275–276
        lance, halberd, mace, morning star 268–269
        longbow, shortbow, javelin 269–270
        sword, dagger, and rapier 267–268
    chivalry 265–266
    gunpowder 279–282
    heraldry and arms 286–292
        achievement, hatchment, canting arms, *impresa* 290
        art of heraldry 286–287
        bar, carbuncle, chevron 289–290
        Bartolus de Saxoferrato 290
        blazon, charge, position 287
        cadency 288–289
        college of arms 290–292
        colors, tinctures, metals, furs 288
        fess, pale, crosses 289
        lion and yale 287–288
    philosophy of war 262–265
    siege techniques and equipment 276–279
    women's arms 282–286
        ladies of manors and lady knights 284–286
        queens and leaders 282–284
warfare and weapons, Islamic **292–311**
    and cultural exchange 74
    heraldry 309–311
    jihad 292–296
    slave-soldiers 296–300
        Almogavares 299–300
        Ghazis 299
        ghilman 296–297
        Ghurids 298–299
        Mamluks 297–298
    weaponry 300–309
        crossbows 307
        dabbabah, darajah, shields, sheds 309
        incendiary weapons 307–309
        lances 302–303
        siege weapons 303–307
        sword, *shamshir, shirkargar, kili* 300–302
warfare and weapons, Jewish **311–320**
    disarmed Jews 319–320
    heraldry 320
    laws on warfare 311–313
    soldiers 313–319
        classical armies 313
        France and Italy 315–317
        Germany 317
        Jerusalem and the Temple 313–314
        Medina, battle in 314–315
        Spain 317–319
        12-century warrior tribes 319
warfare treatises 650
Wars of the Lord, Milhamot Adonai (Gershon) 524
Wars of the Roses 13, 15–16
wassailing 768, 771
water
    farms in Islamic world 233
    in Islamic world 221
    in Jewish magic 450
water clocks 505, 542, 543
water conduit systems 558–559
water distribution 122–123
watermelons
    crops in Islamic world 233
    in medieval European medicine 489
watermills 508–509
wattle and daub 562
Wat Tyler's peasant revolt 192–193

wazirs 226
weaponry. *See under* warfare and
  weapons
weaving
  Flanders and Christian economy
    and trade 197
  guilds 193
  in Islamic world 854–855
Wechsel 642
wedding music
  Jewish 744–746
  secular Christian 721, 724
weddings, Jewish 795–799
weights and measures 199–200, 205
Western Roman Empire ix
  barbarian invasions of 5–7
  growth of Christianity in 3–5
Western schism 23, 24
West Saxon dialect 659
westworks 563
wheelcut glass 621
wheeled transport 544–545
Whirling Dervishes 757
white magic
  in Islamic world 460
  in Judaism 449
White Monks 359
wild boar 777–778
wild individualists 608–609
William, archbishop of Tyre 658
William I the Conqueror (king of
  England) 13, 100, 114
William IX (duke of Aquitaine and
  count of Poitiers) 359, 648, 660
William of Amara 722
William of Malmesbury 657
William of Marra 501–502
William of Ockham 355–357, 425
William of Rubruck 209–210
William the Almoner 509
wimple 863g
windlass 508
windmills 508–509
wine
  in medieval European medicine
    478
  in medieval Jewish medicine
    518–519
  and sumptuary laws, Jewish 178

witches and witchcraft 435–437,
  436, *437*, 461–462
Wolfram von Eschenbach 638, 642,
  663
wolves, trapping of 127, 129
women *120*, *154*
  arms of, in Christian Europe
    282–286
    ladies of manors and lady
      knights 284–286
    queens and leaders 282–284
  Christian 119–120
  in Christian magic 436–437
  in Christian mysticism 415,
    417–429
  and famines in Islamic world 234
  farms, Christian 189
  guilds 194–195
  instruction books for 648–649,
    649
  in Islamic mysticism 453–454
  Islamic vocal artists 752
  Jewish 79–80, 169–171
  and Jewish folk songs 741
  and manuscript art, Jewish 598
  medieval European medicine
    489, 492, 495
  Muslim 153–156
    clothing 850
    in *harim* 153–154
    and inheritance 155
    and marriage/divorce 154–155
    as poets 684–685
    and political power 155–156
    and polygamy 155
    and Quran 156
  overland trade in Islamic world
    219
  and *Pact of Umar* 166
  and sharia 144–145
  as troubadours 640
Women's Secrets (Magnus, Pseudo-
  Albertus) 333, 436–437
woodcuts 577
woodwork 576–577
wool
  Flanders and Christian economy
    and trade 197
  in Islamic world 853

works of wisdom 681
world music 432
worm condenser *511*
  and Christian magic 427
  science and technology in
    medieval Europe 512
wrigglework 580
Wycliffe, John 24, 104

Y

al-Yahudi, Kaula 318–319
yale 287–288
Yarmuk, Battle of 46
yetzer hora 384, 385
Yiddish language 664, 672–673,
  743
Yitzaki, Solomon 370–371
Yom Kippur 803

Z

Zabara, Joseph ibn 481
zahhafah 309
al-Zahrawi, Abu l-Qasim 528–530
zairaja 463
zajal 691
zakat 59
"Zal, Son of Sam" (Firdawsi) 707
zampogna 731
Zayd, Abu 623
Ziryab, Ishaq al-Mawsili 758, 759
ziyar 304–305
ziyarat al-qubur 458
zodiac
  Christian magic 430
  Christian philosophy and religion
    339
  and manuscript art, Jewish 598
  and medieval European medicine
    484
zodiac man 431, *431*
zodiac woman 431, *431*
Zohar Kabbalah 445–447
Zohar mystics 178–179
Zoroastrianism 60
zuhdiyyat 688
zunnar 166
Zwischengoldglas 580